THE CAMBRIDGE COMPANION TO
HORACE

Horace is a central author in Latin literature. His work spans a wide range of genres, from iambus to satire, and odes to literary epistle, and he is just as much at home writing about love and wine as he is about philosophy and literary criticism. He also became a key literary figure in the regime of the Emperor Augustus. In this volume a superb international cast of contributors presents a stimulating and accessible assessment of the poet, his work, its themes and its reception. This provides the orientation and coverage needed by non-specialists and students, but also suggests fresh and provoking perspectives from which specialists may benefit. Since the last synoptic book on Horace was published half a century ago, there has been a sea-change in perceptions of his work and in the literary analysis of classical literature in general, and this territory is fully charted in this *Companion*.

STEPHEN HARRISON is Professor of Classical Languages and Literature at the University of Oxford and Fellow of Corpus Christi College.

THE CAMBRIDGE COMPANION TO
HORACE

EDITED BY
STEPHEN HARRISON
Professor of Classical Languages and Literature, University of Oxford, and Fellow and Tutor in Classics, Corpus Christi College, Oxford

CAMBRIDGE
UNIVERSITY PRESS

CAMBRIDGE UNIVERSITY PRESS
Cambridge, New York, Melbourne, Madrid, Cape Town, Singapore, São Paulo

Cambridge University Press
The Edinburgh Building, Cambridge CB2 2RU, UK

Published in the United States of America by Cambridge University Press, New York

www.cambridge.org
Information on this title: www.cambridge.org/9780521536844

First published 2007

Printed in the United Kingdom at the University Press, Cambridge

A catalogue record for this publication is available from the British Library

ISBN-13 978-0-521-83002-7 hardback
ISBN-13 978-0-521-53684-4 paperback

For Robin Nisbet
sedecim lustris functo
21 May 2005

CONTENTS

Contributors *page* x
Preface xiii

Introduction 1
STEPHEN HARRISON

PART 1: ORIENTATIONS

1 Horace: life and chronology 7
ROBIN NISBET

2 Horatian self-representations 22
STEPHEN HARRISON

3 Horace and archaic Greek poetry 36
GREGORY HUTCHINSON

4 Horace and Hellenistic poetry 50
RICHARD THOMAS

5 Horace and Roman literary history 63
RICHARD TARRANT

6 Horace and Augustus 77
MICHÈLE LOWRIE

PART 2: POETIC GENRES

7 The *Epodes*: Horace's Archilochus? 93
LINDSAY WATSON

8 The *Satires* 105
FRANCES MUECKE

9 The *Epistles* 121
ROLANDO FERRI

10 The *Ars Poetica* 132
ANDREW LAIRD

11 *Carmina*: *Odes* and *Carmen Saeculare* 144
ALESSANDRO BARCHIESI

PART 3: POETIC THEMES

12 Philosophy and ethics 165
JOHN MOLES

13 Gods and religion 181
JASPER GRIFFIN

14 Friendship, patronage and Horatian sociopoetics 195
PETER WHITE

15 Wine and the symposium 207
GREGSON DAVIS

16 Erotics and gender 221
ELLEN OLIENSIS

17 Town and country 235
STEPHEN HARRISON

18 Poetics and literary criticism 248
RICHARD RUTHERFORD

19 Style and poetic texture 262
STEPHEN HARRISON

PART 4: RECEPTIONS

20 Ancient receptions of Horace 277
RICHARD TARRANT

21 The reception of Horace in the Middle Ages 291
KARSTEN FRIIS-JENSEN

22 The reception of Horace in the Renaissance 305
MICHAEL McGANN

23 The reception of Horace in the seventeenth and eighteenth centuries 318
DAVID MONEY

24 The reception of Horace in the nineteenth and twentieth centuries 334
STEPHEN HARRISON

Dateline of works and major political events 347
Works cited 349
Index 379

CONTRIBUTORS

ALESSANDRO BARCHIESI is Professor of Latin at the University of Siena at Arezzo and also teaches at Stanford University. He is the author of books on Virgil and Ovid, including *The Poet and the Prince* (1997) and *Speaking Volumes* (2001), of a commentary on Ovid *Metamorphoses* 1–2 (2005), and of many articles on Latin literature.

GREGSON DAVIS is Professor of Classical Studies and Literature and Andrew W. Mellon Professor of the Humanities at Duke University. His books include *The Death of Procris* (1983), *Polyhymnia: The Rhetoric of Horatian Lyric Discourse* (1991) and *Aimé Césaire* (Cambridge University Press, 1997).

ROLANDO FERRI is Associate Professor of Latin at the University of Pisa; he is author of *I dispiaceri di un epicureo* on Horace's *Epistles* (1993) and of a major commentary on the pseudo-Senecan *Octavia* (Cambridge University Press, 2003).

KARSTEN FRIIS-JENSEN is Associate Professor of Medieval and Renaissance Latin at the University of Copenhagen. His books include *Saxo Grammaticus as Latin poet* (1987) and *Peterborough Abbey* (library catalogue, with James Willoughby; 2001). He has written several articles on the medieval reception of Horace.

JASPER GRIFFIN is Emeritus Professor of Classical Languages and Literature at the University of Oxford and Emeritus Fellow of Balliol College. He is the author of books on Homer and Virgil and of *Latin Poets and Roman Life* (1985).

STEPHEN HARRISON is Fellow and Tutor in Classics at Corpus Christi College, Oxford, and Professor of Classical Languages and Literature in the University of Oxford. He is the author of a commentary on Virgil *Aeneid* 10 (1991) and editor of several volumes including *Homage to Horace* (1995) and *A Companion to Latin Literature* (2005).

GREGORY HUTCHINSON is Professor of Greek and Latin Languages and Literature at the University of Oxford. He has written a commentary on *Aeschylus' Seven against Thebes* (1985), and *Hellenistic Poetry* (1988), *Latin Literature from Seneca to Juvenal: A Critical Study* (1993), *Cicero's Correspondence: A Literary Study* (1998) and *Greek Lyric Poetry: A Commentary on Selected Larger Pieces* (2001). He has just completed a commentary on Propertius Book 4.

ANDREW LAIRD is Reader in Classics at the University of Warwick; he is author of *Powers of Expressions, Expressions of Power* (1999), editor of *A Companion to the Prologue of Apuleius' Metamorphoses* (2001, with A. Kahane) and of *Ancient Literary Criticism* (2006), and has written widely on Latin and neo-Latin literature.

MICHÈLE LOWRIE is Associate Professor of Classics and Co-director of the Poetics and Theory Program at New York University. She is the author of *Horace's Narrative Odes* (1997) and of a wide range of articles on Latin literature, and is currently working on a book entitled *Writing, Performance, and Authority in Augustan Rome.*

MICHAEL MCGANN is former Professor of Latin at the Queen's University of Belfast. He is the author of *Studies in Horace's First Book of Epistles* (1969) and of a number of articles on Latin and neo-Latin poetry.

JOHN MOLES is Professor of Latin at the University of Newcastle. He is the author of a commentary on Plutarch's *Life of Cicero* (1988) and of many articles on Roman literature and culture.

DAVID MONEY is Director of Studies in Classics at Wolfson College and Hughes Hall, Cambridge, and formerly Senior Lecturer in English at the University of Sunderland, and author of *The English Horace: Anthony Alsop and the Tradition of British Latin Verse* (1998). He has been involved in editing a number of neo-Latin texts and has written extensively on neo-Latin poetry.

FRANCES MUECKE is Senior Lecturer in Classics at the University of Sydney. She is the author of *A Companion to the Menaechmi of Plautus* (1987) and of a commentary on Horace, *Satires* 2 (Warminster, 1993). Her wide range of articles on Latin literature includes a major piece on Horace's language and style for the *Enciclopedia Oraziana* (1997) and extensive work in neo-Latin.

ROBIN NISBET is Corpus Christi Professor of the Latin Language and Literature Emeritus at the University of Oxford. His books include commentaries on Horace *Odes* 1 and 2 (1970 and 1978, with Margaret Hubbard) and on *Odes* 3 (2004, with Niall Rudd), and his *Collected Papers on Latin Literature* (1995).

ELLEN OLIENSIS is Associate Professor of Classics, University of California at Berkeley, and the author of *Horace and the Rhetoric of Authority* (Cambridge

University Press, 1998) and articles on Latin poetry. She is currently working on a book entitled *Freud's Rome: Psychoanalysis and Latin Poetry*.

RICHARD RUTHERFORD is University Lecturer in Classical Languages and Literature at Oxford and a Student and Tutor of Christ Church. His many publications include *The Meditations of Marcus Aurelius: A Study* (1989), a commentary on Books 19 and 20 of Homer's *Odyssey* (Cambridge University Press, 1992), *The Art of Plato* (1995), and *Classical Literature: A Concise History* (2005).

RICHARD TARRANT is Pope Professor of the Latin Language at Harvard University. His publications include a commentary on Seneca's *Agamemnon* (Cambridge University Press, 1976), a commentary on Seneca's *Thyestes* (1985), the Oxford Classical Text of Ovid's *Metamorphoses* (2004) and a wide range of essays on Latin literary topics. He is currently working on a commentary on Virgil *Aeneid* 12.

RICHARD THOMAS is Professor of Greek and Latin and Head of the Department of the Classics at Harvard University. His books include a two-volume commentary on Virgil's *Georgics* (Cambridge University Press, 1988), *Reading Virgil and His Texts* (1999) and *Virgil and the Augustan Reception* (Cambridge University Press, 2001). He is currently working on a commentary on Horace *Odes* 4.

LINDSAY WATSON is Senior Lecturer in Classics at the University of Sydney. He is the author of *Arae: The Curse Poetry of Antiquity* (1991), *A Commentary on Horace's Epodes* (2003) and, with P. Watson, *Martial: Select Epigrams* (Cambridge University Press, 2003).

PREFACE

I would like to thank all the contributors cordially for their hard work and good humour through the long editorial process. Contributors have of course been left free to convey their own scholarly views; there has been no imposed editorial ideological line, and attentive readers will find disagreements between contributors on such matters as translation (e.g. of the phrase *carpe diem*) and on the identity of Horace's addressees (e.g. the Albius of *Odes* 1.33 and *Epistles* 1.4 or the Vergilius of *Odes* 4.12).

I would also like to convey my warm gratitude to Michael Sharp and his team at Cambridge University Press, first for offering me the opportunity to undertake this volume and then for their kindness and patience in the course of its preparation, and to Jo Bramwell for her efficient copy-editing.

It is perhaps unusual for a volume to be dedicated to one of its contributors, but the immense contribution of Robin Nisbet to Horatian studies, the great personal and scholarly debts owed to him by the editor and several of the other contributors, and the happy coincidence of his eightieth birthday with the latter stages of this book's assembly make him its natural dedicatee.

SJH
December 2005

STEPHEN HARRISON

Introduction

This volume

The last major synoptic treatment of Horace's whole poetic output was Eduard Fraenkel's *Horace* (1957). A half-century later, the current *Companion* cannot hope to rival Fraenkel's volume in substance, individuality and consistency of vision, but its form of twenty-four chapters by twenty-one different scholars reflects the increased specialism and diversity of modern Horatian scholarship. A vast variety of topics in Horatian studies is investigated in detail in the more than one hundred items on the poet now appearing annually according to the records of *L'Année Philologique*, and it is arguably no longer possible for a single scholar to command the whole range of arguments and issues. Nor is this volume exhaustively encyclopaedic, in the manner of the splendid *Enciclopedia Oraziana* (Mariotti 1996–8), perhaps the most valuable product of the bimillennium of Horace's death, to which much reference is made in our individual chapters. This *Companion* aims to give a lively survey of the state of play in Horatian studies in the first decade of the twenty-first century in a manner which will be useful to students and scholars in other disciplines as well as to scholars working in the field of Horace.

The structure of the volume begins with 'Orientations', which set the background for Horace's poetic achievement. We commence in conventional style from the poet's biography. In chapter 1, Robin Nisbet gives us what can be known or inferred about Horace's life and career, information which is gathered almost wholly from his poems; in chapter 2, Stephen Harrison duly reminds us that poetry is not always a straightforward autobiographical source, and that Horace's self-presentation can be fantastic and conventional as well as realistic.

The second section of 'Orientations' provides an introduction to the repertoire of poetic and political knowledge needed by the modern reader in approaching Horace's work. The importance of Greek poetic models is crucial, both archaic Greek poetry in the lyric and iambic genres (treated in chapter 3 by Gregory Hutchinson) and the aesthetics of brevity and polish of the Hellenistic period (discussed by Richard Thomas in chapter 4). At the same time, Horace's context in Roman literature is also fundamentally important, both in his reactions to predecessors such as Lucilius and Lucretius and in his interactions with his contemporaries Virgil and the elegists (the subject of Richard Tarrant's chapter 5); another central contemporary interaction is that with Augustus and his political framework, both through and without the patronage of Maecenas, dealt with by Michèle Lowrie in chapter 6.

The second section of the volume looks at the individual Horatian poetic genres, beginning with chapter 7, on the early and difficult iambic *Epodes*, by Lindsay Watson. Chapters 8, 9 and 10 separate out Horace's three enterprises in *sermo*, 'colloquial' hexameter poetry – the early *Satires*, treated by Frances Muecke, the middle- to late-period *Epistles*, discussed by Rolando Ferri, and the *Ars Poetica*, usually seen as Horace's last work, here dealt with by Andrew Laird – while in chapter 11 Alessandro Barchiesi turns to the *Odes*, the middle- to late-period lyric work usually seen as the culmination of Horace's poetic career, and the *Carmen Saeculare*, Horace's only known work of public commission for the religious festival of the *Ludi Saeculares* in 17 BC, which is now receiving renewed scholarly attention.

The third and longest section looks at a range of topics and themes of particular importance in Horace's poetry. Ethics are never far from the surface in Horatian verse, and John Moles in chapter 12 surveys the importance of philosophy in general for his work, stressing the range of schools alluded to (not just Epicureanism). In chapter 13 Jasper Griffin points to the importance of gods and religious themes in Horace, arguing that the literary aspect is especially important and that the more elevated the genre the more frequent divine appearances are. In chapter 14 Peter White considers the key topics of friendship and patronage, to some extent co-extensive in the world of Horace and Maecenas, looking at the careful Horatian focus on and elaboration of social relationships as a literary theme. Gregson Davis in chapter 15 tackles the subject of wine and the symposium, showing its key relationship to Horatian value-systems and literary interests. In chapter 16 Ellen Oliensis scrutinises Horace's presentation of issues of gender and erotic desire, Horace being an elite male writing for other elite males; Oliensis stresses the general lack of significant female figures in his poetry and the largely stereotypical presentation of the objects of elite male desire. In chapter 17 Stephen Harrison treats the topic of town and country, relating it to Roman cultural systems and to philosophical ideas, and considering it as the locus of both moral virtue and proper pleasure. In chapter 18 Richard Rutherford surveys the ideas about literature and its function which form a continuous focus for Horatian poetry, especially in the *Odes* and literary *Epistles*; this is paired with chapter 19, in which Stephen Harrison shows some of the key features of Horace's own literary style, looking in detail at three poems from three different genres.

The final section presents five chapters on reception, which as elsewhere in classical studies is achieving a higher profile in contemporary scholarship; these chapters seek as a whole to give a continuous sketch of the afterlife of Horace's poetry, concentrating on English among the vernacular languages. In chapter 20 Richard Tarrant considers the reception of Horace's poetry from immediate reactions through the high Empire and late antiquity to a final coda on the Carolingian period; in chapter 21 Karsten Friis-Jensen takes up the story in the high medieval period, looking at the commentary tradition and its impact on the medieval view of Horace as well as literary appropriation in Latin; in chapter 22 Michael McGann takes us from Petrarch to Ben Jonson via Ariosto, looking at Horace's impact on poetry both in neo-Latin and in the vernacular languages in the Renaissance. Two further chapters fill out the picture: David Money (chapter 23) looks at the rich tradition of Horatianising neo-Latin in the seventeenth and eighteenth centuries in Britain, Europe and the New World, while Stephen Harrison (chapter 24) covers the impact of Horace, still at the centre of the educational system, on poetry in English (including the USA and New Zealand) in the nineteenth and twentieth centuries, with some glimpses at ongoing Horatian imitation in the twenty-first.

Bibliographical resources

Each chapter is equipped with a paragraph pointing to items of further interest on its topic, but here I list a few general bibliographical resources.

Editions, commentaries and translations currently available

[(a) *Satires*, (b) *Epodes*, (c) *Odes* and *Carmen Saeculare*, (d) *Epistles* and *Ars Poetica*]

Latin texts: all works in Shackleton Bailey (1984); (b) and (c) in Rudd (2004); (b) in G. Lee (1998). Free online texts of all the works can be found at http://www.thelatinlibrary.com/hor.html.

English translations: (a) and (d), Rudd (1979b); (b) and (c), D. West (1997), Rudd (2004); (b) G. Lee (1998)

Commentaries:

(a) Book 1: P. M. Brown (1993); Book 2: Muecke (1993)
(b) Mankin (1995); L. Watson (2003)
(c) Book 1: Nisbet and Hubbard (1970); D. West (1995). Book 2: Nisbet and Hubbard (1978); D. West (1998). Book 3: Nisbet and Rudd (2004); D. West (2002). Book 4: Putnam (1986)
(d) Book 1: Mayer (1994); Book 2 and *Ars Poetica*: Rudd (1989); Brink (1963, 1971, 1982).

Bibliography and collections of material

The massive Horatian bibliography for 1936–75 in Kissel (1981) and its supplement for the years 1976–91 in Kissel (1994) are both valuable. See also the survey of Horatian bibliography for the years 1957–87 by Doblhofer (1992). Much good material is now available on the internet (see e.g. <http://www.lateinforum.de/pershor.htm>); especially useful for recent work is the sequel to Kissel (1994), covering the years 1992–2005, published online by Niklas Holzberg in early 2006 at <http://www.psms.homepage.t-online.de/bibliographien.htm>. Very full bibliographical listings are to be found in the already mentioned *Enciclopedia Oraziana* (Mariotti 1996–8), which is always worth consulting if a copy is available.

PART I

Orientations

1

ROBIN NISBET

Horace: life and chronology

Horace says more about himself than any other ancient poet does, and our main source for his life must be his own poems. A subsidiary authority is the ancient *Vita* abbreviated from Suetonius, *De Poetis*;[1] his official posts under Hadrian enabled him to quote the correspondence of Augustus.

From Venusia to Philippi (65–42 BCE)

Quintus Horatius Flaccus was born on 8 December 65 BCE;[2] the Romans cared more than the Greeks for dates and birthdays. His birthplace was Venusia (Venosa) on the border of Apulia and Lucania (*Satires* 2.1.34–5). He recalls the mountains of his homeland (*Satires* 1.5.77–8, *Odes* 3.4.9–16) and the river Aufidus or Ofanto (*Odes* 3.30.10, 4.9.2),[3] but the ties were not to last.

Horace was the son of a freedman, though he himself was born free (cf. *Satires* 1.6.8). Moderns have speculated about Greek or even Eastern roots, but he seems to have regarded himself as a Sabellus or Samnite (*Epistles* 1.16.49, cf. *Satires* 2.1.35–6); his father had perhaps been enslaved as a result of capture in the Social War.[4] The reproach of servile origin rankled (*Satires* 1.6.45–8), but was later exploited by the poet when he wished to exaggerate the humbleness of his background (*Epistles* 1.20.20).

Horace's father was a *praeco* (auctioneer) and *coactor* (*Satires* 1.6.86–7), the middleman who provided credit for the purchaser;[5] it was a profitable business, and like other enterprising freedmen he acquired money and land (*Satires* 1.6.71). He was reluctant to send his child to the local school, which

1 Rostagni (1944).

2 For the year cf. *Odes* 3.21.1 (*consule Manlio*); for the month, *Epistles* 1.20.27; for the day, *Vita* 71.

3 For local patriotism in Italy see Fraenkel (1957) 3–4.

4 G. Williams (1995) 296–313.

5 Fraenkel (1957) 4–5.

was dominated by the hulking sons of hulking centurions (72–3), and he could afford to take him to Rome to be educated in style (76–80); there under Orbilius of Beneventum and other teachers he studied Livius Andronicus and (more agreeably) Homer (*Epistles* 2.1.69–71, 2.2.41–2). Horace gives an affectionate portrait of his father (*Satires* 1.4.105–29, 1.6.81–99), but understandably describes his moral instruction rather than his commercial capacities.

Horace next proceeded to Athens to study philosophy like Cicero's son and other members of the elite (*Epistles* 2.2.45 *inter silvas Academi quaerere verum* 'to seek Truth amid the groves of the Academy'); this was a further indication of his father's prosperity. In a city with such traditions of liberty Caesar's assassination found support, and after Brutus attended philosophy lectures in the summer of 44 BCE (Plutarch, *Brutus* 24.1), Horace joined the Republican cause (*Epistles* 2.2.46 *dura sed emovere loco me tempora grato* 'but the harshness of the times dislodged me from the agreeable spot'); youthful idealism should not be discounted, though later it proved convenient to forget it. In spite of his persistent pose of modesty and idleness, he must have impressed his superiors with his energy and efficiency, and in due course he was promoted to the high rank of *tribunus militum* (*Satires* 1.6.48). This may have carried with it equestrian rank,[6] and seems to have occasioned some jealousy among the well-born young men in Brutus' army.

In the autumn of 42 Horace fought on the losing side at Philippi, when Antony and Octavian, the future Augustus, defeated the tyrannicides Cassius and Brutus. When he says that he shamefully left his shield behind (*Odes* 2.7.10 *relicta non bene parmula*), he is imitating the insouciance of Archilochus,[7] who had abandoned his shield in much the same part of Thrace (5.2 West); and when the Republican army surrendered on Thasos, the second homeland of Archilochus, this may have given him the idea of imitating the most mordant of early Greek poets. When he mentions his part at Philippi, he is often admired for his candour; but in fact he denigrates his own commander (*Odes* 2.7.1–2 *o saepe mecum tempus in ultimum / deducte, Bruto militiae duce* 'you who were often led with me into a desperate crisis when Brutus led the campaign'[8]), and flatters Augustus (*Epistles* 2.2.47–8 *arma / Caesaris Augusti non responsura lacertis* 'arms that could not match the muscle of Caesar Augustus'), though it was really Antony who won the battle. When he says over twenty years later that he had found favour in war and peace with the first men of the city (*Epistles* 1.20.23), some see a compliment to Brutus;[9] but Philippi was not Horace's only campaign (see below).

6 Lyne (1995) 3n. 7 Fraenkel (1957) 11–12. 8 Note how *duce* picks up *deducte*.
9 Fraenkel (1957) 360.

Epodes and *Satires*

Horace obtained pardon from the victors (*Vita* 7 *venia impetrata*), but in the confiscations at Venusia (Appian *Bell. Civ.* 4.3) he lost his patrimony (*Epistles* 2.2.50–1). He says jokingly that he turned to verse because of poverty (2.2.51–2);[10] his first satires must belong to this period, 1.7 (a legal process observed by Horace in Asia) and perhaps 1.2 (a discussion of sexual relationships in the Cynic manner). Grandees like Pollio and Messalla expressed approval (*Satires* 1.10.85), and it was perhaps through their subsidies that he acquired the position of *scriba* at the *aerarium* (*Vita* 8, mentioned immediately after his pardon). The office was an important one,[11] and gave Horace a place in the world that gratified his self-esteem (*Satires* 2.6.36–7).

Apart from his early satires, Horace experimented in the manner of Archilochus with a book of *Iambi* (since late antiquity known as *Epodes*), but his ambiguous origin and new-found caution kept him from attacking important people in either genre;[12] he is content with gibes at an anonymous ex-slave who had become a *tribunus militum* (*Epode* 4), a curious way of compensating for the criticisms of himself. Yet among slighter pieces he wrote two impressive political poems, *Epodes* 7 and 16, expressing horror at the renewal of civil war, presumably the Sicilian War against Sextus Pompeius (38–36 BCE);[13] probably 7 was the earlier, as there the war has not yet begun. The pessimism of *Epode* 16 makes a striking contrast with Virgil's *Fourth Eclogue*, which is dated by Pollio's consulship to 40 BCE; some argue for Horace's priority,[14] others more plausibly for Virgil's.[15] The new Sibylline age gave Virgil his organising principle, but Horace's *altera aetas* is inexplicit by comparison and therefore probably derivative.[16] Both epodes allude to the Parthian menace; this points to a time after their calamitous invasion of Syria and Asia Minor in 40 BCE,[17] which recalled the sixth-century Persian assault on Phocaea (16.17–20). Both epodes, particularly 16, seem to be influenced by Sallust's *Histories*;[18] Sertorius' hope of an escape to the Happy Isles (Sallust *Hist.* 1.103 M) was a moral comment on the state of Rome such as

10 For early experiments in Greek verse see *Satires* 1.10.31–5; for a suggested identification with the Flaccus of *Anth. Pal.* 7.542 see Della Corte (1973) 442–50.

11 Fraenkel (1957) 14–15.

12 For criticism in the *Satires* of the unimportant see Rudd (1966) 132–59.

13 Ableitinger and Grünberger (1971) 60–4; Nisbet (1984) 2–3 = (1995a) 163–9; L. Watson (2003) 269–71.

14 Drexler (1935); Wimmel (1953).

15 Snell (1938); Fraenkel (1957) 50–1; L. Watson (2003) 486–8. For extensive bibliography see Setaioli (1981) 1753–62.

16 Nisbet (1984) 2–3 = (1995a) 163–4.

17 Grimal (1961).

18 Syme (1964) 284–6.

we find also in Horace's poem (16.41–66). If Horace is borrowing from the *Histories*, he might have met the first book by 38, but not in 41.

Horace was out of sympathy with current literary movements, whether of archaisers or of late neoterics (*Satires* 1.10.1–19);[19] but he admired the *Eclogues* of Virgil (1.10.44–5), who was no doubt one of the friends to whom he recited his poetry (1.4.73, cf. 1.10.81). Virgil had recently been taken up by Maecenas, who is not mentioned in the *Eclogues*, and now with his fellow poet Varius he introduced Horace to the great man (1.6.54–61). Horace characteristically exaggerates his bashfulness, an unlikely quality for an ambitious soldier, and eight months later, perhaps early in 37 (see below on *Satires* 2.6.40–2), Maecenas admitted him to the circle of his friends (1.6.61–2). There were practical advantages for both men in the relationship: the politician tamed a potential dissident who had shown dangerous impartiality in *Epode* 16,[20] and the poet found the encouragement, psychological as well as material, that so skilful a manipulator could provide.

Horace's first book of *Satires* derives its political interest from what it does not say. In 1.5 he describes a journey to Brundisium with Maecenas, who was on his way to negotiate the Treaty of Tarentum with Antony (37 BCE); by his literary imitations of Lucilius and his emphasis on warm friendships and trivial mishaps, Horace artfully conceals any political involvement.[21] In 1.9 he tells how a social climber tried to exploit his new friendship with Maecenas (43–60); but his indignant protests themselves show an eagerness to please (48–9 *non isto vivimus illic / quo tu rere modo* 'we don't live there in the way you think'). In 1.6, his most autobiographical poem, he gives an attractive and no doubt exaggerated picture of his simple life (104–31) as he potters around the market and asks the price of vegetables; he thus tries to avert the malice that attended his new success. The thrust of the book is ethical, and in the opening address to Maecenas (1.1) the theme of 'contentment with one's lot' is not just an expression of gratitude but a denial of larger ambitions. The book seems to have been issued about 35 or 34, before Horace's acquisition of his Sabine estate.

The epodes, similarly, become less political for a time. Horace was nearly drowned in the Sicilian War (*Odes* 3.4.28 *nec (me extinxit) Sicula Palinurus unda* 'nor did Palinurus extinguish me with Sicilian waters'); this refers to the storm that wrecked Octavian's fleet off Capo Palinuro in 36,[22] and as Maecenas was present (Appian *Bell. Civ.* 5.99) Horace was presumably in attendance, but in the *Epodes* he says nothing about it. When the tenth

19 Nisbet (1995b) 391–7. 20 Otherwise Griffin (1993) 13.

21 Griffin (1984) 197–8; Du Quesnay (1984) 39–43; Lyne (1995) 17–19.

22 Wistrand (1958) 16–17 = (1972) 304–5.

poem promises an offering to the storm-winds if Mevius is drowned, that reminds us of Octavian's dedication to the winds at Anzio (*ILS* 3279, Appian *Bell. Civ.* 5.48), but typically Horace's enemy is not a man of power but a bad poet (Virgil, *Eclogues* 3.90). When he says that Cupid keeps him from finishing his book of epodes (14.6–8), the excuse means that he is turning to the uncontroversial erotic themes (11 and 15) that were to lead to lyric.

The poems on the hag Canidia (*Epodes* 5 and 17, *Satires* 1.8) are sometimes thought to show personal acquaintanceship with low life, but the series cannot be put back to a time before success had mellowed the poet; *Epode* 3, which mentions the woman, is addressed to Maecenas, and *Satires* 1.8 begins with his renovation of the Esquiline cemetery. Horace talks as if she was a real person (*Epodes* 5.41–8, 17.23, *Satires* 2.1.48), and the ancient commentator Porphyrio alleges that her real name was Gratidia (on *Epode* 3.7); imaginative reconstructions have been attempted, but *Epodes* 5 is too gruesome to be plausible, *Epodes* 17 too literary, and *Satires* 1.8 too farcical. At *Epodes* 5.21–2, where she is described as handling poisons from Hiberia (south of the Caucasus), there is a political gibe that may help to account for her name: Canidius Crassus, suffect consul 40, a leading Antonian and bitter enemy of Octavian, conquered Hiberia in 36 (Plutarch *Antony* 34.10).[23]

The second book of *Satires* continues to dissociate Horace from the political world: the amusing discussion of satire (2.1) is in Rudd's phrase 'shadow-boxing', and the criticisms of gastronomic experts (2.4) and legacy-hunters (2.5), where the poet plays a minimal role, are not related to important individuals. In spite of his display of modesty and simplicity, as when he compares himself to a country mouse (2.6.79–117), we learn that Horace was an *eques Romanus*, perhaps as a result of his position at the *aerarium*; this is made clear when the slave Davus alludes to the poet's equestrian ring (2.7.53). At some stage Maecenas presented Horace with an estate near Licenza in the Sabine hills (2.6.1–5); this gave him not only respite from time-consuming obligations in Rome (2.6.23–39), but a continuing income from his five tenants (*Epistles* 1.14.2–3). He was now bound firmly to the regime by ties of gratitude and loyalty, an important consideration in the crisis that threatened.

It is disputed whether Horace was present at the battle of Actium in 31 BCE,[24] when Octavian defeated Antony and Cleopatra. This corresponds to the disagreement of the sources about Maecenas' whereabouts: the first

23 See Nisbet (1984) 9 = (1995a) 170–1; L. Watson (2003) 197–8.

24 In favour see Wistrand (1972) 293–351; Kraggerud (1984) 66–128; Nisbet (1984) 9–17 = (1995) 171–81. Against, Fraenkel (1957) 71–5. For further bibliography see Setaioli (1981) 1716–28.

Elegia ad Maecenatem says that he was there (45–6), but Appian implies that he was in Rome (*Bell. Civ.* 4.50). The dedication to Maecenas in the first epode reads *ibis Liburnis inter alta navium, / amice, propugnacula* ('you will go in the fast galleys, my friend, amid the towering ships' fortifications'); this is followed by protestations of loyalty from Horace, which would make a strange introduction to the book if the two men had not in fact gone.[25] *Epode* 9 purports to comment on the battle while it is going on, and provides convincing detail about how things looked to a participant. A crucial piece of evidence is 17–18 †*ad hunc*† *frementis verterunt bis mille equos / Galli canentes Caesarem* ('two thousand Galatians turned their snorting horses, singing the praises of Octavian'); here the only plausible reading is *at huc* (cited by Cruquius), for otherwise *verterunt* would mean 'turned in flight', which is incompatible with *canentes Caesarem*.[26] In that case 'hither' shows that Horace was there.

The references to Actium in *Epodes* 1 and 9 are the last datable allusions in the book, which was presumably issued about 30 BCE. The second book of *Satires* seems to have come out about the same time; there is a reference to the settlement of soldiers in 31–30 (2.6.55–6, cf. Dio 51.4.3). The same date suits 2.6.40–2, where Horace says that it is nearly the eighth year since Maecenas included him among his friends; he is looking back to the spring of 37, the date of the journey to Brundisium. We may also note 2.6.38 *imprimat his cura Maecenas signa tabellis* 'see that Maecenas stamps his seal on these writing-tablets'; this indication of Horace's new influence belongs to the time after Actium when Maecenas had charge of Italy and could use Octavian's signet-ring (Dio 51.3.6).

Odes Books 1–3

Horace may have written some of his odes before the Actium campaign of 31, as it is unlikely that the elaborate political poems of 30–27 were his first attempts. The non-political odes do not normally provide a date, but the accident with the tree seems to have belonged to the consulship of Tullus in 33 BCE (3.8.9–12);[27] this suggests an approximate timing for 2.13 and 2.17

25 Nisbet (1984) 10; Du Quesnay (2002) 19; L. Watson (2003) 56–7. Against the general view I take *ibis* to refer to the departure of the expedition (cf. Tibullus 1.3.1), not the attack at Actium (which is supposed to lie in the future), and *propugnacula* to refer to Octavian's ships, not Antony's.

26 Nisbet (1984) 12–13 = (1995) 175–6. La Penna (1963) 54 unconvincingly suggests that *huc* means 'to the side that Horace supports'.

27 Nisbet and Hubbard (1970) 244; E. A. Schmidt (2002) 259–60.

(which may carry with it 1.20). Of the political odes the poem on the Ship of State that is being swept out to sea again (1.14) best suits the period before Actium.[28]

From 30 to 27 Horace concentrated on political poems that in their sensitivity to current ideology show his increasing closeness to the regime. In 1.37 he celebrates the death of Cleopatra (30 BCE) in a way that in its virulence (9–14) must reflect the official verdict; the recognition that she was a courageous and formidable woman (32 *non humilis mulier*) does not reverse this impression. In 1.2 he eulogises the victorious Octavian with the hyperboles of Hellenistic court-poetry. In 3.4 he alludes to the demobilisation of Octavian's army (37–8) and exults over the defeated Antonians with Pindaric allegories about the Giants. In 3.6 he looks forward to the repair of the temples in 28 (as recorded in the *Res Gestae* of Augustus, 20.4); his denunciation of adultery (17–32) seems to be connected with Octavian's first attempt at moral legislation, and the laments of 3.24.33–6 with its failure.[29] In 3.3 he uses mythology to resist the creation of a secondary centre of power in Troy,[30] and in 3.5 he uses the story of Regulus to resist the ransom of the Roman prisoners in Parthia. The name 'Augustus', assumed by Octavian in January 27, is first attested in these two poems.

From 27 to 24, when Augustus was in Gaul and Spain, Horace's political allusions concentrate on foreign wars.[31] In 1.35, the hymn to Fortuna, he looks forward to the invasion of Britain (29–30) and forecasts an expedition against the Arabs (40);[32] he returns to the latter in 1.29 (the ode to Iccius), which must be connected with the campaign of Aelius Gallus in 25 or 24. At 3.8.21–2, which belongs to the spring of 25,[33] he celebrates Augustus' Spanish campaign in the previous year; he also refers hopefully to the rebellion in Parthia in 26–5 (3.8.19–20), but later shows disappointment at its failure (2.2.17–24). In his ode on Augustus' return in 24 (3.14), he greets him not as an imperious conqueror but as a beloved ruler whose illness had threatened the happiness of the poet.

Horace issued the first three books of odes together, and sent copies to Augustus (*Epistles* 1.13.2 refers to plural *volumina*). It has recently been argued that the three books appeared separately,[34] perhaps in 26, 24 and

28 Fraenkel (1957) 158; Syndikus (2001) I. 165–6.

29 Propertius 2.7.1–3, G. Williams (1962); otherwise Badian (1985).

30 Nisbet and Rudd (2004) 36–8 (against the general view); otherwise Fraenkel (1957) 267–9.

31 Nisbet and Hubbard (1970) xxx–xxxiv.

32 For Britain see Syme (1991) 386 against Nisbet and Hubbard (1970) xxviii–xxix. For Arabia, Bowman et al. (1996) 149; Hutchinson (2002) 523n.

33 Nisbet and Rudd (2004) ad loc.

34 Hutchinson (2002).

23; admittedly they show some variation in metrical practice,[35] but, though chronology seems to have played a part in the sequence of the books, there were other factors at work (for instance the alternation of Alcaics and Sapphics at the beginning of Book 2, as well as that book's particular emphasis on friendship). And there are positive objections to the theory: 1.12, which associates Octavian with the great men of the Republic, seems to belong to a later stage (see below) than the semi-divine ruler in 1.2, and 3.8 is hopeful about the rebellion in Parthia, which is over in 2.2 (unless the latter refers to an earlier rebellion).

The date of completion was probably 23 BCE, when Sestius became suffect consul; he was the recipient of *Odes* 1.4, immediately after poems to Maecenas, Octavian and Virgil, and this prominent position could be explained by his office (which is not to imply that this hedonistic poem was written for his consulship). We may also invoke 1.12.45–6 *crescit occulto velut arbor aevo / fama Marcelli* 'the fame of Marcellus grows like a tree with the imperceptible lapse of time'; though that refers not to Augustus' nephew and son-in-law but to his third-century ancestor, the association in the next line with the 'Julian star' (presumably Augustus himself) suggests a date between the young man's marriage to Julia in 25 and his death in the autumn of 23. It is also relevant that the Licinius addressed in 2.10 was certainly Maecenas' brother-in-law,[36] who was killed after an alleged conspiracy, probably in 22 (Dio 54.3.4–5); the tactful Horace would hardly have included the poem in the aftermath of so embarrassing a scandal.

Epistles Book 1

The *Odes* proved less successful than Horace had hoped (*Epistles* 1.19.35–6): he gives as reasons his isolation from the literary cliques (37–40), and jealousy of his success at the imperial court (43–4), but his austere classicism must also have been a factor. Some think the disappointment drove him from lyric poetry to verse epistles,[37] but we should not exaggerate: a poet as versatile as Horace would have wished in any case to move on to another genre. When he introduces his new book with the words *nunc itaque et versus et*

35 Alcaic lines with a short first syllable are commonest in Book 1 (Nisbet and Hubbard (1970) xl); in the third line of the Alcaic stanza the word-distribution *fatalis incestusque iudex* is much commoner in Books 3 and 4 than in 1 and 2 (ibid. xlii); *atque* (normally unelided) is much commoner in 1 than in 3 (Hutchinson (2002) 517–18).
36 The advocacy of the Golden Mean in 2.10 suits the alleged conspirator, who was associated with the Peripatetic philosopher Athenaeus; see Strabo 14.5.4, Nisbet and Hubbard (1978) 152–3.
37 Fraenkel (1957) 365.

cetera ludicra pono (*Epistles* 1.1.10) 'so now I lay aside verses and suchlike trifles', he is humorously suggesting in verse that he has abandoned all poetry, not simply lyrics, in favour of moral philosophy.

The epistles are mainly addressed to congenial and wealthy friends (5 to Torquatus, 16 to Quinctius), a poet like Tibullus (4), a scholar and schoolmaster like Aristius Fuscus (10), sometimes rising young men who could be given tactful advice (2 and 18 to Lollius, 3 to Florus, 8 to Celsus, 12 to Iccius). Horace writes to each with a calculated urbanity that reflects the social hierarchy and the manners of his new class. Maecenas still plays the dominant role, being given the programmatic opening epistle and the defence of Horace's poetry (19) before the epilogue. Most interesting is the seventh poem, where Horace refuses constant attendance on Maecenas; he writes with his usual grace and humour, but at the same time asserts his growing independence.[38]

A date is provided by the autobiographical lines at the end of the book (1.20.19–28), the so-called *sphragis* or seal: Horace says that he completed forty-four Decembers in the consulship of Lollius and Lepidus, i.e. 21 BCE. Elsewhere he mentions Tiberius' mission to Armenia in 20 BCE (1.3.1–2, 1.12.26–7) and the Parthians' submission to Augustus in the same year (1.12.27–8). He also alludes to Agrippa's final conquest of the Spanish Cantabrians (1.12.26), which is assigned by Dio to 19 (54.11.5). If that date is precise, Horace is not referring in his *sphragis* to his most recent birthday, but paying a compliment to his important friend Lollius; the young Lollius addressed in two prominent epistles (2 and 18) may well have been the consul's son.

Carmen Saeculare

Augustus returned in glory from the East in 19 BCE, and now began to take more interest in Horace. At some stage he invited him to be his private secretary (*Vita* 18–25),[39] another sign of the poet's practical abilities, but the offer was wisely declined. Augustus also invited Horace to compose the *Carmen Saeculare* to commemorate the new age (17 BCE); as the inscription in the Museo delle Terme records, *carmen composuit Q. Horatius Flaccus* (*CIL* 6.32323.149). It is suggested that after the disappointing reception of *Odes* 1–3, the perceptive *princeps* brought Horace back to his proper role;[40] and it is true that his feeling of isolation may at last be disappearing (*Odes* 4.3.16 *et iam dente minus mordeor invido* 'and now I am less gnawed

38 Fraenkel (1957) 327–39; Shackleton Bailey (1982) 52–9.
39 Fraenkel (1957) 17–18; Millar (1977) 85.
40 Fraenkel (1957) 382.

by the tooth of envy'). Yet the prosaic Augustus had less understanding than Maecenas of how a poet's imagination works, and the official phrases of the *Carmen Saeculare* (17–20) communicate his social ideals less effectively than the vivid vignettes of *Odes* 3.6.25–44.

Odes Book 4

According to the *Vita* (40–3) Augustus next commissioned poems on the victories of his stepsons, Tiberius and Drusus (*Odes* 4.4. and 4.14), and thereafter induced Horace to produce a fourth book of odes. There may be some exaggeration in this, but it is true that the new book shows the influence of the imperial court: odes celebrate not only Augustus and his stepsons (2, 4, 5, 14, 15) but the young aristocrats who are now coming to the fore,[41] notably Paullus Fabius Maximus, who married the emperor's cousin Marcia (4.1), and Iullus Antonius, who married the emperor's niece Marcella (4.2). The change of emphasis may be connected with the declining importance of Maecenas,[42] who is mentioned only at 4.11.18–20, and, though that poem celebrates his birthday, it is addressed to a fictitious Phyllis. Significantly, Horace no longer mentions his Sabine estate, which he had replaced or supplemented with a house in the more fashionable Tivoli (*Vita* 66), a place celebrated at *Odes* 4.2.30–2 and 4.3.10.

Just as in the earlier collection, some of the non-political odes may have been written early. The invitation-poem to Vergilius (4.12) was probably addressed to the poet,[43] and therefore written before his death in 19; when Horace calls him 'the client of young aristocrats' (who could supply the perfume he asks for) and speaks of his zeal for money-making, that is friendly banter (cf. *Epistles* 1.5.8) that could not have been addressed to anybody in a serious spirit. In the hymn to Apollo (4.6), Horace mentions the *Carmen Saeculare* of 17 as an imminent occasion. In 4.9 he celebrates Lollius, who lost a standard to the Sugambri in 17[44] and may have needed rehabilitation, though the exact date of the poem remains uncertain. In 16 Augustus drove this tribe back without a battle: 4.2, which predicts a triumph that proved unnecessary,[45] must certainly be assigned to that time. The introductory ode to Paullus Fabius Maximus should probably be associated with his marriage

41 Syme (1986) 396–402.

42 Lyne (1995) 136–8, 191; the decline of Maecenas is doubted by G. Williams (1990) 258–75, White (1991).

43 Otherwise Fraenkel (1957) 418n.; G. Williams (1972) 45; Syme (1986) 397 'a merchant, or perhaps rather a banker'.

44 Velleius 2.97.1; Syme (1978) 3–5, 153.

45 Dio 54.20.6; Syme (1986) 398.

to Marcia;[46] Syme puts the date about 16 BCE, when the addressee was already about twenty-nine or thirty, and, though others assign the poem to 11, his consular year, that hardly suits somebody described as *centum puer artium* 'a boy of a hundred accomplishments' (4.1.15). The important Alpine campaigns of Drusus and Tiberius (4.4 and 14) took place in 15 BCE, the return of Augustus from Gaul and Spain in 13 (4.5). The ode to Censorinus (4.8) is assigned by Williams to his consular year (8 BCE),[47] but his attempt to date the completion of the book to that time may not allow enough for the cluster of datable allusions a few years earlier.[48]

At 4.15.6–9, in listing the achievements of the Augustan age, Horace proclaims: *et signa nostro restituit Iovi / derepta Parthorum superbis / postibus, et vacuum duellis / Ianum Quirini clausit* ('and it restored to our own Jupiter the standards torn from the proud portals of the Parthians, and closed the gateway of Janus Quirini when it was free from wars'); he is usually presumed to refer to the Parthian surrender of the Roman standards in 20 BCE and the closures of Janus in 29 and 25. But it is curious that these distinct episodes should be mentioned together both here and at *Epistles* 2.1.255–6 (see the argument below); and as the two closures of Janus did not last, they hardly deserve such prominence years later. It might therefore be relevant that the *periocha* of Livy, book 141, mentions a surrender of standards in 10 BCE; Syme regards this as a mistake for 'hostages',[49] but an abbreviated account in Strabo (16.1.28), if taken literally, implies a similar date. The Parthians had captured standards not just from Crassus in 53 but from Saxa in 40 and Antony in 36 (cf. *Res Gestae* 29.2); it seems possible that the surrender of standards in 20, though much vaunted in literature and the coinage, was less than complete, and that the Parthians had prevaricated to some extent.[50] In that case Horace may be referring to the closure of Janus that was voted in 11 BCE but not enacted after Dacian incursions in the following winter (Dio 54.36.2).[51] This would provide a possible context for the appearance of Book 4 of the *Odes*, for it would be tactless to mention any closure of Janus after the latest proposal had been abandoned; the third closure recorded at *Res Gestae* 13 may not have taken place till 8 or 7 BCE,[52] unless the vote of 11 BC is meant.

46 Bradshaw (1970); Syme (1986) 403.

47 G. Williams (1972) 46.

48 S. J. Harrison (1990) 33 points to activity by Censorinus in 14–13.

49 Syme (1979b) 191–2 = (1984) 1182; (1989) 117–18 = (1991) 445–6. He was ready to put the date a little earlier than 10 BCE.

50 Syme (see previous note) cited *Epistles* 2.1.112 *invenior Parthis mendacior* ('I am found more mendacious than the Parthians'), which he explained by their deceit in diplomacy.

51 Syme (1978) 25.

52 Syme (1978) 25.

Epistles Book 2

In *Epistles* 2.2 Horace addresses Florus as the loyal friend of Tiberius Nero; hence the poem is usually assigned to about 19 BCE,[53] when Florus was with Tiberius on his mission to the East. But when Horace says, 'I told you when you left Rome that I would be too lazy to send you an epistle' (20–2), that is an odd thing to say after he had sent him *Epistle* 1.3; and when he adds an apology for not sending him the odes he had promised (24–5), this promise does not suit the gap in his lyric production between 22 and 18 BCE. These difficulties tell in favour of Stephen Harrison's suggestion that the Epistle to Florus belongs nearly a decade later, close to the Epistle to Augustus (2.1), when the association of Florus with Tiberius could have been repeated in the Pannonian campaign of 12 BCE.[54] When Horace complains that advancing years *tendunt extorquere poemata* (57), 'proceed to wrest poetry from my grasp', his profession of weariness points to the time when the renewed creativity of *Odes* 4 was drying up; as Harrison observes, he claims to have turned from poetry to more serious things, much as at the beginning of *Epistles* 1.1.

Harrison's view finds additional support at 2.2.211 *lenior et melior fis accedente senecta?* ('are you becoming gentler and wiser as old age approaches?'); here Horace is not talking to himself (as is sometimes assumed) but advising Florus to defer to his own greater experience of life (213 *decede peritis*, where *concede* might be clearer). *Accedente senecta* may be a little exaggerated, but implies that Florus will soon cease to be a *iuvenis*; at any rate he is significantly older than the hot-tempered young man of 1.3.32–4 *ac vos / seu calidus sanguis seu rerum inscitia vexat / indomita cervice feros* ('whether it is hot blood or inexperience of life that plagues you both, like wild colts whose necks have not yet felt the bridle'). When the poet warns Florus that he will be pushed aside by *lasciva decentius aetas* ('an age when frivolity is more becoming'), he suggests that Florus is now too old for the concerns of youth (women and wine), and the lyric poetry that describes them; Horace had made a similar point at *Epistle* 1.3.25f. when he advised the young Florus to put behind him the *frigida curarum fomenta* ('the ineffectual comforts for anxiety'), by which he seems to mean the lyric poetry that he has just mentioned (1.3.21).

53 Brink (1963) 184n.; (1982) 552.

54 Harrison (forthcoming, c). Horace accompanied Maecenas both in the Sicilian War and at Actium (see above); Tibullus accompanied Messalla to Aquitania (1.7.9–12) and at the start of his Eastern expedition (1.7.13–16); in the previous generation Veranius and Fabullus may have served with Piso in Spain as well as in Macedonia (Catullus 28 and 47; Syme (1979a) 300–4).

Suetonius tells us that Augustus asked Horace for an epistle (i.e. 2.1) after he had read certain *sermones* (hexameter-poems) that made no mention of himself. This seems a curious comment years after the appearance of the first book of *Epistles*, so Augustus may have been thinking simply of the Epistle to Florus (2.2); it is difficult to put the *Epistle to Augustus* after the *Ars Poetica*, as this was not included in the second book of *Epistles* (see below). Perhaps the compressed account in Suetonius (*post sermones quosdam lectos*) slightly misrepresents Augustus; he may have said 'you write to others', a tactful way of referring to Florus.

The Epistle to Augustus alludes to the *Carmen Saeculare* of 17 BCE (2.1.132–3) and the Alpine victories of Drusus and Tiberius in 15 BCE (252–3, discussed below). There seems to be significance in the opening line, *cum tot sustineas et tanta negotia solus* ('when you bear alone the burden of so many and such great responsibilities'); *solus* would have extra force after the unexpected death of Agrippa, then at the height of his authority, in March 12 BCE.[55] No decisive evidence of date is provided by 16 *iurandasque tuum per numen ponimus aras* ('we erect altars on which oaths are to be sworn to your divinity');[56] this seems distinct from the connection of Augustus' *numen* with the domestic Lares (*Odes* 4.8.34–5), and also from the connection of the Genius Augusti with the local cults of the Lares Compitales.[57]

It seems more significant that the epistle associates the Parthian fear of Rome with the closure of Janus, just like *Odes* 4.15 (see above). In a typical *recusatio* Horace says that he would have liked to celebrate Augustus' military victories (2.1.252–6): *arces / montibus impositas et barbara regna, tuisque / auspiciis totum confecta duella per orbem, / claustraque custodem pacis cohibentia Ianum, / et formidatam Parthis te principe Romam* ('forts planted on mountains and barbarian kingdoms and wars finished under your auspices throughout the whole world, and the gates that shut on Janus, the guardian of peace, and the Parthian dread of Rome in your principate'). Here *arces* refers to the Alpine campaigns of Drusus and Tiberius (cf. *Odes* 4.14.11f. *arces / montibus impositas*) and *tuis auspiciis* to their constitutional position as legates of Augustus (cf. 4.14.15f.); there can be no reference here to the campaigns of the 20s BCE. When Horace goes on to say that wars have been brought to a conclusion throughout the whole world, and refers in the very next line to the closure of Janus, these events surely belong to the same context (cf. *Res Gestae* 13, recording closures of Janus, *cum per totum imperium populi Romani . . . esset parta victoriis pax* 'when throughout the

55 Syme (1978) 173; (1989) 114 = (1991) 442.
56 Brink (1982) 553–4 thinks that the passage may point to a date in 12 BCE or after.
57 Gradel (2002) 115–39, 234–50.

whole dominion of the Roman people peace had been achieved by victories'). Just as in *Odes* 4.15, this passage seems to point to the closure of Janus that was voted in 11 BCE, and suggests that Horace issued the book before the closure was cancelled in the following year.

Ars Poetica

There has been much controversy[58] over the date of the *Epistula ad Pisones*, the so-called *Ars Poetica*; when Horace says that he is writing nothing himself (306), that points either to the gap in his lyric production from 22 to 18 or to the end of his life after *Odes* 4 (say 10 to 8). The ancient commentator Porphyrio, who is knowledgeable elsewhere on prosopography, identifies the recipient with the future prefect of the city, whom he describes as a champion of liberal studies (on *Ars Poetica* 1 *studiorum liberalium antistes*); that means Piso the Pontifex, consul 15 BCE, the son of Cicero's enemy, from whom he must have inherited the great Epicurean library at Herculaneum, and the patron of Antipater of Thessalonica. Piso was born about 48, and the sons who are associated with him in the epistle could have been of the right age (i.e. still being educated) towards the end of Horace's life; they are not attested later, but not all sons of the aristocracy achieved office, as they might prove inadequate or die young. On the other hand, if the poem is put about 18 BCE the recipient would presumably be the consul of 23, of whom no serious literary interests are attested; and if that were the date it is awkward that the poem is separated in the manuscripts from the Epistle to Florus (if the latter is given the conventional date of 19 BCE).[59] When the consul of 15 BCE returned to Rome after crushing a major rebellion by the Thracian Bessi (12–10),[60] a literary epistle would be an unpolitical tribute[61] to his broad culture,[62] much as Augustus was celebrated by *Epistles* 2.1.

Conclusion

Horace died suddenly in Rome on 27 November 8 BCE, soon after Maecenas (*Vita* 74); there is no reason to believe in the causal connection posited by sentimental biographers. Maecenas urged Augustus in his will to remember

58 Brink (1963) 239–43; but see especially Syme (1986) 379–81.

59 Brink (1982) 554–7, modifying his earlier agnosticism.

60 Dio 54.34.5–7; Syme (1986) 333–4.

61 Antipater, less subtly than Horace, wrote a conventional panegyric (cf. *Anth. Pal.* 9.428.3–4).

62 Velleius 2.98.3 comments on his combination of *vigor* and *lenitas*, his love of *otium* and capacity for *negotium*.

Horace as himself (*Vita* 17), and Horace was buried in the Esquiline cemetery near Maecenas' tomb (*Vita* 78–9). This shows that relations between the three men remained outwardly amicable (cf. Dio 55.7.1), even if Maecenas never regained his earlier influence.

Horace describes himself as short (*Epistles* 1.20.24) and fat (*Epistles* 1.4.15), and Augustus wrote to him, with the offensive candour of an emperor, *tibi statura deest, corpusculum non deest* (*Vita* 58–9 'you lack height but not a bit of body'). His hair turned prematurely white (*Epodes* 17.23, *Epistles* 1.7.26, 1.20.24). He describes himself as quick to anger but easily mollified (*Epistles* 1.20.25). Suetonius comments on his sexual intemperance (*Vita* 62), a charge no doubt derived from the poems themselves: Horace lets his Damasippus accuse him of a thousand affairs with both sexes (*Satires* 2.3.325).

Horace's origin left him with some self-distrust and a strong will to succeed: hence the paradoxes of his temperament. He was the son of a south Italian freedman, but presents himself as a model of worldly urbanity. He lacked roots in a community, but introduces to literature a new feeling for locality. He pretends to be lazy and unambitious, but shows practical ability in war and peace. He is hedonistic to an extent that his modern admirers are reluctant to admit, but proclaims the ideals of the Augustan state. His tolerant humanity had a long-term influence on European enlightenment, but he is the most brutally sexist of the Augustan poets. He assumes an air of openness, but calculates precisely how to please (note the careerism[63] commended in *Epistles* 1.17 and 18). Though it is wrong to regard him as unknowable, we must be very conscious that our knowledge of him is less than he would have liked us to think.

FURTHER READING

For studies of Horace with significant biographical detail see especially Fraenkel (1957); G. Williams (1972); Lyne (1995); vol. 1 of Mariotti (1996–8). For important discussions of chronology add Syme (1978) and (1986). See also the commentaries on the *Epodes* by L. Watson (2003), on *Odes* 1 and 2 by Nisbet and Hubbard (1970 and 1978), on *Odes* 3 by Nisbet and Rudd (2004), on the literary epistles by Brink (1963; 1971; 1982). Political and military history of the period is provided by Bowman et al. (1996).

63 For a more charitable view see Mayer (1995).

2

STEPHEN HARRISON

Horatian self-representations

The first person is prominent in all of Horace's work: *ego* and its oblique cases occur some 460 times in the 7,795 lines of his extant poetry. Indeed, the different poetic genres which constitute his output all seem to have been chosen in part because of the primacy of the poet's voice: Lucilian *sermo* with its strong 'autobiographical' element, Archilochean iambus with its 'personal' invective, Lesbian 'monodic' lyric with its prominent 'I', and epistolary *sermo* with its inevitably central letter-writer, further layered in the *Ars Poetica* with the didactic voice of the instructor. In what follows I want to consider some aspects of the poet's self-representation in Horace's work, in particular the deliberate occlusion in his poetic texts of some of the most important events in his biographical life[1] and his sometimes self-deprecating presentation of his poetic status.

The protected poet

Apart from the brief information about his schooling (*Satires* 1.6.71–88, *Epistles* 2.1.69–71), we hear little of the young Horace apart from one memorable anecdote at *Odes* 3.4.9–20:

> Me fabulosae Volture in Apulo
> nutricis extra limina Pulliae
> ludo fatigatumque somno
> fronde noua puerum palumbes
> texere, mirum quod foret omnibus
> quicumque celsae nidum Aceruntiae
> saltusque Bantinos et aruum
> pingue tenent humilis Forenti,

1 For the events themselves see Nisbet, chapter 1 above; for strategies of occlusion see e.g. Oliensis (1998).

> ut tuto ab atris corpore uiperis
> dormirem et ursis, ut premerer sacra
>   lauroque conlataque myrto,
>   non sine dis animosus infans.

I was covered by miraculous birds with fresh leaves in Apulian Vultur as a boy, when asleep tired out with games, having wandered beyond the bounds of the little villa, which was to be a matter of wonder to all those who occupy the nest of high Acerenza and the glades of Banzi and the plough-land of low-lying Forentium, so that I should sleep on with my body safe from dark vipers and bears, covered by a gathering of bay and myrtle, a child of spirit with the gods on his side.

Scholars rightly point out that such myths of miraculous preservation in deadly perils of childhood (very real in the ancient world) belong especially to stories about poets,[2] and the reader may legitimately suspect that this episode may not be wholly autobiographical. Yet the traditional form and likely fictionality of the myth is carefully counterbalanced by the reality effect[3] in the minute details of Apulian landscape: this is the only time that the reader of Horace hears about the homely communities around Venosa. Thus we find a clear combination of fantasy and realism which avoids spilling over into one or the other.

A similar technique seems to be operating in the famous encounter with the wolf at *Odes* 1.22.9–16:

> Namque me silua lupus in Sabina,
> dum meam canto Lalagem et ultra
> terminum curis uagor expeditis,
>   fugit inermem,
> quale portentum neque militaris
> Daunias latis alit aesculetis
> nec Iubae tellus generat, leonum
>   arida nutrix.

For a wolf fled from me though I was unarmed in a Sabine wood, as I was singing of my Lalage and wandering beyond my boundary-stone all free from care, such a monster as the military land of Daunus does not breed in its broad oak-groves or the land of Juba, the dry nurse of lions, produce.

Once again, we may doubt whether such an encounter actually occurred: as commentators observe, the love-struck Horace here enjoys the freedom from harm traditional for lovers, and one might add that the poet is depicted

2 See e.g. Horsfall (1998) 46, citing Lefkowitz (1981).
3 On the 'reality effect' (*effet de réel*) see Barthes (1968).

as an amusing anti-Orpheus (wild animals flee his music instead of flocking to it). But once again an element of fantasy is combined with an element of detailed realism: the incident is carefully located on Horace's Sabine estate or indeed in the wilds near it (matching the boundary-breaking of *Odes* 3.4.10), and though the wolf is implicitly compared with hyperbolic wit to African lions,[4] the reference to the 'land of Daunus' alludes to Horace's birth-region of Apulia.

A similar lack of clarity can be found concerning another incident in Horace's life, his escape from a falling tree. In the continued 'autobiography' of *Odes* 3.4, Horace names this among the three great perils of his life (3.4.25–8), while in *Odes* 2.17 it is seen as the greatest of them, from which he was saved by Faunus and the protection of Mercury, bringing in another deity whose patronage is claimed more than once (see below) for the poet (2.17.27–30):[5]

me truncus inlapsus cerebro
  sustulerat, nisi Faunus ictum

dextra leuasset, Mercurialium
  custos uirorum.

I would have been carried off by a tree-trunk collapsing on my head, had not Faunus lightened the blow, the guardian of men under the protection of Mercury.

In *Odes* 3.8, on the occasion of the Matronalia which seems to have coincided with the time of the incident (early March), he offers an annual sacrifice of thanksgiving for his deliverance, while in *Odes* 2.13 a whole poem is devoted to a curse on the tree and to imagining the trip to the Underworld so narrowly avoided. It is hard to believe that the incident is wholly fictional, and the fact that it is not mentioned in the more sober autobiographical details found in the *Satires* and *Epodes* might suggest that it may well have taken place after 30 BCE; yet the poems offer no fixed date and location for such an important event, a gap which scholars have vainly sought to fill.[6] The symbolic point of the incident (the divine preservation of the protected poet) is clearly more important than its actual place in Horace's life.

The poet at war: Philippi, Naulochus and Actium

Horace fought at Philippi in 42 BCE with the Liberators and against the future Augustus, a record which he does not attempt to conceal (cf. *Satires* 1.6.48,

4 See e.g. Horsfall (1998) 47. 5 See briefly Horsfall (1998) 46.
6 See especially E. A. Schmidt (2002a) 180–1, who dates the tree-fall to 33 BC

1.7, *Odes* 2.7, 3.14.37–8, *Epistles* 2.2.46–8,), though flattering mention is usually made of the righteous might of the other side.[7] The main account of the battle is to be found in *Odes* 2.7, judiciously framed as a welcome for a former comrade (perhaps symbolically named Pompeius) returning to Italy via a post-Actium amnesty (2.7.9–14):

> Tecum Philippos et celerem fugam
> sensi relicta non bene parmula,
> cum fracta uirtus et minaces
> turpe solum tetigere mento;
>
> sed me per hostis Mercurius celer
> denso pauentem sustulit aere . . .

With you I felt the impact of Philippi and our swift flight, shamefully leaving behind my shield, when our courage was broken and those who threatened so touched the lowly ground with their chin; but I was taken away through the enemy's ranks as I panicked by swift Mercury in a thick mist . . .

As commentators have noted, Horace gives a brief and almost mythological account of the battle, and the stress is not on his command of a legion (cf. *Satires* 1.6.48) but on his loss of his shield, which recalls the similar losses suffered by Archilochus and Alcaeus, two of Horace's poetic models,[8] and his protector is Mercury, god of poetry, removing him from the battle in a magic mist like a Homeric hero. Thus Horace's role in a crucial military event is seen through a symbolic and poetic perspective, and we are little wiser about what really happened.

In the list of three main life-dangers in *Odes* 3.4, mentioned above, the falling tree and Philippi are followed by a Sicilian incident (3.4.25–8):

> uestris amicum fontibus et choris
> non me Philippis uersa acies retro,
> deuota non extinxit arbor
> nec Sicula Palinurus unda

I, a friend to your springs and dances [Muses], have not been wiped out by the battle-line turned back at Philippi, the accursed tree or Cape Palinurus in the Sicilian sea.

This is the only allusion to this danger in Horace's poetry. It seems likely that it belongs to the period of the war against Sextus Pompey and perhaps to the campaign of Naulochus (36 BCE), in which a great storm at Cape Palinurus which did considerable damage to Caesar's ships is clearly recorded.[9] If

7 For more detail see Horsfall (1998) 46 n. 38.
8 Cf. similarly Horsfall (1998) 46.
9 See Nisbet, chapter 1 above.

Naulochus is meant here, the final position of this event balancing Philippi at the head of the list might suggest that this time Horace was accompanying the 'right' side of the young Caesar. The non-mention in Book 1 of the *Satires* of any connection with Naulochus is unproblematic, since that book is remarkably reticent about the political situation of the time.[10] But once again an event which was clearly crucial in Horace's life and perhaps significant in his recently established position as *amicus* of Maecenas (Maecenas was at Naulochus, and Horace may well have accompanied him)[11] is recorded in his poetry with tantalising obscurity.

Whether Horace accompanied Maecenas to Actium, on which his poetry gives much more evidence, has been a question much debated by scholars (see Nisbet, chapter 1 above). In the *Epodes*, published soon after the battle and written with the hindsight of Caesarian victory, Horace begins his poetry book with a promise to attend his patron to the battle, and adds to this in the book's central poem what looks like a first-hand report of the battle, both of which strongly suggest that the poet was present with Maecenas. On the other hand, *Odes* 1.37 is cast as a celebration from Rome of the victory at Actium, the capture of Alexandria and the suicide of Cleopatra: like Philippi in *Odes* 2.7, the battle is barely described, and there is no hint of autopsy. Of course, it is more than likely that Horace returned to Italy after Actium and did not go on to the Alexandrian campaign which concluded nine months later (the two are conflated in the ode), but it is surprising that he does not hint at his presence for at least part of the military proceedings he describes. The poetic need for a schematic account of the battle, and the concentration on the end of Cleopatra, here elide any overtly autobiographical reminiscence.

Poet and patron: estates and rewards

Maecenas' gift to Horace of the Sabine estate was clearly a major event in his life, which gave him both financial independence and access to the relaxed rural life which he so often desiderates in his work.[12] But this event is nowhere directly recorded in the poems, and indirect allusions are so vague that an argument has been made that Horace was never given the farm but bought it himself independently.[13]

10 Du Quesnay (1984) attempts to find more political allusions than are normally acknowledged.

11 See Nisbet, chapter 1 above.

12 See Harrison, chapter 17 below.

13 See Bradshaw (1989); Nisbet, chapter 1 above, is surely right not to doubt the gift.

One major piece of evidence usually cited is *Satires* 2.6.1–5:

> Hoc erat in votis: modus agri non ita magnus,
> hortus ubi et tecto vicinus iugis aquae fons
> et paulum silvae super his foret. auctius atque
> di melius fecere. bene est. nil amplius oro,
> Maia nate, nisi ut propria haec mihi munera faxis.

This was my wish: a measure of land not that large, with a garden and a continuous spring of water, and a small stretch of woodland in addition. The gods have done more generously and better than that. That's splendid. I ask for nothing more, Mercury, except to make these gifts truly my own.

Though his gratitude for the estate and incredulity that it is now his are clear, nowhere here does the poet thank Maecenas, who is not even addressed in the poem (though his friendship for the poet is strongly emphasised in 2.6.30–58). And though allusions to the *Sabinum* and its wine are common in odes to Maecenas and can easily be interpreted as elegantly understated thanks (*Odes* 1.9.7, 1.20.1; cf. 3.1.47, 3.4.22), the two further passages which refer to the *Sabinum* could easily be taken as general or non-committal. At *Epodes* 1.25–32, in the opening poem to Maecenas, Horace alludes only vaguely to Maecenas' generosity, though the context of landowning suggests the estate:

> libenter hoc et omne militabitur
> bellum in tuae spem gratiae,
> non ut iuvencis inligata pluribus
> aratra nitantur mea
> pecusve Calabris ante Sidus fervidum
> Lucana mutet pascuis
> neque ut superni villa candens Tusculi
> Circaea tangat moenia:
> satis superque me benignitas tua
> ditavit . . .

Gladly I will serve this war and every war in the hope of your favour, not so that my ploughs may be bound to and rest on a greater number of oxen, or so that my herds may change Lucanian pastures for Calabrian before the burning star rises, or so that my bright villa shining high up at Tusculum may touch the walls of Circe. Enough and more than enough has your kindness enriched me . . .

The comparative *pluribus*, perhaps 'more than I have now [on my estate]', is the only real clue that Maecenas' generosity to Horace has taken the form of land. Equally vague is *Odes* 2.18.9–14, which again makes the point (without direct reference to Maecenas) that Horace needs no more than he has been given already:

at fides et ingeni
benigna uena est pauperemque diues
me petit; nihil supra
deos lacesso nec potentem amicum
largiora flagito,
satis beatus unicis Sabinis.

But I have loyalty and a generous vein of talent, and a rich man seeks my company, poor though I am: I trouble the gods for nothing more, nor do I ask my powerful friend for greater largesse, rich enough with my single Sabine estate.

Again the comparative *largiora* suggests that the rich friend has already shown generosity in the form of the *Sabinum*, and the rich friend is surely Maecenas, but again the overall impression is vague and generalised. As has been recently noted,[14] Horace's indirect approach to acknowledging the gift of the *Sabinum* not only shows delicacy towards Maecenas but also serves to conceal the crudely material workings of the client/patron relationship.

The poet's fame: immortality and self-deprecation

The poet's future fame is a common topic of self-representation in the poetry of Horace's middle and later periods (the *Odes* and *Epistles*). In Book 4 of the *Odes* this topic seems especially serious, perhaps owing to the conscious closure of a poetic career and consequent concern with commemoration, but in *Odes* 1–3 and the first book of *Epistles* the poet rarely treats this theme without some form of concomitant self-deprecation, one of his most attractive self-presenting strategies.

The future fame of the poet is immediately faced in the opening *Ode* (1.1.29–36):

Me doctarum hederae praemia frontium
dis miscent superis, me gelidum nemus
Nympharumque leues cum Satyris chori
secernunt populo, si neque tibias
Euterpe cohibet nec Polyhymnia
Lesboum refugit tendere barbiton.
quod si me lyricis uatibus inseres,
sublimi feriam sidera uertice.

14 See Bowditch (2001).

> The ivy-wreath, the prize of poetic brows, causes me to mix with the gods above, and I am separated by the cool grove and the light-moving bands of Nymphs with Satyrs from the common people, if Euterpe does not hold back the pipes or Polyhymnia shun to tune the Lesbian lyre. But if you set me among the lyric poets, I will strike the stars with my head on high.

The proud boast of divine fellowship, the patronage of the Muses and the ambition to become a member of the classic canon of lyric poets are lofty ideas, but all are punctured by the sting in the tail: the poet will strike the stars with his head, an incongruously literal picture which suggests a nasty headache. As we shall see, the deflation of grand claims is a topic of these Horatian self-promotions.

Similarly two-edged is the famous picture of Horace as a swan in the final poem of Book 2 of the *Odes*. Once again air travel is at issue, and the poet begins by presenting himself as a grand poetic bird soaring immortal above earthly trivialities through the fame of his poetry (2.20.1–8):

> Non usitata nec tenui ferar
> penna biformis per liquidum aethera
> uates neque in terris morabor
> longius inuidiaque maior
> urbis relinquam. Non ego pauperum
> sanguis parentum, non ego quem uocas,
> dilecte Maecenas, obibo
> nec Stygia cohibebor unda.

> Not normal or slender is the wing on which I will be carried, a biform poet, through the clear heaven, nor will I linger longer on earth, but bigger than all envy I will leave its cities. I, the son of poor parents, I who am your guest, beloved Maecenas, shall not perish or be held by the water of Styx.

But in the two central stanzas of this poem this elevated picture is again deflated (2.20.9–16):

> Iam iam residunt cruribus asperae
> pelles et album mutor in alitem
> superne nascunturque leues
> per digitos umerosque plumae.
> Iam Daedaleo ocior Icaro
> uisam gementis litora Bosphori
> Syrtisque Gaetulas canorus
> ales Hyperboreosque campos.

> Now already rough patches of skin settle on my legs; I am being changed into a white bird on top, and smooth feathers are growing from my fingers and shoulders. A tuneful bird, swifter than Daedalus' son Icarus, I shall visit the

> shores of the moaning Bosphorus, the Gaetulian Syrtes and the Hyperborean plains.

The poetic swan here becomes jarringly literal, with the physical details of the process of metamorphosis (rough skin, white hair and feathered fingers and shoulders). It also pursues a dubious flight path: comparing oneself to Icarus is not a recipe for a safe flight (as Horace notes at *Odes* 4.2.1–4), and this perhaps doomed swan will fly not to pleasant climes but to the ship-grave of the Bosphorus, the deserts of Africa and the sterile tundra of Scythia. This is worldwide fame only of a sort; these virtually uninhabited regions are not cultured places or appreciative locales for poetry. Once again immortality is comicised.

A similar approach can be seen in *Odes* 3.30, the mirror-poem to 1.1 and in the same metre, the *sphragis* or seal-poem of the first collection of *Odes*. This begins like 2.20 with broad claims about immortality: Horace's poetic monument will be more durable than the Pyramids and last as long as Roman culture itself. But then the poem turns to more local ideas (3.30.10–14):

> Dicar, qua uiolens obstrepit Aufidus
> et qua pauper aquae Daunus agrestium
> regnauit populorum, ex humili potens
> princeps Aeolium carmen ad Italos
> deduxisse modos.

> I shall be said, where the violent Aufidus roars and where Daunus poor in water ruled over rustic peoples, to have risen to power from humble place, as the first to have brought Aeolian song to Italian measures.

In contrast with the worldwide fame (if dubiously expressed) of *Odes* 2.20, here Horace names the river and mythical king of his own birthplace: his career and rise will be famous in his minor home region, a neat inversion of the common topos that a poet's work makes his marginal home city well known (cf. e.g. Virgil and Mantua at *Georgics* 3.12–15, or Propertius and Assisi at Propertius 4.1.125–6), comically suggesting that he will be appreciated (only?) in the backwoods by local fans. Once again, grand claims are undermined by humour.

The last in this sequence of self-deprecations occurs in the seal-poem to *Epistles* 1. There the poetry book of epistles is comically compared to a slave-boy to be prostituted/sold in the market. It (the boy/book) will lose popularity at Rome and then be exported to the provinces for less discriminating use (1.20.10–13):

> carus eris Romae donec te deserat aetas;
> contrectatus ubi manibus sordescere uolgi

> coeperis, aut tineas pasces taciturnus inertis
> aut fugies Vticam aut uinctus mitteris Ilerdam.

You will be held in affection at Rome until your youthful beauty leaves you; when you begin to be soiled after fingering by the hands of the common mob, either you will go to feed the useless worms in silence, or you will run away to Utica or be sent bound to Ilerda.

Here we can see a comic version of the worldwide fame of *Odes* 2.20: the boy/book goes not to glamorous and romantic locations but as a runaway slave or chain-gang member to two marginal developing towns of North Africa and Spain, both growing under Augustus. Finally, the boy/book will be called on to describe its author to potential buyers (1.20.19–28):

> Cum tibi sol tepidus pluris admouerit auris,
> me libertino natum patre et in tenui re
> maiores pinnas nido extendisse loqueris,
> ut quantum generi demas, uirtutibus addas;
> me primis urbis belli placuisse domique,
> corporis exigui, praecanum, solibus aptum,
> irasci celerem, tamen ut placabilis essem.
> Forte meum siquis te percontabitur aeuum,
> me quater undenos sciat impleuisse Decembris
> collegam Lepidum quo duxit Lollius anno.

When the cooling sun brings more ears close to you, you will say that I, born from a freedman father and in straitened circumstances, stretched my wings wider than my nest, so that what you detract from my family descent you add to my personal virtue; that I pleased the first of Rome in war and peace, that I was of small build, prematurely grey, a sun-lover, swift to anger but easily placated. If anyone happens to ask you about my age, let him know that I completed forty-four Decembers in the year when Lollius took Lepidus as his colleague.

Here in the more relaxed environment of the *Epistles* we find clear ironisation of the grander claims of the *Odes* about its author:[15] the wings too large for the nest surely pick up and play with the poetic swan of 2.20, and the stress on Horace's actual age and birthday is an undermining of lyric claims of immortality – he is a real and ephemeral person who fits the traditional framework of Roman consular dating. This date formula which ends his epistle book amusingly echoes the kind of dating which begins the books of an annalistic Roman history, suggesting perhaps that the first book of *Epistles* is a kind of comic chronicle of his life at Rome.

15 See S. J. Harrison (1988).

Poetry renounced and regained

Finally, I want to turn to some playfully paradoxical statements in Horace's later work, where he claims in verse *sermo* that he is not writing poetry at all, and at the beginning of his return to lyric poetry in Book 4 that he is in fact returning to love. In the first two books of *Satires* the poet sees his writing of the more colloquial *sermo* as a form of poetry close to prose (*Satires* 2.6.17 *saturis musaque pedestri* 'satires and Muse that goes on foot'), and even claims that he is not a 'proper' poet (1.4.39–44):

> primum ego me illorum, dederim quibus esse poetis,
> excerpam numero: neque enim concludere versum
> dixeris esse satis neque, siqui scribat uti nos
> sermoni propiora, putes hunc esse poetam.
> ingenium cui sit, cui mens divinior atque os
> magna sonaturum, des nominis huius honorem.

> First, I shall take myself out of the number to whom I would grant the status of poet: for you wouldn't say it was enough to round off a line of verse, nor would you think that someone who writes material closer to real speech is a poet. You should give the honour of that title to the person who has a more divine spirit and a mouth that will make great words resound.

Here, then, *sermo* is not 'real' poetry, and writing in verse form is not sufficient to be a 'proper' poet; in context, the contrast is with the lofty and truly poetic language of Ennius and his ilk (1.4.56–62).

This claim is taken even further at the opening of the first book of *Epistles* (1.1.7–12):

> est mihi purgatum crebro qui personet aurem:
> 'solue senescentem mature sanus equum, ne
> peccet ad extremum ridendus et ilia ducat.'
> nunc itaque et uersus et cetera ludicra pono,
> quid uerum atque decens, curo et rogo et omnis in hoc sum;
> condo et compono quae mox depromere possim.

> I have a man who often makes my cleaned-up ear resound: 'Be sensible in time and loose the ageing horse, in case he stumbles at the end and over-puffs his sides.' Now accordingly I lay aside poetry and other baubles: the nature of truth and fitting behaviour is my concern, my quest and my whole focus; I store and set aside material to use in due course.

Here the poet claims to give up verse. *Cetera ludicra* might indicate that all that is meant is a change of genre from the more 'frivolous' but also more poetic *Odes* to the more earnest philosophical form of the *Epistles*, consistent with the contrast already seen in the *Satires* between *sermo* and 'real' poetry. This would be supported by *Epistles* 2.2.141–4:

> nimirum sapere est abiectis utile nugis,
> et tempestiuum pueris concedere ludum,
> ac non uerba sequi fidibus modulanda Latinis,
> sed uerae numerosque modosque ediscere uitae.

Clearly to be wise is useful, casting aside trifles, and to leave play to boys as fit for their time of life, and not to pursue words to be set to the Latin lyre, but to learn in full the metres and measures of true life.

But at *Epistles* 1.1.10 *versus* seems to suggest renouncing all poetry whatever, not just outgrowing the youthful delights of lyric poetry. The hollowness of this statement is immediately clear in the poem: not only is it made in an aphoristically well-crafted hexameter, but (as commentators have noted) the programme for the new 'non-poetic' project of philosophical study is cast in terms which can be easily transferred to poetry: *condo* and *compono* are verbs which apply not only to the storage of philosophical wisdom but also to the composition of 'full' lyric verse (*Epistles* 1.3.24 *condis amabile carmen*, 2.2.91 *carmina compono*).[16]

The contrast between *sermo* and real poetry returns in *Epistles* 2.1. There, afflicted by a fashionable poetic fever among ordinary Romans, Horace is tempted to return to the lyric poetry he has left (2.1.109–13):

> pueri patresque seueri
> fronde comas uincti cenant et carmina dictant.
> Ipse ego, qui nullos me adfirmo scribere uersus,
> inuenior Parthis mendacior et prius orto
> sole uigil calamum et chartas et scrinia posco.

Boys and their strict fathers dine with garlands girding their heads and recite poetry. I myself, who proclaim that I write no verses, am found to be a bigger liar than the Parthians and, up before sunrise, demand pen, paper and book-boxes.

Here again it seems difficult to take literally the claim to write no verse: as in *Epistles* 1.1, *uersus* are what Horace is writing here in this elegant *sermo*. The same is true in the *Ars Poetica*, when (306) he undertakes to teach in verse how to be a poet though 'writing nothing myself' (*nil scribens ipse*). In his later *sermones* Horace is clearly playing with the idea of 'poet': in one sense he has renounced traditional poetry, especially the lyric poetry for which he is renowned, and returned to the 'unpoetic' verse of *sermo*, but

16 See Mayer (1994) ad loc.

that renunciation is itself made in elegant verse which exploits poetic devices such as ambiguous metaphor.

An analogous playfulness about Horace's poetic activity is found in the famous prayer which begins *Odes* 4 (4.1.8):

> Intermissa, Venus, diu
> rursus bella moues? Parce precor, precor.
> non sum qualis eram bonae
> sub regno Cinarae. Desine, dulcium
> mater saeua Cupidinum,
> circa lustra decem flectere mollibus
> iam durum imperiis: abi,
> quo blandae iuuenum te reuocant preces.

Are you starting again the wars that have long been in abeyance, Venus? Spare me, spare me, I pray. I am not the man I was under the sway of the good Cinara. Cease, cruel mother of the sweet Cupids, to steer me at the age of some fifty years, already hardened to the bit of your commands; go away to where the charming prayers of young men call you.

This passage presents the poet as entering again the wars of love, using the familiar elegiac conceit of *militia amoris*. This is a heavily misleading programme for this final book of *Odes*: though at the end of this poem Horace professes a passion for the boy Ligurinus, who is again addressed in a brief poem of longing in 4.10, and two further poems allude to erotic elements (4.11 invites the *hetaira* Phyllis to a party, and 4.13 addresses Lyce, grown too old for love), his final book of *Odes* centres on issues of his own poetic status after the *Carmen Saeculare*, on the commemoration of great deeds, especially in war, and on celebrating Augustus and his dynasty. Even this opening poem's interest in erotic matters can be seen as politically significant: Horace asks for Venus to go to the house of the young Paullus Fabius Maximus, who as has been persuasively argued was probably just about to marry Marcia, Augustus' cousin.[17] The return to the world of the *Odes* as the world of love is only apparent: though the pederastic passion for Ligurinus might return Horace to his lyric persona as the Roman Alcaeus, paralleling Alcaeus' passion for the dark-eyed boy Lycus (*Odes* 1.32.11–12), the *hetaira* Cinara is not a figure from the *Odes* but is used by Horace in his later poetry to represent the erotic passions of his youth (*Odes* 4.13.21, *Epistles* 1.7.28, 1.14.33). Once again the poem is playing with its readership: the expected return to the lighter concerns of the earlier collection of *Odes* 1–3 is partial at best, and while making a gesture of return to his earlier

17 See Bradshaw (1970); and Nisbet, chapter 1 above.

concerns *Odes* 4.1 is actually subtly suggesting the different tone of the last lyric book.

Thus we see that in various different types of self-representation, Horace combines strategies of ambiguity and obfuscation, self-deprecation and humour, playfulness and misdirection. The works of one of the most apparently autobiographical poets of antiquity in fact provide a carefully nuanced and often amusingly misleading series of self-presentations, which both exercise and entertain his readership.

FURTHER READING

The traditional biographical approach to first-person statements in Horace is exemplified in Fraenkel (1957), though he is duly sceptical about the information of the ancient biographical tradition on the poet; Fraenkel's line is continued by Levi (1997). Much recent work is more nuanced, arguing that such statements are influenced by rhetorical and poetical strategies of various kinds (G. Davis (1991); Oliensis (1998); E. A. Schmidt (2002a)), and must be treated with suitable scepticism from the biographical perspective (see especially Horsfall (1998), whose approach is close to that taken here). Discussions of the use of 'I' in the Greek lyric tradition which Horace uses in the *Odes* have yielded similar complexities – see e.g. Lefkowitz (1991) and Slings (1990), as have discussions of the first-person voice in Roman satire for the *Satires* – see e.g. Anderson (1982) and the discussion by Muecke in chapter 8 below.

3

GREGORY HUTCHINSON

Horace and archaic Greek poetry

Introduction

Horace proclaims explicitly his use of Archilochus and Hipponax in the *Epodes* and of Alcaeus (seventh, sixth and sixth centuries BCE respectively) in the *Odes* (*Epodes* 6.13–14, *Odes* 1.32, *Epistles* 1.19.23–33). But the relationship of these works to archaic Greek poetry is not easily grasped. They are less closely and pervasively engaged with that poetry than the recently published *Eclogues* are with Greek bucolic; and they discuss their relation to their 'models' less explicitly than the *Satires* do. Is broad difference from the Greek poets significant divergence, or a sign of their relative unimportance? Such questions are trickier because these poets mostly survive in fragments.

The primary aim here is not to compare archaic Greek poetry with Horace, as we perceive both, but to see what function the Greek poetry and ideas of it possess within the Horatian works.[1] Points should be made on both source and target texts. The relevant Greek material is not just naked fragments in neat modern editions. Papyri show abundant metatexts to archaic poetry in circulation: commentaries, lives, treatises.[2] Such works would hardly be ignored, as Horace's evidence confirms, by someone planning to conquer a Greek genre. Scholia – with a marked interest in biography – frequently appear in the margins of lyric texts.[3] Papyri and other material show us things no less essential than fragments: poets' lives, images, critical reputations, the placing of their poems in Hellenistic editions.

1 There is not space here for close textual analyses, or the pursuit of wider contexts.

2 So P. Oxy. 2306–7, 2733, 3711 (all Alcaeus), 2176, 2293, 3722, P. Köln 61; P. Oxy. 1800, 2438; P. Hibeh 173 (3rd cent. BCE), P. Oxy. 2506.

3 So P. Oxy. 1234 + 1360 + 2166 (*c*) (Bod. MS Gr. class. a. 16 (P); 2nd cent. CE; wide margins between columns left by writer of text; Alcaeus), 2387 (1st cent. BCE/1st cent. CE; scholia in various hands), P. Louvre E. 3320/R56 (1st cent. CE; mostly same hand as text), P. Berol. 9569 (*BKT* v(2)3–6; 1st cent. CE; same hand as text; Alcaeus).

Horace's own works are best approached as books of poems with a shape and a strategy, not just as individual poems collected together. Recent scholarship demonstrates the value of so viewing the *Epodes*.[4] But each book of the *Odes* too, even if 1–3 were first published simultaneously, needs to be considered as a distinct entity.[5] It will be shown how each of Horace's books uses archaic poets differently, how each deploys them to fashion an identity and create its own significant structure.

Epodes

Archilochus and Hipponax were the main archaic iambic authors; Archilochus supposedly invented the iambus (cf. *Ars Poetica* 79). Horace annexes the whole archaic literature of the genre, by pointing to both as models (*Epodes* 6.13–14), and marking a special connection with the founder (he avoids Hipponax's metrical hallmark, choliambic lines, lines with 'dragged' end).[6] He goes beyond the Hellenistic poets, who had concentrated on reworking Hipponax. They, however, dramatise the idea of revival: Hipponax appears in a dream or as a ghost (Herodas 8, Callimachus fr. 191 Pfeiffer). Characteristically, the *Epodes* do not present their annexation so directly.

Horace later claims to have followed Archilochus' *numeros animosque*, 'metre and spirit' (*Epistles* 1.19.24–5). The emphasis on metre is notable; and *animos* discourages us from finding in the *Epodes*' narrator a straight anti-Archilochus like Callimachus' peaceable new Hipponax. It will emerge, though, that these two aspects, *numeros* and *animos*, lead in divergent directions.

Archilochus and Hipponax were both famed for anger. Archilochus also seems to invite the listener's admiration or interest for his toughness, bravado and Achillean independence. Hipponax invites amusement at himself. But anger is their crucial feature for Horace.

Their works were divided by metre. Archilochus (in more than one book?): elegiacs, trimeters, tetrameters, epodes (couplets as written in papyri); Hipponax: at least two books of iambi, perhaps at least one further book, maybe including epodes.[7] All but the last of Horace's poems are epodes. Even so there is division by metre: the same all-iambic combination for

4 So Heyworth (1993); A. Barchiesi (2001a); S. J. Harrison (2001a).

5 Argument for successive publication: Hutchinson (2002).

6 Usual in Hipponax's stichic iambic trimeters (contrast Horace, *Epode* 17) and trochaic tetrameters, but not in his epodes. Callimachus makes the first line of the couplet in *Iambus* 5 choliambic.

7 P. Oxy. 4708 now throws some light on the scale of Archilochus' elegiac poems.

1–10; an explosion of new metres, with dactylic elements, in 11–16; stichic iambi (not couplets) in 17. Callimachus' *Iambi* inspire the plain close, and the movement to new metres after the earlier poems.[8]

P. Oxy. 2310 (Archilochus) seems to collocate unconnected iambi. Related epodes appear together in P. Köln 58, but this need not be by design: the epodes dwelt so much on Lycambes and his daughters (one was promised to Archilochus in marriage). It remains notable that the *Epodes* usually avoid placing the same subjects – including politics – consecutively. This is part of their indirectness, in particular as regards narrative.

Narrative had been very important in Hipponax and Archilochus, particularly Archilochus' epodes.[9] Horace here differs strongly, on various levels (including intensity of characterisation for the speaker). How pointed this difference is is shown by animal fables, especially associated with Archilochus' epodes, and used in Callimachus' *Iambi*, and Horace, *Satires* 2.6. Their absence from the *Epodes* is stressed by vestigial comparisons with animals (so *Epode* 6). No *Epode* is straightforwardly narrative; 9 tells of Actium, allusively, 5 of a human sacrifice (it is more like a mime).

Archilochus' epodes included at least one erotic narrative on Lycambes' daughters (fr. 196a). The Lycambes story, recurrent in his poetry, was expanded by biography into a further sensational narrative, with the suicide of the daughters (cf. *Epistles* 1.19.31).[10] The *Epodes* which deal with love and sex offer only fragments of multiple and frivolous stories. The broken oath of 15 is merely a lover's oath; the older woman of 8 and 12 is frustrated, not suicidal. Archilochus' corpus and tradition alike created a super-narrative of his life.[11] Horace's earlier *Satires* Book 1 had been full of biography, and dwelt on the narrator's status and circumstances; the *Epodes* touch on these very little.[12] They are post-Archilochean and oblique.

Instead of narrative and biography, the book as a whole offers a more self-reflexive and metaliterary sequence; here poetry, and relation to the model, and the character of the narrator are combined. Poem 1, like many prologues, both introduces and misleads. We see possible links with Archilochus, but also a considerably modified narrator: not much of a fighter, though willing to accompany his friend to war, and friendly rather than (as in the stereotype of Archilochus) angry and abusive. The first part of the book seems to tease us on its relation to Archilochus; it works towards a trademark outburst of

8 Marked in PSI 1216 by two long lines in the right margin.

9 Cf. Bowie (2001); note also Archilochus P. Oxy. 4708 (myth in elegiacs).

10 On the story and the poetry cf. Carey (1986); C. G. Brown (1997) 50–71.

11 The move from Paros to Thasos will have been crucial for readers of the book(s).

12 Note poverty (11.11); birth-year (13.6, cf. P. Oxy. 2438).

rage. Poem 2 sounds content – but turns out to be spoken by someone else (itself an Archilochean trick). Poem 3 shows mock anger, with Maecenas, on garlic. Much of 4, a brief attack on an unnamed person, is spoken by others. Poem 5 culminates in a verbal attack on the witch Canidia by a character. Poem 6 briefly threatens an attack, and finally mentions (periphrastically) Archilochus and Hipponax: the announcement of the model is delayed, as in the *Eclogues* and *Satires* Book 1, but also achieved.

Poems 7–10 offer Archilochean material (speech to citizens, insults to a woman, battle). In 7 the speaker is impressive; in 8 his impotence appears understandable, the affair sordid. Poem 10 at last offers a full-scale attack, based on an epode probably by Hipponax (fr. 115). The moment is climactic; the enemy is even named. But the cursing discloses no misdeed or story; the reader of the *Eclogues* (3.90–1) takes Maevius' crime to be writing bad poetry. We are in a metaliterary world.

We should be struck by the poet's metrical achievement in 1–10. The couplets of iambic trimeters and dimeters in all ten poems create a special combination of craft and incisive vigour, new to Latin and remote from satiric hexameters. It is particularly potent when depicting anger. It produces a powerful, if elaborately polished, equivalent to Archilochean force; it gives an overwhelming sense of authorial control.

Poems 11–16 explore aspects of Archilochus less apparent before: the narrator's sexual desire (11, 14–15); wisdom and drink (13). The ageing woman (12), the oath (15), the proposal to move city (16), have specific Archilochean associations (fr. 102, 188, etc.). In 11–15 and 17 the narrator now appears weaker and less acceptable. Poem 11, in the metre of Archilochus' narrative of suave seduction (fr. 196a), presents this narrator's passive amorous susceptibility – with self-conscious humour. Poem 12 suggests, through a character's Archilochean direct speech, the narrator's heartlessness: even 'old hags' have a point of view. In 11 and 14 love stops the feeble narrator from writing poems; it was a relative's death that made Archilochus claim that he was not interested in poetry (fr. 215).[13] Poem 16, with the narrator as prophet (*uate* 66), is deflated by 17. In 17, the narrator, afflicted by the witch Canidia, humiliatingly and vainly offers to retract his attacks.

Yet the mention of poetry points to contradictions in 11–17: the narrator *has* finished his book, the reader knows, nor can we swallow (in a poem)

13 In my view L. Watson's somewhat different understanding of *Epode* 11.1–2 (it is writing love-poetry that no longer appeals) suits rather less well the plausible connections with *Epode* 14 and with Archilochus fr. 215, and gives rather less point to the emphasis at the end on friends' advice and stopping love. This narrator does not need to be consistent with his behaviour two years ago. Cf. L. Watson (1983); (2003) 358–60, 363–4.

his lack of interest in poetry. This accentuates a drastic contrast: the good-for-nothing narrator is formally identified (note 15.12) with the poet so brilliantly handling in 11–16 a whole series of metres new in Latin. He mentions his distaste for poetry at the start (11.1–2), in a notably complex three-period metre. Poems 12–16 all begin their 'couplets' with hexameters: Horace is displaying his metrical and poetic range, invading contemporary elegy and the recent *Eclogues*. Callimachus' epodes have no dactylic elements. Poem 17, like 5 using Canidia from the *Satires*, emphasises range beyond this book: stichic iambics besides stichic hexameters. The author's actual command of his creation is apparent in the whole fiction of 17 (including Canidia's closing speech, which ends with the word 'end').

The structure of the book in content and in metre diverges. The result is both humorous (on the level of content) and self-assertive (on the level of art).

Odes Book I

Odes 1 advances beyond the *Epodes*. Horace takes on a more complex tradition. 'Archaic lyric' covers a multitude of dialects, metres and subjects, and various modes of performance. Somewhat as in the *Epodes*, Horace wishes both to encompass the whole tradition, and to appropriate the genre through one paradigmatic author: Alcaeus. The Lesbian poets Alcaeus and Sappho (sixth century) appear from papyrus the most-read lyric poets, apart from Pindar (fifth century), commonly regarded as supreme. When Horace refers to 'Lesbian' poetry in Book 1, he might seem to be modelling himself on both Alcaeus and Sappho. But in 1.32 he connects his tradition specifically with Alcaeus; Alcaeus there embodies amatory as well as symposiastic lyric. Seven poems are known to base themselves ostentatiously on Alcaeus (9, 10, 14, 18, 22, 32, 37), and one on Sappho (13).[14] Yet Horace pushes his distance from his exemplar further than in the *Epodes*.

Alcaeus probably presented himself as Archilochus' successor in activities, ethos and violent emotion (though without Archilochus' dashing charisma). Synesius, *Insomn.* 20, links them in the close relation of poetry and life.[15] Alcaeus' predominant subject-matter was political: he himself, with his brother, was a prime player in Mytilenean politics. In his papyri, some collocations of political poems could be by chance; but sometimes, at least, editors

14 *Odes* 1.31.17–20 (cf. *nec cithara carentem* 20) may more lightly allude to – and contrast with? – Sappho P. Köln Inv. 21351 + 21376.9–20 + P. Oxy. 1787 fr. 1 + 2.10–25 (Gronewald and Daniel (2004a, b), M. L. West (2005)); but the Alcaean lyre emphatically takes over in 32.
15 Cf. Susanetti (1992) 183–4.

have deliberately placed together poems on the same aspect or period of his life (so P. Oxy. 2165, or 2306 with 2734 fr. 6). Notes, commentaries, treatises show that reconstructing his life particularly interested scholars (e.g. scholion on fr. 114; P. Oxy. 2506 fr. 98).[16]

Poem 32 contrasts Alcaeus' turbulent life with the narrator's own inactive existence. This underlines both the slightness of implied narrative about the narrator, and the positive role of that slightness in characterisation. It suits the presentation of this relaxed, middle-aged and supposedly unimportant person that he has nothing to do, and nothing happens to him. Horace is not continuing the anger of Archilochus, Alcaeus and the *Epodes*, as 1.16, in the middle of the book, explains: he is older and gentler and renounces anger and *iambi*.[17] Even in the past, the main events were love-affairs somewhat more intense than his present ones: so 1.5, significantly presented as an allegorical shipwreck – Alcaeus experienced real storms.[18] The present love-affairs push a Sapphic world of shifting attachments towards a humour and a depiction of the ageing male that evoke the self-irony of Anacreon (sixth to fifth centuries). Bereavements, warfare, illness happen to others. Changes of place were crucial to the events, and scholarly reconstruction, of many lyric poets' lives; this book is full of journeys, but they are other people's. The narrator stays put, in retreat but not in exile.[19] There is a philosophical aspect to this quietude, but it is lightly borne.

Let us return to the concerns of the book with its own literary procedures and status. Horace is not really a one-man band, playing all the instruments of lyric: he has transcribed pieces for different instruments on to one. Metrically all is turned into four-line aeolic stanzas. Horace is advancing from the couplets of the *Epodes*, and their range of metrical forms. He had important predecessors: Theocritus adapted aeolic metres (but not in stanzas), the Neoterics used aeolic stanzas (but simpler ones, the Sapphic stanza apart). Sappho's Hellenistic books had been organised by metre – an indication of its perceived importance; mostly, this book juxtaposes

16 For ancient commentary on Alcaeus, see Porro (1994). Liberman (1999) i.xlviii–lx effectively rebuts the firm division which Pardini (1991) posits in the standard edition between poems that touched on strife in Mytilene and those that did not. Probably the nature of Alcaeus' poems made some groupings natural but tight separations between types difficult.

17 This palinode neatly brings in the lyric Stesichorus (6th cent.): fr. 192.

18 Allegory itself is often remarked on in lyric papyri (Alcaeus fr. 306 i col. i, Pindar fr. 6a (g) schol., P. Oxy. 3722 fr. 20.8). 1.14 uses Alcaean allegory to be inscrutable about the narrator's past.

19 Poem 22, beginning from Alcaeus fr. 130b.1 (Burzacchini (1976, 1985)), makes exile notional, irrelevant and Sapphic.

different metres, as usually occurs (perhaps undesignedly) in papyri of Alcaeus.[20]

Horace's book is structured by various displays and links to archaic poetry. The end of 1.1 hopes he may join the lyric canon, but suggests, more ambitiously, that he is embracing it all. Poems 1–9 of Book 1 are all in different metres: this display of range culminates in 1.9, with the first *Alcaic* stanza (Alcaeus' favourite) and the first prominent imitation of Alcaeus.[21] We may compare the final arrival of the *Epodes* at Archilochus and Hipponax in poem 6, and the full imitation (if there are none earlier) in poem 10.

Most of 1.9–23 begin from lines of, or otherwise conspicuously imitate, numerous poets: predominantly Alcaeus, but also Sappho, Pindar, Anacreon and others.[22] Having shown metrical range, Horace is now showing the range of his generic re-creation. Poem 12 starts from Pindar, the model of sublimity, and treats not one occasion but all Roman history; 15 presents myth and 'anterior' narrative, based on Bacchylides (fifth century); 21 evokes choral poetry. Poems 12 and 15 undermine Horace's overt limits of subject-matter: in 6 he eschewed epic and (despite Alcaeus) war.

Metrically, the last part of the book stresses Lesbian poetry: all but three of 25–38 are in the archetypal Alcaic and Sapphic stanzas (the latter popular with both Sappho and Alcaeus). Explicitly, too, Horace speaks of his Lesbian plectrum (1.26.11), and compares himself with Alcaeus (1.32): their lifestyles contrast, but their works are alike to endure. This emphasis on Alcaeus *after* 1.9–23 shows that the specific allegiance is no artistic limitation: it sets the seal on Horace's unification of an unwieldy tradition. One final imitation of Alcaeus (1.37) shows Horace actually rising above his model: starting from Alcaeus' poem on the death of a Mytilenean tyrant (fr. 332), he paints the war with Cleopatra, which involves vast spaces and world events. That rise is played with in the short final 1.38, which dismisses *Persicos . . . apparatus* (Persian armies as well as pompous parties).[23] Poem 37 also takes up 1.2, an apocalyptic poem about recent history, on the margins of the book. Horace's scope again exceeds that of Alcaeus.

20 See P. Oxy. 1234 fr. 1 + 1360 for the same metre consecutively. Cf. Pardini (1991) 260–6. P. Köln Inv. 21351 + 21376 (early 3rd cent. BCE) presents two poems of Sappho in the same metre; a different poem preceded the second in the standard Hellenistic edition (cf. P. Oxy. 1787 fr. 1 + 2.1–9). The new papyrus is not itself an edition of Sappho, the third poem suggests; but it may draw on a metrically arranged edition (even so, it could have excerpted poems that were not consecutive).

21 The name 'Alcaic': Lyne (1995) 98–9. See now Lyne (2005a).

22 Cf. Lowrie (1995). Note how Theocritus 28 begins with a phrase from Alcaeus fr. 129.26.

23 Choerilus of Samos wrote an epic on the Persian Wars (fr. 1–6, 8 Radici Colace, *SH* 314–23); cf. Man. 3.19–21. See further Cody (1976) ch. 1; Fowler (2000) 259–60.

As in the *Epodes*, depreciation of the narrator through the Greek model conflicts effectively with artistic self-assertion. Here, however, the combination possesses ironic charm, all the greater for the paraded achievement.

Odes Book 2

Unlike the *Epodes* and *Odes* 1, *Odes* 2 displays the contrary of range – though its new approach to the genre on a larger view exhibits fresh invention.

Metrically, it restricts variety. Poems 1–11 alternate Sapphic and Alcaic stanzas; 13–20 are all in Alcaic stanzas, with two exceptions (one Sapphic, one other). Poem 18, like 12 not in Sapphic or Alcaic stanzas, begins from conspicuous imitation of a Greek poet (Bacchylides fr. 21): this too is a rarity in Book 2, even for Alcaeus (2.5 is close to Anacreon fr. 417).

Explicit statements on genre and models are few. Poem 1, like 1.2, gives a sweeping vision of recent history, with author and events exceeding Alcaeus; but at the end this is supposed not to suit Horace's Muse, now directly defined as playful and light (*procax*, *leuiore*). Such dirges are said to be for Simonides (sixth to fifth centuries): a disjunction is made within the lyric tradition. In fact 2.2 and 3, and much of the book, are far from light. Poem 13 imagines how Horace might have seen Sappho and Alcaeus in the underworld, had he died. One could suppose both are his models; but Alcaeus seems preferred. The book does not proceed to Alcaean political themes; but the predominance of Alcaics begins here, and love-poetry disappears. The preoccupation with death recalls a symposiastic poem of Alcaeus (fr. 38a). This is a more sombre and moralising version of lyric.

A little more narrative interest accumulates around the narrator. We learn more of his past: his poor parents (2.20.5–6), his fighting at Philippi against Octavian (2.7). His abandonment of his shield connects him to Alcaeus (fr. 401B); mock myth (rescue by Mercury) restores him to his present static repose. He has had a wearying life of travel and warfare (2.6.5–8): this recalls a poem by the ageing Alcaeus (fr. 50). His present age is precisely marked (2.4.21–4), and adds biographical humour to the notional uncertainty in poems 4–12 as to whether he can still experience love; once this is resolved, the theme ceases.

Much more important is a topic also linked with the biography of lyric poets: Horace's death. Many lyric poets were assigned spectacular deaths (Sappho: suicide for love; Pindar: death in his lover's arms; Anacreon: choking on a grape-pip).[24] We have 'almost-scenes' of death escaped, one at

24 E.g. Menander fr. 258 Körte; Valerius Maximus 9.12. *ext.* 7–8.

Philippi (above), one more akin to Anacreon's apt demise.[25] The country-dweller (a motif elaborated in this book) was nearly hit on the head by a falling tree (2.13). The deceased Sappho and Alcaeus (2.13.21–40) invite us to see here a parodic lyric death. There will be an unspoken contrast with Sappho's end. There is also a contrast, taking up 1.32, between Alcaeus' life and the narrator's present life: the narrator knows 'hard pains of war' no longer.

Contemplation of the poet's death also deepens the treatment of death in the whole book. He imagines himself dying in quiet retirement: Septimius will weep at this poet's death (*uatis* 2.6.24). He talks about his own death in consoling Maecenas (2.17). His preaching universal death includes himself – save that at the end, with a humorous twist, he escapes death precisely as a poet. His turning into a bird evokes the self-comparisons of lyric poets (Alcman, Pindar, Bacchylides).

The structure of the book moves it into greater severity, a movement connected with Alcaeus' success (in 2.13). Though the book is more distant from the archaic poets, they enter emphatically in the middle, and shape its concerns.

But 2.19, like 2.20, relaxes the austerity. It is a hymn, the first in Book 2; the narrator has seen Bacchus. Alcaeus' first book had begun with hymns (fr. 307–8, 343, S264 Page); Sappho's began with her encountering Aphrodite (fr. 1). Poem 19 is a quirky one, with the narrator as a ludicrous bacchant. But Horace, like Bacchus, is less limited to *ioci* (fun) than might be thought (2.19.21–8).

Odes Book 3

Book 3, unlike 1, does not abound in obvious imitations, and unlike 1 or 2 does not talk about individual poets; but archaic poets and poetry produce another structure.

The narrator's relation to Alcaeus and Sappho gains further twists, especially as regards audience. The narrator sings to boys and girls (3.1.4); this suggests primarily a development of the role of Sappho, as seen by scholars: a teacher of the noblest girls, approved by the city (S261A fr. 1).[26] But distance from Sappho is marked by the revolted depiction of girls' education

25 Almost-scenes: Nesselrath (1992).

26 Singing 3.1 itself (and beyond) suggests more than just training a chorus. Contrast *Epistles* 2.1.132–8, etc. Of course Sappho is relevant to that conception too (notably so at *Odes* 4.6.31–44); see P. Köln Inv. 21351 + 21376.13–14 (n. 14 above); Battezzato (2003) 37–40. Cf. with *Odes* 3.1.3 Sappho fr. 150?

in dancing and love (3.6.21–4). The narrator's public importance rises: he sings for Augustus (3.4.37–40), and addresses the Roman people (*Romane* 3.6.2, *o plebs* 3.14.1; cf. also 3.24). Even Alcaeus addresses the Mytileneans (cf. scholion on fr. 74) more rarely than he does his comrades.[27]

Augustus has a more dominating presence in this book (thanks to his returning, and approving Horace).[28] In both 3.4 and 3.14 the praise of Augustus is linked with a reminder that Horace had fought against him; he had had parties *not* in celebration of him.[29] We could contrast the 'tyrant' Pittacus – once Alcaeus' ally, then his enemy and his target. Horace, no longer fighting, sings to relax the fighter, and celebrate his return. This is another reworking of the Alcaean role: relaxing his comrades, celebrating his brother's return from fighting in the East (fr. 48, 350).

Poem 9 shows a lighter side of Alcaeus and the narrator, after 1–6: Alcaeus in love with Sappho (cf. the spurious Sappho fr. 137).[30] In 3.27 the narrator, like Sappho, bids a lover farewell. At 3.29.62–4 Horace depicts himself, like Alcaeus, as a sailor in a storm, to be rescued by the Dioscuri (cf. Alcaeus fr. 34, S286 col. ii.1); but the storm is purely notional. In 3.4 the poet actually sketches his biography, now including the tree-crisis (cf. 2.13). A fabled childhood incident links him especially to Pindar (Aelian *VH* 12.45). The rhetoric of the sketch stresses divine aid (cf. Simonides fr. 510 Page); but he appears as a small-scale figure, contrasting with the mighty Augustus. He has no warfare to finish, except warfare with girls; his farewell to such arms (3.26) unconvincingly closes a slender life-story.

In metre, the book begins, like Sappho's first three or four books and *Epodes* 1–10, with poems all in the same stanza, Alcaic (1–6): the opposite extreme from Book 1. It then opens into a range of metres, before settling (17–29) into alternations of *three* stanzas (Alcaic, Sapphic and another); it ends with the same quasi-stichic metre as 1.1 (cf. *Epode* 17). The pattern marks the crucial shift in the book after 6. It also emphasises Alcaeus.[31]

Book and narrator descend after 1–6 (he is nicely cynical in 7); the conspicuous imitation of Alcaeus on female passion in 12, like 9, marks the change. The structure resembles the *Epodes* as regards metre and the narrator: but here the point is neither metrical virtuosity nor deflation. One point is to show, in 1–6, how notional are the boundaries confining the world of the *Odes*. Poem 3, after a long speech by Juno, is declared unsuitable to Horace's

27 Another audience in Book 3 are the addressees of hymns: cult, a vital theme of lyric, now bulks larger. These addressees stress the narrator as poet, drinker and country-dweller.

28 Cf. *Epistles* 1.13. 29 *Odes* 3.14.27–8; cf. 2.7.6–8.

30 For the early origin of this notion, cf. Hutchinson (2001) 188.

31 Poems 1–6 apart, Alcaics open and close 17–29; 29 is particularly long.

iocosae . . . lyrae and *modis . . . paruis* ('playful lyre' and 'little measures'). But 3.4 then uses those little Lesbian stanzas to rise to Pindar and the quintessentially sublime Gigantomachy. In 3.4 the cosmic range of poetry contrasts with the limited poet. Poem 30 stresses Horace's achievement conquering *Lesbian* poetry; but the poem again proudly imitates Pindar, on his poetry as an imperishable monument (*Pyth.* 6.1–14). Horace himself becomes the Delphic victor for whom Pindar made that Delphic 'treasury'.

The book shows new ambition, too, in its prolonged mythological (historical) narratives (3, 5, 11, 27): actually a side of Alcaeus, as in his poem on Ajax's punishment (fr. 298), but one little seen earlier in the *Odes* (1.15 Nereus, 1.37 Cleopatra).[32] Also notable are the long public poem 24, and the powerfully expanded symposiastic 29. Poems 1–6, and 11, 24, 27 and 29, ten out of thirty, occupy two-thirds of the book.

The structure conveys the range and ambition of the book, and of the accumulated *Odes* 1–3. Yet the movement away from 1–6 also accentuates, by contrast with the structure of Book 2, Horatian charm, and the ironic modesty it depends on.

Carmen Saeculare

The *Carmen* presents a climax in Horace's career; but for readers it stands apart from the *Odes*. In what form it was circulated is obscure (an appendix to Book 4?); but even for readers it primarily records a performance. This creates a different relationship with Greek lyric: connection is chiefly with choral performances, not books.

The poem has an unparaded literariness. As a sort-of-paean, it has significant links with Pindar's (Simonides', Bacchylides') paeans, written, as in the papyrus titles, for particular cities.[33] *Paean* D4 graphically depicts Ceos; *Paean* D2 presents the history of Abdera. This poem deals with a vaster city, which dominates the world; its beginning, present and future are encompassed.

The poem is strikingly impersonal. Voiced by girls and boys, and destined for a religious occasion, it avoids subtlety and play, even on the performers (unlike archaic choral poetry). *Odes* 4.6 brings out the difference of the *Carmen* from the *Odes*. Yet the poem itself produces, especially but not only for readers, a sense of Horace's achievement. Implicit is the prestigious commission, recorded in the *Acta* (*ILS* 5050.149). Hellenistic and neoteric

32 Cf. Lowrie (1997) chs. 7–8.

33 Cf. Phlegon *FGrHist* 257 F 37.v.3.18–20; A. Barchiesi (2000) 177–82; (2002) 112–18. The connection of *Odes* 4.6, on the *Carmen*, with Pindar *Paean* D6 is more ostentatious.

ceremonial poems make short stanzas expected, not Pindaric constructions; but the Sapphic stanza surprises (no paeanic refrain), and makes a firm connection with the *Odes* (cf. 4.6.35 *Lesbium*). The dominant divinities are Apollo and Diana; this fits a paean (e.g. Simon. 519 fr. 35), but creates a particular link with the fictive hymn 1.21.[34]

Odes Book 4

Book 4, though with fewer conspicuous imitations than 1, is absorbed by itself and its traditions. It retains its formal Lesbian identity (*Aeolio* 4.3.12, *Lesbium* 4.6.35). It begins, like Sappho's first book, by addressing Venus/Aphrodite, now an enemy, not a 'fellow fighter' (Sappho fr. 1.28). Poem 1 alludes further to Alcaeus (fr. 296b) and Sappho (fr. 31). But 4.9 implicitly draws attention to Horace's whole lyric tradition. *Minaces* ('threatening', 9.7) of Alcaeus' Muses stresses how much Horace has departed from his model. *Si quid . . . lusit Anacreon* (Anacreon's play, 9.9–10), pointing back to 1.32.1–2 *si quid . . . lusimus* (Horace's play), suggests his special affinity with that poet.

The list begins with Pindar and Simonides (9.6–7): the book particularly aspires towards the lyrical summits.[35] This is partly because the poems praising the deeds of Augustus and his family gesture towards fifth-century poetry of praise. Thus poem 4 begins from a comparison with an eagle, a bird important in epinician; opening with a simile is an epinician idea.[36] Families and heredity concern epinician.[37] But no less important is epinician's concern with itself, and its gift of immortality. The fame of the actual poetry, not least this book, is more prominent than in Pindar (cf. 4.8 and 9). Poem 6, which draws on Pindar, dwells explicitly on Horace's fame. Poem 3 sets Horace's fame alongside that of athletes (compare epinician) and generals (compare 4.4, etc.).

Poem 2, a second prologue, alleges the folly for Horace of imitating Pindar; but the language used of both belies the claim.[38] A simile likens Pindar to a river; the device itself acquires sublime, and poetological, associations. The eagle (4.4.1–12) is usually a comparison for the epinician *poet*; Tiberius too is compared to a river (4.14.25–32) – the river by which Horace was born (cf. 4.9.2).

34 On the gods and the ceremony, cf. Feeney (1998) 32–8; P. J. Davis (2001).

35 Cf. A. Barchiesi (1996).

36 Cf. esp. Pindar *Ol.* 7.1–7; Bacchylides 5.16–30 restarts with the eagle.

37 Cf. 4.4.30–2 with Pindar *Ol.* 11.19–20 and P. Oxy. 2438.43–8.

38 Cf. S. J. Harrison (1995a) on the poem.

The narrator's birth is one of the few biographical elements in the book (cf. also 4.3.1–2). His homosexual passion in 4.1, anomalous for *Odes* 1–3, connects especially with Alcaeus (cf. 1.32.11–12 and scholion on Alcaeus fr. 71). His loves are ending, again (4.11.31–4). But the crucial biographical element is fame, and the actual works. A commentary on Sappho, for example, stresses contemporary glory (S261A fr. 1); works are given in many biographies. Horace's own name appears (4.6.44), uniquely in the *Odes*. Someone else speaks it, as in Sappho (fr. 1.20, etc.); but here the point is renown.

After 4.1, the narrator's life of love and drinking, so characteristic in *Odes* 1–3, seems to disappear. Poem 7, of symposiastic type, elides the symposium. Poems 10–13 finally bring these elements back, before more poetry on Augustus in 14–15. Earlier subjects are roughly: poem 1 love, 2–3 poetry, 4–5 *princeps* and family, 6 poetry, 7 near-symposiastic, 8–9 poetry. Partly the reader is being teased: Venus' 'long-suspended wars' (4.1.1–2) have been suspended again (for real wars); love first returns in the very short 10. But 10–13 especially emphasise range. In this book, Horace has unexpectedly developed the grandest side of lyric tradition; but his once standard world is not abandoned. Juxtaposition with the immortality of poetry gives themes like ageing a new poignancy; but the series 10–13 ends with laughter (13.27).

The metrical structure also stresses range. It presents eight different stanzas, only seven Sapphic or Alcaic poems, and, until the last two poems, none in the same stanza consecutively. Variety increases in 7–13. One may particularly contrast the similarly short Book 2.

The emphasis on range is part of the self-glorification. The book celebrates itself, and the whole series of Books 1–4, to which it forms not a coda but a finale.

Each book builds from archaic poetry its own structure, based on the relation, and conflict, between art and the narrator. Each structure is dynamic, and metaliterary. These books are greatly preoccupied with themselves.[39]

FURTHER READING

Standard editions, referred to here: Archilochus, Hipponax: M. L. West (1989–92), I; Alcaeus, Sappho: Voigt (1971), and D. L. Page (1974) (to which 'S' refers); Alcman, Stesichorus, Ibycus: Davies (1991); Bacchylides: Maehler (1982–97); Pindar: Maehler (1987–9), with I. Rutherford (2000) for *Paeans*; other poets: D. L. Page (1962). Tarditi (1968) and Degani (1991) give fuller testimonia for Archilochus and

39 Professor A. Barchiesi and the greatly missed Professor R. O. A. M. Lyne provided valuable discussion and encouragement.

Hipponax. Gerber (1999) and Campbell (1982–93) include translations. The introductions in Hutchinson (2001) set each poet in context. Lives: Lefkowitz (1981) chs. 3, 5, 6. Commentaries of course give a great deal of material: Cavarzere (1992), Mankin (1995) and L. Watson (2003) on the *Epodes*; Nisbet and Hubbard (1970 and 1978) and Nisbet and Rudd (2004) on the *Odes*; Hill's and Thomas's commentaries on *Odes* 4 are eagerly awaited. Recent thinking on the *Epodes* and archaic poetry: see A. Barchiesi (2001a); S. J. Harrison (2001a); Lyne (2005b); *Odes*: G. Davis (1991); Feeney (1993); A. Barchiesi (1996; 2000); Paschalis (2002); Woodman (2002); Lyne (2005a); *Carmen*: A. Barchiesi (2002).

4

RICHARD THOMAS

Horace and Hellenistic poetry

At first sight the early poetry of Horace may appear to be revisionist in comparison with what was happening to Roman literature in the middle third of the first century BCE. The experimentation of Catullus, Calvus and Cinna, for instance, looks programmatically to Alexandria, with each poet producing epyllion and erotic epigram, and with an interest in aetiological topics – some of the chief genres or modes whose development in the third century gives us much of what we consider essential to the Alexandrian poetic achievement. Cornelius Gallus, Propertius and Tibullus created Roman elegy, a genre whose roots are likewise in erotic epigram, Catullan elegiacs and Callimachean poetics; and Virgil's *Eclogues* stand as a comprehensive act of Roman Alexandrianism, tied formally to Theocritus, spiritually to Callimachus, and frequently in a complex polemical relationship to Gallus and the nascent genre of elegy. Next to all of this we have Horace's revival of Archilochean iambic, his new embracing of the Roman genre of satire (if we care to follow Quintilian's ultimately unuseful taxonomy, *satura quidem tota nostra est*, *Inst.* 10.1.93), even his transference to Rome of archaic Greek lyric. All of this might seem to go against the grain. Horatian tastes in the 40s and 30s might on the face of it even seem more Ciceronian than Catullan.[1]

Callimachus, *Recusatio* and *Dichterweihe*

In distinction from the early poetry of Virgil, and from that of Propertius, whose Alexandrianism is very much on as well as beneath the surface, Horatian Alexandrianism emerges more subtly. He would name Callimachus only at *Epistle* 2.2.100, with some irony referring to a writer of elegy,

1 So Hutchinson (1988) 289–91 devotes fewer than two pages to Horace in his 78-page chapter 'Roman poetry' [and Hellenistic poetry].

perhaps Propertius, as 'Callimachus', himself as 'Alcaeus' precisely because that is how Propertius, around the same time, had defined himself (4.1.64 *Romani ... Callimachi*). While Propertius so identified himself, both prospectively at the start of a largely aetiological book of elegies (Book 4), and retrospectively with reference to the poetics of his previous works (implicit in Book 1, stated in Books 2 and 3), Horace on the other hand limits his overt claims to fame to the formal and metrical achievement of having converted the genres of his source models: for the *Satires* Lucilius at *Satires* 1.4.6–7, for the *Epodes* Archilochus at *Epistle* 1.19.23–25, for the *Odes* Sappho and Alcaeus at *Odes* 3.30.10–14, Alcaeus at *Epistle* 1.19.32–33. But in precisely these contexts, he describes his own involvement in those genres in terms that suggest renovation by way of Callimachean poetics, particularly through the expectations of *leptotes* and *techne*, and with a view to writing not for the crowd but only for those on the inside of such poetics (*Satires* 1.10.50–91; *Epistle* 1.19.37–40; *Odes* 3.30.13–14). Nisbet and Rudd have denied the Callimachean possibilities implied by the last of these (*Aeolium carmen ad Italos / deduxisse modos*), where, however, *carmen ... deduxisse* naturally implies a Callimachean treatment of the genre model, as is demonstrably the case in Virgil's adaptation of the *Aetia* preface at *Eclogues* 6.4–5 *deductum dicere carmen* (and later at Ovid *Met.* 1.4 *perpetuum ... deducite carmen*). It is certainly hard to deny the Callimacheanism of Virgil in *Eclogues* 6 or Propertius 2.1.39–42, but many readers have had difficulty seeing beyond Horace's named genre models. This is of course an old prejudice, perhaps not confined to modern readers. Horace himself would draw attention to the under-reading of his verse at *Epistle* 2.1.224–5 *cum lamentamur non apparere labores / nostros et tenui deducta poemata filo* ('when we lament the fact that people don't get our lucubrated poems spun out with slender thread').

Although Horace avoids the naming of Propertius 2.1 and 3.1 and the near-translation we find at the opening of the sixth *Eclogue*, he nevertheless incorporates Alexandrian, and specifically Callimachean, programme words and phrases at a number of prominent beginnings and endings. At *Odes* 2.20.4 his prediction for himself (*invidiaque maior* 'greater than envy') mirrors Callimachus' judgement of his own song at *Epigram* 21.4 Pf. ('his song was better than envy'); at 3.1.1 *odi profanum vulgus et arceo* stakes out a sacral version of the same poet's (*Epigram* 28.4 Pf.) 'I hate everything vulgar'; similar to this is Horace's claim to be distinct from the mob by virtue of his association with the cool poetic grove and choruses of nymphs and Satyrs (*Odes* 1.1.30–32, cf. 32 *secernunt populo*); towards the end of *Satires* 1.10 he enjoins careful composition for poets who want to be read more than once, and by the right people (73–5, cf. 73 *turba*); and in the envoi to the first book of *Epistles*, he expresses anxiety about the book's fate (1.20.11–12 *contrectatus ubi manibus sordescere vulgi / coeperis*). The Callimachean preference for the artful and small-scale (*Aetia* 1, fr. 1.1–9, *Hymn* 2.105–12, *fr. gram.* 465 Pf.) finds precise expression in Horace, and in contexts suggesting a direct engagement with and affiliation to the Hellenistic poet. So at *Satires* 1.4.6–25 Lucilius is to be faulted for writing 200 lines an hour while standing on one foot, as if that were a great achievement. The point is repeated at *Satire* 1.10.9 *est brevitate opus* 'brevity is what's needed'.

Although more oblique than the sixth *Eclogue*, to which it may be alluding by position, the sixth poem of Horace's first lyric collection is a clear instance of the Callimachean *recusatio*, establishing the poet's 'incompetence' in the area of political encomium, as well as in the higher genres, likewise eschewed by Callimachus in the *Aetia* preface (*Aet.* 1, pref. 17–24), Virgil in his *Eclogue*, and Propertius 2.1.[2] Horace's version is in fact as close to the *Aetia* preface as any in Latin poetry – *Odes* 1.6.5–12:

nos, Agrippa, neque haec dicere nec gravem
Pelidae stomachum cedere nescii
nec cursus duplicis per mare Ulixei
   nec saevam Pelopis domum

conamur, tenues grandia, dum pudor
inbellisque lyrae Musa potens vetat
laudes egregii Caesaris et tuas
      culpa deterere ingeni.

We don't try to tell of these things, Agrippa, nor of the bad temper of Peleus' son, who didn't know how to yield, nor two-faced Ulysses' sea travels, nor the savage house of Pelops, big topics for slender types like me, so long as my shyness and the Muse who rules over the unwarlike lyre forbid me to detract from the praises of splendid Caesar and yourself through want of poetic talent.

The display of high-register incompetence proves the point. Epic and tragic themes are lumped together; low-register *stomachus* represents Homeric *menis*; *duplicis* uncomplicates Homeric *polytropos* – as had Tityrus' confusion of the Scylla's and mixing up of Philomela and Procne at *Eclogue* 6.74–81.[3] Moreover, the flip-side of a lack of *ingenium* is an abundance of *ars*, precisely what the Callimachean poet wants. So it is that Horace's theme will be dinner-parties, his battles those of girls against young men, fought, however, with clipped nails – never too serious (1.6.17–20):

2 See Nisbet and Hubbard (1970) 80–3, with references to Wimmel (1960) passim.

3 See R. F. Thomas (1998) 295.

nos convivia, nos proelia virginum
sectis in iuvenes unguibus acrium
cantamus vacui, sive quid urimur,
non praeter solitum leves.

The *recusatio*, and the ultimate presence of the *Aetia* preface and other Callimachean sites, is not confined to this programmatic poem, but is in fact embedded throughout the corpus. *Odes* 2.12 opens with the lyric poet rejecting the suitability of military and mythological themes (1–9). Maecenas is rather to do a prose account of the battles of Caesar (10 *proelia Caesaris*), while Horace will sing of the erotic appeal of Licymnia, probably to be seen as Maecenas' wife Terentia, *pace* those who feel this would be beyond the bounds of taste. Elsewhere (*Odes* 2.1.37–40, 3.3.69–70), Horace recovers his Callimachean stance (*leviore plectro*, *desine . . . magna modis tenuare parvis* respectively) at the close of poems that had become involved in martial and epic themes. Even the *Epistle to Augustus* (2.1) turns out to be a *recusatio*. The poem responds to a real or fictitious protestation from the *princeps* that the poet never addresses him (Suetonius *Life of Horace*). But here too in the end praise of Augustus will have to be done by those who have the poetic stamina, Virgil and Varius for instance (247). Horace is not up to it and again fears detracting:

sed neque <u>parvum</u>
carmen <u>maiestas</u> recipit tua, nec meus audet
rem temptare pudor quam vires ferre <u>recusent</u>.

But your greatness shouldn't get a little song, not does my sense of shame dare to try out a topic that is beyond my strength.

Again, in the world of Callimachus *parvum* is good, while *maiestas* (too big?) can be problematic. Perhaps the final form of the Horatian *recusatio* comes at the end of the return to lyric, *Odes* 4.15, where Apollo interrupts him (as he had Callimachus at *Aetia* fr. 1.21–2 Pf.) and stops him singing of battles and conquered cities, and so his song becomes, somewhat surprisingly, a paean to the *aetas Augusta*. Irony returns at the end as Horace predicts for himself a poem on Troy, Anchises and Aeneas.

Horace would in fact imbed such refusals into the *Satires*, in spite of one view that 'Hellenistic convention is a cock that will not fight in the *Satires*'.[4] The fact is that these poems fundamentally uphold Callimachean principles of composition against the Lucilian looseness that it is Horace's enterprise to trim back, all in the interests of attention to artistry. *Satires*

4 Shackleton Bailey (1982) 75.

1.4 and 1.10 stipulate that Horatian satire is to avoid turgidity and artlessness and will be redirected through the tenets of Callimachean polemics and the principles of brevity, with an emphasis on *techne* and exclusivity.[5] In these poems he even plays on the agricultural context of the Callimachean *recusatio*, in the poem recording the acquisition of his farm. Where the Hellenistic poet was instructed by Apollo to rear his sacrificial victim to be 'as fat as possible' but to keep his Muse 'slender', Horace thanks Mercury for his good fortune, and offers up a prayer: 'make the master's herd fat along with everything else, except his poetic talent (*ingenium*)' (*Satires* 2.6.14–15).

Perhaps the closest intertext with Callimachus comes at *Odes* 4.3.1–16, where Horace, addressing the Muse Melpomene, declares that the one – himself – on whose birth the Muse serenely looked (2 *nascentem placido lumine videris*) will be made famous, not on Rome's Capitoline for success in boxing, chariot-racing or conducting the affairs of war, but rather because of Aeolic song, away from Rome by the waters and groves of Tibur. The Callimachean impulse is evident: at *Aetia* 1 fr. 1.37–8 the poet notes of himself that the Muses do not reject in their old age those 'on whose childhood they looked with benign eye'. Fraenkel ((1957) 449) writes of the 'echo' of Callimachus, who 'in his turn is indebted to Hesiod' (*Theogony* 81ff.). But more is going on here. From the texts cited it is clear, as Fraenkel noted, that Horace is referring to the specific Callimachean passage, but his use of the present participle *nascentem*, where Callimachus simply had the noun, constitutes a direct reference to the Hesiodic text, where the Muses pour sweet dew on the tongue of the one they honour 'and look upon as he is being born' (82). Hutchinson ((1988) 288) also notes that Horace's subsequent mention of the defeat of envy, already noted elsewhere in both authors, is essentially Callimachean: 4.3.16 *et iam dente minus mordeor invido*, 'and now I am less bitten by the tooth of envy'.

This marks a good place of transition from discussion of Hellenistic and Callimachean tags, and programmatic utterances, and overt intertexts, to the more subtle but fundamental Hellenistic principles that underlie Horace's works, and that communicate and renovate those principles in a Roman and Horatian context. *Odes* 4.3, in conflating the Hesiodic proem with the *Aetia* preface of Callimachus, establishes Horace in a tradition that had been operative for him since the first book of the *Satires*. But here, towards the end of his literary career, he provides a demonstration of how that tradition works in its Horatian context. What follows the Hesiodic-Callimachean opening to the poem is a priamel, the signature Horatian means of 'getting started'

5 Scodel (1987).

(as in *Epodes* 1.1–6, *Odes* 1.1, with variations at *Satires* 1.1, *Epistles* 1.1.1–12): the poet on whose birth Melpomene smiled will not be made famous by games, chariot-racing or war (themselves generic as well as professional activities), but rather will be fashioned as noble and known (12 *nobilem* connotes both) through his Aeolic song, in Tibur's idyllic setting. Specification of Tibur renovates the Callimachean trope into an Italian setting. Where Callimachus closed the loop by asserting the Muses' continued support in his old age, Horace gives us Tibur, but in doing so he alludes to the full Callimachean context, for Tibur is to be, in the Aeolic song that secured the status of Horatian lyric *Odes* 1–3, precisely the dwelling-place of the poet in his old age, at least in his wishes (*Odes* 2.6.5–6 *Tibur . . . / sit meae sedes utinam senectae*). That earlier poem, moreover, had implicated Virgilian poetics by putting forward as an alternative retirement-place the Galaesus river and the countryside of Tarentum (*Odes* 2.6.10–12), the river being the locale of Virgil's appealing and literarily mysterious *senex Corycius* (*Georgics* 4.125–48).

The issues of allusivity, poetics and traditional affiliation and distinction again come to the fore in Horace's chief statement of his poetic initiation or *Dichterweihe*. Poetic initiation, particularly where the Muses are involved, suggests a higher register, and that may be the reason that Horace sets his own initiation, in the Hesiodic-Callimachean mode, in the middle of the Roman Odes, at the start of a poem that explores the Pindaric function of Horatian lyric (*Odes* 3.4). His version is also emphatically Italian, making the Roman Odes a good site for this poem. Hesiod encountered the Muses while shepherding on Mount Helicon (*Theogony* 22–9), while Callimachus, at the start of the four-book *Aetia*, seems to have been transported in a dream to Helicon, where he met the Muses of Hesiod (*Aetia* 1, fr. 2 Pf.), who either legitimised his aetiological endeavours, or, as now seems likely, may have continued in conversation with the dreaming poet for the duration of *Aetia* 1–2. In Horace's version, we find the poet first invoking Calliope (*Odes* 3.4.1–4), whose appearance is to be accompanied by vocals, lyre or cithara. The epiphany seems to occur, and Horace finds himself wandering in pious groves (5–8). We are then transported to his youth, with the account of his early initiation, not on Helicon, and not in a dream-journey to Helicon, but while sleeping in his native Apulia on Mount Vultur. Here doves cover him with leaves, a miracle to the locals of Acherontia, Bantia and Forentum, Apulian and Lucanian towns barely known to fame but witnesses to the initiation of this Italian poet (3.4.9–20). As a result Horace belongs not to the Muses of Greece, of Hesiod and Callimachus, but now to the Italic Camenae, as he functions in the fashionable and favoured towns of Latium and Campania (3.4.21–4).

Polyeideia and complexity of voice

This is the essence of Horace's Alexandrianism: visible traces and affiliations, but innovation and originality. So far we have been dealing chiefly with Callimachus, and it has always been the case that the terms 'Hellenistic', 'Alexandrian', and 'Callimachean' blend into each other, particularly in discussions of poetics. It is also the case that Horace resembles Callimachus in a number of ways, first in his practice of *polyeideia*, or the writing of different genres, a practice defended by Callimachus in *Iambi* 13.

There is also something Hellenistic about the voices or personas Horace creates, situated in the establishment of a base voice, a sympathetic personal character that works throughout the corpus. The satires establish this voice, but it is to be found also throughout the iambic and lyric. If we think of the Sapphic, Archilochean or Pindaric voices, for instance, we find an infinitely more straightforward voice or set of voices than those of the lyric Horace. The reading public of Horace met the poet by way of a reported conversation with Maecenas: 'Maecenas, how come nobody can live content with the life chance or intellect has given him, but praise people who get a different break?' (*Satires* 1.1.1 *Qui fit, Maecenas, ut nemo, quam sibi sortem / seu ratio dederit seu fors obiecerit, illa / contentus vivat, laudet diversa sequentis?*). Regardless of addressee, and whether in the *Satires*, *Epistles* or the lyrics, the voice of Horace always speaks to us, and engages us as participants in the game that is Horatian poetry. This conspiratorial and intimate relationship between poet and reader is particularly a feature of all Hellenistic poetry except epic. It is particularly a feature of epigram, in which text and reader are at least putatively in physical contact.[6]

The *Odes* and Hellenistic epigram

It is a notable fact that epigram, erotic, sepulchral, dedicatory or satirical, immensely popular with Catullus and the Neoterics, is not to be found in the Augustan poets. If the poems from Meleager's anthology had been successfully adapted and transferred into the Roman context of these poems, it may be that the genre was felt as having played itself out. There is also the case that elegy had already shown that epigram might be expanded. Propertius 1.1.1–4 translates the homoerotic Meleager 105 Page while launching the Monobiblos, the first book of the elegies.

But epigram remained important as a mine for poetic figures and themes, and the genre is to be found, transformed, throughout the poetry of Horace.

6 See Pasquali (1964) 317–25 for the Hellenistic poets' predilection for talking of themselves.

At times, particularly in the *Odes*, the connection to Greek epigram is straightforward and unmediated. So 4.10, the second Ligurinus poem (*O crudelis adhuc*), for all its textual problems, amounts to little more than an epigram of the type found at *Anth. Pal.* 12.24–41, almost all Meleagrian and therefore available to Horace. But 4.10 has a connection to the opening poem of the book, and the reader who arrives at it immediately connects with the notorious Ligurinus of 4.1 and asks what has happened in the interval – that is in the nature of Horatian intratextuality. Like many of the Greek models, the poem addresses a younger man whose current resistance to the older lover will be a source of regret when the former grows old and hirsute. Likewise 1.5, the Pyrrha Ode, and 3.26 (*Vixi puellis nuper idoneus*) resemble dedicatory 'retirement' epigrams, with Horace giving up the life of the lover, and giving thanks for his salvation. However, in 3.26 we get a creative complication: *vixi* invokes the sepulchral tradition, Hellenistic as well as Roman. This is a doubling that had already occurred in the Greek tradition. In *Odes* 1.20 we have a dinner-invitation poem (*Vile potabis*), and Nisbet and Hubbard rightly point to an example by Philodemus (*Anth. Pal.* 11.44) which was doubtless familiar to Horace. Of course Catullus had already admitted the subgenre to his hendecasyllables (Catullus 13 *Cenabis bene*), and the Catullan intertext (cheap drinking: *vile potabis* / fine dining: *cenabis bene*) is an acknowledgement on Horace's part. Whether Catullus' poem preceded that of Philodemus cannot be known.

Just as epigram is accommodated to larger lyric purposes in the *Odes*, we find different modification in the *Epistles*. So *Epistle* 1.5, at least in its first eleven lines, is indistinguishable from *Odes* 1.20 or Catullus 13; indeed, it is closer to the latter, with the ingredients of the invitation-poem present: a modest, vegetarian meal, a presumably unpretentious wine – unless Torquatus brings a better one – figured with the same future tense (4 *vina bibes*), and the opportunity to talk well into the summer night, since the next day is Caesar's birthday. The poem then continues with a brief *laus convivii*, specification of the details of the party, and a further guestlist, as the poem ends with the admonition that Torquatus drop his legal business (the defence of Volcacius Moschus) and indeed come to dinner. So the invitation, with an attendant exhortation to enjoy the day, is integrated into the collection of *Epistles*. Horace would return to a lyric expression of the theme in *Odes* 4.12, inviting Virgil (or 'Vergilius', for those who do not believe we are dealing with the poet) to a similar party (cf. 16 *nardo vina merebere*).

This process of integration in fact is part of the genre creation that is at the heart of Horatian poetry, and is a mark of its affinity with Hellenistic literature. Hellenistic epigram is itself an expansion of a prior tradition. This is particularly the case with sympotic and erotic in epigram, but also with a variety of other types, as we can now see from the 'Posidippus' papyrus (P. Mil. Vogl. VIII 309). These epigrams, with multiple poems on each of a series of topics (gemstones, bird augury, shipwrecks, statues, etc.), stand as demonstrations of the way subgenres came into being, tied to no performative genre in archaic or classical Greek poetry. We can now see how a poem like *Odes* 1.28, the Archytas ode, is situated precisely in this genre of shipwreck epigrams (*nauagika*).[7]

In his monumental *Orazio lirico* Giorgio Pasquali sought to answer whether the *Odes* looked to archaic Greek, Hellenistic or contemporary literary and liturgical – in the case of hymns – practice. His conclusions were generally mixed but he did in the case of a number of poems show the clear or likely presence of Hellenistic elements. This is particularly the case with erotic poetry: the lovers' exchange and reconciliation in *Odes* 3.9 is indebted to archaic lyric but also to playful exchange such as we find in Philodemus *AP* 5.46; 3.10 is an example of the demonstrably (though not exclusively) Hellenistic genre of paraclausithyron; spiteful poems on aged or ageing women (1.25, 3.10, 4.13), also Propertian (3.25), are found in numerous poems in the Greek Anthology; I have already mentioned 4.10, the poem to the fastidious Ligurinus; 3.7, warning Asterie not to be tempted during the absence of her husband Gyges, shows similarities to Theocritus 3.40–51 and Propertius 2.20 (which like Horace's poem begins with the question *quid fles . . . ?* 'Why do you weep . . . ?). Pasquali is surely right to note that the use of mythological paradigms in all three poems is essentially Hellenistic; the second part of 1.22 to Lalage adopts and transforms the topos of the faithful lover who will endure the elements to continue his *komos* (Asclepiades *AP* 5.64, adesp. 5.168); 2.8, on the perjury on the beloved, shares much with Roman elegy, but also with epigrams of Callimachus (*AP* 5.6 = *Epigram* 25 Pf.) and Dioscorides (*AP* 5.52). Similar claims are made for 2.4 (love of a slave), 1.33 (unreciprocated love), 3.26 (farewell to love), 1.30 (prayer to Venus), and 1.27 (the bashful lover). Some of these poems surely look as much to Roman elegy as to Hellenistic impulses, and, as Pasquali notes, they are all integrated into their new Horatian, lyric contexts, but the Hellenistic essence is present throughout.

Another ode which shows clear signs of Horatian invention in the setting of a specific archaic model that is interrupted and complicated by Hellenistic intertexts is 1.14 (*O navis*). Nisbet and Hubbard point to allegorical treatments, going back to Quintilian, that take the poem as an allegory for the ship of state, a status already apparent in the genre models of Alcaeus

7 See R. F. Thomas (2004) 261–4 for the connections.

(fr. 6, 326). In this reading the ship is enjoined not to go back out on to 'new waves', a reference to civil war, since it is unseaworthy, with planking, mast, stays, keel and sails all worn out, the sailor now lacking trust in its ornate but unreliable decks. Horace's involvement becomes personal in the final stanza:

> nuper sollicitum quae mihi taedium,
> nunc desiderium curaque non levis,
> interfusa nitentis
> vites aequora Cycladas.

> I was once bothered by you and sick and tired of you; now you're my heart's desire, my heavy care, so avoid the waters that are poured among the shining Cyclades.

Although Nisbet and Hubbard note (ad 17, 18) '*taedium* is a lover's word' *desiderium* 'a lover's word for his heart's desire', they insist on the integrity of the political allegory: 'Horace is an ἐραστὴς τῆς πόλεως (['lover of the state'] Thucydides 2.43.1), having previously rejected the view as a 'strange theor[y]' that we might here be dealing with a 'ship of love' allegory.[8] But it is a strange theory only if one does not want it to be true, and the reasons for not wanting it to be true have to do with preconceived views of what Horace could or could not have written. Anderson's argument would have been strengthened had he brought into play, as A. J. Woodman subsequently did,[9] the two Hellenistic epigrams that will have been available to Horace in Meleager's anthology, one by Asclepiades (*AP* 5.161), the other by Meleager himself (*AP* 5.204). If we allow Horace to have read particularly the latter of these two, it becomes impossible to read 1.14 as anything but a poem in this erotic tradition:

> No longer, Timo, do the timbers of your spruce corsair hold out against the strokes of Cypris' oarsmen, but your back is bent like a yard-arm lowered, and your gray forestays are slack, and your relaxed breasts are like flapping sails, and the belly of your ship is wrinkled by the tossing of the waves, and below she is all full of bilge-water and flooded with the sea, and her joints are shaky. Unhappy he who has to sail across the lake of Acheron on this old coffin galley.
> (Loeb trans.)

As Anderson noted, the final couplet of 1.14, mysterious at best with the political-allegorical reading, fits this interpretation: the ship/prostitute is to avoid the waters of the shining Cyclades, because that is where Venus has several cult-places, in reality and in Horace (*Odes* 3.28.13–14 *quae Cnidon /*

8 As proposed by Anderson (1966). 9 Cf. Woodman (1980) 62–3.

fulgentisque tenet Cycladas 'she who inhabits Cnidus and the gleaming Cyclades', the only other appearance of the islands in his poetry.[10] In Catullus 36.15 the final 'cult place' of Venus was Durrachium, the 'tavern' of the Adriatic, already a flesh-pot in the time of Plautus and the source of *Menaechmi* 258–62, and doubtless even more so in Horace's time when it was the port city for the via Egnatia. So it is that, as with other cases we have seen, *Odes* 1.14, unless we forbid readers to see the Hellenistic intertexts (a fruitless enterprise anyway, once they have been pointed out), becomes an exquisite combination of archaic, Hellenistic, and specifically Horatian, Horatian in the surprising empathy for the prostitute whose amorous days are now over, as his own will be in 3.26, 4.1, and in his constant awareness of the fleeting nature of time.[11]

Epodes and iambic

A useful and balanced assessment of the importance of Callimachus and Hellenistic poetry for the *Epodes* has recently been provided by Lindsay C. Watson, in the introduction to his commentary on Horace's *Epodes*.[12] While he rightly notes that the variety of topics in Horace's collection need not point exclusively to the variety of Callimachean iambus (as advertised in *Iamb*. 13, for instance), given that the remains of Archilochus demonstrate similar variety, he nevertheless points to a number of features that indicate the presence of Callimachus, in particular the softening of Archilochean invective that has been associated with the Hellenistic poet's *Iamboi*, and also embraced in *Epistles* 1.19.25 (*non res et agentia verba Lycamben* 'not the themes and the words that goaded Lycambes').[13] Although there are very few identifiable Callimachean intertexts in the *Epodes*, Watson (p. 12) is correct to see in the Horatian *Epode* book a reflection of the 'modernizing iambic *Gedichtbuch*' of the Hellenistic poet whose presence is so abundantly clear in the poetry of the Neoterics and early Augustans.

10 Anderson (1966) 96–7.

11 Jocelyn (1982) 335, who argues against the allegorical reading, claims that 'neither in the life nor in the literature of pagan antiquity did males display sympathy for females exhausted by sexual use'. How he can know this I do not know, nor do I believe it to be true. The allegory is not unrelated to the fact that such empathy is unusual.

12 Cf. L. Watson (2003) 11–18.

13 Catullus may well have shown Horace the way; for Catullus' competing Archilochean and Callimachean invective stances see Wray (2001), esp. chapter 5, 'Code models of Catullan manhood'.

The *Satires* and epyllion

Much of the literary manifesto of Horace was, as we saw, embedded in the *Satires*, particularly in the first book, but we also saw the enactment of this manifesto in the *Epistles*, for instance in *Epistle* 2.1, the *Letter to Augustus*. As in the *Odes*, so in the hexameters, we find not only Hellenistic theory, but also practice, and practice in the area of the quintessentially Alexandrian narrative mode, the epyllion (the term is not ancient but it is a convenient one), as well represented by surviving fragments or works of Callimachus (the *Hecale*, *Hymn* 6, to Demeter), Theocritus (*Idyll* 24, the *Heracliscus*), Moschus (the *Europa*). On the Latin side examples are to be found in the works of the Neoterics: Catullus 64 (the marriage of Peleus and Thetis), the fragments of Calvus' *Io* and Cinna's *Zmyrna*, and later in the Appendix Vergiliana (*Ciris* and *Culex*). Length varies, but the genre does not extend beyond a single book, and the treatment is characterised often by subversion of the heroic, by attention to and delight in artistic perfection and leptotes, and by a disjunction between high register style and the subject-matter at hand. The dactylic hexameter is the preferred mode.

Although Horace famously distinguishes his *Satires* (*Sermones* or 'conversations') from the resounding sort of thing Ennius produced (*Satire* 1.4.38–62), we find epyllion embedded into at least one of these poems, and in one case an entire poem that can best be seen as post-neoteric engagement with this Hellenistic genre. *Satires* 2.6.77–117, the dinner-party narrative of Horace's aptly named rustic neighbour Cervius is an exquisite example of the genre, parallel in style and in disjunction between theme and style to Callimachus' *aetion* of the mousetrap (*Aet.* inc. lib. fr. 177 Pf. = fr. 259 *SH*). The setting, in which hospitality and conviviality are the backdrop for the narrative, is a prominent marker of the genre: Callimachus' *Hecale* (fr. 230–52, Diegesis X–XI Pf.), and the Molorchus inset of the *Victoria Berenices* (*SH* 256–61); Baucis and Philemon at Ovid, *Metamorphoses* 8.626–78. The archetype is Eumaeus at Homer, *Odyssey* 14.410–56.

In Horace's version, the tale begins with a temporal marker (*olim*) in the last foot of the line (79), with the 'Alexandrian' *fertur* closing the next line, in an opening couplet whose chiastic and enclosing elegance and artfully constructed doublets are in marked contrast to the theme: *rusticus urbanum murem mus paupere fertur / accepisse cavo, veterem vetus hospes amicum* ('a country mouse a city mouse is said to have taken into his poor cave, an old host his old friend'). Nothing could be more artful, in marked contrast to the identity of the speaker, and the theme. The journey of the mice to the city is described in high style, with the country symposium (83–9) followed by the moralising *sententia* of the hedonistic town mouse, who suggests that since all the earth's creatures (93 *terrestria*) have been allotted mortal souls (96 *mortalis animas*), they should live for pleasure. They head for town, with a cum-inversum marking the time, a characteristic of high narrative art (100–1 *iamque tenebat / nox medium caeli spatium, cum . . .*), three golden lines in a row (103–5) equal any concentration from Catullus 64, the *Eclogues* or the *Metamorphoses*, and epic language continues to the end of this delightful 41-line epyllion.

Cervius' tale is a compression of an earlier instance of the genre, the journey to Brundisium (*Satire* 1.5), which likewise begins in high style, with mention of hospitality (2 *hospitii*), with epic touches throughout: 9–10 elegant temporal markers, 11 chiastic anaphora, 25 apostrophe, 27–8, 31–3, 40 mini-catalogue invocation to the Muse to recall the genealogy of Sarmentus and Messius Cicirrus before their epic contest, 73–4 metonymy and high-register language, 85, 94 golden or otherly elegant word-order functioning as closural markers. All of this is in marked contrast to the low subject-matter with which it forms a contrast typical of the genre, much of it having to do with bodily function and other matters absolutely outside the bounds of epic decorum (7–8, 18–19, 21–3, 30–1, 56–70, 71–4, 80–1, 84–5). As with the country mouse, we end with philosophical rumination, and with the 104-line epic drawing attention to its great length: *Brundisium longae finis chartaeque viaeque est* 'Brundisium is the end of our long journey and scroll'. The journey is likely to have happened, Octavian's delegation to Tarentum to meet with Antony in 37 BCE, in a world still uncertain as Sextus Pompey's fleet was causing real problems particularly with the Italian food supply. Cornelius Severus was in these years at work producing his epic *Bellum Siculum*, an encomiastic poem on the future *princeps*' achievements. Horace, who does not even mention Octavian, and whose long journey does not even reach its destination of Tarentum, could only manage 104 lines. Politics partially explain things, but ultimately this is the only epic Horace could manage, and for that the poetics of Alexandrianism are largely to be credited.

FURTHER READING

Wimmel (1960) and Cody (1976) are still indispensable for gathering and discussing the instances of Callimachean literary aesthetics in Horace. Scodel (1987) is the standard work on Horace's Callimachean refinement of Lucilian satire, while Freudenburg (1993) extends this topic in his book on the *Satires* in general. Pasquali (1964) is still valuable on the extent and limits of Horace's debt to Hellenistic poetry in the *Odes*, whose general affiliation with Callimachean *leptotes* is well characterised by Santirocco (1986) passim.

5

RICHARD TARRANT

Horace and Roman literary history

Just as Horace appears the most forthcoming of Latin poets on the level of autobiography (see chapters 1 and 2 above), so too his statements of literary preference and affiliation are numerous and, on the surface, unambiguous. Those statements construct a picture that highlights his originality and shows scant regard for his Roman predecessors. He cites the description of Ennius as a 'second Homer' only to mock it, while the comic Plautus is blamed for negligent writing and lack of concern for anything except commercial success; even the satirist Lucilius, the only Roman poet whom Horace acknowledges as a model, receives harsh criticism for his excessive speed of production and consequent lack of polish. Of the leading figures of the generation prior to Horace, Lucretius is never mentioned and the name of Catullus appears only in a jibe at his feeble imitators. Horace's favourable judgements seem limited to a small circle of contemporaries on one hand – Varius, Pollio and above all Virgil – and on the other to the Greek masters whom he took pride in emulating, especially Archilochus, Alcaeus and Sappho.

The foregoing sketch is not a complete travesty, but it offers no hint of the extent to which Horace's poetry is indebted to earlier Roman authors. In seeking to understand that set of relationships Horace's explicit statements will not take us very far: like other Latin poets, Horace signalled his literary allegiances more often through allusion than through overt reference. When critics noted that the main theme of the last movement of Brahms's First Symphony bore a strong resemblance to the 'Ode to Joy' theme in Beethoven's Ninth, Brahms snapped in reply, 'Any jackass can see that!'[1] In the same way, Horace expected alert readers to recognise echoes of earlier Latin poets without explicit signposting.

But Horace's literary pronouncements can also be more actively misleading. Horace approaches Roman literary history not as a disinterested observer but as a participant with his own interests in mind. The result

1 Swafford (1997) 404.

is what Charles Brink calls 'literary history with an ulterior purpose'.[2] In particular, Horace's stated views of his predecessors form part of a contemporary debate in which Horace speaks as a defender of modern poetry. In such contexts Horace is more a polemicist than a historian, and polemic is inseparable from distortion.

The *Letter to Augustus* may serve as an example: there Horace expresses resentment at the unthinking exaltation of older poetry by his contemporaries. Among his targets are the teachers of literature (*grammatici*), who persist in drumming into their students the hoariest remnants of Latin poetry; as evidence he cites his exposure to the works of Rome's oldest attested poet, Livius Andronicus, at the ungentle hands of his teacher Orbilius. Now there is nothing implausible in the picture of schoolteachers assigning texts no longer current – as a high-school student around 1960, I found myself mystified by Walter Scott's *Heart of Midlothian* – and Horace's complaint of the public's fondness for archaic poetry gets some later support from Seneca, who regretted that Virgil had been forced to cater to a public keen on Ennius;[3] nonetheless, Horace's account is far from being the whole story. For one thing, Orbilius and his ilk had no monopoly on setting the school poetry curriculum. Indeed we know of other *grammatici* of the time with an interest in contemporary poetry, e.g., Valerius Cato, author of the neoteric-sounding poems *Lydia* and *Dictynna*, hailed as 'the only one who chooses and makes poets'.[4] The meaning of that phrase has been much discussed, but it probably refers to poets of the present day rather than already established authors.[5] An even clearer example of a *grammaticus* with modernist tastes is Q. Caecilius Epirota, who at the time when Horace wrote was already teaching Virgil and other modern poets to select young men.[6]

Horace could even conceive of his own poetry entering the school curriculum, although he professed to loathe the idea. In *Satires* 1.10.74–5 he claims to be content with just a few readers and says that only a madman would opt for the apparent alternative, to be lectured on in low-class schoolrooms, while roughly fifteen years later, in *Epistles* 1.20.17–18, he ruefully predicts that his new collection of poetry in its doddering old age will be reduced to teaching children in small-town classrooms. However much Horace stresses the sordid details of his work's destiny, the passage still implies confidence that his poetry will survive and make its way into the educational

2 Brink (1971) 481.
3 Seneca quoted in Aulus Gellius *Noctes Atticae* 12.2.10.
4 Furius Bibaculus fr. 6 Courtney *qui solus legit ac facit poetas*.
5 See Nisbet (1995b) 391–3, who suggests that changes in taste had made Cato look old-fashioned by the time of the *Satires*.
6 See Suetonius *De Grammaticis* 16, with Kaster's discussion.

canon – as it soon did: Juvenal 7.225–7 names Horace together with Virgil as authors read in the schools of the *grammatici.*

Horace also foresaw the possibility of his work enjoying a more glorious afterlife. *Odes* 1–3 openly aspire to canonical status on a par with the Greek lyric poets, and indeed the final poem in the collection claims to have obtained it. Horace was not so daunted by the conservatism of the public as to despair of his own poetry's reception at the highest level. The concept of canonicity had recently been given a more tangible form by Augustus' establishment of the Palatine Library with its twin collections of Greek and Roman literature: when Horace speaks of Maecenas 'placing him among the lyric bards' (*Odes* 1.1.35 *si me lyricis uatibus inseres*), the implied image is of a set of rolls being placed alongside those of the canonical lyricists.

Finally, even at a relatively early stage of his career Horace did not lack critical approval. The 'few readers' Horace hopes for in *Satires* 1.10.74 are exemplified by a catalogue of fifteen named individuals, a 'gallery of heavy-weights' in Jasper Griffin's phrase,[7] that includes poets, critics, patrons of literature and political leaders: unless Horace was indulging in wishful thinking – hardly likely in such a prominent passage – he could already count some of the most eminent figures in Rome's cultural life among his admirers. By the time of the letter to Augustus, Horace could expect a favourable hearing from the *princeps* himself – especially if, as Suetonius alleges, the letter was prompted by a complaint from Augustus that Horace had not spoken of him in his previous *sermones.*[8]

When due allowance has been made for strategic omissions and exaggerations, we are left with a core of consistently expressed views that in all likelihood reflect Horace's genuine literary outlook. The salient components are a high regard for originality and adherence to the highest standards of verbal craft, or, in their negative counterparts, scorn for the 'slavish herd' of imitators (*seruum pecus*, *Epistles* 1.19.19) and disdain for careless or uncouth writing.[9] The latter attitude accounts for Horace's harsh remarks about Plautine comedy: in *Epistles* 2.1.168–76 Plautus is criticised for failing to suit his writing to his characters, for overall looseness of style and for valuing financial gain over artistic success;[10] in *Ars Poetica* 270–2 Plautus' audiences are derided for admiring his jokes and metrical displays. Both

7 Griffin (1993) 4.

8 Text and interpretation in Rudd (1989) 1–2. The story is generally believed, but it could be an invention to account for Augustus' absence in *Epistles* 1 and his prominent appearance in *Epistles* 2.1.

9 See also Richard Rutherford's discussion, chapter 18 below.

10 I accept Jocelyn's view (1995) that Horace's judgements centre on style and language rather than plot-construction or characterisation.

passages allude to Plautus' popular appeal, which can in itself constitute a black mark in Horace's book. By contrast, when Horace speaks approvingly in *Satires* 1.10.40–2 of the comedies of his contemporary Fundanius, he refers to them as written texts, *libelli*; either Fundanius wrote comedies to be read rather than performed, or Horace highlights their written quality to elevate them above drama with mass appeal.

Horace's dismissive attitude toward older Roman Comedy did not prevent him from adopting its verbal wit and brio – although credit should also be given to a shared Italian fondness for quick-witted repartee. Some of the most enjoyable passages in all of Horace are the quasi-dramatic dialogues scattered through the *Satires* and *Epistles*: for example, here is part of the conversation between Horace and his persistent companion in *Satires* 1.9.26–8: *interpellandi locus hic erat 'est tibi mater, / cognati, quis te salvo est opus?' 'haud mihi quisquam. / omnis composui.' 'felices. nunc ego resto.'* ('This was my chance to interject, "Do you have a mother, or relatives, who need you to stay healthy?" "Not a one: I've buried them all." "Lucky for them; that leaves me."')[11] The last satire of Book 2, the account of a dinner-party at the home of Nasidienus, is narrated by the comic poet Fundanius and is itself a virtual comedy.[12]

Comedy even colours Horace's satiric autobiography. In *Satires* 1.4.105–29 he claims that he owes his forthrightness in criticising other people's faults to his father's instruction, but that 'father' proves to be modelled on the stern father Demea in Terence's *Adelphoe*. To complicate matters further, Demea is neither a very sympathetic character nor an effective moral teacher; thus what seemed most sincere in Horace's self-portrait takes on an element of fiction and ironic distance.[13]

When it suits his rhetorical purposes, Horace can imply a more positive view of early Latin poetry. In *Ars Poetica* 53–8, he complains that Virgil and Varius are criticised for their verbal innovations whereas Plautus and

11 Other examples include the dialogue of Horace and his critic Trebatius in *Satires* 2.1.4–7, the exchanges between an insensitive host and his polite guest in *Epistles* 1.7.14–19, and the arithmetic lesson of *Ars Poetica* 326–30. Henderson (1999) 210 remarks that Horace's interlocutor in *Satires* 1.9 'comes on like a pimp from the pages of Plautus'; Rudd (1966) 62 notes elements of 'pure Plautus' in *Satires* 1.5; Rand (1937a) 73–4 observed that *Satires* 2.7 – 'a mime . . . but one worthy of Terence' – contains many lines that can easily be recast as comic iambics.

12 As is made clear by Horace's use of *ludi* to describe the goings-on (78); see Muecke (1993) ad loc.

13 Leach (1971) 631 sees an implication that commenting on other men's vices is a Horatian flaw derived from his father's narrow moral training. Freudenburg (1993) 34–9 links the reference to Demea to what he regards as Horace's persona as an inept teacher of virtue.

Caecilius were not, and that he is begrudged his own few additions to the language while Ennius and Cato 'enriched our native language'. In *Satires* 1.10 he claims the right to criticise Lucilius without denying his virtues, and compares Lucilius' own criticism of Accius and Ennius, adding that Lucilius did not consider himself Ennius' superior.

As that comparison suggests, Horace's attitude to Lucilius involved both criticism and respect.[14] In this case an already complex relationship is harder to assess because of the fragmentary state in which Lucilius' works survive: we possess approximately 1,400 lines of what originally comprised thirty books of poetry. The volume of Lucilius' output in fact gives Horace his main basis for criticism: in typically Callimachean terms, Horace laments the 'muddy flow' of Lucilius' writing (*Satires* 1.4.11 *cum flueret lutulentus*, also 1.10.50), the lack of care in revising, the helter-skelter mixing of Greek and Latin (1.10.20–30). The critique is summed up in the image of the older poet dictating 200 lines per hour standing on one foot (*Satires* 1.4.9–10). Having accused Lucilius in *Satires* 1.4 of writing too much, too fast, Horace illustrates his criticism with the following satire. It is well known that Horace's account of his journey to Brundisium has a Lucilian counterpart, a description of a voyage to Sicily. The content and dimensions of Lucilius' narrative cannot be precisely determined, but, since it filled the entire third book of his *Satires*, it probably ran to several hundred lines.[15] Horace's poem, at just over 100 lines, is an implicit rebuke of his predecessor's loquacity, and to underline the point Horace concludes with an ironic apology for his 'lengthy text' (*longae . . . chartae* 104: see Thomas, chapter 4 above).

While claiming to have surpassed Lucilius on stylistic grounds, Horace surprisingly acknowledges him as a superior in satire (*Satires* 1.10.48–9 *inuentore minor*, 2.1.29 *nostrum melioris utroque*). Perhaps Horace was eager to associate himself with Lucilius, for all his faults of style, because Lucilius was the sort of literary figure Horace aspired to be, moving easily among the great men of his time and respected by them. Poetic kinship with Lucilius might therefore dilute awareness of the social gap separating Horace from the exalted company he had succeeded in entering. Horace may also have had self-interested reasons for characterising the content of Lucilius' satires as he does. His two most explicit statements, though not actually inconsistent, present very different pictures of his predecessor's work: in *Satires*

14 A fuller treatment is given by Frances Muecke, chapter 8 below.

15 Friedrich Marx's reconstruction of Lucilius' Sicilian journey provoked A. E. Housman's memorable barb: 'Mr Marx should write a novel. Nay, he may almost be said to have written one; for his notes on book III . . . are not so much a commentary on the surviving fragments as an original narrative of travel and adventure' (Housman (1907/1972) 74/684).

1.4.3–6 Horace plays up the acerbic side of Lucilius' writing and connects his attacks on the powerful with the tradition of Aristophanic comedy, while *Satires* 2.1.30–4 highlight his autobiographical focus.[16] The shift in emphasis probably reveals more about Horace's self-presentation as a satirist than about his views of Lucilius. Horace opens the second book of *Satires* with the implausible claim that his earlier collection had struck some readers as excessively harsh; it is tempting to see Horace's stress in that book on Lucilius' *acerbitas* as a means for him to suggest that his own satires had an edge that they in fact lacked.[17]

Horace's judgements of early Latin poetry are closely linked to the issue of changing standards: in his view, Plautus delighted the audiences of his day because Romans then had no sense of genuinely witty and urbane comic writing. Horace allows that Lucilius would have written more fastidiously if he had lived in Horace's time (*Satires* 1.10.64–71); his more sympathetic attitude may reflect the fact that Lucilius had attracted significant scholarly attention in the previous generation.[18] A likely echo of that critical study is the description of Valerius Cato as a defender of Lucilius in the spurious lines attached to the opening of *Satires* 1.10; the statement that Cato tried to correct Lucilius' poorly formed verses (2–3 *qui male factos / emendare parat uersus*) suggests an awareness that Lucilius' writing no longer met contemporary standards of refinement.[19]

The influence of Lucretius on Horace is less evident than might be expected in light of their shared Epicurean outlook. Lucretius' argumentative rigour and stylistic elevation were far removed from Horace's chosen orbit; the unostentatious but sincere piety that Horace advocates in several of the *Odes* was also at odds with Lucretius' thoroughgoing hostility to religious practice. *Odes* 1.34 even stages a recantation of Epicurean views about the gods, though no biographical inferences can be drawn from that not altogether serious poem.

The mark of Lucretius is most clearly seen in the *Satires*, and indeed *Satires* 1.1 features echoes of Lucretius at three structurally significant points (25–6, 69–70, 119). The first and third of those echoes have long been noticed, but apparently not the middle one: Horace's reference to Tantalus, followed by the address to the reader, *quid rides? mutato nomine de te / fabula narratur*

16 On the slipperiness of Horace's statements about Lucilius see Zetzel (1980) 62. Bramble (1974) 169 more bluntly writes that 'Horace begins the falsification of the Lucilian *persona*'.

17 The depictions of the rabid satirist placed in the mouths of others in *Satires* 1.4.34–8 and 78–9 serve a similar purpose. This is a large and controversial question, with implications for later Roman satire; see further below.

18 See Anderson (1963) 62–9 on the study of Lucilius in the 50s BCE.

19 See also Rudd (1966) 118–24 and Scodel (1987).

('Why do you laugh? Change the name and the tale is about you'), surely recalls Lucretius' argument in 3.978–1023 that the torments of the fabled sufferers in the Underworld represent the emotional anxieties of the living. The first and most conspicuous Lucretian allusion follows a statement of Horace's satiric method that implicitly contrasts him with Lucretius: 'to speak the truth with a smile' (*ridentem dicere uerum* 24). Lucretius is tireless in proclaiming what he takes to be the truth, but he seldom relaxes into a smile while doing so. In keeping with that self-characterisation, Horace modifies Lucretius' famous image of the honey around the rim of the cup containing bitter medicine (1.936–50) into a more benign one, of children given cookies as a reward for learning their ABCs. Horace thus implies that he will share many of Lucretius' therapeutic goals but will adopt a more genial manner in pursuing them.[20]

Lucretius claimed that his project of expounding Epicurean doctrine to a Roman audience was made more difficult by 'the poverty of my native language' (*patrii sermonis egestas* 1.832, 3.260). Horace alludes to the phrase, but in an unexpected way, when he cites Ennius and Cato as having 'enriched our native language' (*Ars Poetica* 57 *sermonem patrium ditauerit*). The fact that Lucretius is not named even as his words are recalled might imply that the kind of abstract philosophical terminology Lucretius strove to create for Latin did not strike Horace as an enrichment of the language.

Catullus is the poet who most clearly foreshadows aspects of Horace's literary persona and writing. Horace shares Catullus' high regard for charm and polish, and his disgust at poetic crudeness. Both poets disparage their own work in terms not meant to be taken literally: Catullus called the collection of poems dedicated to Cornelius Nepos mere 'trifles' (*nugae*) and almost in the same breath prayed that they might survive for more than an age; one could compare Horace's pretence that the *Satires* are closer to versified conversation than to true poetry, contradicted by his insistence on their painstaking composition. The diversity of metre and content that Catullus packed into his slender body of poetry also prefigures the many-sidedness of Horace's work. In fact, Horace at times seems to have taken hints or isolated experiments in Catullus and made them the basis for entire collections of poems. Thus Catullus' poetic letters to friends (35, 65, 68A) may have provided the germ of Horace's first book of *Epistles*, and his four extant poems in lyric metres (11, 34, 51 and 61) were undoubtedly an important stimulus toward the *Odes*.

20 For some other Lucretian allusions in the *Satires* see Rudd (1966) 26, 33, 62–3, 208–9, 251. See also below on *Odes* 4.7.14–16.

The influence of Catullus is most evident in the *Epodes*. As he does with Lucretius in *Satires* 1.1, Horace opens the collection with an unmistakable gesture toward Catullus: his promise to accompany Maecenas to the ends of the earth (1.11–14) evokes the similar willingness that Catullus ascribes to Furius and Aurelius in 11.2–13. The *Epodes* owe much to the invective component in Catullus, who anticipated Horace in blending archaic *iambos* with its Callimachean counterpart.[21] Particular points of contact include scathing images of physically repulsive people (e.g. *Epode* 12 ~ Catullus 69) and poems that lambaste others' failings in manners (e.g. *Epode* 3, pretending to denounce Maecenas for lacing Horace's food with garlic). The erotic epodes frequently echo Catullus' love poetry, though often with a telling shift of tone: so Catullus' Lesbia, 'loved by us as no other woman will ever be loved' (8.5 *amata nobis quantum amabitur nulla*) is transformed into the witch Canidia, 'greatly loved by sailors and merchants' (*Epode* 17.20 *amata multum nautis et institoribus*). In the same poem *tu pudica, tu proba* (40 'how modest you are, how chaste') recalls Catullus 42.24 *pudica et proba*; in both passages the poet pretends to atone for earlier invective with ludicrously inappropriate praise.

Most notably, Catullus is Horace's only significant predecessor in Latin lyric. Although Horace explicitly mentions only Greek models, he pays tribute to Catullus by juxtaposing odes with clear references to Catullan lyrics. *Odes* 1.21, a hymn to Apollo and Diana, invites comparison with Catullus 34, a hymn to Diana, while 1.22 (*Integer uitae*) recalls Catullus' famous adaptation of Sappho (51) both in its metre and in its final lines: Catullus had written of the man so blessed as to watch and hear Lesbia sweetly laughing, *spectat et audit / dulce ridentem* (4–5); Horace, gently deflating his predecessor's romantic reverie, swears that, wherever he may be, he will go on loving Lalage ('the chatterer'), her sweet laughter and sweet talk: 23–4 *dulce ridentem Lalagen amabo, / dulce loquentem*. Horace reintroduces the beloved's talking, present in Sappho but omitted by Catullus, and gives it an ironic twist by linking it to her name and the loquacity it implies.

Catullus' anticipations of Horatian iambic and lyric do not invalidate Horace's claims to primacy in those genres. When a Roman poet claimed to be first (or first in Latin) in a given genre, he did not mean that nothing similar had been written before, but rather that no previous poet had composed a substantial body of poetry that met the formal conditions of the genre. In the case of Catullus and iambic poetry, the latter factor was decisive: Catullus' poetry has many features in common with iambic, and at times he refers to his poems or some subset of them as *iambi*, but as far as we know Catullus

21 See Heyworth (2001); L. Watson (2003) 6, 17–19.

never composed poems in the metres associated with Archilochus, as Horace did in the *Epodes*. Catullus' poems in Sapphic and glyconic metres do qualify as lyric on formal grounds, but they comprised only a small part of a diverse body of poetry, in contrast to the eighty-eight poems in lyric metres that make up *Odes* 1–3.[22] Today we possess only meagre fragments of the lyrics of Sappho and Alcaeus, but in Horace's time their poetry was fully extant. Horace's ambition to become a canonical lyric poet therefore required that he produce a comparable corpus of lyric; by doing so he not only vindicated his claim to be Rome's first true lyricist, but also signalled a shift in aesthetic values away from Catullus' *libellus*, a slender production typical of the first generation of Roman Callimacheanism, in the direction of a consciously monumental work.

Horace's deep knowledge of Catullus and frequent allusion to his poetry show that his sneering reference in *Satires* 1.10.18–19 to the 'ape who knows no songs beyond those of Calvus and Catullus' (*simius iste / nil praeter Caluum et doctus cantare Catullum*) is directed not at the poets themselves but at their unoriginal epigones, who had not learned that the only meaningful way to honour the Neoterics' achievement was to produce work as innovative as theirs had been.[23]

A conspicuous example of Horace's irony in relation to his own poetry is the claim in *Satires* 1.10.40–5 that he chose satire because other poetic genres already had distinguished Roman practitioners: Fundanius for comedy, Pollio for tragedy, Varius in epic and Virgil for the *Eclogues*. Besides showing Horace's respectful treatment of his older contemporaries, the passage also exemplifies the mutually defining element in Triumviral and Augustan literary culture, where statements of poetic aims often acknowledge contemporaries as masters of genres other than the one(s) chosen. Thus Virgil in the *Eclogues* salutes Pollio as a tragedian (8) and Cinna and Varius as generally outstanding (9), and in the *Georgics* looks up to Lucretius for philosophical poetry. In the *Odes* Horace again defers to Varius in epic (1.6) and Pollio in tragedy (2.1), and in a different spirit takes note of Tibullus in elegy (1.33); he even refers to works of historical prose, Pollio's history of the civil wars (2.1) and Maecenas' almost certainly imaginary account of the victories of Augustus (2.12). Catullus had shown a similar interest in recognising the work of friends, though there one gets the impression of a

22 Woodman (2002) locates Catullus' influence on the *Odes* in his appropriation of Sappho's poetry and his creation of a 'dualism of gender' that Horace reproduces in his own way by imitating Sappho as well as Alcaeus (60).

23 See Zetzel (2002), especially 49–50, and Scodel (1987), who situate Horace's remark in the evolving Roman understanding of Callimachean poetics.

group of writers all exploring essentially the same poetic material, whether erotic, personal-invective or learned-mythological. With Virgil and Horace, as later with Propertius and Ovid, there is a much stronger awareness of generic specialisation, which in Ovid takes the form of a profusion of poetic 'canons'.[24]

Horace's literary relationship to Virgil is unique in several respects. Virgil was a close friend, given a place in the *Odes* preceded only by Maecenas and Augustus and there described in unusually warm terms as 'half of my soul' (1.3.8 *animae dimidium meae*). Horace's admiration for Virgil's poetry far transcended the polite regard we may suspect he felt for the work of Varius or Pollio. In addition, the intertwining of their poetic careers creates a pattern of mutual influence. The latter factor makes it difficult at times to determine the chronology of shared motifs or language: the two presumably saw each other often, and in all likelihood discussed or even exchanged drafts of work in progress. Some points, however, seem fairly certain: for example, that *Epode* 16 is Horace's disillusioned rejoinder to the optimism of the Fourth Eclogue, and that Horace's portrayal of Cleopatra in *Odes* 1.37 helped to shape Virgil's depiction of Dido.[25]

Virgil's eminence would in itself have led Horace to challenge him rather than simply deferring to him as *il miglior fabbro*. That mixture of tribute and rivalry can be illustrated from Horace's response to the *Eclogues*, which appeared shortly before Horace's first two published collections, the *Epodes* and first book of *Satires*. *Satires* 1 is indebted to the *Eclogues* for its structure: ten poems in a carefully ordered sequence, with a division into halves signalled by a new invocation at the start of the sixth poem.[26] Explicit references to Virgil are located on either side of the midpoint (1.5.40, 48, 1.6.55) and in a programmatic passage of the last poem (1.10.44–5), where Horace writes that the Camenae of the countryside granted Virgil a style of poetry that was *molle atque facetum*. The terms imply elegance and urbane wit, and alongside the compliment to Virgil they suggest the qualities that Horace himself aimed for in refining Lucilian satire.[27] At the same time, the distinctive character of the *Eclogues* spurred Horace to create for himself a sharply different literary voice, or set of voices: thus the affected pugnacity and scurrility of the *Epodes* are in pointed contrast to the *Eclogues*' air

24 See Tarrant (2002) 15–17, also Rutherford, chapter 15 below.

25 On *Epode* 16 and *Eclogues* 4 see Griffin (1993) 21–2 (admitting no doubt as to Virgil's priority) and L. Watson (2003) 486–8 (cautiously coming to the same conclusion); for Horace's Cleopatra and Virgil's Dido, see Galinsky (2003). Putnam (1996) 314 discusses the influence of *Satires* 1.5 and 2.6 on the *Aeneid*.

26 On this and other structural links see Zetzel (1980).

27 Good remarks in Putnam (1996) 305–7.

of mannered *politesse*, and the aggressively Roman stamp of the *Satires* – typified by the appearance in 1.10.31–5 of Quirinus, the deified Romulus, as their divine sponsor, in place of the 'correct' Apollo – sets them clearly apart from the half-Greek, half-Roman landscapes inhabited by Virgil's shepherds.[28]

Another lesson Horace may have taken from the *Eclogues* is the technique of incorporating diverse or even contradictory attitudes within a single set of poems. For example, the quite different responses offered by *Eclogues* 1 and 9 to the confiscation of land for distribution to veteran soldiers may have served as a model for Horace's procedure in the *Epodes*, in which poems 1 and 9 celebrating the victory at Actium are counterbalanced by poems 7 and 16, which recall the gloomiest phases of the preceding civil-war years. The extremes are wider in the *Epodes*, and the contrast is further sharpened by the fact that all four poems are in the poet's own voice, with none of the distancing that Virgil derives from his pastoral idiom. That shared elusiveness in dealing with political themes enabled Horace and Virgil to engage seriously with contemporary events without becoming propagandists, a goal that each continued to pursue throughout his career.[29]

Virgil seems to have been the first Roman poet to structure his literary career in an ascending order of genres, from the pastoral *Eclogues* to the didactic *Georgics* and, in an especially bold move for a Callimachean, to Homeric epic in the *Aeneid*. Horace did not need Virgil's example to conceive of following the *Epodes* and *Satires* with something more prestigious – his own ambition sufficed for that – but the Virgilian precedent gave him a compelling reason to reject epic in favour of lyric, a more appealing and suitable higher genre. Horace explicitly disclaims epic ambitions in *Odes* 1.6, to Agrippa, but the first ode addressed to Virgil (1.3) makes a similar point through indirection: the perilous sea voyage that Virgil is about to undertake, which prompts Horace to denounce mankind's defiance of god-given limits, is almost certainly a metaphor for the *Aeneid*, and Horace's exclamation *audax omnia perpeti / gens humana ruit per uetitum nefas* (25–6 'audacious at trying out everything, men rush / headlong into the things that have been forbidden')[30] reacts with mock horror to Virgil's transgression of the Callimachean poetics he had espoused in the *Eclogues*.[31] Horace's own poetic progress continued beyond lyric into the *Epistles* – not simply a return

28 Zetzel (2002) sees this differentiation in a somewhat more antagonistic light than I would be inclined to do.

29 On Horace's treatment of Augustus see Michèle Lowrie's essay, chapter 6 below.

30 Translation by Ferry (1997).

31 For this metapoetic reading – not universally accepted – see Santirocco (1986) 27–31.

to satire-style *sermo*, but what could be presented as an upward move into poetry of a philosophical and didactic character.

Virgil is not present by name in *Odes* 4 – the 'Vergilius' addressed in 4.12 can hardly be the poet[32] – but he is twice represented by his creation, the *Aeneid*, already an established classic that has made Aeneas a national hero. The book ends with the prospect of Horace joining a festive throng to sing of 'Troy and Anchises and the offspring of kindly Venus' (4.15.31–2 *Troiamque et Anchisen et almae / progeniem Veneris canemus*), casting the hero of Virgil's epic in appropriately lyric terms;[33] and in the celebrated ode *Diffugere niues* (4.7) Aeneas serves to embody that most Horatian of themes, the universality of death: *nos ubi decidimus / quo pius Aeneas, quo Tullus diues et Ancus, / puluis et umbra sumus* (14–16 'but we, when we go down / where pious Aeneas, rich Tullus, and Ancus have gone, / we're nothing but dust and shade').[34] Those lines also illustrate Horace's assimilation of earlier Latin poetry. Ennius had begun a book of his *Annales* with a line recording the death of 'good king Ancus': *postquam lumina sis oculis bonus Ancus reliquit* (137 Skutsch); Lucretius nearly repeated Ennius' line while giving it a completely different sense: if even a great and good man like Ancus has died, how can we lesser mortals complain of our lot (3.1025)? Horace combines Ancus with another early king, Tullus, and with *pius Aeneas*, i.e., Virgil's Aeneas, acknowledging him as a new Roman icon, but subordinating him to Horace's personal vision, Lucretian in content but with a lyric poet's feeling for tactile imagery. In his undemonstrative but supremely confident manner, Horace subsumes the three leading representatives of the high-poetic tradition in Latin – and does so in a metre half of which consists of dactylic hexameter.

Horace is often portrayed as being cool to the elegiac poetry of his younger contemporaries Propertius and Tibullus, and it may be significant that Horace does not explicitly mention Propertius, a brilliant poet of a very

32 The point remains controversial, but I find it hard to believe that Horace would have called Virgil 'the client of noble young men' (15 *iuuenum nobilium cliens*) or advised him to put aside his 'pursuit of profit' (25 *studium lucri*) or, even if those terms could be explained as spoken in jest, that Horace would have published a jocular invitation to a wine party several years after the addressee's death. The allusions to Virgil's poetry that have led some critics to the opposite conclusion are best understood as playful references to Vergilius' more famous namesake. One could compare the several figures named Gallus who populate Propertius' first book of elegies: none can be identified as Cornelius Gallus, but each reminds us of Propertius' elegiac predecessor.

33 See Lowrie (1997) 348–9 on Horace's accommodation of the *Aeneid* to lyric, and on the effect of the ode's conclusion.

34 Translation by Rosanna Warren in McClatchy (2002).

un-Horatian sort to whom Maecenas made overtures of patronage while Horace was engaged on the *Odes*. Certainly Propertius' declared stance of flippant irresponsibility in the face of Roman social and political orthodoxies is not one that Horace, in any of his literary guises, could endorse. But Horace's treatment of elegiac motifs is largely shaped by his own poetic persona. In the less strictly defined *Epodes* Horace does occasionally adopt the role of the unhappy lover and takes on, at least to a degree, the colouring of an elegist.[35] In *Epode* 11, for example, he depicts himself as still smarting from an affair with Inachia in which he was an impoverished and shut-out suitor, and as now in thrall to the boy Lyciscus and dumb to his friends' salutary counsel. But even there Horace plays ironically with elegiac images of the lover's devotion: when he flings himself upon Inachia's doorstep, the violent language suggests slapstick comedy rather than erotic despair (22 *quibus lumbos et infregi latus* 'on which I smashed my pelvis and side'[36]), and a final twist predicts that deliverance from Lyciscus will come through another attachment, whether to a girl or to a boy.

The dispassionate outlook already visible there is taken further in *Odes* 1–3, where Horace is usually a veteran who looks on love's warfare from a distance.[37] As a consequence, his references to elegy as a genre become deprecatory (1.33 to Tibullus, 2.9 to Valgius) and his handling of elegiac situations more overtly ironic, as in *Odes* 3.10, where he poses as the shut-out lover but ends by warning Lyce that he won't lie on her doorstep in the rain for ever. *Odes* 4, however, complicates the story, beginning with a poem in which Horace's resistance to love finally crumbles in the face of his longing for the young Ligurinus; here Horace evokes not only his lyric models Sappho and Catullus, but also the ethos and language of Propertian elegy.[38] Elsewhere in the book Horace takes up Augustus-related themes that had been handled ironically by Propertius and adopts a different perspective; in particular, as Propertius had plundered *Odes* 1–3 to introduce his new book of elegies, Horace plays off the opening sequence of Propertius' collection at structurally important points. *Odes* 4.2, for example, ends by imagining a triumphant return of Augustus to Rome and the poet's own role as a

35 That is not to deny the significant part played in those epodes by Archilochean iambics and Hellenistic epigram; see L. Watson (2003) 358–63, 458–66.

36 L. Watson (2003) ad loc. rightly declines to see a reference to masturbation.

37 The clearest references to the *militia amoris* are in *Odes* 3.26.2, on Horace's past service, and 4.1.16, where Horace argues that the younger Paullus Fabius Maximus will more properly bear Venus' standards.

38 Compare 4.1.38–9 *iam uolucrem sequor / te* and Propertius 2.26.29–30 *heu! mare per longum mea cogitat ire puella; / hanc sequar*, and *uelocem* in Propertius 1.1.15 (describing Atalanta, but with clear relevance to Cynthia as well).

bystander; the situation resembles that of Propertius 3.4, but while the elegist views the procession reclining in his mistress's lap (15), Horace places himself among the cheering crowd.[39] It is in such deft transpositions of other poets' work to suit his own distinctive voice and stance that Horace's relationship to his Roman predecessors and contemporaries is most fully revealed.

FURTHER READING

I know of no comprehensive treatment of this chapter's subject, but several of its constituent aspects have been usefully discussed elsewhere. Nisbet (1995) vividly recreates the Roman literary landscape of Horace's early career. Jocelyn (1995) explicates Horace's criticisms of Plautus in the context of previous views of the playwright. The literary affiliations of the *Satires* have received particular attention in recent scholarship: on relations with neoteric poetry and Virgil see Zetzel (1980) and (2002), Scodel (1987), and Putnam (1996), more broadly Freudenburg (1993). Helpful commentary on individual poems and passages is provided by Rudd (1989), L. Watson (2003), and Nisbet and Hubbard (1970, 1978) and Nisbet and Rudd (2004). Finally, for readers with Italian, the *Enciclopedia Oraziana* (Mariotti 1996–8) offers detailed studies of Horace's Roman predecessors and contemporaries, with bibliographies that give particularly full coverage to the work of continental scholars; especially commendable are the overview of antecedents and models by Giancarlo Mazzoli (1997) and the discussion of elegy by Alessandro Barchiesi (1997). On Horace and Catullus see very recently Putnam (2006).

39 Putnam (1986) 58–60 (also noting the earlier appearance of the motif in Cornelius Gallus); generally on Horace's 'creative interchange' with Propertius 27–8.

6

MICHÈLE LOWRIE

Horace and Augustus

Given the conspicuous role Augustus plays in Roman poetry from the advent of his power as the young Caesar in the 30s BCE to his death, it is easy to forget the novelty of this feature. No single figure so dominates Republican literature. With virtual monarchy comes a tremendous literary focus. Horace offers a unique opportunity for examining a poetic response to this concentration of power because his oeuvre spans three decades and a multitude of genres. He consistently aims to define his place in this new society, whether as an apolitical individual, or as a poet with a public role. Horace speaks from each genre as an 'I' who is both no-one socially, and a member of the inner circle, though the relative proportion of these positions tilts more to the latter as time advances. Horace's paradoxical status answers to the new possibilities for being a subject and for being a poet under Augustus.

From his earliest to his latest writings, Horace is increasingly preoccupied with the first man in the state. Although Horace fought on the losing side as a military tribune at Philippi, with the start of his poetic career he appears allied to the Augustan camp, whether directly or indirectly through his patron Maecenas. He has been celebrated and condemned as a 'spokesman' for the Augustan programme;[1] he has been exonerated from such commitment as an ironist in an Epicurean vein;[2] it is fiercely debated whether his poetic warnings to the *princeps* constitute praise or blame.[3] However one comes down, Horace's relation to the *princeps* is a long, transformative journey.[4] Augustus

1 Syme (1939) 443–4 is enthusiastic; distaste in Zanker (1988) 158, 169, 176. Fraenkel (1957) 240 is defensive. Doblhofer (1966) measures Horace against panegyric conventions to determine sincerity, but see Nisbet (1969). Brink's (1982) 523–5 assessment of earlier views is brief, but on target.

2 Fowler (1995).

3 Lefèvre (1993) 164; Vidal (1994) 160; Lowrie (1997) 258–65.

4 Fraenkel (1957) 452 on *nos* in *Odes* 4, culminating in the conclusion of *Odes* 4.15, comments: 'Horace at long last came to praise and thank Augustus. He had a long way to go before he was able to speak like that.' Lowrie (1997) chapter 9. D. Kennedy (1992) 33 refers

is important for Horace not only because his coming to power changed the conditions for advancement at Rome. He posed an aesthetic problem: how to represent absolute power and still maintain poetic independence.[5] Horace's solution is perhaps best characterized as studied approach avoidance. Over time, poet and *princeps* develop a collaborative but unequal partnership. A consistent preoccupation is their relative powers.

We are unusually lucky to have a wealth of internal and external evidence for the relation of this highly political poet to his ruler. Substantial agreement exists about facts. Suetonius' life of Horace not only transmits important information, such as that Horace turned down, without alienating the *princeps*, Augustus' request to take up the position of writer of his personal correspondence (*Vita Horati* 10–12), but also quotes verbatim witticisms Augustus made at Horace's expense and extracts from his letters (13–16). The two contributed substantially to the *Ludi Saeculares* ('Century Games'), Augustus by orchestrating the festival, Horace by composing the *Carmen Saeculare* ('century poem'). The poem survives, as does the inscription describing the festival (*Acta*).[6] It attests to the poem's performance on both the Palatine and the Capitoline and reveals its position towards the end of the rites. In the early part of Horace's career, his relationship to Augustus was mediated through Maecenas, Horace's patron and a pre-eminent member of Augustus' 'cabinet'. By the end, Horace addressed Augustus directly in his lyric as well as in the Epistle to Augustus. The jocularity of Augustus' style in the material quoted by Suetonius suggests a high degree of personal intimacy between them as men. Most of the evidence for their relationship, however, derives from Horace's poetry, and the operative question is how the poet represents his ruler. The problematic of the artist and the sovereign cannot be approached from outside poetry or other cultural artefacts. Horace's representations are the perceptible aspects, however manifold, of a multifaceted reality.[7]

Culture both reflects and constitutes reality in an overdetermined process. Augustus' decisions to remove himself gradually from formal powers allowed him to present himself as restoring the Republic (*Res Gestae* 34). His building programme (*Res Gestae* 19–21) reinforced the image of his rule as a refoundation. When Horace advises the Roman people in the sixth Roman Ode (3.6.1–4) to restore the temples and excoriates contemporary marital

to the *Satires*' contribution to 'the process whereby the young Octavian of the proscriptions of the 40s BC was transformed into the saviour of the Republic at Actium'.

5 Fowler (1995). 6 See Pighi (1965) and Schnegg-Köhler (2002).

7 D. Kennedy (1992) generally, with special emphasis on Augustus as an idea, not just a person, 35.

relations, we are confronted with a series of related questions.[8] Did Horace expound his views before or after Augustus began restoring the temples, before or after he began pressing for marriage legislation? Is his emphasis the result of co-operation, of a poet parroting imperial policy, of an emperor picking up on a good idea, of Maecenas mediating between the two, or were these issues generally 'in the air'? The co-operation between Horace and Augustus in the *Ludi Saeculares* was still a decade away. The *Zeitgeist* has fallen out of favour as an explanation, and we cannot recuperate the historical particulars. While my sketch gives priority to Augustus and makes the poetry reflective of his decisions, these responded, however, if not directly to the poetry of Horace and Vergil, then to the cultural matrix in which they flourished. Ideology cannot be pinned down to a single source.

The question is of authorship: who gets to originate ideas and set them in motion? Augustus describes his power as *auctoritas* (*Res Gestae* 34.3), which he contrasts to legal and official *potestas*. Although the poets did not wield political power, their social and intellectual power is a kind of *auctoritas*.[9] It is the power to originate. Horace does not use *auctor* of Augustus; the word rather spans a wide cultural sphere (politics, *Odes* 3.5.46; poetry, *Satires* 1.10.66, *Ars Poetica* 45, 77; philosophy, *Odes* 1.28.14; fashion, *Satires* 2.2.50; abuse, *Satires* 1.4.80). A god can be an *auctor* (*Odes* 1.2.36, 3.3.66), as can a person at a point of origin (*Odes* 3.17.5). *Auctoritas* derives from *augeo*, and it increases with use.[10] I would suggest that the growing confidence with which Horace approaches Augustus over the span of his career is due to his increasing *auctoritas* as a poet. This is more decisive than Maecenas' political fate in fostering a more direct relationship between poet and *princeps*.[11]

Horace's discourse about his ruler must be analysed as poetry, and consequently, nuances of technique will decisively shape his actual representations of Augustus. Peeling off the formal elements will leave a bare skeleton containing many aspects of panegyric. This method has been favoured by those of a historical bent. Horace's value, however, is first and foremost as a poet. Those who insist on weighing his words conversely tend to set his poetry in

8 See Syme (1939) 339 for Horace's *Odes* anticipating reforms; Fraenkel (1957) 261; Nisbet and Rudd (2004) 83, 97, are confident that the poets reflect the 'official attitudes'.

9 Wallace-Hadrill (1997) traces the shifts in *auctoritas* in this period away from aristocrats toward intellectuals under imperial protection without considering the poets.

10 Ernout and Meillet (1939) under *augeo*; Galinsky (1996) chapter 1.

11 Bibliography on the topic of whether or not Maecenas 'fell from favour' and the greater involvement of Augustus in literary patronage after c. 18 BCE can be found in Brink (1995) 276–8.

an independent aesthetic sphere. Best is to take seriously the formal elements as interventions that helped shape his world.

The 30s is the decade of the *Satires* and *Epodes*, and the difference between the two genres is marked. In the *Epodes*, Caesar is the warrior at Actium; in the *Satires*, he is either the (potential) subject or the consumer of poetry. He does appear at *Satires* 2.6.56 in a question posed of Horace about the settlement of retired troops, but Horace's disavowal of privileged intelligence both acknowledges Caesar as a force in the state and removes himself from involvement. The private stance in satire, and the consistent depiction of his participation in Maecenas' circle as non-political, sit as counterpoint to the *Epodes*, where Horace twice (poems 7 and 16) addresses the people to excoriate them for civil war and reveals his personal engagement with the players at Actium (1 and 9). These two strands, man of action and literary material, will be intertwined and developed more fully in later representations of the *princeps*.

In the *Epodes*, Caesar functions as a symbol of power and victory. Horace channels friendship through Maecenas, as he is the addressee of both Actium epodes, but the collection's opening sums up their relative importance: Caesar's name occurs before Maecenas' (1.1–4). Maecenas is Caesar's friend, and Horace is Maecenas', but Horace is not prepared to follow up the chain.[12] Horace's adherence to the Caesarian cause appears only in the context of his friendship with his patron.[13] In *Epodes* 7 (17–20) and 16, Horace attributes civil war to the whole Roman people, with responsibility lying in the mythic past. Such heightened distance exonerates Caesar from responsibility and lends Horace a non-partisan voice, but his allegiance requires Maecenas' company in *Epodes* 9. Caesar's name also precedes Maecenas' in this poem (Cavarzere (1992) *ad loc.*) and articulates the poem (lines 2, 18, 37), but he is not confronted as a topic. Every instance of his name in this collection occurs in an oblique case. Although the war revolves around him, and Horace is happy to give details of the battle (9.19–20, 27–32), Caesar is the subject without being the focus. The party Horace anticipates celebrating at Maecenas' house will be in Caesar's honour (*uictore . . . Caesare*, 9.2); he himself, however, is not imagined as participating.

12 L. Watson (1995) 201; Fitzgerald (1988) 180.

13 Nisbet (1984) 8–9 reads the *Epodes* biographically: after Horace wrote the incendiary *Epodes* 7 and 16, Maecenas intervened. By Actium, he had bought him off with the Sabine farm and Horace remained an 'ingratiating ironist' ever after. Griffin (1993) 13 notes that Horace did not withdraw the poems, but remains within a biographical framework. White (1993) and Bowditch (2001) offer complex understandings of patronage.

Satires 1 is the collection least overtly concerned with Caesar.[14] His name's single occurrence accords him an active role at least potentially as a patron of the arts, but the much discussed *Caesar, qui cogere posset* ('Caesar, who could force', *Satires* 1.3.4) should not be taken out of context: even he would fail at getting Sardus Tigellius to sing on request (5–6). The name occurs by the way, and becomes conspicuous by its absence from the list of Horace's desired audience at the end of *Satires* 1.10. Although Maecenas and his literary friends predominate (81), the powerful men mentioned are Pollio and the Messallas (85).[15] In *Satires* 1.5, the journey to Brundisium, the poet's resolute focus on his own experience and friends (Hortensius, Maecenas, Plotius, Varius and Vergil) tantalises, given the importance of the treaty to be enacted at the journey's end. Antony and Caesar are not even mentioned. Horace coyly embellishes his own social importance, but removes himself from politics. With the opening of *Satires* 2, however, Caesar plays a greater role.

Caesar's potential as a topic for poetry first becomes itself a topic in *Satires* 2.1, where he emerges as a reader whose judgement counts. Horace uses indirection and has Trebatius propose Caesar's deeds to himself (*Caesaris inuicti res dicere*, 'to tell the deeds of unconquered Caesar', 11), and then begs off on the grounds of inability (12–15) (Fraenkel (1957) 149). This technique resembles the *recusatio*: the poet turns a compliment obliquely by modestly declining to write about an important man and makes a show of actual ability with a mini-version of the disavowed material (13–15). Here, however, no request is presented as having been made. The other model Trebatius suggests is not epic, but the example of Horace's satiric predecessor Lucilius, who wrote complimentary poetry about Scipio Aemilianus (16–17). This Horace cannot refuse on generic grounds, and his representation of Caesar as a reader here and at the end of the poem establishes important techniques of both approach and avoidance. Intervention in the world of politics is figured as socially dangerous. Caesar can both attack and protect poets, and the remedy is tact. Poetry must be offered gingerly, at the right time, and the situation handled properly to preclude an adverse reaction (18–20). Horace's metaphor of Caesar as a horse is satiric and lightens the perceived danger, but the issue hangs unresolved. By the end of the poem, however, Caesar is elevated to the absolute judge: if he finds poetry to be good, the poet will get off any putative libel charges – providing his satiric criticism was just to begin with (83–6). Horace defends himself by suggesting

14 DuQuesnay (1984), however, shows the *Satires* to be deeply political, partially through Horace's adoption of a non-political stance.

15 See G. Williams (1994) 395–6 on the social and political status of those on the list.

that Caesar does like his work, and this silences his detractors. His portrait of Caesar progresses from satiric to the praise Trebatius suggests, not fully fledged panegyric, but a depiction of him as *iustum . . . et . . . fortem* ('just and strong,' 16). The light touch is paradigmatic for the genre and emerges again at *Satires* 2.5.62. Tiresias predicts Augustus' advent in language whose portentiousness and panegyric allusion to Apollo's prediction of the advent of Ptolemy in Callimachus' *Hymn to Delos* 166–88, are deflated by the fable about legacy-hunters during Horace's time.

The first collection of *Odes* (1–3) witnesses the first and second Augustan settlements, and brings us to 23 BCE. Although Augustus is a leitmotif in *Odes* 1–3, the overall tonality is rather sympotic, erotic and in the spirit of *carpe diem* ('pluck the day', *Odes* 1.11.8). Horace does not address Augustus directly, or devote any single poem entirely to him.[16] Politics breaks into Horace's quiet and secluded lyric space from the outside, rather than occupying the centre. The dominance of the private, however, is a political stance.[17] Whether this represents a defeatist retreat from Republicanism on the poet's part, or a celebration of the Augustan peace, cannot be resolved. More than anything, Horace's definition of himself in relation to Caesar defines the new imperial subject.

As in the *Epodes*, Caesar is subtly removed from responsibility for the civil wars. In *Odes* 1.35, Horace prays to Fortuna to preserve Caesar as he wages foreign wars (29–32). The subsequent two stanzas lament civil war, but the first person plural (*nos*, 34) lends the entire Roman people the responsibility. A reader can forge the link, but it is in our choice. Caesar's victory is portrayed as the salvation of the state, and he emerges as its saviour (*Odes* 1.2.41–52; 3.24.25–30). In *Odes* 1.37, the omission of Antony and the focus on Cleopatra present the battle of Actium as a foreign war, and the simile comparing Caesar to a hawk casts him in a heroic light. Although the poem's last word is *triumpho*, the focus on Cleopatra's suicide, which prevented her being paraded down the *Via Sacra* in chains, evokes Caesar's triple triumph in 29 BCE in an oblique rather than celebratory fashion. Salvation is expressed negatively, since Caesar drives Cleopatra away from Rome, where Horace has her threatening the Capitoline. As in the *Epodes*, Caesar is predominantly a man of action, though, as in the *Satires*, he comes up, usually indirectly, as a topic of poetry to be disavowed (*Odes* 1.6.11–12, the praise disavowed is mainly Agrippa's; 2.12.10, Horace disavows mythic and

16 Brink (1982) 536 and 547; Feeney (1993) 53–4; Lyne (1995) 195–6; Lowrie (1997) 75–6. The apparent exception of *Odes* 1.2.52 is treated below.

17 Adorno (1991); D. Kennedy (1992) 34.

older historical material, while Caesar is offered humorously as a topic for Maecenas' prose histories).

When Horace does embrace Caesar overtly as a topic for poetry (*Odes* 1.12, 2.9 and 3.25), the poems retreat in some respects from their stated aims. Each occurs in a significant position in the collection. The first closes the Parade Odes opening Book 1,[18] and picks up Caesar from 1.2, where he appears as Mercury on earth. *Odes* 1.12 reserves Caesar for the climactic position, heralded by the poem's opening question (*quem uirum aut heroa lyra uel acri / tibia sumis celebrare, Clio? / quem deum?* 'What man or hero do you undertake to celebrate on the lyre or keen reed, Clio? What god?' 1–3), which Horace answers in chiastic order. The actual treatment of him, however, is distant: hymnic vocatives attach to Jupiter, and Caesar is subordinated to the king of the gods. The technique is similar to that in *Odes* 1.2, whose ending, *te duce, Caesar* ('with you as leader, Caesar') is disorienting. The ablative absolute follows an address to Mercury, who both is and is not Caesar in disguise, so we are not sure who is actually addressed. In *Odes* 2.9, the mid-point of the second book, Horace suggests Augustus as an anti-elegiac topic to Valgius. The first person plural *cantemus* ('let us sing') brings the poet into the celebration of *Augusti tropaea / Caesaris* ('trophies of Augustus Caesar' 19–20), but defers more than a token list of accomplishments to some other poetic production. *Odes* 3.25 corresponds in its position, six odes from the collection's end, to *Odes* 1.6. Horace reverses his earlier disavowal of the *laudes egregii Caesaris* ('praises of outstanding Caesar' 1.6.11), and girds himself up to insert the *egregii Caesaris / . . . decus* ('glory of outstanding Caesar' 3.25.4) in the stars. The poem, however, is more about Horace's inspiration than his *laudandus*. In each case, either some formal element or the poem's focus on poetic choices rather than Caesar himself keeps his praises from occupying centre stage. Whether we view this as decorous and courtly discourse or a reluctance to do what he says depends on our interpretive strategies and commitments.

Caesar often comes up by the way, but this only enhances his power. In a hymn to Diana and Apollo, Horace again reserves the final prayer – to be sung by others – for Caesar. He is to be hymned not personally, but as representative of the Roman state. The proposed prayer is to avert war, famine and pestilence on to foreign enemies, away from *populo et principe Caesare* (*Odes* 1.21.14). This phrase acknowledges Augustus' pre-eminent position, not only with the appellation *princeps* ('first man'), but by his subtly taking the place of the Senate in the regular phrase for the state:

18 See Lowrie (1995) 34 for bibliography on where the Parade Odes actually end.

senatus populusque Romanus.[19] He is not even named at *Odes* 3.24.25, but is intimated with *o quisquis* ('o whoever'). The clarity of the reference emphasises his singularity: whoever wishes to remove civic discord from the state and to have the appellation *pater urbium*, 'father of cities', inscribed on his statues is welcome to rein in immoderate freedom.

In the Roman Odes opening Book 3, Pindaric elevation enables a closer approach to a powerful *laudandus*. Augustus occurs at decisive points, in the opening stanzas of 3.3 and 3.5, and in the mid-point of 3.4, where Gigantomachy allegorises the civil wars. He is 'Augustus' in both framing poems, where Horace intimates his future divinity, and 'Caesar' at the end of the civil wars. Augustus will join the gods in a symposium (3.3.11–12); he is about to disband his troops in 3.4 and turn to the Muses for recreation (3.4.37–40); he will be a god on earth when he has vanquished the Britons and the Persians. These images are peaceful, where peace encompasses foreign but not domestic warfare, and accord with Augustus' indirect presence in the Roman Odes. Horace articulates major pieces of the 'Augustan programme', so that poet and *princeps* appear to operate in tandem, if not yet actually collaborating. The famous *dulce et decorum est pro patria mori* ('it is sweet and honourable to die for the fatherland', *Odes* 3.2.13) is easily excerpted as a gnome, but the sad regret of the surrounding context tempers any apparent patriotism. *Odes* 3.6 in particular heralds the rebuilding of the temples, a traditional view of marriage in anticipation of the Augustan marriage legislation, and a sentimental valorisation of erstwhile virile rusticity. The Roman Odes darkly emphasise failure and the need for moral renewal, and in their wake Horace turns to lighter themes. The effect would be very different had he placed this powerful sequence of poems in a climactic position.

Near mid-position in Book 3, Horace celebrates Augustus' return from Spain in 24 BCE (*Odes* 3.14). His characterisation of Augustus as *uictor* (4) in a foreign war is his closest approach to panegyric in *Odes* 1–3. Formal avoidance, however, still marks his technique. Despite the ceremonial context, Horace does not direct the poem to the honorand, but rather addresses the people (*o plebs*, 1), the virgin boys and girls probably forming a chorus (10), then finally a slave-boy (17), sent to fetch a courtesan for the festivities – or not.[20] He would not have tolerated her resistance when Plancus was consul. This was the year Horace fought as military tribune at Philippi. Puzzling questions abound: Why recall the civil war? Why negate fear of civil disturbance under Caesar (14–16) at this point? Why evoke the appellation

19 Nisbet and Hubbard (1970) ad loc.

20 Brink's (1982) 540–3 handling of the common scholarly division between 'public' and 'private' in this ode should be paradigmatic for this issue.

uniuira ('of one husband') falsely of Livia (5)?[21] We feel a need to decide whether Horace accepts or rejects the ideology. In its support, Livia wears the role of faithful wife; Horace's private celebration at the poem's middle marks his role as lyrist, and his new level of tolerance lays aside his earlier hot-headed Republicanism; now peace averts any fear of external or internal disturbance. For rejection, these elements all recall truths which could go unspoken. Perhaps Horace best encapsulates his age by making it impossible for us to choose between his acceptance of the ideology and his understanding it for what it is.

The emphasis on friendship in *Epistles* 1[22] (published c. 20–19 BCE) makes of Augustus mostly a remote figure. He hovers, a subject of interest, above the easy social interactions between Horace and his addressees. References to his military and state functions are by the way. The first is to Tiberius as his stepson (1.3.2), off on campaign; Augustus' recovery of the standards from the Parthians is 'news' (1.12.28, also 1.18.56); his birthday is a public holiday (1.5.9). His importance makes him a topic Horace identifies but does not adopt. Horace's enquiry to Iulius Florus about the literary activities of Tiberius' entourage shows that he expects others to take up the subject: *quis sibi res gestas Augusti scribere sumit* ('who is undertaking to write of Augustus' accomplishments?', 1.3.7). At *Epistles* 1.16.25–9, several lines offer an example of *laudes Augusti*. Praise is mentioned rather than used, but this technique makes the praise less inoperative than indirect. The juxtaposition of *Iuppiter* and *Augusti* in 29 gives more to the emperor than Horace's obliqueness detracts.

In keeping with the thematics of *Epistles* 1, in several places, Augustus is treated as a powerful friend, but a friend nonetheless. Horace identifies Augustus as his audience more confidently and at greater length than in *Satires* 2.1. An imaginary interlocutor teases him for retaining his writings for Jupiter's ears (*Iouis auribus*, 1.19.43) – the intervening voice adroitly exculpates Horace's gauche allegory. *Epistles* 1.13 purports to instruct Vinnius exactly how to deliver a collection of poems, thought to be *Odes* 1–3, to Augustus, whose name frames the poem (*Augusto* 2, *Caesaris* 18). The poet's ironic worry defuses the potential awkwardness of the book's presentation. Vinnius is a buffer against addressing Augustus directly. This technique attracted sufficient attention to lead Augustus eventually to invite

21 Nisbet and Rudd (2004) ad loc. try to save Horace from a gaffe by taking *unico . . . marito* as 'incomparable husband'. Their parallels use *unice* in a way that would indeed prevent the suggestion of the *uniuira*, but that is not the word Horace chose to use.

22 Kilpatrick's (1986) title is *The Poetry of Friendship*; its importance is defined in xix–xxiv, and it structures the book.

Horace to address him in person, though we do not know when (Suetonius 19–20).

The poetry of the teens represents a new stage in the poet's relation to his emperor. Both contributed actively to the *Ludi Saeculares* (17 BCE) and the most direct treatment of Augustus post-dates this event. Horace continues to deploy familiar techniques for maintaining artistic independence, but their tone changes. The *Carmen Saeculare* does not correspond exactly to the religious rites of the *Ludi*, since Horace prays only to the Olympian and not to the chthonic deities. Fraenkel argues that the poem was not fully integrated into the event ((1957) 364–82), but ignores the games after the poem's double performance on the Palatine and the Capitoline, and his view is exaggerated (Feeney (1998) 32–8). The poem's relation to its socio-political context is not a contest between aesthetic freedom and toadyism. As a work of art, it participates in and comments on a process of citation and innovation authored by Augustus, who consulted many sources in his arrangement of the ceremonies. Horace refers only by innuendo to Augustus (*clarus Anchisae Venerisque sanguis* 'illustrious blood of Anchises and Venus'; Putnam (2000) 5), but the entire poem celebrates the Augustan peace and Horace refers conspicuously to the marriage legislation (17–20). Many deem this stanza inartistic, but these and the surrounding verses participate in a debate running through Augustan poetry on the relation of poetry to the law, and reflect on the festival's status as a singular and repeatable event that partakes in both writing and performance.

After the *Carmen Saeculare*, references to Augustus intensify. *Odes* 4 (13 BCE) comes closer to panegyric than *Odes* 1–3,[23] and Horace addresses Augustus directly several times here and in the epistle bearing his name. Suetonius tells us that both were commissioned by Augustus, and scholars have reviled either Horace himself for acquiescing, or the suggestion of Horatian pandering. At issue are the nuances of *iniunxerit* ('enjoined' 17) and *coegerit* ('compelled' 18). White shows that these are standard words for literary requests ((1993) 65), and furthermore, these words are Suetonius'.[24] Augustus' own words are playfully teasing, though, out of context, their tone is difficult to gauge:

> irasci me tibi scito, quod non in plerisque eiusmodi scriptis mecum potissimum loquaris. an uereris ne apud posteros infame tibi sit, quod uidearis familiaris nobis esse?
> *Vita Horati* 19–20

23 Vidal's (1994) 166 notion that all ambiguity has disappeared is simplistic.

24 An incisive analysis of this passage is Hills (2001).

> Know that I am angry with you because in your many writings of this sort you do not especially speak with me. Or are you afraid that it will be a source of infamy to you with posterity, that you appear to be my friend?

Horace's solutions to imperial suggestion demonstrate artistic integrity, partly by distancing techniques such as folding Augustus as a topic into poetic issues, displacing him from centre stage, and introducing an intervening voice or *laudandus*, but always by the originality of the treatment.

Three clusters of poems in *Odes* 4 concern Augustus, near the beginning (4.2), middle (4.5 and 6) and end (4.14 and 15), and the poet gradually lets his distance go. In *Odes* 4.2, the imagined triumph over the Sygambri in Gaul advances in explicitness over the praise accorded the ruler in *Odes* 1–3, but Horace suggests Iulus Antonius, a poet with Pindaric aspirations, as a surrogate to undertake the celebrations (*concines maiore poeta plectro / Caesarem* 'you, a poet of a greater plectrum, will sing of Caesar' 4.2.33–4). Horace's voice will blend into the people's triumphal slogans (*canam recepto / Caesare felix* 'I will sing, happy at Caesar's return' 4.2.47–8), and the sacrifice he promises symbolises the tenets of Roman Callimacheanism and the poem's own elegance.[25] Praise accrues to Augustus' surrogates Tiberius and Drusus in *Odes* 4.4, where his interest in them is characterised as paternal (27–8). Although *Odes* 4.14 also praises the stepsons as extensions of the emperor's power, starting with 4.5 Horace addresses Augustus in his own voice. The actual vocative in 4.5 is *dux bone* (5, 37), spoken once by Horace directly, once quoted and shared with the people; Caesar's name occurs in oblique cases (16, 27). Although DuQuesnay (1995) argues that the poem was performed in the ceremonies welcoming Augustus back from Gaul, it is hard to pin any utterance down to this event. Augustus has not yet returned at the poem's beginning, and by the end the ceremonies are not localised but spread over Italy among the Roman people. At 4.14.3, Horace finally says *Auguste*, and at 4.15.4 uses a vocative *Caesar*.

The last two odes of Book 4 and the Epistle to Augustus together constitute Horace's final interventions in this relationship, and they take it in different directions, partially for generic reasons. Both, however, praise Augustus more directly than ever before, and both still use distancing techniques. The lyric lauds Augustus' exercise of military power through the agency of his stepsons (*milite . . . tuo* 4.14.9); peace finally dawns with the cessation of civil discord and the subjugation of foreign enemies. Horace reverses the topos of Apollo dissuading a poet from telling of warfare because of his slender genre: now the new age (*tua, Caesar, aetas*, 4.15.4) has adapted itself to a lyric modality

25 G. Davis (1991) 133–43; Seager (1993) 36 sees Horace as grudging.

so that Horace can celebrate it within his genre. Up to this point in his writings, Horace has discursively subordinated his treatment of Augustus to poetic concerns. This veil has not entirely dropped off. *Odes* 4.14 opens with a nod to the state's methods of glorification, inscriptions and *fasti*, and *Odes* 4.15 closes with an image re-creating the *carmina convivalia* ('festive poems') of old. Writing and song, official and familial honour cover the gamut of representational practices. Horace's last lyric word is *canemus* ('we will sing'), but we are left wondering if he includes himself merely as a citizen as at *Odes* 4.2, or whether he lends the celebration his lyric voice. Either way, this voice is subsequently silent. He has finally brought together his art and his sovereign. There is nothing left for him to accomplish as a lyrist.

With *Epistles* 2, however, Horace still has something to say, and this book concerns literature, its practitioners and its cricitism.[26] Augustus is a mere element of history that affected the poet's life in the Epistle to Florus (2.2.48), and he is absent in the *Ars Poetica*. In the Epistle to Augustus, Horace answers the emperor's request by speaking to him about poetry, its history at Rome and the role of the poet in society. The topic suits the addressee, because these issues define concerns shared by both poet and *princeps*.[27] Augustus is praised fulsomely at the opening, but Horace makes a witty transition away from him towards literary history: the great culture-heroes complained that they were not praised in their lifetimes; Augustus is the exception, because he is so praised; but the Roman people is less clairvoyant in other areas, and particularly carps at modern poetry. The poem returns to Augustus at the end, this time with his role as a patron of the arts, where he is identified as the author of the Palatine library and his support of artists, particularly of Varius and Vergil, is acknowledged and contrasted favourably with the tastelessness of Alexander the Great. The poem, however, concludes with Horace declining to write up Augustus' accomplishments (*res componere gestas*, 2.1.251). Horace artfully asserts his independence, even while he recognises that he has in fact praised Augustus in the way here disavowed. His sample of military narrative recalls his final lyrics precisely, even in the words' metrical position despite the difference of metre (*arces / montibus impositas* 'citadels placed on mountains', *Epistles* 2.1.252–3; *arces / Alpibus impositas*, *Odes* 4.14.11–12). Horace's final words to Augustus in both genres are the culmination of a lifetime's attempt to represent a man whose singular position

26 I incline to think that all of *Epistles* 2 post-dates *Odes* 4.

27 A. Barchiesi ((1993) 157 = (2001) 84) stresses the tactful accord between poet and *princeps* in the new discourse of power; Feeney ((2002) 172–3) their shared position of 'classic status' and the 'gravitational pull' between them.

made him an aesthetic challenge. Horace offers praise at the same time as he maintains a position of independence that renders his praise all the more valuable.

FURTHER READING

Before D. Kennedy (1992), much debate revolved around whether Horace was 'Augustan' or 'anti-Augustan', with ambiguity mediating between the two (still in Vidal 1994). These terms are now usually brought up to be dismissed in favour of the idea that Horace's poetry contributed to and benefited from Augustus' ideological hegemony, however the poetry functions and whatever the historical poet intended. The view of poetry as a direct expression of the biographical poet's feelings has also fallen by the wayside, though practitioners persist (Lefèvre (1993) 164–72). White (1993) approaches patronage from a cultural historical, Bowditch (2001) from a Marxist perspective. G. Davis (1991), Lowrie (1997) and Oliensis (1998) focus on the poetry's rhetoric in their analyses of individual poems, many of which involve Augustus. Treatments of Horace's relation to Augustan ideology are La Penna (1963), Seager (1993) and Santirocco (1995); of Horatian panegyric are Doblhofer (1966), Putnam (1990) and Fowler (1995). Horace and Augustus intersect numerous times on religious issues in Feeney (1998); this 28–40, Putnam (2000), Schnegg-Köhler (2002) and A. Barchiesi (2002) offer the most stimulating recent treatments of the *Carmen Saeculare*. Brink (1982) 523–5 evaluates some earlier positions and continues the chapter with a discussion of historical and literary periodisation and Augustanism. Doblhofer (1981) 1922–36 gives comprehensive coverage of the problem up to his time. Lyne (1995) treats all the major issues. Fraenkel (1957) remains classic; see especially 239–97, 364–99, 440–53.

PART 2

Poetic genres

7

LINDSAY WATSON

The *Epodes*: Horace's Archilochus?

Horace's *Epodes* were composed in approximately 42–30 BCE,[1] during Rome's bloody transition from republic to autocracy. Dramatically speaking, the book is set in the run-up to the battle of Actium on 2 September 31 BCE.[2] The *Epodes* were for many years the least regarded of Horace's works. Reasons include a tendency to focus on a few explicitly historical pieces (1, 7, 9, 16) to the relative exclusion of the rest,[3] and a prudish distaste for the explicit sexuality of *Epodes* 8 and 12.[4] In the last two decades, however, there has been a reawakening of interest in these difficult and fascinating poems, with *Satires* 1 the earliest of Horace's works. Three commentaries have appeared since 1992 and there have been a number of important general studies.[5] The current trend is to read the *Epodes* holistically, that is to say as an integral body of verse.[6] This represents a reaction to sometimes over-schematic attempts to divide the book up into balancing pairs[7] and the above-mentioned tendency to privilege the 'serious' poems at the expense of the lighter, more occasional pieces. But the pendulum has perhaps swung too far in the other direction. To embrace a holistic reading is to underplay the polymorphous diversity of the collection – in this respect a direct inheritor of Callimachus' *Iamboi*[8] – and to risk enshrining as

1 Horace began writing verses upon returning to Italy after Philippi (*Epistles* 2.2.50ff.). The latest datable *Epode*, 9, deals with Actium. Allowing some months for revision, we arrive at 30 BC. Kraggerud (1984) holds that the book is designed to be read from a pre- and post-Actian perspective.

2 Du Quesnay (2002).

3 E.g. Fraenkel (1957).

4 Documentation in L. Watson (2003), 36, 40. T. E. Page (1890) and others omit them entirely.

5 See 'Further reading'.

6 Notably Fitzgerald (1988); Oliensis (1991), and (1998) 64–101; Gowers (1993a) 280–310.

7 E.g. Carrubba (1969); D. H. Porter (1995).

8 But see the cautionary remarks of L. Watson (2003) 11–13. Callimachus' *Iamboi*: Dawson (1950); Kerkhecker (1999).

overarching themes certain topics (e.g. the dog star, dyspepsia)[9] of dubious universality.

The title *Epodes* derives from *epodos* sc. *stichos*, 'an epodic verse'. This properly describes a verse which follows or 'echoes' a preceding (usually longer) one, but came by synecdoche to refer to the epodic distich and by extension to a poem composed in a series of such distichs.[10] The most straightforward example of this system is *Epodes* 1–10, composed after the model of Archilochus fr. 172ff. West in a succession of iambic trimeters followed by dimeters. The systems employed for *Epodes* 11–16 are less homogeneous, the metre of the second or 'epodic' verse being broadly speaking different from the first, while in the case of the transitional poem 11, an *Epode* with an identifiably Archilochean metrical forerunner,[11] the second verse is anomalously but permissibly longer than the first. In the final poem, the epodic structure is abandoned for stichic iambic trimeters.

'*Epodes*' is the name by which Horace's book is usually known, but it is by no means certain that this represents the poet's own choice of nomenclature. When Horace speaks of these poems he uses the generic descriptor *iambi*.[12] The issue of title is important. Were it certain that Horace styled his book *Epodi*, it would seem that he was playing on *epode*, 'spell, incantation',[13] in recognition of the pivotal role played by magic in the fabric of the work. Unfortunately the evidence in favour of '*Epodes*' derives from late antiquity, and it is perhaps most judicious to leave open the question of whether Horace labelled his book *Iambi* or *Epodi*.[14] If in what follows the title '*Epodes*' is adopted, this is in deference to convention and house style.

In *Epistles* 1.19, a retrospective of his poetic career, Horace boasted:

> Parios ego primus iambos
> ostendi Latio, numeros animosque secutus
> Archilochi, non res et agentia verba Lycamben

> I was the first to introduce Parian iambics to Latium, adopting the rhythms and the spirit of Archilochus, but not his subject-matter and the words that hounded Lycambes. (23–5)

Horace is apparently saying that he transplanted to Roman soil the metres and ethos of Archilochus, the seventh-century Greek poet of Paros who was

9 Respectively Oliensis (1991); (1998 esp. 80); Gowers (1993a). Other suggested thematic clusters: Büchner (1970b); Fitzgerald (1988); D. H. Porter (1995).

10 Cavarzere (1992) 13.

11 Bremer, Talman Kip, van Erp and Slings (1987) 51–9.

12 *Epodes*. 14.7, *Epistle* 1.19.23, less pertinently *Odes* 1.16.22–5.

13 Cf. Gowers (1993a) 281–2, 288–9; S. J. Harrison (2001a) 176–7; also Oliensis (1998) 69, 76.

14 So Cavarzere (1992) 9–14.

credited with inventing the iambic genre, but did not engage in sustained attacks on a single individual, as Archilochus did in the case of Lycambes, who supposedly promised Archilochus the hand of his daughter Neobule, then reneged upon his undertaking, unleashing in the poet a torrent of vengeful invective which drove Lycambes and his daughters to suicide.[15] Also implicit in this pocket history of the *Epodes*' genesis is Horace's dilution of the extreme virulence for which Archilochus was notorious.[16]

A second piece of evidence for the literary seedbed from which the *Epodes* sprang comes in *Epode* 6 *namque in malos asperrimus / parata tollo cornua, / qualis Lycambae spretus infido gener / aut acer hostis Bupalo*, 'for, most savage against them, I raise my horns to attack the malignant,[17] as did his son-in-law spurned by faithless Lycambes or Bupalus' fierce antagonist'. Here, in a programmatic[18] exploration of the iambic ethos, Horace states that he will respond to provocation in the relentless fashion of Archilochus with Lycambes, or Hipponax, the sixth-century poet of Ephesus, who, in a suspicious replication of the Lycambes story,[19] supposedly hounded to death his enemy Bupalus by the lethal violence of his attacks.

As we have just seen, in his account of his literary models for the *Epodes*, Horace privileges Archilochus. Recent criticism has taken the poet at his word.[20] Hence it will be convenient to examine the *Epodes* through the lens of the archaic Greek poet, while simultaneously holding up to scrutiny the poet's claim to be a Roman Archilochus. For the most pressing challenge which confronted Horace when he took up his iambic stylus was how to make iambus relevant in the socio-historical matrix of first-century-BCE Rome, a process of accommodation which inevitably demanded significant modification of literary and thematic modalities. Moreover, the Archilochean character of the book is overlaid with additional influences in the shape of Callimachus' *Iamboi* (third century BCE) and Horace's immediate predecessor in iambus, Catullus,[21] two vital if not explicitly acknowledged presences in the book.

Archilochus famously declared himself both poet and soldier,[22] and it is no accident that Horace commences the *Epode* book with a piece which revisits the Archilochean motifs of poetry, friendship and war by sea. At

15 L. Watson (2003) 263–4 for testimonia and discussions.

16 Archilochus' virulence: Gerber (1999), testimonia 12, 16–32, 35–6, 40, 42, Cratinus fr. 6 *CGF*. Horace's dilution of same: L. Watson (2003) 4–6.

17 L. Watson (2003) 262–3.

18 Buchheit (1961); E. A. Schmidt (1977) 405–6.

19 L. Watson (2003) 263–4 for testimonia and discussions.

20 Mankin (1995); S. J. Harrison (2001a); and A. Barchiesi (2001a), with the important caution 161. Cf. L. Watson (2003) 4–17.

21 Heyworth (1993).

22 Fr. 1 West.

the same time, in a programmatically significant adumbration of a dominant thematic,[23] he disclaims Archilochean bellicosity and virility, styling himself a *mollis vir*, 'a womanish man', *imbellis ac firmus parum*, 'unwarlike and lacking in strength' and comparing himself to a mother bird which fears for its unfledged chicks but cannot offer them protection against the superior might of predators (10, 16, 19–22).

It has been noted that iambic, in Archilochus' hands, was a potent instrument of social control, articulating and promoting ideals common to the poet and his sodality, and conversely showering with mockery those who deviated from that standard.[24] It has equally been remarked that *iambos* typically arises in times of social change or political stasis:[25] the iambic poet hence feels empowered to preach to the populace at large appropriate behaviour at crucial junctures in their history. It is no surprise to find Horace, in the crisis-ridden 30s BCE, taking up that particular Archilochean mantle: in *Epodes* 7 and 16 he harangues the Romans, in tones of deep pessimism,[26] for their headlong rush into the self-destructive madness of civil war. And in similar fashion, the attack on the loathsome parvenu of *Epode* 4, or the twin broadsides against the superannuated sexuality of the high-born matron of 8 and 12, can be read at one level, not as the expression of personal animus, but as symbolic of the moral deliquescence of the dying Republic.

By adopting a genre a poet simultaneously appropriates that genre's persona.[27] An important aspect of the iambic voice is that it is partial, biased, unilateralist. This dimension of iambus is productively harnessed by Horace, as he moves from outsider to insider over the course of ten years. Returning to Italy 'with wings clipped' after Philippi (42 BCE), where he fought unsuccessfully on the side of the Liberators, Horace found himself deprived of his paternal estate, and, he claims, constrained by poverty to write verses.[28] Among his earliest efforts were the 'civic' *Epodes* 7 and 16, dating, most would agree,[29] to 39–38 BCE. Here the poet's stance is judiciously impartial. 'The Romans' are excoriated *en masse* for their renewed descent into internecine strife. Not a word is said about those responsible for the recrudescence of civil war, the rival dynasts Antony and Octavian, and, less culpably, Sextus Pompey. Instead the blame is placed, nebulously, on an ancestral curse that dogs the race and the tendency of powerful states to consume themselves in an orgy of self-destruction.

23 Discussed under iambic 'impotence' below. 24 Slings (1990) 1–30.

25 O'Higgins (2003) 63. 26 The influence of Sallust's *Histories* has been detected.

27 A. Barchiesi (2001a) 152–3. 28 *Epistles* 2.2.50–4.

29 Kraggerud (1984) 44–65, however, dates 7 to 32, and 16 (p. 136) to around the time of Actium. Similarly Mankin (1995).

Such even-handedness will not last. In 38 BCE, according to the accepted dating,[30] Horace's artistic promise saw him taken up into the entourage of Octavian's man of affairs, Maecenas, with all the obligations to trade mutual benefactions that such a relationship entailed,[31] in Horace's case the composition of politically engaged poetry. *Epode* 4 is revealing of the resultant development. Datable to the months before the final showdown with Sextus Pompey in 36 BCE, the poem is an attack on the inordinate rise to wealth and position of a delinquent ex-slave. In that sense the *Epode* maintains Horace's earlier stance as a promoter of civic hygiene, since the loathsome *arriviste* symbolises the topsy-turvydom and class porousness which characterised the death-throes of the Republic. But on the other hand the concluding revelation that the parvenu has been enrolled as a military tribune on the Octavianic side (17–20) provides the launching-pad for two propagandist messages, one explicit, one implicit: first, an officially inspired misrepresentation of Sextus as a piratical leader of renegade slaves (pointing the irony of the worthless ex-slave's fighting against them),[32] second, the imputation that the Octavianic forces are the morally superior side and should have no truck with the likes of the parvenu. And, by placing the second half of the poem in the mouths of passers-by, Horace makes the citizens, tendentiously, endorse views to which many would not in fact have subscribed.[33]

The apogee of Horace's ideological partisanship is *Epode* 1's thematic twin, *Epode* 9, set in the confused hours following Actium. In keeping with the emergent regime's pretence that the Actian campaign was against a foreign foe, the focus is on Cleopatra, her eunuch minions, symbols of Eastern decadence, and the degradation to which the Antonian soldiers submit by their servitude to both (11–16). The defeated Antony is designated a *hostis*, 'enemy of the state', signifying his alienation from his homeland (27),[34] while the routing of Sextus Pompey from his natal element, the sea,[35] is made a harbinger of definitive success in the present campaign (7–10): an account of Sextus' career egregiously at odds with the facts.[36]

Iambos traditionally blended praise with blame:[37] the dispraise of the Antonians in 9 is framed by enthusiastic endorsements of the Caesarian cause. But the most characteristic generic marker of iambus was undoubtedly its aggressiveness, a feature captured in the association of *iambos* with Greek

30 E.g. Nisbet (1984) 8 = (1995) 169–70. 31 Cf. generally Bowditch (2001).

32 For the misrepresentation see L. Watson (2003) 169–71. 33 Cf. L. Watson (2002).

34 *Hostis* is related to *hospes*, 'stranger'. See further L. Watson (2003) 332–3.

35 Naval successes encouraged Sextus to declare himself Neptune's son: L. Watson (2003) 319–20.

36 L. Watson (2003) 314–5. 37 Nagy (1976); O'Higgins (2003) 66.

iapto, 'hurl a weapon', and an insistence that the poetry of Archilochus, the inventor of the genre, was fuelled by rage: Horace's *Archilochum proprio rabies armavit iambo*, 'furious anger armed Archilochus with the iambic that was particularly his own' (*Ars* 79) succinctly expresses both ideas.[38] The Parian poet's outpourings of hostility were most famously associated with his vengeful attacks upon the Lycambids: but his displeasure was equally vented against others, in tones of varying intensity. Iambic aggression is duly replicated in the *Epodes*. Here too the mood can vary from wry amusement or derisive laughter to unbridled rage. And, also as in Archilochus and iambic more generally, anger can take the form of *aischrologia*, obscene abuse, a key aspect of *iambos* which reflects alike the genre's presumptive origins,[39] its profound misogyny and the scurrility for which Archilochus was notorious.[40] All the women of the *Epodes*, in keeping with the reductionist dialectic of anti-feminism, are objectified as body, or viewed through the filter of their sexual activities. A case in point is the sex-crazed old woman of *Epode* 8, who, in a brutal catalogue of her corporeal parts, is disabused of the notion that she can produce in Horace a flicker of desire:

> to think that you can ask what unstrings my virility, decaying as you are with a long aeon, when your teeth are black and advanced old age ploughs wrinkles into your brow, and there gapes between your shrivelled buttocks an ugly anus like a dyspeptic cow's! But of course I am turned on by your withered bosom and breasts, like a mare's udders, and your flabby belly and skinny thighs tacked on to swollen ankles. (1–10)

The literary pedigree of this thumbnail sketch is too complex to go into here.[41] But certain of the details explicitly advertise their Archilochean pedigree,[42] and the poem as a whole is fed by the further currents of explicitly Roman colouring (11–16) and a Catullan taste for transgressive language.

Thematic variety is a much-studied aspect of the *Epodes*:[43] these incorporate, in addition to poems previously mentioned, a super-hyperbolic squib on garlic gastralgia (3); curses invoking shipwreck and death upon 'stinking' Maevius (10); a rhapsodic account of rural beatitude rounded off by a famously debunking conclusion (2); lengthy treatments of the murderous activities of the nightmarish witch Canidia (5, 17); proto-elegies and lyric

38 Cf. Catullus 36.5 *truces vibrare iambos*, 'hurl angry iambics'.

39 O'Higgins (2003) 84, passim.

40 Misogyny in iambus: O'Higgins (2003) 64–5, 74–82. Archilochean scurrility, especially against women: Gerber (1999), testimonia 18–21, 40.

41 See L. Watson (2003) 288–92 for literary models.

42 See L. Watson (2003) 6–7.

43 E.g. Fedeli (1978).

(11, 13–15) which impart to the second half of the book a notably different character from the first, deliberately problematising its generic identity as iambus. Too often such variety has been ascribed to the influence of Callimachus' richly diverse book of thirteen (or seventeen) *Iamboi*, without a parallel awareness that *iambos* as practised by its archaic representatives Archilochus, Hipponax and Simonides was equally a hodgepodge.[44] In part this was an inevitability, given the highly occasional, 'here and now' character of early iambus: an occasionality which Horace conspicuously strives to replicate. With the partial exception of 2, 6 and 11, all the *Epodes* take their starting-point from a particular moment in time.

It has been remarked that the iambic poet, who victimises others, is himself a victim.[45] Archilochus' attacks upon Lycambes and family, like other of his fusillades, are retributory, that is to say predicated upon offence taken or hurt suffered: in the case of Lycambes the only means of recourse against an irremediable wrong.[46] On one occasion Archilochus complains, 'for you are being throttled by your friends' (fr. 129 West), and both he and Pindar speak, significantly, of his *amechania*, 'helplessness'.[47] Hipponax represents himself as a starveling buffoon, embroiled in a gamut of humiliating situations,[48] and Callimachus too is not free of self-abasement.[49] This aspect of iambus is powerfully developed in the *Epodes*. It has been the focus of important studies over the last fifteen years,[50] critics variously speaking of Horace's self-fashioning as a 'feckless', 'toothless' or 'impotent' iambist, the last term being understood in both a narrowly physiological and a transferred sense. It is argued that the two dimensions come together in exemplary fashion at *Epod.* 15.11–12.[51] Here, threatening to replace with another the congenitally faithless Neaera, who has already discarded him for a more promising mate, Horace fatuously blusters, *o dolitura mea multum virtute Neaera! / nam si quid in Flacco viri est . . .*, 'O Neaera who will suffer much from my firmness. For if there is any manliness in "Floppy" . . .', a self-deflating apostrophe

44 O'Higgins (2003) 60; L. Watson (2003) 11–12.

45 Miralles and Pòrtulas (1983); (1988).

46 Steinruck (2000), 1–14 posits that, in a society with a shortage of marriageable daughters, failure to wed was a disaster for the elite male. Similarly, O'Higgins (2003) 64.

47 Archilochus fr. 128.1, 23.11ff. West, Pindar *Pyth.* 2. 54–6; also Archilochus fr. 88 and 112.3 for the motif.

48 Cf. L. Watson (1995) 189 n. 6, more generally Miralles and Pòrtulas (1988).

49 *Iambus* 3.

50 Fitzgerald (1988); Oliensis (1991); (1998) 64–101; L. Watson (1995) with n. 1.

51 Fitzgerald (1988) 177–8; Oliensis (1991) 124–5; (1998) 74; Gowers (1993) 287. Reservations: L. Watson (2003) ad loc.

unlikely to strike terror into Neaera's bosom.[52] Critics are divided on whether the 'impotent iambist' approach can successfully be applied to every one of the *Epodes*:[53] but it has been plausibly argued that the simile of the bird in *Epode* 1, unavailing in her attempts to protect her fledglings from attack (19–22), is an imagistic adumbration of what becomes a dominant thematic of the book.[54]

Thus far we have considered the *Epodes* from the perspective of Horace's debt to Archilochus. It is time to register some departures from the Archilochean template. A start may conveniently be made with further discussion of iambic impotence. In the biographical tradition, at least, the attacks of Archilochus on the Lycambids, and of Hipponax on Bupalus, were charged with lethal violence. In a symbolic announcement of the potency of his iambic venom, Hipponax's first book of *iamboi* figures Bupalus as a *pharmakos*, 'scapegoat', a ritual which very probably ended in death.[55] Consider now by contrast Horace's third *Epode*, which utilises the traditional iambic motif of the curse.[56] The differences from the archaic prototype are as important as the thematic convergence. This brief piece dramatises an attack of indigestion suffered by Horace after eating a dish over-liberally seasoned with garlic at the house of Maecenas, who apparently finds Horace's sufferings highly amusing.[57] The effects of garlic are ludicrously associated with some of the most deadly substances known to criminology or mythology – hemlock, the incendiary drugs with which Medea smeared her rival's bridal gifts, Hercules' envenomed shirt. According to the absurd (il)logic of the poem, then, Horace has been fatally poisoned by the offending condiment.[58] And what is his reponse? 'If you ever again conceive a desire for such a substance, jesting Maecenas, may your girl block your kiss with her hand and sleep at the edge of the bed' (19–22). Horace's riposte to his 'poisoning' is to invoke upon Maecenas a minor sexual rebuff, moreover at some unspecified time in the future ('if you ever again' . . .). There could not be a clearer example of a toothless curse,[59] a self-contradiction in both imprecatory and iambic

52 Fuller discussion in L. Watson (1995), 194–6.

53 For the across-the-board approach, Fitzgerald (1988); Oliensis (1991); (1998); Gowers (1993a): reservations in L. Watson (1995).

54 E. A. Schmidt (1977), 402–3.

55 Fr. 5–10 West: it is interesting that Bupalus is represented as a public enemy, like various pests assailed by Horace. Scapegoat rituals and death: Bremmer (1983).

56 Notably (?) Hipponax frg. 115 West, the model for *Epode* 10.

57 'Jesting Maecenas' 20.

58 Gowers (1993a), 299–300.

59 Particularly if we imagine that the *puella* who is to deny Maecenas her erotic favours at a future garlicky meal is ensconced on the couch beside him at the present one, which would strongly imply sexual intercourse following the *convivium*. Cf. Roller (2003).

terms: the curses of the dying (for so Horace ridiculously represents himself) were thought to be invested with especial potency;[60] as for iambus, its tendency to disproportion in exacting revenge was often remarked,[61] a pattern laughably nullified here. And this imprecatory toothlessness is emblematic of that blend of assertiveness and weakness which characterises the *Epode* book as a whole: a weakness which Horace develops to a significantly greater degree than Archilochus, elevating it to a cardinal motif of the collection.

So far as we can judge in the fragmentary state of our knowledge, nothing in the pre-existing iambic tradition can have prepared Roman readers for the prominence awarded to magic in the *Epodes*.[62] The two pieces devoted to the activities of the arch-witch Canidia (5, 17) comprise almost a third of the verses in the collection, and it is seen as symbolic of her importance in the literary weave of the whole that Canidia is literally given the last word in the book.[63] Why did Horace develop the theme of magic with such anomalous expansiveness? Some speculative answers may be proffered. At the most basic level this represents an attempt to enhance the thematic parameters of iambus (always a hospitable genre), a process which runs parallel to the generic experimentation so integral to the book. Another instigating factor might have been contemporary politics: Horace paints magic in the vilest colours (in *Epode* 5 Canidia kidnaps a child in order to use his desiccated innards as a love-charm; in 17 her spells reduce Horace to skin and bone while vindictively denying him release in death). This may have as backdrop a push in the 30s by Octavian and his ministers to stamp out magic, and simultaneous attempts to brand Sextus Pompey and his followers as devotees of necromancy (significantly, Canidia is shown practising this in the contemporaneous *Satires* 1).[64]

Another consideration was surely an intellectual fascination with the gruesome arcana of magic; a fascination equally visible in Ovid, Seneca and Lucan, ultimately dependent upon familiarity with books of magic, like those mentioned at *Epode* 17.4–5, which are known to have circulated freely in antiquity and are vestigially preserved in the *Magical Papyri* excavated in Egypt during the nineteenth century. From a literary-historical perspective, Horace may be feeding off Virgil's 8th *Eclogue* or perhaps Catullus, of whom the elder Pliny tantalisingly remarks that he wrote of amatory incantations:[65]

60 L. Watson (1991) 27.
61 Eustathius on Homer *Od.* 11. 227, Lucian *Pseudolog.* 1. *Epode* 10 embodies the pattern.
62 Hipponax fr. 78 West, however, apparently describes a magic procedure to cure impotence (M. L. West (1974) 142f.).
63 Oliensis (1998), 68, 95, further L. Watson (2003) 541: programmatic significance of Canidia's having the exit-line; Cavarzere (1992) ad loc., A. Barchiesi (2001a) 147–8
64 L. Watson (2003) 179–80; Du Quesnay (1984) 38–9.
65 Pliny *NH* 28.19.

more generally the theme of antisocial magic offered a promising canvas upon which to develop that taste for the grotesque which was one of the many inheritances of Hellenistic literature at Rome. Lastly, at a symbolic level, Canidia can be read as the Horatian correlate of Archilochus' *bête noire* Neobule, or alternatively Iambe/Baubo, the presiding genius of iambic:[66] both figures are conspicuously sexual, like Canidia, whose magic is driven by lust.

The prominence of Canidia points up another important divergence from Horace's archaic models. While women had been a perennial target of attack in iambus, for the most part[67] they are denied speech (iambus likes to silence the opposition).[68] By contrast Horace gives his females expansive opportunities to express themselves. Canidia speaks at length in *Epode* 5 and the dialogic 17, while 8 and 12 report respectively at first and second hand the strident protests to Horace of the sexually affronted *matrona*. It is not, however, to be supposed that, by giving his female characters such extensive air-time, Horace precisely empowers them. Rather, he both empowers them by granting speech and simultaneously disempowers them by the unloveliness of the characters which their words disclose. Horace invests them with the anger and sexual jealousy which were held to be peculiarly female vices,[69] not to mention a profound lack of self-awareness which makes them appear ridiculous – and Horace too for becoming embroiled with such.[70]

Horace, it was noted, claimed that his version of iambus moderated Archilochus' ferocity, a contention which might seem disingenuous to modern readers of 8 and 12, with their irate female-driven phallocentrism and explicit crudities. Horace, however, had a precedent for this claim in the shape of his generic predecessor Callimachus.[71] Moreover, one might reflect upon the anonymity of the target(s) of 8 and 12, which dilutes somewhat the force of the poet's attack, particularly when compared with the *First Cologne Epode* of Archilochus (fr. 196a West), which named and sexually shamed Lycambes' daughters. Further, it is arguable that Horace's language in the sexual *Epodes* is not as robust as in the more colourful fragments of Archilochus,[72] than whom Hipponax is still coarser.[73]

The point comes into sharper focus if one compares the extremes to which *libertas*, 'frank speech', ran in Catullus,[74] who, *pace* Horace, has a valid claim

66 For the sugggestion, A. Barchiesi (2001a) 152. Iambe/Baubo: O'Higgins (2003) 37–57.

67 Exceptions: Archilochus fr. 196a, 23, Hipponax fr. 25 West.

68 O'Higgins (2003) 64, 73.

69 Harris (2003).

70 Cf. L. Watson (1995) 190–4 for the poet's ridiculousness in 8 and 12.

71 Cf. L. Watson (2003) 5–6.

72 So S. J. Harrison (2001) 174.

73 Cf. M. L. West (1974) 28.

74 Cf. A. Barchiesi (2001a) 158–60.

to be considered Rome's first iambic poet.[75] Horace, it has been argued,[76] consciously sanitises the pugnacity of his *Satires*, eschewing the devastating aeschrology which Catullus drew from the language of the street, and a similar process may be at work in the *Epodes*. At all events, *Epodes* 8 and 12 pale by comparison with some of the more cloacal outpourings of Catullus, such as poems 37 or 97, or – especially interesting because written in the metre of *Epodes* 1–10 and a direct continuation of the Roman iambic tradition as represented by Catullus and Horace – the little-regarded *Catalepton* 13, an astonishing sexually based dissection of an unidentified Luccius.

Lastly, some features of the *Epodes*, whether Archilochean or not, which there is no room to discuss here: Horace for the most part attacks type-figures, the presence of whom in Archilochus is a deeply contested issue;[77] the architecture of the *Epodes*, which divide into two metrically demarcated and unequal parts, each poem, 13 excepted,[78] having its thematic partner, either within its own half or across the internal divide (1 and 9, 7 and 16, etc.);[79] 'imbrication' or leakage of motifs from one *Epode* to the next;[80] the *Epodes* as a locus for generic problematisation, an issue metapoetically explored in 11–17;[81] the iambist as both insider and outsider (Archilochus allegedly the son of a slave-woman Enipo but articulating the ideals of the elite symposium,[82] Horace the freedman's son with a conduit to the most important men in Rome); the foregrounding of the poet's likes and dislikes, a feature common to Archilochus, Catullus and Horace (in the *Epodes* perhaps taking over some of Catullus' exclusivity);[83] the metrical legacy of Archilochus and Callimachus.[84]

FURTHER READING

Of recent commentaries, Cavarzere (1992) is first rate, with a useful bibliography on each poem; Mankin (1995) helpful but idiosyncratic, especially on chronology; L. Watson (2003) fullest, offering the first detailed exegesis of the magical *Epodes* and featuring an interpretive essay on each *Epode*. The most important general studies are

75 Heyworth (2001). 76 Ruffell (2003).

77 See conveniently O'Higgins (2003) 72, with nn. 68–70.

78 D. H. Porter (1995) 129. 79 Carrubba (1969) reviews various schemata.

80 Henderson (1987) 112, 116; L. Watson (2003) 23–8.

81 Generic hybridisation in the *Epodes*: Leo (1900); Heyworth (1993); A. Barchiesi (1994); S. J. Harrison (2001).

82 Archilochus Enipo's son: fr. 295 West. Archilochus and the symposium: Bowie (1986).

83 Catullan exclusivity: Krostenko (2001). But Catullus, like Horace, may have felt himself an outsider too: Tatum (1997).

84 L. Watson (2003) 43–5.

Fitzgerald (1988); Watson (1995); Gowers (1993a); and Oliensis (1991/1998): the last two sometimes pursue interpretive trajectories having little basis in Horace's text. On generic hybridisation A. Barchiesi (1994) and S. J. Harrison (2001a) are mandatory, as are Fraenkel (1957) and Nisbet (1984/1995) on the political *Epodes*. On the latter Kraggerud (1984) is provocative but stimulating. Among studies of individual poems, noteworthy are Du Quesnay (2002) on 1, Cairns (1975) on 2, Buchheit (1961) and Dickie (1981) on 6, Wagenvoort (1956) on 7, L. Watson (1983) on 11, Lowrie (1992) on 13, Watson (2001) on 14, and Reynen (1964) on 16. Grassmann (1966) is most informative on the 'erotic' *Epodes* 8, 11, 12, 14 and 15 and their literary background. Fedeli (1978) usefully surveys the Hellenistic and neoteric background to the *Epodes*. Hanslik (1958) discusses the contested issue of whether Maecenas and Horace were at Actium.

8

FRANCES MUECKE

The *Satires*

Magnam rem puta unum hominem agere. Praeter sapientem autem nemo unum agit, ceteri multiformes sumus.

Consider it a great thing to play the role of one man. But nobody except the wise man plays a single role; the rest of us have many parts.
(Seneca, *Epistles to Lucilius* 120.22)

The first monograph in English devoted exclusively to the *Satires* appeared as recently as 1966. On reflection, it is perhaps not surprising that this was presented as 'an effort to revive interest in Horace's *Satires*'.[1] Much to the taste of the eighteenth century,[2] the *Satires* had inevitably been swept aside in the age of Romanticism. Even in the mid-twentieth century, under the lingering influence upon later criticism of the Romantic interest in individuality, Eduard Fraenkel's powerful voice had dismissed a considerable proportion of the two books as immature and ineffective Lucilian experiments, and Patrick Wilkinson (in a book on Horace's lyric poetry written for non-specialists) had felt obliged to explain why he did not get much enjoyment from the hexameter works.[3]

In the generation or two that have now passed since Rudd brought the *Satires* back into the mainstream of Latin literary studies, there have been enormous changes in this field, and, far from being neglected, the *Satires* have been recognised as offering much scope to current interpretive approaches, where emphasis is placed on dynamic relationships within genre and literary history, on the ideological dimension and on reintegration of the cultural and the political.

Horace's *Satires*, with their engagement with Roman social life, their problematisation of their genre, their flaunting of powerful patrons, and their setting in the politically uncertain period of the young Caesar's consolidation

1 Rudd (1966) 1.

2 Brower (1959) 163 dubs Horace a 'culture hero' of the eighteenth-century elite; more recently on Pope see Stack (1985) and Martindale and Hopkins (1992). In eighteenth-century Germany 'Wieland felt a very strong affinity with Horace's personality, especially as this is expressed in his *Satires* and *Epistles*': Curran (1996) 183.

3 Fraenkel (1957) 101; Wilkinson (1945) 5–6.

of power, are no longer marginalised, yet still elusively evade any attempt to pin them down. Probably the greatest change in the reading of the *Satires* has been in the evaluation of the figure of Horace himself.

Autobiography, *personae* and personality

Horace's presence is pervasive in the *Satires*, but in different ways: as first-person speaker in the 'diatribe' satires in Book 1, as 'example', as narrator of his own experiences, as defender (or celebrator) of his own social or literary position, as victimised interlocutor of a 'satirist' figure in Book 2. Introduced without much circumstantial background in the opening three satires, the 'I' is gradually built up to become a seemingly autonomous inhabitant of a vividly realised world, as more and more incidents and people from Horace's own life are made part of the texture of his work. The process is cumulative, and involves both selection and omission.

In any attempt to tell Horace's life, evidence for crucial early episodes will be drawn from the *Satires*: his birth at Venusia (2.1.34–9), his education at Rome (1.6.71–8) despite his relatively modest family background (1.6.71) and low social origins as a freedman's son (1.6.6, 45–6). Further events closer to the time of writing are documented in the poems; we might even say they are in a way their *raison d'être*: his meeting with and entering into a relationship with Maecenas, his patron and one of the young Caesar's closest supporters (1.6.54–62, 2.6.40–2), his accompanying him on the embassy to Tarentum, along with two other young and important poets, Virgil and Varius, now his friends (1.5.27–33, 39–42), the gradual growth in intimacy and *impegno* of the bond with Maecenas, and the benefits received, notably the estate in the Sabine hills (2.6, 2.7). There are other more private episodes, or teasing glimpses of them: his sex-life (1.3, 1.5, 2.7), his life off duty and on duty (1.6, 2.6), his father's care for his education and moral formation (1.4, 1.6). The *Satires* offer more of such biographical information than any of his other works, and the habit of extracting it for historical purposes will die hard.

Similarly, the *Satires* were long taken as direct expressions of the author's personality – his ideas, attitudes and viewpoints, his humanity. The idea that any such literary expression is unmediated by genre, ideology or rhetoric has now gone, and correspondingly there is less agreement as to the lineaments of the authorial figure being projected. Despite the great amount of attention that has been given (*post* Fraenkel and Rudd) to the rhetorical divorce of the historical figure of the author from his presentation of himself in his poems, and to his artistically constructed satiric voice (his *persona*), two recent studies demonstrate, in their very different ways, that the 'autobiographical' element, in the widest possible sense, is a 'disturbing' part of the fabric of the *Satires*, the source of a perpetual ambiguity 'which cannot be eliminated by any critical intervention'.[4]

A stumbling-block for criticism in this regard has been the co-existence, especially in book 1, of satires of varying lengths, structures, and modes. Some are moralising 'sermons' (1.1–3), some are anecdotes or narratives (1.5, 7, 8, 9), and some are justifications of Horace's life or writing (1.4, 6, 10). The disparity between the satires of 'self-revelation' and the more 'satirical' satires prompted varying reactions. Fraenkel's influential enthusiasm for the 'faithful, detailed, and lively picture of [Horace's] own personality and his world' was accompanied by an unconcealed distaste for the 'diatribe' satires: 'the earliest satires with their diatribes on conventional topics and their somewhat mechanical invectives against a number of more or less shadowy characters'. Horace, he argued, discovered his own voice in the 'free self-presentation' of 'the most perfect poems of the two books of *sermones*'.[5]

Rudd, on the other hand, began his book with the claim that the collection of Book 1's 'reputation must stand or fall by the diatribes'.[6] The 'diatribe' satires are versions of the kind of moral discourse commonly labelled with this term, the popular philosophical diatribe itself being characterised by its moral themes, serio-comic approach and vivid and direct language. In Rudd's reading they have the qualities of humaneness, lightness of touch, subtle structural control and originality in their use of commonplace material. Nevertheless, he too contrasts the first satires, where we learn little about the poet himself, with 1.6, 'in which the diatribe has been made the medium of a personal declaration'.[7] Anderson's version of Horace's satiric *persona*, a concept he was influential in establishing in interpretation of the *Satires*, as 'a Socratic satirist probably quite unrepresentative of [Horace] himself', was based on the diatribe satires.[8] The satirist is 'a smiling teacher of truth about important ethical matters'. This *persona* is 'cumulatively achieved'. Horace gives a general impression of the satirist in the first three satires before 'letting him speak about himself'.[9]

Anderson had downplayed the 'self-portraiture' later in Book 1, but Zetzel redressed the balance, by tracing the development of a single *persona* within the book from 'a voice that is all but disembodied' in the first three poems to 'an increasingly vivid picture of the speaker'. He also added the important idea that the book as a whole, when the poems are read in sequence,

4 The quotations are translated from Cucchiarelli (2001) 9. See also Gowers (2003).

5 Fraenkel (1957) 103, 101. 6 Rudd (1966) 1. 7 Rudd (1966) 35.

8 Anderson (1982) 29. 9 Anderson (1982) viii, x.

yields a kind of autobiographic narrative: 'a description of the speaker's progress from outside the circle of Maecenas to inside it'.[10] This first version of Horace's 'master narrative . . . of [his] career' in *Satires* 1, his ascent of the social ladder by means of both his character and his poetry, is explored with great perceptiveness by Oliensis.[11] McNeill relates Horace's concern with self-presentation even more directly to the inevitable dilemmas of his relationship with Maecenas, seeing the new approach which arose through bringing this relationship into the foreground as 'one of his greatest poetic innovations': 'his thematization of his relationship with his patron as a focus for his private concerns and social challenges sets him apart from his contemporaries in the Roman literary world'.[12] McNeill attempts, as he admits, to reconcile irreconcilable positions (the biographical and the rhetorical), or, we might suggest, he attempts to work within 'the discernible gap between the poet and his poetry'.[13]

A further challenging move in describing the nature (and literary background) of Horace's satiric *persona* was made by Freudenburg. He argued that the *persona* of the diatribe satires is 'incompetent' in the handling of Greek popular philosophy (and that therefore the diatribe satires are parodies of diatribe).[14] The satirist is also a buffoon, imported from the comic stage.[15] Freudenburg thereby took issue with the assumption, shared by most previous critics, that Horace meant his moralising to be taken seriously at some level, even if not the literal, and to portray himself as a tactful, genial advocate of moderation and discrimination behind the pose of critic of others. In contrast, Freudenburg shows us a brilliant poet, in supreme control of the range of often contradictory literary traditions he is manipulating, displacing our attention on to the inadequacies of the satiric speaker. The latter is consistently characterised in the diatribe satires alone as *doctor ineptus*, but in the perspective of the book as a whole is as changeable as Proteus. For in the satires from 1.5 onwards, including those usually thought most personal, the satirist adopts a variety of inconsistent roles – 'frivolous clown' in 1.5, 'unassuming philosopher' and 'noble advisor to Maecenas' in 1.6, 'tactless jesters' in 1.7 and 1.8, coming close to one aspect of his 'real' self (worthy friend of Maecenas) only in 1.9.[16]

In Book 1 the reader's search for 'Horace' among the shifting population of dogmatic moralists and characters from the comic stage (including his father

10 Zetzel (1980) 68–9. Freudenburg (1993) 198–211 further explores the progressive arrangement of Book 1, while Cucchiarelli (2001) 92–102 traces the change of Horace's voice from the first, aggressive, diatribe satires: it is hollowed out by irony.

11 Oliensis (1998) 14, and chapter 1. 12 McNeill (2001) 31. 13 McNeill (2001) 7.

14 Freudenburg (1993) 27. 15 Freudenburg (1993) 32–3.

16 Freudenburg (1993) 203–9. On the *doctor ineptus* see also his chapter 1.

in 1.4), perpetually frustrated, can never be abandoned. This multiplicity of *personae* is made concrete in the dialogic structure of Book 2, where (except in 2.2 and 2.6) the role of adviser, satirist or *doctor ineptus* is given to a cast of other figures in conversation with an interlocutor. The displacement that is constantly gestured towards in Book 1 – we cannot help asking if the satiric mask fits our poet – seems to be accomplished in Book 2, where the poet lays aside the mask of abusive satirist – but not the theme of self-characterisation and external reactions to the image he presents. Criticism, self-defence and implicit self-justification are still present: in the defence of himself as satirist (2.1) and friend of Maecenas (especially 2.6), in the alternative models of reaction to material loss (Ofellus 2.2, Ulysses 2.5), and in the close-to-the-bone exposés of the satirist's personal failings by Damasippus and Davus (2.3, 2.7).[17] The implications of Horace's shift of discursive mode between the two books will be considered in the next section.

From Book 1 to Book 2: genre and poetics

We have seen above how a generic approach allows critics to escape from the biographical fallacy: the poet's personality in the poems depends on the requirements of his own and his readers' inherited expectations of satire. This does not mean that the question of genre itself is straightforward. Genre, in that it demarcates a particular aspect of human experience, is where the literary tradition and the poet's own responses to his world intersect. In recent work the issues of generic dependence and contemporary literary controversy which Horace himself raises in his literary satires (1.4.10, 2.1) have been shown to have a sophisticated theoretical hinterland.[18] The literary tradition itself has been broadened to include, along with the acknowledged model, Lucilius (fl. c. 129–c. 101 BCE), not just the Callimacheanism of the previous generation, the Neoterics, with its new stylistic polish and refinement, but also the *De rerum natura* of Lucretius. Zetzel reads Horace's choice of the Roman models, Lucilius and Lucretius, as a way of turning poetry to an engagement with social and ethical issues of contemporary significance.[19] In contrast, Ruffell argues that the generic context should be widened to include a range of forms of popular invective (elite and non-elite), which Horace excludes in his creation of his literary tradition, a move which uncovers 'the role of Horace himself in establishing and policing generic boundaries'.[20]

The (ironically exaggerated) story Horace tells of himself is of a radical reorientation of satire from public, social, engagement to private meditation

17 Oliensis (1998) 57; Cucchiarelli (2001) 156–61.
18 Freudenburg (1993).
19 Zetzel (2002) 46–52. Cf. Freudenburg (185–235).
20 Ruffell (2003) 40.

(1.4.1–6, 133–40). In the opening poem of the more inwardly directed second book Horace even pushes back into his generic model this identification of satire as a private site of personal reflection:[21]

> ille velut fidis arcana sodalibus olim
> credebat libris neque, si male cesserat, usquam
> decurrens alio neque, si bene; quo fit ut omnis
> votiva pateat veluti descripta tabella
> vita senis.

> In the old days, he entrusted his secrets to his books, as though to faithful friends, having no other outlet whether things had gone well or ill. The result is that the whole life of the man of old is open to view as if sketched on a votive tablet. (2.1.30–4)

The loss of most of Lucilius, who survives only in short fragments, unfortunately means that our picture of Lucilius must be largely based on what Horace tells us. More concerned to point out differences rather than similarities, Horace claims modifications both in style and in focus. In Horace's hands the genre becomes one which matches his talents, the informality of *sermo* (conversation) enabling a skilful blend of philosophical reflections, literary criticism and parody, snatches of autobiography, anecdotes and personal vignettes of friends and enemies.

In comparison with the prolixity of his generic model, Lucilius, who left thirty books, Horace in his first book, his debut, deliberately emphasises brevity. Sparing of speech in person (1.4.18), he makes *breuitas* the first of his stylistic requirements of the modern satirist (1.10.9–15). In practice, Horace's first book is a miniaturisation of Lucilius.[22] It reproduces Lucilius' chaotic multiplicity of subject-matter – political, social, philosophical, literary, erotic, autobiographical – tremendously compressing and condensing it. It may be the case that greater consistency of focus accompanied the brevity, that is, that Horace made single poems out of topics that Lucilius used in combination with others.[23] A paradoxical result of this would be the evident diversity of the satires in Book 1. Lucilius' writings – a capacious grab-bag of a number of interrelated comic-satiric genres – must have offered many possibilities for Horace to develop. When he chooses to present his selections or 'fragments' in a small compass, isolated from the great flowing river which was Lucilius (1.4.11), it is as though he were making a provocative display of the incoherence of the genre as he had inherited it.

21 Cf. G. Harrison (1987). 22 Cucchiarelli (2001) 146.
23 Cucchiarelli (2001) 20 n. 19, 43 and n. 93.

The implicit 'plot' of Book 1, and a number of ensuing thematic and verbal interconnections, work against the genre's intrinsic disunity, while leaving intact the impression of experimental variety.[24] At first sight nothing could be more different from Virgil's *Eclogues*, with their elaborate symmetries and structural rings across a book of ten poems.[25] Nevertheless, Book 1 does present some correspondences in arrangement.[26] But while Horace is acutely aware of the exquisite artistry of the *Eclogues*, and lays claim to his own (generically appropriate) version of Callimacheanism (1.10.31–5, cf. Virgil *Ecl.* 6.3–5),[27] his unruly material, mundane ethos and 'pedestrian' style resist, at least initially, too high a degree of assimilation of such patterns.

Satires 1.4 raises the question of the outspoken satirist's unpopularity and presents Horace's satire as both more artistically polished and less publicity-seeking than that of Lucilius. The earlier satirist's public engagement, his comic exposure of malefactors, is recognised as an essential feature of the genre (1.4.1–6, cf. 1.10.3–4), but not the only one, and not necessarily the dominant one. The transition from satire as written by Lucilius to that written by Horace is aligned with the shift from the personal attack of Old Comedy to the staging of foolish and ridiculous excess in New Comedy.[28] *Satires* 1.10, imagined as an afterthought answering objections to the earlier poem, and functioning as an epilogue to the whole book ('Off with you, boy; add this at once to my little volume' 92),[29] proudly claims an elite audience. The book's central core (1.4–1.6) focuses on Horace as satirist and friend of Maecenas, with *Satires* 1.5 (modelled on Lucilius' own 'Journey to Sicily') playing the double role of example of the production of the 'new Lucilius' as well as of (ironic) demonstration of the insignificant position of Horace in Maecenas' entourage.[30] Horace in the last line of this satire makes a mock apology for its length ('Brindisi marks the end of this long tale and journey' 104). Not long even by Horatian standards, it must have been considerably shorter than Lucilius' relaxed ramble.

As well as being more inward-looking – Rudd called it 'a walled garden'[31] – Book 2 takes new directions in formal structure and theme. The new preoccupation with food and dining allows Horace to exploit a topic that not only has a punning connection with philosophy (*sapiens* 'wise, of good taste' 2.4.44, cf. Plautus *Cas.* 5, Cicero *Fin.* 2.24), but is also linked through

24 See Freudenburg (2001) 24 'an odd jumble'.

25 See Putnam (1996) on 'generic rivalry' with the *Eclogues*.

26 Rudd (1966) 160–1. See also Rudd (1976); Zetzel (1980).

27 Zetzel (2002).

28 Hunter (1985) 486–90.

29 Translations from Book 1 are those of Rudd (1979b).

30 See Gowers (1993b).

31 Rudd (1966) 131.

metaphor with satire itself, for *satura* was felt to mean a 'mixed dish' as well as 'stuffed full'.[32] In Book 1 Horace set the ethical ideal of moderation and contentment with what is enough (*satis*) against insatiability as a root cause of unhappiness and other evils (esp. 1.1), and his poetics of brevity and artistic discipline against the superabundance of the garrulous Lucilius.[33] But now the advocate of brevity, and sufferer of writer's block (2.3.1–16), allows the previously rejected copiousness of a Stoic preacher (cf. 1.1.120–1) to swell a satire to 326 lines. Another satire, unique in the corpus, marries cynical epic burlesque (Odysseus' consultation of Teiresias from Homer *Od.* 11) with mock didactic instruction in the contemporary Roman 'art' of legacy-hunting. *Satires* 2.4, likewise a parodic 'art', this time of dining, is also more overtly didactic than anything in Book 1. Horace's strategy is to exaggerate, in the mouths of other speakers, the dogmatic, homiletic, element of diatribe, from which he had begun to retreat in Book 1. The implicit split between Horace and his diatribe pose becomes an explicit split between Horace and a third-person spokesman for the doctrine, an abdication that points to a 'crisis' in the satiric attitude and has given Book 2 prominence in recent analysis of Horace's negotiations with his genre.[34]

Satires 2.2 is interestingly transitional. Horace portrays himself as giving a formal lecture, but disclaiming authorship of his lecture's diatribe content (*nec meus hic sermo est*, 2.2.2) which has come from Ofellus, a rustic sage. Similar in theme, and ending with the words of another farmer, Arellius, who tells the famous fable of the town mouse and country mouse, is *Satires* 2.6. But not only is *Satires* 2.6 not a dialogue, it is also without a dramatic setting or contextualising addressee. The monologue with its prayers to Mercury and Ianus has lyric touches at times, but the poem as a whole, with its unexpected twists and turns, brilliantly exemplifies the stylistic and imaginative suppleness that Horace brought to his hexameter poetry.[35]

The first satire of the new book reproposes the issue of choice of genre and generic model, now vividly personalised through the depiction of Lucilius' friendship with Scipio and Laelius (2.1.71–4). In the first book (4, 10) Horace had constructed an image of Lucilius as too fond of invective and coarse humour, too open in his diction to vulgarisms and Greek, his writing muddy and diffuse, his versification rough – and staged his own emergence as a new, more polished and decorous writer:[36]

32 Coffey (1976) 11–18.

33 Gowers (1993a) 126–35. For self-reflexive metaphors in the food satires, 2.4 and 2.8, see 135–79.

34 Cucchiarelli (2001) 95.

35 Ludwig (1968) 311.

36 See Rudd (1966) 97–124. On Roman poets' 'staging' of their choice of genre see Conte (1994) 120.

> hoc erat, experto frustra Varrone Atacino
> atque quibusdam aliis, melius quod scribere possem,
> inventore minor; neque ego illi detrahere ausim
> haerentem capiti cum multa laude coronam.

This form had been tried by Varro of Atax and others without success and was therefore one which I could perhaps develop – though always inferior to its inventor. I wouldn't presume to snatch from his head the crown which he wears with such distinction. (1.10. 46–9)

The sentiment expressed towards Lucilius, *inventor*, is respectful – we note the swift dismissal of minor predecessors – but coexists with a hint of comic scurrility. Alongside the epigone's high-flown, traditionally poetic acknowledgement of the path-breaker as crowned with glory (cf. Lucretius 1.117, 926), we may catch an echo of Euripides' rude attempt in Aristophanes' *Frogs* to dethrone Aeschylus and claim primacy through physical violence (*Frogs* 777–8). The context is playful, too. In lines 40–5 Horace has stated that other important genres have already found outstanding contemporary exponents, implying that he had to take what was left, if he wanted to enter the poetic arena. Nevertheless, the whole passage is coloured by the Callimachean contrast in 36–7 between the swollen epic of 'the turgid Alpman' and his own lighter verse, or private poetic play (cf. 1.4.137–9).

The first critical exploration of the dialogic technique of Book 2 was that of Anderson. He offered the widely adopted term *doctor ineptus* as a label for the new chief character, one of the category of surrogate speakers, or would-be-experts, by whom Horace 'is crowded off the stage'.[37] For Anderson, even as the character Horace endures their misguided attacks, Horace the author ironically exposes the blindness, folly, delusion or fanaticism of his interlocutors. Anderson emphasised the philosophical dimension of the new form. The introductions to three of the satires (2.2, 2.4 and 2.8) contain allusions to similar liminary moves in Platonic dialogues,[38] and at 2.3.11–12 Plato is named among the group of Greek authors (the others are Menander, Eupolis and Archilochus) who are Horace's 'companions' as he writes the *Satires* (and *Epodes*).[39] In Book 1 Anderson discerned a Socratic satirist, a teacher who 'tried to guide mistaken people from extreme error towards a modest happiness';[40] in Book 2, he argued, Horace adopted the dialogic strategy of Plato as author, inviting the readers themselves to criticise the foolish speakers (42). The Socratic/Platonic analogy is particularly useful

37 Anderson (1982) 42, cf. 13–49. 38 Fraenkel (1957) 136–7.
39 On the generic demarcation from the *Epodes* see Cucchiarelli (2001) 119–86.
40 Anderson (1982) 46.

for the combination of the new narrative structure with a variety of didactic modes in Book 2.

Subsequently Oliensis argued that Horace in Book 2 not merely steps away from the role of satirist, but that he undermines it, and not only in the case of the surrogate satirists of Book 2, the diatribists Ofellus, Damasippus and Davus, but also, retrospectively, in his own case as satirist in Book 1.[41] Ofellus, Damasippus and Davus all have circumstances in their lives which have led to their becoming 'satirists'. Ofellus has been dispossessed of his farm, Damasippus is a bankrupt, whose conversion to philosophy has furnished him with an instrument of revenge (2.3.296–9), and Davus is a slave, whose situation allows him to perceive the moral slavery of his master (2.7): 'By situating his satirists as he does, Horace exposes satire for what it "really" is: not a disinterested revelation of timeless philosophical truths, but a consolation prize awarded to life's losers.'[42] If, she suggests, satire is shown to be a means of repairing one's fortunes, then this is a reason why Horace no longer wears the mask of satirist in Book 2, while continuing, of course, to write satire – he is now a made man. But if the point of Book 2 is the rewriting of Book 1, after this exercise there is nowhere else to go, and Horace ceases to write in this genre.

Another attempt to come to grips with this problem is one which sets the shift from Book 1 to Book 2 within a reinterpretation of the 'genre question' itself. Freudenburg argues that subsequent Roman satirists, in their relationship to Lucilius, were dealing not simply with a literary inheritance, but with anxiety about the loss of Rome's Republican identity, 'an identity that was heavily influenced, and emblematized, by Lucilius'.[43] It is simply not possible for Horace, given his status and the realities of his own political and social world, to be a Lucilius, and to replicate his predecessor's trademark freedom of speech (1.4.5, 2.1.62–8), but far from concealing this, he makes it the driving force of his satire. By the time of Book 2 (30 BCE), just after Actium, satire may be less welcome to Horace's patron, and more disturbing to his readers. In 2.1 he raises the legal and political implications of continuing to write satire, and refuses to be intimidated, only, surprisingly, to vacate the position of satirist for the rest of the book. Developing Oliensis's readings of Ofellus, Damasippus and Davus as losers in society, Freudenburg throws more emphasis onto the repressive aspects of the new world after Actium, and identifies the central question of Book 2, thrown into relief by its difference from the first book, as that of coping with 'the

41 Oliensis (1998) 41–63. 42 Oliensis (1998) 53. 43 Freudenburg (2001) 3.

totalitarian squeeze'. Book 2's 'most salient defining feature, in fact, the key to its relational identity, is that contrast with the first book'.[44]

Politics and ethics

The provocative argument just ruthlessly and all too blandly summarised comes to conclusions strikingly at variance with an earlier and highly influential essay on Horace's *Satires* in their political environment. The methods and presuppositions of these two studies are as tellingly different as their conclusions. Freudenburg finds satire which unveils the workings of power beneath the poems' surface of conformity.[45] Du Quesnay saw the collection of Book 1 as supporting those in power.[46]

Du Quesnay began by challenging the prevailing view that the *Satires* were apolitical.[47] It had long been recognised that they contain very few references to the dramatic events of recent history, the civil wars, or the leading players in the uncertain times in which they were written – that is, apart from their dedication to Maecenas, the young Caesar's friend and supporter. Most striking in this regard is 1.5, with its studious disregard of the political importance of the journey on which the poet tags along. As Du Quesnay pointed out, *Satires* 1 was the first book dedicated to him to come from Maecenas' patronage of a group of new poets, another of whom was Virgil. Maecenas is not simply the dedicatee. He is kept before our eyes as the great man whom Horace has come to know and of whom he can provide telling glimpses. These add up to an impression of moral integrity, restraint and civilisation.

In his study Du Quesnay set *Satires* 1 in its political context, which he defined as the years 38–36 BCE, when the young Caesar and Maecenas were involved in war in the West against Sextus Pompey, winning support in Italy, and laying foundations for the future. Included in the analysis is a consideration of the propaganda war of these years, the issues and the terms of the debate between those competing for power. Viewed in this light, the satires are seen to have a political dimension: to a certain extent some of the names deployed can be associated with negative attack on political targets, but, more importantly, *Satires* 1 constructs a positive image of Maecenas,

44 Freudenburg (2001) 73, cf. 71–124.
45 Freudenburg (2001) 117.
46 Du Quesnay (1984).
47 Rudd (1966) 37; see also Griffin (2000). Lyne (1995) 12–20 argues that Horace constructs an apolitical image as part of a policy of 'image-management': he had been on the wrong side in the civil war of 42 BCE.

the young Caesar and the values they represent. This image is not just at the service of Horace's portrait of himself but is a calculated attempt to win over his readers to the new ruler.

The question arises, then, why Horace chose to write satire, or at least to follow Lucilius, and here Du Quesnay offered an explanation which Freudenburg was later to complicate. Lucilius, as we have seen, is the emblem of Republican free speech, and famous as a practitioner of abusive invective. Horace's satires contain very little personal abuse or direct political attack. Horace's satire therefore is a modification of his predecessor's in precisely that aspect which characterised him, not so much to criticise Lucilius, but to distinguish himself from the political motivations of more recent supporters of Lucilius. Horace redefines 'Lucilian *libertas* as something morally responsible', inviting 'the inference that the Triumvirs are opposed not to true *libertas*, which is traditional and responsible, but rather to licence, the irresponsible, malicious and divisive exercise of freedom with which true *libertas* is wrongfully confused by those who oppose them'.[48]

Du Quesnay's ingenious argument is built on a finely detailed reading of the historical context but based upon a questionable assumption: if the young Caesar expected his friends to help him win support for his cause, he states, 'it is scarcely credible that . . . Maecenas, his closest friend and adviser, should publish and distribute a work which was irrelevant to the needs and preoccupations of himself and his friends'. Even if we concede the point of relevancy (or resonance), we need not make the next step to political propaganda.[49] But Du Quesnay's demonstration of the usefulness of relating the ethical concerns of the satires to the broader context of contemporary ideology has been a lasting contribution.

In contrast, Freudenburg spends hardly any time in establishing the historico-political context of the *Satires*. His prime focus is the generic tradition, and within each poem, its images and intertexts. His mode of interpretation is one which seeks to expand the range of 'relevant' intertexts and allusions. Once seen, the presence of these non-satiric texts is used to 'make us reconsider any prepackaged notions we might have about what satire looks like and how it goes about its "straightforward, moral" work'.[50] So Freudenburg expands the poetic and ideological context by establishing meaningful relationships with texts outside the genre (for example, Catullus,

48 Du Quesnay (1984) 23, 30. See Cucchiarelli (2001) 92 'to imitate or not to imitate Lucilius is a political act'; Ruffell (2003) 38–40.

49 D. Kennedy (1992) 30, esp. 34–6, introduced the fruitful concept of the 'integrationist text'.

50 Freudenburg (2001) 39.

Virgil's *Eclogues* and *Georgics*, Ennius' *Annales*). It is through analysis of particular nodes of tension or contradiction that he tries to uncover the implicit political motivations behind the poet's modes of expression.[51]

Recent readings of the poetics and politics of the satires have destabilised the independence of the satirical/moral element, the 'telling of the truth with a smile' (1.1.24). It was once asserted that 'Horace brought the philosophical discourse into satire as an essential motive'. Philosophy for him was 'a means of grasping personal experience and using it to come to an understanding of the multi-faceted world and the human heart'.[52] These days the question asked is why, in a specific political and cultural context, Horace turned satire away from political invective towards quietism and witty, but unthreatening, moral criticism.[53]

Even before this new take there was no agreement as to the part played by the philosophical topics.[54] Are they simply hackneyed and convenient topics for a satirist, to a certain extent prescribed by the genre, or are they an element of substance, part of what gives the *Satires* their claim for our attention?[55] Does Horace's perception and handling of the moral ideas 'in complex but successful structures of thought'[56] justify taking him seriously as a moral philosopher, or does the satirist (that is, the *persona*) show 'a degree of overt incompetence which both destroys his credibility as a moraliser and seriously questions any direct analogy with Bion, Socrates or any true philosopher'?[57] Does Horace align himself with a particular philosophic system? And if so, for what reason? For example, recently the *Satires*' positioning of the Stoics as antagonists has been interpreted through the lenses of both politics and poetics.[58] Attention to these questions is further encouraged by the role and importance of philosophy in *Epistles* 1, even if the significance and depth of this are likewise disputed, for the *Epistles* are 'an organic continuation of the *Satires*'.[59]

The point is well made that the poet is not to be identified with the diatribist of the first three satires, nor are these satires simply versions (or parodies) of diatribe.[60] They are new *satiric* creations, full of vivid images and comic

51 E.g. Freudenburg's discussion of 2.1.13–15, (2001) 82–92.

52 Knoche (1975) 83.

53 As is done by Ruffell (2003) 37–8.

54 This whole issue receives separate treatment in Moles, chapter 12 below.

55 E.g. Shackleton Bailey (1982) 35: 'His ideas on the subject are neither original nor profound nor wide-ranging.' Rudd (2000) is also sceptical.

56 Armstrong (1964) 96, see also Armstrong (1989) 31.

57 Freudenburg (1993) 27, partly building on a long tradition of perceptions of incoherence in the arguments of *Satires* 1.1–3. See also Freudenburg (2001) 15–23.

58 Du Quesnay (1984) 33 (politics), and Freudenburg (1993) 132–84 (poetics).

59 Fraenkel (1957) 310.

60 Hunter (1985) 480; Cucchiarelli (2001) 95, cf. 15.

vignettes, their genre marked by allusions to Lucilius. This symbiosis of comic satire and moral reflection is suggested by the passage in which Horace portrays his father's teachings (which embody a method of learning how to 'live better' from the faults of others), as the impulse that lies behind his own satiric writings (1.4.103–40, cf. 1.4.115–6 'A philosopher will give you reasons / why this is desirable and why that is better avoided').[61] The same satire enacts a shift from the public and political free speech of Old Comedy and Lucilius to a philosophical idea of free speech between friends (1.4.103–6, 129–33): a key element of the satires' ethical theory. This was a new development of Hellenistic philosophy, discussed in the contemporary Roman context in the Epicurean philosopher Philodemus' *On Frankness*.[62]

Likewise Book 2, which, overall, is more philosophical than Book 1, contains another passage which seems to put ethical discussion at the heart of Horace's life. Appropriately for this book so centred on dialogue and dining, the setting is dinner-party conversation:

> And so conversation arises, not about other people's villas and town-houses, nor whether Lepos dances badly or not, but we discuss what has more relevance to us and not to know is an evil: whether it is wealth or virtue that makes men happy; or what leads us to friendships, self-interest or rectitude; and what is the nature of goodness and what its highest form. (2.6.70–76)

Here the language is more technical than in *Satires* 1.4, and the references are to specific problems of recognisable schools, canvassed, for example, not long before, in Cicero's philosophical works. The opposed theories on friendship of the Epicureans and Stoics are contrasted and here is the only place that Horace uses the technical term *summum bonum* ('highest good'). In the text an effect of incongruity arises from the attribution of sophisticated ethical theorising to Horace's rustic neighbours – they are philosophers in spite of themselves. The reader, however, may be led to see a parallel with Horace's own *sermones* ('conversations'), which deal with everyday-life experiences but nonetheless point to a more specifically philosophical context.

It is hard to tie Horace down to a particular philosophical school, partly because the values taught – such as the mean (1.1.106–7, 2.4–11, 27–30), consistency (1.1.1–22, 3.4–19), the simple life (1.1.59–60, 74–5, cf. 1.6.110–31) and the importance of friendship (1.3, cf. 2.6.75) – were commonly held, and partly because, in the *Satires*, this ethical common ground, freed from any comprehensive physical and metaphysical system, is enmeshed with

61 See Schlegel (2000) 93–119; Hunter (1985) 490; Freudenburg (1993) 34–5.

62 Hunter (1985) 488; Konstan (1997).

specific instances of human conduct.[63] Far from being guided by the exposition of abstract ideas, the reader is kept alert by linguistic detail: technical terms, metaphorical allusions to philosophical issues, Lucretian language. In the first book, *Satires* 1.3.96–114 is a rare example of an extended polemic which uses theories associated with particular schools, the Epicurean view that justice was a result of historical development being opposed to the Stoic belief that there is a natural, not conventional, distinction between right and wrong. The comic-satiric context involves an element of mockery even of the side the satirist advocates.[64] Similarly, there is marked and amusing discrepancy between the lowly domestic detail of Horace's Epicurean retirement in *Satires* 1.6.111–31 and the 'sweet' life of Lucretius' Epicurean hero, secure and independent in the citadel of wisdom (*De Rerum Natura* 2.1–13).[65]

In 2.2 Horace is the teacher, but the content of his lecture, on the simple life, appropriately comes from a rustic 'philosopher', Ofellus.[66] In 2.3 the Stoic doctrine of Stertinius (reputedly the author of 220 volumes of treatises) is relayed to Horace through the mouth of the recent convert Damasippus, who now feels empowered to serve out advice and criticism to others in his turn. The source of the slave Davus is even less reliable. In 2.7, a poem which is a kind of resumé and reversal of the diatribe satires of Book 1 in particular, Davus turns against his master Stoic topics and argumentation he has gathered from the doorkeeper of that same Stoic Crispinus from whom Horace had earlier dissociated himself. Davus is the last surrogate satirist in the *Satires*, echoing the comic, philosophical and Lucilian elements of the genre.[67] Davus tellingly shows that Horace fails to live up to the ethical teachings of his own satires, but his own authority is simultaneously undermined. Nevertheless, it is suggestive that he uses a temporary concession of freedom of speech (*libertas*) to discourse on the Stoic ideal of spiritual freedom, to a Horace, who is accused, at the next-to-last moment, of himself manifesting those very failings on which he has earlier preached – discontent, inconsistency, pursuit of married women, gluttony, lack of independence – and whose reaction is to betray the normal touchiness of the satiric victim.[68]

The indirect mode of Book 2 can be used as a clue for interpreting the *doctor ineptus* of Book 1. Damasippus' and Davus' characters and motivations clash with the Stoic doctrine they have opportunistically appropriated, and so an ironic distance is set up between the speaker and the morality he

63 Lucilius did not confine himself to ethical philosophy (Knoche (1975) 50).

64 Freudenburg (1993) 26–7 is right to notice a comic lowering of tone in 107–10.

65 For a contextual analysis see Armstrong (1989) 277–9.

66 I follow Kiessling and Heinze (1967) ad loc.

67 Cucchiarelli (2001) 157.

68 Evans (1978) 307–12. For a political interpretation see Ruffell (2003) 62–4.

propounds, without, I believe, totally discrediting the notion of a search for values on which it is based. Similarly, in Book 1 there is an ironic gap between the poet and the *persona* in the 'diatribe' satires. Nevertheless, the humour and parody through which the poet constantly dissociates himself from the surface meaning of the text do not amount to a repudiation of the *persona* nor of the possibility that the poem as a whole might contain serious moral reflection.[69]

With this we have returned to our opening topic, for the philosophical dimension of the *Satires* will appear differently according to whether we focus on Horace the poet, the satiric *persona*, or the self-image of Horace presented in the poems.

FURTHER READING

There has been no monograph in English devoted to the *Satires* as a whole since Rudd (1966). The *Satires* tend to be treated in the context either of Roman verse satire, or of Horace's oeuvre as a whole. In the first category Coffey (1976) is sound and rich in detail, while Freudenburg (2001) attempts an adventurous reframing of the satiric genre in the context of social poetics. Chapters on *Satires* 1 and 2 by Gowers, and on philosophy and satire by Mayer in Freudenburg (2005), complement what has been presented here.

Books on Horace which contain lively and stimulating readings of the *Satires* are Armstrong (1989) and Oliensis (1998), the latter an original tracing of the evolution of Horace's self-presentation. McNeill (2001), focusing mainly on the *Satires* and *Epistles*, breaks away from the developmental, genre-by-genre approach to use the notion of 'rings of audience' to shape his sympathetic and sensitive inquiry. Compulsory (and delightful) for those with Italian is Cucchiarelli (2001).

That the *Satires* are complex and subtle poems was emphasised by Zetzel (1980). Freudenburg (1993) explored in great detail their literary and intellectual background and setting in contemporary literary debates. Zetzel (2002) is another interesting and sophisticated approach to the *Satires*' place in the literary history of their time.

Recent commentaries (with translation) of Books 1 and 2 respectively in the Aris and Phillips series are P. M. Brown (1993) and Muecke (1993). Commentaries by Gowers (Book 1) and Freudenburg (Book 2) are in progress for the Cambridge Greek and Latin Classics series.

69 Here I have been helped by Gale (1997) 90. Cf. Armstrong (1989) 40–1.

9

ROLANDO FERRI

The *Epistles*

Our manuscripts of Horace and his ancient commentators know two different books of *epistulae* in the corpus of his poems.[1] What is thus called the 'first book of Epistles' (*epistularum liber primus*) in the manuscripts is a collection of 20 hexameter poems of varying length, from 13 to 112 lines, which were published by Horace in the year 20 or 19 BCE, and probably composed during the three or four preceding years.[2] A second 'book of epistles' comprises two much longer poems addressing Iulius Florus and Augustus, and devoted mainly to literary topics (though the letter to Florus, the older of the two, is still very close to the first book). These later poems, to which the longer *Ars Poetica*, or *Ad Pisones* (*AP*), is sometimes attached as '*Epistle* 2.3', are less clearly identifiable as letters, and they altogether belong in a tradition different from that of the first Book. The two 'books' therefore call for separate discussions, and we shall concentrate first on Book 1.[3]

The practice of presenting a poem as a letter in verse, rather than as a song performed before an audience at a symposium or a religious celebration, is early, and cross-generic, spanning from lyric to elegy: it has been recognised in Sappho and Solon (to Mimnermus), and even some among the *epinicia* of Pindar and Bacchylides are commonly treated as poetic epistles.[4]

In the Hellenistic age an important change has occurred, because poems are often referred to as written documents, physical objects which can be

1 The reliability of the MS evidence relating to the title of this work has been questioned in Horsfall (1979a), with counter-arguments by Jocelyn (1979) 145–7 and Rudd (1979a) 147; but the joint evidence of the MSS, the ancient commentators and the poems themselves is decisively in favour of the traditional title.

2 For discussions about the date of the work cf. McGann (1969) 86–7.

3 It is in fact not certain that Horace ever intended to publish these longer poems as a book: for a discussion cf. Brink (1982) 555, with reference to earlier discussions. For the closeness of 2.2 to Book 1 cf. W. R. Johnson (1993) 155–7.

4 Cf. Pindar *Isthm.* 2, *Nem.* 3, *Pyth.* 1 and 2, which the ancient scholia called an *apostolikē ōdē* (cf. sch. *ad Pyth.* 2 Drachmann inscr. e 6b). Cf. Tedeschi (1985) 35 n. 20.

addressed and delivered to someone. In this context, it must have been relatively natural, even for texts not exhibiting formal markers of epistolarity, such as initial and final salutations, to become in some sense epistolary. However, among extant poems of this age, texts explicitly presented as sent messages are few, mainly some epigrams accompanying gifts, invitation billets (*AP* 11.44), and love letters (*AP* 5.9).[5] At Rome, before Horace, poetic epistles are found in Catullus and Propertius, and in the Corpus Tibullianum;[6] even some of Horace's odes, for example *Carmina* 1.20 and 4.12, two invitation poems, fall into the category.

Perhaps more importantly for Horace, one of the satires of Book 5 of Lucilius' *Satires* began as a letter to an inattentive friend, scolded by the poet for failing to enquire about his health. It is not certain, however, how the epistolary beginning evolved in the rest of the poem. The fragment we possess leads quickly to a discussion of *homoeoteleuta*, and the suspicion arises that the epistolary beginning was only a pretext, an original device excogitated to satisfy the variety requirements of the genre of satire.[7]

Yet, notwithstanding the importance of recent formal precedents, especially neoteric, an entire book of poems purporting to be a collection of private letters was a novelty among ancient poetic genres, and one which Horace must have initiated with some determination.

Horace has chosen to present the *Epistles* as a collection of real letters, and the framework of an epistolary exchange is maintained consistently and repeatedly asserted. Apart from the deployment, ably varied, of standard formulae of salutation at beginning and end of the letters (*Epistles* 8.1, 6.67, 10.1), Horace alludes to prior exchange with his correspondents, answers requests or complaints (*Epistle* 12), imparts admonitions, expects answers or visits (*Epistles* 3.30, 5.30, 10.49, 15.25), gives and seeks information, and adapts the tone and content of the letter to the personalities and interests of his interlocutors.[8] The pretence of a real letter is kept up by even

5 It is sometimes suggested that Hellenistic love elegy adopted epistolary speech conventions more extensively, paving the way for the relatively significant occurrence of poetic epistles in Roman elegy and Ovid: cf. Leo (1901) 323; Abel (1930) 124. For verse letters in Sappho cf. Haight (1948) 525–40; in Theocritus and the *Anthology* cf. Page (1978) 71; Rosenmeyer (2001) 100–10.

6 Cf. for example Catullus *Carmina* 13 (a dinner invitation), 35 (an excuse to compliment a friend's poem), 65 (a variant of the prefatory epistle of dedication), 68. For Propertius cf. 1.11, 3.22 and 4.3. For other examples cf. Leo (1901) 323–5; Kroll (1924) 217; Fedeli (1980) 267.

7 Cf. Fiske (1920) 432; Puelma-Piwonka (1949) 138.

8 For a useful catalogue of the epistolary features and conventions, and a comparison with Cicero's use of them, see Allen et al. (1978) 124–30. Trapp's description of the epistolary features in the work as merely 'patches of epistolary colouring' ((2003) 23) is, in my view, too restrictive.

jumbling up together unrelated, or tenuously related, topics, in imitation of the miscellaneous character of real correspondence (cf. *Epistle* 12.20–9).[9]

In contemporary or near-contemporary Latin poetic books, for example in Catullus or Propertius, the inclusion of the occasional letter was a device deployed to create a different pathetic background for the main themes of friendship, love, separation and infidelity (as most characteristically in Propertius 1.11 and 4.3, or in Catullus 35). More generally, the choice of the epistle tied in with the Callimachean and generally Hellenistic fondness for minor poetic genres, in which more intimate, life-like pictures of personal relationships could be drawn, and where even the little things and mundane details of life could be given a space (cf. Catullus 13, the invitation poem).

Yet an entire book of sole letters, as Horace chose to publish now – not letters as diversives in a book of satires and epigrams, or poetic epistles among sublime lyrics – aimed at telling a different story about the poet's newly chosen path in life. Horace wanted to show himself enfenced in his world of philosophy, letters and friends, engrossed in occupations more pressing and important than poetry. Indeed, he now proclaims to 'give up poetry, and all other *bagatelles*' (*et uersus et cetera ludicra pono*) in order to devote himself to philosophy, and the form of the private document he has elected is consistent with this programmatic statement.[10] As the envoi (20) will elaborate more explicitly, the *Epistles* (Horace affects to believe) were not even meant for publication: they have 'run away' from the poet's boxes, like a delinquent slave longing for a better life – a fictional scenario which is also an important poetic manifesto.[11]

In this way, the very choice of communicative medium relates to the poet's newly chosen stance, and of his *persona*. Horace expresses himself in a distant and indirect form, looking away from the readers of the book, facing only his private addressees, as if he wished to situate himself at some remove from Roman society. Future readers are – the last poem will drive the point

9 Although, more commonly, each letter is devoted to a single topic, a practice which was recommended by epistolographic theory: cf. [Demetrius] *De Elocut.* 231. On the *Epistles* and ancient theory cf. S. J. Harrison (1995b) 57–60. Our source is mainly [Demetrius] *De Elocut.* 222–35, stressing the need for simplicity of argument, brevity and sincerity; for Demetrius, letters are 'the image of one's soul'.

10 Of course the *Epistles are* poems, but Horace plays up a paradoxical, covertly polemical motif of his *Satires* (cf. *Satires* 1.4.39–40): his *sermones* are unpoetic *vis-à-vis* the more high-flown, elevated registers of epic and tragedy.

11 On the implications and literary precedents of the final poem cf. Kiessling and Heinze (1930) 190; Macleod (1979) 23–4; Citroni (1986) 111; Pearcy (1994); Oliensis (1995); D. H. Porter (2002).

home – eavesdroppers, unforeseen listeners overhearing a muffled sound of confessions, complaints, exhortations.

Also importantly, a number of letters claim to be despatched from Horace's country estate or some other location away from Rome (2, 7, 10, 13), and several others are compatible with the same setting (16, 18). Horace elaborates a new scenario for his letters, different from the fairy, diaphanous, poetic landscape of the *Odes* (*e.g. Carmina* 1.17, 2.6).[12] Founding a new genre, the *Epistles* set up their own landscape, out of time, dilapidated, yet self-sufficient like the philosophy which Horace now wants to be his way of life. The poet sits and waits behind the crumbling pillars of *Vacuna*'s temple (10.49 *post fanum putre Vacunae*), a name conjuring up timelessness, emptiness, leisure; he lives in a shady valley, enclosed by a crown of mountains, which he calls *latebrae dulces*, a 'sweet hideout' (16.15); the nearby village is wrinkled with frost (18.105 *rugosus frigore pagus*); happiness now for Horace is a path of life which hides away (18.103 *fallentis semita uitae*); of his friends, the melancholy Albius drags himself wearily through solitary woods (4.4), another seeks oblivion in godforsaken corners in Asia (11).[13] The town vignettes of so many brilliant satires, most memorably in *Satires* 1.6, 1.9, 2.6, have almost entirely disappeared.[14]

If the model of the new genre was the prose, non-literary letter, it would be crucial to know what books of prose letters were in circulation at the time and how they helped to shape Horace's project. Leafing through Cugusi's (1970; 1979) collection of all known letters from the third century to the end of the Republic, it comes as something of a surprise to encounter the names of some 150 personages on record for writing letters. In fact, the surprise is mitigated by a look at the correspondence of Cicero, which shows how widespread and routine writing and reading letters were for many upper-class Romans: the *Epistles* certainly presuppose the routine practice of letter-writing as a natural activity for Horace's readers. But granted that writing letters was an ordinary activity, we cannot point to published books of real spontaneous

12 On the theme of landscape in Horace cf. Mayer (1994) 46–7.

13 On the spatiality of the *Epistles* cf. De Pretis (2002) 116–21. On melancholy in the *Epistles* cf. Kilpatrick (1986) 112.

14 It is sometimes suggested that the *Epistles* express a reaction against the rise in popularity of elegy in contemporary Rome. It is true that, to some extent, Horace's epistolary *persona* is cut out to be the reverse of the elegiac poet. The elegiac poet sees philosophy as the pursuit of his old age; elegy, especially in Propertius, is town poetry; the elegiac poet devotes his whole life to a single, all-embracing passion. Horace preaches self-sufficiency, the *autarkeia* taught by Hellenistic philosophers; the *Epistles* shy away from town living, and philosophy has replaced poetry. On the anti-elegiac elements of the *Epistles* cf. McGann (1969) 97–8; Syme (1986) 177; La Penna (1993) 265; Pearcy (1994) 460.

letters, sincere giveaways of their writers' feelings, at Rome, before Horace's *Epistles* or Cicero's *Ad Atticum*.[15]

The *Epistles* are perhaps, among the works of Horace, the work that has been most consciously planned and set up as a book: the letters gain enormously from being read one after the other, indeed, they require a continuous reading, in which even backslidings, second thoughts, contradictions are parts of a planned overall effect on the reader (see below).[16] At the same time the montage of the book, with its variety of correspondents and themes, is designed to communicate a sense of discontinuity and fragmentation. This is done with two aims in mind: on the one hand, to impart to the work the casual spontaneity of the document; on the other, the gaps in the continuous narrative create a tension about what has been left outside the book, for us to imagine: the story behind, the real lives and moral predicaments of the poet and his follower-friends.[17] This very curiosity about the people of the *Epistles*, the author and his respondents, is a vehicle used to enhance the protreptic impact, the message of the work.

But who are the people of the *Epistles*? Horace showed, even by his selection of correspondents, how much his book of letters should pose as a private and personal document. Horace by now seems to have been on a fairly firm footing with Augustus, even a 'star' of the Augustan literary establishment. The *princeps* wanted him on his staff, as a private secretary (cf. Suetonius *De Poetis* p. 44 Reifferscheid), and the clout and status of Horace were to be given public recognition by the prestigious commission to write the *Carmen Saeculare* for the celebrations of 17. Yet the *Epistles* do not open up a window into the world and thoughts of the great and good; the addressees of the work, apart from Maecenas, seem to have been mainly second-rank

15 Cicero alludes to his publication project in *Att.* 16.5.5, but he does not seem to regard publication of private letters as a bold, unprecedented innovation, demanding special justification (H. Peter (1901) 8, however, stresses the lack of parallels at Rome for Cicero's decision). Whatever letters Cicero ended up publishing in his lifetime, they are certain to have been literary showpieces, not the more revealing letters to Atticus. Shackleton Bailey (1965) 59–60 suggests that some of the recommendation letters and some other such literary *tours de force* would have been included in that book (such as *Fam.* 5.12 on writing history, or *Fam.* 7.1 on the theatrical shows given by Pompey). There is an early example (1st cent. BCE) of a *uolumen* of letters pasted together from the private archive of a certain Macedo in Cavenaile (1958) n. 247.

16 Good points about the poems' reciprocal relationships in McGann (1969) 99–100; Armstrong (1989) 124–33.

17 On the arrangement of the book in general cf. Mayer (1994) 48–51. A design or even the progression of a narrative have sometimes been recognised: cf. Maurach (1968); McGann (1969) 33–87; Armstrong (1989) 117–35; Ferri (1993) 127–31; W. R. Johnson (1993) 66–71; D. H. Porter (2002).

individuals. The book does not include letters to politically influential personages, or to protagonists of the Roman poetic and intellectual stage such as, say, Pollio, Agrippa, Vergil, Varius. Apart from Albius, perhaps the poet Tibullus, only minor figures turn up, some unidentifiable (16, 17), others with more definite personalities: a young man with a good family background (2, 18), friends from older days (9, 10, 11), aspiring writers, perhaps young (3, 8), a would-be natural philosopher, now managing Agrippa's estates in Sicily (12), a Lucanian notable (15, Numonius Vala), and Horace's own bailiff (14). This stands in some contrast with several of the *Odes*, and most notably with Book 4, where crucial figures of the imperial house and other representatives of the nobility are given great importance.[18]

Writing to relatively undistinguished friends, who had not attained public eminence, was then a deliberate choice: the book sets up its own ideal society of friends who become prime targets of the book's moral search for wisdom. Although the poet reaches out to them to meet their requests and respond to their moral predicaments, none of them upstages the poet or hijacks the content of the letter by a prepossessing personality.

For all the miscellaneous, plural features of the *Epistles*, the work is kept together by a major unifying feature: a concern for ethics, as applied to all situations in life, the *uiuere recte* or 'right living'; it is this unifying thread that permeates and binds together what may appear sometimes difficult to reconcile with a monolithic reading of the work, such as, in *Epistles* 17 and 18, the advice on how to gain favour and ingratiate themselves with powerful patrons, apparently at odds with the great stress on freedom and self-sufficiency advocated in most other epistles.[19] Horace's attitude as a teacher is that of a more advanced fellow student, eager but tolerant and often uncertain about the best answer to the problem at hand, even open to better suggestions, if any come to mind (cf. *Epistle* 6.67–8): there is not just one way of life he can recommend, although he has his own predilections.[20]

Around this ethical core, the *Epistles* build up a determined didactic programme, for which Horace must have drawn inspiration from the model of the Greek philosophical letter. Collections and anthologies of letters, mostly spurious, went under the name of several Greek philosophers, from Socrates onwards:[21] by far the most significant of them for Horace must have been the

18 Discussions of the social status of Horace's addressees in the *Epistles* in Allen et al. (1970); Syme (1986) 395–6; Lana (1989) 48–54; Perutelli (1993) 205–18; White (1993) 46–7, 223–39.
19 Cf. Macleod (1979).
20 On philosophical relativism in the *Epistles* cf. Moles (2002) 148–9; on 'disjunctive truth' and the use of doxographies cf. Armstrong (1989) 117–8.
21 On the collections of letters of Greek philosophers cf. Trapp (2003) 27–30, with full bibliography. On Epicurus' letters cf. Gigon (1980) 128–32; Angeli (1993) 11–27; critical text

correspondence of Epicurus, not only for the great appeal Epicureanism had for Horace throughout his poetic career,[22] but also for the intrinsic charm of Epicurus' letters, which were to be an important model also for Seneca's *Letters to Lucilius*.

Epicurus used his correspondence as a means to keep contact with his closest friends and disciples scattered by the Hellenistic diaspora, in a way which calls to mind the role of epistolography for early Christian communities. Epicurus' correspondents spanned a social spectrum as wide as or wider than Horace's, from old disciples who had become powerful ministers and needed reminding that happiness was but a simple thing, to women and children. Epicurus succeeded to interweave in his letters the personal and affectionate with the theoretically challenging, and was capable even of speaking of himself in humorous, captivating tones.[23]

The epistolary medium could then, and with good precedent, both serve as a protreptic, and afford an opportunity for the expression of one's true self and self-analysis. Indeed, autobiography and self-confession are part of an 'effective protreptic tactic',[24] making for a more gripping and convincing message exactly because that message does not resonate from the serene heights of superhuman wisdom, but is pronounced down below amid the fray by one who is only a little farther along the way.

Like Seneca in his *Epistulae ad Lucilium*, Horace presents himself as a man still in search of illumination, not as perfect, and much of the appeal and comedy of the *Letters* derives from Horace's dwelling on his own neuroses, his dissatisfaction, his sudden changes of mind (cf. *Epistles* 8.3–12, 15.42–6). The persuasiveness his words carry for his addressees is sustained by the manner in which Horace sits next to them and discloses his inner thoughts and anguishes. So, for example, Horace endeavours to cure the elusive Bullatius of his compulsive travel mania by showing that he sometimes feels the same drive to get away from it all: 'You know, Lebedus: it's lonelier than Gabii / or Fidenae: and yet, o to live just there,/ and forgetting and forgotten by my friends (*oblitusque meorum, obliuiscendus et illis*) / from the distant shore look down at Neptune raving', only to conclude that 'crossing the sea is a change of air, not heart. / A busy idleness drives us: in ships and cars / we seek the good life. What you seek is here, / or at Ulubrae, so long as your

with Italian facing translation in Arrighetti (1960) 383–437. On the influence of Epicurus' letters in the *Epistles* cf. Heinze (1919); Dilke (1981) 1844–6.

22 On Epicureanism in the *Epistles* cf. Macleod (1979) 22, 26; Moles (2002).

23 Among the fragments where warmest details of personal relationships emerge cf. 44, 65, 113, 114, 120, 122 Arrighetti. Fragment 122 closely corresponds to *Epistle* 1.70–3, and 35 to *Epistle* 8.1 (philosophic salutation formulae).

24 Cf. S. J. Harrison (1995b) 59.

heart is calm' (11. 7–10, 27–30, trans. Macleod; *Ulubrae* was a village on the edges of the Pomptine marshes, the quintessence of desolation).

Older treatments of the *Epistles* tended to stress their similarity with the earlier collections of satires, in metre, style, presentation of argument, and choice of topics, sometimes minimising the originality of the new book.[25] Indeed, the link with the *Satires* is very important, and close echoes of the earlier collection are numerous and significant. Several satiric themes are picked up in the *Epistles*, although the crudest and most diatribic have been left behind: there is no talk of the right kind of sex (*Satires* 1.2), or of legacy-hunting (2.5), almost no literary parody. But above all, the poetic mask donned by Horace is different. The poet no longer strolls about the city, seeking out occasions for laughter or censure at the expense of ridiculous maniacs, or even of himself; and the choice and treatment of a topic are conducted with a friend's wish or need in mind, not as points on the diatribic agenda.

One significant example of the redeployment of familiar themes and atmospheres in different colours in the new genre is letter 15. A medical prescription sets the poet on a journey towards a spa, less fashionable than his usual summer haunts, and the poet asks a friend to write back with information about the climate, the roads, the people, the drinking-water, very important for a convalescent – but his friend is not to bother about the local wines: he is sure not to care greatly about those, and will bring some from his best reserve to keep himself in good spirits.

The garrulousness and longwindedness of *Epistle* 15 are a masterwork of studied pretence: the periods flow in a rambling sequence, in which the main request for information is interspersed with parenthetic digressions, adding chatty and unnecessary though memorable details (in a flash forward, the surprise of the poet's equipage at the unexpected turn when they reach the familiar Baiae-Cumae junction, the spite and anger of the neglected holiday towns personified): it all seems to go on for ever.

The letter starts as a real document responding to a practical need: we may even wonder why such a mundane, even frivolous letter was included. A suspicion glimmers through as we wend our way through the embarrassed contortions of the letter, the starts and jolts of the syntax. Then the poet picks himself up, and rounds off the ramble with a story and a confession: does Vala know that notorious glutton, old Maenius, so ready to pillory the profligate when money is out, and so quick to throw aside all aloofness and

25 A handy catalogue of the most significant points of contact between *Epistles* and *Satires* is in De Pretis (2002) 99–107, with some earlier bibliography. On metrical and stylistic differences between *Epistles* and *Sermones* cf. Mayer (1994) 11–36.

turn into an Epulon when money is in again? He is no different from him now.

We encounter here some familiar satiric elements: the Lucilian comic vignette of Maenius (naming and shaming was a feature of Lucilius), the theme of gluttony, and that of *non aequabiliter uiuere*, living inconstantly, not in peace with one's inner self.[26] In *Satires* 2.7.22–38 Horace let Davus caricature exactly this tendency of his to slip into inconsistent habits, donning and shedding the garb of the self-sufficient wise man as the occasion required. On an evening with no prospects of grand invitations, Horace sets off dining frugally at home on greens, when a late call from Maecenas makes him get up and rush to join his patron's party, his appetite whetted by the pleasures of the rich man's table. The satire made the most of the motif of the repentine, unabashed change from philosopher to parasite, highlighted by the anger and desolation of Horace's poor clients left without a meal. The satiric sketch, beautiful as it was, was a successful comic gag, brilliantly acted, with the poet himself putting in a magisterial appearance. In the letter, a similar motif is treated with more emphasis on the psychological realities of self-analysis and self-discovery. The context is serious (the poet has really been ill, and some cure is justified), and the old satiric elements make way into the text only gradually: first, the targets of humour seem to be an implacable doctor, his longsuffering patients, and a couple of slighted holiday resorts, wounded in their pride, while Horace goes on with his queries about how best to prepare himself for this southward trip; the open avowal of Horace's condition surfaces only later, as if the poet had come to the realisation of his inconsistency while writing. In this way, the exposure of vice is dramatised as part of a process of self-discovery and reflection, and the letter acquires psychological depth.

The letter stands in a neat contrast with the preceding poem, in which Horace chided his bailiff, who did not appreciate the frugality of life in the country, for wanting a change: Horace has now fallen prey to the same restlessness and dissatisfaction with poor living.[27] The diptych of 14 and 15 also provides a good example of the moral open-endedness of the work, without undermining the serious engagement of the core message: the *Epistles* as a whole proclaim the urgency of virtue, but prepare for the inevitability of relapse.

The two poems of the second book mark the transition to another subgenre of epistolary writing, namely the literary-critical and theoretical essay in epistolary form, which at Rome seems to have been initiated by Varro,

26 A traditional satiric theme: cf. Fraenkel (1957) 90–7; La Penna (1993) 180–1.

27 Good analysis in Armstrong (1989) 126.

perhaps Horace's most important source for the historical sections in *Epistle* 2.1. The letter to Florus (*Epistle* 2.2), apparently the earlier one, begins as an apology for not writing poems any more (and is therefore sometimes taken to pre-date Book 4 of the *Odes*, i.e. 17 BCE; for the dating see chapter 1 above). In the context of this apology, however, Horace gives sharp precepts on how, in his view, poetry should be written (cf. esp. 109–25). The letter unfolds through various layers of argument, set against a background of *Epistles* 1 ideology: in the end, it is always better to do philosophy than to write verse (141–216). The much later letter to Augustus (*Epistle* 2.1, composed perhaps as late as 12 BCE) reacts against the blind preference which Horace's contemporaries accord to archaic Roman poetry, especially to what Horace describes as tacky theatrical shows, presumably revivals of older dramas. In these poems the epistolary scenarios of Book 1 fade almost to insignificance: epistolary commonplaces do occur, such as the elaborated proemial apology for being a bad correspondent in *Epistle* 2.2.20–5, but the world from which these letters emanate is no longer the moral landscape of Book 1, and has nothing of the voyage of self-discovery and self-analysis in which Horace engaged himself and his correspondents then. The old epistolary atmosphere of intimacy and meditative loneliness has been left behind, and in one memorable passage Horace describes with graphic detail the impossibility of being a poet in the Roman city bustle, where one's peace is continually threatened by the rushing about of men, animals and vehicles (*Epistle* 2.2.65–76).

FURTHER READING

Epistles 1, 'Horace's strangest . . . and least talked-about book' (W. R. Johnson (1993) ix), have been well served by commentaries (the most important of them are Kiessling and Heinze (1930); Mayer (1994); and Fedeli (1997a)); and contributions dealing with individual aspects of the work, above all its philosophical sources, are good and numerous: cf. in particular Traina (1991); Moles (1995; 2002); and Armstrong (2004). Yet few general studies have been devoted to the collection as a whole, or to its generic and literary affiliations. This lack of sympathy for the work is partly a result of the embarrassment felt by scholars at negotiating the literariness of the book – an embarrassment fuelled by some older critics' tendency to emphasise the significance of the biographical elements in the work. To what extent are the *Epistles* more than an incoherent collection of threadbare, moralistic topoi? How do they rise above the individual concerns of Horace and his addressees?

Among modern attempts to rescue the *Epistles* from this impasse La Penna (1949) and McGann (1969) stand out. La Penna (1949) offered a perceptive and appealing 'melancholy' reading of the *Epistles* tinged by contemporary French existentialism. McGann, in new-critical vein, gave a coherent interpretation of the *Epistles* as a book, which he tried to situate in contemporary Roman literary discourse. Among brief overall presentations of the *Epistles* as a book, most incisive and insightful is

Armstrong (1989). Other monographs devoted entirely to the *Epistles* are Kilpatrick (1986), a poem-by-poem presentation highlighting possible Ciceronian elements, especially in the centrality of the friendship theme, and Ferri (1993), who attempted to read the *Epistles* within the tradition of the didactic genre, viewing the book as a response to Lucretius. Also important, idiosyncratic as it may be, is Johnson's fascinating reading of the *Epistles* (1993), as an obsessive study in freedom, culminating in Horace's realisation of the inadequacy of its various hypostaseis.

Other treatments of the refashioning of letter-writing conventions in Horace are Morris (1931); Allen (1972); Ferri (1996); and De Pretis (2002). De Pretis (2002), in particular, offers a sophisticated assessment of the genre of the *Epistles*, with good insights about cross-generic elements in the collection, the poet's *persona*, and the literary context to which the *Epistles* respond. S. J. Harrison (1995b) provides a welcome comparison with epistolographic theory, and probes the plausibility of Horace's acquaintance with it.

10

ANDREW LAIRD

The *Ars Poetica*

The title '*Ars Poetica*' ('The art of poetry') was very possibly attached to Horace's verse letter to the Pisones before we find it used by Quintilian at the end of the first century CE.[1] That title hints at the universal status of this didactic poem as a pre-eminent, authoritative and, in every sense, 'classical' manual on the composition of poetry. The *Ars* provided an object of imitation, as well as a code of practice, for Renaissance poets and playwrights; it continued to be the paradigm for neo-classical literature and aesthetics; and even some modernist writers of the twentieth century responded, or else owed something, to its prescriptions.[2] There is no doubt that this single composition by Horace – at 476 hexameters his longest – has exercised far more influence than any of his other individual poems, and more even than his collections of poems. The later reception of *Ars Poetica*, like that of Plato's *Republic*, is of far more consequence than its significance for the period in which it was originally produced.

At the same time, the recent tendency to consider Horace's poem on poetics as a 'literary epistle' points to the way in which it can be imagined in

1 Quintilian, who also calls it the *liber de arte poetica* 'book on the art of poetry' (*Institutio Oratoria* 8.3.60), quotes this single poem on eight occasions (cf. Index of Russell's Loeb Quintilian iv) – more frequently than any other single poem of Horace, and almost as many times as he quotes from all four books of the *Odes*. The stature of the *Ars Poetica* for Quintilian is affirmed by the prominent reference to the work in his Preface (2), where Quintilian claims to have applied Horace's recommendation to his own *prose* treatise. For detailed discussion of the poem's title in antiquity, see Fischer (1991) 5–16.

2 The manifestos of the Imagist movement, penned by Ezra Pound in the early 1900s and reprinted in Jones (2001), bear comparison to some sentiments in the *Ars*. Willett (1964) 270 records Brecht's unsurprisingly negative verdict on the account of how poetry should arouse emotion in *Ars* 99–103: 'I must say there is only one word for such an operation: barbaric.' For medieval and Renaissance reception and imitation, see the 'Further reading' recommended at the end of this chapter.

an original context: as a poem in the oeuvre of a major Augustan writer, who refined and built on a longstanding tradition of Aristotelian and later Hellenistic poetic theory.[3] The placing of the *Ars Poetica* after the *Epistles* in modern editions is not based on its position in the manuscripts (where it frequently comes after the *Odes*), but rather on its date of composition, generally agreed to be around 10 BCE.[4] The contents of this exceptional work can be understood in terms of learning and tastes which belonged, not merely to Rome towards the end of the first century BCE, but to Horace himself. Horace's confident grasp of both Greek and Roman literary history led him to express views, about tragedy, epic and some other forms of poetry, which could be idiosyncratic and playful. Moreover, those views may have been further conditioned by the specialised interests of the original addressees of the poem.[5]

Thus the *Ars Poetica* cannot escape being regarded bifocally: as a provocative and vital source for a range of ancient theories, and also as a kind of literary 'Magna Carta' for norms and principles that were earnestly applied to literature, drama and other art forms well into the eighteenth century. The *Ars* is a difficult text to introduce in its own right, and it is frequently presented to new readers in relation to something else – to Horace's own poetic practice and his views on poetry expressed in other works (e.g. *Satires* 1.4, 1.10, *Epistles* 1.2, 2.1, 2.2); to Roman epic and drama; to Aristotle's or Callimachus' poetic theories; to Augustan *mores*; or to conceptions of art and literature in later times that have been determined by Horace's precepts.

In fact most introductions present the *Ars* in relation to the ideas of a lost Hellenistic writer of the third-century BCE, Neoptolemus of Parium, who is widely supposed to have shaped Horace's outlook on poetry in this text.[6] That supposition rests on a remark by Pomponius Porphyrio, an ancient commentator on Horace in the early 200s CE:

3 For Fraenkel (1957) 125 n. 3 'the *Epistula ad Pisones* [is] misnamed *De arte poetica*'! Brink (1963) 154 n. 1, in response to this remark, noted a 'tendency to underestimate its theoretical purpose and character'. Armstrong (1989) 154 and Rudd in his Penguin translation (1979b) have no qualms about calling the poem 'Epistles 2.3' in volumes which are aimed at general readers.

4 Following Dilke (1958): compare Rudd (1989) 19–21 and Syme (1986) 379–81. On a largely stylometric basis, Fischer (1991) concurs with those scholars who seek to put back the date of the *Ars* to 23–20 BCE, although it is hard to see the *Ars* as chronologically prior to *Epistles* 2 in thematic terms.

5 For discussions of the identity of the Pisones, see n. 9 below.

6 Brink (1963); Innes (1989); Russell (1973); Rudd (1989); Kilpatrick (1990).

> In quem librum congessit praecepta Neoptolemi τοῦ Παριανοῦ de arte poetica, non quidem omnia, sed eminentissima. Primum praeceptum est περὶ τῆς ἀκολουθίας.[7]
>
> In this book [the *Ars Poetica*] Horace has put together precepts of Neoptolemus of Parium concerning the art of poetry, by no means all, but the most outstanding. The first precept is *Concerning the natural succession* [of words or ideas].

Although Porphyrio shows detailed knowledge of a wide range of recherché Greek texts, this is the only occasion on which he mentions Neoptolemus in his commentary on Horace's complete works. The mention is made *à propos* of the opening verse of the *Ars Poetica*.

Some of Neoptolemus' precepts are preserved in a fragmentary treatise, *On Poets*, by a later Greek author, Philodemus. Philodemus of Gadara, who was possibly Virgil's teacher, had come to Rome in the 70s BCE. There is in fact an independent link between Philodemus and the *Ars Poetica*. Cicero's famous speech *Against Piso* indicates that L. Calpurnius Piso, a young man (*adulescens*) in the 70s BCE, was Philodemus' patron.[8] That man's son, L. Calpurnius Piso Caesoninus, was appointed as *Praefectus Vrbi* by the emperor Tiberius. It seems to be this Piso whom Horace's commentator Porphyrio identifies as the primary addressee of the *Ars Poetica*. Such an identification may be right or wrong but it is certainly significant that this identification is made *immediately* before Porphyrio's mention of Neoptolemus quoted above.[9]

The publication of the fragments of Philodemus' *On Poets* in 1918 led to further evidence about Neoptolemus (along with a good deal of conjecture!) being brought to bear on the *Ars Poetica*. From Philodemus, it appears that Neoptolemus commended unity and coherence, as does Horace (*Ars Poetica*

7 For the text see Holder (1894) 162. Porphyrio's Latin commentary on the *Ars Poetica* is not hard to read, and is more succinct than its modern counterparts, as it runs to only sixteen pages.

8 Cicero *In Pisonem* 68–72, 74. Nisbet (1961) offers commentary on these passages and his Appendices III 'Piso and Philodemus' and IV 'Piso and the Villa of the Papyri' at 183–8 are relevant. See also Janko (2000) 1–10.

9 Porphyrio's commentary (n. 7 above) begins as follows: *Hunc librum, qui inscribitur de arte poetica, ad Lucium Pisonem, qui postea urbis custos fuit, eiusque lib<e>ros misit; nam et ipse Piso poeta fuit, et studiorum liberalium antistes. In quem librum congessit praecepta Neoptolemi.* [This book, which is inscribed 'On the art of poetry' he sent to Lucius Piso – who afterwards was made guardian of the city – and to his children. For Piso was also a poet himself and a *doyen* of liberal studies. In this book Horace has put together precepts of Neoptolemus]. Brink (1963), and more accessibly Rudd (1989) 19–21. Fischer (1991) 52–9 considers this testimony for the recipient of the *Ars* in depth to reach a different conclusion.

1–23, 152). From Philodemus, it appears that Neoptolemus conjoined skill (*technē*) and power (*dynamis*) as properties of the poet, as does Horace: *ars* ('skill') and *ingenium* ('natural talent') are famously discussed together in 408–11. And from Philodemus it also appears that Neoptolemus held that the poet should combine charm with moral instruction, as does Horace (99–100, 333–4, 343–4). It should be emphasised that none of these tenets was unique to Neoptolemus, and that the theory and practice of Roman authors, including Lucilius, Lucretius and Varro, had already accommodated comparable ideas from Greek sources.

However, it is further argued that Horace deliberately applied to the *Ars Poetica* a tripartite structure attributed, via Philodemus, to Neoptolemus' treatise. Neoptolemus' actual discrimination between 'poem' (*poiēma*: equivalent to diction or style), 'poetry' (*poiēsis*: a conception of content, plot and character), and 'poet' (*poiētēs*: attention to the role and moral responsibility of the poet) fused the Hellenistic interest in verbal style with an emphasis on the grander composition which was more Aristotelian.[10] Not a single Alexandrian poet or theorist is actually named by Horace, though, and there has been disagreement about the way in which this tripartite schema might be reflected in the *Ars Poetica*: while the *poiētēs* is obviously the subject of verses 295–476, the situation of the distinction between *poiēma* and *poiēsis* in verses 1–294 has been much debated – and one might doubt whether it should be applied at all.[11] The perilous role of guesswork in the construction of scholarly edifices is highlighted by Umberto Eco's scenario of papyrologists, in a future epoch, who conclude that 'Singing in the Rain' must have been composed as a fertility ode to be sung by a chorus of young girls.[12] The imposition of the now celebrated poem/poetry/poet schema on the *Ars Poetica* could, after all, reflect an inclination that is quite modern – to knock the unco-operative contents of this composition into a shape that orderly minds find more justifiable or appealing.

Commentators and translators of the *Ars Poetica* divide up the texts of their editions or renderings into constituent units, irrespective of the degree to which they invoke Neoptolemus. Different systems of thematic division point to different ideas about the 'overarching' or 'underlying' structure for the poem. All agree that Horace's argument moves from a consideration of artistic content and technique (*ars*) in 1–294 to an account of the poet (*artifex*) which runs from 295 to the end of the poem. The view that

10 Brink (1963) 55.

11 Innes (1989) 259–60 is moderately sceptical. Although I resist referring to the *Ars Poetica* as a treatise, the comparisons made in Innes (1995) = (2005) to Longinus should be noted.

12 Umberto Eco's 1959 essay 'Fragments' is translated in Eco (1993) 21.

poiēma – matters of poetic style as opposed to content – can be isolated as Horace's main concern in verses 45–118 is prevalent, though not universal.[13] Otherwise, breakdowns of the poem's contents have varied considerably on matters of detail: a useful reminder that a text's structure is never an intrinsic property waiting to be discovered, but something that readers attach to it themselves.[14] As long as this is understood, a clear overview of the *Ars Poetica* is bound to be useful for anyone who is new to this enigmatic work:

1–23	Unity and consistency
24–58	Skill needed to avoid faults
59–72	Fashions in words
73–98	Metre and subject
99–118	Emotion and character
119–78	Choice and handling of myth
179–201	Some rules for dramatists
202–19	Development of tragedy
220–50	Satyr-plays
251–68	The need for technical perfection in metre
269–74	Greek models
275–84	Inventiveness of the Greeks in drama
285–94	Inventiveness of the Romans
295–322	The poet
323–90	Greek and Roman attitudes
391–407	Poetry and its social uses and value
408–52	Art and nature
453–76	The mad poet

These are the section headings which Donald Russell used in his 1972 translation.[15] The synopsis they provide is no more authoritative than any other, but it is helpful because, by giving less emphasis to the idea of an overall structure, it shows reasonably well how each subject leads comfortably into the one that follows, by an association of idea and theme. Indeed, Horace's associative connections are made so effectively that people do not always agree on which specific verses mark the transitions in the poem's argument.

13 Brink (1963) 31 tabulates the analyses of Norden (1905), Jensen (1918), Rostagni (1930) and Immisch (1932). These can be compared to the tabulation in Rudd (1989) 21–3, and to the synopsis of headings from Russell and Winterbottom (1972) 279–91, quoted above.
14 Laird (2000) 143–6. This remains so even in the case of ancient authors who had a firm conception of the contents of their treatise – as Horace no doubt would have done: cf. Brink (1963) 3–14 on *technologia*.
15 Russell and Winterbottom (1972) 279–91.

This system of associative connection could be a far more important respect in which the influence of Neoptolemus is at work – through the principle of *akolouthia*: the 'natural succession' or 'consistency' that Porphyrio identified as the explicit concern of the poem's opening.[16] On this level Horace practises what he preaches about unity and consistency (1–23) in the *Ars Poetica* to a remarkable degree. By way of demonstration it can be shown here that the poem's end can even be united and made consistent with its beginning.

The *Ars Poetica* ends with a derisive caricature of the mad poet. He is presented as akin to an invalid suffering from various sicknesses ('accursed scabies, jaundice, fanaticism, or Diana's wrath' 453–4). A few lines later, this figure is compared to a caged bear (472–4), which mutates without warning into a blood-sucking leech (475–6). The sudden change has disturbed commentators: for Brink it is 'startling' and Rudd deems it 'disconcerting'. Yet that rapid conjunction of ideas and images involving sickness and hybridisation of the human with the bestial does recall the humorous supposition at the beginning of the *Ars Poetica*. There, Horace's addressees are asked to imagine (1–4) 'a painter who wanted to join a horse's neck to a human head, and then clothe an assemblage of limbs with various feathers, so that what started out at the top as a beautiful woman ended in a hideously ugly fish'. Horace points out that such a pictorial hybrid would prompt derisive laughter (5), and that, if it were to appear in a poetry book, it would be symptomatic of an invalid's delirious dreams (6–9). This subtly themed ring-composition makes it clear enough that the products of an undisciplined mind are as sick and grotesque as the poet who produces them.

Verses 6–9 perhaps have a further reflexive significance. They call attention to the mock application of such bad practice to the very poetry book we are now reading:[17]

> credite, Pisones, isti tabulae fore librum
> persimilem cuius, velut aegri somnia, vanae
> fingentur species, ut nec pes nec caput uni
> reddatur formae.

Credit, dear Pisones, that a book whose features are conceived fantastically like a sick man's dreams would be similar to that picture in such a way that neither the foot nor the head of the shape give its due as a unity.

16 The Greek word *akolouthia* ('a following on') also seems to be a critical term (Dionysius of Halicarnassus *On Composition* 22, Longinus 22.1) which denotes a natural sequence of words, ideas or argument.

17 Brink (1971) 86 notes that the placing of six words before the word *si* ('if') in the first verse of the *Ars* is a 'violation of the law of unity'.

The financial connotations of the words *credite* ('Credit') and *reddatur* ('give its due') suggest that the poet is playfully seeking an advance which will not be redeemed at the *end* (*pes* 'foot') of this book, or here at the *beginning* (*caput* 'head'). At its start and finish, Horace could be warning us, the *Ars Poetica* itself is going to look like the sort of chimaera he has been describing – the ploy of using such a device to characterise discourse in a reflexive manner actually goes back to Plato, a debt that Brink's detailed commentary does not identify.[18]

Later on there is a more adventurous use of the word *pes* (also a metrical 'foot' in Greek and Latin verse) to which Alessandro Barchiesi has recently drawn attention. Horace is giving an account of the origin of iambic poetry (79–80):[19]

> Archilochum proprio rabies armavit iambo
> hunc socci cepere pedem grandesque coturni

> Rage armed Archilochus with its very own iambus: this foot was clad in the shoes of comedy and the grand boots of tragedy.

The innovation here is that the normally metaphorical metrical 'foot' has become the *primary object of reference*: the 'human foot', by contrast, has turned into an illustrative vehicle of comparison.[20]

The *Ars Poetica* is full of mischievous wordplay, sophisticated conceit and surprising transitions. It should never be forgotten that the initial verses of the poem lead the first-time reader to believe that they herald a didactic poem about painting: later Latin writers were inspired to write Horatian didactic poems on that subject.[21] Horace's own interest in the visual field is, however,

18 Plato plays such a figurative game with the notion of an *eikōn* ('likeness') in *Republic* 487e–488a. Socrates explains to Adeimantus that the question he is asking requires an *eikōn* by way of reply. 'I don't think you're accustomed to use *eikones* in what you say,' is Adeimantus' sarcastic reaction. Socrates does more than reply with his habitual iconic analogy – he uses another *eikōn* to characterise the one he says he is compelled to produce: an image of painters who make goat-stags and other hybrid animals which is vengefully *meta*-iconic in itself. The original chimaera is described at Homer *Iliad* 6.181. Plato's illustration of Pan in *Cratylus* is comparable – with a connection to Virgil's *Fama*: Laird (1999) 301–5.

19 A. Barchiesi (2001a) 144–7. On Horace's *iambus*, see Lindsay Watson in this volume, chapter 7.

20 A. Barchiesi (1994) 135–8 is also vital for any footnote on this subject.

21 Charles Du Fresnoy's *De Arte Graphica* ('On graphic art') is one outstanding and highly influential example, now translated and annotated in Allen, Haskell and Muecke (2005). See David Money in this volume (chapter 23) on Latin imitations of Horace in the seventeenth and eighteenth centuries.

maintained beyond these initial verses. His formulation of the famous tags *pictoribus atque poetis* (10) and *ut pictura poesis* (361) accumulated an after-life all of their own in art-historical and iconological theory.[22] What is more, the opening discussion of unity and consistency in the *Ars* is centred on *ekphrasis* (or visual description) and the role of the 'purple patch' (14–19) – yet another Horatian coinage which has become common currency:

> inceptis gravibus plerumque et magna professis
> purpureus, late qui splendeat, unus et alter
> adsuitur pannus, cum lucus et ara Dianae
> et properantis aquae per amoenos ambitus agros
> aut flumen Rhenum aut pluvius describitur arcus.
> sed non erat his locus.

> Serious and ambitious designs often have a purple patch or two sewn on to them just to make a good show at a distance – a description of a grove and altar of Diana, the meanderings of a stream running through pleasant fields, the River Rhine, a rainbow: but now there is no place for them.

This apparently uncontroversial assertion that description is a form of detachable digression was quoted by Servius and endorsed by many other ancient authors.[23] Here again, though, Horace is playing with the text we are reading. The passage presents what is at once a list of poetic topoi *and* a sequence of brief impressions of the scenes in themselves, which constitute 'virtually the only ecphrases in the whole of Horace's *oeuvre*'.[24] The meta-literary game is signalled at the end of this quotation. Descriptions of places in Latin poetry are commonly heralded by the expression *est locus* ('There is a place'). Here, in talking about the place of descriptions of place in poetry, Horace amusingly negates the cliché *est locus* with *non erat . . . locus* ('there is *no* place'). [25] As with the word *pes* in 79–80, there is a slippage between the literal and the metaphorical, and between sign and signified, in the application of a routine technical term.

22 R. W. Lee (1967); Gage (1973); Hardie (1993).

23 Servius on *Aeneid* 10.653; Quintilian *Institutio Oratoria* 4.3.12–13; Demetrius *On Style* 108; Lucian *How to Write History* 57. Passages about *descriptio* are treated in a discussion of narrative transition in M. Barchiesi (1987) 13–111. For modern theoretical accounts see Genette (1982) 127–46; Fowler (1991) = (2000).

24 Hardie (1993) 122.

25 A lengthier discussion of this condensed and complicated passage with further bibliography is in Laird (1996) 91–4, which also considers its significance for visual art at 91–2. Hinds (2002) 125–30 applies some of those observations to the *locus amoenus* in Ovid. M. Barchiesi (1987) 29 considers the *est locus* / *loco è* / *luogho è* motif.

While the *Ars Poetica* is clearly far more than a versified technical treatise, it would be wrong to give the impression that its main appeal lies in an abundance of clever flourishes. C. O. Brink shrewdly characterised the *Ars* as 'a work of the imagination that makes a poetic symbol out of literary theory' and enjoins readers of the work to make sense of that theory.[26] The poem contains much astute observation that can be appreciated by today's readers for insight not only on ancient thinking but also on ideas about literary expression which have broader significance. For example, at 93–7, having made a prescriptive distinction between the comic and tragic styles ('everything must keep appropriately to the place it is alloted' 92), Horace concedes that characters in comedy may sometimes speak with more elevated eloquence and, conversely, that characters in a tragedy can occasionally move the spectator more directly by using the prosaic language of everyday life. This flexibility makes sense in terms of modern thinking (and even some postmodern thinking) about genre: its 'rules' are certainly there, but those rules are there to be broken.[27]

Horace's recognition that poetry can copy real-life diction involves the clarification of another theoretical issue in the *Ars Poetica*. The ancient rhetorical notion of *imitatio* (or *mimēsis*) – as the adoption of the style of an earlier author – is generally regarded as categorically distinct from the semantic conception of *imitatio* – as the linguistic representation of objects – which is found in Plato and Aristotle.[28] But *Ars Poetica* 317–18 nicely show how the imitation of models and imitation-as-representation come together:

> respicere exemplar vitae morumque iubebo
> doctum imitatorem et vivas hinc ducere voces.

I will order the learned imitator to look to the model of life and morals, and draw his utterances living from there.

The phrase *doctum imitatorem* ('learned imitator') presupposes both the priority of imitating models and the necessity of the imitator being well versed in those models. In telling the imitator to look at the exemplar of life and to draw living voices from there, Horace is actually suggesting that the imitation of life in poetry comes down to the imitation of real-life utterances.

26 Brink (1971) viii.

27 Compare the opening of Derrida (1981), a famous essay on 'The law of genre'. Rudd (1989) 34 is not so happy with Horace's position here, but the fact of the matter is that generic mixing or 'inclusion' (Cairns (1972) 89–90, 158–9) is a hallmark of most, if not all, literary texts including the *Ars Poetica*: there is an interesting discussion of its genre in Frischer (1991) 87–100.

28 The *Oxford Classical Dictionary* article on *imitatio* makes no attempt to connect these divergent usages.

This provides the link between the two ancient conceptions of *imitatio*.[29] Literary language may imitate life, but it must imitate everyday language in order to do so.

The fact that a Renaissance Latin commentary on the *Ars Poetica* by the renowned Florentine humanist Cristoforo Landino was illustrated throughout by examples of *Virgil*'s poetry shows how Horace's work can inspire literary criticism as well as literary theory.[30] And there may indeed be some specific appraisals of Virgil and other authors lurking in the *Ars Poetica* itself, which remain to be uncovered. Even if the composition of the *Ars* were to go back to the early 20s BCE (see note 4 above), it is not inconceivable that Horace was already familiar with parts of the *Aeneid* as a 'work in progress'. This could be suggested by the well-known discussion of epic beginnings in relation to epic verisimilitude in the *Ars Poetica* (147–52) – even though Horace is ostensibly talking about Homer:

> nec gemino bellum Troianum orditur ab ovo:
> semper ad eventum festinat et in medias res
> non secus ac notas auditorem rapit, et quae
> desperat tractata nitescere posse relinquit,
> *atque ita mentitur, sic veris falsa remiscet,*
> *primo ne medium, medio ne discrepet imum.*

> He does not begin the Trojan war from the twin egg; he is always making good speed towards the end of the story, and carries his hearer right into the midst of it as though it were already known. He leaves out anything which he thinks cannot be polished up satisfactorily by treatment, *and thus tells lies, and mixes truth with falsehood, in such a way that the middle squares with the beginning and the end with the middle.*

The main point of this passage is made in the last verse quoted (152): the plausibility of a story is intimately bound up with the mechanics of plot construction.[31] Rostagni and Brink saw that verses 151–2 pick up the way Horace opened this discussion of the use of myth in poetry at 119:

> aut *famam* sequere aut sibi convenientia *finge*

> Either follow *hearsay* (*fama*) or *make up* a consistent story.

29 The important treatment of *imitatio* in Russell (1979) 3–5 would appear to corroborate this interpretation of the passage. On *Ars Poetica* 133 *nec desilies imitator in artum* ('nor will you jump down as you imitate, into a hole'), Russell comments (at 4) that 'it is difficult to believe that Horace did not mean us to have both senses [of *mimēsis*] in mind'. Laird (1999) 310–18 reviews some theoretical implications of this.

30 See Pigman (1990).

31 Laird (2006) considers this passage in relation to Aristotle *Poetics* 1460a.

What did not interest those commentators is the remarkable similarity between Horace's description of the 'lying' epic poet in 151–2 and Virgil's personification of *Fama* ('Rumour') in *Aeneid* 4.188–90:

> tam *ficti* pravique tenax quam nuntia *veri* . . .
> . . . *pariter facta atque infecta canebat*

> clinging on to her *fiction* and slander as often as she tells the *truth* . . . *she was singing things done and not done in equal measure.*

Horace's apparent evocation of the Virgilian figure of *Fama*, occurring as it does in a discussion of plot construction, yields a significant critical insight on the *Aeneid* which has eluded its subsequent devotees: *Fama* actually contributes to the *formal structuring* of Virgil's poem, by effecting, and rendering plausible, some crucial transitions in the poem's narrative.[32] In this respect at least, the fabrications of the singing figure of Rumour may be aligned to those of the epic singer himself.

The *Ars Poetica* is far more of a guide to inform the judgement of readers and audiences than the manual for practising writers it pretends to be. The antiquarian forays into the origins of Greek literary genres (73–85, 202–84) show this well enough – the portrayal of the poet (295–476) also emerges from an assessment that is based more on reception and reading than it is on literary production. Evaluation, as well as being prominent in ancient writing on rhetoric and oratory, was very much part of the original Hellenistic notion of 'criticism': the judgement (*krisis*) of poems was a fundamental activity for grammarians. Through the *Ars Poetica*, Horace transmits the canons of Hellenistic evaluation to later literary traditions in Europe and beyond.

Two general ways in which the *Ars* can be viewed were pointed out at the beginning of this discussion. If it is historicised, it appears to be *descriptive* and also *iconoclastic*: Horace concentrates on Greek literature (202–67) at the expense of Roman achievements in epic, love elegy and lyric; he explains away the myth of the inspired poet (391–407); and he attaches more importance to hard work than to natural talent (408–52). If on the other hand the *Ars Poetica* is conceived as the basis of Renaissance and early modern aesthetic theory, it becomes *prescriptive* and *classical*, as its emphases on unity (1–23), refinement and verbal elegance (24–72), decorum (73–201) and the imitation of good models (268–74) are foregrounded. The scholarly fascination with the original innovation of the work is bound to compete with the enduring appeal of its classicism.[33] In a poem entitled 'Arté Poética', a

32 *Aeneid* 4.666, 7.104, 9.474, 11.139.

33 Classicists have been surprisingly reluctant to explore the idea of 'classicism', which ultimately derives from a socio-economic category (Aulus Gellius *Attic Nights* 19.8.15);

modernist tribute to Horace's verse epistle, Jorge Luis Borges sums up these two sources of the work's appeal in terms of the feeling that overwhelmed Ulysses – who here seems to stand as a reader (or even as an arbiter) of classical literature – on his return home: :

> They say that Ulysses, sated with marvels,
> Wept tears of love at the sight of his Ithaca,
> Green and humble. Art is that Ithaca
> Of green eternity, not of marvels.[34]

In the end the 'marvels' of the *Ars Poetica's* quality in its ancient context mean little in relation to its permanent value for all time – a value which is tantamount to that of art itself.

FURTHER READING

Translations are to be found in Russell and Winterbottom (1972) 279–91; Rudd (1979b); Dorsch and Murray (2000) 98–112; and Kilpatrick (1990). Of editions of the Latin text with commentary, Rudd (1989) is the most accessible and reassuringly pragmatic in its approach. The commentary of Brink (1971), which follows Brink (1963), a volume of 'Prolegomena' on Horace's literary epistles, is admirably detailed, and will have more appeal to readers once they are familiar with the poem and the issues it raises. The Italian edition of Rostagni (1946) is still valuable. Of general accounts, Russell (1973) = Laird (2006), is an excellent survey, which takes the importance of reception into account. G. Williams (1968) 329–57; Innes (1989); and Grube (1965) 238–52 also offer very useful overviews. Fischer (1991) is an analytical but controversial investigation of the title, dating and genre of the *Ars*. On specific aspects and the reception of the *Ars Poetica*: Dilke (1958) on dating; Wiseman (1988) on satyr-drama; Jocelyn (1995) on Horace and Plautus; Herrick (1946) on Horace and Aristotle in the Renaissance; R. W. Lee (1967) and Gage (1973) on legacies of *ut pictura poesis*. Vida's *De Arte Poetica* first published in 1527 (G. Williams 1976) and Dufresnoy's *De Arte Graphica*, printed in Paris in 1668 (ed. Allen, Haskell and Muecke 2005), are early modern Latin verse treatises modelled on Horace's *Ars*, which have been highly influential in their own right. The extensive bibliography of primary works from 1650 to 1800 in R. Murray (1974) demonstrates the enormity of Horace's influence on later neo-classical poetics. For further bibliography on the *Ars* see Brink (1963), 273–86 and (1971) 524–7; Kilpatrick (1990) 111–16, and the general bibliographies mentioned in the Introduction to this volume.

Fleischmann (1974) is a useful general account; Porter (2006) represents an important new departure.

34 Originally from *El Hacedor* (1960), trans. W. S. Merwin in Borges (2000) 137.

II

ALESSANDRO BARCHIESI

Carmina: Odes and *Carmen Saeculare*

Oliver Lyne, in memoriam

Modernity hit downtown Berlin on 3 October 1760, driven and unstoppable like a cannonball. Actually, it was a cannonball. The Russian gun established a very provisional record for long-distance bombing of a city, just at the end of the Seven Years War. The Prussian Horace, Karl Wilhelm Ramler, rose to the occasion. He was ready for it. Thanks to his favourite poet, he knew how to sing about private and public destinies, and the unforeseen dangers of life; he knew that the best poetic strategy for a successful lyric was none other than apostrophe:

Ode *Auf ein Geschütz*
(*Lyrische Gedichte*, Reuttlingen 1782, 69)
Ode to a Cannon
O du, dem glühend Eisen, donnernd Feuer
Aus offnem Aetnaschlunde stammt,
Die frommen Dichter zu zerschmettern, Ungeheuer,
Das aus der Hölle stammt!

O thou, whose glowing iron and thundering fire
Come from Etna's open jaws,
To shatter virtuous poets – monster,
That comes from Hell itself!

War technology made progress over the next 150 years, and at the end of this cycle another poet steeped in Horace realised that gas attacks were making traditional lyric not only impossible but poisonous: however, he still needed Horace to make this contradiction felt:

My friend, you would not tell with such high zest
To children ardent for some desperate glory,
The old Lie: Dulce et decorum est
Pro patria mori.
(Wilfred Owen, *Dulce et decorum est*, 1917)

This had been the quotation whispered by Quentin Battye as he fell mortally wounded during the Great Mutiny on the Delhi ridge, as R. S. Conway had mentioned in his appropriative talk 'Horace as Poet Laureate' (1903).

How was Horace himself upgraded to such prominence? He was more important as a lyric author in modern Europe than he had ever been in Roman culture. His rise as a model of lyric in the early modern age seems to be connected to a strategic positioning: occasions in life, mediating between private and public. Thus Ramler is helped by Horace to triangulate between the personal response of the 'pious poet', the communal spirit of Prussia, and the occasional effect of the Russian blitzkrieg. The other substantial reason is that Horace was widely read as a text that guarantees access to 'one of us' – the people who really matter in this world: the modern, European, middle-aged, male, empowered citizens of a nation-state. The concept of literature as a way of meeting exceptional individuals of the past has later been exposed as a tendentious and pathetic fiction. (How and why are certain individuals more important than others? The worst possible canon is a canon of 'very important *persons*' – not just texts – of the past.) In the history of this misconception, a significant one for European culture, Horace has a place *qua* lyric poet, as well as poet of epistles and satires.

The success of his lyric has to do with the perception that there is 'one of us' behind the poems: an 'honorary Englishman' and an ideal club man (Don Fowler) for an English reader; an upwardly mobile southern Italian intellectual if you happen to be a southern Italian intellectual; a Harvard man of the world if the reader is E. K. Rand:

> Horace is the prince of club men . . . he is a pleasant counsellor, a perfect Freshman adviser, always at home, always at leisure, ever ready to pour out for us a glass of one of the mellower brands and to expound the comfortable doctrine of *nil admirari* . . . The *sprezzatura* of the Renaissance, French wit in any period, Oxford reserve, and, rightly understood, Harvard indifference, these are the links in a golden chain.[1]

Those are of course self-serving stereotypes, but Horatian lyric has been instrumental in answering some of the crucial issues in European intellectual history: How can we design a worldly ethics as separated from a religious one? Is it possible to be a Christian with Epicurean inflections? Equally important, Horace is one of the few classical authors for whom it would make some sense to attempt a psychological biography:[2] for all our diffidence, we

1 Rand (1937b) 31 (quoted in Fowler (1993) 269, a fundamental discussion).

2 On the idea of *morale mondana europea* see La Penna (1969); on psychology and the literary career, Traina (1993).

have to admit that this possibility is related to a very personal tone of voice in his published work. Yet before we return to personality and individual voice, we have to face the specific textual nature of the *Odes*: the enormous importance of form.

Lyric form: models, metre, collection

When Horace asks to be classified among the *lyrici vates* (1.1.35) he is being innovative and surprising on various levels. *Lyricus* had still been used as a Greek word, in Greek letters, by Cicero, while after Horace it is already normal as a genre indication (presumably as a consequence of the *Odes*) in Ovid's Latin. In Hellenistic Greek, *lyrikos* had become the standard learned expression for the more traditional *melikos* or *melopoios*, a poet of songs. The request itself is both ambitious and unrealistic:[3] by the late second century BCE, and presumably much earlier, the corpus of the old 'lyric' poets in Alexandrian editions had become the approved canon of the Big Nine. The youngest (and most admired) of the Nine was Pindar, active more than 400 years before Horace, and it was proverbially impossible to be included in the canon (1.1.35 *inseres*) after it had been closed for ever, and sealed with the number of the Muses: even Corinna, the famous Greek poetess, had become 'tenth' in the shortlist only at a metaphorical level. As is often the case in Horace's work, the relationship to classical Greece expresses ambition but also occludes competition with Republican Roman culture: as 'lyric' predecessors, Catullus, and even Laevius, not to mention the forgotten heroes of Republican scenic *cantica*, had been important and are now voluntarily eclipsed. The main thrust of the argument is elegant *eironeia*: 'Like my Greek models, I will be a classic and reach for the sky – if you shelve me among them, Maecenas', but the undercurrent is self-serving: 'Unlike Catullus and the others, *I* will be the first of the lyric poets in Latin.'

On the other hand it is a fact that the nine poets of the canon are all demonstrably present in Horace: they undergo a further selection into fragmentary models.[4] Horace's approach to the Greek tradition is unashamedly formalistic. He can transplant into Latin, with Catullan precedent, the strophic metres of the poets from Lesbos, Sappho and Alcaeus, and so he proceeds to write 'Aeolian' poems. The effort contributed by Horace is about perfecting a clear and repeatable metrical pattern, and making it work in a different

3 Feeney (1993) 41–2.

4 For details on the Greek models see Hutchinson in this volume (chapter 3) and my piece on Roman receptions of Greek lyric in F. Budelmann (forthcoming), *The Cambridge Companion to Greek Lyric*.

language. Pindar, by contrast, is impossible to imitate because his system is based on triadic stanzas that tend to be unique to each composition, not stabilised and repeatable like the Alcaics and Sapphics. The difference is enhanced *in vitro* at 4.2.11–2 [Pindarus] *numerisque fertur / lege solutis*, with *lege solutis* filling up the regulated measure of the *Sapphic* strophe in the standard 'autonomous' format[5] of the *adonius*, precisely when the reference is to the uncontrollable triadic structures, spillover effects and proliferating variety of cola in Pindar. We are reminded that the most conspicuous adaptation in Horace's handling of the Alcaic and Sapphic strophe is the systematic introduction of a caesura (see below) – in his hands the Greek metre is certainly not lawless; it undergoes a process of regulation and even mechanisation. (On consequences for the issue of musical performance, see below.)

The Alcaic and Sapphic strophes form the most substantial part of the *Odes* (37 Alcaic, 25 Sapphic, out of 103 poems, plus the *Carmen Saeculare* in Sapphics; a total output of 205 Sapphic stanzas and 317 Alcaics; most of the Asclepiad-based systems are also found in Alcaeus, cf. Nisbet and Hubbard (1970) xxxviii–ix), and their importance is so great that most people accept that four-line groupings are valid also for poems in (di)stichic metres. In fact, the number of lines of every Horatian ode is a multiple of 4: the so-called 'Meineke's law', the only exception being the problematic 4.8. This does not happen in the *Epodes*, even when some metres overlap with epodic systems used in the *Odes*, and in the *Epodes* Horace's praxis presupposes intense and formalistic study of Archilochus as much as the *Odes* bear witness to intense and formalistic studies of Alcaeus/Sappho and their learned editions. In other words, the Aeolic stanzas become a normative model even for non-Aeolic lines. Ironically, the idea that Alcaics and Sapphics are four-liners is not a natural fact, but the product of a rather artificial interpretation. There is much to be said, in the Greek tradition, for an interpretation as a three-line stanza with a final line formed by two cola, but the four-line interpretation was made canonical by the regular editorial praxis of the Alexandrians, and this is confirmed by an examination of the manuscript tradition of Horace, one that presupposes a learned edition in a book-roll format, with a graphic grid specifically designed to represent the strophic arrangement on the page, and clearly itself the result of a self-editing activity by Horace himself.[6] Even the names 'Alcaic' and 'Sapphic' for the two kinds of strophe are likely to

5 Cf. what West labels 'the Sapphic effect': D. West (1998) 33. The context in 4.2 is, however, the longest sweeping phrase in Horatian Sapphics.

6 On the grid and the *mise en page* cf. C. Questa in Mariotti (1996–8) I. 329–44; on the idea of 'self-edition', Rossi (1998) 165.

pre-date Horace and to be relevant to his programmatic allegiance to the two poets.[7]

Behind these formal issues there is a hyper-formalistic aspect: it is all about the music – the absent music. All the metrical and formal choices are motivated and conditioned by the choice to reinvent Greek lyric without its osmosis between the verbal and the musical.[8] The music is present (and richly so) at the level of *theme*, not of *performance*, just as, as we shall see, the treatment of time in the poems provides a thematic ersatz, a thematisation, of the missing performance culture. The 'live' performance of the *Carmen Saeculare*, intervening between the publication of Books 1–3 and of Book 4, only reinforces the distinction between text and song: Book 4 is frequently fascinated by various aspects of choral performance, but it refers to the *Carmen* as the true realisation of this ideal in Rome, and the *Carmen* was pointedly excluded by the self-edition of that book.

Insisting on formalism only means that the opus is presented to us initially as the expression of a coherent formal language: I am not implying that Horace had no interest in the Greek poets as 'wholes', as personalities, as texts endowed with biographical depth.[9] In fact, he wants the *Odes* to express a consistent sense of the self, and even a sense of a career: as if the *Odes* were episodes.

Variation is combined with coherence: Alcaics and Sapphics are dominant and become signature forms, but sequences of two to three consecutive poems in the same metre are very unusual (1.16–17, 1.26–7, 1.34–5, 2.13–5, 2.19–20, 4.14–5, all in Alcaics; 3.24–5 in Asclepiads; and as a case apart, the grand sequence of 84 Alcaic stanzas usually called the 'Roman Odes' and printed as poems 1 to 6 of Book 3[10]). Variation is in fact maximised at the beginning of Book 1 and then never again, as if to ensure that readers of the collection grasp the entire spectrum of metrical forms and their Greek pedigree before entering a process of selection and concentration: the so-called 'parade odes', showing nine examples of different metres, the sequence culminating with 1.9, the first Alcaic poem, followed by 1.10, the first repeated metre, in Sapphics like 1.2.[11] After this initial display of variation, the collection accepts a growing amount of uniformity and discipline, until, as we

7 Cf. Lyne (1995) 98–9; and Woodman (2002) 214 n. 9. Against attempts to downplay the importance of Sappho alongside Alcaeus in Horace's 'Aeolic' programme, see Woodman (2002) 53–64.

8 Rossi (1998) 164–71.

9 Cf. Macleod (1983) 245, 249, 257–8; A. Barchiesi (1996) 5–8.

10 On the history of the debate on poem division see Heyworth in Pecere and Reeve (1995).

11 On other links between 1.2 and 1.10 via Alcaeus and his Alexandrian edition, see A. Barchiesi (2000) 172.

mentioned, the grand topics and serious political references of the Roman Odes are matched by the regular use of the most frequent measure, the Alcaic stanza, and the *Carmen*, although external to the collection, confirms the versatility of the Sapphic stanza. The most interesting metrical innovation, in this context, is the routinisation of a pause after the fifth element in Sapphic and Alcaic hendecasyllables, when caesura had been non-existent in the Greek authors: this gives Alcaic and Sapphic lines a regular but also monotone pace, one that would be intolerable in a cantata, and belongs to a text as a place where structures are regularised and the pleasure of order dominates over the need for modulation. Then it is surely significant that the caesura becomes much more mobile in the Sapphics of the *Carmen Saeculare* (once again the watershed) and remains mobile in the late Book 4,[12] now that the poet has been through the watershed of a song-and-dance event.[13]

The study of compositional arrangement also confirms that the lyric work is a textual opus where a culture of performance still resonates. There have been many studies of structure and ordering of poems, and some are sceptical, with reason, about far-fetched nuances and symmetries. As a definitive objection, it has been asserted that the design cannot have affected the text of the individual poems once they had been fixed in writing, since that was a *ne varietur* because of the complexity of lyric metres, but this is to overestimate the technical difficulty of Aeolic rhythms, and, more importantly, Horace knew perfectly well that it was possible, without rewriting one syllable of the authorial verses, to create effects of positioning and complex linkages by editing *other people's work*, and that in a culture of the book the *mentalité* of readers is the decisive factor.

The important point is surely that Horace is aware of the potential of books as devices for additional signification; but it is also important to note that he has resisted the impact of book-form on the autonomy of individual poems.[14] He must have learned from epigram collections, but he also resists their model of pan-textualism: he wants every poem to be marked by a different occasion and addressee.

Those considerations do not excuse indifference toward hidden, implied continuities among poems: the addressees of 2.1–3 are respectively Pollio, the great historian of the civil wars in the Roman world, Sallustius, son of Pollio's main predecessor, and Dellius, adventurer and historian of Antony's

12 Rossi (1998) 171–5, a crucial argument against the *Odes* as librettos.

13 All this presupposes intense direct study of Greek metre through the colometry made systematic and available to non-professional readers by the Alexandrian editions, but it is not clear whether Horace had a specific metrical theory as a guide: identifying this theory is deemed impossible in the influential discussion of Heinze ([1918] 1972) 227ff.

14 This important aspect is well argued by Krevans (1984); see also Santirocco (1986).

Parthian wars, the other half of the *orbis Romanus*. The poems remain, of course, very different from each other, but their author is the editor.

Lyric unity: I and thou

The tendency to disregard addressees, especially in New Criticism, has been a snag for interpretation. One exception, in that generation, is the admirable attention in Nisbet's commentaries to inflections in ethical arguments and existential or political topoi as pointers towards individual addressees and their taste or agenda. In close readings, the erasure of pronouns is a mistake, even when it is a shortcut towards convincing symbolism.[15] Ironically, in the meantime, criticism of modern lyric[16] had come to reappraise apostrophe: Ramler was right, it seems, in his Horatian address to the cannon. Lyric is poetry that says 'O'; apostrophe defines lyric as a genre. We can see the trend at work already in the early transmissional history, since headings of the type '*Ad Maecenatem*' must have been inserted very early on as ways of singling out poems in the books.

Lyric can be tentatively (transhistorically) defined as *a first-person utterance whose performative conditions are reconstructed by a 're-performing' reader*, who typically positions herself somewhere in a continuum whose extremes are a generic voice and some individual idea of the author. Extreme positions are of course possible: one can certainly prefer a *very* author-centred reading. To choose a painfully clear example, if one knows that Celan wrote *Todesfuge* while in a Nazi labour camp, it is likely that a re-performance of the poem will include a memory of its compositional context. Even formal aspects will be affected, for example the way one re-performs the heavy metrical pattern at the beginning – a mnemotechnics of suffering and fatigue; it will thus be easy to stay away from unfair appropriations, such as aestheticism, or the decision to include the poem as a metrical example in German textbooks of metre, or the comment that it should be forbidden to write lyric poetry after Auschwitz.

In less clear-cut cases, readers will opt for a very generic reading, for instance when we are in love and perform a love song from the point of view of our present situation, taking for granted some sort of loose assimilation between the composition of the song and its performance, but without much interest in the specifics of the author's love-life. In order to play the blues, a blues singer does not have to feel blue, but to convey to the audience the idea

15 Dunn (1995) 165–76 (with good points against different 'closures' imposed in turn by New Criticism, textual, and by New Historicism, cultural).
16 Culler (1981); Lowrie (1997) 20–4.

that he knows about that certain feeling and is able to perform it. Most re-performances of lyric will happen somewhere in the intermediate spectrum between those extremes: the idea of an author in a specific, unrepeatable occasion, and 'some' notion of the author as the source of the utterance.

Not for the last time, we see the importance of apostrophe. The figure creates 'poetic events', makes something happen, exposes that event as based on verbal devices,[17] and by its artificial status invokes the supplement of tradition and convention, precisely when it is so 'direct'.

Lyric opposes the missing context (e.g. a longer conversation, a history of previous contacts: Horace sometimes writes about divine epiphanies, but never about first-time encounters with humans) to a sense of textual wholeness (incipit is marked, closure strategic). Ironically, Greek poetry did not come to the Romans in fragments as it reaches us, but Horace does turn his models into fragments: models become initial mottoes, poems never presuppose a complete one-on-one imitation.[18] The only complete poem we have from Greek monodic lyric, Sappho 1, has been reduced to a fragment to be incorporated into *Odes* 4.1.

The whole ideology of Horatian lyric is 'phonocentric', according to the illuminating definition by Michèle Lowrie:[19] it centres on the presence of a voice, and occludes writing and reading as the foundational practice.

The poet 'does not meditate or introspect but exhorts, questions, invites, consoles, prays, and orders . . . As Horace's *Odes* profess to be directed at somebody, they naturally use the techniques of rhetoric.'[20]

The prevalent modes of discourse associated with his lyric are admonition, persuasion, greeting, farewell, praise and consolation: they all have some relationship to address and are different from soliloquy or epic narrative; they are also different from the modes of discourse typical of the iambic poems in the *Epodes*: in the *Epodes* discourse is closer to speech-act, and typical modes include curse, abuse, oath, magic spell and straightforward questioning.

If we combine the idea of re-performance with the preferred types of utterance, what is the result? He does not re-create an act of meditation (although a certain inwardness was important in turning Horace into a leading influence in European modernity); instead, he re-creates an act of communication, often with a temporal marker, framed by an occasion. Now it is hard to be

17 Culler (1997) 76–7.

18 Cavarzere (1996); Feeney (1993) 44–5 on mottoes as imitation of Greek originals *and* of the learned practice of cataloguing their poems by incipits.

19 Lowrie (1997) 58 and 75–6, usefully adapting the Derridean concept of 'logocentrism'.

20 Nisbet and Hubbard (1970) xxiv. See also G. Davis (1991).

more precise about the semiotic status of those lyric utterances. Is it more like a melancholic 'This is what I might / should have said' (Smith (1979): fits the epideictic aspect of ancient lyric rather well)? Or is it the classical insight of lyric situations as overhearing (John Stuart Mill), minus its Romantic overtones?[21] Dialogic (Heinze) is an even more difficult category, available in too many versions, and confusing, because it would merge lyric with the epistolary mode.

Thoughts about the reprocessing of Greek lyric in its reception history can help.[22] After some time, through re-performance and canonisation, the reception of lyric becomes almost an act of quotation: 'those were the words of old, immortal Sappho', against the backdrop of the new performance occasion. Sappho's success among male authors (including Catullus and Horace – contrast the charming pieces by Posidippos on Sappho in women's private lives, *Epigr.* 8.24, 9.2 B.–G.) shows that the difference can be a source of aesthetic pleasure. Other categories of song (often, so-called choral songs) were marked as occasional by paratexts, accessible to Horace as such: 'for the Aeginetans, at Delphi'. In short, Horace knew that lyric works in a series of re-performances at growing degrees of separation from a point of origin – and that being at the point of origin would not terribly matter.

Perhaps, with such a self-conscious strategist, we can make progress by focusing on things he does not do. In general, he moves away from effects of writtenness – they are Alexandrian and neoteric.[23] He absorbs much of epigram culture but stays at an arm's length from speaking objects (contrast Catullus) and from ecphrasis (contrast most other Augustan poets),[24] and from (a related issue in terms of representation) the new Rome of Augustus and its monuments.[25] He avoids self-consciousness of the text as a detachable written object, and pits the coherence of utterance and song against the alternative of other authors as 'writers' (1.6.1 *scriberis*). Only later is writing as an authorial activity reinscribed in the Pindaric praise poetics of Book 4, as it never was in the Alcaic-Sapphic poetics of Books 1–3 (cf. 4.8.21, 9.31). He never confuses melic poetry with epistolarity.[26] He dislikes static forms of discourse, static form being an obvious link with the epigram, a rejected model from which he learns so much: he experiments with very subtle forms of dynamic (not static) ring-composition, gliding from

21 Oliensis (1998) 5–6.

22 For Horace and Greek lyric see Hutchinson, chapter 3 above.

23 At the level of book composition, cf. Krevans (1984), on resistances against the 'written' texture of the tradition culminating in the Bucolics and in Horace's own Book 1 of *Satires*.

24 Hardie (1993). 25 Dyson-Prior (1995); M. Jaeger (1995).

26 Note Ferri in this volume, chapter 9, on 'epistolary' moments in Pindaric poetry.

argument to image, then to argument again.[27] He avoids naming himself: the only example, 4.6.44, points outwards, towards the *Carmen Saeculare*, which is anonymous but is in turn ascribed to Horace by a public inscription.

As an author, he eschews travelling (a significant link with the self-representation of Callimachus): other people do travel and migrate, but Horace is bound to fixed spaces, especially some sort of suburban/heartlandish countryside. Most places mentioned with affection, with the intention of immortalising them, are within a day trip from central Rome (Tibur, the Anio, Bandusia, the Sabine farmland, the Soracte), and some of the unnamed locales look like suburban villas rather than urban mansions: so lyric is not urban, the way satire is. Horatian lyric celebrates and monumentalises places that people in his generation would link to Republican *otium* and philosophical dialogues in prose. In fact, if we want to look at his poetic originality, we have to study a certain striking coherence in the representation of time and of space.

Coherence in time and space

In terms of time-perception, Horace differs from all Greek poets known to us: he works on the interplay, or clash, between 'the impersonal grid of the state's time'[28] and the subjective perception of individual experience (4.13.14–16 *tempora quae semel / notis condita fastis / inclusit volucris dies*). So he intensifies what we call the subjective element of time by bringing in the culturally specific, Roman resource of public time-reckoning. Greek lyric had been achieving similar effects by the common strategy of contrasting linear human time-perception and recursive, cyclic time: in practice, by linking the themes of ageing and of seasonal return (itself another conceptual pair that Horace loves to rewrite in some of his best poems, such as 1.4 and 4.7).

He is also unique in ancient lyric for his love of setting the time in calendrical terms – not just the rhythm of seasons that are a perennial resource from Simonides to Kavafy. The poem I have just mentioned, 1.4, a combination of a spring song with *Totentanz*, is actually for Sestius the consul of 23 BCE (23 is our language, but for a Roman the year was identified as the Year of Sestius Consul): a very economical and intense way of indicating the publication year of the collection (the dedication to Sestius being in fact our main evidence for that date) exactly when time becomes a problematic, existential content of his poetics.

27 For a refined example of close reading see Tarrant (1995) 32–49 ('*da capo*' structures).

28 Feeney (1993) 58: a splendid discussion at 57–60.

Poem 8 of Book 3 provides a date,[29] 1 March 25 BCE, for the symposion: how frequent is this in a poem? I am not aware of any equivalent in Greek poetry. This poem as a poem and as a symposion in fact celebrates the anniversary of the tree incident that had been described in 2.13.1ff., and *consule Tullo* at 3.8 11–12 allows a dating of 33 BCE – not only an accident but a locus in the text of Horace is now being situated in time! We also have celebrative, public versions of anniversaries: in 4.14.34–40 the Alpine victory on 1 Sextilis 15 BCE 'commemorates' an Alexandrian victory on 1 Sextilis 30 BCE: the *domus Augusta* controls time,[30] the grid of time links public and private.[31] We also receive updates on the age of the poet at the moment of writing: over forty in 25 BCE = 2.4.23–4; about fifty = 4.1.6, both times with the very Roman measure in *lustra*.[32] The point is not just an obsession with time, but a search for marked, single occasions and for marked, ritualised times of life: it also matters that a number of occasions are therefore special but also repeatable (anniversaries, festivals), and therefore eminently lyrical times if we think about (re-)performance.

Those superficial instances are more than skin-deep if we realise that this is the poet of *carpe diem*, the most misquoted Latin tag ever, scandalously mistranslated 'Seize the day' not only on spring-break shirts but also in professional books by classicists. It is *carpere* (*Carmen Saeculare* 1.11.8), not *rapere* (*Epodes* 13.3) or *capere* (*Carmen Saeculare* 3.8.27) or *sumere* (*Epistle* 1.11.23): it conveys not rushed pleasures but the attempt to slow down the present, as if by plucking and grazing.[33] If we consider how time is interiorised in the *Odes*, we may conclude that for the poet time is the part of him that is outside his full control.

Defensive control over anxieties is also crucial to the representation of space: the equivalent of *carpe diem* is the defensive *angulus*,[34] a protected economy based on patronage, separated from the centre and far from the borders: far enough to be fenced from the satiric mess and rat-race of the capital, and absolutely remote from exotic wars. The new state is a warlike empire, but warlike at the borders; often barbarians and exotic images are controlled by the poem structure, imprisoned in the outer frame of the song,[35] while the Romans are made doubly safe now that war is not civic

29 Nisbet and Rudd (2004) 124–5; Nisbet and Hubbard (1978) 201.

30 T. S. Johnson (2004) 187.

31 The coexistence of public and private has been a crucial aspect for controversies on sincerity: cf. Fraenkel (1957); La Penna (1963); Lyne (1995).

32 Nisbet and Hubbard (1978) 76 on parallels: in Greek epigrams by Philodemus and Asclepiades, most unusual in lyric tradition.

33 Traina (1986) 227–52.

34 Cf. 2.6.13 sg. and the analysis of Traina (1985) 16–19.

35 On the imperialist poetics of 'margins', Fowler (1995) 257; Oliensis (1998) 111–13.

but professional. Hence the irony of the tree incident, a static in-house danger, when death strikes at home through one's private property, and targets Horace who, as a poet, has a professional habit of seeking shelter under trees, *sub tegmine*. The poet does not travel, or hawk around his skills; it is the friends who offer patterns of departure and return, particularly useful in a genre that needs to demarcate significant occasions within the temporal continuum of private life.

The addressees

If one has to choose, Heinze's *The Horatian Ode* (1923) is perhaps the single most important short text on Horatian lyric.[36] It must have been one of the first papers on Latin poetry to be a consequence of the rise of literary criticism, accepting the idea that a literary theory of modernity is inescapable and needs to be integrated with philology. Heinze also accepts the important idea that the genesis of 'new' Latin studies must be influenced from 'new' Greek studies and take for granted the influence of Greece over Rome. Finally, his paper is still important because he has an appetite for generalisation that is absent from the more empirical and fragmented Nisbet and Hubbard and Fraenkel. His argument proceeds in five easy steps:

1. In the *Odes*, there is always the same lyric voice, which is 'he himself' in terms of voice. At least, there is compatibility with his persona: he, Q. Horatius Flaccus, might have said, or can be imagined as saying, such words as . . . Very few episodic exceptions (none of them, as it happens, in the Alcaic or Sapphic metre): 1.15, the narrative on Paris, with no reference to the modern, Roman world; 1.28, the speaker is the spirit of a dead sailor addressing Archytas of Tarentum; 3.9 is amoebaean, thus containing utterances by Lydia as well as 'Horace'.
2. There are almost always addressees.
3. The addressees are not absent in the sense that epistolary addressees are, and the ode frequently strives to influence and modify the addressee, without the ceremonies of written communication and contact.
4. Therefore there is a limited space and interest for what 'we' tend to imagine as lyric: the expression of inwardness, as a progress towards the modern idea of lyric.
5. The poem is not imagined as text and is consistently offered as 'live' and 'musical'.

36 Reprinted in the (unpleasantly titled) collection *Vom Geist des Römertums*, Heinze (1972); never translated into English or French; Italian edn with preface, Santini (2001).

The upshot of the five principles is: Horace is singing to his addressees. Equally important is the next step: 'It is all a fiction.' It is a necessary step, especially for those who agree that Horace is not a performance poet and does not compose for musical recitals. This conclusion by subtraction reveals what Heinze's true agenda had been all the time: understanding Roman lyric through opposition to Greek lyric (artificial following after natural, and obsessed with it) and through incomplete analogy with modern lyric (personal and inward expression, the quintessence of modernity, had been limited by rhetoric and praise).

The weak aspect of Heinze's thesis is this absolute opposition between Greek and Roman, Roman and European (esp. point 4). The problem is not so much the existence of individual exceptions: some of the objections made on this count against Heinze are not serious, since they presuppose verisimilitude as the standard, or focus on poems that are clearly, like 1.1, the odd ones out. There are also advantages. This kind of abstract formalism helps us to realise a certain coherence in the way Horace balances the use of the second person with forms of deixis. Explicit deixis of a dramatic kind is very low, while the second person is ubiquitous. Even in sympotic poems, there are very few examples of demonstrative deixis (otherwise only 'bland' deictic pointers such as '*nunc*', '*huc*'): the only examples I know are both, as it happens, about trees:[37] 2.11.13–14 *cur non hac sub alta vel platano vel hac / pinu iacentes . . . potamus*; 2.4.22 *neque harum, quas colis, arborum*. It did not have to be that way. There are three poems in Catullus that would probably qualify as lyric in the modern sense, 65, 68 and 101: the first two are very rich in address, but they are clearly epistolary, while 101 is very rich in deixis but the only interlocutor is dead and buried.

The thesis also works well in linking the form of discourse with thematisations of occasion through time-frames (anniversaries, festivals, sacrifice, arrival and departure). Where the approach ceases to work is in the neat oppositions to modern lyric, at the price of devaluing apostrophe in the modern genre, and to Greek lyric, constructed as a poetry of presence, by ignoring re-performance, the metapoetic atmosphere of *symposia*, and the effect of Hellenistic textualisation on Horace.[38]

A socially grounded approach is not really an answer to Heinze;[39] it is a radically alternative route: in Heinze's ultraformalistic terms it makes no

37 On the possible significance, A. Barchiesi (2005) 155–7.

38 Still very much an open debate, cf. the different projections of the dualism in W. R. Johnson (1982); Miller (1994).

39 In the fundamental revision by Citroni (1995a) 271–376; Edmunds (2001) 83–93 triangulates between Heinzian formalism, Citronian sociology and deconstruction.

difference whether the addressee is a tree, a ship, a slave, a prostitute, a millionnaire, a consul or Agrippa. Where those approaches agree, in a constructive way, is in stressing that addressees always matter: compare for example the absence of addressees in two strikingly exceptional poems, 2.15 and 3.24, where moralising is tough and post-Sallustian, and the involvement of individuals is necessarily absent: it is instructive to try to imagine those poems as a difficult no-man's land between the Roman odes and the regular 'second-person' poems, especially the sympotic ones.

The sociological approach has its own rewards: a statistics of characters in the *Odes* is a highly useful control of literary interpretation. Greek names are erotic, often women; they also sound real, if we compare the epigraphical record.[40] Greek male names tend to occur in eroticised atmospheres, especially when Horace is a spectator of other people's love affairs. Private friends with verifiable citizen names are eroticised only indirectly, via a Greek proxy. Private friends are never really a group, and here we must contrast neoteric coteries, even the *Epodes*, and the whole sympotic tradition. To talk about a circle of friends is not really a helpful metaphor, not realistic,[41] yet to a certain extent the *form* of the *Odes* does construct the centrality of one person – Horace: the power belongs to the author who plays fast and loose with biographies and interactions, in spite of modesty. Even the 'club' idea, then, has its own justification. The restrictive field in which *amici* are invited to play, songs of wine and/or love, colours their presence, restricts information. The names are frequently significant and motivated in a positional kind of way, even when they are referential: the addressee of 2.16, the ode on tranquillity, Grosphus, has a name which is the Greek for 'a javelin', and the name follows after a mention of the restless Medi with their quivers (6–7 *Medi pharetra decori / Grosphe* . . .). At the social level, we can verify a certain coherence in the selection of addressees. In the *Odes*, Horace does not routinely sing for the aristocracy of *nobiles*.[42] There is a polarisation between a careful selection of top dedicatees, strategically placed at the beginning of Book 1 and at the end of Book 3, and dominant in Book 4, versus a larger group of 'friends', mostly *homines novi*, or loosely definable as elite but not senatorial or very prominent in politics. There are careful differences of genre: with the *Epistles*, addressed to a group of younger elite Romans, excluding protagonists of politics and the cultural scene;[43] with the panoramic, multi-tier society of satire; with the world of the *Epodes*,

40 Lyne (1980) 198 sg. 41 White (1993) 82–3.

42 Nisbet in Woodman and Feeney (2002) 81, quoting Syme (1986) 382–95.

43 See Ferri in this volume, chapter 9.

consisting basically of Maecenas plus anonymous targets and figureheads, and weak specifics on undistinguished 'friends'.

On philosophy and love

The other significant context for the interpretation of the *Odes* is the diffusion of Greek philosophy. In general, Horace (just like Virgil) depends on Greek prose, not only poetry. Perhaps the most direct way to approach this context is a reading of *Satire* 1.4. In that foundational poem, his father (the satiric poet now remembers) understood the importance of philosophical education and had him schooled; but there is more: his father is actually 'reformed', obviously in retrospect, through Greek philosophy (Plato's *Laws*, in particular).[44] The son is now translating his father's image into the kind of cultural capital that had been made available by him.

The absorption of ethical debate into life and into lyric has one important side-effect: Horace is perhaps the first Roman *litteratus* who does not have a relationship of intensified pathos, of *Pathetisierung*, *vis-à-vis* his chosen Greek models. This tendency had been characteristic of Roman developments throughout Republican history, and holds true, with various degrees and inflections, in tragedy, comedy, epic and personal poetry. Horace's inversion of the trend is a pointed one and has to do with his ambitious revision of the society of letters and of politics in Rome: his favourite attitude is 'more ethics, less pathos'. He is programmatically less passionate than Sappho, less violent than Archilochus or Alcaeus, less grand than Pindar, less vicious than Anacreon. His poetry privileges ethos over pathos, in spite of occasional sallies into Dionysiac territory.

Polemical too is the approach to love, and here elegy is the foil. In contrast with elegy, we find little pragmatics of seduction, little *Werbung*; the polemical substitute is an emphasis on the confessional mode, on the precariousness and mobility of desire, and on other people's love affairs. Once again the intersection with Time is important. The anti-elegiac mode is based on rotation and change, a different vision of love in time, open to relativism, ready to compare and contrast previous and present opportunities for love.[45] As if to enhance the opposition, the poet, after focusing on desirable women in *Odes* 1–3, decides to alternate women *and boys* in Book 4, now that the unpaederastic Propertius, and perhaps the young Ovid, are probably the most visible love poets in Rome. Lyric love can be observed from its margins: it

44 Citroni Marchetti (2004); on the importance for Boccaccio, Marchesi (2004) 58–66. On ethics and lyric, Macleod (1983) 225–91.

45 Labate (1994), developing Lyne (1980) 204, 215.

begins and ends (1.19.4 *finiti amores*) and starts again (3.9.17 *quid, si prisca redit Venus / diductosque iugo cogit aeneo*) or moves to another object: *vacui sive quid urimur* (1.6.19) – in elegiac terms like being simultaneously inside and outside the genre, impossible although tempting for the elegist (compare Ovid, *Amores* 1.1.26 *uror, et in vacuo pectore regnat Amor*).

The symposion

Greek lyric was in large part composed for the symposion, and in even larger part consumed and re-performed in sympotic situations. Horace depends on this model of social interaction, and on its real-life Italic adaptations, for a majority of his poems, and almost all of them are compatible with a sympotic performance of some kind. Yet, as we saw, there are differences: unlike Greek lyric, his texts are not dependent on musical performance, and the circulated text does not mirror the actual circumstances of performance. The difference should not be exaggerated, as it has been in Heinze and also later: Greek sympotic poetry easily becomes meta-sympotic, and references to the 'original' occasion become very effective markers of 'literariness' once the poem is being re-performed. But then of course epigram is in a sense closer – no music, sympotic and emphatically textual – yet Horace does not want to be nailed to that tradition either. In particular, Horace often mentions or implies 'symposia for two' in some of his most characteristic and programmatic poems (especially in Book 2): if we want to imagine some Roman cena and/or symposion as a frame, then the picture offered by the poem is selective and streamlined. As we saw, the use of time, space and occasion thematises precisely the loss of a communal musical performance.

An approach to the Horatian symposion as a symbolic fiction is on the other hand a mistake, if we are implying that real symposia were 'real life' because they had nothing to do with symbolic exchange. The Roman symposion was in fact the place for exchange among unequal individuals:[46] the traffic included material gifts, rewards in terms of power, visibility, intellectual success, protection, continuation of 'friendship'; the interactive behaviour could move through a spectrum of flattery and praise, vituperation and mockery, entertaining performance and poised self-control: a social game. Horace's game is about outstripping, paring away the social structure of the Roman cena-cum-symposion: hence the importance of programmatic poems like 1.38 and 4.1, and of the restricted use of deixis.

One final difference is significant if we think about Horace's intensive and distinctive cultivation of a professional career. Symposion culture had been

46 Roller (2001) 146–54.

about an in-group where the audience is filled by potential performers. In Horace, there is very little openness to this potential confusion of the amateur and the professional. Of course, even in the *Odes*, fellow poets do exist, but they are never 'insiders' of the genre: we glimpse epic and elegiac authors of the Roman world, such as Virgil, Tibullus, Valgius, and surely there are other implicit presences, but there is no sense that other voices of poets can be active *within* the symposion context. (Iullus Antonius in 4.2 is a confirmation that no 'school of lyric' is forthcoming.[47]) If Greek poets perform live, it must be Hades (2.13.21ff.). Horace is alone[48] and the surprising success of the *Carmen Saeculare* is a confirmation by exception. The only point where the poet names himself in the *Odes* is in fact a reported speech[49] by one of the performers of the *Carmen*: *'vatis Horati'* (4.6.44). The final adonaean is a replacement for the final adonaean of the *Carmen*, where the social function of the performance – praise – had been stated by the chorus, without any mention of the author, who can be named only in the public inscription: *dicere laudes* (*Carmen Saeculare* 76).

FURTHER READING

Commentaries on individual books of the *Odes*: Nisbet and Hubbard (1970) and (1978) and Nisbet and Rudd (2004) are indispensable on the first three books; useful also are D. West (1995); (1998); (2002), again on books 1–3; and G. Williams (1969) on Book 3; Quinn (1980) on the complete *Odes*. A commentary on Book 4 on the scale of Nisbet, Hubbard and Rudd is a desideratum: Putnam (1986) is important. In languages other than English, Kiessling and Heinze (1964) is still influential; Italian commentary by Romano (1991: includes the neglected *Carmen Saeculare*); Syndikus (1972–3) on the complete *Odes* is also very rich and balanced.

The crucial books for the history of interpretation are Heinze (1972) (includes seminal early twentieth-century discussions of the lyric genre and of metre); Pasquali (1964) (reprint of the 1920 edn, with rich updates); Fraenkel (1957). Recent volumes of essays with emphasis on evolving critical approaches are Klingner (1965); Pöschl ([1970] 1991); Cairns (1972); Macleod (1983); G. Davis (1991); Lowrie (1995); and Oliensis (1998). Important and accessible collections of essays: Ludwig (1993); Rudd (1993b); S. J. Harrison (1995d); *Arethusa* 28, special number on Horace (1995); Woodman and Feeney (2002); Paschalis (2002). Historical contexts: La Penna (1963) and (1969); Griffin (1985); Armstrong (1989); White (1993); Lyne (1995); Bowditch (2001).

Selected topics: allusion and 'mottoes': Cavarzere (1996); reception: Edmunds (1992); Martindale and Hopkins (1993); book structure: Santirocco (1986); poem division: S. Heyworth in Pecere and Reeve (1995) 117–48; symposion culture:

47 And he may even be an epic poet: S. J. Harrison (1995a) 118–22.

48 On programmatic 'uniqueness' of the *Carmen Saeculare*, Barchiesi (2002).

49 Mention of the author's name in reported speech is in fact a Sapphic preference, cf. fr. 1.19–20; 65.5; 94.5; 133.2 LP.

O. Murray (1990): Murray in Rudd (1993b) 89–105; Roller (2001) 135–53; Dunbabin (2003); Mindt (2006); metre: Rossi (1998); patronage: Saller (1982); White (1993); addressees and social context: White (1993) (summarising what is known of the social status of identifiable 'friends'); Citroni (1995b); style: Wilkinson (1945); Traina (1985); philosophy and ideas: Traina (1973) and (1986); *Carmen Saeculare*: Feeney (1998); Putnam (2000); Schnegg-Köhler (2002); praise: T. S. Johnson (2004); love: Lyne (1980); Labate (1994); Horace and Catullus: Putnam (2006).

On comparing different theories and ideologies of lyric, B. H. Smith (1978); W. R. Johnson (1982); Culler (1997), with further selective bibliography; on the relationship with Greek lyric, see Hutchinson in this volume (chapter 3), and the forthcoming *Cambridge Companion to Greek Lyric* (ed. F. Budelmann). The entire territory is covered by the impressive *Enciclopedia Oraziana* (Mariotti 1996–8): deplorably, the work is very difficult to find even in specialised libraries.

PART 3

Poetic themes

12

JOHN MOLES

Philosophy and ethics

In his later poetry, Horace himself spins a narrative about these controversial topics. Poetry can be 'useful', 'delightful', or both (*Ars Poetica* 333–4). It has 'useful' ethical functions (*Epistles* 2.1.126–31). Writing 'well' (technically and morally) requires 'wisdom' sourced from Socratic and Platonic philosophy (*Ars Poetica* 309–22): Socratic writings provide the poet's basic material; life is like a drama, but different social roles have appropriately different 'duties', 'parts' and 'characters'. Here the poetic representation combines the 'is' and the 'ought', and traditional Peripatetic literary theory is overwritten by the moral relativism of the Stoic philosopher Panaetius (who greatly influenced late Republican Roman philosophy).[1] 'Philosophy', both in its broadest sense and in the narrow sense of specific philosophies, informs Horace's own poetry.

Epistles 2.2.57–60 itemises Horace's range:

> What do you want me to do?
> Moreover, not all men admire and love the same things.
> *You* rejoice in lyric, this one delights in iambics,
> That one in Bionian 'conversations' and their black salt.

The *Satires*

Horace has written 'lyric', 'iambics' and 'conversations' (= 'satires'). Why the emphasis on Bion, the largely Cynic ('doggish') philosopher?[2]

The *Satires* parade numerous satiric predecessors, models and exemplars without naming Bion,[3] but Horace here advertises his reading of Bion: 'black

Translations are mine. Presentation and documentation are minimalist, Moles (2002) reworked. Nothing denies multiplicity of poetic meaning. Readers are assumed to want to read Horace. I thank Emily Gowers, Stephen Harrison and Tony Woodman.

1 Cicero, *De Off.* 1.107ff., 124ff.; McGann (1969) 10ff.

2 Kindstrand (1976) (useful but uncritical); *OCD* 3rd edn (1996) 243 (sharper).

3 E.g. 1.4, 1.6, 1.10, 2.1, 2.2, 2.3.11–12, 2.6.

salt' refers both to the salt fish sold by Bion's father and to Bion's 'abrasive' wit.[4] 'Conversations' glosses 'diatribes', or 'informal philosophical talks', a form associated with Bion.[5] The Roman satirist Lucilius 'rubbed the city down with much salt' (*Satires* 1.10.4) and was 'of wiped [keen] nose' (1.4.8), just as Bion's father 'wiped his nose with his elbow':[6] Lucilius is Horace's 'satirical father'.

Crucial is *Satires* 1.6 (beginning the second half of Book 1):

Bion F1, 2, 16 Kindstrand	Horace
The philosopher Bion addresses King Antigonus Gonatas (whose names imply 'high birth').	The poet-philosopher Horace addresses Maecenas, himself of the noblest birth.
Antigonus asks Bion where he comes from and who his parents are.	At their first meeting, the question of Horace's background arises.
Bion, favourite of Antigonus, has been criticised by jealous rivals for low birth.	Horace, favourite of Maecenas, has been criticised by jealous rivals for low birth.
Bion gives much information about his father.	Horace gives much information about his father.
Bion admits that his father was a freedman and that he himself had been enslaved.	Horace repeatedly describes himself as son of a freedman.
Bion's father wiped his nose with his elbow.	Maecenas does not turn up his nose at unknowns (Maecenas is another 'literary father').
Bion's father was branded on his face.	The highborn Laevinus was 'branded' by the Roman people.
Bion's mother was of dishonourable status: a prostitute.	Octavian's public supremacy prompts the question whether he was dishonoured by an unknown mother (Octavian is another 'father').
Bion's father was a customs officer.	Horace's father was a tax-collector.
Bion's master bought him for sex.	Horace's father kept Horace pure.
Bion asks to be considered on his own merits; Bion tells Antigonus, in the case of friends, to examine not where they are from but who they are.	Maecenas holds that a man's father does not matter, provided he himself is a free man.
Antigonus chooses friends.	Maecenas chooses friends.

(*cont.*)

4 DL 4.46; F1A Kindstrand; T15–18 Kindstrand.

5 *OCD* 3rd edn 463; T8A–B Kindstrand; p. 168 below.

6 F1 Kindstrand.

(*cont.*)

Bion F1, 2, 16 Kindstrand	Horace
Bion boasts of his parentage.	Horace will never regret such a father.
Bion: 'these are the things concerning *me*'.	Horace: 'now I return to myself'.
Antigonus rules many well, Bion himself.	Maecenas' ancestors commanded great legions, a Roman legion once obeyed Horace, and Horace now does as he pleases.
Bion rejects rhetoric.	Horace celebrates the education his father secured for him.
Bion rejects wealth and extravagance for simplicity and ease.	Horace rejects wealth and extravagance for simplicity and ease.

Horace mobilises a whole series of items to accentuate the Bion analogy.[7] His reworking of Bion's father's 'branding' enlists Bionian diatribe under satire's 'branding' function (1.4.5, 106).

Readers are challenged to detect Bion's presence. The successful are retrospectively congratulated (*Epistles* 2.2.60), the unsuccessful re-challenged. The challenge is alike literary ('spotting the allusions') and moral/philosophical (discerning Horace's distinctive moral/philosophical stance).

Two passages in *Satires* 1.1 ambivalently acknowledge Cynic diatribe. In 13–14 (where Horace curtails examples), 'all the other examples of this *genre*, so many are they, could *wear out the talkative* Fabius', the italicised words gloss the Greek 'genre' of 'diatribe' (literally, a 'wearing away' of time in 'talk').[8] Lines 23–7 gloss Cynic 'pedagogic', 'serio-comic' didacticism:[9] 'Besides, not to run through the subject with a laugh like a writer of jokes – although what forbids telling the truth with a laugh? Just as coaxing teachers sometimes give little cakes to children, to make them want to learn the first elements – nevertheless, putting playfulness aside, let us seek serious matters.' A further Cynic 'marker' comes in 2.1.84–5: 'what if someone has *barked* at a man worthy of abuse, himself untouched by blame?' And the witch Canidia (~ *canis*) articulates another 'doggish' voice within the collection.[10]

7 The historical circumstance of his father's being a freedman (G. Williams (1995)) will have contributed to Horace's inspiration.

8 Gowers (2004) 54.

9 Kindstrand (1976) 209, 47f.

10 *Satires* 1.8.48, 2.1.48, 2.8.95; Muecke (1993) 293; Mankin (1995) 300; Oliensis (1998) 68f.

Thus Horace presents his *Satires* as 'Bionian', 'Cynic' and 'serio-comic' 'diatribe'. Hence much basic Cynicism, of content and style;[11] jibing at pretentious Stoics;[12] and emphasis on 'unofficial' moral authorities such as Horace's father, Ofellus and Cervius.[13] Book 1.4, Horace's defence of his own milder satire, rejecting the 'blackness' of malevolent criticism (85, 91, 100) or himself as a biting dog (93), functions as a redefinition, rather than a negation, of such Cynicism (cf. Lucilius' 'wiped nose' and the 'branding' motif).

What of the strong Epicurean strand, both of doctrine and of allusions to Lucretius, greatest Epicurean poet of the previous generation?[14] Since Cynicism influenced Epicurean ethics and Epicureanism appropriated diatribe, Cynic and Epicurean positions sometimes intermix, as in 1.2 on 'easily available sex'. Elsewhere, they differ, Horace favouring the less extreme Epicurean position. In 2.2.53ff. Ofellus' simple living is the mean between gross, 'wolfish' gluttony and sordid, '*doggish*', parsimony. Book 1.1's gestures to Cynic diatribe are punningly redefined by the Epicurean moral '*sati*ety' which this Horatian '*sati*re' advocates and which its very length instantiates (119–21).[15] Horace's teasing citations, in an Epicurean erotic context (1.2.92–3, 121–2), of Philodemus, Greek poet, literary critic and Epicurean philosopher, whose circle included Horace's friends and fellow poets Plotius, Varius and Virgil (1.5.40; 1.10.81), look programmatic of that Epicurean strand. Horace actually *was* the fellow Epicurean of Plotius etc. and of Maecenas,[16] a fact constantly alluded to, and reflected in, his poetry (however ironically). The extended punning on his own name (*Horatius* ~ *hora*) in 2.6[17] makes Horace the personification of the Epicurean principle *carpe diem*, though Epicureans, too, can be satirised (2.4). And there are other important philosophical influences, including mainline Stoic, Panaetian Stoic, Peripatetic and (in Book 2) Platonic dialogue.[18]

Philosophical programmes, then, can be presented piecemeal and unsequentially, implemented, Romanised, incompletely descriptive, ironised, redefined, subverted, etc.: but they must be recognised.

11 Esp. *Satires* 1.1–4, 1.6; Freudenburg (1993) 8–27, 78–82, 216–29.

12 E.g. *Satires* 1.1.120, 1.2.134, 1.3.96 ff., 2.3.

13 *Satires* 1.4.105ff., 1.6, 2.2, 2.6.

14 E.g. *Satires* 1.1.74–5, 1.2.111–12, 1.3.76–7, 97–114, 1.5.44, 101–3, 1.6.128–31, 2.2.14–20, 25, 2.6.93–7.

15 *Lucretius* 3.938, 959–60; Epicurius *Sent. Vat.* 88; fr. 69 Bailey; note that this criterion targets Lucretius as well as Cynics.

16 Armstrong (2004); Maecenas' Epicureanism: André (1967) 15ff; Maecenas' *Symposium* (*Odes* 3.21) included Virgil and Horace.

17 Reckford (1997); also *Satires* 1.6.119ff.

18 Surveys: Muecke (1993) 6–7; Gowers (2004).

The *Epodes*

Epodes and *Satires*, contemporaneous and generically affiliated (both being 'blame poetry'), have many links, including the 'doggish' Canidia[19] and the Greek poet Archilochus, part of Horace's satirical reading (*Satires* 2.3.12) and the *Epodes*' main inspiration.[20]

Crucially, *Epode* 6 runs:

Why do you worry unoffending strangers,
A cowardly dog when facing wolves?
Why not, if you really can, turn your empty threats here
And attack me, who will bite back?
For, like either the Molossian hound or the tawny Laconian, 5
A force friendly to shepherds,
I'll drive through deep snow with ear upraised,
Whatever beast goes before.
You, when you have filled the wood with fearful voice,
Sniff at the food thrown you. 10
Beware, beware! For I raise my ready horns most savagely against the wicked,
Like the spurned son-in-law of faithless Lycambes or Bupalus' keen enemy.
Or, if anyone attacks me with black tooth,
Shall I weep unavenged like a child?

In this fable, one dog represents the malice of the iambic tradition's negative version (13), which attacks the innocent and defenceless (1) but is cowardly in the face of the strong (2–4, 10), becoming all bark and no bite (9f.). The other (Horace) bites back (4, 13–14), defends the community (6, 11), and, now also bull-like, charges the wicked (11). Its literary and moral ancestors are Archilochus and Hipponax (12), whose notorious aggressiveness is harnessed to Cynic moralising.[21] Thus the *Epodes* integrate Cynic 'doggishness' into the iambic tradition of 'biting', producing a genre which serves the common good, attacks the wicked and manifold forms of moral 'beastliness', and defends the weak, including the poet himself, but which is also serio-comic (Horace's '*upraised* ear' being deflated by his name *Flaccus* ~ 'floppy').[22]

As with the *Satires*, this Cynic programme does not make the collection solidly Cynic. Many of the poems deploy general 'hard–soft', 'public–private', 'business–leisure', 'manliness–unmanliness/womanliness', 'virtue–pleasure' (etc.) contrasts, which are sometimes given philosophical colouring.

19 *Epodes* 3, 5, 17.
20 As *Epistles* 1.19.23–5 retrospectively reveals (cf. *Epistles* 2.2.60 on Bion).
21 Dickie (1981) 195–203; *Epode* 6 resembles *Satires* 1.4 and 2.1 (esp. 47ff.).
22 Generally: Fitzgerald (1988); Oliensis (1998) 68ff.

In the *Epodes*, as elsewhere, 'soft' philosophical colouring denotes Epicureanism, 'hard' Stoicism, Cynicism, or both (Cynicism influenced Stoicism even more than it did Epicureanism, hence Cynic and Stoic ethics sometimes cohere, sometimes diverge).

Epode 1 introduces the contrasts:

'Virtue' (etc.)	'Pleasure' (etc.)
Life 'oppressive' if Maecenas does not survive.	Life if Maecenas survives 'pleasant'.
Public engagement/'war'/'labour'	'Leisure'/'unfitness for war'
	'Leisure' only 'sweet' if Maecenas present
'Men'	'Softness'
Travelling to the extreme north, east and west	Staying put
'Bearing labour'	Not bearing labour
'Strength'	'Insufficient strength'
Lack of fear	'Fear'

None of these is automatically philosophical, but the emphasis on 'labours' and travels to the Caucasus and extreme West evoke Hercules, Stoic hero. Consequently, 'pleasure', 'leisure', 'sweetness', 'softness', etc. are 'attracted' into the Epicurean colouring that they have in philosophical contexts. Exploration of the demands of friendship in crisis is underpinned by a contrast between Stoicism and Epicureanism, resolved by Horace's combining of public and private obligations.

Epode 2 has similar contrasts and lightly Epicureanises the countryside (19, 37–8, 40). *Epode* 3, on Maecenas' garlic, contrasts 'hardness' (4) and Hercules' sufferings (17) with Maecenas' girl. *Epode* 4, on the upstart, contrasts 'hardness' (4, 11) and 'softness' (1).[23] The boy victim of *Epode* 5 tries to 'soften' (14, 83–4) the witches' savagery (4) and 'labours' (31). In 8, Horace's 'strength' is 'unmuscled' (2), his impotence 'urged on' (7) by the woman's 'soft' belly (9); Stoic tracts fail to 'stiffen' Horace (who, symbolically, cannot 'sustain' his Cynic/Stoic 'hardness'), and the only useful 'labour' is *fellatio* (hardly a Herculean task).

Epode 9 reworks the contrasts of 1. The closing lines – 37–8 'it is pleasurable to dissolve care and fear for Caesar's affairs in the sweet Loosener' (Bacchus) – give the celebratory symposium an Epicurean flavouring, hence

23 Read sympathetically, the upstart recalls Horace (cf. *Satires* 1.6) as (ironically) 'suffering Cynic-Stoic hero'.

its opposites a Stoic one. In turn, 19–20 ('though *urged* to the left, the poops of the hostile ships *hide* in harbour') exploit Epicureanism's passive and negative associations. As in 1, Stoicism and 'good' Epicureanism coexist (hence Epicurean celebration of Octavian's Stoic valour), but 'bad' Epicureanism smears Antony and Cleopatra.

In 10, the shipwrecked Maevius emits 'unmanly' wailing (17). In 11, Horace no longer takes 'pleasure' in writing poetry, smitten by 'oppressive' love and fire for 'soft' boys and girls, a frequenter of 'hard' thresholds. *Epode* 12 finds Horace sniffing out odours more shrewdly than 'a keen dog where the pig [= vagina] lies hidden' (philosophical animal imagery – 'dog' = Cynic, 'pig' = Epicurean – is again burlesqued: so much for poem 6), his penis 'dissolved', 'soft' for one act only and 'inert'. *Epode* 13 Epicureanises the symposium (3–4, 9–10, 17–18). In 14, the 'soft inertia' of love for a freedwoman has prevented Horace from completing his promised iambics, just as Anacreon wept for love in 'unelaborated' feet. In 15, the unfaithful Neaera will suffer from Horace's 'manhood', 'if there is anything of the *man* in *Flaccus*' (pun). The politically escapist and extravagantly Epicurean 16 redeploys, in contrast to 1, the themes of 'manliness' (2, 5, 39), 'labours' (16), 'sweetness' (35), 'softness' (37), and 'womanliness' (39). *Epode* 17 finds Horace suffering 'labours' (24, 64) worse than those of Ulysses (16) or the dying Hercules (31–2), through the witchcraft of Canidia, in a final 'authority' struggle between the iambic tradition's 'two voices'.

The ingenious patterns Horace creates from these basic contrasts, philosophical and general, contribute substantially to the collection's poetic texture.

Odes 1–3

Ode 1.1 programmatically weaves philosophical threads: the renewed Bion–Antigonus paradigm;[24] the 'choice of life' motif; structural imitation of *Satires* 1.1; evocations of the diatribe theme of 'discontent' and of 'endurance of poverty'; hinted reconciliation of public life/duty/reward/Stoicism and private life/pleasure/emotion/Epicureanism (Maecenas as Horace's 'sweet glory' [2]); and links between philosophical material and addressee.

Into this higher genre, diatribe sporadically injects low-life energy: heated moralism (serious or ironic), down-to-earth illustrations, mockery of pretension and folly, and paradoxical inversions of worldly values.[25] It suffuses 2.15 (encroachments of luxury-building), 2.18 (vanity of riches in contrast

24 Further *Odes* 2.18.12–14, 3.16.37–8.

25 E.g. *Odes* 1.3.9ff., 1.16.9ff., 1.31.6, 2.2.13ff., 1.28.4ff., 2.14.21ff., 3.16.25–8, 3.29.55–6.

to Horace's poverty) and 3.24 (futility and destructiveness of Roman luxury contrasted with Cynic primitivism).

Stoicism is the dominant philosophical presence in few odes. In 1.22 the sage's 'weaponlessness' is the paradigm for Horace's inviolability as lover/love-poet. Ode 1.29 twits Iccius for eyeing the treasures of Araby over those of Panaetius and the Socratics. Ode 2.2 contrasts Sallustius' 'tempered' use of wealth, self-rule and philosophical kingship with Eastern potentates. In 3.2, military endurance and prowess, political greatness (especially that of Augustus) and political discretion (including Horace's) variously manifest Virtue. Ode 3.3 subsumes Augustus' political consistency under Stoic tenacity of purpose.

Epicureanism is the dominant presence in more than twice as many odes. Epicurean *carpe diem* feeling inspires symposia or holidaying as antidotes to wintertime, time passing (1.9, 3.29), preoccupation with the future (1.9, 1.11, 3.29), mortality (1.9, 2.3), hard times (2.3), cares (2.11, 2.16), anxieties over life's necessities or foreign wars (2.11, 3.8, 3.29), and luxury (1.38, 3.29), and as exhortations to love and pleasure (1.9, 1.11, 2.3). The simple Epicurean life is advocated in 1.31, 1.38, 2.16 and 3.1, where it is strikingly preferred to the lives – whether good or bad in their kind – of kings (who must include Augustus), politicians and landowners (who must include Maecenas). By contrast, 1.34's spoof recantation of Epicureanism introduces reflections on Fortune's power.

Another important group juxtaposes Stoic and Epicurean, in varying relationships of tension. Ode 1.7 praises Plancus' 'virile' Stoic 'labours' in war and politics, while counselling periodic immersion in 'softening' Epicurean symposia. Ode 1.32 superimposes Stoic and Epicurean colourings on Horace's public and private[26] lyric voices (similarly 1.31, 2.13.25–8), warranting generalisations about public~Stoic and private~Epicurean. In 1.37 (a poem framed by legitimate Epicurean celebration), Cleopatra's base Epicurean association with 'un-men', 'sweet' fortune and 'softness' (cf. *Epodes* 1 and 9) is succeeded by Stoic 'nobility', 'unwomanliness', rejection of 'the hidden', daring, serenity, bravery and deliberated suicide. Ode 2.7 urges a returned Republican die-hard to forget a shared past of misguided Stoic 'virility' through Epicurean 'sweetness' of friendship and celebration. Ode 3.1, generally Epicurean, envisages a hierarchical Stoic universe. Ode 3.2, generally Stoic, piquantly mixes the two in the famous 'It is sweet and glorious to die for one's country' (cf. 1.32.13, 15, 1.1.2). Ode 3.16 combines Stoic incorruptibility, Epicurean satisfaction with little, gratitude to Maecenas and teasing. In 3.21, tough Stoic types are not immune to wine and

26 The punning 'Latin'/'latent' evokes Epicurean 'hiddenness'.

the poem guys earnest philosophical Symposia, while simultaneously honouring both Maecenas' *Symposium* and Messalla's 'sweet' poetry. Horace's seduction campaign (3.28) deploys the Epicurean symposium against Lyde's 'Stoic citadel'.

Exceptionally, 2.10 advocates the Peripatetic golden mean as a remedy for political troubles.

Thus about a third of the *Odes* are varyingly philosophical, though their impact spreads further. The tone ranges from solemn (2.10, 3.2, 3.3) to flippant (1.22, 3.28). Proportionately, Stoicism lags far behind Epicureanism, which characteristically has the last word and with which, whether as temporary expedient or choice of life, Horace regularly identifies,[27] though not in a 'professional' way (cf. 1.34, 3.1, 3.2, 3.16). Epicureanism dominates 3.1 (the first 'Roman Ode'), a challenge redoubled by the corresponding, also Epicurean, 3.29. Yet, while Stoicism can be mocked (1.22), so can Epicureanism (1.34), and Stoicism generally receives great respect (1.7, 1.37, 2.2, 3.2, 3.3). 'Both – and' formulations (1.1.2, 1.32.13, 15, 3.1, 3.2.13, 3.16) further complicate the picture. Importantly, Epicureanism could celebrate stable rule as guarantor of Epicurean 'quiet' (something of this in 1.7, 2.7 and 3.1, as in the *Epodes*). Horace implicitly claims a 'Stoic voice' as well as an Epicurean (1.1.35, 1.31, 1.32, 2.13.25ff., 3.2). There is, then, a strong pull towards the Epicureanism Horace had espoused since the 30s, but an avoidance of the exclusive commitment alien to his temperament (or its representations), to his role as Augustan *vates*, and to the collection's literary, political, social and philosophical fecundity.

Other questions.

First, the relationship between content and addressee (including implicit addressees and referents). The two may complement – Stoic odes to Stoics (1.22 to Fuscus, 1.29 to Iccius, 2.2 to Sallustius), Epicurean odes to Epicureans (3.8 and 3.29 to Maecenas) – or contrast (2.7 Epicurean solution to Pompeius' 'Stoic' problems; 2.11 Epicurean exhortation to Stoic Quinctius). Other relationships are unclear (2.3 to Dellius; 2.10 to Licinius; 2.16 to Grosphus). If addresses are formally honorific, do philosophical exhortations function as concealed praise for what addressees are doing anyway, or as genuine admonitions? Admonition of other readers is always possible. Of addressees explicit and implicit, there is much concealed praise (Plancus in 1.7, Sallustius in 2.2, Augustus in 3.2 and 3.3, Messalla in 3.21). But there is also teasing (e.g. Iccius in 1.29, Quinctius in 2.11) and admonition: 2.7 ('forget the past'), or 2.10 (whoever its addressee). Slipperiest are odes addressed to, or implicitly referring to, Maecenas (1.1,

27 Again, *hora* ~ *Horatius*: *Odes* 1.9.20, 2.16.32, 3.8.28, 3.29.48.

2.18, 3.1, 3.16, 3.29). Granted encomium, affection and gratitude, teasing is certain, jibing plausible, criticism – as morally protreptic – apparent. Such frankness was traditionally permitted to symposiastic companions and moralising poets, and demanded by Cynic and Epicurean[28] conceptions of friendship.

Second, integration of philosophy into the collection. As in the *Epodes*, Horace is consistently ingenious. Thus the non-philosophical 1.6 rejects, as a poetic theme, the wanderings over the sea of the duplicitous Ulysses. Ode 1.7 implicitly likens the mature Plancus to the sea-wandering and complex Ulysses, imbues him with Stoic virility and endurance, and recommends periodic Epicurean retreats to the shade. Ode 1.8 has the youthful Sybaris, hitherto enduring of dust and sun, lurking, unmanned in a shady brothel. Odes 1.9 and 11 reactivate 'good Epicureanism' in Horace's own erotic campaigns.

Epistles 1

The book begins (1.1–20):

Told of in my first Camena [Muse], to be told of in my last,
I've been spectated enough and already been given my discharge staff,
Maecenas, are you seeking to enclose me again in the old school game?
My age and mind are not the same. Veianius,
His arms fixed to Hercules' doorpost, lies low, hidden in the country, 5
So that he may not so often have to beg the people at the end of the arena.
There is one who constantly imparts loudly into my purified ear:
'If you're sane, loose the ageing horse in time, so that
He may not fail at the end laughably and strain his flanks.'
So now I put aside both verses and all those other games: 10
What is true and what befits is my care, this my question, this my whole concern:
I am laying down and putting together things that I can bring out presently.
And, in case by chance you question, under what leader, at what hearth I protect myself,
Not told to swear to the words of any master,
Wherever the storm snatches me, I am carried in as a stranger-guest. 15
Now I become active and drown myself in political waves,
Guard of true virtue and its rigid attendant,
Now I furtively slip back into the precepts of Aristippus,
And I try to subdue things to me, not me to things. 19

Horace, it seems, has retired from the 'old game' of 'verses', likened to gladiatorial games (1–10), and his 'new game', suiting his age (4), is

28 Armstrong (2004) 281f., 287f.

philosophy, which totally absorbs (11). As to philosophical master, he oscillates between Stoics (16–17) and Aristippus (18–19). The latter follower of Socrates may seem a surprising choice, because no 'Aristippean' school survived in Horace's day, but, as will emerge, the ambiguities of Aristippus' thought facilitate wide coverage of philosophical issues, and his chequered career, subject of amusing anecdotes, furnishes suggestive parallels with Horace's own.

The whole passage flaunts the poet's philosophical erudition. 'Game' (3) can apply to philosophical 'schools'; 5 glosses Epicurean 'hiddenness'; 7 evokes Socrates' 'divine voice', in its familiar 'deterrent' role. The verb translated as 'im*parts* loudly into' (*personet*) canvasses Panaetius' theory that individuals can play legitimately different 'parts' in life's 'drama'. The absoluteness of 11 suits philosophical conversion. 'What is truth?' is *the* philosophical question. 'What befits' glosses Panaetius' category of 'the appropriate'. Horace's and Maecenas' 'questions' (13) suggest Socratic dialectic. Philosophy is a 'storehouse' for the future (12). The sectarian religious imagery of 13 suggests philosophical exclusiveness. 14 echoes the Academic non-commitment of Cicero, *Tusc.* 4.7 ('but let each man defend what he feels; for judgements are free: we will maintain our principle and be bound to the laws of no single teaching'), and contrasts with Epicureans' oaths to Epicurus' doctrines. Horace's oscillations (15–19) recall Socrates' wanderings in search of knowledge (Plato, *Ap.* 22a). Line 15 echoes Cicero, *Ac.* 2.8 ('carried in to whatever teaching, as if in a storm'). 'Stranger-guest' glosses Aristippus' claim to be a 'stranger-guest' everywhere (Xenophon, *Mem.* 2.2.13). Line 16 conveys Stoicism's commitment to political life, 17 its characteristic imagery of warfare and hardness. Contrastingly, 'drown myself in political waves' suggests the 'sea of troubles' rejected by the Epicurean. 'Guard' and 'attendant' (17) image Virtue as king, glossing Stoic 'kingship'. Line 18 adapts Cicero, *Ac.* 2.139 ('I see how agreeably pleasure caresses our senses: I slip to the point of assenting to Epicurus or Aristippus'). 'Furtively' echoes 'lies low, hidden' (5), suggesting the side of Aristippus aligned with Epicureanism. Line 19 glosses, via the yoking metaphor, Aristippus' characteristic boast, 'I have, but I am not had' (DL 2.75). The combination of that yoking metaphor, of the horse metaphor for Horace's rejected verses (8–9) and of the name 'Aristippus' (= 'best at horses' or 'best horse') recalls the contrasting horses of Plato, *Phaedr.* 246bff. And beneath the general contrast of 16–19 lies Hercules' choice between Virtue and Vice/Pleasure and their corresponding roads, a choice put to Aristippus (Xenophon, *Mem.* 2.1.21–34) and alluded to in Cicero, *Ac.* 2.139 (cf. also 6). Retrospectively, 'enclose' (3) glosses Aristippus' refusal to 'enclose himself' in any political state (Xenophon, *Mem.* 2.1.13).

First question: the status of the *Epistles* – self-evidently *philosophy*, are they *poetry*? Line 10 creates a key ambiguity. 'Verses' can mean '*lyric* poetry', a young man's game (4), 'the *old* school game' (3), 'enclosure' into which Horace avoids by writing philosophical hexameters. But 'verses' can also mean 'all poetry', 'philosophy' suits older men, and 'conversational' hexameters can be represented – archly – as prose.[29] Neither interpretation quite works, since, both in this poem and in later ones, Horace repeatedly brings the *Epistles* into relationship with other genres. The ambiguity/illogicality is fruitful: Horace both does and does not fulfil Maecenas' request; the *Epistles* both are poetry and are not poetry, but philosophy; they both are and are not a radical departure, whether in relation to Horace's earlier poetry in general or in relation to his earlier philosophical poetry; and philosophy itself is something that both can and cannot be dissociated from both texts and life. These ambiguities bear on central questions about social dependency or independence, the value of poetry and of books (including *Epistles* 1), and the practice and practicability of philosophy.

Second, figures in a philosophical landscape. Lines 16–19 construct a complex polarity between orthodox Stoicism/virtue/consistency/political involvement and Aristippus/adaptability/pleasure/political disengagement. Panaetian Stoicism (7), Socrates (7), and 'country' Epicureanism (5) are further possibilities. Subsequent poems unpack this complex polarity and feature these philosophical figures. For example, 1.2 contrasts Virtue/Wisdom/Ulysses/Stoics/Cynics (17–22) and Pleasure/Folly/Companions/Phaeacians/Epicureans (23–31), and ends with a practical Panaetian compromise (70–1). In 1.3 the addressee and his friends may be behaving like Phaeacians/vulgar Epicureans, and the unifying thought is that true wisdom involves concord/friendship with oneself, one's fellows, one's fatherland and the universe (28–9), a Panaetian formulation. *Epistle* 1.4 again recycles the polarity but now favours Epicureanism. In 1.5, Augustus' birthday allows a busy man to implement Epicurus' advice.

Third, addressees and other characters. *Epistles* 1 is a philosophical drama (7), whose poems present a series of dramatic situations in which 'characters' 'play' the different philosophical parts outlined above (as in *Ars Poetica* 309–22), in accordance with known philosophical preferences or psychological appropriateness, and whose purpose is 'right' or 'kingly' 'living' (1.60).

The most important character is Horace himself *qua* letter-writer. Of his stated parts, the orthodox Stoic is illustrated by *Epistle* 1 itself, with its ironic concluding endorsement of the 'sage' – a category that still includes Horace (106–8), and by 1.16 (where Horace the poet honours the magnificence

29 E.g. *Satires* 2.6.17 and Harrison, chapter 2 above.

of the Stoic ideal), and Aristippus by 1.17,[30] while Horace's inconsistency appears repeatedly.[31] He has also unstated parts: that of Socrates and Panaetian relativist (7). The former is illustrated by further passages in *Epistle* 1 and elsewhere,[32] the latter throughout the collection.[33] Horace's appearance in later poems as an Epicurean[34] derives partly from the 'pleasure' side of Aristippus but also from the less explicit, but ultimately more substantial, Veianius analogy. Lines 14–19 and 7, then, introduce 'the dramatic Horace' at the start of the drama, the complexity of whose role allows the practical exploration of a wide range of philosophical possibilities, as on a first encounter with philosophy, whereas 4–6 adumbrate 'the real Horace', ever more drawn to Epicureanism.

Of other characters, Lollius, 'freest of men', receives one epistle (1.2) which is appropriately Cynic-Stoic, and in another (1.18) is warned against 'unmixed freedom' of manner. Both the sombre Albius (1.4) and the Epicurean Torquatus (1.5) get Epicurean letters. The Stoic Fuscus, city-lover, learns of Epicurean country pleasures (1.10). The Stoic Quinctius is shown the high stakes of Stoic conduct in Augustan Rome (1.16).

As with the *Odes*, the question arises whether addressees (as opposed to other readers), while honoured, are also admonished, even criticised. Granted Horatian irony, wit and teasing, criticism is an indispensable element of serious moralising addressed to individuals. Maecenas, Lollius, Florus, Albius, Iccius, Quinctius and Scaeva all receive protreptic criticism: as, indeed, does Horace himself.

Fourth: philosophical conclusions. While high-falutin philosophy is predictably mocked (1.12), only one philosophy is strongly criticised: Cynicism, whether Diogenic (1.17) or modified within society (1.18.6–8), and, as against these, 1.2 is quite strongly Cynic (or Cynic-Stoic). Otherwise, two main strands. First, Socratic non-commitment and Academic, Panaetian and Aristippean relativism legitimatise not just flexibility within philosophies but choice between philosophies. This shrewd insight acknowledges that individual personality influences philosophical, political and social choices. It becomes increasingly clear that Horace's personal choice is Epicureanism. But this is itself the second strand, for the Epicurean note sounds ever more insistently and comes at the end of 1.18, an analysis of the difficulties and dangers of friendship with the great and the last strongly philosophical poem of the collection. When Horace tells Lollius, amid all his preoccupations, to

30 *Epistle* 1.17.35 ~ 20.23 (of Horace's own political career).

31 E.g. *Epistles* 1.76, 2.3–5, 7.1–2, 8.2–12, 10.49–50, 14.12–13, 15.

32 E.g. *Epistle* 1.18.96, 100.

33 E.g. *Epistles* 2.70–1, 7.98, 10.42–3, 14.44, 17.29.

34 E.g. 4.15–16, 5, 7.45, 10, 11.22 ff., 16.15, 17.6–10, 18.104 ff.

keep up study of philosophy, the list of alternatives (96ff.) resumes the main philosophical choices examined in earlier poems, and Horace then (104ff.) confesses his own, Epicurean, choice. But even within the list, there is an Epicurean bias, and the total emphasis recalls Veianius, in an Epicurean ring-structure similar to *Odes* 3.29 ~ 3.1. Even for Lollius, the Epicurean secret life seems the better way.

The final period

From Horace's first poems, and almost throughout his poetic corpus, the Epicurean life offers an alternative to public life. And from *Odes* 3.30 ('I have completed a monument more lasting than bronze') onwards, much of Horace's poetry seems valedictory. (Apparently) disappointed by the (apparent) fact that few readers – Augustus notably excepted– appreciated the *Odes* (*Epistles* 1.13, 1.19), and (apparently) pressurised by Maecenas (*Epistles* 1.1.3), Horace produced *Epistles* 1. The book ends with endorsement of Epicurean retreat, with thoughts about the remainder of life, and with retrospective glances at *Satires*, *Epodes*, *Odes* and *Epistles* themselves.[35]

Whatever their relative chronology, the poems of Horace's last decade read similarly. To an importunate Florus (*Epistles* 2.2), Horace explains why he can no longer write poetry. There are retrospective glances at *Epistles* 1, *Odes*, *Epodes* and 'Bionian conversations'.[36] But the poem is itself such a 'conversation', with internal Bionian diatribe and philosophical reminiscences. Thus 'I was nourished in Rome ['strength'] and learned philosophy in Athens' (41–5) echoes Bion's 'I am Borysthenite [= 'strong'] by birth and learned philosophy in Athens',[37] and '*Bio*nian' suggests 'bio-'. The poem ends with appeals to the Epicurean life, with the Bionian/Lucretian image of departure from the feast of life, and with renewed back-references to *Epistles* 1 and to the *Satires*, right back to *Satires* 1.1.[38] Like *Satires* 1.1, *Epistle* 2.2 is itself a feast (57ff.), but now the feast is nearly over. No more poetry, then, but philosophical poetry advocating a philosophical life for what remains of life and specifically both an Epicurean life and an Epicurean departure from it. A 'life-conversation', indeed.

35 *Epistles* 1.18.104ff., 1.19, 1.20.

36 E.g. *Epistles* 2.2.1–19 (~ *Epistles* 1.20), 47 (~ *Odes* 2.7.15f.), 55–7 (~ *Epistles* 1.1.4, 10), 59–60, 99, 141–2 (~ *Epistles* 1.1.3–4, 10–11), 175–9 (~ *Odes* 2.3.17–24; ~ *Satires* 2.2.132ff.), 199–200 (~ *Epistles* 1.1.15f.), 204 (~ *Epistles* 1.2.71).

37 F1A Kindstrand.

38 *Epistles* 2.2.198; F68 Kindstrand; *Epistles* 2.2.213–16 ~ *Satires* 1.1.118–21 ~ Lucretius 3.938 and *Epistles* 1.1.2–4, 7–8, 10.

At Augustus' request,[39] Horace added *Odes* 4: unphilosophical, except for the spring poem 4.12, which invites 'Virgil', 'client of noble youths', to 'wash away the bitterness of cares' in wine, to 'put aside the study of gain' and, 'mindful of the dark fires, mix, while you may, brief folly with your counsels; to be unwise in the right place is sweet'. Horace's 'sweet' 'unwisdom' is Epicureanism, the 'unwise wisdom' of 1.34.2. 'Virgil's' contrasting 'counsels' are public Stoicism. Naturally, this impossibilist vision of stealing time with the dead Virgil creates bitter-sweet pathos. But the serio-comic alignment of the Epicurean friend with Stoicism (through the *Aeneid*), with 'clientship to noble youths' (Octavian?) and with 'study of gain', ruefully recalls the philosophical, moral and political compromises that Virgil had made in his life – and that Horace himself is still making. This perfectly poised philosophical focalisation could hardly be more disconcerting.

To a reproachful Augustus,[40] Horace explains why he is no longer writing poetry (*Epistles* 2.1), reviews the relationship between poets and rulers, especially that of his own poetry to Augustus *qua* world ruler, and emphasises their intertwined *Nachleben*.

The *Ars Poetica*, part response to a request, part general literary treatise, stresses the philosophical nature of poetry and ends with the end of life, recalling both the end of the *Letter to Florus* and the end of *Satires* 1.1, the first poem of Horace's first published collection.[41]

Notwithstanding counter-factors (the *Carmen Saeculare*, the irony that disavowal of poetry occurs within writing what – on one level – obviously remains poetry, and Horace's apparent admission that, while claiming to be writing nothing, he is still writing),[42] the cumulative impression of Horace's last decade is that he would rather not write: he is old and tired, he would rather just live – or die. 'Enough' of poetry, of material things and of life. That 'enough' is itself an Epicurean stance and one that looks back all the way to the close of the first Satire. In the end, it seems, living the philosophy he had favoured since the beginning of his poetic career was more important than writing, even than writing about the philosophy, and Epicureanism proved to be the main thread, not just of his poetry, or even of his philosophy, but of his life.

Spinning a yarn? Only a construction? With Horace, the boundaries between construction and life, while demanding exploration, are finally elusive.[43] But such questions do not – here – matter finally. Horace's representation of the role of Epicureanism in the pattern of his life is sufficiently

39 Suetonius *Hor.* (Loeb edn 2.486).

40 Suetonius *Hor.* (Loeb edn 2.486–8).

41 *Ars Poetica* 476 'full' ~ *Epistles* 2.2.214 ~ *Satires* 1.1.119–20 ~ Lucretius 3.938.

42 *Epistles* 2.1.111 (also ~ 2.1 itself).

43 See e.g. Harrison, chapter 2 above.

plausible to have protreptic force, a force enhanced, not diminished, by his constant ironies, playfulness, equivocations and inconsistencies. He paints a far more realistic picture than most 'proper' philosophers of the ups and downs of practising philosophy in everyday life. Granted obvious differences of density and intensity, Horace's philosophising, essentially school-based, but broad-minded, benign, frequently humorous, and formally self-revelatory, can justly be compared with the philosophising of the two best philosophical teachers of pagan antiquity: Seneca, whom he influenced, and Plutarch.

FURTHER READING

The close, parallel-text translations of Bennett (1927), Fairclough (1929), P. M. Brown (1993) and Muecke (1993) are the best for non-Latinists. All relevant philosophical matters are fully covered in *Oxford Classical Dictionary*, 3rd edn (Hornblower and Spawforth (1996)). Attractive accounts of Horace as moralist: Rudd (1993b); Russell (1993) (comparing Plutarch). 'Horace-*philosophus*' survey: Mariotti (1996–8) II. 78–98. Scholarly controversy: 'pro'-philosophy: Macleod (1979); S. J. Harrison (1995b); Moles (2002); Armstrong (2004) (valuably linking Horace with Philodemus but, arguably, neglecting epistles' internal logic); 'anti'-philosophy: Mayer (1986); (2004); Rudd (1993b). Of commentaries, on the *Satires*, Lejay (1911), P. M. Brown (1993) and Muecke (1993) are all philosophically responsive, Brown and Muecke especially helpful. On the *Epodes*, Mankin (1995) and L. Watson (2003), otherwise outstanding, minimise philosophy; on *Odes* 1–3, Nisbet and Hubbard (1970), Nisbet and Hubbard (1978) and Nisbet and Rudd (2004) excel, philosophically and otherwise. On *Epistles* 1, Mayer (1994) is unsympathetic to philosophy, but presents much evidence; similarly, Brink (1963, 1971, 1982) on the literary epistles. General studies include Fiske (1920) (controversial, but full of matter); McGann (1969) (seminal on *Epistles* 1); and Ferri (1993) (important on Horace and Lucretius).

13

JASPER GRIFFIN

Gods and religion

For Horace, as for all serious Roman poets, the choice of poetical form in which to compose meant selecting a model from those bequeathed by the great writers of Greece. It was to Greek models that Horace, approaching the composition of lyric verse, naturally and explicitly turned.[1] That had important implications, not only for the manner but also for the content of the work.

Greek lyric poetry, from its origins, was intimately connected with the cult of the gods. Poems were occasional, produced for specific events, often ritual in nature. Later on, when the Alexandrian scholars set out to produce collected editions of the works of the lyric poets, by now regarded as classics, they were faced with the task of finding an intelligible system by which to arrange the mass of poetry produced for different occasions and without thought for subsequent or collected publication. One of the solutions they found was to separate the poems by the type of religious occasion for which they had been produced. Thus with Pindar the hymns, maiden songs, paeans, dithyrambs, etc., were each grouped into separate books. Only the four books of epinicians, alas, his victory songs for athletes, survived the end of antiquity. They were grouped by the festival at which the victory had been won: Olympia (Olympians), Delphi/Pytho (Pythians), etc.[2]

When Horace decided to compose a substantial body of short lyric poems, he faced two immediate needs: to identify a range of subject-matter, and to find an appropriate level and style. He went back, he claims, behind the more recent Greek poets, Callimachus and the Hellenistic writers who had been in vogue in the previous generation, their names ostentatiously dropped by Catullus and his contemporaries. The names of Callimachus and Catullus each occur once in Horace, both times in a disobliging context:

1 That is made clear immediately: in his very first ode Horace refers to his 'Lesbian lyre', *Odes* 1.1.34 *Lesboum barbiton*. On this, see Feeney (1993) and Hutchinson, chapter 3 above.
2 Cf. Pfeiffer (1968) 181ff. A few odds and ends were placed at the back of the *Nemeans*.

Epistles 2.2.100 and *Satires* 1.10.19. Callimachus and Catullus are no longer explicitly in vogue, but their influence is still important. Horace continues to favour the short poem over the long, and to criticise earlier poets like Lucilius for sloppy technique. While many traces of Hellenistic influence did in fact colour his lyric, and the poet remains attached to the small scale and to verbal refinement, Horace does not parade Callimachus as source or influence but, on the contrary, explicitly claims as his models the archaic poets. Already in the *Epodes* he is evoking Archilochus. In the *Odes* he sometimes assumes the persona of Alcaeus, but with full freedom to echo and imitate other archaic and early classical masters: Sappho, Anacreon, Bacchylides, Pindar.[3] His friend Virgil, in a career in some ways parallel, was working his way back from a Hellenistic model in his *Eclogues*, first to Hesiod, and finally to Homer himself.

When Horace applied his mind to these archaic poets, he was inevitably struck by the religious setting, form and content of so much of their work. In the seventh ode of his first book he speaks of poets who devote themselves to different places: to Thebes, made famous by Bacchus; or Delphi, made famous by Apollo; or Athens, city of the virgin goddess Pallas: very many, again, will be speaking of Argos and Mycenae, in honour of Juno. The places and the deities naturally go together, and praise for either naturally suggests the other. That was all the more important, because some of his readers had actually visited the Greek sites and were familiar with their more prosaic modern reality. The divine was to lend them an aura of remoteness, rarity, legend: in short, of poetry.

Horace's lyrics were not, of course, produced for actual cult performance, until his success as a literary man led to his receiving the unique commission to compose a *carmen* for the Secular Games in 17 BCE.[4] With the rest of his output, we are dealing with something different: with literary evocations. In the words of Gordon Williams, 'The reason why Horace's hymns are, in general, so successful is that he made a virtue of their being no longer functional. The hymn became a form adaptable to a wide range of emotional effects that achieve remoteness and universality from the actual blending of Greek and Roman elements.' It is natural to see an analogy in the way that literary echoes can transform and glorify events in the poet's own life, or at least can render them less prosaically verifiable, less accessible, less ordinary. In his cradle, he tells us, he was covered with leaves by protective birds – like Stesichorus; he left the field of Philippi wrapped in a cloud by a god, like a hero in Homer, but shamefully leaving his shield behind – like Archilochus and Alcaeus (*Odes* 3.4.9ff., 2.7). Religious references and

3 See further Hutchinson, chapter 3 above. 4 See further Barchiesi, chapter 11 above.

religious colouring, too, can function for Horace as a special kind of literary allusion, helping to elevate his work, to enrich it with depth of literary background, and to make it impossible for the reader to press for the plain truth of facts and events.

Thus, it might be asked: how did it come about that Q. Horatius Flaccus, a young officer in the armies of the Liberators, now appears on the Caesarian/Augustan side? The innocent and unrevealing answer comes: 'Why, it was a god who managed it; Mercury snatched me away, hidden in a cloud' – an allusion to Homeric poetry and Homeric theology; 'at the time, of course, I was terrified' (*paventem*, 5. 14). 'And I abandoned my shield' – another literary allusion. After so disarming a performance, who is gauche enough to press the question: How, and on what terms, did you make peace with the winning side? Another beautifully poised, charming, and uninformative brush with the theme: *Epistles* 2.2.41–52. Horace tells us only that 'reckless poverty drove me to write poetry', and that friends introduced him to Maecenas (*Epistles* 2.2.49ff., *Satires* 2.6.40ff.). Again it was poetry, we are to believe, and poetry alone, that did the trick.

It is, of course, from a god that Horace derived his inspiration. That clearly was important to him. He is telling us: 'I am not just one of Maecenas' young men, low-born but clever, as I may have depicted myself, with irresistible self-deprecating charm, in *Satires* 1.4, 1.6 and 2.6: plump, irascible, but essentially good-natured. Far from it! I am the successor to great classics, marked off as special by a direct link to the divine.' In the very first ode several Muses join to assist his song (1.1.30–4, cf.1.36, 2.12.13ff.); he may indeed speak as a priest of the Muses (3.1.3). They have protected and patronised him from his childhood (3.4, cf. 4.3).[5] Without the Muse his poetic achievement has no value (1.26.9–10 *nil sine te mei/prosunt honores*).

Other deities are no less vital. Sometimes it is the cruel mother of the Cupids who instructs him (*Odes* 1.19, 4.1), sometimes a visitation and ecstasy from Bacchus (*Odes* 2.19, 3.25):[6] unambiguous assertion of his exceptional nature. A less obvious example shows how skilfully he turns such material to account. 'When I am on my country estate, the god Faunus gives me special protection'; *di me tuentur, dis pietas mea / et musa cordi est*, 'the gods protect me, they love my virtuous life and poetic work'; so surely, my charming and musical Tyndaris, you will join me there for a *soirée musicale*, and a glass of wine, and no risk of jealous violence, as there is with your regular boyfriend (*Odes* 1.17)? The apparently religious opening mutates deftly into a scene from real life, or something adroitly fashioned to resemble it.

5 On Horace's construction of his divine patronage see Harrison, chapter 2 above.

6 See further on these two poems Davis, chapter 15 below.

A minor god, of an amusingly rustic sort; and a bit of culture, too, as a pretty girl sings of an erotic theme from Greek poetry, in a cool spot, out of the heat. The commonplace round of picnic and pick-up[7] is gilded with literature and the divine.

It would be inept to ascribe to the poet some unique or quasi-monotheistic relationship with one particular deity. At an exalted moment he insists that it is Phoebus, first and chief addressee of the *Carmen Saeculare*, who has granted him inspiration, technique and fame as a poet: *spiritum Phoebus mihi, Phoebus artem / carminis nomenque dedit poetae* (*Odes* 4.6.29–30). But three poems earlier it was the Muse, she who could, if she chose, make mute fishes musical, who gave him any poetic power and recognition that he may have enjoyed (4.3.21–4):

totum muneris hoc tui est,
quod monstror digito praetereuntium
Romanae fidicen lyrae:
quod spiro et placeo, si placeo, tuum est.

This is wholly your gift: that passers-by point me out as the lyric poet of Roman verse. That I live and find favour, if I do find it: that is your gift.

But in the last poem of Book 4 he will return to Apollo. He is the god who warned Horace off epic! But that is a literary allusion, too: this time, to a celebrated tag of Callimachus: 'When I tried the grand scale in poetry, Apollo told me to stick to the small and chiselled' (Callimachus, fr. 1 Pfeiffer). Again, the interpretation of a divine passage is distanced and blurred, as the reader picks up a mildly learned reference. Since Virgil's sixth *Eclogue*, the motif had (of course) been a very familiar one. Horace is not dazzling us with erudition, but he is making it hard for us to read his tone without ambiguity.

By that stage of his life Horace was confidently asserting that poetry, far from being a mere cultured extra, had a positive practical value to the community. It taught excellent moral lessons, warning the rising generation to avoid wrongdoing, and edifying grown men, too.[8] Poetry is fertile in moral exhortations and examples; equally valuable, without a poet neither boys nor girls, however chaste and virtuous, would know how to address the gods in prayer (*Epistles* 2.1.123–3):

Castis cum pueris ignara puella mariti
disceret unde preces, vatem ni Musa dedisset?

7 Cf. Griffin (1985), chapter 5, 'The pleasures of water and nakedness'.

8 For Horace on poetry see further Rutherford, chapter 18 below.

We can go further. It is verse which has the power to appease the gods of life and death: *carmine di superi placantur, carmine Manes* (*Epistles* 2.1.138).

It is actually true, or in this exalted vein of verse it can be asserted as true, that it is to the poets that we are indebted for all the arts of civilised life (*Ars Poetica* 396ff.). That assertion involves some sleight of hand. Italic traditions existed which gave an important place to *vates* and *carmina* in Italian life in the old days; or perhaps still, in secluded places, untouched by Greek art and thought, and still possessing that indigenous home-spun excellence which Octavian/Augustus, and his favoured writers, admired and extolled. I am thinking, of course, primarily of Virgil, Horace and Livy.[9] The *carmina* of pre-literate Italy, the sort of thing which old Cato, for instance, thought it important to intone when performing certain agricultural operations (*De agri cultura* 132, 134, 139–41, n. 160 [in the case of a dislocation]: 'This spell will make it well. Start to croon: Motas vaeta daries dardares astaaries dissunapiter.' Such mumbo-jumbo Italian jingles were *longe longeque remoti* from the Hellenised and exquisite verses of Horace. But all alike are *carmina*, a word which, like *vates*, had a nicely poised double aspect, looking both to Italy and to Greece: that made them favourites for the complex purposes of Horace and Virgil, and here our sophisticated poet glides smoothly on, to the assertion that his type of poetry, too, could serve a religious function. After all, as he will say in a poem composed, probably, at a date not very distant, it was (in Greek terms) a singer, priest and mouthpiece of the gods, who first taught us the benefits of civilised life: Orpheus, *sacer interpresque deorum* (*Ars Poetica* 392). Sophisticated thinkers had worked to bridge the gaps between art, religion and philosophy; such figures as Orpheus came in handy, as being philosophers and lawgivers as well as singers. Italic rituals, Greek poetry and initiatory religion, and Horatian lyric, now all go beautifully together, the reader unaware of any awkward jolt of inconcinnity, as Horace passes smoothly from one gear to another.

It was natural for a lyric poet, in such a tradition and such a position, to think of writing religious verse. Religious forms appealed to Horace from several angles and for several purposes. The Greek lyric poets had bequeathed a treasury of religious poetry, in the ritual forms of hymns, paeans, dithyrambs, partheneia, prosodia and the like; those classic works explored the nature of the gods and their relationship with their worshippers, as well as imparting moral instruction and warnings. They were impeccably classic, unquestionably poetic, rooted in something real but clearly distinct from prosaic ordinary life. They provided the questing poet with models for the

9 *Carmina* and related matters are illuminatingly discussed by Brink (1982) 156–7.

manner, and material for the content, of his own poems.[10] On the one hand, then, there was the inheritance of Greece. On the other, there was the desire, felt with various degrees of urgency at different times by all the Augustan poets, to play a part in the life of their society. The desire was partly, doubtless, internal; but it was also encouraged and sharpened from without by the expectation of Romans, and especially of Maecenas and Augustus, that literature should possess practical value, both moral and political. Only cynics might think of anything so crude as 'propaganda'.[11] Horace, whose artistic conscience, while not as finely exigent as that of Virgil, was none the less keen and perceptive, thus found himself struggling to bridge the potential divide that always threatened high Augustan art: the risk that the Greek and the Italian sides might split embarrassingly asunder, the borrowed form and its applied decoration, however beautiful, proving ultimately incompatible with sturdy Italic content and contemporary Roman relevance.

It seems clear that Horace began with very little sense that specifically religious feelings or arguments were of great importance. The first book of his *Satires* tackles, in a manner which curiously combines the boisterous and the evasive, various moral and social faults: avarice, discontent with one's lot, unsympathetic judgements on the defects of friends, foolish pride in one's ancestry. Gods are remarkable for their absence. Moral standards come, not from religion, but either from a popular version of contemporary philosophical preaching, or from native common sense, while examples and illustrations are drawn from literature. In book 2 he tackles, at considerable length, such themes as pretentious gourmet taste in food, or dishonest legacy-hunting, or doctrinaire Stoicism. Again, the gods are hardly mentioned. That might be thought a pure matter of form, the personal deities being reserved for more 'poetical' settings; but in the *Epodes*, where he is approaching the poetic forms that he will perfect in the *Odes*, the situation is hardly different. 'Night and Diana' (Hecate) are invoked at *Epode* 5.51, but by a witch at her hideous and grotesque work, and the invocation will be in vain. In 15 we hear of an oath sworn by 'the power of the great gods', but it was an erotic oath only, and it has been lightly broken, as in 17 the appeal to the witch Canidia 'by Proserpina and the godhead of Diana' (Hecate again) is contemptuously disregarded.

10 Cf. Syndikus (1972–3) II. 243: the gods in these poems 'sind nicht zufällige und irgendwie beliebige Gestalten der Tradition, sondern Vorstellungen, die die Menschen damals über den Alltag erhoben, die das Leben geistiger und bedeutender zu machen vermochten'.

11 The theme receives masterly handling in chapter 30, 'The organisation of opinion', of Syme (1939).

What, then, is there of religious language in the *Epodes* that is not trivial or slighted? The poems on the battle of Actium, where we might expect to find the personal gods, remembering *Aeneid* 8 and Propertius 4.6, very noticeably do not feature them (1, 9). That is true even of the evocation of a Roman triumph, 9.21ff., envisaged purely as a spectacle. There are a couple of impressive poems on the guilt of Rome and its punishment. In *Epode* 7 Horace speaks of it in terms of 'fate' and fratricide, the distant killing of Remus and the recent civil wars: *sic est: acerba fata Romanos agunt / scelusque fraternae necis*, 'so it is: Rome is being hag-ridden by cruel destiny and the guilt of fratricide'. *Epode* 16, with its powerful depiction of the present peril and imminent ruin of Rome, speaks of guilt – *impia perdemus devoti sanguinis aetas* (16.9) – 'Rome will be ruined by a wicked generation of accursed ancestry' – but finds no place for a deity until the very end, when the poet, urging instant flight from the coming doom of Italy, speaks of an unknown land in the West, reserved by Jupiter long ago for the virtuous (16.63f.): very remote, we may feel, and pretty insubstantial, too. All told, a thin total, in the *Epodes*, of references to serious religion. Instead, we find the grim alternatives of fatalism and necromancy.

What of the poet's later work in non-lyric form: the *Epistles*? Here Horace professes to be in earnest on serious topics (*Epistles* 1.1.11): *quid verum atque decens quaero et rogo et omnis in hoc sum*, 'I am inquiring into the nature of truth and morality, wholly absorbed in the search.' He does indeed discuss such central themes as the control of anger (1.2), moderation in lifestyle (1.5) and the preservation of serenity (1.6).[12] Again, the personal gods appear seldom and have no serious role. When the poet speaks of the contribution of Greece to the cultural life of Rome, what interests him is the Greek influence on culture, not on cult (*Epistles* 2.1.156–7): *Graecia capta ferum victorem cepit et artes / intulit agresti Latio*, 'Greece, conquered, led her uncouth conqueror captive and brought the arts to a Latium uncivilised.' The poetry of Homer, we hear, is a more valuable guide to conduct than philosophy (*Epistles* 1.2.1ff), let alone religion; cf. *Ars Poetica* 120–51, a notably fuller and more sympathetic treatment of both epics than Horace ever gives to the teachings of any philosopher; and when Horace uses Homer as a source for moral teaching, the Homeric gods are one element which goes unmentioned. If we had only Horace's account of the *Iliad* and *Odyssey*, we should hardly guess that the gods played an important role. They are not, it seems, a natural resource to invoke, when the poet is talking seriously about morality, whether in the early *Satires* or in the late *Epistles*.

12 On philosophical topics in the *Epistles* see Moles, chapter 12 above.

We might indeed press the line which immediately precedes that just quoted. 'Now that I am older,' says Horace, 'like an aged horse fit to be released from further service', *nunc itaque et versus et cetera ludicra pono*, 'now I am laying aside poetry and all the other frivolities' (*Epistles* 1.1.10). Among those *ludicra*, one must suppose, were the personal gods: along with the passion (or pretence) of sexual love, and with attacks on alleged enemies, and with those carefully manicured indecencies which had seemed *de rigueur*, when he was the Roman Archilochus, or Hipponax, or Bion of Borysthenes; along, that is, with so much of the 'Horatian' wardrobe, which had served a talented poet in need of material. And out, with the rest, went the divine apparatus, which, like the rest, had played an important role in the *Odes*.

Horace, then, spent much of his poetical career at a level which did not involve the gods of cult. Wilkinson is doubtless not far from the truth in saying, 'For Hellenistic poets Hymn and Dedication had become conventional literary forms'; he perhaps goes a little further when he adds that Horace 'was not religious in our sense of the word'.[13] Who are 'we'? And at moments Horace, self-confessedly not one to be held to rigid consistency, starts a lyric poem from the statement that a startling experience, thunder from a clear sky, has converted him from unbelief to orthodoxy (*Odes* 1.34). That, too, is part of his range. But he also composed a large body of poems – noticeably, they are in the higher genres – which did address them and make them central. We saw that the very first of his *Odes* placed him under the personal patronage of the Muses, of Euterpe and Polyhymnia. But that is not all. Horace there tells us that he loves, is exalted by, 'the chilly grove and the frivolous[14] choruses of Satyrs and Nymphs': they are what 'distinguish him from the masses' and set him among the lyric poets. *Secernunt populo*: the phrase repays reflection – an echo, subdued but revealing, of Callimachus and Catullus (e.g. Catullus 95). At another moment he will casually identify himself with the *populus* (*Ars Poetica* 153: *tu quid ego et mecum populus desideret, audi*, 'Listen to what I want, and what the populace wants, too'. Horace makes no claim to consistency. If we try to make him consistent, the joke is on us. It is the divine apparatus which marks him off as special, as a poet. No reader, surely, imagined that Q. Horatius Flaccus actually spent his time, for choice, in chilly mountain groves, any more than they envisaged him at home with the Satyrs and Nymphs placed there by mythological fantasy. That all went with the poetic persona, ever since Hesiod reported

13 Wilkinson (1944) 27.

14 Nisbet and Hubbard (1970) do not translate or comment on this epithet (*leves*).

encountering the Muses on Mount Helicon – which was at least near where he, unlike Horace, actually lived.

But the presence of the poetic gods was a great part of what distinguished Horace's more ambitious poems. We have glimpsed the essential reasons. His Greek models constantly addressed the gods; and Horace urgently needed something which would give acceptable form to his claim that he, the dependant of Maecenas, the familiar figure in society, the freedman's plump and dapper son,[15] really was someone very special, a great poet. Supernaturally inspired, he was the author of poems that would endure as long as Rome itself: more lasting than brass, more lofty than the Pyramids (*Odes* 3.30). That claim needed Melpomene to crown him with the well-earned bays of Apollo, in the last words of the poem, and of the book, and of the three-book collection (3.30.15–17):

> sume superbiam
> quaesitam meritis et mihi Delphica
> lauro cinge volens, Melpomene, comam.

Muse, assume the pride which your merits justify: with full consent circle my head with the Delphic garland of bay.

Horace makes the boldness of that boast fully, even aggressively, explicit (*Odes* 2.20.5–10):

> non ego pauperum
> sanguis parentum, non ego quem uocas,
> dilecte Maecenas, obibo,
> nec Stygia cohibebor unda.
>
> iam iam residunt cruribus asperae
> pelles, et album mutor in alitem . . .

The son of humble parents, the protégé of Maecenas, he will not be confined to the world of the dead but pass the River Styx, assuming supernatural form as a swan, Apollo's favoured bird; he will soar above the earth, surviving death, his poems known to the whole world. Already, he cries, he feels incipient metamorphosis: 'The rough skin on my legs is shrinking, as I am changed into a white bird . . .'

A sophisticated and self-conscious poet, writing for a sophisticated and self-conscious reader, can give satisfying form to a deeply felt aspiration only

15 Despite the ingenious doubts raised by G. Williams (1995), I think one passage, *Epistles* 1.20.20–3, shows that this really is what Horace means, not a subtly expressed claim to distinguished Italian ancestry. Cf. Griffin (2002) 316 n. 19.

in the imagery of classical religion and classical legend. It may even be felt that the aspiration has been so strong as to lead this most tactful of poets, in this remarkable passage, rather beyond the limits of irony or good taste; but we can perhaps compare, for the strangeness of the boast, Yeats's splendid 'Sailing to Byzantium':

> Once out of nature I shall never take
> My bodily form from any natural thing,
> But such a form as Grecian goldsmiths make
> Of hammered gold and gold enamelling
> To keep a drowsy Emperor awake . . .

Usually, however, Horace mingles self-assertion with real, or mock, modesty more urbanely: in proportions which he makes it very difficult to measure.

Thus Horace makes varied and subtle use of the divine machinery to illuminate and elevate aspects of his personal life, from change of party to erotic affair and poetic inspiration. But he is not simply a poet of private life. On the contrary, he is determined to do justice no less to the side of Alcaeus which dealt with politics and war. As he says, comparing Sappho and Alcaeus as they sing among the dead (*Odes* 2.13.29–32):

> utrumque sacro digna silentio
> mirantur umbrae dicere, sed magis
>   pugnas et exactos tyrannos
>   densum umeris bibit aure volgus.

> The song of both is admired by the shades in the reverent silence it deserves, but the crowd is denser where their ears are drinking in the tale of war and the fall of tyrants.

The audience for martial and political verse, that is, was – rightly – larger than that for love poetry. Alcaeus, not Sappho, was the greater poet.

The commission to compose the *Carmen Saeculare* in 17 BCE confirmed the freedman's son as a religious poet and gave him laureate status. It showed him also as a master of the loftiest style of political utterance. The falling birth-rate, and the Senate's wholesome legislation to promote it; problems of agriculture, of education and public morality, of foreign policy and national prestige: such are the subjects which receive magisterial treatment, along with elegantly orthodox allusions to the gods.[16] Horace evaded, indeed, the invidious honour of pressure to compose a national epic (*Odes* 1.6, 2.12, 4.2), but Maecenas made it clear that he hoped for patriotic verse, and doubtless Horace himself felt some wish to contribute to the carefully orchestrated

16 On the poem see the subtle piece by A. Barchiesi (2002).

national mood of regeneration. Poets could not fail to be flattered, when the *princeps* himself declared that they had something to contribute at a turning-point in the history of their country. Horace in his maturer years liked to meditate, not without complacency, on the social role of poets and poetry, and he gives religious functions first place; see, for instance, *Epistles* 2.1.124ff., insisting that a poet is *utilis urbi*. Prominent among the services listed are the composition of prayers and the assuaging of possible displeasure on the part of the gods. The mention of a chorus glances at his own *Carmen Saeculare*.

So it was that Horace composed, and placed prominently, a whole set of odes on centrally religious themes, in forms deriving, directly or indirectly, from cult.[17] Book 1 opened with a poem presenting him under the personal patronage of the Muses. The second poem is in his very grandest manner, appealing to Jupiter to cease his anger, all too well though Rome has deserved it by the recent civil wars. Several deities are suggested as possible intermediaries for the supreme god: Apollo, perhaps, or Venus, or Mercury – who, it may be (the poet is careful not to overstep a certain boundary), is already present in the form of Caesar's avenger, the youthful Octavian. May his reign be long, and may he triumph in foreign wars (1.2.41ff.)! There follows, with neat and effective variation, a poem to a friend, the poet Virgil, about to set off on a voyage. The collection of the *Odes*, we are immediately shown, is to combine the public and the personal, in focus and in tone. But matters are not so simple. The poem opens with prayer, to Venus and the Dioscuri, to safeguard the traveller – since, it emerges unexpectedly, crossing the sea is an instance of human presumption, like Prometheus' theft of fire. We mortals persist in wrongdoing; we oblige Jupiter to use his angry thunderbolts (1.3). Virgil was a real person, Horace's friend, embarking on a trip; how real is the rest – the protection of named deities, the sins of Prometheus and Daedalus, Hercules' defeat of death, the thunderbolts of Jupiter? Horace's smooth construction and urbane style make it impossible to be sure, and inept to press the question.

Near the end of this same book he will offer a retraction of his earlier religious indifference (1.34). The poet has undergone conversion: evidently Diespiter was manifesting himself. Of course, he will go on expressing something similar: e.g. 2.8, 4.7. Thunder and lightning from a clear sky! But let us not be too credulous. Up to now, says Horace, he has not been assiduous in his devotions. Why not? For two reasons: he was too stingy (*parcus*, the very first word), and he has been applying himself to the study of a wisdom

17 Cf. Griffin (1997) for a discussion of the poet's artful exploitation of this device.

(technical philosophy) which is really madness; in fact, it is his expertise that has led him astray:

> parcus deorum cultor et infrequens
> insanientis dum sapientiae
> consultus erro . . .

The exquisite verbal art elegantly takes back what it says at the very moment of utterance; but, clearly, only a simpleton would press it for autobiographical confession. And the next poem is addressed to a very different divinity, the goddess Fortuna. After a recital of her powers, conventional perhaps rather than inspired,[18] the poet turns deftly to a prayer for Our Leader: may Good Fortune bring him safely home! He concludes by deploring civil war and irreligion. Horace liked and repeated this turn, from an opening in [good old] religious terms, with apparently personal participation, to eulogy of the regime: thus *Odes* 1.21, 1.37, 2.9, 3.4, 3.8. The shape is reversed in 3.14, which opens with Augustus and then turns to a party; a poem like 2.7 is very closely allied to it.

An occasion or incident of cult serves often as the springboard, the starting-point, from which he can develop a typically Horatian lyric.[19] The turn can be personal, or political, or both. 'Girls, praise Diana, while you, boys, praise Apollo: and ask them to avert war from Caesar and his Roman people' (1.21). 'What is an appropriate prayer to Apollo, on a specially significant day? Not wealth but health, sanity and poetry' (1.31, cf. also 1.32). 'My vow shall be paid with feasting and music, since my friend is come safely home!' (1.36). 'How is it that I, unmarried, am celebrating the Matronalia? Come on, Maecenas: enjoy yourself, and relax for a while those heavy civic responsibilities!' (3.8). 'A religious procession shall greet our Caesar, safely recovered and returned home!' (3.14). 'Where are you rushing me, Bacchus? In some remote spot, inspired, I shall sing of Caesar's glory' (3.25).

The poet plays a virtuoso set of variations on such transitions and developments. He also composes 'hymns' of an apparently more straightforward character; not that they are necessarily easier to interpret. Thus 1.10, a little hymn to Mercury, very neat and charming, evocative of Alcaeus; is there more?[20] Or 'Venus, forsake Cyprus and take up residence with the delightful

18 'H's ode, though ambitious, is inferior to his general level' is the comment of Nisbet and Hubbard (1970) 388.

19 On Horace's use of the motif of festivals, see Griffin (1985) 101.

20 'Horace's ode must be regarded primarily as a literary imitation, yet it is noteworthy that on three other occasions he writes as if he had a close relationship with Mercury', is the guarded comment on 1.10 of Nisbet and Hubbard. Horace has no intention of making it easy for us, and wherever his heart may be, it is certainly not worn on his sleeve.

Glycera!' (1.30). And 'Faunus, visit my estate kindly, in return for the honours we pay at our artless festival!' (3.18). 'Diana, god of the wild, to you be this tree dedicated!' (3.22). And so on: not his most weighty productions, but charming, as they give ancient poetic conventions new twists and new relevance, and allow the lyric poet to give us artfully stage-managed glimpses of his life (which is, of course, poetical and special).

It remains to glance at what Horace surely intended as the pearls of his lyric output: serious and substantial creations, with an important role for the gods. These, after all, were the compositions which earned him the right to the ancient title of *vates*,[21] and which secured him that weighty commission, the *Carmen Saeculare*, an element in a very grand state ceremony, and public recognition as a serious moral and religious writer. *Odes* 2.19 and 3.25 state Horace's claim to be a true poet in terms of a unique relationship with Bacchus. Elsewhere, the Muses and Apollo support the same aspiration, one dear to the poet's heart. The gods appear in 1.12, in a Pindaric priamel. What god, what hero, what man, shall the poet praise? Among the gods, Jupiter; among heroes, Hercules and the Dioscuri; among men, the Julian *gens* and Our Leader, conqueror of the Parthians, and (under heaven) ruler of the world. The utterance aims high, and the mythological religion is crucial.

The 'Roman Odes' of book 3.1–6 are exceptionally rich in named gods. Jupiter is pervasive: 3.1.5–8, 2.29, 3.6, 4.42ff., 5.1f. It is Juno who announces to the listening gods the doom of Carthage and the destiny of Rome (3.3.17–68). The Muses marked Horace out for a special career (3.4.9ff.); they give sage counsel to Augustus, whose power resembles that of Jupiter himself (3.4.37ff.), and who is closer at hand (3.5.1–4). It is because of offences against the gods that Rome has suffered so terribly (3.6.1ff.). In Book 4 the great patriotic poems, notably 4.5 and 4.6, tend to call on the same divine machinery; in 4.14 the stepsons of Augustus achieved their triumphs 'with Augustus providing his forces, his plan, and his gods' (*te copias, te consilium et tuos / praebente divos*). The *princeps* has his own divine protectors. The last *Ode*[22] opens with an Apollo out of Callimachus, hails Augustus' benign rule and moral reformation, and finishes with a vision of the ideal Roman family singing of Troy and Anchises and the offspring of kindly Venus (*Troiamque et Anchisen et almae / progeniem Veneris canemus*). A miraculously blurred phrase leaves the final chord unresolved. 'The offspring of Venus': is Aeneas meant, or Augustus, or the whole Roman people? All are descended from that kindly goddess: no more talk now, of course, of *mater saeva Cupidinum*, 'the cruel mother of the Cupids' (*Odes* 1.19.1). Again,

21 On *vates* and *sacerdos* in Horace see Lyne (1995) 184f.

22 On this poem, see Griffin (2002).

Horace feels no obligation, and little inclination, to consistency; none of the three (surely) is to be excluded. Horace succeeds in blending the *Aeneid*, and Augustus, and myth, and history, and religion. And that is right. His religion is, in a way, a thin subject; he was hardly what we think of as a religious man. But he could combine it most skilfully with the other colours on his palette, and he could achieve with it the most marvellous effects.

FURTHER READING

All commentators and writers on Horace must touch on his religious poetry. Oksala (1973) goes through the poems systematically, in what he justifiably calls 'a systematic complete presentation of the religious and mythological passages in Horace' (7). There is much of interest in G. Williams (1968) and in Galinsky (1996). Eduard Fraenkel's learned *Horace* (Fraenkel 1957) is rewarding on many of these poems. Especially recommended is chapter 30, 'The organisation of opinion', of Ronald Syme's classic *Roman Revolution* (Syme 1939).

14

PETER WHITE

Friendship, patronage and Horatian socio-poetics

Horace addressed poems or otherwise paid compliments to over sixty of his contemporaries, and he treated of social relationships in every sort of verse he wrote.[1] He thus created a more detailed representation of his milieu than we have from any other Roman poet except Martial. And although Horace put on show only about half as many people as Martial, on average he gave them more exposure. They tend to have firmer identities outside his text as well, since they belong to a comparatively well-documented period of Roman history.[2] They are the available data from which a historian can hope to draw some inferences about one poet's social position in late first-century Rome. From Horace's standpoint, too, they were a kind of raw material, but less as facts about his life than as symbolic elements in a constant poetic reprocessing of it. Both perspectives are relevant to the subject of this chapter.

Profiling Horace's relationships

To begin from a socio-historical perspective, Horace's relationships can be characterised first of all in terms of the activities ascribed to the people

I am grateful for improvements to this essay suggested by Stephen Harrison and Robert Kaster.

1 Certain and less certain connections of Horace are catalogued by White (1993) 224–39. Syme (1986) 382–402 surveys *nobiles* in Horace.

2 Porphyrio on *Satires* 1.3.21 and 90 cites writers 'on persons in Horace' from whom scholiasts like himself drew an erratic mix of good and bad information. The Suetonian Life of Horace, on the other hand, contributes little information about social relationships, since Suetonius is interested in Horace's relationship with Augustus and Maecenas to the disregard of almost everyone else. The discovery of inscriptions or other documents might at any time throw new light on relations between Horace and a number of his friends, but details accumulate slowly. In the past half-century, finds have clarified the identity of Aelius Lamia and his brother, carried the senatorial career of Numonius Vala down closer to the period of his acquaintance with Horace, and revealed that Viscus also befriended the author of the so-called Gallus fragment, but little more.

involved in them. In *Epistles* 1.17 and 18, paired letters of advice that have been described as Horace's own version of a *De Amicitia*,[3] he emphasises the time that they spend in each other's company. They dine and party together, share pastimes and confidences, and accompany each other on trips and to holiday retreats. The same or similar activities figure in narratives in which Horace depicts his own experience of Roman social life, and they underlie occasional poems in which he invites others to drink or dine with him, bids them goodbye or welcomes them home from their travels, and congratulates or commiserates with them.[4] This intense socialising is what the Romans meant when they spoke of enjoying *convictus*, or 'life in common', as Horace does in his boast of 'having lived with the great' at *Satires* 2.1.76.

It is consistent with the kind of engagements they have that Horace can refer to himself and those he celebrates as *amici* or 'friends'. He applies the word to these relationships more than twice as often as all other terms combined, and without apparent regard for status differences. 'Friend' is how he describes himself in relation to, among others, his junior protégé Septimius, the influential knight Maecenas, the senators Pollio and Messalla, and the prince Tiberius.[5] Especially in the lyrics, where Horace's language is most laden with implication, he sometimes highlights his choice of words. The book of *Epodes* opens with a salutation to '*amice . . . Maecenas*', *Odes* 2.9.5 again features the rare syntagm of vocative *amice* plus proper name (*amice Valgi)*, and in *Odes* 2.6 and 7, *amicus* is reserved for the final position of the closing line.[6] But although Horace uses the word assertively, his language was not out of line with that of his contemporaries. Augustus himself testified to a friendship with Horace,[7] and, throughout Roman literary history, friendship language was the standard idiom in which relationships between writers and the elite were described. The language implies that they were voluntary associations based ideally on sentiment,[8] however diverse their particular manifestations might be.

Modern readers of Horace have been more inclined to understand these relationships in terms of literary patronage than of friendship, however. In principle, nothing prevents a friend from occupying the position of a patron

3 Macleod (1979) 19.

4 For example, narratives: *Satires* 1.5, 1.6.47–64, *Epistles* 1.7.25–8; invitations: *Odes* 1.20, *Epistles* 1.5; propemptika: *Odes* 1.3, 1.29; homecoming: *Odes* 1.36, 2.7; congratulations: *Odes* 3.19.10–11; commiseration: *Odes* 1.24, *Epistles* 1.14.6–9.

5 *Odes* 2.6.24, 3.8.13, *Satires* 1.10.85–7 and *Epistles* 1.9.5.

6 See Storch (1970) on Horace's play with friendship language in the *Odes*.

7 Suetonius *Vita Horati* p. 297.31 and 298.6 Roth.

8 Konstan (1995) 340–1: 'For Horace . . . to be a friend meant to engage in an elective and mutual relationship based on altruistic generosity that transcends differences of status.'

or a client at the same time, and *patronus* and *cliens*, being good Latin words, should reflect the truth of Roman social relations as faithfully as the word *amicus*. Yet it is now generally recognised that the Romans rarely invoked them in literary contexts. Not only that, but Latin sources reveal little about the working of patron–client ties generally during the late Republic and early Empire.[9] Lacking a clear Roman model of patronage, classicists have therefore borrowed from sociologists and defined patronage in the abstract, as an asymmetrical personal relationship of some duration which involves the reciprocal exchange of goods and services.[10] The definition is not perfectly tailored to the shape of Roman society, less because it does not cleanly demarcate the institution of patronage from marriage or slavery than because it does not explain relationships at the top of society in which the asymmetry ratio fluctuates. It would be difficult to apply to the dealings between Cicero and Atticus, for example.[11]

But it can be applied to some of Horace's literary relationships. A clear-cut case is his tie with Maecenas, which lasted from an initial meeting in the year 38 to the death of both men in 8. The inequality between them is emphasised in Horace's avowal that in conversation he used to call Maecenas his 'father' and 'king' (*Epistles* 1.7.37), and he describes himself to Maecenas in turn as a 'friend who depends on and looks to you' (*Epistles* 1.1.105). Elements of an exchange are discernible on both sides. Apart from supplying the kind of boon companionship already noted, Horace honoured Maecenas with mention in 26 of his 162 poems. Moreover, in the *Epodes* and in the first book of the *Satires*, the *Odes* and the *Epistles*, Maecenas is addressed before anyone else, making him effectively the dedicatee of the respective books. He also elicits more fulsome invocations than anyone else, as, for example, 'O Maecenas, scion of ancestral kings, my bulwark and my sweet ornament' (*Odes* 1.1.1–2), 'Maecenas, proud ornament and mainstay of my affairs' (*Odes* 2.17.3–4), 'Maecenas, descendant of Etruscan kings' (*Odes* 3.29.1–3), 'Maecenas, hailed in my earliest muse as you shall be in my last' (*Epistles* 1.1.1–3). No-one else in Latin literary history was as lavishly and consistently advertised by any poet.

On the other side of the exchange, Horace points to one benefit that he received when he proclaims Maecenas the ornament of his affairs. Close association with Maecenas brought him to public attention, and that in

9 Brunt (1980b) 441: 'Modern accounts of patronage . . . conceal how elusive is the evidence for its strength. The references to it are somewhat rare; and it is not conspicuous where we should most expect to find it.'

10 So Saller (1982) 1, whose definition remains standard.

11 For these difficulties with the current conception of patronage, see Eilers (2002) 1–18.

turn probably contributed to the success of his poetry.[12] But he makes his frankest reference to benefits received when he tells Maecenas that 'you made me rich' (*Epistles* 1.7.15). Since the root sense of the word he uses for 'rich' (*locuples*) is 'rich in land', Horace may have in mind the gift of property and specifically of his Sabine farm.[13] But here and elsewhere, his references to Maecenas' generosity are forthright without being concrete.[14] They do not indicate the value of the gifts received, what form they took or when Horace received them. But if a detail in the Suetonian *Life* (p. 297.8–9 Roth) can be trusted, Horace did not have to rely on Maecenas for basic subsistence. About four years before they met, Horace had already wangled a pardon for fighting at Philippi, and a salaried clerkship that installed him in 'the status group which lies just below the rank of *eques*'.[15] Subsequent largesse from Maecenas and others is best seen as an enhancement of his income rather than the foundation of it.

Aside from Maecenas, however, Horace's only documented benefactor is Augustus, who according to Suetonius 'enriched him with a couple of grants' (p. 297.34 Roth). Curiously, Horace himself gives no hint of these grants, even when extolling Augustus' generosity to his fellow poets Vergil and Varius (*Epistles* 2.1.245–7). Maecenas is the only source of benefits he openly acknowledges. But while he downplays material rewards in the case of his own relationships, he takes them for granted in relationships involving others. *Epistles* 1.17 and 18, the two letters of advice mentioned earlier, assume that anyone who cultivates a rich friend will be angling for gifts in return. Horace all but confesses to the same motivation himself when he declares that 'brazen poverty compelled me to write verse' (*Epistles* 2.2.51–2). Since literary activity *per se* could not generate an income, he can only have been thinking of the *entrée* it provided to the company of the well-to-do. Over half of the sixty-plus persons celebrated in his poems are identifiable as prosperous knights or senators. Although none but Maecenas and Augustus is known to have supplied economic benefits, Horace's silence

12 Horace claims to find the attention burdensome at *Satires* 2.6.40–58 and *Epistles* 1.19.35–45. Maecenas may have tried to promote Horace's reputation as vigorously as he did Vergil's (Seneca *Suasoriae* 1.12, 2.20, 3.5).

13 Bradshaw (1989) rightly insists that Horace does not unambiguously describe the Sabine farm as a gift from Maecenas and that the scholiasts, who do, cannot be proved to have possessed information independent of Horace's words. Cairns (1992) 107–9 is equally right to say that the conventional view may nevertheless be correct.

14 *Odes* 2.18.11–14, 3.16.38, *Epodes* 1.31–2 and *Epistles* 1.7.15–45.

15 Purcell (1983) 126. Horace's secretarial position, like the pardon, must have been gained through influence, presumably exerted by now unidentifiable friends from the early years of his climb in Roman society.

about Augustus' gifts stands as a warning not to assume that no-one else did.

Still, the fact that Horace rarely adverts to material aspects of the exchange between him and his friends suggests that these preoccupied him less than they do us. Possibly tact played a part in his reluctance to speak of benefits. *Satires* 2.6, in which he extols his Sabine farm without remarking that Maecenas gave it to him, has often and perhaps correctly been interpreted as an exquisite adaptation of a poem of thanksgiving. Maecenas would have known the identity of the donor, after all. But Horace also seems to distance himself from other conventions that we associate with the poetry of patronage. Although, as mentioned earlier, some of his poems could be classified as occasional verse, most often the occasion is but the thinnest pretext for a poem. The first book of *Epistles* provides many examples. Horace also does not promise to immortalise friends in his poetry, and he generally refrains from puffing their literary productions in the way that poets like Martial do. When he alludes to work by Maecenas and Tibullus, for example, it is to imagined rather than actual writings.[16] Even his most specific homage to poetry written by friends (*Satires* 1.10.40–5) functions within the context of an argument about his own work.

One aspect of social attachments which Horace does emphasise, especially in his early work, is that they engage him as much with groups as with individuals. Some of his most memorable vignettes are of groups, as when he describes the writers and magnates who frequent Maecenas' house (*Satires* 1.9.48–52) or the cronies desperate for amusement during a dull journey (*Satires* 1.5) or dinner-party (*Satires* 2.8). Not surprisingly, shared interests in poetry often provide the focus: about twenty of Horace's friends can be identified as writers of verse. He says that he was first taken to Maecenas by poet friends (*Satires* 1.6.54–6). He claims that he limits readings of his work to groups of friends (*Satires* 1.4.73), and it is just such an audience that he evokes at the end of *Satires* 1.10, where he ticks off the names of fifteen fans. The collective appetite for poetry among his friends also inspired the image of the literary smorgasbord he develops at *Epistles* 2.2.58–64.

Literary exchanges in this milieu flow in many directions, unlike the exchange of material goods, which flow from richer to poorer. The compliments that Maecenas received from Horace were reciprocated by compliments he made to him in prose and poetry of his own.[17] Recitations of verse were as likely to be staged by rich men before dependent friends as vice

16 *Odes* 2.12.9–10, 1.33.1–4, *Epistles* 1.4.3. The reference to Varius at *Odes* 1.6.1–2 also concerns an imagined rather than an actual poem.

17 Büchner (1982) 132 nos. 2 and 3, and Servius Auctus on Vergil *Aeneid* 8.310

versa, a situation on which Horace comments at *Ars Poetica* 419–25, and poets whom he praises include the senator Pollio as well as his peers Vergil and Varius. Horace represents himself as being both a recipient and a source of literary requests and literary criticism.[18]

Since these interactions and the communal framework in which they take place are not obviously explicable in terms of patronage, it would be helpful to have supplementary models of exchange to deal with them.[19] Alternatives are all the more desirable because we have so few data in which to ground the basic postulates of patronage. If largesse defines a patron, strictly speaking only two of the people connected with Horace qualify. With few can we be sure that he had long-lasting relationships, and to many whose social standing was plainly higher (the senator Valgius, for example) he does not exhibit the deference that would suggest an association on unequal terms. The conventional model presumes too much in Horace's milieu that we cannot observe, and explains too little that we can.

Socio-poetic perspectives

The selection of friends presented in Horace's poems differs in some respects from the set he would be expected to have acquired in real life. As noted earlier, more than half of those he invokes are senators and knights, who made up only a small fraction of society overall. Other categories seem under-represented. Horace cites no Roman women among his friends, apart from pseudonymous and possibly fictitious lovers. He identifies only one compatriot from his Apulian homeland and only two among the comrades whom he followed on to the losing side during the civil war.[20] Although *grammatici*, the teacher-critics who were the academics of his day, played a vigorous part in contemporary literary life, Horace professes to disdain them and numbers one at most among his set.[21] Dozens of Greek poets and intellectuals sojourned in Rome during his lifetime, but they too scarcely figure among the

18 Requests to Horace: *Epodes* 14.1–8, *Epistles* 1.1.1–10 and 2.2.24–5; from Horace: *Odes* 2.9.17–24, 2.12.9–12; criticism received: *Ars Poetica* 438–42; offered: *Epistles* 1.3.15–20. But Horace does not allude to any of the three literary requests that Suetonius says he received from Augustus (p. 297.35–298.11 Roth).

19 A communal interpretation of the Roman literary milieu (with Horace in a cameo appearance) recurs in Ovid *Tristia* 4.10 and is developed for the era of Pliny by Guillemin (1929).

20 But Ofellus, the Apulian sage of *Satires* 2.2, is thought by many readers to be fictitious. The comrades-in-arms are Brutus and the Pompeius of *Odes* 2.7.

21 Disdain: *Epistles* 1.19.39–40. Scholiasts at *Satires* 1.9.61 and *Epistles* 1.10 identify Aristius Fuscus as a *grammaticus*.

associates he names. The only Greeks in evidence are a diplomat in whose company he once journeyed, a doctor, and perhaps his booksellers and a landowner in Sicily.[22] While it cannot be proved that the friends he advertises do not correlate closely with the friends he had, that seems a plausible surmise, given the apparent biases in our sample. Horace's selectivity extends also to what he reports about the relationships that he does advertise. He rarely alludes to benefits or literary requests and he skirts other conventions of praise poetry. His poems are at best an imperfect mirror of his activities and attachments in society.

Not that most readers have supposed differently, of course. But over the past generation, as critics have stressed the constructedness of every facet of Latin poetry, they have argued that it is no less true of the prosopography than of anything else in Horace's poems. From the critical perspective that Zetzel (1982) sketched as 'the poetics of patronage', a relationship treated in poetry carries a meaning intrinsic to the poem or book, which may or may not correspond to an external reality.

Social relationships can be transmuted into poetic material in any number of ways, but critics have discussed three aspects in particular of their treatment by Horace. In the view of some, the abiding preoccupation with friends and friendship in his works reflects an effort to integrate his social experience into a philosophical ethics, or at least to question his experience in that light. Various philosophical schools had produced accounts of friendship, of which Horace could not have been ignorant.[23] He says that as a young man he studied ethics in Athens (*Epistles* 2.2.43–5). His poems sometimes flaunt a familiarity with philosophical doctrines, and in one passage he imagines himself and his Sabine neighbours debating 'whether utility or right draws us to friendship' (*Satires* 2.6.75). He tells the Pisones that the study of philosophy can aid a writer to create characters who effectively imitate the roles and duties of real-life people, including 'what one owes to friends' (*Ars Poetica* 312).

It is thus not unreasonable to suspect some influence of philosophy on Horace's own representation of friendship. But even in the *Epistles*, where he comes closest to intimating a philosophical project, consensus about it has been elusive. Mayer has reminded us that philosophers appropriated much of the existing lay language of moral evaluation.[24] The moral terminology of the poems does not by itself establish a philosophical debt, therefore, much less discriminate among positions of the different schools. The vagueness

22 *Satires* 1.5.2, *Epistles* 1.15.3, 1.20.2 and *Odes* 2.16. The booksellers and the landowner are not certainly Greek.

23 See J. Powell (1995) for a survey.

24 Mayer (1986) 60.

of the language is further complicated by Horace's intellectual stance. In the programme poem of the *Epistles* he declares that his approach to philosophy is eclectic (1.1.11–19), which means that an idea he borrows may not have the same ramifications for him as it did in a putative source. The problem can be illustrated by the minor motif of choosing worthy friends that is common to Horace and to Cicero's *De Amicitia*.[25] 'Worthiness' is one of those terms of moral approbation that is susceptible of many applications. Cicero brings it up when he talks about the importance of testing friends over time, about the criteria of trustworthiness and sweet temper, about balancing old friends and new friends, and about virtue as the foundation of affection. Horace speaks about choosing worthy friends in the contexts of contrasting character with social status, real goods with sham goods, and artistic talent with the lack of it. Horace and Cicero might not have quarrelled with each other's statements. But even where their language is similar, they seem to be talking to different purposes. And Horace's philosophical purpose overall is at least not transparent. Two critics of the *Epistles* concluded in the same year that 'Cicero . . . provides a paradigm for Horace in both the theory and practice of friendship' and that Horace 'is not interested in aligning himself with ethics as his contemporaries understood the word . . . he rejects philosophy'.[26]

But whether or not philosophy provided Horace with an organising scheme for poetry about friendship, it certainly contributed a tone that he was able to exploit. In the first place, since Lucilius, too, had been in the habit of salting his social commentary with philosophical allusions, Horace posted a generic marker every time he followed suit.[27] It also served to impart an air of expertise to one of his key modes of discourse, which was the dispensing of advice. In both Horace and Lucilius, in fact, philosophy complements the theme of friendship in authorising this discourse. The one lent intellectual authority, while friends had also the moral duty to give each other advice.[28] But the trappings of philosophy could be as useful for the purpose as the substance.

A second approach to Horace's presentation of social relationships makes use of a micropoetic lens and examines how the naming of particular addressees contributes to meaning within the poem or work. A frequently

25 Horace *Satires* 1.6.50–64, *Epistles* 1.7.22–4, 1.9.4, 1.18.78 and 2.1.229–47, and Cicero *De Amicitia* 62–8 and 78–85.

26 Kilpatrick (1986) x and Mayer (1986) 62–3. The argument continues unabated: Moles (2002).

27 Mayer (1986) 60 n. 16 and Gärtner (2001) 103–4.

28 A commonplace, compare Lucilius 611 Marx, Cicero *De Amicitia* 44 and 88 and Horace *Satires* 1.4.132.

cited early example is Zetzel (1982), which is exemplary also for its clarity in articulating premises. Zetzel argues that in Book 1 of the *Satires*, Maecenas symbolises the goal in an episodic narrative of progress by Horace from outside to inside an artistic haven. But the pair Maecenas and Horace are 'only a vehicle for discussing the role of the poet in society' ((1982) 95). In the *Odes*, a different pattern is discerned. The first poem of Book 1 leads off with an invocation to Maecenas and takes his approval as the measure of artistic success. Book 3 winds up with another poem about poetry in the same metre, but with no mention of Maecenas, who has been displaced to the immediately preceding piece. For Zetzel, the displacement is part of Horace's point, as the finale celebrates a poetic triumph which has placed him 'beyond the need for any mortal patron' ((1982) 96).

Philologists have long been accustomed to comb through the background of Horace's dedicatees for details which might bear on the poems and vice versa. Zetzel's essay illustrates how a poetics-oriented criticism differs: language and organisation of a work alone determine relevance, and details have a strictly poetic purpose. In a similar vein is an essay by Gold (1992), who again examines the introductory poems of the *Satires* and the *Odes*. She emphasises that Maecenas is not the only one addressed in them, however. The poems posit a series of internal and external addressees, and Gold discusses the effects that Horace obtains by playing one against another. Other critics have suggested that Maecenas functions as an idealised figure of the general reader.[29]

The logic of this approach entails that the *persona* of an addressee should be no less stylised than the *persona* of the poet, and in one case fiction is unmistakable. The addressee of *Epistles* 1.20 is not a person but a book figured as a person. Almost as plainly imaginary are the interlocutors in some of Horace's erotic pieces (like Pyrrha, Lydia and Ligurinus) and in *Epistles* 1.14, a meditation on inconsistency and content directed to his slave bailiff. In a few other poems as well, critics have sometimes suspected that the persons invoked (like Ofellus in *Satires* 2.2, Bullatius in *Epistles* 1.11, and Scaeva in *Epistles* 1.17) are too perfectly suited to the topic to be real.

Nevertheless, most critics have shown less readiness to treat as poetic fiction what Horace says about his addressees than what he says about himself. Perhaps one cannot shake both poles at the same time without experiencing something like vertigo. In any event, the critic who has made the most comprehensive effort to interpret Horace's addressees poetically has also wanted them to stay firmly put in history: 'the space of private relations in Horace . . . cannot be systematically reduced to a mere fictitious pretext

29 Pomeroy (1980) 38; compare Dunn (1995) 171.

for introducing content of more general validity: it has its own reality and value'.[30] Surveying the dedicatees and interlocutors in all of Horace's works, Citroni in some measure balances the historical and the poetic by postulating two 'levels of audience'. On one level, the poems address real situations in the lives of real contemporaries who are meant to find them pertinent. On another, the poems aim at a general reader to whom, through the figure of the interlocutor, Horace communicates on broad issues of politics, poetry or ethics.

While it appears that the figure of the addressee functions somewhat differently in the satires, lyrics and epistles respectively, it is now taken for granted that the addressee is integral to the argument of the poem. In principle, the same should be true for the way groups are presented in the poems. Divergent poetic aims must have something to do with the contrast between the high-toned and raffish presentations that Horace offers of Maecenas' entourage in *Satires* 1.9 and 2.8. These presentations in turn diverge from the aura of sophistication that Maecenas lent to conversation between himself and his friends in a literary dialogue he composed.[31] But critics have so far been less concerned with the poetics of collective representations than with individuals.[32]

A third trend in recent criticism focuses not on Horace's philosophy of friendship or on individual addressees but on imagery. Images are the stock-in-trade of poets and pre-eminently of Horace, who relies on them to convey his most complex observations about social relations. Often his vehicles are illustrative personalities imported from life, literature or history. Among the more developed portraits are Tigellius, the entertainer friend of Caesar who serves as the lead-in to a discussion of friendship in *Satires* 1.3, Maenius, the bankrupt but buoyant Lucilian scrounger to whom Horace compares himself in *Epistles* 1.15, and Ulysses, who in *Satires* 2.5 is imagined in a post-war role as the hanger-on of a rich and vulgar freedman.[33]

But Horace's imagery extends beyond such *exempla* to the associative language characterising relationships that he depicts. This is the area that has been most intensively explored in recent critical writing. Since the word *amicus* is directly related to the Latin word for 'love', it was easy for Horace to transpose social intercourse into an erotic key. Oliensis (1997) has discussed the analogies he draws between attendance on a magnate and courtship of

30 Citroni (1995b) 279. 31 Servius Auctus on Vergil *Aeneid* 8.310.

32 See, however, the remarks by D. Kennedy (1992) 32–3 and Cucchiarelli (2001) 95–7.

33 Others include Aristippus (*Epistles* 1.17.11–29), Eutrapelus (*Epistles* 1.18.31–3), Davus, 'master's slave friend', in *Satires* 2.7, the anonymous would-be friend of Maecenas in *Satires* 1.9 and Philippus and Mena in *Epistles* 1.7.

a mistress, and the overtones of prostitution he gives to the role of dependent friend. Another image that Horace frequently evokes is the parasite or buffoon. Damon (1997) has shown that in these passages his aim is not to delineate a distinct social type, but again to comment on the plight of dependent friends, to which the stereotype of the parasite holds up a distorting mirror. Fitzgerald (2000) treats Horace's play with language that assimilates friendship to slavery, and Bowditch (2001) studies his manipulation of economic imagery to contrast the forms of exchange in which friends engage.

Yet these are only a few among many images in a repertoire that develops Horace's view of social relationships more elaborately than any of his other themes. He also finds illustrative material in political campaigns and comic plots, in the frog, the mouse, the fox, the horse and other protagonists of animal fable, and in real-life figures such as gladiators, legionaries, beggars and kings.[34] What distinguishes these images, apart from their sheer fertility, is the degree to which they are left to interpret themselves. It has long been recognised that, at transition-points in an argument, Horace often neither sums up nor recommences, but deliberately blurs a change of subject that occurs without warning.[35] His images likewise challenge the reader because the point of them is frequently unstated. After a friend complained of receiving no new poems, for example, Horace responded at *Epistles* 2.2.26–40 with a story about a soldier who refused to risk his life for prize-money once he had enough for retirement. The story begins and ends with no indication of its relevance. Although context makes the point fairly clear in this case, in others it is less so, and most notoriously in *Epistles* 1.7 to Maecenas. The centrepiece of this poem, whose argument is conveyed almost entirely through parables, is the story of Philippus the aristocrat and Mena the auctioneer. Horace tells it by way of excusing his failure to spend more time in Maecenas' company, and he gives to his characters traits which heighten their resemblance to Maecenas and himself. Yet both behave badly, and Mena's life is ultimately ruined by Philippus' careless attentions. Horace leaves it to the reader to determine whether the pair are adduced as analogues or as antitypes of Maecenas and himself, or as something in between.

The tactic of not explicating images allowed Horace to broach in this guise concerns about social attachments with which he could not confront his interlocutors directly. Many of his images, like the two stories just cited, foreground the theme of personal autonomy. Prominent throughout his work, it is crucial to his treatment of friendship. Another theme which surfaces

34 *Satires* 1.6.24–52, 2.5.91, 2.3.314–20, 2.6.79–117, *Epistles* 1.7.29–33, 1.10.34–8, 1.1.2–6, 2.2.26–40, 1.17.13–15 and 58–9.

35 Horace's 'gliding transitions' were first analysed by Cauer (1906).

more often in images than anywhere else is the harm that is apt to befall the weaker partner of a pair. It is present in the fables of the city mouse and the country mouse and of the frog and the calf, in comparisons Horace draws between himself and a gladiator or soldier, and in his reminiscence of the magnate Eutrapelus, who lavished presents on 'whomever he wished to harm'.[36] A case could be made, in fact, that through imagery Horace consistently offers a more negative assessment of friendship than in his more expansive pronouncements on the subject.

Finally, socio-poetic studies of friendship in Horace have helped to crystallise a perception that friendship is not merely a focus in itself but also a framework in terms of which Horace presents other subjects. That is most obviously true for the subject of poetry, but it is true for others too, and especially politics. Discourse relating to friends is one element which clearly bridges the conventional dichotomy between public and private themes in Horace. It would be worth knowing more about why it works this way.

FURTHER READING

The best approach to understanding the social background implied in Horace's works is through two papers by Brunt (1980a; 1980b), on *amicitia* and *clientela* respectively. Brunt provides a broad, inductive account of what the Romans meant when they spoke of friendship and patronage. But it is important to realise, as Eilers (2002) emphasises, that there is a certain disconnect between what modern scholars understand by patronage and what the Romans understood by it. Whether Horace in particular enjoyed relationships of friendship or patronage (or both) with those he advertises remains controversial. Konstan (1995) comes down on the side of the former in an essay preliminary to his study of friendship in the ancient world (1997).

On the whole, however, recent critics have found it more productive to discuss the creative use that Horace made of social relationships than to discuss how they should be labelled. There is now an abundance of studies that focus on the intersection of Horatian poetics with themes of friendship and attachment. Among the most stimulating are Macleod (1979) on Horace's 'poetry of ethics', Zetzel (1982) and Citroni (1995b) on the function of the addressees within the poems, and Oliensis (1997) on the application of erotic imagery to relations between friends.

36 *Satires* 2.6.79–117, 2.3.314–20, *Epistles* 1.1.2–6, 2.2.26–40 and 1.18.31–6.

15

GREGSON DAVIS

Wine and the symposium

The topic of 'Wine and the symposium' constitutes a major preoccupation of Horace's poetry from the early *Epodes* to the late *Epistles*. It is therefore crucial to an understanding of his underlying system of values. The main focus of this condensed treatment will be on the *Odes*, with occasional glances at pertinent passages from the *Epistles*. Since wine is seldom mentioned in Horace's lyric corpus outside of the context of the symposium, the convivial odes will receive prime attention in what follows.

Before summarising the typical content and structure of the Symposium Ode, it is useful to consider the arrangement of the poems with respect to the theme of wine-drinking. The collection of odes in Book 1 is framed by opening and closing poems that give prominence to the leitmotif of wine. Thus the dedicatory poem to his patron, Maecenas (*Odes* 1.1), which presents the programme of the *Odes* as a whole, takes the rhetorical form of a priamel in which the climactic term features the poet-speaker's choice of a Dionysian community of Nymphs and Satyrs dancing and singing together in a sacred grove and crowned with ivy (29–34). The main vocation championed by the speaker is the composition of lyric poetry in the tradition of Archaic Greek (Lesbian) lyric, but the setting is consonant with the sympotic muse, since the presence of the Bacchic entourage is hardly conceivable without wine-induced *ekstasis*. In the concluding ode of Book 1 (*Odes* 1.38) Horace foregrounds the banquet wreath (*corona*) as an emblem for his lyric values (aesthetic and philosophical) in a dense poem that functions as a virtual thematic signature:

> Persicos odi, puer, apparatus,
> displicent nexae philyra coronae;
> mitte sectari, rosa quo locorum
> sera moretur.
>
> simplici myrto nihil adlabores
> sedulus curo: neque te ministrum

dedecet myrtus, neque me sub arta
vite bibentem.

I detest Persian paraphernalia, my boy, wreaths woven on linden bark displease me; stop trying to track down those rare places where a late rose lingers on. Take care that in your zeal you work no extra ornament into the plain myrtle: myrtle is most fitting both to you, as you serve, and to me, as I drink, beneath the dense vine.

Since the last word of the poem (and the *liber*) is *bibentem* ('drinking'), the poet leaves the reader with a self-portrayal that is clearly emblematic for the whole book. Although the only participants mentioned are the speaker and his addressee, the attendant slave, the occasion implied by the *corona* is presumably a symposium.

Within these framing odes the sympotic theme is recurrent, whether as metonymy or as full-blown event. As illustrations of the former we may cite the hilarious ode addressed to the personified wine-jar (3.21), and the short encomium of the vine (1.18). Both of these poems operate as powerful metonymic references to the pleasures of the symposium, as their final scenes disclose – in the former case, Bacchus, Venus and the Graces are requested to be present at a prolonged symposium; in the latter, the speaker invokes the infamous wedding-feast that ended in a drunken brawl between Lapiths and Centaurs as an admonition against over-intoxication in convivial settings.

The staple constituents of Horace's version of the literary symposium are conventional and derivative of the Greek tradition.[1] While the core of the ensemble is the sequence of feast followed by extended drinking-party, other standard features of the symposiastic complex are demonstrably no less important. Of these we may distinguish three interrelated activities: (i) social intercourse between friends (mainly in the form of witty and entertaining conversation), (ii) poetic performance (the exchange of songs accompanied by music) and (iii) erotic interplay. All three of these activities are nurtured by wine.

The social aspect (i) is crucial to the very definition of the occasion as a *sym*-posion ('drinking *together*'). Horace favours the terms *sodales* and *amici* to refer to the social group, which is modelled on the Archaic Greek *hetairia*. In an early example of the genre, *Epode* 13, the apostrophe to the *amici* is salient (*rapiamus, amici / occasionem de die* 'let us snatch, my

1 For an astute review of the evidence (mainly extra-literary) for Roman convivial norms, see Roller in Donahue (2003). Certain key practices shared with Greek symposia (e.g. reclining posture, presence of female courtesans) were apparently in vogue among Roman elites as early as the third century BCE.

friends, the opportunity from the day' 3–4). The centrality of the social bond receives ironic formulation in the first, programmatic Ode (1.1), in which the absence of drinking companions in a famous scene is salient (19–22):

> est qui nec veteris pocula Massici,
> nec partem solido demere de die
> spernit, nunc viridi membra sub arbuto
> stratus, nunc ad aquae lene caput sacrae.

> There is the person who neither refuses cups of aged Massic wine, nor shrinks from taking off a section from the compact day, now with limbs outstretched beneath the green arbutus, now by the gentle source of a sacred spring.

This picture of the solitary *vinosus* is appealing at first blush, and many commentators have been seduced into seeing it as a mirror for the poet's own life-habits. The rhetorical context, however, precludes such a superficial reading, for the undeterred tipster is part of the elaborate 'foil' of an opening priamel that begins with the intrepid Olympic victor and ends with the fanatic hunter. The appealing element in the tipster scene – the imbibing of a vintage wine – is all the more ironic as foil because it takes place outside the framework of convivial intercourse. The entire representation of lifestyles preferred by others is 'capped' by the vocation of the poet, who enjoys a rather select company of Dionysian followers – a sympotic setting that trumps all others and is conducive to poetic performance.

If social interaction is the *sine qua non* of the authentic symposium, the sharing of poetic performance (ii) among the gathering of *amici* is no less essential as a core activity. When Horace in a typical gambit invites a *hetaira* named Lyde to join him at a feast, he anticipates an exchange of musical performances (*Odes* 3.28.9–12):

> nos cantabimus invicem
>   Neptunum et virides Nereidum comas;
> tu curva recines lyra
>   Latonam et celeris spicula Cynthiae.

> We in our turn will sing of Neptune and the Nereids' sea-green hair; you will sing in exchange on the curved lyre of Latona and the darts of swift Cynthia.

Lyde's initial song (celebrating the chaste Diana as opposed to the amorous Neptune) is a deliberately tantalising serenade that precedes erotic engagement (Venus, we soon learn, is reserved for the final climactic song). Although the speaker elides mention of other participants besides Lyde, we know from the occasion he announces at the opening of this ode – the feast of the Neptunalia – that it was the custom for outdoor banquets to be held in improvised huts on the banks of the Tiber. Lyde, in any event, conforms strictly to the paradigm of female *hetairai* with Greek names who populate the Horatian *convivium*. Such *hetairai* are invariably typecast as accomplished musicians who are also adept at witty conversation. As is the case with the Greek symposiastic model, the male *sodales* in Horatian symposia are entertained by skilled musician-courtesans who engage in poetic exchanges with them.[2]

The presence of courtesans is by definition linked to love-making (iii). The presence of Eros is an equally critical component of the drinking-party, and Horace makes it clear that the professional *hetairai* he routinely includes in his symposia are conceived as sophisticated erotic partners, as well as skilled entertainers. For instance, the Licymnia of *Odes* 2.12, an artful courtesan who is also a gifted dancer, is portrayed in a closing vignette as inflaming her partner with tantalising erotic play.[3] Wine and sexual desire are endemic to the Greek sympotic institution that receives a Roman inflection in the Horatian *Odes*. As we saw above in the case of Lyde, in which the goddess of love is invoked in the finale, Venus and her son Cupid are either explicitly invoked or are presumptive presiding deities at Horatian parties, along with the god of wine, Dionysus. Sexual desire is a common conversational topic in the Horatian convivium at a certain peak in the potations. The erotic inclinations of a youthful *amicus* at a banquet are the subject of teasing banter on the speaker's part in *Odes* 1.27, where the occasion is a very riotous drinking-party that threatens to get out of hand. After calling on the *sodales* (line 7) to behave in a less disorderly fashion, the speaker goes on to challenge a love-sick *puer* to reveal his erotic flame to the inebriated guests in a playful dialogue.

In addition to the basic constituents of the *convivium*, as we have adumbrated them, Horace adopts a few of the ancillary rituals of the drinking-party *à la grecque*. Chief among these is the convention of the *magister bibendi* – the *amicus* who is appointed to regulate the proportions of water to wine to be dispensed from the mixing-bowl that occupied the centre, symbolically and spatially, of the *triclinium*.[4] In the Soracte Ode (*Odes* 1.9) the person who controls the wine is given a Greek name that bespeaks his

2 Horace here represents himself as singing to the accompaniment of the lyre at a symposium, but it would be rash to infer that the *Odes*, in general or in part, were intended to be actually performed at banquets. In the absence of solid extra-literary evidence the issue remains *sub iudice*. O. Murray (1985) makes a tentative case for occasional performance, but acknowledges (44) that 'for the sympotic image to work, it is only necessary to believe in the possibility of performance'.

3 For the unconventional interpretation sketched here see G. Davis (1975).

4 See Lissarrague (1990) 19–46.

function, 'Thaliarchus' ('ruler of the revels'). In the ode to Sestius (*Odes* 1.4) Horace warns his friend that, once dead, he will no longer be eligible for selection by the lot that determines the *regna vini* ('kingship over the wine'). Elsewhere the convention is alluded to in anonymous terms, as in *Odes* 2.7.25–6, where the poet asks, in anticipation of a wild celebration, 'whom will the Venus dice-throw designate as master of the drinking-bouts?' (*quem Venus arbitrum / dicet bibendi*?). Here the play on the name 'Venus' (signifying both goddess of love and the highest throw of the dice) allows Horace to conjoin the erotic element with the ritual apportionment of the wine. In another ode the lyric speaker refers to the changing ratios of wine to water in the imagined symposium he is advocating (3.19.11–18).

The master of the revels presided over the *quantity* of the wine consumed by the guests (a function of its differential dilution with water). The *quality* of the wine, however, is a no less valued coefficient of the sympotic experience, and Horace pays due attention to this dimension in the convivial odes. Thus he frequently mentions the vintage of the wine and even, on occasion, its precise age. Since the finest wines were, then as now, relatively expensive, the poet often proclaims his wish to savour the best vintages when accepting invitations to dine at the villas of the wealthy, such as his patron and friend, Maecenas. Conversely, he was not above urging his wealthy guests to be generous in the gift of rare wines when he himself was to be the host. The motif of refined wine-selection for a proposed party is handled with sophisticated humour by the lyrist. An entertaining example occurs in the ode to Vergil (*Odes* 4.12),[5] who evidently shared his taste for *grand crus*. Horace's invitation anticipates Vergil's predilections for vintage Campanian wines, and is couched in the kind of gentle banter that is the very hallmark of close friendship (13–20):

adduxere sitim tempora, Vergili,
sed pressum Calibus ducere Liberum
si gestis, iuvenum nobilium cliens,
    nardo vina merebere.
nardi parvus onyx eliciet cadum,
qui nunc Sulpiciis accubat horreis,
spes donare novas largus amaraque
    curarum eluere efficax.

The time of year has brought on a thirst, dear Vergil; but if you, a protégé of noble youths, are eagerly anticipating draughts of Bacchus pressed at Cales, you shall best earn such vintage wine with a precious nard. A wee onyx will

5 This ode has generated widespread misinterpretation on the part of critics who ignore its telling allusions to Vergil's poetry.

draw forth a wine jar, which at the the moment rests in the storerooms of Sulpicius – a jar wide enough to sponsor new hopes and efficient in washing away bitter anxieties.

The poet-connoisseur slyly suggests that the quality, no less than the quantity, of the wine is a major vector of enhanced sympotic pleasure.[6]

The essential constituents of the Horatian symposium, as we have outlined them, recur within a coherent structural framework throughout all four books of *Odes*. The full-blown Symposium Ode is typically binary in structure, with the second part comprising two subsections. The first part, which may be labelled 'Scene', presents a vivid picture of change drawn from nature; the second, the 'Response', consists typically of philosophical reflections (insights in the form of gnomic expressions, or *sententiae*), and a Prescription, which offers a solution to the human predicament articulated in the Scene and often made explicit in the gnomic section.[7] These elements of a skeletal structure are, of course, analytical: they constitute a nexus of topoi that do not follow a rigid sequence, but frequently overlap, and are sometimes abbreviated or left implicit. In the most dense instantiations the logical connections between these topoi are elided in a sparse, paratactic presentation. As to content, the Prescription is, invariably, the sympotic solution: the addressee, and by extension, the audience of posterity, are enjoined to drink wine as a consolation for the harsh exigencies of human life.

To illustrate the schema in operation, let us briefly analyse the first convivial ode in Horatian lyric: *Odes* 1.4. The Scene is introduced in the opening, expository description (lines 1–4):

Solvitur acris hiems grata vice veris et Favoni,
  trahuntque siccas machinae carinas;
ac neque iam stabulis gaudet pecus aut arator igni,
  nec prata canis albicant pruinis.

Vicious winter is being loosened by the pleasing change of Spring and the West Wind, and the windlasses are hauling the dry keels; and no longer does the

6 Apart from the issue of connoisseurship *per se*, Horace occasionally makes reference to the vintage of particular wines (in terms of provenance as well as age) as a way of alluding to social and political events. Nisbet (1959) ably discusses this dimension in regard to the Epistle to Torquatus (*Epistles* 1.1). See further E. A. Schmidt (2002a) 248–65, along with the review by S. J. Harrison (2002b). In the 'Cleopatra' ode (1.37) the contrast between Egyptian and Roman symposia (and the values they embody) is reflected in the pejorative opposition between the respective vintages consumed: Maeotic (Eastern and decadent) versus Caecuban (Italian and superior). I am indebted to Stephen Harrison for this astute observation.

7 For a detailed description of the schema outlined here, see G. Davis (1991) 145–67.

herd take pleasure in the stables and the ploughman in his fire, nor do the meadows turn white with hoar-frost.

The change (*vice*) from one season to the next (in this case from winter to spring) defines the Scene, and it is precisely the process of change – symbolised in the procession of the seasons – that is basic to the 'argument' in the discourse of the *convivium*. Horace articulates the Response in the succeeding four lines in a manner that contrasts the exemplary with the inappropriate. Thus the goddess Venus along with the coterie of Nymphs and Graces models the correct response – leading off the dancing and singing in the outdoors – while her unenlightened spouse, Vulcan, is at work lighting up the fire in the forges of the Cyclopes. The divine actions prepare the way for the poet's injunction, which is expressed in terms of what is appropriate (*decet)* to the spectacle of seasonal vicissitude, viz. the symposium (9–12):

nunc decet aut viridi nitidum caput impedire myrto
aut flore terrae quem ferunt solutae.
nunc et in umbrosis Fauno decet immolare lucis,
seu poscat agna sive malit haedo.

Now it is fitting to bind one's gleaming head either with green myrtle, or with the flowers that the loosened earth engenders; now it is fitting to sacrifice to Faunus in shady groves, whether he demands a lamb or prefers a kid.

The convivial argument is further buttressed by a gnomic reflection on human transience:

pallida Mors aequo pulsat pede pauperum tabernas
regumque turres. O beate Sesti,
vitae summa brevis spem nos vetat inchoare longam.

Pale Death beats with even footstep on the huts of the poor and the towers of royalty. O fortunate Sestius, the short span of life forbids us to entertain hope of immortality.

The Prescription is elaborated by means of an oblique, negative formulation. Though it is not actually enunciated, it is subtly implied in the culminating vignette; for, by listing the principal joys that the addressee will miss in the underworld, Horace cleverly gives us a vignette of the happy life, which is symbolised in the choice of a *magister bibendi* and the pleasures of Eros – metonyms for the symposium (16–20).

The basic schema we have outlined here is no sterile formula; rather it functions as a fertile template that the poet of the *Odes* uses to articulate a cogent philosophical outlook. That outlook is derived from two principal sources that coalesce in the *Odes*: the lyric ethos first expressed in robust form in the archaic poetry of Archilochus (and elaborated in Lesbian melic verse), and the Hellenistic philosophy of Epicureanism. The appropriateness of wine-drinking as supreme emblem of the lyric worldview flows from the underlying premise of man's need for consolation in the here and now, which, in turn, is grounded in a prior acceptance of the ephemeral nature of human existence. Horatian wisdom (*sapientia* and its cognates are frequent in his lyric discourse) takes the shape of an enlightened hedonism in which the spectre of mortality serves as foil for the valorisation of the pleasures of the convivial lifestyle.

The ode that famously encapsulates this view of *sapientia* in the terse phrase, *carpe diem*, merits a brief analysis (*Odes* 1.11):

> tu ne quaesieris (scire nefas) quem mihi, quem tibi
> finem di dederint, Leuconoe, nec Babylonios
> tentaris numeros. ut melius, quidquid erit, pati!
> seu plures hiemes seu tribuit Iuppiter ultimam,
> quae nunc oppositis debilitat pumicibus mare
> Tyrrhenum. *sapias, vina liques*, et spatio brevi
> spem longam reseces. dum loquimur, fugerit invida
> aetas: carpe diem, quam minimum, credula postero.

> Do not ask (it is wrong to know) what end the gods have assigned to you or what to me, Leuconoe, and do not dabble in Babylonian calculations. How much better it is to endure whatsoever will be, whether Jupiter has allotted us more winters or whether this is our last that now wears down the Tyrrhenian sea against the opposing rocks. *Be wise: decant the wine*, and prune back long hope to a short span. Even as we speak, envious time will have fled. Pluck the day, trusting as little as possible to tomorrow.

The Scene here unfolded is nothing less than the human lifespan measured by the annual cycle of the seasons. Winter is the privileged season in this ode, primarily because of its association with death, or at least the waning of life. This variant of the schema involves a double deployment of the Prescription: the first enjoins the female addressee, Leuconoe, to relinquish the desire to know or predict the moment of one's death (1–3); the second, which follows the scene of the winter storm, carries the exhortation to wine-drinking (*carpe diem*). Crucial to the closing injunction is the premise that the symposiastic stance embodies wisdom (*sapias, vina liques*). Thus the prescription to imbibe is grounded in the insight that the illusion of immortality (*spes longa*) is deeply debilitating in its impact on our capacity to achieve the good life.

It would be fundamentally misleading to conclude from the stark juxtaposition of wine and wisdom here (*sapias, vina liques*) that Horace is promulgating a simplistic or reductionist ethos. The proper consumption of wine, for the poet of the *Odes*, is best understood in the context of the sophisticated philosophical doctrine of the 'mean'. The doctrine is most completely expounded in Aristotle's *Rhetoric*, but in its Epicurean inflection, to which Horace was most immediately heir, moderate consumption of food and drink enhances life's 'kinetic' pleasures – a far cry from the 'mindless hedonism' that characterises certain poems in the Anacreontic tradition.[8] Of course Horace is not above portraying himself, with deliberate tongue-in-cheek, as a 'pig from Epicurus' sty' (*Epistles* 1.4.16), but he does so with humorous intent and in full awareness of the fact that the popular belief regarding Epicurean over-indulgence at banquets blatantly contradicts the teachings of the founder.

The heart of the doctrine of the 'mean', as Horace articulates it in his lyric,[9] consists in advocating, not a rigid adherence to an arithmetic rule (e.g. an invariable middle course between polar extremes), but rather a flexible approach that takes into account the nature of the occasion. When the occasion is a symposium, the doctrine is especially subject to nuance; for, while admitting the need for flexibility, the lyrist eschews certain outer limits of behaviour that pose a threat to the peace of the social gathering. Chief among these is the outbreak of physical violence in the form of brawls (*rixae*) or downright battles (*pugnae*). We have already alluded to the negative mythological example of the battle of the Centaurs and the Lapiths which erupted at a wedding-feast. The example occurs towards the end of an ode that begins with the advice, 'Plant no tree, Varus, in preference to the sacred vine' (*nullam, Vare, sacra vite prius severis arborem*, *Odes* 18.1). The poet inveighs against those who transgress the limit of moderation in imbibing the gifts of Dionysus (7–11):

> ac ne quis *modici* transiliat munera *Liberi*
> Centaurea monet cum Lapithis rixa super mero
> debellata, monet Sithoniis non levis Euhius,
> cum fas atque nefas exiguo fine libidinum
> discernunt avidi.

And lest anyone transgress the precious bounds of *Bacchus who observes limit*, he should be warned by the brawl between Centaurs and Lapiths, which was

8 On the Aristotelian concept of the Mean in relation to its Horatian adaptation, see G. Davis (1991) 167–72; on 'kinetic' pleasures see Long (1986) 65–6; the phrase 'mindless hedonism' comes from M. L. West's discussion of the Anacreontic tradition (M. L. West (1990) 275). On Epicurus' viewpoint on the banquet see his *Letter to Menoeceus* (Arrighetti (1960) 106–17).
9 The doctrine is most fully articulated (with illustrations) in the form of the 'golden mean' (*aurea mediocritas*) in *Odes* 2.10.

fought out over unmixed wine; warned also by the not-so-gentle treatment that Bacchus metes out on the Sithonians, when in their rapacity they discriminate right from wrong by the thin line of their desires.

In many odes the deplorable proclivity to violence is ascribed, in accordance with the ethnic stereotyping of the day, to Thracian or Scythian barbarians. Consider the following stern remonstrance that ushers in *Odes* 1.27:

natis in usum laetitiae scyphis
pugnare Thracum est: tollite barbarum
morem, verecundumque Bacchum
sanguineis prohibete rixis

To fight with wine-cups created to serve our enjoyment is a Thracian habit: away with so rude a custom and defend Bacchus, who knows shame, from bloody brawls.

Violence connected with aggressive sexual pursuit or jealousy is roundly condemned by the pacific poet as disruptive of the social harmony of the banquet, as he makes clear in the closing lines of *Odes* 1.17, which are aimed at reassuring the addressee, Tyndaris, that she need not fear that the jealous Cyrus will attack her if she joins the poet in his secure bucolic retreat:

hic innocentis pocula Lesbii
duces sub umbra, nec Semeleius
cum Marte confundet Thyoneus
proelia, nec metues protervum

suspecta Cyrum, ne male dispari
incontinentis iniciat manus
et scindat haerentem coronam
crinibus immeritamque vestem.

Here you shall drink beneath the shade goblets of harmless Lesbian wine; nor will Bacchus, son of Semele, mix it up in battles with Mars; nor shall you, under suspicion, have to fear that bully Cyrus, lest he should cast upon you – no fair match – his unchecked, violent hands, and tear apart the wreath clinging to your hair and your undeserving raiment.

While violence and 'barbarian' excess are abjured as absolutely off limits in the *convivium*, Horace elsewhere sanctions heavy drinking among the *sodales* if the occasion demands it. Extraordinary public events, such as the death of Cleopatra (*Odes* 1.37), or even private ones, such as the unexpected return of a close comrade from the battlefield (*Odes* 2.7), call for a more than normal degree of inebriation.[10] As Horace puts it incisively in the form of an adage to his friend Vergil (*Odes* 4.12.28): 'it is a pleasure to act unwisely *on occasion*' (*dulce est desipere in loco)*. Though on the surface this sentiment may appear contradictory to the values he espouses in the doctrine of *aurea mediocritas*, Horace's advice to his fellow poet and friend clarifies the relativity of the concept (*in loco*). On the other hand, there are some odes in which the pretext advanced for extreme indulgence in the cups verges on the specious. In the Epistle to Torquatus, for instance (1.5), the poet is not above using the excuse of Augustus' birthday to invite his aristocratic friend Torquatus to a symposium that will last all night. In eager anticipation of the event the host launches into exaggerated praise of the gifts of inebriation (14–18):

potare et spargere flores
incipiam, patiarque vel inconsultus haberi.
quid non ebrietas dissignat? operta recludit,
spes iubet esse ratas, ad proelia trudit inertem,
sollicitis animis onus eximit, addocet artes.

I'll begin the drinking and the strewing of flowers, and I'll allow myself to appear even as imprudent. What does inebriation not unseal? It discloses the hidden, bids hopes to be realised, shoves the coward into the fray, takes away the burden from troubled minds, teaches skills.

The governing idea that the symposium is emblematic of a life securely anchored in philosophical insight is basic to the argument of the ode addressed to Plancus (*Odes* 1.7). In the final summational vignette the mythical epic hero Teucer is refashioned into an unlikely lyric avatar whose resilience in the face of a catastrophic event (expulsion from his homeland on his return from the Trojan War) is exemplary in its philosophical viewpoint. Teucer is represented as donning a convivial wreath and exhorting his comrades to adopt the sympotic solution to the problem of acute misfortune (21–32). In its underlying message his embedded speech recapitulates the message introduced by the poet earlier in the ode, where wine-drinking is put forward as a universal icon of Horatian *sapientia* (15–21):

albus ut obscuro deterget nubila caelo
saepe Notus neque parturit imbres

perpetuos, sic tu *sapiens* finire memento
tristitiam vitaeque labores

10 D'Arms (1995), addresses the issue of insobriety and decorum in Roman drinking-parties. On Horatian *modus* and its transgression, cf. La Penna (1995).

molli, Plance, mero, seu te fulgentia signis
castra tenent seu densa tenebit

Tiburis umbra tui.

As Notus often turns to white and wipes away the clouds from a dark sky, nor brings forth showers continuously, so you *in your wisdom* remember to put an end to the sadness and the toils of life, Plancus, with a mellow unmixed wine, whether you are detained by the camp gleaming with standards or by the dense shade of your beloved Tibur.

The counsels conveyed separately by the speaker to Plancus and by the lyric surrogate, Teucer, to his companions are perfectly congruent with Horace's deeply cherished conviction that the sympotic lifestyle is based on an internal, universally valid, value-system that is independent of place and circumstance.

Outside of the strictly convivial contexts that we have illustrated above, Horace occasionally invokes the god Dionysus, under his Roman name, Bacchus, in self-reflexive odes that humorously affirm the bond between the intake of wine and poetic inspiration. As we saw in the climax of the inaugural ode cited above, Horace insinuates the central figure of the wine-god, Dionysus, without actually naming him: the references to honorific ivy-wreaths and to the emblematic entourage of Nymphs and Satyrs provide transparent clues to the identity of the deity who is primarily responsible for his poetic success. His lyric canonisation is represented as doubly contingent on the co-operation of the Muses Euterpe and Polyhymnia, along with the critical approval of his patron, Maecenas (*Odes* 1.1.29–36).

Horace introduces Bacchus by name in two hilarious odes that reaffirm the essential link between the blessings of the wine-god and poetic effusion. The prelude to *Odes* 2.19 describes an epiphany of the god as a privileged experience that guarantees the speaker's state of genuine ritual possession (*ekstasis*):

Bacchum in remotis carmina rupibus
vidi docentem (credite posteri)
Nymphasque discentis et auris
capripedum Satyrorum acutas.

euhoe, recenti mens trepidat metu,
plenoque Bacchi pectore turbidum
laetatur, euhoe, parce Liber,
parce gravi metuende thyrso!

I have seen Bacchus teaching poems on remote cliffs – believe me, posterity – and the Nymphs, his pupils, and the pointed ears of the goat-footed Satyrs. Euhoe, my mind quivers with a novel fear and a wild ecstasy agitates my

> heart, fully possessed by Bacchus: euhoe, be gentle, Liber; be gentle, O god to be feared for your heavy *thyrsus*!

Implied in the hymn to the god that Horace goes on to pronounce in tones that recall the chorus of Euripides' *Bacchae* is the fancy that he has been granted a grandiloquent poetic voice as a direct result of his wine-induced transport. The function of Dionysus as the god whose transubstantiation in the wine engenders a bold poetic excursion is even more salient in *Odes* 3.25, where the inebriated bard is again foregrounded as ritually possessed and thereby authorised to explore novel poetic terrain in a high stylistic register:

> Quo me, Bacche, rapis tui
> plenum? quae nemora aut quos agor in specus
> velox mente nova?

> Where, O Bacchus, are you taking me, fully possessed by you? Into what groves, into what caverns, am I being driven, at such speed, with a mind that is new?

The rhetoric of Bacchic possession serves to proclaim the credentials of a poet who is contemplating an encomium on the grand theme of Augustus' exploits. In the enhanced state of creative frenzy, which is simultaneously a state of intoxication, Horace compares his wild poetic journey to that of a Thracian Bacchant, and he ends the poem with a vow that reconfirms the innate bond between devotion to the wine-god and high poetic utterance:

> nil parvum aut humili modo,
> nil mortale loquar, dulce periculum est,
> O Lenaee, sequi deum
> cingentem viridi tempora pampino.

> Nothing trivial or in a pedestrian manner, nothing mortal in tone shall I utter. It is a sweet danger, O Bacchus-of-the-winepress, to follow your godhead, crowning my temples with green vine-leaves.

Thus the poet whose signature is the light-hearted sympotic lyric justifies his departure into a more elevated generic territory by re-pledging his fealty to the god of wine.

FURTHER READING

Horatian convivial poetry in its generic dimension is ably discussed by O. Murray (1985). The collection of essays edited by the same author (Murray 1990) is an invaluable source of information on many facets of the symposium as a social institution in Greek, Roman and Etruscan cultures. The iconography of the conventional Greek banquet (the model that Horace partially transposes in his *Carmina*) is brilliantly analysed by François Lissarrague (1990). The role of the professional *hetaira* in Greek life and thought (and, by extension, of the erotic theme in Greek and Roman literary representations of food and the sympotic lifestyle) is wittily illuminated by Davidson (1998). On the main forms of entertainment at Greek symposia, the article by Pellizer (1990) provides a coherent overview. Many *realia* associated with the Horatian banquet (including wine-connoisseurship) are succinctly described in the encyclopaedic article 'Vino', Fedeli (1997b).

On the strictly literary interpretation of the Horatian sympotic ode, see the insightful synopsis by Steele Commager (1957). The rhetorical economy of Horace's deployment of convivial motifs and their philosophical interconnections are discussed at length in G. Davis (1991), especially chapter 3: 'Modes of consolation: *convivium* and *carpe diem*'.

16

ELLEN OLIENSIS

Erotics and gender

Horace has always been a poet more for men than for women. By comparison with the contemporary poets whose work we know (Virgil, Tibullus, Propertius, Ovid), Horace shows relatively little interest in the life of love, which is where Latin literature tends to locate its women. Though Horace is, for most readers today, the poet of the *Odes* above all, it is worth remembering that roughly half his poetry consists of the hexameter *Satires*, *Epistles* and *Ars Poetica*, poems in which women have at most a marginal existence. And this marginalisation is not an accidental but a constitutive feature of the hexameter poems, thickening their characteristic 'men's club' atmosphere. At the end of his debut collection, *Satires* 1, Horace submits his poetry to the judgement of his ideal readership, a star-studded list of masculine proper names (Maecenas, Virgil, Pollio, et al.) forming the strongest possible contrast to the nameless females (distant ancestors of Hawthorne's 'damned mob of scribbling women') who seek instruction from Horace's poetaster-rivals: 'As for you, Demetrius, and you, Tigellius: go and whine to your classroom of ladies in armchairs' (*Demetri, teque Tigelli, / discipularum inter iubeo plorare cathedras*, *Satires* 1.10.90–1). A similar exclusion marks Horace's last venture in hexameters, the *Ars Poetica*, which opens with Horace inviting his (male) friends to join him in laughing at an ineptly imagined painting of a monstrous female nude – thus from the very outset casting men as the knowing critics, and women as the matter but not the producers or consumers of (Horatian) art.

Until relatively recently, scholarship has tended to follow suit. There have been critics, men and women, to espouse, with varying degrees of warmth, Ovid's feminism and what might be termed Virgil's Didonianism. But those interested in resistant or alternative models of gender and desire have found little to attract them in Horace's poetry. To the extent that feminists have laid claim to Horace, it has been mostly in the service of exposing the aggressively gendered dynamic in which Horace's poetry seems quite wholeheartedly to participate.[1] By contrast, when the topic 'Horace as a love poet' is broached, the emphasis typically falls not on gender roles (which the reader finds already distributed, as it were) but on Horace's characteristic blend of urbane detachment and erotic susceptibility, the chief aim being to defend the (philosophical, emotional, aesthetic) value of the love poems.[2] Thus to write heatedly about gender is to oppose Horace, while to write dispassionately about desire is to identify with him.

Gender

Across Horace's poetry, gender roles are distributed along broadly predictable lines. Elite Roman girls are meant to mature into virtuous matrons, Roman boys into capable householders as well as hardworking participants in the varied business of the *res publica* – prudent lawyers, honoured senators, valiant soldiers. But there is also a class of men and women of less secure social status and less clearly differentiated gender (slaves, freedmen, freedwomen: 'feminised' subordinates) who pour the wine, play the music and supply the erotic interest at the parties at which Horace's good Romans take a well-deserved break from the stresses of public life. The identity of the poet is likewise hard to pin down. The venomous but avowedly ineffectual epodist, the relatively soft-spoken satirist, the courtly moraliser who puts in regular appearances in the *Odes*:[3] these personae embody a masculinity implicated in a shifting social hierarchy not readily reducible to the polarity of subordinate and master, feminine other and masculine self. In every case, gender is not only an attribute but a predicate: something that can be asserted or denied, or even (however tendentiously) simply shrugged off.

In the hexameter poetry, with its nearly all-male cast (hapless lovers, faithless friends, social climbers, etc.), the emphasis falls on the relations men sustain with themselves (e.g., self-restraint) and with other men (e.g., loyalty) – not with women. The masculine bias is most pronounced in the first book of *Epistles*, one of Horace's most engaging and innovative works, produced, perhaps not coincidentally, during the height of the love-elegy craze at Rome. While the elegists were celebrating and deploring their erotic entanglements, Horace was conducting his life in a set of verse letters to men on the capacious theme of how to live – a theme that does not, in Horace's

1 E.g. Richlin (1992) and chapters 4 and 7 of Henderson (1999).

2 E.g. Lyne (1980) 190–238.

3 I do not have space here to fill out, much less defend, these characterisations; my hope is that the other chapters in this *Companion* will help my readers put these and other claims in context.

view, call for any extended discussion of how or how not to love.[4] Horace's chatty letter to his fellow author Albius, whom many have been tempted to identify with the elegist Albius Tibullus, has nothing to say about love in particular, while the dinner-party to which he invites Torquatus in *Epistles* 1.5 features wine, friendship and conversation, but no women (and, as befits this hexameter genre, no song). Where sex does crop up, it is chiefly framed as an economic issue: what Horace terms, in a letter to his up-and-coming friend Lollius, *damnosa Venus* (*Epistles* 1.18.21), financially ruinous sexual desire. It is for men that Horace holds up the mirror of his hexameters, a mirror that reflects Horace's fluctuating personae while also recurrently encouraging the reader to check his own moral and social character before sallying forth into (or out of) the world: 'Is your heart free of vain ambition? free of the fear of death, and anger? Dreams, the terrors of magic, marvels, witches, ghosts in the night, Thessalian prodigies – do you laugh at all this? Are you thankful for the sum of your birthdays? Do you forgive your friends?' (*Epistles* 2.2.206–10).

One consequence of the relegation of 'real' women is the re-emergence of women as figures for how men should or should not behave with each other. In *Satires* 2.7, Horace's slave accuses Horace, his purportedly 'free' master, of dancing servile attendance on his eminent friend Maecenas, and also (and at much greater length) of being at the beck and call of the women to whom he is sexually 'enslaved'; it has been persuasively argued that the second, relatively frivolous charge displaces anxieties raised by the first.[5] The same anxieties send *Epistles* 1 repeatedly back to the theme of *virtus*, the quality that defines a *vir*, man-liness: something that is always imperilled by one man's (potentially servile or effeminate) subordination to another, for example Horace's to Maecenas. Horace's epistolary defence rests first on the philosophical meditation on the conditions for self-ownership that runs through the collection (a theory of *virtus*), and second on two politely disobliging letters in which he declines to do what Maecenas wants him to do (*virtus* in practice). In one of these, Horace even casts himself as a long-absent Ulysses opposite Maecenas' increasingly impatient Penelope: like Ulysses, Horace is a liar (*mendax*, *Epistles* 1.7.2), and he too will return 'home' to the tune of the swallow's song (*hirundine prima*, 13). A less savoury identification shows up in a pair of letters warning aspiring friends-of-the-great to shun the role of *meretrix* (courtesan or prostitute: *Epistles* 1.17.52–7,

4 Or, for that matter, how to interact with women on any other basis. I am aware of the danger of filtering the topic 'gender' through the topic 'erotics', as if the one inevitably implied the other.

5 Bernstein (1987).

1.18.1–4). Mercenary and untrustworthy, the *meretrix* embodies the vices of the false friend; the true friend finds his reflection instead in the loyal *matrona* (1.18.3–4). But either way, the comparison of the aspiring *amicus* to a woman compromises his *virtus*, the crucial term about which *Epistles* 1.17 draws ironic circles (Horace's crass addressee evidently fancies himself a conquering hero) and which *Epistles* 1.18 redefines as a middle course between servile accommodation and macho self-assertion (*virtus est medium vitiorum*, *Epistles* 1.18.9): an amiable pliability that remains just this side – the virile side – of effeminate softness.[6]

On those rare occasions when women take centre stage in Horace's hexameters, they appear as desirable sexual objects or repulsive sexual subjects, caught up in a discourse that is still more about men than about women. In *Satires* 1.2, a poem long subject to decorous truncation by bowdlerising editors, mankind's propensity to behavioural extremes is further illustrated by men's tendency to pursue the wrong sort of women: too low (sordid, promiscuous) or too high (married, aristocratic). It is the latter, 'romantic' desire for the unattainable that is the focus of Horace's Epicurean critique, which recommends appeasing the sexual appetite with objects either readily attained or already possessed – a slave-girl or boy, for example (116–18). Whereas the penis is personified and endowed with a voice, with which it irritably reproaches its over-fussy proprietor (68–71), the object of desire is dehumanised – compared to a horse (best to look it over thoroughly before purchasing the merchandise, to make sure that all's sound, 86–90), or a golden goblet or luxurious dinner (unnecessary frills, like high status in a woman, to the satisfaction of an appetite, 114–16). And at the satire's comic climax, where Horace counterpoints his own carefree sex act with an anxiety-fraught adulterous encounter, his naked obscenity does without not only the trappings of romance but even the object, grammatical and sexual: 'And I don't fret, while I'm fucking (*dum futuo*), that her husband may come hurrying back from the country, the door fly open, the dog bark . . .' (127–8).

In *Satires* 1.8, a statue of the phallic god Priapus (another talkative penis) takes over from the satiric speaker to tell us about two scary witches who have been practising magic in his garden, drawn by the lingering spirits of the dead (the garden, formerly a graveyard, belonged to Maecenas, as Horace's readers would have known). The moral checklist quoted earlier included witches among the dark fears a philosophically sound man ought to be able to laugh off, and this satire is indeed funny, albeit mostly at the expense of the speaker, who ultimately frightens the witches out of his garden, not with any glorious virile display, but with a fart of terror. Yet in the end it is the

6 On Horace's bid for freedom in *Epistles* 1, see further W. R. Johnson (1993).

discomfited witches who are presented to us as the proper targets of laughter, as they run off shedding false teeth and hair and magic accoutrements, a sight to provoke 'a lot of laughter and joking' (*cum magno risuque iocoque videres*, 50) in Priapus' imagined audience. Though Priapus is himself a mere hunk of wood (*truncus*, 1) shaped by a sculptor and given voice by the satirist, it is the witches whose bodies are here seen to be subject to disintegration, as if their comical 'truncation' could compensate for the satiric speaker's own.[7]

This aggressive but only semi-effectual Priapus could be the tutelary divinity of Horace's *Epodes*, published around the same time as the second book of *Satires*, soon after the victory of the young Caesar over Antony and Cleopatra near Actium in 31 BCE. Whereas the satirist pointedly overlooks the upheavals of the 30s, the epodist builds them into the framework of his book, which is anchored from the start in the uneasy ebb and flow of current events: the first poem shows Maecenas pledging allegiance to Caesar on the eve of Actium, an example Horace follows by pledging allegiance in turn to Maecenas (*Epodes* 1.1–14; though he readily concedes he may be reckoned 'unwarlike and not steady enough' for the battle to come, *imbellis ac firmus parum*, 16). It is in part this new engagement that brings women into new prominence. Relatively unthreatening targets, women give the epodist a way of managing the free-floating anxieties of civil war. The witches banished by Priapus in *Satires* 1.8 reappear in two epodes, exulting in purported triumph over their masculine victims – in the dramatic sketch of *Epodes* 5, a little boy; in the dialogue of *Epodes* 17, the final poem of the collection, Horace himself. These lurid fantasies of emasculating witchcraft are complemented by two remarkably obscene poems levelled against sexually rapacious women to whose challenge Horace has failed to rise; Horace retaliates by representing them as grotesque assemblages of disgusting body-parts, smells, and sounds, unredeemed by the trappings of elite status and discourse they parade (*Epodes* 8, 12). In poems such as *Epodes* 11 (a rueful confession of Horace's erotic susceptibility) and 15 (a half-hearted threat directed against an unfaithful mistress), the collection also offers the first samples of what we might recognise as Horatian 'love poetry': if Horace's hexameters represent a radically un-elegiac or even anti-elegiac world, his epodic couplets not only superficially mimic the elegiac couplet but admit something resembling 'elegiac' content.[8] *Epodes* 11 and 15 are

7 This paragraph resumes Henderson (1999) 186–91. On Horatian truncation, see further Gowers (1993b).

8 With Epode 11 Horace starts incorporating elegiac metrical material into his 'epodic' couplets; see A. Barchiesi (1994).

certainly engaging scenes from an erotic comedy. Yet when read alongside the obscene invectives of *Epodes* 8 and 12 and the witch-haunted dramas of *Epodes* 5 and 17, these light-hearted representations of erotic humiliation can also register as another, differently styled expression of masculinity under threat.

What helps hold together the miscellaneous material of the *Epodes* is their common stress on masculine impotence, variously manifested as Horace's unwarlike shakiness, his sexual inadequacy, his emotional inconstancy, and also as the uncontrollable civil violence deplored in poems such as *Epodes* 7 and 16.[9] Whereas what Horace gives us in the *Satires* is a world from which (but for the satires discussed above, and bit appearances elsewhere) women have already been effectively banished, what the *Epodes* dramatise is the ongoing labour of expulsion, which might guarantee, if it were ever completed, the *virtus* of the men remaining behind. The context of the civil war, in particular the battle of Actium, is critical: it is above all Cleopatra whose blend of sexual allure and political expertise energises the repulsion of Horatian obscenity.[10] Though he glances at both Sextus Pompey and Antony in *Epodes* 9, and intermittently launches energetic assaults against other (significantly non-elite) men (the upstart ex-slave of *Epodes* 4, the 'stinking Maevius' of *Epodes* 10), it is against the sexually unrestrained women in whose bed he unaccountably keeps finding himself that Horace unleashes his most violent invectives. Just as Cleopatra gave the young Caesar a way to reconfigure the final phase of Rome's prolonged civil strife as a war against an external foe, so the women of the *Epodes* allow Horace to 'go to war' without doing irreparable damage to the civic fabric.

This differentiation also informs Horace's *Odes*. Though the *Odes* do satirise, sometimes gently and sometimes quite harshly, the varied vices of men – the greed of the landowner, the discontent of the rich, the self-indulgence of the lover, the inconsistency of the philosopher-turned-soldier – Horace reserves his nastiest attacks for women. The famous ode on Cleopatra (*Odes* 1.37) overlooks Antony, focusing instead on the vices of the emasculating queen, mad with ambition and drunk on hope (a propagandistic caricature famously discarded by the end of this brilliant poem, however).[11] Women whose desires have outlived their attractiveness are likewise excoriated as out of touch with (social) reality (*Odes* 1.25, 3.15, 4.13; it is worth pointing out that there are no comparable poems to *pueri delicati*

9 See Fitzgerald (1988), with L. Watson (1995), the latter conveniently resuming recent scholarship in an attempt to save Horace's reputation.

10 Henderson (1999) 104.

11 On contemporary representations of Cleopatra, see Wyke (1992).

past their prime). The differential treatment of the 'girls and boys' (*virginibus puerisque*, *Odes* 3.1.4) to whom Horace addresses the ambitious sequence commonly known as the 'Roman Odes' is particularly striking. While Horace in *Odes* 3.5 condemns the surviving soldiers of Crassus' army (conquered by the Parthians roughly thirty years earlier) for abandoning their Roman upbringing and 'going native', when he looks around the contemporary Roman scene in *Odes* 3.6 what really catches his eye is the immoral behaviour of the girls, who go from bad (before marriage, when they cultivate Greek dancing and other pernicious arts of seduction) to worse (after marriage, when they begin their strings of adulterous liaisons). Though the same ode also castigates the complaisant husband (the young wife rises to join her lover 'not without the complicity of her husband', *non sine conscio / . . . marito*, 3.6.29–30; Horace has in view Augustus' programme of moral legislation, which would soon make such complaisance illegal), the grammatical and rhetorical focus remains on the misbehaving wife. Further, whereas *Odes* 3.2 elaborates a positive model of masculine, military *virtus* for the boys in the audience, there is no comparable model set before the eyes of the girls, unless we count the stern mother who bred up Roman soldiers in the rustic past, lamented as a long-lost ideal near the end of *Odes* 3.6.

That ideal has been recovered, or is at least within reach, by the time we reach the *Carmen Saeculare*, the hymn Horace wrote for performance by a chorus of boys and girls (the same, as it were, to whom he addressed the improving images of the Roman Odes) at Augustus' Secular Games of 17 BCE. The Games were designed to announce the new age inaugurated by the implementation of Augustus' programme of moral reform, which included laws criminalising adultery, penalising citizens who failed to marry and providing incentives to encourage the production of offspring.[12] The boys and girls in the chorus accordingly join in asking the appropriate divinities to watch over 'mothers' and to foster the decrees of the senatorial 'fathers' concerning 'the yoking of women and the marriage law productive of new offspring' (*Carmen Saeculare* 13–20). From the fertility of mothers the chorus passes to the fertility of the good earth, and thence to a comprehensive prayer for the good of the community: 'Gods, give upright morals to the teachable young, rest to the elders at ease, property and offspring and every adornment to the race of Romulus' (45–8). The girls might locate themselves among the 'teachable young', whom Horace, usurping or mediating the role of the gods, has already provided with 'upright morals' (insofar as the performers of the hymn 'are' the boys and girls morally (re-)formed by the Roman Odes, Horace is celebrating his own as well as Augustus'

12 A good overview is in Galinsky (1996) 128–40.

achievement). Yet the implicit message of the hymn, which moves centrifugally from domestic to imperial space (subsequent stanzas will take up the imperial victories of Augustus), is that the girls are to efface themselves behind or within the unmarked masculine community, to which (gods willing) they will one day contribute 'property and offspring'. And indeed by the end of the poem they have decorously vanished: we are left with the prayers of 'men' and 'boys' (*quindecim . . . virorum*, 70: the college of priests; *puerorum*, 71: the chorus).[13] Desire has naturally no place in such a hymn, unless it be the communal desire that finds expression in prayer.

Erotics

Viewed from the perspective of normative gender roles, desire figures chiefly as the enemy: it makes men soft. So Horace reproaches Lydia for 'destroying' Sybaris by turning him away from the toughening proto-military exercises in which he once excelled (*Odes* 1.8) and advises the elegist Valgius, trapped in the endless repetitions of his mournful couplets, to master his emotions and adopt a more virile poetics (*Odes* 2.9). The superior vantage-point Horace adopts in odes such as these helps confirm his own masculine poise. Knowledge is 'hard', ignorance 'soft'; the innocent or amorously blinded always find themselves at a disadvantage. Horace's love poetry is typically the poetry of experience, not innocence – of diagnosis, not bafflement. In *Epodes* 11 Horace lucidly describes his own propensity for serial infatuations, one erotic entanglement severed but simultaneously replaced by another, and in *Odes* 1.33 he analyses the plight of the elegist Albius (Tibullus?), forlorn at a rival's success, as one instance of our universal tendency to love the scornful and scorn the loving. One of Horace's most knowing and inflexibly virile pieces of erotic rhetoric is the sweet talk of *Odes* 1.23: three stanzas addressed to a girl who shuns his advances out of misguided fear, clinging to the mother and childhood she has (so he asserts) outgrown.[14] The innocent Chloe is as timid as the shuddery prey whose springtime jitters fill the middle stanza: 'for whether the approach of spring bristles in the shifting leaves, or green lizards push apart the brambles, [the fawn] trembles, heart and knees' (5–8). And Chloe's suitor proceeds to underscore the analogy in the act of disavowing it: 'yet I am not, like some fierce tiger or African lion, chasing you to break you' (9–10). In so far as this is a poem not just about gender but of desire, its erotic energy is generated first by the agitation of the

13 The commentaries offer various palliatives, without, however, banishing the rhetorical asymmetry.

14 On this poem see Ancona (1994) 70–4.

landscape, rustling with imminent sexual knowledge, and then by the final image of predation – delicate foreplay, as it were, followed by a fantasy of sexual assault.

But the ode to Chloe is exceptional. Elsewhere in Horace's poetry, desire finds its opening not in the virile certitude this poem deploys but in the discovery or creation of uncertainty. Even the famous 'Pyrrha' ode (*Odes* 1.5), a quintessential song of experience, the ironic musings of a survivor of the storm of love, opens not with knowledge but with questions: what perfume-soaked stripling is forcing his ardent attentions on you now, Pyrrha? Granted, the answer doesn't matter. Whoever it is, Horace knows his future: he will experience the same reversal, marvel at the same transformation, suffer the same shipwreck, as all Pyrrha's other lovers, Horace among them. And yet the very form of the question, along with the amused criticism of the young lover's naïvety that it conveys, opens up the possibility of desire. Is Horace perhaps proposing himself to Pyrrha as a candidate for a different kind of affair, an urbane affair of experience? The possibility glanced at in this ode is brilliantly dramatised in the dialogue of *Odes* 3.9, which culminates in the proposed reunion of the estranged speakers, against their better judgement and despite the supposedly superior attractions of their current partners (the authenticity of desire is thus guaranteed by its refusal to listen to reason). But my point is that it is the rhetorical instability of the Pyrrha ode, its indeterminate temperature (warm or cool?), that generates its erotic appeal.

Though Horace often deplores the unmooring of identity produced in those who succumb to desire, this unmooring is a crucial part of his poetics. Horace knows how to make the most of waywardness. Consider the final stanza of the ode to the forlorn Albius, ousted by a rival (*Odes* 1.33.13–16):

> ipsum me melior cum peteret Venus
> grata detinuit compede Myrtale
> libertina fretis acrior Hadriae
>   curvantis Calabros sinus.

I myself, when a better Venus was in pursuit, was held fast in welcome shackles by Myrtale, a freedwoman more violent than the Adriatic that makes the Calabrian coastline curve.

The self-inclusion is rhetorically effective: Horace's detached perspective on mismatched desire is the fruit of bitter experience. Yet the specificity of the final image, set as it is in a centrifugal syntax (Horace's sentence, though complete with *Myrtale*, spins outward from there), works to derail the poem from its instructive conclusion, sending Horace and his readers back inside the experience of desire. *Acrior*: Myrtale is 'more violent' (like a stormy sea) but also 'more passionate' (unlike her presumably sedate rival) and 'sharper, more pointed' (in contrast to the alluring curves the sea carves out of the coast). Though rejected by Horace's good judgement as inferior to a 'better Venus', Myrtale, even in recollection, seduces him into lingering once more over the enticing landscape of her oxymoronically angular curves.

One recurring figure for this seductive confusion of qualities is the girlish boy, smooth-cheeked and long-haired, marked out by his 'softness' (*mollitia*; cf. *Epodes* 11.4, 24) as a fit object of desire for men, yet himself on the verge of manhood, and potentially attractive to women as well. An ode contemplating a girl named Lalage (*Odes* 2.5), whom the hyper-masculine speaker objectifies as an unbroken heifer or unripe grape not yet ready for virile consumption, ends by swerving away toward less certain images of lovers past: fugitive Pholoe; Chloris with her white shoulder gleaming like the moon's reflection in the sea; and finally Gyges, a boy who, if set down in a group of girls, could confound judgement, with his flowing hair and sexually ambiguous (still beardless) face. A *discrimen obscurum*, Horace calls him: an uncertain distinction, a shadowy division. It is the suspenseful hesitation of the syntax and image that makes the reader stick, ensnared by the poem, as the speaker by his fugitive memories.[15]

A similar oscillation or chiaroscuro informs *Odes* 4.1, in which the now ageing poet sets out to persuade Venus to leave him alone (he is too old for love; his friend Maximus will be a more effective campaigner; etc.), only to be swept back by questions of desire (*Odes* 4.1.33–40):

sed cur heu, Ligurine, cur
manat rara meas lacrima per genas?
cur facunda parum decoro
inter verba cadit lingua silentio?
nocturnis ego somniis
iam captum teneo, iam volucrem sequor
te per gramina Martii
campi, te per aquas, dure, volubilis.

But why, alas, Ligurinus, why does the infrequent tear slide down my cheek? Why does my eloquent tongue trip midspeech into unseemly silence? In my dreams at night, now I've got you, and now I chase you flying across the grassy Field of Mars, chase you, hard heart, through the Tiber's fluent stream.

Unlike Gyges, more girl than boy, the Ligurinus of Horace's dreams is located in a Roman space, the Field of Mars, and is engaged in improving and approved Roman activities: he is toughening himself up, racing and

15 Cf. Sutherland (1997) 40.

swimming as the Sybaris of *Odes* 1.8 was wont to do, before Lydia whisked him away into the shadows of her bedroom. The same location sets off the glamour of Enipeus in *Odes* 3.7: 'Take care Enipeus doesn't find more favour with you than he should', Horace warns Asterie, and then adds, seductively, 'though no other skilled at handling a horse is as admired as he is on the grassy Campus, and no other swims as fast as he down the Tuscan river' (22–8). Who is out there looking on appreciatively or swooningly as the young men strip down to work out on the Field of Mars and to plunge their hardened bodies into the lambent Tiber? In *Odes* 1.8 Horace may be reproaching Lydia not only for softening up the virile Sybaris but also or chiefly for depriving his admiring fans of their accustomed pleasure.[16]

One critic has suggested that the perfected virility – the agility, strength, corporeal mastery – of Ligurinus and his kind represents the ultimate (narcissistic) object of desire for the Roman man.[17] Yet for Horace, the axis of desirability is less 'virile versus feminine' than 'young versus old'. The young desire, and are desirable. The old desire too, alas!, and what they desire, in Horace's poetry, is chiefly the fugitive image of their lost youth. This image gleams out of Horace's excuses to Maecenas in *Epistles* 1.7 (25–8): 'If you want me never to go away, you will have to give me back my unflagging stamina, the black curls framing my brow, my sweet eloquence and becoming laughter, and my tipsy laments at the flight of that reckless girl Cinara.' Horace links compliance with Maecenas' desire to a resumption of his lyric persona (*Odes* 1–3 had been published a few years earlier). Yet these lines paint Horace not only as a young lover but also as a youthful beloved, object as well as subject of desire, like the beautiful boys he elsewhere celebrates, suited for the embraces of men as well as women. It is as if Horace had taken fugitive Cinara's place, leaving Maecenas to sob alone in his disconsolate cups.

We are at liberty to domesticate the image by reading it allegorically, as a response to Maecenas' request for more lyric poetry (such a request is the implied background of the refusal Horace metes out to Maecenas in the first of his epistles). But we can also reverse the direction of our interpretation and take the image as an emblem of the erotic appeal of Horatian poetry. We are encouraged to do just that by the envoi to *Epistles* 1, Horace's wittiest exposition of his poetry's desirability. In this reluctant send-off, Horace personifies his book as an attractive boy foolishly intent on marketing his charms to the world at large. The book is at once a beloved slave, determined

16 As remarked by Leach (1994) 338, it may be these exercises that caught Lydia's eye in the first place.
17 Desbordes (1979) 80.

to run away from his doting master (as Horace has run away from his own 'master', Maecenas), and a surrogate son, a diminutive, portable 'Horace' whose peregrinations will perpetuate Horace's name and image, and disseminate his pleasurable products, in the world and into the future. Though the realist poet of the *Epistles* imagines the material book rapidly ageing, it is safe to say that the only body that has any hope of remaining perpetually fresh, young and desirable is the transmaterial 'body' of Horace's poetry.[18]

The channelling of desire into poetry also shapes Horace's last love-poem. In *Odes* 4.1, the ageing Horace insisted to Venus that 'no woman or boy' (*nec femina nec puer*, 29) could turn his head any more. If Ligurinus is the boy who immediately proves Horace wrong, the Phyllis of *Odes* 4.11 (which follows, not by chance, a second ode to 'cruel' Ligurinus) is the woman (*femina*, 34, a rare noun in Horace's poetry). Horace's household is getting ready for a party, the altar is wreathed in anticipation of the sacrifice of a lamb; Phyllis is summoned to attend. The party marks a great event in Horace's year, the Ides of April, the birthday of 'my Maecenas' (19), who occupies a place of honour in the poem's central stanza. It seems Horace has a bit of reluctance to overcome on Phyllis' part, since he goes on to insist that the young man she has her eye on is not for her – Telephus is already taken, held fast by a wealthy, sexy girlfriend (*puella*, 22). Think of the sad fate of Phaethon and Bellerophon, Horace advises, and don't overreach! What is left for Phyllis, it seems, is Horace. And what is left for Horace is Phyllis, or rather her answering, desirable voice (31–6):

> age iam, meorum
> finis amorum
>
> – non enim posthac alia calebo
> femina – condisce modos, amanda
> voce quos reddas; minuentur atrae
> carmine curae.

> Come now, last of my loves (I won't warm to another woman after this), learn the measures well so you can render them with your lovely voice; black cares will diminish with song.

This close reworks the final stanza of an earlier poem from *Odes* 4, in which Horace imagines a newlywed proudly recalling her role in performing Horace's own *Carmen Saeculare* (4.6.41–4):

18 The distinction between the book and the work it carries is crucial to Catullus 1, an important model for the Horatian envoi; see Fitzgerald (1995) 38–42.

> ego dis amicum,
> saeculo festas referente luces,
> reddidi carmen, docilis modorum
> vatis Horati.

When the age brought round the holiday, I rendered a song dear to the gods, having learned the measures of the bard Horace.

The points of contact are very numerous,[19] and they incline me to propose that Horace is not just placing himself again in the role of lyric instructor[20] but revisiting, from a different angle, the Secular Games, with the anniversary of Maecenas' birth in place of the civic *saeculum*, and a modest blood sacrifice (not a normal component of Horatian drinking-parties) in place of the splendid offerings that punctuated the Augustan ritual. Horace's poems usually downplay the contributions of slave labour to aristocratic leisure, but this poem has its own reasons for reversing that decorous policy.[21] The slave-'girls mixed with boys' (*mixtae pueris puellae*, 10; *puellae* in the sense of 'slave-girls' is a notable anomaly) who race about getting the house ready for the party reconfigure the elite boys and girls who formed the double (not mixed) chorus that performed the *Carmen Saeculare*. It is as if the whole stable hierarchical world envisioned and wishfully prolonged by the communal hymn were darkening and shifting before our eyes.

Whereas the *Carmen Saeculare* rigorously demarcates gender roles, this ode, as the 'mixing' of boys and girls emblematically suggests, repeatedly confounds them. The slight dislocation involved in inviting Phyllis to a party honouring Maecenas (why isn't the poem addressed to Maecenas, as several earlier Horatian invitations are?) invites us to ponder the relation of the 'last' of Horace's 'loves' and the patron he elsewhere addresses as his poetic alpha and omega (*Prima dicte mihi, summa dicende Camena*, *Epistles* 1.1.1). Some suspect that Horace's advice to Phyllis serves as a tactful reminder to a purportedly overreaching Maecenas, who may have permanently offended Augustus some time in the period preceding *Odes* 4 – hence, we are told, the absence of any poem dedicated directly to Horace's patron.[22] Yet if Maecenas

19 *Amicum* ~ *amanda*, *reddidi* ~ *reddas*, *carmen* ~ *carmine*, *docilis* ~ *condisce*, *modorum* ~ *modos*; following the *Carmen Saeculare*, both odes adopt the Sapphic stanza.

20 So Quinn (1980) ad loc.

21 Only in the second book of *Satires*, where he has particular reasons for advertising his elite status, does Horace give us a comparable impression of the slaves who crowded his house. The closest parallel within the *Odes* (and it is not very close) is *Odes* 1.19, where plural *pueri* tote the necessary equipment for Horace's sacrifice to Venus (13–15).

22 O. Murray in Rudd (1993b) 103.

did fall from favour, it would be more in Horace's manner to rewrite this history than to rehearse it. Far from aping Augustus and excluding Maecenas from the party, Horace here represents *himself* as the one who has fallen from favour: his beloved Maecenas is, it seems, otherwise engaged. This would align Maecenas with Phyllis' Telephus, and Horace with Phyllis, as two disappointed lovers who may find solace in each other. Whereas Ligurinus reflects a younger self, Phyllis (a *femina*, not a *puella*) looks more like the mature Horace of the present.[23] The moment of identification across the gender divide – untinged, for once, by anxiety or hostility – is peculiarly moving. The 'lovely voice' Phyllis is called upon to supply is also the voice with which Horace's readers reanimate his poetry, thereby diminishing their own black cares.

FURTHER READING

There is a wide-ranging account of Roman and Horatian sexual *mores* and humour in Richlin (1992). Henderson (1999) provides seminal discussions of gender issues in the *Epodes* (chapter 4) and *Satires* (chapter 7) as well as suggestive comments on the gender dynamics of *Odes* 3.22 (chapter 5). Gender is intermittently foregrounded by Oliensis (1998) (especially chapters 2 and 5). On gender roles in the *Odes*, see Leach (1994) (focusing on *Odes* 1.8) and (in French) Desbordes (1979) (a systematic overview tethered to *Odes* 3.12). On Horace's poetic 'bisexuality', see Woodman (2002).

There are several useful overviews of 'Horace as a love-poet', most recently Arkins (1993) (partly resuming but not superseding the sympathetic accounts of Reckford (1959), Boyle (1973), and Lyne (1980)). Putnam (1986) illuminates the workings of desire across *Odes* 4. Current studies of individual love-poems typically include some consideration of gender roles (especially the distribution of power between lover and beloved); see, e.g., T. S. Johnson (2003); Sutherland (1997). Ancona (1994), the only book-length study of Horatian desire, offers an intelligent critique of the then scholarly status quo as well as thoughtful readings of a series of odes, focusing on the interplay of desire and temporality. On Horatian homoerotics, see Oliensis (1997). On the erotics of Horatian poetic form, see Lowrie (1997) chapter 7 (esp. 304–14); Oliensis (2002).

23 And as a poet, Horace identifies with Sappho as well as with Alcaeus: Ancona (2002); Woodman (2002).

17

STEPHEN HARRISON

Town and country

The tension and interplay between town and country form a key theme in Horace's poetry, and have significant philosophical and ideological implications. This chapter seeks to explore this important poetic material and its presentation in the different genres and periods of Horace's output.

A divided existence?

The theme of town and country appears in the first programmatic poem of Horace's first poetry book, *Satires* I (35 BC) – *Satires* 1.1.8–9:

> agricolam laudat iuris legumque peritus,
> sub galli cantum consultor ubi ostia pulsat;
> ille, datis vadibus qui rure extractus in urbem est,
> solos felicis viventis clamat in urbe.

> The expert in law and statute praises the farmer, when a client knocks on his door at cock-crow; the farmer, dragged from country to city on court surety, cries that only those who live in the city are happy.

This split between urban and rural life, here couched in the ironic context of criticising *mempsimoiria*, discontent with one's own lot, and applied to lifestyles paradigmatic of the two environments, is a major Horatian topic. Like most Romans of the first century BC, Horace's existence, both practical and poetical, oscillated between *rus* and *urbs*: the tension between his natural inclination for the quiet life in the country, with its peaceful space for reading, writing and thinking, and the bustle of Rome, with its round of social and other duties, is often brought out in his work. In the first book of *Satires* Horace himself is firmly located in Rome, perhaps something of a necessity for a satirist seeking to attack the excesses of his own society, but in the second we find him dividing his time between Rome and the Sabine estate, clearly presented to him by Maecenas in the gap between *Satires* I and

Satires 2 (35–30 BC; the estate is not alluded to in *Satires* 1).[1] In 2.6, which famously begins with warm praise of the Sabine estate (an indirect but real thanks to Maecenas), we find the contrast of town and country life carefully articulated, first through Horace's own movement from the (non-satiric) peace of one to the (satire-engendering) maelstrom of the other (2.6.16–26):

> ergo ubi me in montes et in arcem ex urbe removi,
> quid prius inlustrem saturis musaque pedestri?
> nec mala me ambitio perdit nec plumbeus auster
> autumnusque gravis, Libitinae quaestus acerbae.
> Matutine pater, seu Iane libentius audis,
> unde homines operum primos vitaeque labores
> instituunt – sic dis placitum – tu carminis esto
> principium. Romae sponsorem me rapis: 'eia,
> ne prior officio quisquam respondeat, urge.'
> sive aquilo radit terras seu bruma nivalem
> interiore diem gyro trahit, ire necesse est.

So when I have moved myself away from the city to the hills and to my citadel, what should I first illuminate with my satires and my pedestrian muse? [For there] no wicked ambition destroys me, or the leaden south wind, or the oppressive autumn, all gain for Libitina the goddess of bitter mourning. Father Matutinus, or (if you prefer it) Janus, from whom men draw the earliest labours of work and life, you be the beginning of my song. You rush me off to Rome to give surety: 'Hey, get on with it, in case anyone else gets in first with a dutiful response.' Whether the north wind is scraping the earth or winter is dragging the snowy day in a narrower circle, I have to go.

Here the need to get on with (unattractive) urban business (note the reappearance of law) is contrasted with the sage-like contemplation of country life. The philosophical aspect of country life (for its Epicurean colour see below) is clear in the conversation at Horace's country dinner-table with his unpretentious country friends, not idle city chit-chat but discussion of the real moral issues of life (2.6.70–6); and of course it is as part of that discussion that the famous fable of the town mouse and country mouse emerges (2.6.79–116).

In this celebrated story the town mouse invites the country mouse to visit in return for earlier hospitality, and a contrast is made between the rough but carefree life of the country and the sybaritic but perilous existence of the town: the town mouse cannot tolerate the rough diet of the country, but the gourmet feast of the mice in the town is interrupted by terrifying domestic dogs, and the country mouse returns thankfully to his unsophisticated but

1 See Nisbet, chapter 1 above.

peaceful rural life. The fable has sometimes been taken as an unalloyed condemnation of the life of the town in favour of that of the country, but this is too schematic a view: the dangerous luxury of the city has at least some attractions for Horace, as his slave Davus says in the next poem, which presents Horace with a number of home truths (2.7.28–32):

> Romae rus optas; absentem rusticus urbem
> tollis ad astra levis. si nusquam es forte vocatus
> ad cenam, laudas securum holus ac, velut usquam 30
> vinctus eas, ita te felicem dicis amasque,
> quod nusquam tibi sit potandum.

At Rome you long for the country; in the country you praise the absent city to the stars in your fickleness. If it happens that no-one has invited you to dinner, you commend your vegetables free from care, and, as if you would have to be tied up to go anywhere, you congratulate yourself and feel good that you don't have to go out drinking.

Just so Horace attends the very different urban dinner of the pretentious gourmet Nasidienus in *Satires* 2.8, though he and the other guests ultimately leave in indignation.

This split personality is well brought out in the fable of *Satires* 2.6. There the trite hedonistic exhortations of the town mouse have clear amusing traces of the sympotic, *carpe diem* Horace of the *Odes*, at least some of which were written in the 30s[2] – cf. 2.6.93–7:

> carpe viam, mihi crede, comes, terrestria quando
> mortalis animas vivunt sortita neque ulla est
> aut magno aut parvo leti fuga: quo, bone, circa,
> dum licet, in rebus iucundis vive beatus,
> vive memor, quam sis aevi brevis.

Hit the road, comrade, believe me, since earthly creatures have mortal souls by lot and there is no escape for death for either small or great: so, my good fellow, while you can, live happy in pleasant circumstances, and live mindful of how brief your life is.

Horace, perhaps, is both the town mouse and the country mouse.

In the *Epodes* of 30 BC Horace's own country life is again prominent, though once more not without some irony and complexity. In *Epode* 1 the moderate size of Horace's Sabine estate (referred to delicately and implicitly) is contrasted with the ambition to possess vast land-holdings as an emblem

2 See Nisbet, chapter 1 above.

of self-restraint and self-sufficiency (see further below), but it is in *Epode* 2 that we find the most overt praise of rural life (2.1–8):

> Beatus ille qui procul negotiis,
> ut prisca gens mortalium,
> paterna rura bubus exercet suis
> solutus omni faenore
> neque excitatur classico miles truci
> neque horret iratum mare
> forumque vitat et superba civium
> potentiorum limina . . .

Happy he who, far from business, like the ancient race of mortals, works his ancestral estate with his own oxen freed of all debt interest, and is not aroused as a soldier by the fierce trumpet and does not shudder at the sea's rage, and avoids the forum and the proud thresholds of greater citizens.

Following directly on Horace's just-mentioned moralising praise of the *Sabinum* at the end of *Epode* 1, this seems to strike the same note of uncomplicated commendation of modest rural life; but of course the poem ends with a famous twist which reveals that these lines are spoken not by the poet but by Alfius, a rapacious money-lender whose dreams of country retirement are unrealistic and even hypocritical (1.67–70). This satirises Alfius' greed, but also takes the edge off his rapturous praise of country life, with an amused glance at the *Georgics* and *Eclogues* of Virgil;[3] this in turn raises the question of whether the Horace who, in the *Epodes*, is elsewhere closely bound to the city of Rome is serious about his rustic idyll. Of the remaining *Epodes*, none has an explicitly rural setting (*Epode* 13 is a possible exception); *Epode* 16 uses a dark version of the moralising contrast of town and country, fearing that the great city of Rome will destroy itself and become a rural home for beasts again (16.10), and offering the ironic solution of a rustic paradise in the Isles of the Blest, the miraculous pastoral features of which again ironise elements from Virgil's *Eclogues*.[4] In the sometimes fragile world of the *Epodes*, the security of the rural idyll is rarely straightforward.

Rustic and urban ideology

We have already considered some uses of the town-and-country contrast as a moral emblem. As I have argued elsewhere,[5] Roman writers often spoke of

3 On these echoes see L. Watson (2003) ad loc.

4 See again L. Watson (2003) ad loc.

5 See S. J. Harrison (2005a).

the present as corrupt, and of Rome's past as a prelapsarian golden age; the inhabitants of the imperial metropolis looked back with some nostalgia to the supposedly pristine morals and lifestyle of the early Republic, and Rome's imagined beginnings as a primitively virtuous rustic community. This attitude sometimes emerges in Horace, for example in the contrast of decadent current Romans with their peasant ancestors at *Odes* 3.6.33–48:

> Non his iuuentus orta parentibus
> infecit aequor sanguine Punico
> Pyrrhumque et ingentem cecidit
> Antiochum Hannibalemque dirum;
>
> sed rusticorum mascula militum
> proles, Sabellis docta ligonibus
> uersare glaebas et seuerae
> matris ad arbitrium recisos
>
> portare fustis, sol ubi montium
> mutaret umbras et iuga demeret
> bobus fatigatis, amicum
> tempus agens abeunte curru.
>
> damnosa quid non inminuit dies?
> aetas parentum, peior auis, tulit
> nos nequiores, mox daturos
> progeniem uitiosiorem.

> Not such were the parents of the army which stained the sea with Punic blood, and laid low Pyrrhus, great Antiochus and the accursed Hannibal; but they were the manly issue of peasant soldiers, well versed in turning the soil with Sabine mattocks and carrying sticks cut to the will of a severe mother, when the sun changed the shadows cast by the mountains and unharnessed the yokes from tired oxen, bringing on the kindly time of rest with its departing chariot. What has time which brings only loss not diminished? The age of our parents, worse than our grandparents, brought forth us, more wicked, set in due course to spawn an even more vicious stock.

Here Horace strikes a traditional Roman note in the sometimes untypical Roman Odes; but the moral dimension of the country is more commonly articulated in Horace's work within the frame of Hellenistic philosophy.

Both Epicureanism and Stoicism, the chief philosophies of first-century-BC Rome, presented significant doctrines related to nature: Stoics famously claimed to live 'in accordance with nature' (Cicero *Off.* 3.13), that is, according to virtue and the natural laws of reason, while Epicureans saw in a proper understanding of nature and of the material universe the key to moral certitude and felicity, and commended the quiet life of withdrawal and contemplation (all well exemplified in Lucretius' *De Rerum Natura*).[6] In *Epistles* 1.10, in a poem to the Stoic town-lover Fuscus, urging him to come to the country, Horace amusingly argues for the rural life as the Stoic ideal (*Epistle* 1.10.12–14):

> viuere naturae si conuenienter oportet,
> ponendaeque domo quaerenda est area primum,
> nouistine locum potiorem rure beato?

If [i.e. as you Stoics claim] it is right to live in accordance with nature, and a site for locating a house is the first thing to seek, do you know a place preferable to the happy country?

Here Horace is urging on the Stoic Fuscus the Epicurean life of country retirement, arguing that it is the truly 'natural' life, amusingly perverting the normal view that the Stoic life should be one of political action (alluded to at *Epistle* 1.1.16); this is one of several allusions to Stoic doctrine in the poem.

Epicureanism is of course Horace's natural mode (see Moles, chapter 12 above), and in the *Epistles* we find several allusions to Epicurus' doctrine of *lathe biosas*, 'live your life without attracting notice': e.g. 1.17.10 *nec vixit male qui natus moriensque fefellit*, 'and he who has escaped notice in being born and dying has not lived badly', or 1.18.103, commending the *secretum iter et fallentis semita vitae*, 'the concealed journey and the path to a life which escapes notice'. The rural links of this Epicurean precept, implicit in these two references, are openly deployed in the Epistle to Tibullus (1.4.1–7):[7]

> Albi, nostrorum sermonum candide iudex,
> quid nunc te dicam facere in regione Pedana?
> scribere quod Cassi Parmensis opuscula uincat,
> an tacitum siluas inter reptare salubris,
> curantem quicquid dignum sapiente bonoque est?
> non tu corpus eras sine pectore; di tibi formam,
> di tibi diuitias dederunt artemque fruendi.

Albius, candid judge of my *sermones*, what should I say you are doing now in the district of Pedum? Writing something to outdo the works of Cassius of Parma, or creeping silently through the healthy woods, concerned about all

6 For the details see Long and Sedley (1987) I. 125–39 and I. 423–9.

7 For Tibullus as the 'Albius' addressed here, see e.g. Nisbet and Hubbard (1970) 368. (Mayer (1994) 133 is perhaps unnecessarily sceptical given that an elegist is involved.)

> that is worthy of a wise and good man? You were never a body without a heart; the gods have given you beauty, riches and the skill to enjoy them.

Though Tibullus is greeted first as a man of literature, a critic and poet in the Callimachean mould,[8] Horace turns swiftly to his philosophical cogitations in the quiet of the country, and the stress on the enjoyment of pleasures is plainly Epicurean. Here as often in the *Epistles* the epistolary situation feeds naturally into the contrast of town and country. Horace is often in Rome, and writing to correspondents in the country (1.4, 1.14) or (more often) vice versa (1.2, 1.7, 1.10, 1.16): this sets up the virtues of the country as a common topic, and in 1.14 we find a whole poem, addressed to Horace's farm supervisor, in which (as in 1.10) Horace's desire for the country and his addressee's desire for the city are set against each other. The theme is established early on (1.14.10): *rure ego viventem, tu dicis in urbe beatum*, 'I say that he who lives in the country is happy; you, he who lives in the city', and the poem takes a reasonably sympathetic view of the supervisor's longing for city delights amid rural hardships, but it is clear that the rural life is to be preferred for men of culture and distinction like the poet.

The opposition of the city as place of imposed duty and attendance, and the country as place of free, leisured life, is brought out especially well in the Epistle to Maecenas (1.7). Here the poet paradoxically deploys Maecenas' gift to him of rural property and independence as an argument for not coming this time for irksome and unhealthy urban attendance in the summer; Maecenas has given him willingly the freedom to refuse requests from him, which makes the gift even more valuable. As in *Satires* 2.6, the principle is illustrated by an apt story: Philippus' casual and capricious encouragement of and help to the urban waster Mena in the purchase of a Sabine estate predictably ends in disaster.[9] This is a negative parable for the relationship of Horace and Maecenas: Maecenas, Horace implies, is a more generous and discriminating patron, giving his friend an appropriate gift without strings or obligations, which enables him to achieve the true independence which Mena can never attain from Philippus, an independence which does honour to Maecenas even when Horace refuses patronal requests to return to Rome. Thus the theme of town and country is used to illustrate the moral dignity of the potentially money-oriented relationship between Horace and Maecenas, and to illustrate the true meaning of freedom and friendship.[10]

8 *Opuscula* suggests elegant small-scale works.
9 See Horsfall (1993) for a full treatment of the poem.
10 On Horace's capacity to obscure his economic relations with Maecenas see Bowditch (2001).

The pleasures of town and country

The presentation of the city as the locus of cares, anxiety and danger, and of the country as the place of pleasure, is a dichotomy not always maintained in the works of Horace. Much of the sympotic colour of the *Odes* is urban, and the majority of the pleasurable celebrations there described seem to take place in Rome.[11] Symposia in the country are not unknown, however, and here again we see the country represented as the antidote to urban excitement and stress in a strikingly modern mode. In *Odes* 3.8, for example, Maecenas is invited to spend the Matronalia festival with Horace, it seems in the country, since Horace intends to sacrifice a goat (3.8.6–7), which will provide relief from political concerns (3.8.13–17):

> sume, Maecenas, cyathos amici
> sospitis centum et uigilis lucernas
> perfer in lucem; procul omnis esto
> clamor et ira.
>
> mitte ciuilis super urbe curas.

Take a hundred ladles of wine to celebrate your friend's safety and stretch the wakeful lamps to the dawn; let all shouting and passion be far away. Leave aside your political cares for the city.

Cares for the city's political situation are to be left behind in the city itself, along with urban noise and contention; here again we have the idea of Epicurean rural tranquillity, fittingly wrapped up with sympotic pleasure and the celebration of friendship, further key Epicurean ideas for Horace.

In *Odes* 3.29 Maecenas is again invited to leave behind his urban concerns in Rome and visit Horace in the Sabine country for a symposium (3.29.1–12):

> Tyrrhena regum progenies, tibi
> non ante uerso lene merum cado
> cum flore, Maecenas, rosarum et
> pressa tuis balanus capillis
>
> iamdudum apud me est: eripe te morae
> nec semper udum Tibur et Aefulae
> decliue contempleris aruum et
> Telegoni iuga parricidae.
>
> fastidiosam desere copiam et
> molem propinquam nubibus arduis,
> omitte mirari beatae
> fumum et opes strepitumque Romae.

11 See Davis, chapter 15 above.

> Etruscan descendant of kings, for you I have had for some time at my house mellow wine from a cask as yet untapped, Maecenas, with flower of roses and balsam to be pressed over your hair: tear yourself from delay, and don't always just look at damp Tibur and the sloping territory of Aefula and the ridges founded by Telegonus the parricide. Leave behind the plenty which leads to disgust and your mass of house neighbouring the clouds on high, and stop being stupefied by the smoke, wealth and noise of rich Rome.

Here once again the simple and moderate delights of a country retreat are offered as an antidote to the excesses of the city in materialism, noise and stress. Later on in the poem we find that again Maecenas is specifically invited to lay aside or at least moderate his political concerns for Rome and the troubles on its distant borders amid the more measured tempo of country life (3.8.17–48): once more, then, the tranquillity of the country is set against both the literal turmoil of the city and the metaphorical turmoil of high politics.

The relationship between city, country and symposium can be framed in different ways in the *Odes*. In *Odes* 1.9, for example, the magnificent rural sight of Soracte from what seems to be a Sabine symposium[12] stimulates the poet to reflections shared with his young wine-pourer, who, like the farm supervisor of *Epistles* 1.14, is eager for the pleasures of the city his master has left behind. The snows on the mountain famously remind the poet of mortality and lead to the inevitable *carpe diem*, here transferred to the young wine-pourer (1.9.13–24):

> Quid sit futurum cras, fuge quaerere, et
> quem fors dierum cumque dabit, lucro
> adpone nec dulcis amores
> sperne, puer, neque tu choreas,
>
> donec uirenti canities abest
> morosa. Nunc et Campus et areae
> lenesque sub noctem susurri
> composita repetantur hora,
>
> nunc et latentis proditor intumo
> gratus puellae risus ab angulo
> pignusque dereptum lacertis
> aut digito male pertinaci.

12 Though Soracte is arguably visible from the Ianiculum (Nisbet and Hubbard (1970) 116), the point of its naming here is surely to locate the poem outside the city and in the Sabine country; see D. West (1995) 41.

> Cease to seek to know what will be tomorrow, and put in the plus column whatever the fortune of days brings, and, my boy, do not spurn sweet love-affairs or dancing, for as long as morose old age stays away from your green vigour. Now let the Campus and the squares and gentle whispers at night at the appointed hour be your goal, now the pleasant laughter from the inmost corner that betrays a hidden girl, and the love-pledge snatched from the arm or the finger of unconvincing resistance.

Here the city is contrasted as the locus for the youthful games of love with the rural Soracte: the *canities*, white/grey hair, which will come to the boy in time (17) is already there for the snow-topped mountain and (by implication) for the ageing poet, for whom rural contemplation has now replaced urban adventure.[13]

Rural inspiration

We have already seen how the country is established in Horace's mature work as the place for writing and contemplation. In the *Odes*, with their lyric interest in the figure of the poet and the nature of his inspiration, we find the country increasingly presented as the starting-point for poetry, as urban culture had been for the attacks of the *Satires* and the *Epodes*. In the very first ode, Horace's claim to special poetic status is joined with a rural landscape of inspiration (1.1.29–32):

> Me doctarum hederae praemia frontium
> dis miscent superis, me gelidum nemus
> Nympharumque leues cum Satyris chori
> secernunt populo . . .

> The ivy-wreath, the prize of poetic brows, causes me to mix with the gods above, and I am separated by the cool grove and the light-moving bands of Nymphs with Satyrs from the common people.

Again, in the address of the Muse Calliope in *Odes* 3.4, country and non-Roman locations are invoked as associated with the Muses and therefore with Horace's poetic impetus (3.4.21–4):

> Vester, Camenae, uester in arduos
> tollor Sabinos, seu mihi frigidum
> Praeneste seu Tibur supinum
> seu liquidae placuere Baiae

13 On 1.9 see the interesting treatment by Edmunds (1992).

It is as yours, Muses, as yours that I am lifted up into the lofty Sabines, whether cool Praeneste is my pleasure, or spread-eagled Tibur, or clear-watered Baiae.

Likewise, it is in a rural location that Horace claims to have seen Bacchus and heard him singing as an inspiration for his own poetry (2.19.1–4):

Bacchum in remotis carmina rupibus
uidi docentem, credite posteri,
Nymphasque discentis et auris
capripedum Satyrorum acutas.

I have seen Bacchus teaching songs among distant crags (believe me, you who come after), and the Nymphs learning them, and the sharp ears of the goat-footed satyrs.

But rural inspiration can be enlisted for particular purposes in the Odes. In *Odes* 3.25, the country and its capacity to engender poetic novelty are interestingly joined with a strongly Roman theme, the praise of Augustus (3.25.1–8):

Quo me, Bacche, rapis tui
plenum? Quae nemora aut quos agor in specus
uelox mente noua? Quibus
antris egregii Caesaris audiar
aeternum meditans decus
stellis inserere et consilio Iouis?
Dicam insigne, recens, adhuc
indictum ore alio.

Where are you taking me off to, Bacchus, full of you? What groves, what caves am I being driven to, moving swiftly in this strange state of mind? In what grottos shall I be heard practising to place the eternal glory of great Caesar among the constellations and the council of Jupiter? I shall tell of something outstanding, fresh, something unspoken yet by any mouth.

The wild landscape of Bacchic inspiration (perhaps influenced by Lucretius)[14] is here harnessed to civic purposes, and, though Augustus here is not specifically an urban figure, the conjunction of culture and nature is a striking effect, showing how the sometimes private poetic landscape can be enlisted for more nationalistic and public poetry.

More common, however, is the presentation of the country as a place of moderation and restraint which matches the moderation and restraint of the more Callimachean side of Horatian poetics.[15] At the close of the first

14 See Nisbet and Rudd (2004) 305.
15 On Horace and Callimachus see Thomas, chapter 4 above.

Roman Ode (3.1) we find Horace looking to his Sabine estate as a model for moderation which covers poetic as well as material ambition (3.1.45–8):

> cur inuidendis postibus et nouo
> sublime ritu moliar atrium?
> cur ualle permutem Sabina
> diuitias operosiores?

> Why should I laboriously build a hall with doorposts to envy and with lofty ceiling in the latest style? Why should I exchange my Sabine valley for riches which are more burdensome?

Here the Sabine estate is clearly presented as a model for material and moral restraint in response to general greed and transgression, but there is also a sense in which the moderate lifestyle it represents reflects Horace's moderation of poetry in the Roman Odes, despite their weighty and dignified subject-matter.

The same idea is pursued in another lyric closure at *Odes* 2.16.33–40, where Horace's poetic poverty is contrasted with the wealth of the great landowner Grosphus:

> Te greges centum Siculaeque circum
> mugiunt uaccae, tibi tollit hinnitum
> apta quadrigis equa, te bis Afro
> murice tinctae
> uestiunt lanae; mihi parua rura et
> spiritum Graiae tenuem Camenae
> Parca non mendax dedit et malignum
> spernere uolgus.

> Around you low a hundred herds of Sicilian cattle, for you the mare ready for the chariot sends up its whinny, you are dressed in wools twice dipped in African purple; to me a true Fate has granted small lands, and the modest breath of a Greek Muse, and to be able to reject the hostile crowd.

Here the exclusivism of the true poet, set apart from the crowd (see 1.1.32 above) is specifically joined with limited wealth: restrained material consumption, as often in Horace, is matched by restrained and refined Callimachean poetry, measured by art and not by size.

Thus the theme of the contrast between town and country can be seen as a frequent and central concern in the poetry of Horace. Through this dichotomy a number of poetic themes are focused: the poet's own physical interchange and mental dilemma between the two locations and the Epicurean character of the country; their functions as locations of different types of pleasure and the role of the country as the locus of real relaxation;

and the role of the country as an inspiration for poetry and of the Sabine estate as a symbol for poetic and material moderation.

FURTHER READING

Troxler-Keller (1964) provides the basic account of Horace's poetic treatment of landscape; on the poetic symbolism of the countryside in Horace (especially the Sabine estate and the *fons Bandusiae*) see E. A. Schmidt (2002a) 117–53, and for the ode on Soracte (1.9) see Edmunds (1992); for briefer accounts see G. Williams (1968) 671–5 and La Penna (1993) 129–35. On Horace, Lucretius and the Epicurean aspect of the country, Ferri (1993) 81–131 is especially helpful; on the 'pastoral impulse' at Rome in the first century BCE and the interest of an urbanised culture in nature, see Leach (1974) 51–70; for the self-construction of the Romans as a peasant race softened by urban luxury, see S. J. Harrison (2005a), and on the contrast of town and country in Roman satire (including *Satires* 2.6) see S. H. Braund (1989).

18

RICHARD RUTHERFORD

Poetics and literary criticism

Study of Horace as a critic of literature normally and justifiably focuses on the *Ars Poetica* and on the two 'literary' epistles of Book 2, to Augustus and Florus; sometimes the three poems in which Horace discusses the satiric genre are also brought into the picture (*Satires* 1.4, 1.10, 2.1).[1] But the poet's comments on other writers and on literature in general are not confined to these works; nor is the subject-matter of those poems restricted to literature. In this chapter I try to present a broader view, and consider a number of recurring preoccupations which can be traced in Horace's writings from first to last.

We need be in no doubt that Horace was familiar with the terminology and conceptual framework of ancient literary criticism.[2] He described himself as learning the perils of anger from studying the *Iliad* at Rome (that is, in his schooldays: *Epistles* 2.2.41–2); elsewhere he shows full awareness of the moralising readings of both Homer's poems (*Epistles* 1.2).[3] His splendid characterisation of Pindar runs through several of the categories into which that poet's work was divided in the Alexandrian edition. He aspires to join the ranks of the lyric bards (alluding to the 'canon' of Greek *lyrici* established by Hellenistic editors); he draws on Aristotle's *Rhetoric* for his characterisation of the different age-types, and also uses ideas derived (perhaps at some remove) from the *Poetics*; he alludes to Aristarchus as the model of the judicious critic.[4] As we might expect from so bold a metrical innovator, he is

I am grateful to the editor, and to Dr D. C. Innes, for comments on a draft of this essay.

1 See e.g. Grube (1965) 231–55; more fully Brink (1963) 153–209. See also Innes (1989).

2 On near-contemporary figures, and the general intellectual background, see esp. Rawson (1985), chapters 4, 8, 18. Since her survey much has been published on Philodemus in particular: see esp. Obbink (1995) (index s.v. Horace); Armstrong et al. (2004).

3 On Stoic readings of Homer see Long (1992). For further examples of epic or tragedy used as the springboard for moralising lessons see *Satires* 2.3.128–41, 187–223, *Epistles* 2.16.73–9, 18.41–5.

4 *Odes* 4.2.1ff., 1.1.35, *Ars* 156–74 (cf. Aristotle *Rhetoric* 2.1389b–90b); 450.

familiar with discussions of metrical usage, and seems to exploit Hellenistic theories about the relation of Lesbian lyric to iambic.[5] Like Virgil, he is evidently acquainted with the commentary tradition which underlies our scholia on Greek authors, especially Homer: thus *duplicis* in *Odes* 1.6.7 presumably reflects his choice of one interpretation of the disputed adjective *polutropos* in the proem of the *Odyssey*;[6] and the cynical treatment of Penelope in *Satires* 2.5 probably springs from Hellenistic controversy over her attitude to the suitors (cf. Seneca *Letters* 88.8). Similarly, the reference in one passage to *mascula Sappho* clearly hints at ancient discussion of her sexual orientation.[7] Yet his attitude to scholarly debate, like that of many poets, can be mocking and dismissive. Who first composed elegy among the Greeks is a vexed question: 'the schoolmasters are in dispute, and the case is still under litigation' (*Ars Poetica* 78). Sharper still is the sardonic use of the Grecism *critici* at *Epistles* 2.1.50–1 (Ennius is a sage and valiant and a second Homer, 'so the *cognoscenti* declare').[8] Although Horace is well informed about critical discourse, he often treats the experts' debates lightheartedly or satirically. Even those themes which are most fully developed in his work – such as the generic hierarchy, the value of Greek models or the importance and dangers of imitation – are creatively adapted to his own context and purposes.

Besides learning from books, Horace evidently valued the interaction and exchange of ideas with contemporaries. Tibullus is thanked for his frank criticism of Horace's *sermones* (*Epistles* 1.4.1); a well-known passage at the end of the first book of *Satires* lists a further dozen or so names of readers (poets among them) whose judgement Horace esteems (candour is also ascribed to one of these, Furnius). At the end of the *Ars Poetica* tribute is paid to another friend, Quintilius, who knew how to give advice free of flattery (438–44). In the same poem we see Horace offering himself as a potential reader to the younger Piso (385ff.). Elsewhere he performs at a distance something not far from that role for Florus and the other young poets in Tiberius' entourage (*Epistles* 1.3). Although Horace has many harsh things to say about recitations, he admits that he does take part in them, though only among friends and under pressure (*Satires* 1.4.73); we can guess that, as in the Catullan circle, partial drafts or particular poems first found receptive ears in that context. The ode to Pollio is clearly a reaction to recitations from the great man's *History* (*Odes* 2.1: note 18 *auris*, 21 *audire*). This context may also

5 E.g. Fraenkel (1957) 346–7. 6 Pfeiffer (1968) 4, 37.
7 *Epistles* 1.19.28; cf. Sappho T1, 2, 19, 20, 22 and 49 Campbell.
8 Cf. Feeney (2002) 178.

explain some of the links that have been seen between the poetry of Horace and his contemporaries (esp. *Odes* 3.3, which echoes themes important in the unpublished *Aeneid*).[9]

So much by way of background. In what follows I consider four themes which seem central to Horace's thinking about literature: genre-consciousness, the parallel of life and art, perfectionism, and the poet's ethical and social responsibilities. The topics are related and recur in varying combinations; they surface in different ways in different works. Generic context and addressee make a difference: Horace speaks more technically and indulges in more polemic against individuals in the hexameter poetry than in the *Odes*, and the manner he adopts when addressing a youthful acolyte like Florus differs from the tone in which he writes to Maecenas, let alone Augustus. It also makes a considerable difference at what stage in his career Horace is writing: he naturally takes a more tentative approach in his earlier works, for all their boldness, whereas in the poetry of his maturity he speaks with greater authority: the bard of the *Ludi Saeculares* is a figure of laureate status, proud of his achievements (*Odes* 4.3), and we can reasonably assume that by that date many Roman readers would be interested to know what he had to say about poetry. Despite all these reservations, however, we shall see that the continuity in Horace's thinking is considerable.

Genre and cross-generic criticism

Horace, like all the Augustans, is acutely conscious of generic distinctions and relationships: indeed, his listing of the major genres in the *Ars Poetica* is a key text for ancient assumptions about literary forms.[10] This concern has a number of aspects. First, he is strongly aware of his own choices of genre and of writing in a tradition. This is partly signalled by homage to the founder(s) or the most significant figures of the genre in question: Lucilius in the satires, Archilochus and Hipponax in the book of iambi; in the *Odes* Alcaeus receives special mention. Second, knowledge of the generic 'rules', flexible though these were, is considered essential for any poet: diction, metre and subject should be appropriate to the genre chosen. Here genre is intimately bound up with another key concept of ancient criticism, that of decorum or propriety. Third, neither reverence for one's predecessors nor respect for decorum is incompatible with a willingness to criticise and a

9 However, Nisbet and Rudd in their commentary (2004) follow Feeney (1991) 125–6 and others, assuming that the similarities are due to an Ennian source.

10 *Ars Poetica* 73ff. Other important passages include Ovid, *RA* 374–89; Martial 12.94. For a broader discussion of the importance of these topics see R. B. Rutherford (2005) 6–11.

desire to outdo those distinguished models. Even when the echo of a model is particularly close, the allusion can be seen as a challenge. In *Odes* 1.37 Horace's opening, the famous *nunc est bibendum* ('now is the time to drink'), echoes Alcaeus' celebration of the death of his enemy Myrsilus (fr. 322 L–P). The well-read reader will anticipate that in Horace's poem, too, a tyrant is dead. But the echo is a form of one-upmanship: the faction-fighting and party politics of tiny Lesbos in the sixth century are dwarfed by the significance of the victory and the death which Horace is about to praise, a landmark in Mediterranean history, which settles for years to come the destiny of the Roman world, a fact already obvious to Horace and his contemporaries.

This aspiration to outdo one's model is more explicit in the case of Lucilius (see section on 'Perfectionism' below), a Roman predecessor: perhaps the Greek classics need to be treated more cautiously, but even here Horace claims to have improved on Archilochus, civilising and taming the older poet's aggression. It is now widely recognised that Latin imitators often embody a form of criticism in their reworking of model texts. If we had the whole of Lucilius' third book, in which the poet narrated a journey to South Italy and Sicily, we would be better equipped to assess Horace's sustained imitation in *Satires* 1.5: as it is, we can at least see that he tightened up the narrative, eliminating repetition and the use of Greek words or clumsy expressions; also, the Horatian poem takes up only 104 lines, whereas Lucilius apparently spent a whole book on the journey.[11] All of this is in line with Horace's criticisms of Lucilius elsewhere in *Satires* 1.

We see in Horace a keen awareness of the relationship between genres and their 'ranking' in the hierarchy. In the ancient world there was not a fixed and universally accepted hierarchy of literary forms, but a loose grouping of 'high' genres (epic, tragedy, sometimes history) in opposition to 'low' (epigram, satire, iambic, much elegy). The status of lyric was attractively ambiguous, for lyric poetry was itself an inclusive form embracing a great variety of poets and types of poem. It made a great deal of difference whether a poet was imitating Pindar or Anacreon: as Horace does both, he can represent the *Odes* as inspired, ambitious and prestigious poetry, or as trivial and frivolous. It is perhaps more characteristic of him to adopt the role of a lesser writer, admiring more ambitious artists but modestly disclaiming any ability to scale the poetic heights. This is of course typical above all of the *recusatio* or polite refusal. *Odes* 1.6 is a well-worn example (1.6.5–12):

11 *Paucis* in 1.5.51 is pointed; also 104 (even 104 lines are seen by Horace as amounting to a *longa charta*).

nos, Agrippa, neque haec dicere nec gravem
Pelidae stomachum cedere nescii
nec cursus duplicis per mare Ulixi
    nec saevam Pelopis domum

conamur, tenues grandia, dum pudor
imbellisque lyrae Musa potens vetat
laudes egregii Caesaris et tuas
    culpa deterere ingeni.

We do not attempt, Agrippa, to speak of these things,
nor of the bad temper of Peleus' son who did not know
how to yield, nor of the voyages of Ulixes the double-dealer,
    nor of the savage house of Pelops.

We are too slight for these large themes. Modesty
and the Muse who commands the unwarlike lyre forbid us
to diminish the praise of glorious Caesar and yourself
    by our imperfect talent. (trans. D. West)

Here the principle of propriety comes into play: Horace as a lyric poet cannot do justice to these majestic themes, but would mar them with inappropriate or inadequate language: the use of *stomachum* and *duplicis*, which convey a sense of Homer's subject-matter but lower the tone below the appropriate epic level, is calculated to demonstrate this.[12] Of course, Horace protests too much: in the stanza which follows this extract he expresses himself in suitably grandiose terms, as though to show that he could do it if he wanted.[13] The *recusatio* is both apologetic and self-assertive: the author can have his cake as well as eat it.

When Horace comments on another poet or another genre, it is frequently in order to establish his own position in relation to these. Often he declares his own inferiority, but there is usually a submerged note of self-promotion nonetheless. A fine example (which also includes Horace's longest description of an earlier poet) is the opening of *Odes* 4.2, the praise of Pindar.[14] Here the Greek lyricist is presented as beyond rivalry: to emulate him is perilous. Horace is again playing the *recusatio*-game, rejecting (it seems) an invitation to compose Pindaric verse for a given occasion. After the splendid period in which he sings Pindar's praises, Horace contrasts the Dircaean swan with the humble, low-flying Matine bee, engaged in its productive labour just like Horace (*operosa parvus / carmina fingo*, 'small as I am, I shape painstaking poetry'). But not only has the resonant eloquence of his description itself

12 See further Ahern (1991). 13 So too esp. *Epistles* 2.1.250–9.
14 S. J. Harrison (1995a).

imitated the manner of Pindar; the very image of the bee as a symbol of poetic composition derives from that poet (*Pythian Odes* 10.54, fr. 152). Thus while praising Pindar as an unapproachable genius, and explicitly contrasting his own undertakings, he also claims a kind of affinity with his great predecessor.

Odes 2.1, addressed to Pollio, is in some ways parallel.[15] On the one hand Horace expresses admiration for Pollio's momentous historical theme and powerful narrative style (which for a few stanzas he brilliantly emulates). On the other hand, he warns that the subject is potentially dangerous: the ashes are still warm. At the end of the poem, breaking off and upbraiding his Muse, he urges her to turn away from such gloomy material (suited to Simonidean dirges) and return to the delights of love and the cave of Venus. The lyric poet has paid tribute to the tragic historian; but the conclusion implies that Pollio's work is all very well, but almost too lugubrious to give pleasure for long. To put it in these terms is of course to exaggerate – the ode is, after all, in honour of Pollio; but the change of direction in the final stanza does allow a glimpse of an alternative path, a further perspective.

To sum up, Horace's handling of genre-contrasts and related topics is rarely detachable from his concern with his own work and its status in relation to that of others, including his own predecessors.

Life/art analogies

One feature of Horace's literary criticism which has received much attention is his Callimachean preoccupation with the big / small antithesis, the opposition between short, subtle, sophisticated craftsmanship and crude, over-inflated, bombastic work. Especially interesting are the ways in which he creates analogies between the way this antithesis works in literature and the ways it figures in life: style mirrors lifestyle, and vice versa. Poets were traditionally poor; philosophers advocated simple fare; satirists are preoccupied with images of appetite and gross self-indulgence. Horace draws on all these conceptions and plays many variations on them.[16] One passage which makes the parallel particularly clear is *Odes* 2.16.33–40, where the contrast of Grosphus' wealth and Horace's relative poverty is patent: the accumulation of clauses, the hundred herds, in opposition to the *parva rura* ('small fields') that constitute Horace's property and the '*spiritum . . . tenuem*' ('slender breath') of Horatian poetry. *Tenuem*, of course, evokes the Callimachean

15 For an excellent recent account, see Woodman (2003) 196–213.
16 See further Mette (1961); Bramble (1974), esp. 156–64; Cody (1976).

'slender muse'; the reference to scorning the malicious mob also echoes Callimachus, recalling at least two passages in which the poet declares his superiority to envy. Thus the passage expresses and endorses Callimachus' ideals, while extending them to the poet's own way of life.

This complex of ideas is found throughout Horace's oeuvre. The *Satires* provide particularly clear illustrations. In the first poem of Book 1, much is made of the idea of 'sufficiency': enough is enough, in both poetry and life. The avaricious man is never satisfied: he prefers to take from a huge heap of supplies rather than a small one; he would sooner draw the same amount of water from a big river than from a small spring. Again we observe imagery that Callimachus had applied to poetic activity transferred to an ethical context. But the literary application is not forgotten. Early in the poem Horace emphasises that the examples of human discontent are numerous enough for him to go on indefinitely: *loquacem / delassare valent Fabium* ('enough to tire out long-winded Fabius' 1.1.13–14); at the end of it he recurs to the same idea, in a passage that brings the two sides together (116–21):

> inde fit ut raro, qui se vixisse beatum
> dicet et exacto contentus tempore vita
> cedat uti conviva *satur*, reperire queamus.
> iam *satis* est. ne me Crispini scrinia lippi
> compilasse putes, verbum non amplius addam.

> This is why we can rarely find anyone who says he's lived a happy life and who, when his time is up, departs content, like a satisfied guest. That's enough; in case you think I've plundered the sore-eyed Crispinus' desk, I shan't add a word more.

Just as the avaricious man needs to curb his desires, so the satirist needs to keep his diatribal eloquence within bounds. *Satur* and *iam satis est* echo the earlier *nil satis est* (62). It is hard to resist the suspicion that there is also a play on the name of the genre, perhaps indeed a paradox: since the term *satira* is so often connected with the idea of a platter or a type of food, diverse and abundant,[17] Horace's drive for self-restraint is in a kind of tension with the sprawling excesses of the genre.

More explicit combination of life and art, and more aggressive use of food metaphors, can be seen in one of the passages attacking the epic poet Furius (*Satires* 2.5.39–40): *pingui tentus omaso / Furius hibernas cana nive*

17 Diomedes *GLK* 1.485, quoted e.g. in Coffey (1976) 12–13: note esp. *a lance quae referta variis multisque primitiis*, 'from a platter which is stuffed with many various types of produce', and *sive a quodam genere farciminis, quod multis rebus refertum*, 'or from a type of sausage, because it is stuffed with many things'.

conspuet Alpis, 'swollen with rich tripe, Furius bespatters the wintry Alps with white snow'. The inflated bombast of the inept epic poet is internalised as fattening and ill-digested food; the poet is like his work.[18] This idea, too, is widespread in Horace: similarly Plautus is disparagingly described as being like the clowns and parasites whom he puts on stage in his plays (*Epistles* 2.1.170–6), and Pollio makes his audience's ears ring with the blaring of trumpets (that is, describes the trumpet-call to battle in his History, *Odes* 2.1.17–18): in the last case the merging of author and text is made still more natural by the fact that Pollio himself has played a part in the events he narrates.

Perfectionism

Horace is a stern critic of others' work. In the *Ars Poetica* he remarks that 'neither men nor gods nor booksellers can tolerate the existence of mediocre poets' (372–3). He evidently thought that there were far too many people writing too much (*Satires* 1.4.141–2, and esp. *Epistles* 2.1.108ff.), and the hexameter poems are studded with caustic references to inferior writers.[19] He is particularly harsh on mere imitators, of himself or others (*Epistles* 1.19); though respect for tradition is vital, imitation alone is not enough. The man who can only croon the lyrics of Calvus and Catullus is dismissed as an 'ape' (*Satires* 1.10.18–19).[20] Even writers of considerable standing can be quite caustically handled: Tibullus, whose judgement Horace esteemed, is mocked for his 'pitiful elegies' (*Odes* 1.33), and Valgius similarly is urged to pull himself together and 'put an end at last to your sentimental laments' (*Odes* 2.9.17f., cf. 9). It is plausible that Horace, who relished brevity and variety of tone, found erotic elegy tedious and self-indulgent.[21] Already in the *Epodes* elegiac motifs (derived from Gallus?) are humorously deployed and juxtaposed with the more dynamic note of iambic aggression

18 Nisbet and Hubbard (1978) on *Odes* 2.1.17–18; cf. *Satires* 1.10.36.

19 *Satires* 1.4.21f. on Fannius; *Epistles* 1.4.3, 1.19.19–20.

20 A highly controversial passage, since it is unclear whether the condemnation of the imitator extends to the original poets. Horace himself echoes Catullan phrases, but in altered contexts. See Zetzel (2002) for a highly suggestive though necessarily speculative reading of Horace's attitude to the neoteric movement.

21 Elegy is traditionally a mournful genre: cf. *Ars Poetica* 75 (*querimonia*), Nisbet and Hubbard (1970) on *Odes* 1.33.2. That erotic lamentation can easily be overdone seems also to be the implication of his comment on Sappho at *Odes* 2.13.24ff. (note esp. 24 *querentem*), a passage in which more space and higher approval are given to Alcaeus; this is, however, a much-discussed passage (interesting comments in Woodman (1981) 165, detecting a conflict in Nisbet and Hubbard's assessment; Feeney (1993) 49).

(*Epodes* 11, 15); in the *Odes* the stock situations of the elegiac lover are regularly parodied (e.g. 3.10).[22]

His judgements of older literature are much more detailed. The criticisms of Lucilius in the *Satires* foreshadow a broader and more ambitious assault on older Latin poetry in the Letter to Augustus. He complains of Lucilius' casual attitude to poetic composition: for all his merits, he wrote too quickly and easily, and at excessive length; also, his readiness to include Greek words and phrases marred the purity of his work. The complaint about long-windedness is widespread: quality is more important than quantity, but Crispinus (*Satires* 1.4.13–19) and the bore of *Satires* 1.9 are blind to this. When Horace renews the criticism of Lucilius in *Satires* 1.10 he introduces a more challenging point, one which involves seeing Latin literature historically. Granted, Lucilius' poetry represented an advance on his predecessors, men unfamiliar with Greek models; nevertheless, Lucilius himself found fault with Ennius and Accius, and if Lucilius were alive today he would apply stricter standards, he would prune and edit his work more. Latin has developed, and poets must set themselves more exacting targets (cf. *Ars Poetica* 290–4). Even Homer can be criticised: Horace is annoyed (*indignor*) when the master falls short of his normal excellence, though conceding that some falling-off is to be expected in a lengthy work (*Ars Poetica* 358–60). It is interesting to contrast the opinion of Ovid, that a face is more attractive for a mole, and still more that of Longinus, for whom flawed magnificence is to be valued far more highly than dull consistency (*On the Sublime* 33).

The question of poetic standards is closely related to the issue of the poet's audience. Here Horace appears uncompromising. Again the principle is that 'small is beautiful' – large audiences are unwelcome, whereas a select group of informed judges will be more discriminating. He disdains recitations (*Satires* 1.4.71–8, esp. 73–4, 1.10.73ff., *Epistles* 1.19.41f.), and does not want his works to endure exposure in bookshops or suffer from the hands of sweaty readers (*Satires* 1.4.72); his preferred critics are men of taste and culture (*Satires* 1.10.81ff.). He does not court his audience, or woo the academic critics (*Epistles* 1.19.39–40); the worst that can befall the escaping book of epistles is to become a school text (*Epistles* 1.20, cf. *Satires* 1.10.75). In lyric mode he declares his hostility to the *profanum volgus*, and seeks the seclusion of a sheltered grove (*Odes* 3.1.1, 1.1.32). There is, however, a contradiction in Horace's position, for as a poet he naturally seeks to be as widely read

22 Nisbet and Hubbard (1970) xvi–vii. The relationship between Horace and elegy has often been discussed: see e.g. Otis (1945); Commager (1962) 31–41. The silence on erotic elegy in the *Ars* is eloquent.

and as famous as possible (e.g. *Odes* 2.20, playfully paralleled at *Epistles* 1.20.13),[23] and as a satirist he needs to speak to a wider public if his claims to act as a critic of society are to have any meaning. The self-mocking humour of one of the passages on this theme shows Horace to be aware of the tension in his position (*Satires* 1.10.74–7):

> an tua demens
> vilibus in ludis dictari carmina malis?
> non ego; nam satis est equitem mihi plaudere, ut audax,
> contemptis aliis, explosa Arbuscula dixit.

> Or are you crazy enough to prefer your poems to be dictated in paltry schools? Not me; it's enough for the knights to applaud me, as Arbuscula, contemptuous of others, dauntlessly said when hissed off the stage.

The affectation of contempt for popular applause is clearly a self-defensive pretence in the mouth of an actress; by quoting the words of a female, and a theatrical performer, and applying them to himself, Horace deflects accusations of elitism and deflates his own fastidiousness.

These topics – the contrast between older poetry and new, the need for exacting standards and the importance of a select and discriminating audience – are revisited and united in the Letter to Augustus. There Horace insists that older Latin literature is over-valued; moderns should not be dismissed for their novelty, but judged by their quality. 'I am annoyed when something is blamed, not because it is crudely or inelegantly written, but because it is recent' (*Epistles* 2.1.76–7). His criticisms of earlier poetry are polemical and not altogether fair: the slapdash composition of Plautus is condemned, but no mention is made of Terence, a far more careful and refined artist, whose plays Horace quotes and alludes to elsewhere. The polemic is driven by Horace's own critical agenda: he attacks the ancient in order to vindicate the modern. We may doubt whether he would have ventured such a bold assault earlier in his career, and in particular before the publication of the *Aeneid* made clear that the Augustan age would be seen as a high point in the history of Latin literature.[24] A further contrast, which becomes more explicit as the poem advances, is between the spectator in the theatre and the reader in his study. Public taste has been degraded by extravagant theatrical spectacle; processions and visual display, even the costumes of the performers, distract the audience's attention from the words the actors have to utter (182ff.). Augustus was a keen enthusiast of the theatre, but Horace

23 S. J. Harrison (1988).

24 This is not to deny that Virgil had his detractors; cf. Tarrant (1997).

presses upon him the claims of the non-dramatic poet. The *princeps* needs to become more of a good Callimachean reader.[25]

The poet in society

For Horace, neither literary creation nor literary criticism exists in a vacuum. The poet has a duty to his art, but also a responsibility to society. In the earlier oeuvre the emphasis falls more on the art. In the *Satires*, for all the enthusiastic praise of Lucilius as a lambaster of public immorality, it is hard to see Horace as living up to the same standards of bold outspokenness.[26] Horace advises not the city but individuals. A particularly telling passage is the defence of satire in *Satires* 1.4.78ff., where the poet replies to the accusation that he takes pleasure in injuring others, and this is the motive for his writing. Rather than asserting the moral role of the satirist and the need to speak out about bad men, Horace prefers to shift the accusation into one of personal maliciousness: the situations envisaged involve the dinner table, not the forum (80–1, 81 *amicum*, 86–91, 95); the weighty apostrophe *Romane* (85) is deceptive. Satire becomes more personal and ethical, less antagonistic and less political. The justification draws on ethical discussions going back to Aristotle,[27] but the explanation must go deeper, relating to Horace's low status and the uncertainty of the times.

Ethics, then, provides a safer battleground than social or political comment directed at the great issues of the day. Most relevantly to literary criticism, Horace comments ironically on his fellow poets and their habits. His criticisms are presented dramatically and by implication in *Satires* 1.9, where the bore represents everything that is unsuited to the cultivated circle of Maecenas: self-satisfied conceit, composition with an eye on speed and quantity, pushiness, insensitivity, self-interest. The proper way for someone seeking to win Maecenas' approval is indicated through counter-example, and made explicit in Horace's mild protest (*Satires* 1.9.48–52):

> 'non isto vivimus illic
> quo tu rere modo; domus hac nec purior ulla est
> nec magis his aliena malis; nil mi officit, inquam,
> ditior hic aut est quia doctior; est locus uni
> cuique suus.' 'magnum narras, vix credibile!'

'We don't live there on the basis you're assuming; no household is as honourable as that house of his, or so remote from vices like these. I tell you, it's

25 On Horace's Callimacheanism see Thomas, chapter 4 above.

26 Cf. the contrast between the two poets in Persius, 1.114–18.

27 Cf. Dickie (1981).

nothing to me if one man is richer or more learned than I am; each individual has his own assigned place.'
'What you say is extraordinary; it beggars belief!'

The bore is anonymous, perhaps a mere type, but, being a poet, he is a type particularly relevant to Horace, almost a caricature or reversed image of the author. In the Epistle to Florus and his friends, Horace deals with real people and offers more explicit advice on poetry itself: by this stage he is an established figure, able to instruct younger men. Although enquiring about their poetic efforts, he cautions them against faults which he evidently thinks them likely to fall into: Titius is warned against bombast, Celsus against plagiarism.[28] Ethics and poetry are intertwined, as is natural in the most philosophic book Horace wrote.[29] Florus himself is urged to follow his natural bent and leave poetry for philosophy (as Horace represents himself as doing or wishing to do in the first poem of this book). It goes with this that poets are increasingly seen as a vain and temperamental lot (*Epistles* 1.13, 1.19.19ff., 41–7, 2.2.89–105).

With the second book of epistles we encounter a more positive vision of the poet. Partly this reflects Horace's higher standing (especially perhaps after the *Ludi Saeculares*); in 2.1 it doubtless also corresponds to the interests and attitudes of Augustus (cf. Suetonius *Div. Aug.* 89). Literally at the centre of *Epistles* 2.1 is the passage in which Horace outlines the value of the poet to the community: he guides the young towards virtue, removes or warns against vices, recounts virtuous deeds, gives consolation and comfort, trains choirs to sing hymns to the gods (124–38). This is of course an idealised vision, suited to the lofty addressee; it does not adequately describe what Horace's own poetry does or could be thought to do; and the description is not free of more whimsical elements (esp. 122–3). Yet it would be a mistake to suppose that it does not form part of Horace's conception of poetry: this is shown by the analogous passages in the other literary epistles. In 2.2 the writer's task is again outlined (109–25). In that passage the focus is on the choice and use of words, the poet's duty to enrich and purify the language, but this task is described in terms which associate the writer with the functions of the state: he will act as a censor, dismissing and including those words which have earned such treatment.[30] Here admittedly the political imagery is used to illuminate the labour of the artist rather than vice versa. Finally, the *Ars Poetica* devotes extended attention to the qualities and duties of the poet

28 On this poem (*Epistles* 1.3) see Macleod (1983) 265–6; Hubbard (1995).
29 On philosophy in *Epistles* 1 see further Ferri, chapter 9 above, and Moles, chapter 12 above.
30 On the question of the poet and diction see further *Ars* 47–72.

(306ff.): morality, rooted in philosophic study, must form the foundations (309–11), and the best poet will instruct even as he gives pleasure. A notable passage outlines a sequence of poets as cultural heroes and benefactors or civilisers of the community (391ff., naming Orpheus and others). It is because Horace holds such high standards and sets such store by poetry that he is hostile to verse which breeds dissension or malice: the frankness of the old Fescennine verses was corrupted into licence, and had to be restrained by law (2.1.145–55). In the *Satires* he evaded warnings of the dangers of *mala carmina* with a jest (*Satires* 2.1.80–6); by the time of *Epistles* 2 he himself is endorsing the constraint of literature by law. Fortunately Horace died too soon to see this legal suppression of poetry re-enacted, with the exile of the libellous Cassius Severus and of Ovid.[31]

I have tried to show that Horace's literary-critical thinking looks in two directions – inward, at the verbal and stylistic quality of the work of art and its intertextual relationship with other literature, and outward, at the impact of the writer's work on society. We might say that the one approach focuses more on form and style, while the other gives more priority to content, and especially to a didactic aspect. The first might be loosely labelled Callimachean (or neoteric?), the second Augustan. Ancient literary criticism always felt a strong gravitational pull towards the moral-didactic interpretation of literature, often oversimplifying the moral content genuinely present in the work. Readers of Horace's treatment of the Homeric epics, mentioned at the start of this paper, will know that Horace is no exception. But this can hardly be an adequate summary of all Horace's thinking on literary matters. I have already noted that his account of the virtues of the poet includes some humorous touches: it is no very high praise of the bard to assure the reader that he refrains from defrauding his ward, or that he lives on pulses and black bread (2.1.122–3). An elusive irony runs through many passages where poetry is under discussion: Horace is concerned to avoid being seen as too proud or portentous.

Moreover, the more definite and demanding his claims for poetry, the more he is concerned to distance himself from the poetic profession: satire is no true poetry, according to *Satires* 1.4; he himself has resigned from the poetic lists, and will serve merely as a whetstone for others, according to the *Ars Poetica* (301–5). There are analogies here with the treatment of philosophy in the *Epistles*: there, wisdom is a goal which the poet is constantly failing to reach, and his own imperfection and inconsistency are thematised in the collection. Where poetry is concerned, we may be less ready to accept that Horace is not up to the task. Perhaps indeed there is a sense in which the

31 Cf. Seneca, *Contr.* 10, preface. See further Ruffell (2003).

rules and the prescriptions are deliberately flouted: Horace is bolder and more innovative than the *critici* would approve. The *Ars Poetica* itself offers an example: it is no accident that such stern advice on the need for harmony and unity should be placed in a poem which to most readers seems bafflingly diverse and disharmonious. In the *Ars* he affects to be finished with poetry, writing as an outsider.[32] There is surely a paradox here, similar to that in Plato's *Phaedrus*: just as Plato criticises writing within a written dialogue, so Horace disclaims the status of poet within a poem. It is not surprising that Horace's precepts prove inadequate as a summary of his practice: the wings of poetry will always outstrip the plodding pursuit of criticism, even the best, the poet's own.

FURTHER READING

On many aspects of Horace's literary criticism, especially as regards the long literary epistles, the first recourse will naturally be to the commentaries and discursive essays in Brink (1963; 1971; 1982), but the work is somewhat indigestible. The much shorter commentaries on the literary epistles by Rudd (1989) may be found more accessible (Kilpatrick (1990) has an essay on each of the long epistles). A broad account of Horace's critical position, with extensive citations from throughout his oeuvre, is provided by Commager (1962) chapter 1. For literary criticism in the *Satires*, Rudd (1966) is still a reliable guide; for more detail on background, see also Freudenburg (1993). A very penetrating paper on Horace's poetry and status in his later career is Feeney (2002). On genre, besides the classic treatment by Kroll (1924), there is a valuable essay by A. Barchiesi (2001c): see also S. J. Harrison (forthcoming, a), which focuses on Virgil and Horace. On assimilation of literature and ethical lifestyle see Mette (1961); Bramble (1974); Cody (1976).

32 The complexities of the *Ars Poetica* are discussed in Andrew Laird's chapter in this volume (chapter 10). In general, I consider the disclaimer at 306 (*nil scribens ipse*, 'writing nothing myself') to be clearly disingenuous. Horace's own poetic concerns recur constantly in the poem, though doubtless also blended with the literary ambitions of the Pisones. On how this works in detail in one area, see the interesting discussion by Innes (2002) 20–7.

19

STEPHEN HARRISON

Style and poetic texture

Horace's carefully crafted poetic style, fundamentally influenced by the Callimachean aesthetics of brevity, elegance and polish, was already recognised as such within a century of his death:[1] a character in Petronius' *Satyrica* (118.5) refers to *Horati curiosa felicitas*, 'Horace's painstaking felicity of expression'. Both this verbal craft and its structural analogue, Horace's careful construction of his poems, have been well discussed in recent scholarship; his main contribution to Roman poetic language has been seen as the art of careful combination of traditional and innovatory elements, including an admixture of 'unpoetic' and colloquial language,[2] while his brilliant poetic architecture[3] and impressive manipulation of complex Greek lyric metres in the *Odes* have been a constant subject of study.[4] Though some have played down Horace's use of imagery, it is clear that it is rich and detailed.[5] Careful scholarly collections of material illuminating Horatian poetic language are readily available, especially in the great commentaries of recent years;[6] in this chapter I would like to try to convey something of Horace's stylistic and poetic virtuosity in a form accessible to both specialists and non-specialists, by brief close examination of three relatively short poems from the three main literary kinds in which Horace worked: iambus, lyric and hexameter *sermo*.[7]

1 On Horace and the Callimachean aesthetics of the Hellenistic Greek period see Thomas, chapter 4 above; on the ancient reception of Horace see Tarrant, chapter 20 below.

2 For the issue of colloquial language in Horace see e.g. P. Watson (1985) and Bonfante (1994).

3 See e.g. Syndikus (1995); Tarrant (1995); and S. J. Harrison (2004), all with further references.

4 See Barchiesi, chapter 11 above.

5 For playing down see e.g. Nisbet and Hubbard (1970) xxii; for more emphasis see e.g. D. West (1967).

6 See details in 'Further reading' below.

7 The translations of the three poems are my own.

Iambus: *Epode* 10

Mala soluta navis exit alite
  ferens olentem Maevium.
ut horridis utrumque verberes latus,
  Auster, memento fluctibus;
niger rudentis Eurus inverso mari
  fractosque remos differat;
insurgat Aquilo, quantus altis montibus
  frangit trementis ilices;
nec sidus atra nocte amicum appareat,
  qua tristis Orion cadit;
quietiore nec feratur aequore
  quam Graia victorum manus,
cum Pallas usto vertit iram ab Ilio
  in inpiam Aiacis ratem.
o quantus instat navitis sudor tuis
  tibique pallor luteus
et illa non virilis eiulatio
  preces et aversum ad Iovem,
Ionius udo cum remugiens sinus
  Noto carinam ruperit.
opima quodsi praeda curvo litore
  porrecta mergos iuverit,
libidinosus immolabitur caper
  et agna Tempestatibus.

The ship, freed from its moorings, moves out under bad omen
Conveying stinking Maevius.
South Wind, make sure you batter both sides
With bristling waves;
May the black East Wind, as the sea turns over,
Carry away the cables and splintered oars;
May the North Wind rise up, strong as when
It shatters the trembling holm-oaks high on the mountains;
And may no friendly star appear in the darkness of night,
When grim Orion sets.
May he be carried on an ocean as stormy
As that which met the victorious band of Greeks,
When Pallas turned her wrath from Troy's burning
To the sinful ship of Ajax.
What a sweat is in store for your crew
What clay-like pallor for you
And that unmanly wailing
And prayers to a heedless Jupiter,

When the Ionian bay, roaring like a bull
Under the soaking storm-wind, smashes your keel!
And if a rich carcass on the curving shoreline
Lies stretched out to pleasure the gulls,
A lustful goat and a lamb
Will be offered to the Storm-Gods.

This poem, based on a preserved archaic Greek iambic text, curses an enemy, possibly the poet Maevius of Virgil, *Eclogue* 3, perhaps for a sexual offence.[8] As always with Horatian poems, structure is important, and here it is bipartite; the main curse on Maevius, a single sentence in seven epodic couplets (1–14), is capped by a section of imaginative *Schadenfreude* (15–24) in five further couplets.[9] Some ring-composition is also evident, as so often in Horace's poetry;[10] the evocation of storms in the opening line is picked up by the poem's last word, and the abusive reference to Maevius as 'stinking' in the poem's second line is picked up in its penultimate line with the reference to a he-goat, traditionally also high in odour.[11] The names of the winds are also carefully distributed: the third, fourth and fifth pairs of lines each contain one wind-name, covering three cardinal points of the compass: the missing fourth is the west wind, which would blow Maevius where he wants to go (the reference to Ionia shows that this is an eastwards voyage). The proper names referring to the legendary storms after the fall of Troy are also carefully distributed in the sixth and seventh pairs of lines: the strategic placing of names is a common decorative effect in Horace's poetic texture, and the effect here, as often, is to convey much in little, rapidly keying the reader into a familiar mythological episode.

Careful word-order is a key feature of Horace's style at all levels. The third and fourth lines are almost enclosed by the noun/adjective pair meaning 'bristling waves', perhaps mirroring the prospective swamping of the ship by the water, but certainly wholly inverting normal Latin word-order, which would place the two words together. The verb at the end of line 6 is followed immediately by another verb in the same mood at the beginning of a new clause in line 7 (*differat; / insurgat*), again a spectacularly unprosaic word-order; both the sixth and the eighth lines begin with words related to breaking (*fractosque*, *frangit*): the wind's shattering of holm-oaks is clearly mirrored in the splintering of oars – the mighty trees and the slender wooden oars are both to be broken by storms. Note too how the rising of the North Wind (*insurgat*) matches the fall of Orion (*cadit*), with the two opposite verbs at

8 For these issues and much else on this poem see Watson (2003) 338–57.

9 For the metres of the *Epodes* see e.g. L. Watson (2003) 45–7.

10 See Tarrant (1995).

11 See *Odes* 1.17.7.

opposite ends of successive clauses: in both cases the movement of the cosmos is hostile to Maevius, whether upwards or downwards. This hostility of the landscape is repeated in the metaphor of *remugiens*, which brilliantly turns the bull-identity often used of the sea-god Poseidon/Neptune to personify the Ionian shore as violently opposed to Maevius and his ship.

Epic tone is a particular feature in this poem. The evocation of the storms associated with the returns of the Greeks from Troy recall the (lost) Greek cyclic epic of the *Nostoi* in which those returns were narrated, and the phrase *Graia victorum manus* strikes a lofty tone with the poetic *Graia* and the enallage (transfer of epithet) with *manus* (it is the victors and not the band who are primarily Greek).[12] The 'clay-like' pallor of Maevius' fear picks up a well-known Homeric phrase (*chloron deos*),[13] while the 'unmanly wailing' perhaps presents an ironic version of the song of the Sirens: Maevius, who has none of Odysseus' aplomb under pressure, succumbs where Homer's hero had famously resisted female utterance at sea, indeed actively mimics the Sirens himself as an effeminate coward. The prospect of the corpse feeding the birds is also a familiar idea from Homer, used several times in battlefield threats from which these lines gain some menacing tones, though the specification of somewhat unpoetic seagulls is a nice local twist.[14] Commentators have noted this cluster of epic material around the figure of Maevius; it might be worth suggesting that it can be connected with *Eclogue* 3.90, where the poetry of a Maevius is condemned, to argue that Maevius is a bad epic poet. Perhaps violence metaphorically done by Maevius to the tradition of epic poetry is here literally turned against him.

Lyric: *Odes* 1.22

Integer uitae scelerisque purus
non eget Mauris iaculis neque arcu
nec uenenatis grauida sagittis,
  Fusce, pharetra,

siue per Syrtis iter aestuosas
siue facturus per inhospitalem
Caucasum uel quae loca fabulosus
  lambit Hydaspes.

12 See L. Watson (2003) 351; on enallage as an epic feature see conveniently Conte (2002) 5–64.

13 See L. Watson (2003) 350.

14 On the Iliadic echoes see L. Watson (2003) 352. The *mergus* is found elsewhere in Horace only at *Satires* 2.2.51.

Namque me silua lupus in Sabina,
dum meam canto Lalagem et ultra
terminum curis uagor expeditus,
  fugit inermem,

quale portentum neque militaris
Daunias latis alit aesculetis
nec Iubae tellus generat, leonum
  arida nutrix.

pone me pigris ubi nulla campis
arbor aestiua recreatur aura,
quod latus mundi nebulae malusque
  Iuppiter urget;

pone sub curru nimium propinqui
solis in terra domibus negata:
dulce ridentem Lalagen amabo,
  dulce loquentem.

He that is untainted in life and unsullied with crime
Needs no Moorish javelins or bow
Or quiver teeming with poisoned arrows, Fuscus,

Whether he is about to march through the sultry Syrtes
Or the Caucasus hard to strangers, or the domains
Lapped by the Hydaspes of story.

For a wolf fled from me, all unarmed, in a Sabine wood
As I sang of my Lalage and wandered
Beyond my boundary-stone, all freed from cares,

Such a monster as the soldierly South does not breed
In its wide oak groves, nor the land of Juba,
That dry nurse of lions.

Set me on the sluggish plains where no tree
Is refreshed by a summer breeze, on the side of the world
Oppressed by mists and an evil sky,

Set me under the chariot of the Sun where it comes too close
In the land forbidden to habitations:
I will love my Lalage with her sweet laugh, her sweet voice.

Once again structure is crucial: here we have three pairs of stanzas, and ring-composition between the first and last pairs, which both deal with journeys to distant parts of the world, while the central pair of stanzas is located much nearer to home on Horace's Sabine estate. This overarching structure is underlined at the verbal level by the echo of *aestuosas* (5) and *aestiva* (18), sharing the root *aest-*, 'heat', and also reinforced by clear intertextual echoes of two famous poems of Catullus, the only two extant Catullan poems in this same metre of the Sapphic stanza, near the opening and at the close of Horace's ode.[15] The alternative exotic locations of the second stanza (*sive . . . sive . . . vel*) clearly recall the equally distant destinations evoked for the potential journey of Furius and Aurelius at Catullus 11.1–8 (*sive . . . sive . . . sive . . . seu*, in a similar Eastern travelogue of India, Arabia, Parthia and Egypt), while the 'sweet laughter' of Lalage in the poem's penultimate line recalls the same phrase of Lesbia at Catullus 51.5. This encapsulation of the only two poems of Catullus in a Lesbian stanzaic metre[16] represents both homage to a formal predecessor and an implicit assertion that Horace's own *Odes* outdo Catullus' lyric poems in their thoroughgoing use of the complex Aeolic lyric metres only occasionally ventured by his predecessor: where Horace claims to be the first to produce Lesbian lyric in Latin, what he means is that he is the first to do it consistently in a whole collection.[17]

The first stanza shows typically Horatian density of poetic texture. The two phrases of the first line balance each other not just in their elegant and poetic genitives but also in chiastic ABBA word-order;[18] the semantically similar terms *integer* and *purus* (expressing purity by negative and positive means respectively) thus frame the poem's opening line. The negative list of what the virtuous man does not need is carefully varied with three different terms (*non . . . neque . . . nec*); all the words for weapons are located at the ends of metrical lines, increasing in length and phonetic weight (*arcu . . . sagittis . . . pharetra*); and the African location implied by *Mauris* perhaps puns on the name of the addressee Fuscus, a *cognomen* which can mean 'dark-skinned'.[19] *Gravida* shows a brilliantly ironical use of the metaphor of life-giving pregnancy for a quiver teeming with death-dealing poisoned arrows. Once again, word-placing is a vital effect: in the second stanza the location of the long adjectives *aestuosas, inhospitalem* and

15 On Horace and Catullus see further Tarrant, chapter 5 above and Putnam (2006).

16 For the metres of Horace's odes in general see Nisbet and Hubbard (1970) xxxvii–xlvi.

17 See Hutchinson, chapter 3 above.

18 See Nisbet and Hubbard (1970) 264 for these details (and much else on this poem).

19 See *Satires* 2.8.14 *fuscus Hydaspes*, a dark-skinned slave with an Eastern name (a name indeed found in *Odes* 1.22).

fabulosus at the ends of the three successively metrically identical lines of the Sapphic stanza is a clear effect of co-ordination of colourful epithets which all point in the same direction of hostile and mysterious landscapes, while the proper names are again carefully distributed – one more or less at the beginning of the stanza, one at the end and one near the middle (*Syrtis*, *Caucasum*, *Hydaspes*).

The grandeur of expression in this first stanza fits its historical resonances. The Moorish javelins, bow and poisoned arrows are hard to place in a specific context other than that of barbarian enemies of Rome, but the journeys of the second stanza evoke memories of great historic marches by Cato Uticensis and Alexander,[20] suiting the military expression *iter facere*.[21] Horace's much more domestic escapade in stanzas 3 and 4 is marked by ironic use of the military and expeditionary terminology of the first two stanzas: he marches not to the ends of the earth but only just over the borders of his estate, and his close encounter is comic, momentary and unhazardous. The term *expeditus* perhaps recalls the use of this adjective for light-armed troops,[22] while *inermem* and *militaris* are clearly military. The mention of the 'land of Juba' is another safe containment of the perilous landscape of the opening stanza: Juba II was the safe and loyal client-king of Mauretania, and his mention suggests that the Moorish spears of line 2 have been tamed in Rome's interest, though the opening out to a more distant location also looks forward to the renewed far places of the final pair of stanzas, and the sequence of proper names *Sabina . . . Daunias* (Horace's native region of southern Italy) . . . *Iubae tellus* draws us southwards from the metropolis to the periphery of the Roman Empire. As commentators note, the mention of lions here recalls Juba's prose work on that topic, while the phrase *arida nutrix* neatly frames a typically Horatian oxymoron in the compact metrical unit of the adonean (the last, short line of the Sapphic stanza); the nurturing metaphor of *nutrix* applied to exotic lions neatly picks up the perverse use of the imagery of pregnancy earlier in *gravida* (line 3).

The last pair of stanzas is held together with the same initial phrase, underlining like the initial word-pair *sive . . . sive* in lines 5–6 the idea of alternative destinations. Sluggish plains and relieving winds are neatly contrasted with each other in word-order as in sense by the balanced noun–adjective pairs *pigris . . . campis / aestiva . . . aura*, again separated against natural Latin order. This symmetry is continued in the last stanza, not just with the

20 See Nisbet and Hubbard (1970) 265–7. 21 Caesar *Gall.* 1.7.3, Livy 27.13.4.

22 Caesar *Civ.* 1.42.1, Livy 5.16.3. I here adopt Bentley's conjecture for the transmitted *expeditis*.

obvious balance of *dulce ridentem . . . dulce loquentem* (the last phrase again exposed in the adonean to stress its etymological play on the name of Lalage, 'chatterer'), but also with the pair *nimium propinqui* and *domibus negata*: these adjectival phrases (as often in Latin poetic language) look like translations of Greek compound adjectives: *nimium propinqui* suggests a rendering of a Greek adjective beginning with *hyper-*, 'excessively',[23] while *domibus negata* seems to pick up Herodotus' similarly ethnographic *aoiketos* (2.34), 'uninhabited' (literally 'with no houses').

Sermo: *Epistles* 1.12

Fructibus Agrippae Siculis quos colligis, Icci,
si recte frueris, non est ut copia maior
ab Ioue donari possit tibi; tolle querellas;
pauper enim non est cui rerum suppetit usus.
Si uentri bene, si lateri est pedibusque tuis, nil
diuitiae poterunt regales addere maius.
Si forte in medio positorum abstemius herbis
uiuis et urtica, sic uiues protinus, ut te
confestim liquidus Fortunae riuus inauret,
uel quia naturam mutare pecunia nescit
uel quia cuncta putas una uirtute minora.
Miramur, si Democriti pecus edit agellos
cultaque, dum peregre est animus sine corpore uelox,
cum tu inter scabiem tantam et contagia lucri
nil paruum sapias et adhuc sublimia cures;
quae mare compescant causae, quid temperet annum,
stellae sponte sua iussaene uagentur et errent,
quid premat obscurum lunae, quid proferat orbem,
quid uelit et possit rerum concordia discors,
Empedocles an Stertinium deliret acumen?
Verum, seu piscis seu porrum et caepe trucidas,
utere Pompeio Grospho et, siquid petet, ultro
defer; nil Grosphus nisi uerum orabit et aequum.
Vilis amicorum est annona, bonis ubi quid dest.
Ne tamen ignores quo sit Romana loco res,
Cantaber Agrippae, Claudi uirtute Neronis
Armenius cecidit; ius imperiumque Prahates
Caesaris accepit genibus minor; aurea fruges
Italiae pleno defundit Copia cornu.

23 Though I cannot find an exactly matching Greek word: cf. e.g. *hypermēkos*, 'too long'.

Iccius, if you have proper enjoyment
Of the Sicilian yields you collect for Agrippa
No greater abundance can be given you by Jupiter.
Cut your complaints: no-one is poor who has the use of plenty.
If all is well with your stomach, your midriff and your feet
A king's wealth will add nothing more.
If you happen to live on a frugal diet of herbs and nettles
Though surrounded by ready-made dainties
That way you will lead a smooth course of life
Even though Fortune's clear stream suddenly gild you,
Either because money cannot change your nature
Or because you think that everything is inferior to virtue supreme.
Do we wonder that Democritus' flocks ate up his poor fields and crops
While his mind was in flight away from his body,
When you, surrounded by such itching and contagion of wealth
Show no small wisdom and still care for elevated things:
The causes which keep down the sea, what controls the year,
Whether the stars orbit and wander by themselves or under orders,
What presses the moon's sphere down to darkness, what brings it out,
What the discordant harmony of things means and can accomplish,
Whether Empedocles is raving – or the sharp mind of Stertinius?
But whether it's fish, or leeks and onions that you slaughter,
Make use of Pompeius Grosphus, and if he asks for anything, give it freely;
Grosphus will beg for nothing that is not true and fair.
The price of friends is cheap when a good man has a need.
To let you know how the Roman state is faring,
The Cantabrian lies low through the might of Agrippa,
The Armenian through that of Claudius Nero;
Phrahates has accepted on his knees the laws and power of Caesar:
Golden Abundance pours forth the corn of Italy from a full horn.

Verbal ring-composition is once more important here, not only tying the poem together but also identifying a key theme: *fructibus* and *copia* in the opening two lines (with the additional wordplay of *frueris* in line 2)[24] are echoed with brilliant effect in *fruges* and *Copia* in the closing two lines, pointing to the idea of production and plenty as the central idea of the poem, while the mention of Iccius' patron, Agrippa, in the poem's opening is picked up with the notice of his victory in Spain at the close. Iccius' philosophical credentials would already be known to readers of *Odes* 1.29, where his ethical interests are subordinated to the financial lure of an Eastern expedition; this poem reprises the same dilemma of wisdom against materialism for

24 The so-called *figura etymologica*, where a noun and verb in partnership share the same root.

Iccius when surrounded by the wealth of Sicily. The concatenation of proper names in the opening line rapidly establishes the identity and location of the addressee and his affiliation to Agrippa, a technique often used at the beginning of Horace's epistolary poems (cf. e.g. 1.11, 1.15); the implicit comparison between Jupiter and Agrippa as sources of gifts for Iccius, brought out by the use of the two names in balance, is light and amusing and helps to set the tone of the poem.

Horace's deployment of the flexible hexameter of *sermo* is much more relaxed than his engagement with the tight lyric metres of the *Odes*, and this is clear from such features as syntactical breaks near the end of metrical units, such as the comma one syllable before the end of line 5 or the sentence-end close to the end of line 3, something generally avoided by loftier hexameter technique (e.g. in Virgil).[25] But the longer line can be used equally artistically to interact with the sense: line 4 presents a self-contained sententious one-line summary of a moral idea, an effect repeated at line 24 and often used in the *Epistles* for pithily highlighting precepts.[26] Likewise, repetition can still be used for literary point: beginning both line 10 and line 11 with *vel quia* not only points up a debt to Lucretian didactic technique[27] but also nicely balances two equipollent explanations, with the key contrasting terms *pecunia* and *virtute* set against each other in similar positions in successive lines. This effect is continued in lines 14 and 15, where the opposing words *contagia* and *sublimia* are again placed in clear contradistinction in the same metrical position, stressing the same contrast between the corruption of wealth and wholesome philosophical pursuits; the metaphor of disease in *scabies* and *contagia* looks as often in the *Epistles* to the image of philosophy as healer of the soul's sickness caused by excessive material consideration.[28]

Humour and familiar tone are important characterising features of the *Epistles*, and come across in this poem partly through lexical choice: the amusing listing of body-parts in line 5 begins with the *venter*, stomach, too vulgar to be named in the *Odes*, while the allusion to nettles, *urtica*, in line 8, picks out this humble plant for the only time in Horace's output. The entertaining anecdote of Democritus' disastrous attempt at farming is another natural locus for lexical lightness: the diminutive *agellos* in line 12 (a usage limited to hexameter *sermo*) might suggest both non-extensive holdings and sympathy for the ravaged fields, while *peregre est animus* characterises the lofty philosophical idea of the flight of the mind with an amusingly colloquial

25 On the hexameter of Horatian *sermo* see conveniently Mayer (1994) 13–32.

26 See S. J. Harrison (1995b) 51–3.

27 See Mayer (1994) 197.

28 See S. J. Harrison (1995b) 54–7.

turn of phrase (his mind is 'out to lunch').[29] Similarly, the speculations on Iccius' diet – luxurious fish or ascetic leeks and onions – is entertainingly coloured by the hyperbolic *trucidas*, 'slaughter', picking up the Pythagorean idea that eating other creatures is tantamount to murder but using a melodramatic word found elsewhere in Horace only of Medea's infanticide (*Ars Poetica* 184).

Style again works closely with content in another way in lines 16–20, where the listing of topics in indirect questions follows a traditional model for summarising the contents of a poetic work: the repetition of *quid* (varied once by *quae*) gives headings within a programme of study for Iccius in his philosophical investigations of the natural world, and symmetry is again an important effect: *quid* begins two successive lines (18–19), *quid temperet annum* (16) is exactly balanced in placing and phrasing by *quid proferat orbem* (18), and the neat paradox *concordia discors* summarises Empedoclean cosmic theory in another Horatian oxymoron.

The list of philosophical topics is nicely balanced by another list in the poem's concluding lines, this time of Roman victories. This epistolary news-report cleverly manipulates proper names once again: two defeated parties, *Cantaber* and *Armenius*, are placed at the beginning of successive lines, and line 27 both begins and ends with the names of conquered Roman enemies (*Armenius . . . Phraates*), while the break between line 27 and line 28 is also the break between the Parthian king and his Roman conqueror (*Phraates / Caesaris*). Word-order can even express political diplomacy here: line 26 shows a nice equipollence between the two main candidates for the imperial succession at the time of writing (c. 20 BC): Agrippa, Augustus' deputy, and his stepson Tiberius (Claudius Nero). In addition the list-structure which knits this final section together is the unifying metaphor of corn and productivity, with which, as we have seen, the poem began: *annona* in line 24, the technical term for the price of corn, is echoed in *fruges* in 28.[30]

These brief and superficial analyses show, I hope, something of the density of Horatian poetic texture, and of the detailed way in which poetic effects are achieved through the manipulation of vocabulary, verbal design and symmetry, metrical effects and imagery.

FURTHER READING

D. West (1967) offers the liveliest introduction to Horace's use of verbal style and poetic effect; two older books written under the influence of the New Criticism, Collinge (1961) and Commager (1962), also contain much important analysis of

29 For the colloquial tone of *peregre est* see Plautus *Stich.* 739, *Trin.* 149, Seneca *Contr.* 7.4.5.
30 See Mayer (1994) 201.

the *Odes*, especially in terms of structure and imagery, as do several pieces in S. J. Harrison (1995d). For a more recent overview and useful scholarly bibliography on Horatian poetic style see Muecke (1997), and the rest of the major section of which it forms the chief part in the *Enciclopedia Oraziana* (Mariotti (1996–8)). But most useful are the detailed Horatian commentaries of the last generation: see Nisbet and Hubbard (1970) and (1978); Nisbet and Rudd (2004); L. Watson (2003); Brink (1971) and (1982); and Mayer (1994).

PART 4

Receptions

20

RICHARD TARRANT

Ancient receptions of Horace

Propertius to Statius

The immediate impact of Horace's poetry, especially *Odes* 1–3 and *Epistles* 1, can be measured by the reactions of his two most creative younger contemporaries. Propertius was acutely sensitive to new developments in Latin poetry, and his third collection of elegies, which probably appeared within a year or two of *Odes* 1–3, eagerly responds to this new literary phenomenon. In his opening lines he recalls Horace's self-characterisation in *Odes* 3.1.3 as the 'priest of the Muses' (*Musarum sacerdos*) and his claim in 3.30.13–14 to have first adapted Greek lyric to Roman verse, and cheekily applies both attributes to himself as an elegist; the following elegy continues to appropriate material from *Odes* 3.1 and 3.30, most obviously in comparing the immortality won by poetry to such ephemeral monuments as the Pyramids (3.2.19–26). Horace's assertion of immortality in *Odes* 3.30 was also evoked by Ovid at pivotal points in his poetic career, first in the final lines of *Amores* 1.15 (perhaps originally the coda to the fifth and last book of *Amores*), then at the end of the *Remedia Amoris* (811), signalling Ovid's move away from lighter elegy to the larger forms of his mature years, the *Fasti* and the *Metamorphoses*,[1] and most explicitly in the epilogue to the *Metamorphoses* (15.871–8), where the words *si quid habent ueri uatum praesagia*, 'if there is any truth to the prophecies of poets', are probably intended to signal the allusion to another poet's prediction.

Ovid was one of Horace's few rivals in moulding Latin verse into an utter naturalness of expression, and countless echoes show how thoroughly he had absorbed the older poet's work.[2] There is no evidence of a personal connection between them, but Ovid's statement in *Tristia* 4.10.49 that 'Horace with

1 As suggested by S. J. Harrison (2002) 84.

2 Useful collection of material in Zingerle (1869–71).

his many metres beguiled my ears'[3] could imply that he attended Horace's recitations of his poetry, which according to *Satires* 1.4.73 were restricted to friends. The two did, however, move in some of the same circles and had friends in common; one was Paullus Fabius Maximus, depicted by Horace in *Odes* 4.1 as a highly eligible bachelor (perhaps in connection with an approaching marriage), for whom Ovid wrote the actual wedding-song (*Epistulae ex Ponto* 1.2.131–2).[4] In that ode Horace also cited Fabius' eloquent protection of defendants (14); the exiled Ovid appealed to him for precisely that service (*Epistulae ex Ponto* 1.2.67–70), surely with a rueful reminiscence of Horace's line.

The publication of *Epistles* 1 may have helped to inspire the elegiac verse letters of Propertius (4.3) and Ovid (the *Epistulae Heroidum*), which were probably written in the immediately following years, but the content and manner of those epistolary elegies owe little to Horace. The example of a collection of verse letters to friends, however, may have been important in shaping the framework of Ovid's exile poetry. In particular, Ovid probably took from *Epistles* 1.20 the image of the poetry book as a slave eager to see Rome and transformed it into the motif that animates the opening poems of *Tristia* 1 and 3, where the collection is a child of the poet setting out for the city his parent can no longer visit. On a larger scale, Alessandro Barchiesi has shown that *Tristia* 2, a long letter to Augustus largely taken up with literary issues – in particular, Ovid's defence of the *Ars Amatoria* – should be seen as a counterpart to Horace's letter to Augustus.[5]

As we proceed further we may follow Quintilian (10.1.93–6) in assessing Horace's influence in terms of individual genres. Little needs to be said about the *Epodes*, since iambic as a distinct genre is virtually invisible after Horace. Propertius addressed an elegy (1.4) to a friend named Bassus, almost certainly the Bassus whom Ovid recalls from his youth as famous for iambics (*clarus iambis*, *Tristia* 4.10.47), but Quintilian (96) names no writer of *iambus* later than Horace, and the iambic elements in Martial owe more to Catullus than to the *Epodes*. A partial exception should be made for the *Ibis*, a bizarre product of Ovid's exile excoriating an unnamed and probably fictitious enemy; Callimachus is the primary model, but some influence from the *Epodes* is likely as well.[6]

3 *Tenuit nostras numerosus Horatius aures*. By a fine irony, the closest parallel to Ovid's punning use of *numerosus* (not just 'harmonious' but also 'composing in many metres') is the *numeri innumeri*, the 'uncountable metres', that were said to mourn the death of Horace's *bête noire*, Plautus; cf. Aulus Gellius 1.24.3.

4 See Syme (1978) 143–5.

5 A. Barchiesi (2001b) 79–103.

6 So briefly S. J. Harrison (2002) 93.

Horace's example was important for later satire, but not to the exclusion of Lucilius. That is partly due to Lucilius' renewed popularity in later periods: Quintilian (93) reported that Lucilius still had admirers in Flavian times, the most ardent of whom preferred him not only to other satirists but to all other poets. The prominent role that Horace had given Lucilius may also have helped keep the fame of the older poet alive; more specifically, the emphasis Horace placed on Lucilius' outspokenness (*libertas*) made that an issue to be confronted by later satirists.[7] For Persius and Juvenal, Horace does not so much supersede Lucilius as offer another way of doing satire; for example, Persius claims that both Lucilian acerbity and Horace's milder form of criticism are beyond his reach (1.114–18). Despite that assertion, Horace remained a constant presence for Persius – one count registers nearly 80 reminiscences in the 134 lines of his first satire.[8] Persius' thumbnail sketch of Horace as a satirist – 'as his friend laughs, Horace slyly puts his finger on his every fault; once let in, he plays about the heartstrings'[9] – comes closer than any other description to capturing his unique blend of play and earnest. For Juvenal, who measures his satire more in Lucilian than in Horatian terms, Horace is nonetheless both a generic model and a school author like Virgil, too familiar to need mentioning by name: thus he can express the idea 'themes worthy of Horatian satire' by the elliptical 'themes worthy of the Venusine lamp' (1.51).[10]

The *Odes* are among the works of literature that so successfully embody their form as to render imitation in the strict sense impossible. To the best of our knowledge, no Latin writer in the next 400 years composed a body of lyric poetry comparable to the *Odes*; given Horace's disdain for imitators, he may not have been entirely displeased by the absence of successors. Yet paradoxically the *Odes* enjoyed the longest and richest ancient reception of any of Horace's works.

Horace seems for reasons not now recoverable to have been disappointed in the initial reception of *Odes* 1–3, but the response of one reader could hardly have been more gratifying. Augustus was prompted to commission a grand ceremonial ode to mark the celebration of the Centennial Games in 17 BCE; the *Carmen Saeculare* must be one of very few works of Latin literature mentioned, along with its author, in an official state inscription. If Suetonius is to be trusted, the *princeps* was also the driving force behind

7 The topic is central for Freudenburg (2001). 8 Hooley (1997) 29.

9 *Satires* 1.116–17 *omne uafer uitium ridenti Flaccus amico / tangit et admissus circum praecordia ludit.*

10 *Venusinus* alludes to Horace, *Satires* 2.1.35, and the image of the lamp compliments Horace by implying that his polished poems required labour extending far into the night. See S. M. Braund (1996) ad loc., and for Horatian echoes in Juvenal 1 see Woodman (1983).

Horace's second, and final, collection of lyrics. From that point onward, Horace's position as Rome's premier lyricist was assured.

There appears to have been something of a vogue for Pindaric-style lyric following the publication of *Odes* 1–3, perhaps because that form of lyric had been less fully exploited by Horace than the personal mode of Alcaeus and Sappho. In *Epistles* 1.3.9–13, Horace predicts (not without irony) that a young man named Titius will soon win public notice for his Pindaric compositions. A more conspicuous figure is Iullus Antonius, whom Horace in *Odes* 4.2 proposes (again with some irony) as fitter than himself to produce a Pindaric ode celebrating Augustus' return to Rome in 13 BCE. (Iullus, the son of Mark Antony, was executed in 2 BCE for adultery with Augustus' daughter Julia.) Ovid's catalogue of poets active at the time (*Epistulae ex Ponto* 4.16.27–8) includes a Rufus, *Pindaricae fidicen . . . lyrae*, a play on Horace's self-description as *Romanae fidicen lyrae* in *Odes* 4.3.23. Imitation of Horace, along with Pindar, by these younger poets is highly likely, but nothing specific can be said.

The two aspects of the *Odes* most prized by ancient opinion are their metrical virtuosity and consummate verbal artistry. Quintilian, who regarded Horace as almost the only Roman lyric poet worth reading, explained that judgement as follows: 'He can be lofty sometimes, and yet he is also full of charm and grace, versatile in his Figures, and felicitously daring in his choice of words.'[11] Such capsule evaluations were the stock-in-trade of *grammatici*; a generation before Quintilian, Petronius parodied the genre while offering a superior version of it when he had the poetaster Eumolpus praise Horace's *curiosa felicitas*, the felicitous phrasing that is the product of much effort (*Satyricon* 118.5).[12]

Horace's lyric metres quickly became the object of academic study, for example, in the treatises of Caesius Bassus, a mid-first-century metrical theorist and writer of lyric poetry (also a friend of Persius and the dedicatee of his sixth satire), named by Quintilian as Horace's only rival.[13] Bassus was an exponent of *deriuatio*, a procedure by which established metres could be

11 *Nam et insurgit aliquando et plenus est iucunditatis et gratiae et uarius figuris et uerbis felicissime audax* (10.1.96, Loeb translation by D. A. Russell). Quintilian's *felicissime audax* is an echo of one of Horace's own literary judgements, on the tragic poetry of the Republic: *nam spirat tragicum satis et feliciter audet* (*Epistle* 2.1.166); Quintilian makes into a straightforward compliment what for Horace had been a highly ambiguous form of praise ('it was all daring and luck', Brink (1971) ad loc.).

12 Eumolpus is offering his inept version of a Horatian *Ars Poetica*; see Conte (1996) 68–72, also 124–30 for the Petronian *Cena Trimalchionis* in the light (or perhaps better, the shadow) of Horace's *Cena Nasidieni* (*Satires* 2.8).

13 Text in Keil (1874) 255–72.

altered, through the addition or omission of syllables, to generate new metrical patterns; the results of such a process can be seen in several choral odes of Seneca's tragedies *Oedipus* and *Agamemnon*, in which predominantly Horatian metrical cola are combined in polymetric non-stanzaic lyrics.[14] Senecan drama also contains odes in actual Horatian metres such as Sapphics, along with freer and arguably more successful treatments of favourite Horatian themes. Citations of Horace in Seneca's prose works are, however, remarkably rare, perhaps because they would not be as immediately recognisable as lines from the *Aeneid* or the *Metamorphoses*.

Statius' collection of occasional poems, the *Siluae*, contains one example each of the lyric metres with which the *Odes* were most often associated, the Alcaic and Sapphic stanzas (4.5 and 4.7 respectively). Those isolated lyrics constitute an *hommage* to Horace rather than an attempt to rival him as a lyricist, but Statius' relationship to Horace extends well beyond the poems in Horatian metres; in fact he often displays his dexterity by evoking Horatian phrases in a different metrical setting: thus *Siluae* 2.1, a poem of consolation to Melior on the death of a favourite slave-boy, renders the commonplace 'we shall all die' as follows: *ibimus omnes, / ibimus: immensis urnam quatit Aeacus umbris* (218–19 'we shall all go, we shall go; Aeacus shakes his urn for numberless shades'), combining the repeated *ibimus* of *Odes* 2.17.10 (where it refers to Horace and Maecenas), Aeacus as judge of the dead from *Odes* 2.13.22, and *omnes* and *urna* from *Odes* 2.3.25–6; all three Horatian odes are in the Alcaic metre, but Statius' reworking flows seamlessly in hexameters.

Statius' lyrics are representative of the Flavian interest in Republican and Augustan authors. Pliny (*Epistles* 9.22) praises the work of a friend, Passennus Paulus, who wrote elegies modelled on those of Propertius (from whom he claimed descent), then took up Horatian lyric and had equal success in replicating its qualities. On the evidence of Pliny, lyric at this time was reckoned among the lighter poetic genres in which cultivated amateurs might engage: in *Epistles* 3.1.7 he recalls that the eminent Vestricius Spurinna, thrice consul, composed *lyrica doctissima* in both Latin and Greek, and in 5.3.2 he couples reading lyric poets with attending comedies and mimes and appreciating risqué Sotadean verses.

Late antiquity

Horace retained his standing as a school author throughout late antiquity, and it is not surprising to find him frequently evoked by the major Latin poets

14 For a metrical analysis of the *Agamemnon* choruses see Tarrant (1976) 372–81.

of the period, such as Claudian and Ausonius. Two extant commentaries, remnants of a larger body of ancient Horatian scholarship, are additional evidence of Horace's place in the late-antique curriculum: one consists of large portions of the commentary of Pomponius Porphyrio (late third century?), while the other is a miscellaneous body of material put together perhaps in the fifth century, to which in fifteenth-century manuscripts is attached the name of Helenius Acro (*c.* 200 CE), author of a lost commentary on Horace.[15] As it has come down to us, Porphyrio's commentary is arranged in a non-chronological order, with the *Odes* first, followed by the *Ars Poetica*, then the *Epodes*, *Satires*, and *Epistles*; that order (with minor variations) is also common in medieval manuscripts of Horace, and the *Odes* are still placed first in modern texts of Horace. The privileged position of the *Odes* may reflect their greater prestige in later periods, or the general antique admiration for Horace's metrical mastery: pseudo-Acro begins with an elaborate account of Horace's lyric metres, and prefaces the commentary on each ode with a metrical analysis.

Near the end of his life Aurelius Prudentius Clemens, often called the first great Christian poet, published a collected edition of his poetry. Although most of his poems were written in hexameters, Prudentius framed the edition with two sets of hymns in diverse metres, including some used by Horace, and added an introductory poem in which he implicitly cast himself in the role of a Christian Horace.[16] The *praefatio* recalls Horace both in its metrical form (a three-line stanza made up of Asclepiads in ascending order of length) and in the poet's self-portrayal: Prudentius notes his advanced age as Horace had done in *Odes* 4.1.6, and professes to turn aside from frivolous pursuits to the proper use of his literary gifts, as Horace had claimed to do in the opening of the *Epistles* (1.10–11). Prudentius also weaves together allusions to the *Odes*, giving them a negative colour by associating them with the secular life that he is now foreswearing: thus *lasciua proteruitas* (10) combines *Odes* 1.19.3, *lasciua licentia*, and 5, *grata proteruitas*, and *male pertinax* (14) is lifted from *Odes* 1.9.24, where it describes a girl's 'poorly resisting' finger, and is reapplied to the 'wrongly stubborn' desire for victory, *uincendi studium*.[17] Prudentius similarly reinterprets Horatian motifs in other poems: for him it is the martyr's death that is *dulce* and *decorum*,[18] and the vocative *dux bone*, 'blessed leader' (*Odes* 4.5.5, 37) is transferred from Augustus to Christ.[19]

15 On these collections see Nisbet and Hubbard (1970) xlvii–li.
16 The reading of Horace and Prudentius in conjunction is in fact attested by the mid-fifth century; cf. Sidonius Apollinaris, *Epistulae* 2.9.4.
17 See Witke (1968); Palmer (1989) 8–16.
18 Roberts (1993) 49; Palmer (1989) 148–51.
19 Opelt (1970) 208.

Shortly after 527 CE, the ex-consul Vettius Agorius Basilius Mavortius corrected his copy of Horace with the assistance of his teacher Felix; their activity is recorded in a subscription that follows the *Epodes* in several ninth-century manuscripts.[20] Mavortius was a descendant of Vettius Agorius Praetextatus, a prominent pagan senator of the late fourth century and himself an energetic corrector of classical texts, but the family had in the interim converted to Christianity; as it happens, Mavortius' name appears in a contemporary owner's note in the Codex Puteanus of Prudentius, and it is an attractive speculation that 'Rustic' capitals were used in that manuscript (a virtually unique occurrence for a Christian text) to match the script of Mavortius' Horace.[21] For Mavortius, Horace and Prudentius were both part of a classical heritage that stood in acute need of help to survive. Earlier in the same decade Boethius, imprisoned in Pavia, had composed his *Consolation of Philosophy*, arguably the last major work of classical Latin literature. Boethius used the ancient form known as Menippean satire, in which sections of prose alternate with verse portions; in the poetic parts of the work Horace, sometimes filtered through Senecan tragedy, provides the most frequent classical source of inspiration.

In the eighteenth and nineteenth centuries, Horace was closely associated with a fund of memorable phrases, such as *simplex munditiis* or *splendide mendax*; today perhaps only *carpe diem* has a comparable fame, and its Horatian source is usually forgotten. The evocative power of particular phrases may have already been part of Horace's appeal in antiquity, as suggested by Propertius' and Ovid's adaptations of *exegi monumentum* or Prudentius' Christianising of *dulce et decorum est pro patria mori*. But Horace was also remembered for certain core themes and values, among them self-sufficiency, inner contentment, and fortitude in the face of danger and death. A passage from one of the 'Roman Odes' (3.3.1–8) held a particular attraction for poets of several centuries:

> Iustum et tenacem propositi uirum
> non ciuium ardor praua iubentium,
> non uultus instantis tyranni
> mente quatit solida neque Auster,
>
> dux inquieti turbidus Hadriae,
> nec fulminantis magna manus Iouis:
> si fractus illabatur orbis,
> impauidum ferient ruinae.

20 On the Mavortius subscription see Tarrant (1983) 185, and in general on such late-antique readers' notes see Reynolds and Wilson (1991) 39–43.
21 Questa (1996) 340.

The man who knows what's right and is tenacious
in the knowledge of what he knows cannot be shaken,
not by people righteously impassioned
in a wrong cause, and not by menacings

of tyrants' frowns, nor by the wind that roils
the stormy Adriatic, nor by the fiery
hand of thundering Jove: the sky could fall
in pieces all around him, he would not quail.[22]

Seneca in *Agamemnon* 593–603 has a chorus of captive Trojan women wistfully describe the peace attained by one who can escape the longing for life and face death without fear:

nullus hunc terror nec impotentis
procella Fortunae mouet aut iniqui
  flamma Tonantis.
pax alta nullos ciuium coetus
timet aut minaces uictoris iras,
non maria asperis insana Coris, . . .
non urbe cum tota populos cadentes
hostica muros populante flamma
  indomitumue bellum.

No fear moves him, no storm
of raging Fortune or the fire
of the hostile Thunderer.
That deep peace fears no crowds
of citizens, no victor's menacing anger,
no sea driven wild by harsh storm winds,
no fall of peoples with their whole city
as enemy fire destroys their walls,
no unconquerable war.

Prudentius, *Peristephanon* 4.5–12, sees the collapsing world and the hand that wields the thunderbolt in terms of the Last Judgement and the salvation of the just:

Plena magnorum domus angelorum
non timet mundi fragilis ruinam . . .

Cum deus dextram quatiens coruscam
nube subnixus ueniet rubente
gentibus iustam positurus aequo
  pondere libram

22 Translation by Ferry (1997).

> A house filled with glorious saints does not fear the collapse of a fragile world . . . when God will come, brandishing his brilliant right hand and resting on a crimson cloud, to establish for the nations the balanced scales of justice.

Boethius, *Consolatio* 1 *metrum* 4, though farthest removed from Horace in time, most closely reflects the Horatian perspective; his words, written under sentence of death, are testimony to Horace's continuing power to console and fortify:

> Quisquis composito serenus aeuo
> fatum sub pedibus egit superbum
> fortunamque tuens utramque rectus
> inuictum potuit tenere uultum,
> non illum rabies minaeque ponti
> uersum funditus exagitantis aestum . . .
> aut celsas soliti ferire turres
> ardentis uia fulminis mouebit

> He who keeps composure in a life well-ordered,
> who thrusts underfoot fate's arrogant incursions,
> confronts with integrity both good and evil fortune,
> succeeds in maintaining an undefeated outlook –
> he will not be moved by the wild threats of ocean
> spilling out and churning up waves from deep recesses . . .
> nor by the thunderbolt, which often blazing fiercely
> reduces to rubble the loftiest of towers.[23]

Carolingian postscript

Nearly all classical Latin authors went through a period of hibernation between the mid-sixth century, when the copying of classical texts slowed to a halt, and their rediscovery at some point in the Middle Ages.[24] Horace's dormancy was relatively brief. While generally overshadowed as an influence by Virgil and Ovid, he remains a presence in the classicising poets of the early sixth century, such as Maximian in Italy, Dracontius in North Africa and Avitus in southern France; for example, Avitus' epic on the Creation and Fall neatly applies Horace's lines on the return of spring, *redeunt iam gramina*

23 Translation by Walsh (1999). Walsh (118) notes that Philosophy, who has banished the Muses of poetry from Boethius' cell, repeatedly echoes Horace's *Odes* in her own verses. Could Boethius have recalled *Epistles* 1.1.10, in which Horace claims to set aside 'poetry and other trivial pursuits' (*uersus et cetera ludicra*) to devote himself – in hexameter poems – to the pursuit of truth and proper behaviour?

24 See L. D. Reynolds (1983) xv–xxxi for an overview.

campis / arboribusque comae ('grass now returns to the fields / and leaves to the trees' *Odes* 4.7.1–2) to the changeless state of Paradise, *stant semper collibus herbae / arboribusque comae* ('grass stands for ever on the hilltops / and leaves on the trees' 1.228–9).[25]

Although Ludwig Traube dubbed the tenth and eleventh centuries the *aetas Horatiana*, situated between the *aetas Vergiliana* of the eighth and ninth centuries and the *aetas Ouidiana* of the twelfth and thirteenth centuries, in fact Horace played a substantial role in the ninth-century revival of interest in classical literature, and by the end of the century was among the classical poets most firmly established in Carolingian literary culture.[26] The precise date and circumstances of his re-emergence are not clear.[27] Literary figures of the 780s and 790s, such as Alcuin and Paul the Deacon, were familiar with the name of Horace (or 'Flaccus') as an eminent poet of antiquity, like Virgil or Homer, but evidence for direct knowledge of his work at that time is inconclusive.[28] The mention of *Ars Poetica* in a booklist of the 790s has often been taken to show that a copy of Horace was then in the court library of Charlemagne at Aachen, but that hypothesis has recently come under challenge.[29] Most early Carolingian citations and imitations appear to be of passages previously quoted by patristic writers or grammarians (Priscian in particular), or excerpted in *florilegia*.[30] Carolingian compositions in metres associated with Horace, such as the Sapphic stanza, are in themselves not proof of direct knowledge, since those metrical forms had also been used by Prudentius and Boethius.

The place of Horace in Carolingian monastic culture is reliably demonstrated from the middle of the ninth century onward by extant manuscripts. Six manuscripts of Horace can be dated with some assurance to the ninth century; that number exceeds the surviving ninth-century copies of Lucan,

25 *Odes* 4.7 may have been particularly well known in later times: both Dracontius and Avitus echo Horace's *mutat terra uices* (3).

26 For a reassessment of Traube's dictum from a different perspective, see Vollmann (1996). Traube was thinking of Horatian satire as the focus of medieval imitation; cf. Bischoff (1971).

27 The following summary has benefited from the judicious discussion by Stella (1998).

28 See Ogilvy (1967) 162–3 for a list of possible echoes and imitations by Alcuin.

29 Villa (1992) argues instead that the booklist in Berlin Diez B Sant. 66 records part of the contents of an Italian library with roots in late antiquity, for example the Chapter Library in Verona.

30 Horatian lines appear in two ninth-century prosodic *florilegia* (i.e., collections of isolated verses illustrating the correct metrical quantity of key words): Mico of St Riquier's *Opus prosodiacum* and the anonymous *Exempla diuersorum auctorum*; see Munk Olsen (1979) 57–64.

Juvenal, Statius' *Thebaid* and Terence,[31] and to it should be added two ninth-century copies of Porphyrio's commentary on Horace. It was long ago suggested that knowledge of Horace was introduced to the continent by Irish monks;[32] while that hypothesis can no longer be entertained, the involvement of insular scribes in the circulation of his works is beyond doubt. One of the earliest surviving copies is Bern Burgerbibliothek 363, written in an exuberant Irish minuscule in a continental scriptorium[33] and representing a distinctive form of the Horatian text.[34] Lombardy, a region with close ties to Irish foundations, is the certain or likely origin of two other early copies, Paris BnF lat. 7900A (c. 900, Milan), and its relative Milan, B. Ambros. O 136 sup. (s. ix/x).[35] Vatican Reg. lat. 1703, probably the earliest extant copy, originated in Alsace, probably Weissenburg; the manuscript was written before 849, since it contains annotations in the hand of Walahfrid Strabo, who died in that year.[36] The two remaining ninth-century copies are of French origin, London BL Harley 2725 (s. ix^{4})[37] and Paris BnF lat.10310 (s. ix–x). In addition to those surviving copies, a text of Horace is recorded in a library catalogue of Lorsch compiled shortly after 860.[38] Analysis of textual variants in the early witnesses rules out descent from a single source and argues instead for the survival into the Carolingian period of at least two ancient exemplars, if not three.[39] Where those exemplars had been preserved and how they became the basis for the ninth-century transmission cannot yet be determined, but it seems likely that in the case of Horace, as with several other classical authors, a central part was played by books imported from Italy to the north.[40]

By the third quarter of the century, direct knowledge of Horace among Carolingian writers was no longer a rarity. A single example will suffice, that of Heiric of Auxerre (d. c. 876), called by Traube the most learned poet

31 Two manuscripts previously assigned to the ninth century (e.g. by Tarrant (1983) 183), Leiden B.P.L. 28 and Paris lat. 7972, should probably be dated to the tenth century.

32 Winterfeld (1905).

33 Bischoff (1994) 125 tentatively suggested St Gall.

34 'The superficially disordered and unsophisticated codex preserves much ancient and good material,' Brink (1971) 4; Brink's description also fits the extracts from Ovid's *Metamorphoses* that the manuscript contains.

35 On Paris 7900A see Villa (1979) 35–41; the Ambrosian manuscript was ascribed to N. Italy or S. France by Bischoff (1994) 164.

36 Bischoff (1994) 122. Walahfrid may have encountered Horace near the end of his life, since his poetry does not display certain knowledge of him.

37 Bischoff (1994) 114–15.

38 Glauche (1970) 28; McKitterick (1989) 185–91. Horace has the catalogue number 429, and is immediately preceded by Juvenal and Lucan.

39 Brink (1971) 29.

40 L. D. Reynolds (1983) xxii–xxiv.

of the century.[41] One of his poems, a rebuking address to his poetry book (*allocutio ad librum*), takes its inspiration from Horace's *Epistles* 1.20. As Prudentius and Avitus had done before him, Heiric deftly transfers Horatian expressions to Christian contexts: in his *Life* of St Germain of Auxerre, he applies Horace's appeal to Venus at the start of *Odes* 4, *rursus bella moues? . . . parce, precor* ('are you stirring up war once again? . . . spare us, I beg') to a resurgence of the Pelagian heresy (4.378–82), and makes the claim of Lydia in *Odes* 3.9.15 that she would die twice for her lover's sake (*pro quo bis patiar mori*) into an attribute of the saint ready to die twice over for the sake of the Lord's commandments (5.369 *bis . . . mori propter domini praecepta paratum*).

Horace had been a staple of the school curriculum in antiquity, and he soon became a school author for the Middle Ages as well. The earliest explicit reference comes from shortly before 1000, when Gerbert of Aurillac, the future Pope Sylvester II, was lecturing on Horace in the schools of Reims; since Persius and Juvenal are mentioned in the same context, the work in question was probably the *Satires*.[42] But there are indications that scholastic interest in Horace had already begun in the ninth century. One such piece of evidence is the imposing collection of texts in Paris 7900A, in which Horace appears along with Lucan, Juvenal, Terence and Martianus Capella, each provided with copious annotation, ancient or medieval. It is very plausible that the collection was intended for scholastic use of some kind.[43] The Paris manuscript also exemplifies another medieval practice with a possible scholastic intent, marking the text with musical notation, or neumes. Nearly fifty neumed manuscripts of Horace have been registered, dating from the ninth to the twelfth century; while the functions of neuming can only be guessed at, one likely purpose was to assist in the memorisation and explication of Horace's lyric metres.[44]

A link between Horace and music is appropriate for a poet whose lyric poems were by generic convention 'songs' (*carmina*) and who pointed with pride to his control of complex 'measures' (*modi*). One of the most impressive examples of Carolingian religious poetry is a hymn in honour of John the Baptist beginning *Vt queant laxis*, written in Sapphic stanzas and generally ascribed to Paul the Deacon.[45] The poem's language is Prudentian rather than Horatian, but it has at least a circumstantial connection to Horace,

41 Traube (1896) 421. 42 Glauche (1970) 63. 43 Glauche (1970) 36.

44 Full study by Wälli (2002); see 165–9 for Paris 7900A, 245–50 for Vatican Reg. lat. 1703; also Ziolkowski (forthcoming).

45 Principal editions include Duemmler (1881) 83–4 and Szövérffy (1964) 186–8, who calls it 'perhaps the best hymn of the early Carolingian period' (186). The attribution to Paul the Deacon is not secure, and the hymn is markedly superior to Paul's other religious poetry.

since, in the earliest extant source, Bern 363, only a few folios separate it from Horace's *Odes*. The hymn was soon set to a melody that would make its first stanza famous in the history of music, because the notes corresponding to the initial syllables of the six half-lines outline a scale in ascending order:

> UT queant laxis REsonare fibris
> MIra gestorum FAmuli tuorum,
> SOLve polluti LAbii reatum,
> Sancte Ioannes.

In the eleventh century Guido of Arezzo turned the resulting series of syllables into a mnemonic device in teaching music and produced the solfege system that with minor adjustments is still in use today. This chain of connections ends with a direct link to Horace: in an eleventh-century Montpellier manuscript (Ecole de Médecine 425 H), *Odes* 4.11 is neumed with the melody of *Vt queant laxis*.[46]

A single Carolingian manuscript unites several moments in Horace's medieval and modern reception. Florence, Bibl. Laur. lat. 34.1, is an elegantly written tenth-century codex with copious marginalia.[47] It was purchased by Petrarch in Genoa in 1347 and contains nearly 250 annotations in his hand.[48] In the 1930s, the conjunction of Horace and Petrarch made the Florence manuscript an icon of that glorious Italian past that the Fascist regime was assiduously promoting. A meticulously exact facsimile was published with an accompanying essay by the eminent Latinist Enrico Rostagno; in his peroration, Rostagno quoted the *Carmen Saeculare*, *possis nihil urbe Roma / uisere maius* (11–12 'may you see nothing greater than the city of Rome'), and claimed that Horace's wish was even then being brought to fruition through the energies of Il Duce.[49] Today Mussolini's vision of a restored Roman Empire is only a memory, but the codex remains, and with it the testimony of a great medieval lyricist's regard for his ancient predecessor.

FURTHER READING

Only isolated aspects of this topic have so far received detailed treatment. A. Barchiesi (1993) cogently places Ovid's *Tristia* 2 in relation to Horace's *Letter to Augustus*. Horace's influence on later satire is explored by Hooley (1997) and Freudenburg (2001). Witke (1968) and Palmer (1989) discuss Prudentius' use of Horace.

46 Ziolkowski (2000) 80 n. 16; Wälli (2002) 156–60, 279–81.
47 Reproduction of folio 27 verso in Chatelain (1884–1900) pl. 87.
48 See M. Feo (1998) 405–7.
49 Rostagno (1933) 39.

Ziolkowski (2000) offers an overview of the medieval practice of setting classical poetry to musical notation, and Wälli (2002) provides photographs of all manuscripts of Horace containing such notation. More detail on the ninth-century manuscripts of Horace is available in Tarrant (1983). For readers with Italian, the essay by Stella (1998) on Horace in ninth-century Carolingian writers in the *Enciclopedia Oraziana* can be warmly recommended.

21

KARSTEN FRIIS-JENSEN

The reception of Horace in the Middle Ages

'Note that Horace wrote four different kinds of poems on account of the four ages, the *Odes* for boys, the *Ars Poetica* for young men, the *Satires* for mature men, the *Epistles* for old and complete men.'[1] Every epoch will try to form its own image of the author behind a widely diffused school text, and medieval readers of Horace were no exception. The quotation belongs to a twelfth-century scribe who managed to compress one particularly influential medieval understanding of Horace the poet into a formula. Horace's friend and fellow poet Virgil became famous in the Middle Ages for his all-embracing prophetic wisdom, and their younger contemporary Ovid for a conflict with the Emperor Augustus that was intriguingly connected with his love-life. Horace was not the stuff that prophets or expert lovers are made of, but instead he became the embodiment of a typical human being who had lived through the stages of life and had written about them in turn for the benefit of people of his own age group. For medieval readers believed that the sequence of Horace's works found in most complete manuscripts, the one outlined in the quotation, did in fact represent the chronology of Horace's oeuvre, in the way that complete manuscripts of Virgil do. Moreover, a well-known passage in Horace's *Ars Poetica* (156–78) speaks eloquently about the ages of man and how important it is for the poet to make individual characterisations of them. Therefore Horace had simply followed his own good advice both in his art and in his life.

In many respects medieval education in the Latin West stood in the tradition of imperial Rome, and in both epochs extensive reading of poetry was regarded as an effective didactic tool. The canon of authors varied, and, for a period in late antiquity and in the early Middle Ages, Christian poets were preferred over the pagan canon of imperial Rome. However, the school

1 Bruxelles, Bibliothèque royale, 10063–5, fol. 79v: *Nota: Oracius fecit quatuor diuersitates carminum propter quatuor scilicet etates, odas pueris, poetriam iuuenibus, sermones uiris, epistulas senibus et perfectis*; see Hajdú (1993) 232.

curriculum that was introduced into the cathedral schools of Germany and France in the second half of the tenth century and which spread to England and elsewhere concentrated on the pagan Roman poets. This pagan canon was not seriously challenged during the later Middle Ages, even if some 'modern classics' such as Walter of Châtillon's *Alexandreis* (from the 1180s) supplemented it. The original cathedral-school education, which Stephen Jaeger characterises as a 'school of manners and letters',[2] had its golden age in the eleventh century. One may well ask how the reading of pagan poets might contribute towards such a programme.

The poets who belonged to the ancient Roman canon had status as authorities in the fields of prosody, linguistic usage and style. But could they teach Christian pupils morally good behaviour as well? In a series of articles Philippe Delhaye discussed the question from a twelfth-century point of view, but his results have also been applied to the preceding century. Delhaye points to the existence of a concept of a non-theological morality which could also be found in pagan authors, and this morality was normally named *ethica*.[3] That is why the introductions (*accessus*) to medieval commentaries on the pagan Roman poems almost invariably claim that their texts 'belong to that part of philosophy called *ethica*'. To interpret poetry in moral terms was certainly not alien to classical antiquity, but medieval interpreters normally went further than the ancients. This insistence on the moral aspect of pagan literature was often a way to justify the reading of it, one suspects, as Delhaye argues.

The fortune of the pagan authors had fluctuated, but even in the high and late Middle Ages, when they were actually a staple element in the school canon, warning voices were often heard, and at all times the pagan classics had some inveterate enemies. One of the original warning voices belonged to St Jerome. His own education had included the pagan classics, which he cherished. However, when he felt that the salvation of his soul was at risk, he once wrote: '"What harmony can there be between Christ and the devil?" What has Horace to do with the Psalter?'[4] This cry resounded through the centuries, and one of those who heard it was the Burgundian historiographer Rodulfus Glaber, who in the 1030s told the story of a heretical movement in Italy that was crushed by fire and sword. Its originator was a certain Vilgardus of Ravenna, an assiduous student of grammar: 'One night some demons assumed the likeness of the poets Virgil, Horace and Juvenal. They appeared before him and perfidiously thanked him because he dedicated

2 For instance C. S. Jaeger (1994) 53–75. 3 Cf. e.g. Delhaye (1958), in particular 71ff.
4 St Jerome, *Epistles* 22.29 (quoting 2 Cor. 6.14): '"qui consensus Christo et Belial?" quid facit cum psalterio Horatius?'

himself so lovingly to the works in their books, and because he was such a successful messenger of theirs to posterity.'[5] One might claim that Vilgardus' demons were not the real Virgil, Horace and Juvenal, but Rodulfus' warning against reading the pagan poets of the school curriculum seems clear enough.

Manuscripts, commentaries, glosses

In western Europe Horace was among the most widely read Roman poets throughout the Middle Ages. One of our best connoisseurs of the classical tradition, Birger Munk Olsen, is even inclined to see precisely the eleventh century as 'the veritable *aetas Horatiana*':[6] he thus defends a part of Ludwig Traube's famous sweeping statement about dividing the eighth to thirteenth centuries evenly into the ages of Virgil, Horace and Ovid. Eleventh-century manuscripts containing Horace's *Odes* (a total of 50) are more numerous than the corresponding manuscripts of Virgil's *Aeneid* (46), and almost five times as numerous as manuscripts of Ovid's most popular work, the *Metamorphoses*. In terms of figures the *Odes* and the *Aeneid* are closely followed by Horace's own hexameter poems, and not far behind are Juvenal's satires and Terence's comedies. Virgil, Horace, Juvenal and Terence were in fact highly recommended authors in the school canon that was established in the late tenth century, as witnessed by contemporary schoolmasters such as Gerbert of Aurillac and Walter of Speyer.[7] From the ninth to the sixteenth centuries about 850 manuscripts of various works of Horace have been preserved.[8] Virgil was probably the most popular Roman poet in the Middle Ages, and in comparison manuscripts of his works number about 1,000. The main groups of Horace's poems (*Odes*, *Ars Poetica*, *Satires*, *Epistles*) seem to be rather evenly balanced against each other through the centuries, but in-depth statistics exist only for the period before 1200. However, of the total number of manuscripts of Horace, about 400 belong to the fifteenth century, that is, a period when Renaissance humanism influenced patterns of reading.[9] The *editio princeps* of Horace's works was printed in about 1470.

Important evidence for how a text was studied can be deduced from the manuscripts themselves, in particular from the ancillary material in them

5 Rodulfus Glaber 2.23 *quadam nocte adsumpsere demones poetarum species Virgilii et Oratii atque Iuuenalis, apparentesque illi* [sc. Vilgardo] *fallaces retulerunt grates quoniam suorum dicta uoluminum carius amplectens exerceret, seque illorum posteritatis felicem esse preconem*.

6 Munk Olsen (1996) 3, 17.

7 Cf. e.g. Munk Olsen (1991) 30f.

8 See Villa (1992–4), and Villa in Mariotti (1996–98) I. 319–29; pre-thirteenth-century manuscripts are described in Munk Olsen (1982–9) vols. I and III:2.

9 Friis-Jensen (1995b) 229.

accompanying the basic text, such as marginal commentaries and glosses. We know that many medieval manuscripts of Horace transmit older commentaries in their margins, most often the late-antique compilation known as Pseudo-Acro. This is an interesting and significant indication of the level of seriousness with which Horace was studied. On the other hand only commentaries actually composed in the Middle Ages can offer us specific information about medieval interpretations or changing attitudes. Medieval commentaries on Horace normally pretend to exist in a timeless continuation of his own pagan world, and topical references to Christianity and to contemporary events or facts are rare. Likewise, such moralising as can be found is often rather discreet. However, some commentaries from around 1100 combine frequent references to the medieval Christian world with explicit moralising, and even now and then, anachronistically, turn Horace into a monk.[10] This attitude is most likely a conscious pedagogical strategy.

Glosses in Latin are a regular feature of manuscripts of Horace throughout the Middle Ages, and Suzanne Reynolds has made a special study of the strategies of reading they reveal.[11] About twenty mainly eleventh- and twelfth-century manuscripts of the texts of Horace are provided with glosses in Old High German.[12] German-speaking students translating Latin texts must have had a harder time than their French and Italian fellows, due to the greater distance between their mother tongue and Latin, and the glossing of difficult words was a solution. These glosses are of great interest to linguists, but first of all they confirm that Horace was studied diligently in this period. The same may be said about vernacular glosses in French and English that appear in English manuscripts of Horace, mainly in the thirteenth century.[13]

The *Odes* and *Epodes*

'It should be known that Horace did not observe such great diversity or variety in his works without reason. For he took into consideration the various ages and the various circumstances of human life, and that is why he gave such great variety to his oeuvre. For first he composed his lyrics, and in them, speaking to the young, as it were, he took as subject-matter love affairs and quarrels, banquets and drinking parties. Next he wrote his *Epodes*, and in them composed invectives against men of a more advanced

10 See Friis-Jensen (1988) 89; cf. Bischoff (1981) 266.
11 S. Reynolds (1996) passim, and with further references.
12 Siewert (1986). 13 Hunt (1991) 63f.

and more dishonourable age.'[14] All traces of devilry are absent in this Horace who appears in the *accessus* to the French standard commentary on his *Satires*, probably composed in the mid-twelfth century.[15] Instead we meet an appealingly human poet, at the outset presumably a young man, who possesses the gift of expressing the feelings of his own age group in his poetry, including love. The fact that his poems also carry a moral message is suspended until the mention of the *Epodes*, but it goes without saying and will be repeated in the *accessus* to the *Odes*.

We know that the chronology of Horace's oeuvre presented here is all wrong, and yet the naïve simplicity of the model has its own attraction. Besides, youth and lyrical poetry tend to go together in many literatures, even when love is not the main theme, which means that the association may after all reflect some sort of socio-psychological truth. Moreover, since medieval commentators on *Epistles* 1.1.10 with some right interpret that passage as the older Horace's farewell to lyric poetry in favour of more philosophical reflections, it looks as if there may be a time for everything in a poet's life, both love poetry and philosophy. This 'times of life' topos, as Peter Dronke calls it in a context of late twelfth-century rhythmical poetry, may also imply that youth in general has a right to be in love, an appealing thought for all young people.[16]

There exists a considerable number of medieval commentaries on the *Odes*; few have been studied in detail. They are all anonymous, but in one of them there is a reference to an older commentary by a 'Master Alfred' (*magister Aluuredus*), probably a twelfth-century Englishman.[17] A group of related commentaries transmitted in twelfth-century manuscripts can be located to northern France and England, and it is highly probable that they reflect the doctrines of an influential eleventh-century teacher or commentary. Another commentary on the *Odes* may be traced back to a scholastic environment on the borders of France and Germany, possibly the Liège region, which flourished in the late eleventh century.[18] Originally these commentaries all began with an *accessus* (some are now fragmented), and more *accessus* have been transmitted on their own. There is a high degree of redundancy regarding

14 Marchionni (2003) *accessus* 1.1, 'Sciendum est Horacium non sine ratione tantam operum diuersitatem, uarietatem obseruasse: siquidem diuersas etates et diuersos humane uite status considerauit, ideoque adhibuit operi suo tantam uarietatem. Primitus enim lirica composuit, ibique quasi adolescentibus loquens amores et iurgia, commessationes et potationes materiam habuit [cf. *Ars Poetica* 83–5]. Deinde epodon condidit et ibi in homines fortioris et turpioris etatis inuectiua composuit.'

15 Marchionni (2003) xiii. 16 See Dronke (1976) 204ff. 17 Friis-Jensen (1997a) 64f.

18 St Gallen, Stiftsbibliothek 868, s. xii 1/2; cf. Bischoff (1981) 263ff.; Siewert (1986) 216; Friis-Jensen (1997a) 56f.

the information presented in these *accessus*. One of the recurring pieces of information is particularly interesting. The key concept for the entire genre of lyrical poetry is claimed to be variety (*uarietas*), both in metre and in subject-matter. The connection between variety and the lyrical genre is an etymology, unfortunately false, defined for instance thus: '[The name] "lyrics" is derived, as Isidore tells, from *lirin*, that is from variety' (*Lyrica ut dicit Ysidorus apo ty lirin, id est a uarietate*).[19] The metrical variety of Horace's lyrics was a didactic challenge that was met in the form of metrical glosses, as well as being a constituent of the lyrical genre, false etymology or not: several of Horace's imitators in the Middle Ages focus very much on his metrical variety. Some *accessus* also emphasise the original meaning of the words *carmen* and *oda*, thereby pointing to the convention that Horace's lyrics were written to be sung.

There exists evidence that medieval singers took up this challenge. In a recent monograph Silvia Wälli has analysed the melodies or neumes to a number of Horatian texts from the Middle Ages which carry musical notation. There are 48 instances of neumatic notation to 26 different texts, one of which is the *Carmen Saeculare*, two are *Epodes*, and the rest *Odes*. The manuscripts belong to the eleventh and twelfth centuries, and most of them are French and German. One of Horace's *Odes* (3.12) has also found its way into the manuscript of the *Cambridge Songs*, an eleventh-century singer's textbook, even if not all its texts are provided with neumatic notation. Silvia Wälli regards the musical notation as support for orally transmitted melodies, and she ventures a guess that performances of these songs cannot have been restricted to school audiences.[20]

A sign of Horace's popularity is the large number of quotations from all his works found in almost every genre of medieval Latin literature.[21] Another witness to Horace's influence in the Middle Ages is the numerous imitations of his poems found in quantitative Latin poetry. Horace's lyrics, too, were often made the object of imitation, but modern critics perhaps rather unfairly tend to be disappointed by the results when they do not recognise their own worldly and immensely sophisticated Horace.[22] All medieval students of Horace were sincere Christians, and many of them members of the clergy. These facts are naturally reflected in their poetry, even when they write with Horace in mind. Another important influence on the language and metrical technique of medieval writers of quantitative lyrics was

19 St Gallen, Stiftsbibliothek 868, s. xii 1/2, p. 13, referring to Isidore of Seville, *Orig.* 3.22.8, 8.7.4; cf. Friis-Jensen (1993) 280ff.

20 Wälli (2002) 345, 354.

21 See e.g. Quint (1988), in particular 47–124.

22 Cf. e.g. Stotz (1998).

the religious poetry of St Ambrose, Prudentius and their many followers. A medieval writer of (for instance) Sapphic stanzas would be familiar with the rich tradition of religious Sapphic poetry originating in Prudentius.[23] He would have absorbed prosodic and verbal formulaic patterns from this tradition, and it was neither possible nor desirable for him to ignore them completely when he tried to imitate Horace.

Recently David Daintree has attempted to single out poems in Sapphic stanzas inspired by Horace from the corpus of Carolingian poetry edited in the *Poetae Latini Aevi Carolini*.[24] By establishing a minimum list of criteria for Horatian prosody and practice he concludes that Horace's lyrics were available to, and directly influenced, at least three ninth-century poets writing in Sapphic stanzas, namely Walahfrid Strabo, Sedulius Scotus and Notker Balbulus.[25] This is an interesting and very convincing attempt to go beyond the sphere of verbal borrowings from Horace as evidence of imitation. Walahfrid, Sedulius and Notker were contemporaneous with the earliest preserved manuscripts of Horace. The eleventh and twelfth centuries, the heyday of cathedral-school education with its canon of pagan poets, produced a much larger number of poets in Western Europe who imitated Horatian lyric.

Two Sapphic stanzas by Alphanus of Salerno (d. 1085) may serve as an example of how Christianity can be fused with Horatian spirit.[26] Alphanus belonged to a noble Lombard family from Salerno and was educated in the famous schools of his home town. As a mature man he became a monk in Monte Cassino, and later archbishop of Salerno. Alphanus wrote religious and personal poetry in lyrical forms, in this case an ode in twenty Sapphic stanzas addressed to a boyhood friend, the schoolmaster William of Aversa. William had prospered through his teaching in the Norman settlement of Aversa but finally took monastic vows, and Alphanus praises the ideal of poverty. The ode contains verbal borrowings from Horace and an eight-stanza-long animal fable to prove his point, in the manner of Horace's *Satires* 2.6. Alphanus concludes the poem on a personal note:

Sic suos mundus perimit sequaces,
Cuius omnino metuenda dona
Dedicant regis uice purpuratos

23 Cf. Stotz (1998). On Prudentius and Horace see Tarrant, chapter 20 above.

24 For Horace in the Carolingian period, see further Tarrant, chapter 20 above.

25 Daintree (2000) 901; Stella is rather more cautious in the cases of Walahfrid and Sedulius; see Stella (1998) 162; Mariotti (1996–8) III. 474.

26 F. Lo Monaco gives a detailed survey of Alphanus' relations with Horace in Mariotti (1996–8) III. 85–91.

Pauperiei . . .
Non mihi marsupia plena nummis
Non honor desunt epulaeque regum,
Dum Ceres detur simul et Caleno
Plena diota.[27]

Thus the world destroys its followers, and its utterly fearsome gifts destine those clad in kingly purple to poverty . . . I need no purse full of coins, no worldly dignity nor kingly dishes, as long as there is bread and a full jar of Calenian wine on the table.

Alphanus expresses the ideal of monastic poverty by contrasting it with the risky possession of worldly riches, and he uses the word *mundus* in its full Christian sense of 'the secular world'. However, the rest of the phrasing and his line of thought evoke Horace. In Horace, poverty is often a positive concept, meaning 'frugal living', in one instance called 'honest poverty' (*probam . . . pauperiem*, *Odes* 3.29.55f.). When Horace contrasts the rich and the poor, as he often does, the rich are often simply called 'kings', and he emphasises the precarious nature of their position. Alphanus' final two lines show a gentle irony worthy of Horace: the symbols of frugality are bread and a full jar of, presumably excellent, Calenian wine on the table.

The most prolific and systematic medieval imitator of Horace's lyrics was a monk from Southern Bavaria known as Metellus of Tegernsee. About 1170 he wrote a huge collection of poems forming a complete life, passion and miracles of St Quirinus, patron saint of the monastery of Tegernsee. The first part contains odes, and in its heading Metellus claims that these odes are 'composed in different metres after the fashion of Horace', *odæ . . . ad instar odarum Flacci Oratii diuerso metri genere editæ*;[28] note the allusion to the keyword of the lyric genre, *diuersitas*. Metellus in fact first imitates all Horace's metres, and then he goes on to the lyric metres of Prudentius and Boethius not found in Horace. In his own special way Metellus thus demonstrates that metrical diversity is central to the emulation of the ancient lyrical poets. Metellus also borrows words and phrases from Horace in a systematic way, but he manages to restrict Horatian influence to the surface of the text, as it were, while his odes remain naïvely devout in spirit.

27 Alphanus of Salerno, *Carmina* 19.69–72, 77–80, Lentini/Avagliano, *PL* 147, 1261d; for *epulae regum* contrasted with pauperies cf. for instance *Satires* 2.2.45, for *Calenum* (sc. *uinum*) e.g. *Odes* 1.20.9 and 1.31.9, for *diota Odes* 1.9.8; lines 73–6 (left out here) contain a massive borrowing from *Odes* 1.22.6–10; cf. F. Lo Monacho in Mariotti (1996–8) III. 87, 90; Friis-Jensen (1993) 290f.

28 See Metellus of Tegernsee (1965) 172; Metellus' relations to Horace are discussed by Jacobsen ibid. 53–100 and by G. Orlandi in Mariotti (1996–8) III. 355f.

In general, medieval imitators of Horace's lyrics seem mainly to restrict themselves to personal poetry addressed to friends, or perhaps we are just better able to recognise the signs of Horatian imitation in these poems. Few Horatian love lyrics in quantitative metres exist, and that holds even more true for civic poetry. The historian Saxo Grammaticus inserted dialogue poems in a variety of quantitative lyrical metres into the legendary part of his *History of Denmark* (c. 1200), claiming that they were translations of vernacular poetry. Horace was among his models, as a number of convincing verbal borrowings (mainly from the *Odes*) proves.[29] One of Saxo's poems (7.4.5) is a lover's persuasion in Sapphics, and that should be enough to make us think of Horace. In the more than 100 years between Saxo Grammaticus and Petrarch it seems that imitations of Horace's lyrics in quantitative metres were rare. On the didactic front John of Garland's *Parisiana Poetria* from about 1220–35 teaches all Horace's metres, with specimens written for the occasion.[30] However, for the following period one must go to Italy to find new treatises that contain comprehensive instruction in quantitative lyric metres, according to Jürgen Leonhardt.[31]

Writers of rhythmical Latin lyrics also imitated Horace on the verbal level. These borrowings are sometimes difficult to recognise as such because the metrical dimension is absent. Space does not allow us to discuss a related and interesting question: if the keyword of the Horatian lyrical genre is 'variety', could medieval writers of Latin lyrics in that case have found it legitimate to adopt a rhythmical metre and still want their poem to be regarded as Horatian in its entirety?[32] This question poses itself in even more radical form in the case of the great transitional figure of Petrarch (1304–74). Petrarch loved Horace, not least his *Odes*; he wrote a letter to Horace in the form of a Horatian ode, and he imitated Horace's *Epistles* in his own Latin verse letters. There are also clear borrowings from Horace in Petrarch's carefully composed collection of lyrics in Italian, the *Canzoniere*.[33] Is it possible that Petrarch believed so completely in the medieval Horatian principle of variety that he saw his collection of vernacular lyrics as a Christian and modern counterpart to Horace's collection of *Odes*? Among various pieces of evidence, one seems to possess particular force. In Petrarch's Latin *Eclogue* 4, with the title *Dedalus*, the main character Tirrenus, who clearly is a mask for Petrarch himself, once received a lyre as a gift from its maker, Dedalus.

29 Cf. e.g. G. Orlandi in Mariotti (1996–8) III. 468ff.

30 See John of Garland (1974) 198–218.

31 Leonhardt (1989) 124–7.

32 See Friis-Jensen (1993) 293–8; an obvious candidate is the Archpoet, for whom cf. S. J. Harrison (1997) and V. de Angelis and G. Orlandi in Mariotti (1996–8) III. 94f.

33 M. Feo gives a detailed survey of Petrarch's relations with Horace in Mariotti (1996–8) III. 405–25.

In the course of the poem a certain Gallus tries to persuade Tirrenus to hand over the lyre to himself, but in vain. There are good arguments for an identification of Dedalus with Horace, and in that case the allegory must mean that Petrarch acknowledges his profound debt to Horace the lyrical writer, most likely in the *Canzoniere*.[34]

The *Ars Poetica*

'He next wrote his book about the *Ars Poetica*, and in that instructed men of his own profession to write well.'[35] Medieval interpreters of Horace's *Ars Poetica* all shared the view that the poem is entirely didactic, and accordingly they refrained from the usual classification under *ethica*. Horace's poem, together with commentaries on it, was actually used as the main introduction to the writing of poetry until the new, independent 'arts of poetry' began to appear in the late twelfth century, and it remained popular during the later Middle Ages. Horace's *Ars Poetica* can only with difficulty be forced to yield clear-cut pieces of advice for the budding poet, but eleventh- and twelfth-century commentators actually managed to elicit these. Their method was to interpret Horace's text very firmly in the light of ancient rhetorical doctrine. This tendency was already found in the late-antique commentary tradition, and it is very pronounced in the *Vienna Commentary* from the eleventh century, the earliest full-scale commentary on the *Ars Poetica* that has been edited and studied so far.[36] Its main source for rhetorical doctrine is the pseudo-Ciceronian *Rhetorica ad Herennium*, which became popular in the eleventh century. The rhetorical interpretation of Horace developed even further in the French *Materia Commentary* (from c. 1125–75), the standard commentary on the *Ars Poetica* for the later Middle Ages, and probably also the 'missing link' between Horace and the new arts of poetry.

The most interesting feature of this commentary is a rather heavy-handed interpretation of the first thirty-seven lines of the *Ars Poetica* as the doctrine of the six vices of poetic composition and their respective virtues, an interpretation which exists in embryonic form in earlier commentaries. This doctrine is first defined at length in the *accessus*, and then pointed out in Horace's text. The first four vices are the following: 1. 'incongruous arrangement of parts', 2. 'incongruous digression in speech', 3. 'obscure or incongruous brevity',

34 See Friis-Jensen (1997b) 89–96.

35 Marchionni (2003) *accessus* 1.3, 'Deinde de arte poetica librum scripsit ibique sue professionis homines ad bene scribendum instruxit.'

36 Zechmeister (1877), who dates it to the ninth century; for the later dating see e.g. Friis-Jensen (1990) 322.

4. 'incongruous change of style'.[37] Except for the fourth vice, all six have corresponding virtues defined by changing the adjective 'incongruous' into 'congruous'. The concept of 'congruence' is clearly related to the general concept of appropriateness or decorum, which is so important in Horace. Some of the precepts are easily connected with rhetorical doctrine, for instance the first rule with that part of rhetoric called 'arrangement' (*dispositio*), and the fourth rule with the part called 'elocution' (*elocutio*). In the *Materia Commentary* the fourth rule comprises an exposition of the three levels of style and the faults connected with them, a doctrine known for instance from the *Rhetorica ad Herennium* and already associated with Horace in the *Vienna Commentary*.[38]

The first independent 'art of poetry' was written in prose by Matthew of Vendôme about 1175, and there can be no doubt that he used the *Materia Commentary* for parts of his doctrine. The same holds good for Geoffrey of Vinsauf, both in his prose treatise on poetics and in his versified *Poetria Noua* (c. 1208–13) – its title alone proclaims Geoffrey's ambition to emulate Horace's *Poetria Vetus*, as it was sometimes called to distinguish it from Geoffrey's work. Matthew and Geoffrey no longer saw the point in studying Horace's complex and difficult text with the help of a modern interpreter, and they offered a much simpler model in their own works. A later commentator on Geoffrey's *Poetria Noua* simply claims that Geoffrey succeeded in 'explaining fully the art of poetry which Horace had taught confusedly and compendiously'.[39] Geoffrey was the first writer of poetics among many to discuss the concepts of amplification and abbreviation of a text, a doctrine with very little foundation in ancient rhetoric. It is possible that Geoffrey's point of departure was the second and third Horatian rules of poetic composition, as discussed in the *Materia Commentary*, 'incongruous digression in speech', 'obscure or incongruous brevity' and their corresponding virtues.[40] Other central medieval poetological doctrines that originated in a rhetorical interpretation of Horace's *Ars Poetica* are: natural versus artificial order,[41] and propriety in the characterisation of sex, age, social standing and nationality.[42]

37 In the terminology of the *Materia Commentary* (Friis-Jensen (1990)), they are the following: *1. partium incongrua positio*, *2. incongrua orationis digressio*, *3. brevitas obscura/incongrua*, *4. incongrua stili mutatio*.

38 Cf. Quadlbauer (1962) 32–53.

39 See Woods (1991) 63 n. 30 'ut artem poeticam posset (sc. Gaufridus) declarare perfecte quam Oracius nimis confuse et compendiose docuerat.'

40 See Friis-Jensen (1990) 327; (1993) 371–5.

41 See e.g. Quadlbauer (1962) 32f.

42 See Friis-Jensen (1993) 382–5.

The new arts of poetry flourished in the thirteenth century, and for all we know they may have influenced the popularity of Horace's *Ars Poetica* negatively. However, new manuscripts of the *Ars Poetica* as well as of older commentaries on it, such as the *Materia Commentary*, were produced in considerable numbers, as late as in the fifteenth century, and new commentaries were composed in the thirteenth and fourteenth centuries,[43] before humanist scholarship took over.

The *Satires* and the *Epistles*

'Later he added his book of *Satires* (*sermones*), in which he reproved those who had fallen a prey to various kinds of vices. Finally he finished his oeuvre with the *Epistles*, and in them, following the method of a good farmer, he sowed the virtues where he had rooted out the vices.'[44] The author of the *Sciendum Commentary* on the *Satires* acknowledges the close relationship between Horace's *Satires* and his *Epistles*, the more so as he believes them to have been written in succession.

One of the most successful imitators of Horace's *Satires* in the Middle Ages, the German author from about 1100 calling himself Sextus Amarcius, seems to have been influenced by a similar view. In his huge hexameter work in four books (with further subdivisions), which probably carried the Horatian title *Sermones*, the first two books exemplify vices, and the two last mainly virtues. Amarcius explains the division himself at the beginning of Book 3: 'With my defamatory song I have so far advised against dangerous and sordid behaviour for those who enjoy the gift of the Holy Spirit; now my aim is to attract to the virtues those called back from the path of vices.'[45] This statement has been interpreted as a veiled reference to the *Satires* and *Epistles* of Horace, each of which comprises two books and shows differences in style comparable to those of the two halves of Amarcius' *Sermones*.[46] The linking of the didactic functions of Horace's *Satires* and *Epistles* found in the *Sciendum Commentary* seems to support this interpretation of Sextus Amarcius' work.

43 Cf. Villa (1992) 39–42.

44 Marchionni (2003), *accessus* 1.6–7, 'Postea librum sermonum addidit, ubi diuersis generibus uiciorum irretitos reprehendit. Ad ultimum opus suum in epistolis terminauit ibique ad modum boni agricole uiciis extirpatis uirtutes superseminauit.'

45 Sextus Amarcius (1969) 3.1–4 'Hactenus infestas infami carmine sordes / Dissuasi flatus sancti karismate functis, / Nunc ad uirtutes uiciorum calle reductos / Allicere est animus.'

46 See Jacobsen (1978) 207f; cf. Quint (1988) 180, and F. Stella in Mariotti (1996–8) III. 92f.

The twelfth-century standard commentary on Horace's *Epistles* called the *Proposuerat Commentary* is an advocate of the life-and-works concept of Horace also found in the *Sciendum Commentary*, and it rephrases its basic metaphor, claiming that 'in the present work Horace, following the method of a good farmer, sowed the virtues when he had previously in his *Satires* rooted out the vices'.[47] These two commentaries are several times found together in the manuscripts and seem to originate in the same French scholastic environment. The *Proposuerat Commentary* interprets the opening of *Epistles* 1.1 as the mature Horace's renunciation of the lyric poetry of his youth in favour of poetry that has an unadulterated moral message: '[Horace] writes this first letter to Maecenas, and excuses himself with the words that he ought not to write any further lyric poems, offering a valid reason . . . The reason is that since he has changed in age, he accordingly ought to change his mind for the better'.[48]

The *Epistles* mark the culmination of Horace's development as a writer, since his conscious choice of this genre makes it possible for him to devote himself to moral philosophy and to the dissemination of its doctrines. In this way Horace manages to begin his career as a whole-hearted singer of love and youth and still end up as a kind of sage. The conversion from youthful lyrics to mature moral poetry may again be one of the archetypal literary themes, but there is reason to believe that in the medieval Latin West it often carried Horatian associations.[49]

An example of a medieval writer who must have been influenced by this Horatian life-and-works model is Marbod of Rennes, for many years head of the cathedral school at Angers, and bishop of Rennes from 1096. He wrote poems in several different genres, but his 'conversion' is proclaimed in a collection of ten philosophical and satiric hexameter poems that must be seen in some sense as a Horatian entity. The first poem of this cycle is a dedicatory letter to a fellow bishop, in which he renounces the frivolous and flashy poetry of his youth. According to Marbod, youth and mature age make different claims on the poet: 'Moreover, it was proper for the young man to sing about cheerful matters which manifest reason teaches us must

47 *Proposuerat Commentary on Horace's Epistles*, accessus, 'cum enim prius in sermonibus uicia extirpasset, consequens erat ut in hoc opere ad modum boni agricole superseminaret uirtutes' (Paris, Bibliothèque nationale, lat. 5137, s. xii/xiii, fol. 39rA).

48 *Proposuerat Commentary on Horace, Epistles* 1.1.1, 'Hanc . . . primam epistolam scribit ad Mecenatem, excus[s]ans se quod amplius lirica non debeat scribere, pretendens competentem rationem . . . Est autem hec ratio, quia scilicet mutauit etatem, debet igitur mutare animum in melius' (Paris, Bibliothèque nationale, lat. 5137, s. xii/xiii, fol. 39rA).

49 Cf. the above section on the *Odes*, with n. 16.

be denied to the mature man: *his* words must be spiced with moral flavour and must oppose vices with a stern face.'[50]

Towards the end of the Middle Ages, Dante builds a monument to the medieval cult of Horace's friend Virgil in his *Divine Comedy*. However, even though Virgil had been chosen as Dante's guide through Hell and Purgatory, he still belonged among the virtuous but unbaptised poets in the first circle of Hell, and this is where he and Dante encounter Homer, Horace, Ovid and Lucan (*Inferno* 4.88ff.). To Dante, Horace is *Orazio satiro*, an epithet that probably reflects a special status for the *Satires* and the *Epistles* in the later Middle Ages. As we have tried to show, this is not true for the eleventh and twelfth centuries, when the *Odes* seem to enjoy an equal popularity.

FURTHER READING

The *Enciclopedia Oraziana* (Mariotti 1996–8), particularly vol. III, comprising Horace's later *fortuna*, is a mine of information about how Horace was read and imitated in the Middle Ages. The information is organised in a series of articles, mainly on individual writers. Two older collections of material about Horace's *Nachleben* still have some use as surveys, Manitius (1893) and Stemplinger (1921). For references to new literature the section on 'Fortleben, Horatius' in *Medioevo latino* (Leonardi 1980–) is very useful. Literature on pre-thirteenth-century manuscripts of Horace and of commentaries on his works is listed in Munk Olsen (1982–9), and supplements are given in Munk Olsen (1991–2002). Literature on 'classical scholarship', including commentaries on Horace, from the ninth to the fifteenth centuries is given in Friis-Jensen, Munk Olsen and Smith (1997). Kindermann (1978) is an interesting attempt to provide a survey of medieval notions about satire as a genre, and much of the book is relevant for Horace. An important survey of the medieval commentary tradition with an anthology of texts is given in Minnis and Scott (1988). The monographs by Quint (1988) on the medieval reception of Horace, Leonhardt (1989) on the quantitative metrical tradition in the Middle Ages, S. Reynolds (1996) on medieval reading and Wälli (2002) on Horatian texts with neumes are all interesting contributions to important aspects of the study of Horace in the Middle Ages.

50 Marbod of Rennes (1984), capit. 1.47–50, 'Praeterea iuuenem cantare iocosa decebat, / Quod manifesta seni ratio docet esse negatum, / Cuius morali condiri uerba sapore / Conuenit et uitiis obsistere fronte seuera'; Leotta's commentary in this edition gives a full report of the many Horatian borrowings.

22

MICHAEL McGANN

The reception of Horace in the Renaissance

Introduction: Petrarch to Jonson

Nothing prepares us for Petrarch's conversation with Horace. It is not just a matter of quotations, adaptations or echoes. He creates a Horatian self-portrait – of a man with few needs and a gift for friendship, who does not seek social advancement, finds the city unpleasant and enjoys a life of withdrawal, but unlike Horace is a Christian and a tormented lover. And nothing in Horace anticipates Petrarch's drastic comparison of reading Horace (and other favoured writers) with the process of digestion or with roots penetrating his marrow (*Familiares* 22.2.12–13).

One of the constants in the reception of Horace had been, and would long continue to be, the importance of the *Ars Poetica*, which during the sixteenth century was joined as a canonical text by Aristotle's *Poetics*.[1] Milestones marking developments in that reception are few between Petrarch's death in 1374 and the 1460s. Perotti's treatise on the metres of Horace and Boethius was written in 1453, and during the following decade there were courses of lectures in Florence, Rome and Verona. Horace was first printed around 1470, as was Perotti's handbook. The ancient commentaries followed and, in 1482, a contemporary one by Landino. Also in the 1480s Politian lectured on Horace in Florence.

Apart from scholarship, Horace is mainly present in quattrocento Italy through the composition, by poets such as Filelfo, Pontano, Politian, Marullus and Crinitus, of Latin lyrics that are Horatian in metre, language

1 In Robortello (1548) a commentary on the *Poetics* was juxtaposed with a prose paraphrase in Latin of *Ars Poetica*. See Stillers (1988) 107–24, 142–3; and in general Herrick (1946); Weinberg (1961); and Norton (1999). On the medieval reception of the *Ars Poetica* see Friis-Jensen, chapter 21 above.

or theme.[2] Flaminio and Torquato Tasso continued this tradition into the sixteenth century, which was also an age of translation.[3] Vernacular experiments in classical lyric were few in Italy (though Torquato's father Bernardo should be mentioned), being discouraged by the dominance of Petrarch. In France a complete printed text first appeared in 1501, Lambinus published his great edition in 1561 and Montaigne made constant and creative use of Horace in quotation. Both the Latin poetry of Macrin and others and the French of the Pléiade, above all of Ronsard and Du Bellay, register the lively presence of Horace. The Pléiade looked back to Pindar also, and towards the end of the century Chiabrera in Italian and the German Paulus Melissus in Latin derive from it Pindaric as well as Horatian inspiration. In Germany, where there were lectures on Horace from the 1450s and a complete edition was published in 1492, Conrad Celtis wrote a Latin *carmen saeculare* for 1500, which with four books of *Odes* and a book of *Epodes* was posthumously published in 1513. The vernaculars were dominant in Portugal and Spain, and in the sixteenth century Horace was present there in the work of Sá de Miranda, Antonio Ferreira and Garcilaso. And in Poland, where Celtis had studied and taught in 1489–91 and had located the first of the four love affairs narrated in his *Amores* (published in 1502),[4] Jan Kochanowski later wrote lyrics in both Latin and Polish that show the pervasive influence of Horace.

In England and Scotland the reception of Horace took place in a context of literature rather than of scholarship, and creative imitators, at pains sometimes to obscure their relation to a classical text, could make it difficult to establish the nature and extent of its reception.[5] How Horace, Henryson the Scottish schoolmaster and Wyatt the Tudor diplomat relate to one another in their versions of the fable of the two mice has been viewed very differently.[6] Skelton's polyglot parrot is more forthright about his reading: after proclaiming loyalty to Henry and Catherine, he weaves Horace's *vis consili expers mole ruit sua* ('force without counsel collapses under its own weight', *Odes* 3.4.65) verbatim into his speech, warning the royal couple and probably criticising Wolsey (*Speke, Parrot* 40–2).[7] In *Medicinable Morall* (1566) Horace's earliest English translator Thomas Drant interestingly juxtaposed

2 McGann (1995; 2004); Mastrogianni (2002); Filelfo's *Odes* and a first volume of Pontano's *Lyric Poetry*, edited respectively by Diana Robin and Rodney Dennis, have been announced by the *I Tatti* Renaissance Library.

3 In Germany, however, Horace was not translated until well into the seventeenth century: Stemplinger (1921) 113.

4 Rupprich (1970) 523–4, 609–10.

5 Burrow (1993) 40.

6 P. Thomas (1964) 264; D. Gray (1979) 133; M. Powell (1983) 119–20; Burrow (1993) 40.

7 Heiserman (1961) 131–3; Walker (1988) 78–9.

translations of *Jeremiah* and the *Satires*, which as a pagan work he said he approached with the ruthlessness shown by the ancient Hebrews to beautiful foreign captives.[8] Another coming together of Horace and the Bible took place in the same year, when the Scot Buchanan published his paraphrases of the *Psalms*.[9] In *The Faerie Queen*, Spenser, exceptionally, introduced to a northern fairyland divinities more at home in the world of the *Odes*.[10] (The well-disposed and amused tolerance of Horace's Sabine neighbours (*Epistles* 1.14.37–9) was very different from the view of the incomer taken by the Irish who destroyed Spenser's castle in 1598.)[11] It is unclear how wide or deep Shakespeare's reading of Horace was.[12] There may be some connection between Cleopatra's final serenity in *Anthony and Cleopatra* (5.2.233–7; 275–85) and *Odes* 1.37.21–32.[13] More telling is the similarity between Jessica's being told in *The Merchant of Venice* not to listen to 'the wry-necked fyfe' nor to 'thrust [her] head into the public street' (2.5.30; 32) and *Odes* 3.7.29–31, where Asterie is warned against 'the song of the plaintive pipe' and forbidden 'to look down into the streets'.[14] With Jonson, to whom with Drayton may be credited the beginnings of the English classical ode,[15] there is no problem of 'small Latin' when in 1601 he convincingly puts Horace and other Augustans on stage in *Poetaster* (see below).

Petrarch: Lalage and Laura

Three of Petrarch's sonnets are noteworthy for their close, and complementary, links with Horace, *Odes* 1.22.[16] This (see chapter 19 above) begins with the assertion that no matter where the upright man goes (outlandish places are mentioned) he need carry no weapons to defend himself (1–8). The poem gives an example: a monstrous wolf has fled before the speaker (let us call him Horace) as he wandered in a Sabine wood without weapons or cares, singing of Lalage (9–16). The personal note is continued in the remaining

8 Drant (1566); Braden (1978) 12. 9 McFarlane (1981) 286.
10 *Faerie Queene* 6.10, esp. 21–2. Cf. Erickson (1996) 67.
11 Judson (1945); Shepherd (1989).
12 Material for consideration of the question may be found in Baldwin (1944) and Thomson (1952). Martindale and Taylor (2004) has very little on Horace.
13 Westbrook (1947). Neither Baldwin (1944) nor Thomson (1952) makes this connection. For a discussion of a possible stylistic link see C. and M. Martindale (1990) 161.
14 Baldwin (1944) 507 dismissed the similarity as 'growing naturally out of parallel customs'. Cf. Thomson (1952) 32. For a subtle discussion of passages in *Timon of Athens* and *Epistles* 1.19 see Adair (1998).
15 Herford and Simpson (1925) 394–406; Maddison (1960) 290–304; Trimpi (1962) 192–204; Hardin (1973) 1–9, 136–45.
16 This group of poems was studied by Maggini (1950). See also Petrie (1983) 94, 144, 203.

eight lines of the poem, where Horace returns to the no-matter-where theme of the beginning (5–8). Using imperatives, 'put me (*pone me*) . . . where . . .', 'put (*pone*) me beneath . . .' (17–21), he declares that whether in a cold wasteland or in an uninhabitable sun-scorched region, he will continue to love the 'sweetly laughing, sweetly speaking Lalage' (23–4).

The three sonnets draw on different parts of the ode. In *Canzone* 145 *pone me* is reproduced almost letter for letter as *ponmi*, which is used to structure the whole sonnet (1, 3, 5, 7, 9, 12) just as *pone* (*me*) structured the last two stanzas of the ode. Petrarch offers a much wider range of alternatives, of which the most striking is at line 11: *libero spirto od a' suoi membri affisso* ('with my spirit free or attached to its limbs'), which seems to envisage an out-of-the-body experience, for which Horace offers no precedent. The last pair displays a Petrarchan concern with reputation: 'with fame obscure or glorious' (12). Laura is not referred to in this sonnet, but her effect on Petrarch is brought out in the concluding two lines, which correspond to, and contrast with, Horace's declaration of continuing love for Lalage: Petrarch says, 'I shall be as I have been, I shall live as I have lived, prolonging my fifteen years of sighs' (*continuando il mio sospir trilustre* 13–14). Nothing here of sweet laughter or talk.

They are reserved for *Canzone* 159, as indeed is the name Laura: *in selve mai qual dea / chiome d'oro sí fino a L'AURA sciolse?* ('What goddess in the woods ever loosed hair of gold so fine to the breeze?' 5–6). But all her beauty is, shockingly, 'guilty of his death' (*la somma è di mea morte rea* 8). He does not dwell on this thought, but immediately turns to a more distanced mode in the sestet, where a seeker after 'divine beauty' is introduced. His quest will be in vain if he does not see the sweetness of 'her' sidelong glance (9–11). Distance is maintained in the final tercet, but the darkness of line 8 returns as killing is associated with sighs and Horatian sweet talk and laughter: 'he who does not know how sweetly she sighs and how sweetly speaks and sweetly laughs does not know how Love heals and slays' (12–14).[17]

There are three elements in the ode which do not appear in these two sonnets: the solemn opening with its virtuous traveller, the dangerous wood, and the carefree, singing poet. Only the first of these is absent from *Canzone* 176, which opens with 'inhospitable and savage woods', where there is the dangerous presence of armed men (1–2); Petrarch travels free from care (*vo securo io*, 3) and later sings of 'her' (5–6). Her name almost appears

17 Foscolo (1953) 241–2 described Horace as being merely 'gay and gallant', in contrast to Petrarch, who (unknowingly) reignited the fire of Sappho, fr. 199 D. L. Page (1968), which Horace had extinguished. Noferi (1962) 269 observes a clear reference in Petrarch to Catullus 51, 4–5, as well as to Horace, but see Ludwig (1990) 187–8. Cf. Bosco (1965) 149.

at line 9, *L'ORE* ('the breezes'), the form perhaps determined, ominously, by the need to rhyme with *orrore*, 12. While apparently dangerous, neither wolf nor armed men worry the poet lovers. Horace is completely carefree and happy; not so Petrarch. One thing undermines his sense of security, 'the Sun with its rays of living Love' (3–4). That Sun is Laura. As he speaks of his song about her, he interjects a cry, 'oh my thoughts without sense!' (*o penser' miei non saggi!*): he is not facing the reality of his relationship with her (5–6). The rest of the sonnet is concerned with the fact that physical separation from Laura does not remove the threat she poses to his equanimity (6). He thinks he sees her among 'ladies and damsels', but it is only a clump of trees (7–8). The hallucination is auditory, too, as he hears her in the sounds of the countryside – the rustle of leaves in the breezes that embody her name, the sough of the wind on the hilltops and the murmur of a stream (9–11). This open landscape, however, pleases him less than the relief from Laura's oppressive nearness to be found in the spookiness of a dark wood (12–13). But the complexity of his feelings about Laura does not allow him to find unalloyed pleasure there. He is cut off from the physical sun, the light of which is the medium of his daytime visions of her, and this is welcome, but it also causes him (and here the ambiguity of his position in regard to Laura becomes clear) to lose too much of *his* Sun (*dal mio Sol troppo si perde*) (14), that Sun which he has said can alone frighten him (3–4).

It may seem strange that Petrarch, for whom love is overwhelmingly an unhappy experience, should have found the Lalage ode so congenial. A few points can be made. Horace actually represents himself here as being, like Petrarch, a practitioner of love poetry (10). *Dulce ridentem . . . dulce loquentem* ('sweetly laughing . . . sweetly speaking' 23–4) seems to anticipate the sound of vernacular poetry even if Petrarch's *ride* ('laughs') rhymes with the ominous *ancide* ('slays'). Lastly there is the part played by the sun in the last stanza of the ode. In 21–2 it is 'too close', forbidding civilised human life (*in terra domibus negata*). Those lines cannot have failed to speak to Petrarch, for whom the sun both in itself and as Laura is destructive as well as life-giving. In these sonnets the balance inclines largely to the side of the harmful, excessively close sun. At the beginning of 145 it 'slays (*occide*) flowers and grass' (1) just as in 149 Love is capable of 'slaying' (*ancide* 12) his victims. Love and the sun (or better the Sun, who is Laura) come together in 176, where the poet's sense of security is threatened only by that Sun with its (her) 'rays of living Love' (3–4). Finally the balance shifts a little in the sun's (or rather *his* Sun's) favour as he confesses that too much success in avoiding that threat may be achieved at the price of losing too much in his relationship with Laura (14). Hardly as forthright as Horace's *Lalagen amabo* (23), but still an acknowledgement, however grudging, that he cannot live without her.

Ariosto: Maecenas and Ippolito d'Este

The surviving satires of Ludovico Ariosto, which formally are epistles, belong to his maturity, corresponding to the *Epistles* in Horace's career.[18] Ariosto could look back over a life very different from Horace's. His nine siblings, widowed mother and well-connected but probably impecunious father,[19] who drove him to the study of law (6.154–9) at an age more appropriate to the writing of poetry, contrast strongly with Horace's humble origins and indebtedness to his father (the only member of his family he mentions) for his liberal education. Ariosto's devotion to a simple life (e.g. 2.13–27) seems, unlike Horace's, to be hard won as he acknowledges his 'vast greed for ownership', which only a realisation of the vanity of human desires can overcome (3.187–207). Again, unlike so many of Horace's poems, these satires are not suffused with thoughts of friendship, whether affectionate, critical or gently teasing. *Satire* 7.127–38 is exceptional: if he went to Rome, he would have cultured men to talk to (he names eight) and someone to escort him over the seven hills, guidebook in hand. The passage recalls Horace, *Satires* 1.10.81–8, which incorporates *honoris causa* the names of fifteen 'scholars and friends'. If *Satire* 7 was written to be the last in Ariosto's collection, the parallel is even more striking, since the passage in Horace concludes his first book. Both men had patrons: Maecenas and Ippolito and Alfonso d'Este. In contrast to the overwhelmingly favourable view which Horace gives of his relations with his patron Maecenas, Ariosto portrays both d'Estes as difficult – demanding and not punctilious about supporting their man (1.88–93, 97–108, 238–43, 4.175–201). None of the satires is addressed to either brother, whereas Horace directs three epistles and two satires to Maecenas. Nevertheless, it is in Horace that Ariosto finds a template for dealing with the clash between Ippolito and himself about his unwillingness to be with him in Hungary (*Satires* 1).[20]

Horace's seventh epistle is about the relationship between friends of unequal status. He had told Maecenas that he would spend a few days in the country, but has been proved a liar. He has been missing all August, in

18 See in general Grimm (1969). Ariosto's satires can be conveniently read, in Latin and in English, in Wiggins (1976). An earlier satirist, Filelfo, is considered by Haye (2003) as Lucilian and Juvenalian rather than Horatian.

19 Wiggins (1976) 77 n. 2.

20 Grabher (1967) 101–13 gives a useful account, but without mentioning Horace.

the autumn he intends to avoid unhealthy Rome, in the winter he will be beside the sea, and only in the spring will he revisit his friend (1–13). It is not clear whether the epistle is to be thought of as being in response to, or a pre-emption of, a protest from Maecenas. It deals with gifts, gratitude and the obligations which gifts may be thought to create. The gist of his explanation is that he is afraid of falling ill, and, if he is never to leave his friend's side, Maecenas must do the impossible by giving him back the constitution, looks and disposition of youth. If Maecenas is going to use his gifts to control him, they must be given back (25–36). Almost three-quarters of the epistle is not direct statement or argument, but is in the form of what Ariosto calls *essempi*, an animal fable (29–33), a little speech taken from the *Odyssey* (40–3) and two anecdotes, one timeless (14–19) and the other attached to a historical person (46–95).

Ariosto also deals with a difficult situation between men of unequal rank. Cardinal Ippolito has asked the poet to accompany him to his see in Hungary, and he has refused. He writes not to Ippolito, but to his own brother Alessandro and a friend, who are with the cardinal. The ostensible purpose of the poem is to enquire how Ariosto's stock stands with the cardinal and his court. However, having claimed that he dealt truthfully with Ippolito (unlike 'lying' Horace), he proceeds to repeat the reasons that he gave, any one of which should have sufficed. Like Horace, he begins with his health, but, as might be expected in a work more than two and a half times as long, he goes beyond climatic problems to mention wine, food and its preparation. If he were to make his own arrangements, it would cost money, and (the first mention of gift or salary) he has not had enough from the cardinal to pay for self-catering. The argument modulates into a discussion of how far his poetry is valued by Ippolito. Anything he has received has come to him not because of his verses, which he might just as well consign to the privy, but for being a hard-riding courier (19–114).

He raises the delicate question of gifts and liberty in the context of an address to Marone, another client of Ippolito's, who, he warns, will lose his freedom as soon as he receives a benefit. If Marone wishes to dissolve the connection, the best he can hope for is that the cardinal will take his gifts back while preserving good relations (*con amore e pace* 115–26). Now that he has raised in connection with someone else the question of recovery of gifts by the donor (not restitution by the recipient as in Horace), he can more easily speak of its happening to himself. That possibility, however, displeases him less than the prospect of losing Ippolito's love (a rare hint of past affection) and being hated by him. Fear of this is why he has never, from the time that he was refused permission to stay in Italy, appeared before him (127–38).

The atmosphere lightens (the effect is comparable with Horace introducing an episode from Homer into the epistle) as he conjures up from his own *Orlando Furioso* the figure of Ruggiero, ancestor of the d'Este, recalls how little his celebration of his deeds has been appreciated at court and declares himself unfit for the duties of a courtier. These may bring wealth, but at a cost. His studies would suffer, and it is these he must thank for feeding his mind, saving him from feelings of envy and teaching him satisfaction with a simple life (139–89).

Conscious that he has wandered off the point, he calls himself back, a Horatian touch (190–2, cf. *Satires* 1.1.108). There is a second reason: his family is vulnerable and needs him at home. And he himself is old – forty-four and bald. His brother who is with the cardinal may offer Ludovico's literary services, but there will be no travelling to the Danube. On the other hand (and here Horace's demand that Maecenas do the impossible is recalled), if he could have back the fifteen years he has spent in the service of Ippolito, he would even cross the Don. But if the undependable payment of seventy-five *scudi* a year is thought to give the cardinal the right to treat him like a slave, he must learn that the poet would rather live patiently in poverty.

There follows immediately an *essempio*, based on Horace's animal fable, expanded from five to fifteen lines (247–61). Horace tells of a fox creeping through a crack in a corn bin, devouring the corn so that she grew too fat to escape and being told by a weasel that she must leave the bin as thin as she was when she entered. The lesson for Horace is that, if challenged with this story, he should pay everything back (29–34). Ariosto's version is truer to the facts of natural history, with donkey and mouse replacing fox and weasel. The crack in the bin becomes a hole in a wall. Horace's 'thin' little fox becomes a donkey 'whose thinness showed every bone and sinew', and the fox's 'full body' becomes the donkey's 'belly larger than a great barrel'. Unlike Horace, Ariosto supplies a motive for his donkey's struggle to escape: 'fearing that his bones might be smashed', presumably by the owner of the corn. Horace's weasel simply says that the fox must get thin to get out; Ariosto's mouse is more specific: 'You need to begin vomiting up what you've got in your body and come back thin' (*che ritorni macro* 260; cf. Horace's *macra . . . repetes*). Vomiting violently represents the act of discarding with which both poets are concerned. Calling Ippolito *sacro*, 'sacred', an adjective regularly applied to the College of Cardinals, used here perhaps with an eye also to the meaning 'cursed', which Latin *sacer* can have, Ariosto says that if Ippolito believes that he has bought him, it would not be painful for him to give his gifts back (262–5). The conclusion is harsh, but the break is serious: they have not met since his unsuccessful request to be allowed to stay in Italy. Horace is more emollient. After telling a disturbing story of a great man whose help, given perhaps with a degree of malicious anticipation, sets a friend on a road leading from contented and moderate busyness to driven ruin so that he begs to return to his former state, he refrains in the concluding lines from explicitly aligning the story with Maecenas and himself, but simply states that if a former state of affairs is superior to the present, there should be a return to what has been abandoned. In the end it is a matter of insight.

There are differences between the poets' situations. Horace admits that he was deceitful and makes no reference to any reaction of Maecenas, while Ariosto has been frank and recognises that Ippolito may call him faithless and seek to recover his gifts (4, 127–35). Each poem advances two reasons or clusters of reasons for the writer's decision. For Horace it is a matter of health (3–9) and a feeling that he has grown old (25–8). These are supplemented by the observation, deriving from two of the *essempi*, that there is a lack of fit between himself and life with Maecenas (44–5; 96–8). Ariosto's reasons are health or more generally lifestyle (25–93) and family responsibilities (196–216). Interwoven with these are allusions to his role at the court of Ippolito: he is fit for nothing there except composing unappreciated celebratory poetry (85–108, 139–42, cf. 226–31); he is useless as a personal servant, and it is no longer appropriate that he should be an unwilling courier (142–56; *non si convien più* 156). Amusingly, he is physically too large to help Ippolito with his boots and spurs (*perch' io son grande*), whereas Horace implies that he is 'small' and says that 'small things' (not 'royal Rome', where Maecenas belongs) are appropriate to him (44–5). He makes no mention of duties owed to Maecenas (except implicitly that of joining him), and in particular says nothing about writing poetry for him. (Of course he is in a phase of not writing 'real poetry', *Epistles* 1.1.10.) Maecenas indeed is shown as singularly passive in the epistle, his reactions not being even surmised. The epistle gives no clue to the nature of life in the great man's company, while the satire is richly informative about the personnel and workings of a princely court. The difference may be connected with generic expectation, but it is likely that Horatian discretion also played a part.

Jonson: Horace on stage

When at the age of twenty-eight, in 1601, Ben Jonson staged *Poetaster*, he had passed through experiences reflecting Horace's life at many points.[21] Neither was socially advantaged, Horace's father having been a freedman, while Jonson was the posthumous son of a minister and the stepson of a master bricklayer. Horace was educated above his station, and Jonson's

21 Riggs (1989) 76–8.

education went beyond the needs of his stepfather's business. In his early twenties Horace fought as an officer at Philippi, while the youthful Jonson soldiered in the Low Countries. Horace portrays himself as a redoubtable fighter with the pen as his weapon (*Satires* 2.1.34–46). Jonson's pugnacity, evidenced in war, also landed him in prison after a fatal duel. But he fought with the pen also, and in *Poetaster*, set in Augustan Rome and performed by the Children of the Chapel, he delivered an attack on his enemies, lawyers and players as well as fellow dramatists, in which Horace himself, with Virgil and Augustus, states the timeless principles on which moral poetry may be written in a moral community.[22]

The play is remarkable for the amount of translated material that it contains. Ovid *Am.* 1.15 (1.1.39–80, largely a translation by Marlowe), Horace *Satires* 1.9 (3.1.1–3.7) and 2.1 (3.5.1–140, probably composed for the folio edition of 1640) and Virgil *Aen.* 4.160–88 (5.2.56–97) are only the most substantial passages. The characters Virgil and Ovid speak translations of lines which 'they' as poets have composed, and *Satires* 2.1, being in dialogue form, simply becomes a scene between Horace and Trebatius. *Satires* 1.9 needed a more thorough adaptation.[23] Most of the original is in dialogue, but it has a narrative thread, which had to be dispensed with in the play. Jonson's version more than compensates for these minor excisions, for, at 286 lines, many of them prose, it is considerably longer than its model, with 78 lines.

Some of this expansion can be seen as assisting the audience. The scene begins with a new character, who declares confidently that he will begin an ode to Maecenas. (This corresponds to Horace's modest 'totally absorbed in some trifle or other I was pondering' (2), though no-one in the audience would at first hearing be likely to realise this.) Crispinus, who has the role of Horace's unnamed persecutor in the satire and represents John Marston, enters with words spoken aside that identify the other character as Horace, 'an excellent poet', and make clear what lies behind the encounter: since Maecenas loves Horace, Crispinus will self-promotingly 'fall into his acquaintance' (3–6). Nothing corresponds to this speech in the satire, which does not reveal the other man's agenda until 43–8. Jonson continues to expand the beginning of the satire as he introduces the opening of the ode, a vaguely Horatian drinking-song which assimilates writing to drinking: 'I drink as I

22 Erskine-Hill (1983) 108–21, 169–70; J. Martindale (1993) 50–1, 54–8; Steggle (1998) 121. For Donaldson (1997) 191, Jonson's great poets live 'out of time, or equally in all times'. Timeless above all is *Ars Poetica*, which occupied Jonson over so many years. See Dutton (1996) 13–21; McCanles (1992) 37, 89–92; Donaldson (1997) 191; Stewart (2000) 177–84. For a general study see Enck (1966) 70–88.

23 Parfitt (1976) 50–4, 117–19.

would write, / In flowing measure, filled with flame, and spright' (8–12).[24] Later, in another addition, Crispinus plays the connoisseur of architecture and praises the street as 'polite and terse', another assimilation, of buildings to literary style (32–3).

Towards the end of the encounter, where there has been a great deal of talk about coiffure and clothes (not in Horace) (45–56, 67–76), Horace's friend Fuscus enters, but refuses to take the hint that he should rescue him (3.2.1–22). In Jonson he says limply that he does not want to interrupt his conversation (20–2). In the satire Fuscus' response is mischievously imaginative: 'I'll talk to you at a better time. Today's the thirtieth Sabbath. Do you want to offend the circumcised Jews?' 'I've no religious hang-ups,' says Horace. 'But I do,' says Fuscus. 'There are lots of us weaker vessels. Please forgive me. Another time' (68–72). Why did Jonson omit this vivid passage? It may be worth recalling that seven years previously the Jewish doctor Roderigo Lopez had been executed on a charge of plotting, on behalf of Spain, to poison the queen.[25] Was a light-hearted mention of a Jewish festival, even an invented one, too risky?

Perhaps the most interesting scene involving Horace is where Augustus asks about Virgil (5.1.75–141).[26] His question, which is very explicit about social position, gives offence to Horace: Maecenas, Tibullus and Gallus are 'gentlemen', ranking higher than Virgil, whose profession they share; Horace is 'the poorest' and therefore liable to feel envy (75–8).[27] Horace's reply, as Augustus later acknowledges, shows a 'free and wholesome sharpness' (94): Augustus is speaking 'after common men' when he assumes that poverty has as baneful an effect on a 'knowing spirit' as riches on 'an ignorant soul' (79–83). Horace claims that his soul is 'as free as Caesar's' and that his knowledge will enable him to give 'virtuous merit' its due (88–93). Accepting the rebuke, Augustus abandons the distinction and asks 'loved Horace' for his 'true thought of Virgil' (94–9). Horace uses the image of distillation to give a moral appraisal of Virgil's pure spirit (100–7). Gallus sees a fastidious purity in his verses also (108–15), and Tibullus, returning to the image of distillation, acknowledges his relevance to 'all the needful uses of our lives', so that when a man recalls any serious lines of his, he is able to breathe forth Virgil's *spirit* (116–23). Turning back to Horace, now called, in contrast to Virgil, 'material' (his work has substance), Augustus asks about Virgil's

24 It was not an unconsidered trifle; see Cain (1995) on 3.1.8–12.

25 Roth (1964) 143–4.

26 Cain (1995) 15–18.

27 Duncan (1979) 131, 136, assigns Horace a middle position, superior in morals to Ovid and inferior in every respect to Virgil, but overshadowed by Ovid in most of the play, and by Virgil in Act 5; Barton (1984) 81; Steggle (1999) 121–2. Talbert (1945) places Ovid at the centre of his discussion of *Poetaster*. See now Hardie (2002a) 97–105.

learning. It is not a matter of recondite words or recherché information, says Horace, but a summation of human knowledge, 'a direct, and analytic sum / Of all the worth and first effect of arts'. His poetry, 'so rammed with life', 'shall gather strength of life' and with time win ever more admiration (129–38).

This is a discussion of subtlety, linguistic power and moral seriousness. It is opened and closed by Horace, who, having spoken with a frankness even more striking than that displayed in 'his' seventh epistle, characterises Virgil in terms that do justice not only to his spiritual qualities, humane learning and poetic vitality, but also to his own independence of spirit, moral earnestness and critical insight.

Epilogue

In 1610 George Sandys, son of an Archbishop of York, poet and future Treasurer of Virginia, travelled to the Holy Land.[28] In *A Relation of a Journey* he tells how he arrived in Lesbos, speaks of its produce and quotes in translation *Odes* 1.17.21–2:

> Here underneath some shadie vine,
> Full cups of hurtlesse Lesbian wine
> Will we quaffe freely: nor yet shall
> Thyonian Liber with Mars brawle.[29]

In adding to his narrative a 'continuous flow of literary allusions', Sandys was a pioneer of travel literature.[30] Although the passage attests to the harmlessness of Lesbian wine ('not so headie as the ordinarie') and is not strictly an evocation of the island, it is tempting to see in Sandys a forerunner of eighteenth-century tourists recalling ancient texts at classical sites, where 'our memory', as Horace Walpole put it, 'sees more than our eyes'.[31]

FURTHER READING

Sowerby (1994) is a useful study of the reception of the classics in sixteenth- and seventeenth-century English poetry. A somewhat earlier *terminus a quo* would have been welcome, but a certain view of the periodisation of English literature may have discouraged this. (The title, which refers simply to 'Renaissance poetry', is misleading.) The book is helpful to the general reader in including accounts of ancient genres and an outline of the classical world.

For book-length studies of Horace in European literature it is necessary to go back to the opening decades of the twentieth century, which saw two ambitious surveys by

28 R. B. Davis (1955); Haynes (1986). 29 Sandys (1973) 15–16.
30 R. B. Davis (1955) 90. 31 T. Gray (1935) I. 160–1.

Stemplinger (1906; 1921). The former, which contains a great deal of material about Ariosto, Du Bellay and Ronsard, delivers more than its title seems to promise, and the latter is noteworthy in taking a thematic rather than a geographical or chronological approach. Ludwig (1993a) is an up-to-date, substantial and focused discussion of the subject, and Martindale and Hopkins (1993) contains a number of useful papers. The extensive sections on the reception of Horace from the medieval to the modern period and in different countries in the *Enciclopedia Oraziana* (Mariotti (1996–8) III. 81–612) also contain much useful and up-to-date material.

Curcio (1913) gives a long and detailed chronological account of Horace's presence in Italian literature over 600 years; for Petrarch there is Petrie (1983). Menéndez Pelayo (1951) is a massive resource for writing in Spain and Portugal. Milosz (1969) provides a way into Polish literature, and Glomski (1987) contains detailed discussion of Kochanowski. English satire, to which ancient, medieval and contemporary European traditions contribute, has been studied by J. Peter (1956) and Hester (1982). There has been much important work on the presence of Horace in the Latin poetry of the period, particularly by scholars writing in German (Schäfer (1970; 1976); Gruber (1997); Auhagen (2000)) and French (Schmitz (1994), which is a significant supplement to Lebègue (1936); Galland-Hallyn (2001)). Stillers (1988), which includes an excellent bibliography, makes an important contribution to the study of literary theory in Italy during the Renaissance.

23

DAVID MONEY

The reception of Horace in the seventeenth and eighteenth centuries

At the start of our period, in 1601, Ben Jonson identified himself with Horace, in *Poetaster*;[1] exactly 200 years later, in a soil barely scratched by Elizabethan adventurers, an anonymous author in Philadelphia's *Port Folio Magazine* chose to translate a sonnet of Charlotte Smith, the English Romantic, into five stanzas of Horatian Sapphics.[2] Between those two moments – one celebrated, one obscure – lies a vast, disparate mixture of receptions. The central part of our period is often called the 'Augustan Age' – sometimes a contentious term:[3] to what extent is it a Horatian age? It is not always profitable to try to distinguish specifically Horatian attitudes from a more general and pervasive neo-classical culture. The concept of politeness was to become influential, alongside the ideal of retirement from urban chaos; for Alexander Pope, as for Jonson, Horace was a means of self-fashioning. Both moralists and libertines could seek instruction in his works. Neo-Latin, alongside many vernaculars, continued as a medium of creative imitation. There follows a series of snapshots, from Britain and beyond, to illustrate at least some aspects of our poet's extraordinary cultural impact.

Translating, reading and editing

John Ashmore, in 1621, was the first to publish a selection of Horace's odes in English. He translated 17 of them (3.9 three times). Sir T[homas] H[awkins], in 1625, 'had rather teach Vertue to the modest, th[a]n discover Vice to the dissolute . . . [and not] take unhappy draughts, from the troubled and muddy waters of *Sensuality*'. Hawkins admits the 'lesse morall' 3.9 with reluctance, and only 'for Iul. Scaliger's sake, who much admireth it'. Ashmore

1 Cain (1995) 10–14; Money (1998) 15–17; Erskine-Hill (1996a) 135; see McGann, chapter 22 above.

2 Kaiser (1981) 274: published 14 March 1801.

3 Erskine-Hill (1983); Weinbrot (1978); Levine (2002).

approached it with gusto: 'In Fortunes lap, who then, but I, / By *Venus* luld-asleep did lie?' (from the third, looser version). Ashmore's version of *Odes* 1.5 (too immoral for Hawkins) is full of passion; his 'doublet wringing wet, and cod-piec't breeches' pack more punch than the 'dropping weeds' favoured by Milton and others.[4] Herrick tackled 3.9, as well as mixing 2.14 with other odes in a fascinating adaptation.[5]

Horace was popular among Restoration translators,[6] most notably Abraham Cowley, the earl of Roscommon, and Thomas Creech. Dryden's version of *Odes* 3.29 was much admired, and his 'Britannia Rediviva' imitated *Odes* 1.2.[7] Probably the most successful eighteenth-century translator was Philip Francis, who particularly impressed Dr Johnson.[8] His edition borrowed occasional odes from earlier writers, such as *Odes* 4.3 from Francis Atterbury, Jacobite bishop and friend of Pope; his note praises both Atterbury and the original, which is 'delicate and natural . . . noble and elegant . . . flowing and harmonious . . . Such is the Judgement of all the Commentators, but Scaliger is so charmed with it, that he assures us he would rather be Author of it, than be King of Arragon.'[9]

A more controversial figure was Christopher Smart, who produced both prose and verse translations; one way in which he 'consciously strove to emulate the urbane Roman was by using the current modes of speech of polite and impolite London society'.[10] He also sometimes experimented in classical quantities: thus *Odes* 1.38 'in the original metre exactly' – 'Thee the prompt waiter to a jolly toper / Hous'd in an arbour.'[11] For 1.11 and 1.18 he adopted archaic English fourteeners, but 'for convenience of printing, one line is severed into two'.[12] Since the resulting alternation between four- and three-foot lines would look quite normal to a modern reader, the note serves to emphasise Smart's curious mix of pedantry and accessibility. Earlier, Smart had updated *Odes* 2.4 as 'The Pretty Chambermaid': 'Atrides with his captive play'd, / Who always shar'd the bed she made.' Amusing though it is, this also reflects a casual attitude towards servants' chastity that was being challenged in the 1740s: Smart's chambermaid is more *Shamela* than *Pamela*.[13] Some Horatian obscenity, however, was too much for Smart: he omits *Odes* 4.10 entirely (as if it had never existed, confusingly renumbering later odes), and silently suppresses the end of 4.1. The boy Ligurinus could not be presented

4 Money (2004a); Ashmore (1621); Hawkins (1625).
5 Carne-Ross and Haynes (1996) 81–5; Erskine-Hill (1983) 173–4.
6 Gillespie (1992).
7 Gillespie (1993); Erskine-Hill (1996a) 183–4.
8 Money (2002) 207.
9 Francis (1753) II. 170. Selections in Carne-Ross and Haynes (1996).
10 Sherbo (1979) 37.
11 Sherbo (1979) 39.
12 Sherbo (1979) 57.
13 Carne-Ross and Haynes (1996) 190–2; Sherbo (1979) 23; Richardson's *Pamela*, 1740, satirised in Fielding's *Shamela*, 1741.

in what Smart hoped (unsuccessfully)[14] might become a textbook. Ligurinus, decorously handled, was acceptable to both Creech and Francis: but neither of them could stomach the ugly picture of female lust in *Epodes* 8 and 12. Creech's publisher prints the Latin, with facing page blank; that of Francis omits both, only a gap in numbering revealing Horace's shameful secret.[15] Pope, meanwhile, makes Ligurinus a woman, but is otherwise risqué.[16]

In comparing Horace to Pindar, Sir Edward Sherburne had to 'declare the horrour I conceive of these two Poets most disorderly love of Boys'; he also highlighted the poet as playboy: 'Horace before his Death, caus'd several Glasses, or Mirrors to be plac'd on every side of his Chamber, that he might at once see divers Lascivious Postures, and entertain himself to the last with voluptuous Thoughts.'[17] Despite these moral lapses, the comparison tends to favour Horace: in the words of Sherburne's French model, he offers 'plus de douceur . . . et beaucoup moins de défauts'.[18]

In France, bowdlerisation was quite normal; Jérôme Tarteron, translating the hexameter works into prose, declared: 'Je supprime ce qu'il y a de deshonneste.'[19] Pierre de Marcassus began to translate the odes at the age of eighty, in 1664, and finished in two months.[20] While one expurgated manuscript turned Pyrrha (*Odes* 1.5) into 'La Fortune',[21] Etienne de Martignac dared to describe Horace's method: 'il la peint comme une coquette qu'il est dangereux d'aimer . . . car enfin on voit que cette dame avoit l'art d'attirer des Amans malgré son humeur volage'. And his prose version offers a woman ready for dangerous intrigues: 'Pyrrha, qui est ce beau mignon si parfumé d'essences, qui vous embrasse étroittement dans vôtre agréable cabinet parsemé de roses?'[22]

Horace also appeared in popular fiction. Marie-Catherine Desjardins's *Les Exilez de la cour d'Auguste* (1672) was often reprinted, with several English versions. Superficial, but of 'immense popularity', it vulgarised her Roman characters, 'reducing them to the size of the personalities of her readers'.[23] But she could still include genuinely Horatian sentiments, as in Cornelius Gallus' speech, alluding to *Odes* 4.9: 'The Fame of a Poet is oftentimes as

14 Poverty impelled him, like Horace: P. Wilson (1982) 80; Sherbo (1979) 39.

15 Creech (1718); Francis (1753). Their first editions were in 1684 and 1743–7 respectively.

16 Stack (1985) 109, 90–4.

17 Sherburne (1696) 35; cf. Suetonius, *Life of Horace*.

18 Marmier (1962) 52.

19 Tarteron (1694) s.*4^{r}. 'Mais ses traductions sont mauvaises', Le Moyne (1800) III. 182. Dacier does face up to the issue: Stack (1985) 80.

20 Marmier (1962) 45, 404. Le Moyne (1800) 2.266. Another fast worker was Oldisworth: Erskine-Hill (2000) 108.

21 Marmier (1962) 45.

22 Martignac (1696) 1.[s. a]v–vi, 19.

23 Morrissette (1947) 174.

necessary to signalize the glory of Heroes, as their own virtue; And those, who now admire the Valor of Achilles, had perhaps never heard of his Name, had not the Pen of Homer eterniz'd it.'[24] A more serious thinker, like Shaftesbury, could cite Horace frequently, 'because he is now so much in esteem, and by this will appear an Air of Gallantry and Humour', while defending his reputation, despite the 'corrupting Sweets' of a 'poisonous Government'.[25]

Horace was good business, generally attractive to the taste of the public (whether buying scholarly editions, cribs or scurrilous imitations) and profitable for booksellers. In the first half of the eighteenth century, the period covered by Foxon's catalogue (1975), there were well over 100 imitations of individual Horatian poems, quite apart from complete editions: 61 based on *Odes*, 8 on *Epodes*, 2 on *Carmen Saeculare*, 20 *Satires*, 28 *Epistles*, and 10 on *Ars Poetica*, including *the Art of Cookery* of the gazetteer William King (1708), who also produced an Ovidian *Art of Love*.[26]

Compared to this Horatian outpouring, we find seventeen items for Ovid (covering translations and imitations of all works, several of them 'burlesque'). Virgil's *Eclogues* inspired ten imitations; there are four burlesque or modernised Homers. Of the other satirists, Persius inspired six imitations, and Juvenal seven, including Samuel Johnson's famous imitations of Juvenal 3 and 10, and a Latin imitation of Juvenal 3 by Jabez Earle (1724).[27] Nicholas Rowe, poet laureate, adapted *Odes* 3.9 for a humorous picture of the reconciliation of Congreve and the publisher, Jacob Tonson.[28] There were seven individual imitations of *Odes* 4.5, including [Jane Brereton], *The fifth ode of the fourth book of Horace, imitated: and apply'd to the King. By a lady* (London, 1716). Thomas Neale used *Odes* 1.37 to celebrate victory at Ramillies, 1706. In the following year Lewis Maidwell's *Comitia lyrica* used all of Horace's metres in praise of Godolphin, paraphrased in English by Nahum Tate. A similarly ambitious multi-metre effort, its title clearly signalling practical ambitions, was [Anon.], *A Poem dedicated to the Queen, and presented to the Congress at Utrecht, upon declaration of the peace. Writ in Latin, that foreigners might more easily understand and celebrate the transcendent virtues of her Britannic Majesty* (London, 1713).

At home, in the Sacheverell crisis of 1710, *Horace turn'd Whigg: or, a low-church ode* imitates *Epode* 7. Frank Stack, illustrating Pope's context,

24 Desjardins (1679) 198. Cf. Anon., *Le poète courtisan ou les intrigues d'Horace à la cour d'Auguste* (1705): Mariotti (1996–8) III. 546.

25 Klein (1994) 110, 187. Shaftesbury and Dacier: Stack (1985) 117–22.

26 Foxon (1975) I. 356–9.

27 Foxon (1975) I. 543–4, 844, 353–4, 566, 393.

28 Poole and Maule (1995) 350–1.

has stressed the numbers of other imitators in the 1730s, especially George Ogle.[29] John Boyle, earl of Cork and Orrery, attempted *Odes* 1.5: an attempt satirised in the same year, 1741, by the anonymous *Pyrrha, a cantata . . . Not by John Earl of Orrery*. Horace was called up naturally for contemporary purposes: e.g. *An allusion to the tenth ode of the second book of Horace; On a report of . . . H[enry] F[ox] quitting all public employments, and, in a religious fit, retiring to H[olland] H[ouse]* (London, 1757).

All of these – and many more examples could be given – reflect a degree of cultural ubiquity: Horace was never far away. The poet James Thomson had five editions, in a 'modest' classical library; the fictional Tom Jones could give 'feeling recitations'; James Douglas, a notorious eighteenth-century collector, had nearly 500 Horace-related titles.[30] Throughout our period, new editions piled up, almost every year; in 1612, two in Leiden (Elzevier, Raphelengius), one in Frankfurt; in 1699, Utrecht, Barcelona, Cambridge.[31] Periodicals played a large part in moulding taste, and Horace was often found at the head of essays, especially in *The Spectator*.[32] He was a 'Master of refined Raillery', 'a Man of the World throughout', with a 'strong Masculine Sense' – unlike Ovid.[33] His praise of moderation displayed 'a pretty sober Liveliness', and he offered a useful starting-point for moralising: 'Horace in my Motto says, that all men are vicious, and that they differ from one another, only as they are more or less so.'[34] In Boston, John Lovell's *The Seasons. An interlocutory exercise at the South Grammar School, June 26. 1765*, Edmund Quincy's *A treatise of hemp-husbandry* (also 1765), and Sir Richard Hill's *An address to persons of fashion* (1767) were all dignified by Horatian mottoes. Other Americans in the same period alluded naturally to Horace; the Charleston library had Francis's translation.[35] There were fine editions from the Foulis press (1760), and Baskerville (1762 and 1770); John Pine engraved the entire text in copperplate (1733–7).[36] Cheaper editions abounded. The young Wordsworth read Horace and Boileau; he owned a copy of Smart's prose translation, and translated *Odes* 3.13; a consciously Horatian

29 Stack (1985) 21–3, 249–51, 281–3.
30 P. Wilson (1982) 70, 76.
31 Bijker (1996): 26–39 (17th cent.), 41–67 (18th cent.); Mills College (1938) 25–37 (17th cent., items 256–391), 37–79 (18th cent., items 392–863).
32 Bond (1965) 5. 225: 'roughly a third' of mottoes, more than any other source. Cf. Goad (1918) 298–9, 336–9; Sherbo (1979) 13–14.
33 Bond (1965) v. 113 (*Spectator* 618, 10 November 1714).
34 Bond (1965) III. 129, IV. 461 (*Spectator* 312, 27 February 1712; 548, 28 November 1712 – using *Satires* 1.3.68–9).
35 Gummere (1963) 2; Raven (2002) 366. Raven's own motto is *Epistles* 1.2.27. Cf. Ronnick (1994): a Puritan almanac, 1647, alluding to *Odes* 1.2.9.
36 Gaskell (1952); Washington (1997) uses Pine's illustrations.

preference for classical simplicity as opposed to false ornament affects his maturer work, including the preface to *Lyrical Ballads*.[37]

French editions were influential in England: Francis's notes regularly cite them. Most important was that of André Dacier, with his 'vigorous defence of the classics as bastions of civilisation'.[38] But unquestionably the greatest textual critic to work on Horace in this period was Richard Bentley (who, a month before his death in 1742, elected Smart to a university scholarship). Bentley was an acerbic and controversial character, ridiculed in Pope's *Dunciad*, lauded by foreign scholars (who had less experience than his compatriots of his rancorous side). His Horace (1711) is claimed as 'the foundation document of the new "philology"'.[39] He introduced numerous bold conjectures, with a clear view of how to approach textual problems, even if some conclusions were unconvincing. There would always, though, be a majority of scholars and readers for whom textual matters remained, in Highet's provocative phrase, 'a glorified form of proofreading'.[40] In the various skirmishes of the 'battle of the books', Bentley's opponents tended to hold their own.[41]

Approaches to lyric

Horace reached the peripheries of Western culture; Thomas Morris, in 1761, imitated *Odes* 2.16:

> Ease is the wish too of the sly Canadian;
> Ease the delight of bloody Caghnawagas;
> Ease, Richard, ease, not to be bought with wampum,
>   Nor paper money . . .
> O think on Morris, in a lonely chamber,
>   Dabbling in Sapphic.[42]

Also in 1761, Harvard welcomed George III in Latin verse.[43] John Beveridge (1703–67), a Scotsman who emigrated to America in 1752, corresponded with friends in Latin odes.[44] Benjamin Young Prime (1733–91) wrote 160 lines of Sapphics (far longer than any ode of Horace's) in 1751 to his teacher Aaron Burr, father of the future vice-president. He recalls reading with Burr the attacks on bad morals in the satires, and the good morals celebrated

37 Wu (1993) 17, 51, 76, 122, 165–6; Carne-Ross and Haynes (1996) 37–8, 214–5.
38 Weinbrot (2001) 183. 39 Brink (1986) 71. 40 Highet (1949) 496.
41 Levine (1991); Money (1998) 77–85. 42 Lonsdale (1984) 498–500, lines 5–9, 39–40.
43 Inspired by Governor Francis Bernard, stepson and editor of the poet Anthony Alsop: Money (1998) 63–8.
44 Kaiser (1984) 104–19.

in the odes.[45] An anonymous Philadelphia poet of 1775 addresses an ode to George Washington: *Te vocat Boston (ubi dux iniquus / Obsidet cives miseros)*,[46] 'Boston calls you, where an unjust general besieges the unhappy citizens.' When Kentucky became the fifteenth state, in 1792, a newspaper elegist declared that a new pyramid of stars would defeat the ravages of time, in language resonating with echoes of *Odes* 3.30 (as well as the opening of Martial's *Liber Spectaculorum*).[47]

John Parke published his version of the *Odes* and *Epodes* in 1786, dedicated to Washington. He led a regiment at the battle of Monmouth, in June 1778, but then, in true Horatian fashion, resigned from the army in October 1778, in the middle of the war, to enjoy rural life 'far from arms and camps retir'd'. His style is vigorous and eccentric. Poor Ibycus' wife, in *Odes* 3.15, is 'Lewd as a goat'. In 1776, Parke imitated *Odes* 3.29 from the army camp, turning *fumum et opes strepitumque Romae* into 'Th' eternal buz of merchandise and care, / The smoaky town and its corrupted air'.[48] At the eastern periphery, in Russia, Horace could be judged alongside a French imitator: *Horatium imitando superat Malherbius* ('Malherbe surpasses Horace in this imitation'). No class can escape death (*Odes* 1.4.13–14): *Et la garde qui veille aux barrières du Louvre / N'en défend pas nos rois.*[49] In Croatia, a vigorous neo-Latin tradition produced Junius Restius, a Horatian satirist, and some odes of Titus Brezovatsky, in response to the turmoil of the Revolutionary and Napoleonic wars. Mathias Petrus Katancsich's *Fructus Auctumnales* (Zagreb, 1791) are full of Horatian Sapphics and Alcaics.[50] An earlier Croatian, B. Bolic, lamenting a Ragusan citizen, felt like a flying swan propelled by Horace.[51]

Most nations had their 'Horaces'; Friedrich von Hagedorn (1708–54) 'was called in his day "the German Horace", but was influenced by English poetry as well as classical models'.[52] Lessing's *Die Rettungen des Horaz* (1754) defended Horace's moral character, while Francesco Algarotti's *Saggio sopra*

45 Kaiser (1984) 90–6. 46 Kaiser (1984) 166–7. 47 Kaiser (1984) 190.

48 Kaiser (1965) 228–30; Carne-Ross and Haynes (1996) 33.

49 Murav'ev (1995) 67; on Malherbe: Marmier (1962) 147–54; Maddison (1960) 277–84. Cf. Busch (1964) 106–11 on Murav'ev's classicism, and on Antioch Kantemir, translator and imitator, 51–3.

50 Vratovic (1998); Ijsewijn and Sacré (1998) 69.

51 Josifovic (1966) 41; adapting *Odes* 4.2. Cf. Hungarian imitators: Waldapfel (1935); Mariotti (1996–8) III. 610.

52 Garland (1997) 324. Cf. Klopstock's odes: 471–2. For Hagedorn and Horace, and the reception of Horace in the German Enlightenment in general, see E. A. Schmidt (2002b).

Orazio (1760) treated him as *un filosofo e un intellettuale*.[53] The great Dutch poet Vondel (1587–1679) produced a prose translation of the *Odes* and *Ars Poetica*. Metastasio tackled the *Ars Poetica* (Venice, 1781–3), while Boileau's Horatian imitations remained widely influential. The edition of Marolles (1652) *fait l'éloge de l'* aurea mediocritas *horatienne*.[54] Voltaire and Diderot could take inspiration from Horace – and be satirised in Horatian Latin in the *De Celibatu Ecclesiastico* (Padua, 1791) of a conservative priest from Treviso, Ubaldo Bregolini.[55]

In seventeenth-century Italy, an Italian pope and an English exile wrote large quantities of Horatian Latin odes; the latter, James Alban Gibbes, was a rather conceited physician, deliberately setting out to match Horace's achievement – not without some success, since he was made an imperial poet laureate in 1667: he received an Oxford MD, never before granted to an English Catholic, in return for his laureate regalia.[56] Maffeo Barberini, Pope Urban VIII, wrote elegant biblical paraphrases, and odes on other topics, such as gout.[57] He was patron, as cardinal, of John Barclay, who introduces him as a character in *Argenis*, the age's most celebrated Latin novel.[58] His moral purity made him attractive to some eighteenth-century readers, *cum Poesis optimos in usus instituta, in pessimos subinde rapiatur* ('since poetry, instituted for the best purposes, is frequently snatched for the worst').[59]

Edward Hannes, an English physician-poet, wrote: *non ego cederem / Libens vel Urbano, vel ausae / Grandia Sarbivii camoenae* ('I would not freely cede to Urban, or the muse of Sarbiewski, who dares great things').[60] Even more famous than Urban, as a Latin religious poet, was the 'Polish Horace', Maciej Kasimierz Sarbiewski, often known simply as Casimir. Cowley, Henry Vaughan and other English writers imitated his works. He gives a vision of heaven: *Auro prata virent; arbor crinitur in aurum* (in Hils's charming version, 'Each blade of grasse was gold, each tree was there, / A golden Periwig did weare').[61] The terrible goddess, fortune, can be treated as a wayward girl: *Riserit? vultum generosus aufer. / Fleverit? dulci refer ora risu* ('Laughs shee? turne bravely away thy face. / Weeps shee? bring't back, with smiling grace').[62] Sarbiewski's third epode is a 'palinode' providing a

53 Garland (1997) 522–3, 691; Mariotti (1996–8) III. 575.
54 Beugnot (1999) 210.
55 Mariotti (1996–8) III. 514–8, 546; on Bregolini: Ijsewijn and Sacré (1998) 68–9.
56 Money (2004b).
57 Urban VIII (1634) 238–40.
58 Barclay (2004) I. 24–5; e.g. criticising Calvin, I. 266–75.
59 Urban VIII (1726) s. a3r.
60 Urban VIII (1726) x–xi; Hannes (1721) 265; on Hannes (d. 1710), Money (1998) 52.
61 Hils (1953) 92–3 (ode 4.30).
62 Hils (1953) 44–5 (ode 3.4; cf. 2.7, 2.8).

religious response to *Epode* 2 (one of the most influential of Horace's poems in the period, with its theme of the 'happy man').[63]

The Renaissance Latin tradition (see McGann, chapter 22 above) continued in our period, and in some places, such as Britain, greatly expanded. Ode-writing grew in popularity: here are a few examples, from over 100 university verse collections, containing many thousands of Latin poems (and quite a few in Greek, Hebrew and English).[64] Oxford's 1736 collection saw a particularly high proportion of Horatian lyrics: 30 odes (12 each in Alcaics and Sapphics), out of a total of 86 poems. Edward Coke, son of Baron Lovell, adapts *Odes* 1.2 to reflect modern concerns about European war, a return of the bloody age of Charles. It is unclear, from his formulation, which Charles is meant: perhaps primarily Charles I (with the simultaneous Thirty Years War), with echoes of Emperor Charles V, the more recent Charles XII of Sweden and possibly the future danger of the Young Pretender, then aged sixteen, and already an anti-Hanoverian warrior.[65]

Writers of English also turned naturally to Horatian commonplaces; James Parry, commoner of Merton, later a barrister, began:

> What Friendly muse will teach my Lays
> To emulate the *Roman* fire?
> Justly to sound a *Caesars* praise
> Demands a bold *Horatian* Lyre:
> Yet, tho' unworthy I attempt the task,
> Inspired by Loyalty, no other Muse I ask.[66]

In 1700, Oxford contributors produced 26 odes (fully 22 of them Alcaic), out of 145 poems; in 1762, 15 (8 Alcaic) out of 114. In the earlier seventeenth century, there had been somewhat fewer odes, and a greater fondness for epodic or other less usual metres: in 1613, 16 lyrics (3 Alcaic, 6 Sapphic) out of 247 contributions, in 1619 only 5 out of 216.

Cambridge writers produced not dissimilar proportions: in 1748, 20 odes out of 78 contributions (thirteen Alcaic, six Sapphic), though there had been far fewer in 1736. In 1641, there had been only 7 lyricists (5 Alcaic) out of 103. One of them was Samuel Collins, provost of King's, a very prolific contributor; he uses *Odes* 3.9 (*Donec gratus eram tibi*) as a model for

63 Hils (1953) 124–35. Carne-Ross and Haynes (1996) 485–7, 499–503 (Vaughan). On the theme, and Sarbiewski in general, see Røstvig (1954–8); Ulcinaite (1998); Urbanski (2000); Money (2006).

64 H. Forster (1982); Money (1997); (1998) 229–49.

65 Oxford University (1736) s. B2^{r}. For recent controversies over Jacobite links to Charles XII, see MacKenzie (2002).

66 Oxford University (1736) s. L2^{v}; Money (1997) 81.

dialogue between England and Scotland: *Donec foedere mutuo / Immotaque fide firma cohaesimus / Dulci copula vinculo, / Sprevissem Annibalis jure, soror, minas* ('While we were joined in a mutual treaty and unmoved faith, a firm bond with a sweet chain, sister, I would rightly have scorned a Hannibal's threats').[67]

In Cambridge's 1697 volume, there were 15 odes (8 Alcaic, 6 Sapphic) out of 125 poems. Benjamin Wyllys, BA, fellow of King's, addresses a male friend in 18 Sapphic stanzas, borrowing his opening from *Odes* 4.11 (*Est mihi nonum* . . .); the nine-year-old vintage is appropriate to celebrate peace after a nine-years war – better than Belinda has tasted, though she is *Cara permultis, mihi praeter omnes* ('Dear to many, to me above all'). Fellows were not allowed to marry, and not encouraged to fornicate: Belinda may be one of Cambridge's less respectable citizens. French wine can now be imported again, and they can get peacefully sozzled in French company, *Dum mero Boini simulantur undae, et / Castra Namurci* ('While the waters of Boyne are imitated in wine, and the citadel of Namur'). While drinking to peace, even to Louis XIV, Wyllys recalls William's victories: the Boyne, 1690, and the recovery of Namur, the great fortress on the Meuse, 1695. He borrows *Odes* 3.8.17 (*mitte civiles*); Prince Eugene of Savoy has defeated the Turks at the battle of Zenta, 1697: *Ipse Sultanus fugit et Sabaudi / Signa Gradivi* ('Even the Sultan himself flees the standards of the Mars of Savoy').[68]

Anthologies of Renaissance Latin, edited by Atterbury (1684) and Pope (1740), both contained a selection of odes, presented for an 'Augustan' readership.[69] A French anthology, also of 1740, included odes of Pierre-Daniel Huet (1630–1721), alongside Bernard de la Monnoye, and Fraguier, whose Latin was said to display *elégance* and *urbanité*.[70] Huet reminds Louis XIV that lasting fame cannot be achieved without poets.[71] Edward Popham's collection of English Latinists, first published at Bath, 1774–6, ranges from pious paraphrase to secular diversions, with odes by Gray and John Jortin, and Isaac Hawkins Browne to the painter Highmore.[72]

There was much debate over the usefulness of different lyric forms for modern writers. Regular, four-line stanzas naturally owed much, however indirectly, to Horace; he was 'the perfect model' for love lyrics.[73] More irregular, or longer, stanza forms became associated with Pindar, although the

67 Cambridge University (1641) s. ¶4^{r-v}; Hunter and Money (forthcoming).

68 Cambridge University (1697) s. Aa2^{v}–Bb1^{v}; this and other odes discussed in Money (2003). 'Gradivus' (short 'a'): unusual, but with classical precedent.

69 Money (1998) 98–105.

70 Le Moyne (1800) II. 140.

71 Anon. (1740) 120–2, ode 5. Cf. Marmier (1962) 391–8.

72 Popham (1779) 293–4; Money (1998) 212, 227–9.

73 Richmond (1964) 229; Scodel (1998).

distinction can be artificial – many 'Pindaric' odes are quite Horatian in content. Gabriello Chiabrera, another member of Urban VIII's circle, had attempted both styles in Italian.[74] Though there were many other predecessors, Cowley came to be seen as the archetypal English exponent of Pindaric looseness; Corbet Owen's Latin *Carmen Pindaricum* (containing Horatian allusions) had some success.[75] Addison considered 'Pindaricks' to be 'monstrous Compositions'.[76] Steele put it more gently, imagining a scene on Parnassus: 'I saw *Pindar* walking all alone, no one daring to accost him till *Cowley* joyn'd himself to him, but, growing weary of one who almost walk'd him out of Breath, he left him for *Horace* and *Anacreon*, with whom he seemed infinitely delighted.'[77] Horace was a better companion for an Augustan stroll. Aphra Behn 'revises Cowley's Horace in daring fashion'.[78] Thomas Gray is a fine example of the mixture: a writer of Latin odes, as well as Pindarics notable for their Horatian moral sentiments, and a famous *Elegy* that is really a Horatian lyric. Samuel Johnson made complex use of Horatian satire and lyric in '*Gnothi Seauton*' and his odes from Skye,[79] while Cowper lamented the loss of the 'Royal George' (1782) in Latin as well as English.

Long Latin odes preceded Milton's *Lycidas* on its first appearance, and Milton himself retained Horatian links throughout his career. His version of *Odes* 1.5 has attracted both supporters and detractors.[80] While in Italy Milton acquired 'a kind of Horatian signature', allowing Horatian fondness for song to obscure more carnal aspects of his model.[81] The opening of *Paradise Lost* 7 echoes *Odes* 3.4; indeed, 'there are, throughout *Paradise Lost*, many strong connections to the Roman odes in general'.[82] But, characteristically, Milton offers a challenge as well as an allusion; he calls on a different Muse, and rejects pagan mythology: 'The meaning, not the Name I call' (line 5).

Matthew Prior, poet and diplomat, appeared particularly Horatian; as James Parry put it, 'The *British* Lyre's unstrung, Now *Prior's* muse is fled.'[83] Elizabeth Tollet, in 'The Triumvirate of Poets', thought of Addison as a Virgil for 'this Augustan Age', Pope as Homer, while 'In *Prior Horace* shines, sublimely great'.[84] Tollet's own imitation of *Odes* 2.10 presents Horatian morality for the prudent classes:

74 Maddison (1960) 178–83; Highet (1949) 235–6, 245–6. 75 Money (2004c).
76 Bond (1965) II. 128 (*Spectator* 160, 3 September 1711).
77 Bond (1965) IV. 329 (*Spectator* 514, 20 October 1712).
78 Scodel (2002) 186: on Behn's adaptation of *Odes* 1.5 cf. Doody (1998) 65.
79 Money (2002) 200–8. 80 Carne-Ross and Haynes (1996) 57–8, 88–9.
81 C. C. Brown (1991) 340; Scodel (2002) 108. Cf. Finley (1937). 82 Talbot (2001) 22.
83 Oxford University (1736) s. M1ʳ. On Prior: Goad (1918) 90–116, 360–79; Prior's Spenserian Horace: Radcliffe (2000) 131n.
84 Tollet (1755) 56. On Tollet: Londry (2004a); (2004b); Lonsdale (1989) 96–102.

Fondly, my Friend! does proud Ambition soar,
And Danger tempt with an unwearied Flight:
Fondly does Fear still keep the humble shore,
Whom whistling winds and beating surges fright.

Whoever wisely keep the golden Mean,
Nor he to smoaky Cottages retires,
Nor he in envied Palaces is seen:
Too low he sinks not, nor too high aspires.[85]

And when her brother returns from Bruges, Tollet anticipates restrained refreshment:

Quos procax nobis numeros, jocosque
Musa dictaret? mihi dum tibique
Temperent baccis Arabes, vel herbis
Pocula Seres.[86]

What verses and jokes might the bold Muse dictate to us, while for you and me the Arabs flavour cups with [coffee] beans, or the Chinese with [tea] leaves.

Horatian neo-Latin also had its risqué side: Benjamin Loveling composed an elegant Sapphic catalogue of the Drury Lane and Covent Garden prostitutes, and admires a lady 'of salacious memory' on her deathbed.[87] Similarly coarse vigour, on occasion, combined with a far more sophisticated range, was displayed by Anthony Alsop (d. 1726). According to Thomas Hearne, Alsop 'was looked upon to be the best Writer of Lyric Verses in the World'.[88] He found Latin verse a convenient medium for the expression of subversive ideas, for an audience of sympathetic friends. In a marriage ode of 1695, Alsop expressed his hopes for Jacobite revolution: *En! tempus instat, en! veniet dies, / Cum rursus in Coelum caput efferet / Nomen Stuartorum* ('Look – the time is at hand, look, the day will come, when the name of Stuart will again raise its head to heaven').[89] The Scot Archibald Pitcairne was another Jacobite who used Horace's metres for seditious purposes.

Andrew Marvell's Latin *parodia* on *Odes* 1.2 reflects a Renaissance tradition of close imitation.[90] (Philip Bouquet, professor of Hebrew, was to go further, parodying *Odes* 4.2 in Greek Sapphics.)[91] But it is Marvell's English 'Horatian Ode upon Cromwell's Return from Ireland' that has attracted the

85 Tollet (1755) 8–9. 86 Tollet (1755) 84. Musa procax: *Odes* 2.1.37.
87 Loveling (1741) 49–52, 79–83. 88 Money (1998) 54.
89 Money (1998) 141. Horace on a Jacobite print: Clark (2002) 134.
90 Haan (2003) 19–56. 91 Money and Olszowy (1995) 558.

greatest critical attention, focused particularly on his sensitively nuanced depiction of Charles I's execution, reflecting Horace's Cleopatra in *Odes* 1.37. 'Perhaps our critical perplexity over the ambiguities . . . richly reveals how meaning can only be figured and fixed in all the variegations of persons and moments.[92] Erskine-Hill, however, is rather more robust: 'It is hard to see why a tradition concerning the Ode's poised neutrality should have arisen, only to be demolished by later commentators who rediscover a Cromwellian stance well known before.'[93] Marvell turned to Horace, not for some grand public gesture, but in a private, personal attempt 'to grasp the meaning' of events;[94] the ode was suppressed, and not widely published until 1776.[95]

Satirical applications

Most of the examples above have illustrated responses to the *Odes*, many of them unfamiliar to modern readers; *Satires*, *Epistles*, and *Ars Poetica*, however, all had a huge impact on critical thinking and poetic practice in the period. This, too, was not entirely a vernacular activity: Latin satirical dialogues recited at university occasions, such as *Bellus Homo et Academicus*,[96] could be reprinted and reach a wider audience. But major English authors dominate the debate. Horace could form part of a discourse of 'politeness', in which his approval was sought for civilised lifestyles and literary fashions. He was also appropriated for scurrilous personal abuse. Rochester could see himself as Horatian, loathing the rabble, sexually ambivalent, devoted to friendship, drinking and sharp wit.[97] Rochester's 'Allusion to Horace' formed part of a feud with Dryden, who himself absorbed and refashioned Horace's critical precepts.[98] Roscommon – whom Dryden praised – could celebrate 'our Old *Horatian* way',[99] but there was rarely agreement about the implications. Updated for modern purposes, Horatian satire was too contemporary, too edgy, for that.

Alexander Pope is a central figure in 'Augustan-age' reception. Pope's Horatianism is not confined to his direct *Imitations*: it also informs such works as *The Rape of the Lock*,[100] and his *Essays* (and, one might argue, a quite Horatian Homer). A Horatian concept of correct poetic decorum is implicit in his decision to 'versify' and modernise the old-fashioned satires

92 Sharpe and Zwicker (2003) 21. 93 Erskine-Hill (1996a) 160n.
94 Friedman (1993) 299. 95 Stapleton (1993) 32; A. J. N. Wilson (1969).
96 Popham (1779) 140. 97 Chernaik (2000); Hammond (2000); Ferraro (2000).
98 Kupersmith (1985) 97–101; Hammond (1993).
99 Womersley (1997) 108. 100 Rosslyn (1993) 193.

of Donne – ironically, Pope himself can appear forbidding to many modern students.[101] Pope attracted and fostered bitter controversy; personal enmities were part of the reason, but also the boldness of his poetic creativity. As one enemy suggested, he might have been safer

> Had he in modern language only wrote
> Those rules which *Horace*, and which *Vida* taught;
> On *Garth* or *Boileau's* Model built his Fame.[102]

Patronage, and the poet's relationship to powerful men, were delicate topics for Pope's circle. Pope and Gay wrote jointly to Swift, in 1727: 'Horace might keep his coach in Augustus' time, if he pleas'd, but I won't in the time of our Augustus.'[103] When he turned, as a mature and independent poet, to Horatian imitation, Pope was exploring his own relationship with Horace (whose Latin he pointedly placed alongside his own English) and with contemporaries. Pope's position could be subtly equivocal.[104] His approach to *Epistles* 2.1, speaking to George II in sifting layers of irony, has particularly impressed modern critics.[105]

While Pope's brilliance made him an outstanding individual example of creative reception, others selected varying approaches. That vigour remained undiminished in the 1790s. There was often a mixing of influences, as is neatly implied by the pseudonym of 'Horace Juvenal', chosen by the author of *Modern manners: a poem* (1793); the same can be seen in William Gifford's *Baviad* (1791) and *Maeviad* (1795). 'D. M.' offered appropriate representatives of old and new, in *Ancient Rome and modern Britain compared. A dialogue, in Westminster Abbey, between Horace and Mr Pope* (1793).

As we have seen with Tollet, female authors could be inspired by Horace; as the century closed, Anna Seward published her *Original sonnets on various subjects, and odes paraphrased from Horace* (1799). Charlotte Smith, not in most respects (despite her Philadelphian admirer's enthusiasm) especially Horatian, still chose to quote from Pope's imitation of *Odes* 4.1: 'For me the vernal garland blooms no more.'[106] She perhaps develops her own melancholy type of Horatian sensibility, turning from thoughts of spring to man's lot:

101 Schakel (1993); as Waller might have predicted: Money (1998) 9–11.
102 Guerinot (1969) 241.
103 Erskine-Hill (2000) 194; on Swift, cf. Kupersmith (1995); Goad (1918) 441; Schakel (2001).
104 Noggle (2000). 105 Rudd (1994); Stack (1985) 150–97.
106 C. Smith (1993) 16: *Elegiac Sonnets* VI, 'To Hope'.

Ah! poor Humanity! So frail, so fair,
Are the fond visions of thy early day,
Till tyrant Passion, and corrosive Care,
Bid all thy fairy colours fade away![107]

And she can address her lyre, which sets her apart from the crowd:

For all the anxious Sons of Care,
From Bishopsgate to Temple Bar,
To my young eyes seem'd gross and sordid.[108]

Glimpses of Horace can be caught in far-flung places. Goethe, who believed in the healthiness of classicism,[109] admired Sir William Jones's work on oriental poets, while doubting the appropriateness of his classical comparisons. The temptation, however, was natural: 'we may well be reminded of Horace when reading Hafiz'.[110] Novalis, the German Romantic, responded to a 'visionary quality' in Horace.[111] Yet, as I have suggested in this chapter, it is not just a matter of a few great authors aligning themselves with a distinguished predecessor. Use of Horace's verse-forms, allusion to his sentiments, and emulation (or criticism) of his lifestyle were all extremely widespread; despite the considerable challenges of imitating Horace in Latin, a large number made the attempt. The interest shown in Horace by so disparate a readership, and by so many satirists and lyric poets, now mostly forgotten, is perhaps the strongest evidence for his significance in the culture of the seventeenth and eighteenth centuries.

FURTHER READING

There are good selections from various translators in Carne-Ross and Haynes (1996); Poole and Maule (1995); discussions in Ogilvie (1981); Sherbo (1979); Edden (1973); theories of translation: Steiner (1975); Classe (2000); France (2000) 3–38; on allusion, Ricks (2002); history of translation: Gillespie and Hopkins (2005).

On British Latin, see Money (1998); Bradner (1940); and, for the early seventeenth century, Binns (1990); some scientific odes, Fara and Money (2004). For an introduction to neo-Latin in general: Ijsewijn (1990), Ijsewijn and Sacré (1998); there is an extensive annual bibliography in the journal *Humanistica Lovaniensia*. A Jesuit anthology: Thill and Banderier (1999); emblems, L. Forster (1981). For European reception, see articles on nations and individuals in Mariotti (1996–8) III; Highet (1949) remains wide-ranging and spirited, Showerman (1922) gives a simple introduction; studies of particular countries include Marmier (1962) for France, Killy (1981a) for Germany.

107 C. Smith (1993) 13–14: *Elegiac Sonnets* II; cf. 34, 70.

108 C. Smith (1993) 310–12.

109 Stephenson (2002) 61.

110 Bell (2002) 210.

111 Carne-Ross and Haynes (1996) 36.

Relevant Cambridge *Companions* have more space than is available here for English neo-classical poetry: Corns (1993); Zwicker (1998). Several essays in Martindale and Hopkins (1993) are devoted to this period (a review: Braden (1994)). On Ben Jonson: J. Martindale (1993); Helgerson (1993); for Marvell and his contemporaries, see Norbrook (1999); Nuttall (1993); Sharpe and Zwicker (1987; 1998; 2003), Chernaik and Dzelzainis (1999). Some more detailed essays: Abraham and Wilding (1999); L. Hopkins (2001); Loxley (1994). A useful annotated anthology is Dawson and Dupree (1994). For satirists: Kupersmith (1985); Weinbrot (1988); town and country mice: D. Hopkins (1993); Rochester: Fisher (2000); Ballaster (1998); Boileau and Pope: Wood (1985). On Pope, Stack (1985) is excellent; other discussions in Rudd (1994); Sowerby (1993); Erskine-Hill (1981); (1983) 291–349; (1996b); more specific essays: Ferraro (1993); Richardson (2000); Rogers (1992); Greason (1977); a brief introduction, aimed at teachers: M. E. D. Brown (1993). Terry (2001) discusses canon-formation. Goad (1918) has valuable appendices.

24

STEPHEN HARRISON

The reception of Horace in the nineteenth and twentieth centuries

This chapter looks at the literary reception of Horace in poetry in English (primarily but not exclusively produced in the United Kingdom) in the nineteenth and twentieth centuries, and the early years of the twenty-first. It does not treat the use of Horace's verse in literary prose texts,[1] or discuss scholarly work on the poet in these periods.[2]

From the Romantics to the Victorians

Horace was popular among both general and scholarly readers in Victorian England.[3] The centrality of Horace to the curriculum of the newly influential elite English 'public' (private) schools[4] was clearly one root cause of this popularity, along with the reception and construction of Horace as an honorary English gentleman who represented the values of the male Victorian English elite.[5] Horace was not a new element in English culture; he had been important in the eighteenth century, and though the Romantics might revolt against the tyranny of being taught Horace at school, they still admired him, a tension which comes out well in Byron's famous lines (*Childe Harold* Canto IV (1818) 77), motivated by the sight of Soracte in Italy and consequent recall of *Odes* 1.9: 'Then farewell Horace, whom I hated so, / Not for thy faults, but mine.'[6] The Romantic link of literature and landscape is also seen in Wordsworth's desire to explore 'Sabine vales' following

1 For a study of the use of Horace in Thackeray's novels see Nitchie (1918).

2 For some discussion of twentieth-century Horatian scholarship see Fowler (1993) and S. J. Harrison (1995c); I hope to do more work on the nineteenth-century material. The scholarly literature stimulated by the bimillennia of Horace's birth and death is well surveyed in *Enciclopedia Oraziana*, Mariotti (1996–8) III. 615–58.

3 For Horace in Victorian British culture see Vance (1997) 175–93.

4 See Stray (1998), and for a case study see Gaisser (1994).

5 See S. J. Harrison (forthcoming, b).

6 On Byron's Soracte encounter see Edmunds (1992) 71–5.

'a wish / To meet the shade of Horace by the side / Of his Bandusian fount', combining an allusion to *Odes* 3.4 with one to *Odes* 3.13 in his *Memorials of a Tour of Italy* (1837), and Keats, generally more interested in Hellenic culture, could echo Horace in the opening of one of his most famous poems, *Ode to a Nightingale* 1.1–4: 'My heart aches, and a drowsy numbness pains / my sense' clearly echoes *Epodes* 14.1–4, in its initial position as well as in its theme.

Victorian Horace: translations

Translations of Horace became an important feature of the UK literary landscape for the first time in the nineteenth century. John Conington, the Corpus Professor of Latin at Oxford, produced versions of the *Odes* (1863) and the hexameter works (1870). These had some success, but more widely read and reprinted was the 1860 translation of the *Odes* (extended to the complete works by 1881) of Sir Theodore Martin, biographer of Prince Albert. Conington used plainer language than the more flowery Martin, and also tried to reproduce more faithfully the basic shape of the Latin metre, though both used the quatrain stanza to mirror Horatian stanzas, as we can see if we compare their versions of the opening of *Odes* 1.5:

What slender youth, besprinkled with perfume,
Courts you on roses in some grotto's shade?
  Fair Pyrrha, say, for whom
  Your yellow hair you braid,
So trim, so simple! (Conington)

Pyrrha, what slender boy, in perfume steep'd
  Doth in the shade of some delightful grot
Caress thee now on couch with roses heap'd?
  For whom dost thou thine amber tresses knot

With all thy seeming-artless grace? (Martin)

Both also bowdlerised, omitting, for example, the erotic *Odes* 1.25. (Martin also omitted the 'obscene' *Epodes* 8 and 12, and the *Epodes* were wholly ignored by Conington.)[7] Martin also in his comments tried to provide mid-Victorian equivalents for the Horatian social context, thus implying the usually assumed similarity between the English elite classes and aristocratic Romans:[8] *Odes* 1.8, reporting on urban amours in Rome, he maintained,

7 For the general Victorian 'down' on the *Epodes* see e.g. Wickham (1874) 326 (arguing that these are clumsy and unpleasant early poems).
8 See e.g. Hingley (2000).

has 'value as a picture still true in all its main features of "modern habits and manners, and of the amusements and lighter occupations of the higher classes of society in England" '.[9] The translation of Horace seems to have been particularly favoured by retired statesmen, perhaps imitating his famous literary *otium* or leisure: the version of 1869 by Lord Lytton (the novelist and politician, Secretary for the Colonies 1858–9) was several times reprinted, and Horace was also translated by W. E. Gladstone, the quintessential eminent Victorian, in a version at least partly written in Gladstone's last days of office as Prime Minister and published in 1894, very soon after his retirement at the age of eighty-five.[10]

Horatian appropriations in Victorian poetry

The undoubtedly central place of Horace in Victorian literary culture did not prevent criticism. Matthew Arnold in 'On the modern element in literature' (1857) sees the 'gentlemanly' Horace as 'inadequate', representing the middlebrow taste of the Philistine bourgeoisie whom Arnold hoped to direct to the superior joys of Hellenism, and as lacking key Victorian virtues: 'If human life were complete without faith, without enthusiasm, without energy, Horace . . . would be the perfect interpreter of human life.'[11] Nevertheless, the younger Arnold had indulged in Horatian pastiche in his 'Horatian echo' (1847), which addresses a friend advising him not to worry about politics, in a clear echo of the opening of *Odes* 2.11.[12] Arnold's friend Arthur Hugh Clough likewise made some use of both *Odes* and *Epistles* in his epistolary *Amours de Voyage* (1858), which ends with an envoi which plainly echoes the closing poem of Horace's *Epistles* 1 (1.20):

> So go forth to the world, to the good report and the evil!
> Go, little book! thy tale, is it not evil and good?
> Go, and if strangers revile, pass quietly without answer.
> Go, and if curious friends ask of thy rearing and age,
> Say, I am flitting around from brain unto brain of
> Feeble and restless youths, born to inglorious days:
> But, so finish the word, I was writ in a Roman chamber,
> When from Janiculan heights thundered the cannon of France.

Horace's personified book proclaims its author's age and origins (1.20.19–28), while Clough's gives its own autobiography under questioning, but the

9 Martin (1860) 283. 10 Lytton (1869); Gladstone (1894)
11 Arnold (1970) 74. 12 See Allott and Allott (1979) 58–60.

link is clear and a marker of the Horatian strand in Clough's epistolary work.[13]

The practice of Horatian pastiche, like that of Horatian translation, became extensive in the nineteenth century, with some interesting adaptations to Victorian social and intellectual contexts.[14] The most distinguished example of these *vers de société* is Tennyson's 'To the Rev. F. D. Maurice', which like Arnold's 'Horatian echo' neatly inserts real current affairs into the literary frame; Thackeray's version of *Odes* 1.38, Horace's address to his wine-pourer urging simple party practices, neatly replaces the dubious boy with an address to 'Lucy', perhaps a maid, and this widespread habit of imitating single Horatian odes suggests a shared cultural capital and Horace as 'one of us' (i.e. upper-class English male). The enormously (and deservedly) popular 'version' of the medieval Persian *Rubaiyat of Omar Khayyam* (1859) by Tennyson's friend Edward Fitzgerald, 'the Bible of Victorian agnosticism', has more than a touch of Horace about it. The stanzas and rhyme-scheme generally derive from the Persian *rubai*, but the quatrains inevitably recall the stanzas of the *Odes*, as does the narrating first person of the world-weary, ageing epicurean Omar himself, mixing sympotic exhortation and *carpe diem* with splendid moralising and *memento mori* nihilism.[15]

One perhaps unlikely translator of Horace is Gerard Manley Hopkins, often seen as a forerunner of Modernism in English poetry for his difficult and involved style. Hopkins' earlier poems of the 1860s include translations of two very different famous Horatian odes – *Odes* 1.38, the light but reflective address to his wine-pourer turned by Thackeray, and *Odes* 3.1, the ponderous first Roman Ode. Both preserve original quatrain stanzas, with 1.38 also attempting the short last line of the Sapphic stanza:

> Ah child, no Persian-perfect art
> Crowns composite and braided bast
> They tease me, Never know the part
>   Where roses linger last.
> Bring natural myrtle, and have done:
> Myrtle will suit your place and mine;
> And set the glasses from the sun
>   Beneath the tackled vine.

Not all Victorian poetic appropriators of Horace were men. I conclude this section with the opening of Christina Rossetti's striking sonnet, 'A study

13 Vance (1997) 190–1 notes a different Horatian echo in Clough's work (of *Odes* 3.2).
14 For more on the poems mentioned in this paragraph, see Vance (1997) 175–93 and S. J. Harrison (forthcoming, b).
15 See Turner (1989) 102–5.

(a soul)', written in 1854 but not published in her lifetime.[16] Rossetti's depiction of a woman apparently bent on death begins with a version of *Odes* 1.19.5–6, describing the 'sheen of Glycera [a *hetaira*] who shines more purely than Parian marble' (*Glycerae nitor / splendentis Pario marmore purius*), and makes clear use of Horace's picture of Cleopatra's suicide in *Odes* 1.37:

> She stands as pale as Parian statues stand:
> Like Cleopatra when she turned at bay,
> And felt her strength above the Roman sway,
> And felt the aspic writhing in her hand.
> Her face is steadfast towards the shadowy land,
> For dim beyond it looms the land of day:
> Her feet are steadfast: all the arduous way
> That foot-track hath not wavered on the sand.

The reluctant admiration for the grand act expressed in the Horatian poem here becomes a feminist assertion of a (fallen?) woman's determination to go through with a similar resolution.

Horace in the 1890s

Horatian influence was so general that it could reach into the most unlikely literary corners of Victorian England. The most famous poem of the 1890s poet Ernest Dowson (1867–1900) shows Horace transposed into the perhaps notably un-Horatian arena of low and obsessive physical passion. *Non sum qualis eram bonae sub regno Cynarae* (published 1896) appropriates *Odes* 4.1.4 as its title ('I am not the man I was under the sway of the kindly Cinara').[17] Cinara is mentioned only a few times by Horace, each time very briefly and with gentle nostalgia (also at *Odes* 4.13.21, *Epistles* 1.7.28, 1.14.33), as a former flame of his long-distant youth; Dowson, not yet thirty and destined to die before reaching thirty-three, turns Cynara/Cinara into a Swinburnian figure representing the pain of lost love which cannot be extirpated by mere physical self-indulgence (lines 7–12):

> All night upon mine heart I felt her warm heart beat,
> Night-long within mine arms in love and sleep she lay:
> Surely the kisses of her bought red mouth were sweet:
> But I was desolate and sick of an old passion,

16 To be found conveniently in Rossetti (2001) 758.
17 The name is properly spelled 'Cinara' in Latin and is usually so printed in modern texts of Horace.

When I awoke and found the dawn was gray:
I have been faithful to thee, Cynara! in my fashion.

A rather more conventional version of Horace, though perhaps with some erotic undertones, is to be found in the well-known version of *Odes* 4.7 published almost simultaneously by A. E. Housman in 1897: as so often in English versions, Housman retains the quatrain stanza structure of the original, and draws out its plangent and elegiac elements which fit his own poetic *persona*, with a closure which shows typical Housmannian emphasis on renounced male friendship and resigned fatalism:[18]

Night holds Hippolytus the pure of stain,
Diana steads him nothing, he must stay:
And Theseus leaves Pirithous in the chain
The love of comrades cannot take away.

Edwardian and Georgian Horace

Quite different was the use of Horace in the Edwardian/Georgian period by Kipling and Newbolt, which shows the enlistment of Horace in British imperial ideology. Kipling first engaged with Horace at school, and his juvenile poems include a comic rendition of *Odes* 3.9 into Devonshire dialect. Many years later he wrote perhaps the most famous parody of Horace's *Odes* in 'A translation' (1917), where he brilliantly takes off the strangeness of the poet's lyric style and especially its extraordinary word-order.[19] Horace could also be appropriated by Kipling for imperialistic purposes: this comes through most strongly in the story 'Regulus' (1917) in the school collection *Stalky and Co.*, where the class under Mr King works through *Odes* 3.5 and becomes (unusually) interested in the poem's message: [Mr King] 'Regulus was not thinking about his own life. He was telling Rome the truth. He was playing for his side.' Sir Henry Newbolt, most famous for his Lucretian-titled poem '*Vitai Lampada*' ('Play up, play up, and play the game'), also knew Horace well, and produced a version of *Odes* 1.7, '*Laudabunt alii*' (1907), where Horace's Tibur is metamorphosed into Newbolt's native Devon, the addressee Plancus into an Edwardian soldier and the Homeric world of Teucer's exile into Drake's heroic proto-imperialism:

You too, my friend, may wisely mark
How clear skies follow rain,

18 For these qualities in another Housman poem see S. J. Harrison (2002c).
19 For this poem and a good account of Kipling's engagement with Horace generally see Medcalf (1993).

And lingering in your own green park
   Or drilled on Laffan's Plain,
Forget not with the festal bowl
To soothe at times your weary soul.

When Drake must bid to Plymouth Hoe
   Goodbye for many a day,
And some were sad that feared to go,
   And some that dared not stay,
Be sure he bade them broach the best
And raise his tankard with the rest.

At the zenith of the British Empire, Horatian imitation was a natural vehicle for nationalistic poetry. This was famously undermined in the next generation by Wilfred Owen, who in '*Dulce et decorum est*' (1917) cited in a poem's title and refuted in its climax Horace's famous declaration (*Odes* 3.12.13 *dulce et decorum est pro patria mori*) that death for one's country was both sweet and glorious:

My friend, you would not tell with such high zest
To children ardent for some desperate glory,
The old Lie: Dulce et decorum est
Pro patria mori.

It is hard to find uses of Horace in other First World War poetry, presumably because war is not a major theme in his work.

Horace and the Moderns

The continuing central role of Horace in Anglophone elite education until the 1960s ensured further allusion and appropriation in modern British and American poetry. In 'Out on the lawn I lie in bed' (1933), W. H. Auden adapts the Horatian sympotic ode, in a similarly stanzaic poem addressed to a friend, to the fragile contemporary world of the 1930s:

And, gentle, do not care to know,
Where Poland draws her Eastern bow,
   What violence is done;
Nor ask what doubtful act allows
Our freedom in this English house,
   Our picnics in the sun.

This plainly picks up the beginning of Horace's ode to Quinctius (2.11.1–4), in which the addressee is asked 'not to ask what the warlike Cantabrian and

Scythian is planning with the Adriatic between us': in both poems warlike stirrings in distant parts can be ignored for the sake of current pleasure, though Auden's version has a typically dark and ironic sense of the precarious and dubious status of that momentary peace.

Auden returned to versions of the Horatian ode in his later poems. Two occasional pieces, 'Lines to Dr Walter Birk on his retiring from general practice' (1970) and 'A toast' (written for William Empson's retirement in 1971), use what is plainly a version of the Sapphic stanza, with its three identical lines followed by a much shorter fourth, in poems dedicated to old friends in the Horatian mode, and to this same period belongs 'The Horatians' (1968). Here, in a poem which again recalls in length and quatrain stanza the form of Horace's *Odes*, Auden imagines a modern Horace and his ilk as countrymen, loving 'a farm near Tivoli / or a Radnorshire village', points out the Church as the modern Maecenas as patron/employer of poets: 'how many have / found in the Anglican Church / your Maecenas who enabled / a life without cumber', and concludes with stanzas admiring Horatian moderation and resignation and character:

> You thought well of your Odes, Flaccus, and believed they
> Would live, but knew, and have taught your descendants to
>   Say with you: 'As makers go,
>   Compared with Pindar or any
>
> Of the great foudroyant masters who don't ever
> Amend, we are, for all our polish, of little
>   Stature, and, as human lives,
>   Compared with authentic martyrs,
>
> Like Regulus, of no account. We can only
> Do what it seems to us we were made for, look at
>   This world with a happy eye,
>   But from a sober perspective.'

Here, with allusions to *Odes* 4.2 (where Horace contrasts his own poetry with the grander style of Pindar) and *Odes* 3.5 (where Regulus is presented as a great patriotic martyr), Auden seems to class himself with Horace and his descendants as careful poetic craftsmen and thoughtful observers of the world.

Another British poet from the 1930s concerned with Horace was Louis MacNeice, like Auden a teacher of classics in his early career.[20] MacNeice produced some interesting translations of individual *Odes*, especially his

20 See Arkins (2000).

version of *Odes* 1.4 (1936–8; in a metre close to Thomas Gray's *Elegy in a Country Churchyard*), from which I cite the first stanza:

> Winter to Spring: the west wind melts the frozen rancour,
> The windlass drags to sea the thirsty hull:
> There is no longer welcome to beast or fire to ploughman,
> The field removes the frost-cap from its skull.

Here the sharp, personifying imagery ('rancour', 'thirsty hull', 'frost-cap from its skull') is effective in renewing Horace's ode for the translator's Audenish times, and perhaps reacting against Housman's more sentimental version (see above). At the end of his career, MacNeice, like Auden, turned to address Horace in 'Memoranda to Horace' (1962), which, like Auden's 'The Horatians', links the modern and ancient poets: both have a realistic attitude to life, and both know when to pursue private pleasure and retirement. The poem begins with doubt about whether Horace can be appreciated in the modern future, but then echoes Horace's own self-immortalisation from *Odes* 3.30 in reasserting his permanence:

> Yet your image
> 'More lasting than bronze' will do: for neither
> Sulphuric nor other acid can damage,
> Let alone destroy, your Aeolian measures
> Transmuted to Latin – *aere perennius*.

On the other side of the Atlantic, Robert Frost as poet of nature has sometimes been aptly compared with Horace. One poem which has been particularly picked out is the early 'Hyla Brook' (1916), which focuses on a temporary winter stream on Frost's New Hampshire farm.[21] This poem seems to echo Horace's poem to the *fons Bandusiae*, a spring on his own Sabine estate (*Odes* 3.13), especially in its ending:

> A brook to none but who remember long.
> This as it will be seen is other far
> Than with brooks taken otherwhere in song.
> We love the things we love from what they are.

Frost's reference to 'brooks taken otherwhere in song' seems to mark the intertextuality, and his brook's status as 'a brook to none but who remember long' seems to play wittily on Horace's promise to immortalise his spring (*Odes* 3.1.13 'you too will become one of the well-known springs', *fies nobilium tu quoque fontium*). Lyric was not the only Horatian genre Frost echoed:

21 See Bacon (2001).

he has been persuasively said to have revived the Horatian literary *sermo* in some of his longer poems.[22] Perhaps most Horatian of these is 'The lesson for today' (1941), where Frost follows the tradition of the Horatian literary epistle in combining the history of literature (here looking back to the poets of medieval Latin) with moral lessons for the present day.

Of Frost's United States contemporaries, Ezra Pound, using only occasional glancing allusions to Horace in *Personae* and the *Cantos*, published at the end of his career a few striking translations from the *Odes*; I cite the opening of his 3.30:[23]

> This monument will outlast metal and I made it
> More durable than the king's seat, higher than pyramids.
> Gnaw of the wind and rain?
>   Impotent
> The flow of the years to break it, however many.

Pound's prowess as a linguist is shown in some sound-echoes of the original ('king's seat' ~ *regalique situ*, 'impotent' ~ *impotens*) and close attention to its metaphors ('gnaw of the wind and rain' ~ *imber edax*). The Briton Basil Bunting (1900–85), who lived for some years in the States and was a Pound protégé, had many Horatian qualities (note the significant titles of his collections *The First Book of Odes*, 1965, and *The Second Book of Odes*, incorporated in his *Collected Poems*, 1968), and his carefully crafted, brief nature-poems strongly recall Horatian lyric, for example the early (1924) first item in the *First Book of Odes*:

> Weeping oaks grieve, chestnuts raise
> mournful candles. Sad is spring
> perpetuate, sad to trace
> mortalities never changing.

The link with Horatian spring odes (1.4, translated by MacNeice, above, and 4.7, translated by Housman, above) is irresistible. Unsurprisingly, Bunting wrote several translations of Horatian odes, including a lively version of *Odes* 1.13 (from 1931):

> Please stop gushing about his pink
> neck smooth arms and so forth, Dulcie; it makes me sick,
> bad-tempered, silly: makes me blush.
> Dribbling sweat on my chops proves I'm on tenterhooks.

The stark physicality of Horace's symptoms of jealousy are amusingly rendered in modern idiom, and the substution of 'Dulcie' for the

22 See Brower (1963), chapter 3; and Tomlinson (1993) 242.

23 From Pound (1970).

original's 'Lydia' could allude to 'Glycera', which it translates, another erotic object in Horatian erotic odes (e.g. 1.30). Much later (1971), Bunting also wrote a version of *Odes* 2.14 (to Postumus) which again frames the Horatian point with firm physicality and (this time) in a Horatian quatrain format:[24]

> You can't grip years, Postume,
> that ripple away nor hold back
> wrinkles, and soon now, age,
> nor can you tame death . . .

Other poets from this generation who have produced interesting versions of Horatian odes or other poems are the Americans Robert Lowell and J. V. Cunningham, and the Briton C. H. Sisson, whose modernisation of the *Carmen Saeculare* is especially notable.[25]

Living Horace

Translations of Horace remain popular in current poetry in English. The US poet and translator David Ferry has done lively and expansive complete translations of the *Odes* (1997) and of the *Epistles* (2001); as a sample of the latter I cite the opening of *Epistles* 1.1:

> Maecenas, you were the first to be named in the first
> Poem I ever wrote and you'll be the first
> To be named in the last I'm ever going to write,
> So why on earth, Maecenas, do you persist
> In trying to send a beat-up old timer like me
> Back into the ring?

Another complete translation of the *Odes* has recently been produced (1998) by the late Guy Lee, with his typical accuracy, wit and euphony, shown for example in the opening of *Odes* 3.30:

> I've achieved a memorial that will outlive bronze,
> Higher-class than the royal rubble of the Pyramids,
> Which no blustering north wind, no eroding rain
> Will have power to destroy, nor the innumerable
> Succession of the years and the swift flight of times.

But perhaps most notable in recent years is the complete translation of the *Odes* by thirty-six poets from either side of the Atlantic, edited by

24 From Bunting (2000).
25 Texts in Carne-Ross and Haynes (1996); some discussion in Tomlinson (1993).

J. D. McClatchy; elsewhere I have picked out the versions of Evan Boland, Heather McHugh and Charles Tomlinson for praise, and it is a highly diverse and stimulating collection which cannot be surveyed here.[26]

I conclude with some samples of contemporary versions in which poets appropriate Horace in their own work; interestingly, these range across all the genres and not just the ever-popular *Odes*. Michael Longley, well known for his brilliant lyric miniaturisations of Homer, has, in 'After Horace' and 'The mad poet' in *The Ghost Orchid* (1995), juxtaposed witty, brief versions of the beginning and the end of the *Ars Poetica* which combine translation with ironic commentary; I cite the first stanza of 'After Horace':

> We post-modernists can live with that human head
> Stuck on a horse's neck, or the plastering of multi-
> Coloured feathers over the limbs of assorted animals
> (So that what began on top as a gorgeous woman
> Tapers off cleverly into the tail of a black fish).

Even more miniaturised, Peter Reading's encapsulation of the Horatian sympotic/erotic ode is typically blunt and ironic ('Horatian', 1997):[27]

> *Nunc est bibendum*
> (then address the issue of
> cheesy pudendum)

The US poet August Kleinzahler, in *The Strange Hours Travelers Keep* (2003), presents several pastiche Horatian epistles, including one addressed to Maecenas ('Epistle VIII') which ironically attacks Horace's favoured country life in his own voice, while the New Zealander Ian Wedde has in *The Commonplace Odes* (2003) produced a collection of updated Horatian odes which uses Horace as the filter for the 'tension . . . between the marvellous, surreal details of ordinary life, and the great themes of human existence'. The beginning of 'Epode: a conversation', the opening poem of the collection, makes this clear:

> In these days of late autumn I know the poet only
>   As the fortunate man who
>   Free from cares on cool mornings
> Praises the commonplace world.
>   On just such a morning
>   It's Quintus Horatius Flaccus I invoke . . .

26 McClatchy (2002), reviewed in S. J. Harrison (2003).

27 From Reading (1997).

In the United Kingdom, the *Epodes*, relatively neglected in Horatian translation generally, have been brilliantly transposed to 1950s working-class steel-town Teesside by Maureen Almond as part of her collection *The Works* (2004). This vivid relocation cleverly matches the grit, wit and sense of precarious existence important to the original context of the poems, for example in 'Trafalgar Street men', her version of *Epode* 2, put into the voice of cynical and grasping landlords urging the joys of the steelworks:

> 'It's a lucky man who can follow
> his dad into the works,
> tread in his footsteps, use his know-how
> and not get into debt.
> Why would you need an education
> or little bits of paper?
> You won't be buying and selling shares
> or knocking at Number Ten . . .'

Versions of Horatian poems continue to appear regularly in the classical reception journal *Arion*,[28] and Horace, it seems, is alive and kicking in contemporary poetry in English on both sides of the Atlantic.

FURTHER READING

The best further reading to pursue is of the poems mentioned in this chapter, which can necessarily be only summarised or briefly cited here. Vance (1997) provides a good survey of the Victorian reception of Horace in the United Kingdom; S. J. Harrison (forthcoming, b) more on the Victorian use of Horace; Tomlinson (1993) a more eclectic view of his influence in twentieth-century poetry. Carne-Ross and Haynes (1996) provide a useful anthology of translations across all English literature with a good range from the periods discussed here, while McClatchy (2002) presents a complete *Odes* translation by a wide range of living poets. Among more specialist articles, Rudd (1991) presents a brilliant analysis of Tennyson's reworking of *Odes* 3.29 in 'To the Rev. F. D. Maurice', while Gaisser (1994) shows the centrality of Horace's Roman Odes in Victorian education. An impressive range of material on the reception of Horace in modern literary culture is also to be found in the *Enciclopedia Oraziana*, Mariotti (1996–8) III. 81–612.

28 See <http://www.bu.edu/arion>.

DATELINE OF WORKS AND MAJOR POLITICAL EVENTS

KEY LITERARY EVENTS		KEY HISTORICAL EVENTS	
50s BC	Catullus and Lucretius writing poetry	65 BC	Horace born in S. Italy
		49–5	Civil War, won by Julius Caesar
40s BC	Cicero writes most of philosophical works	44	Assassination of Julius Caesar and posthumous adoption of his great-nephew Octavius ('young Caesar', the future Augustus)
		42	Young Caesar defeats Republican forces (including Horace) at Philippi
		42–1	Land confiscations in which Horace and others suffer
?38	Virgil's *Eclogues* published	38–36	Renewed civil war of young Caesar against Sextus Pompey
38–37	Horace comes under patronage of Maecenas		
35	Horace, *Satires* 1 published		
30	Horace, *Satires* 2 and *Epodes* published	32–30	Young Caesar fights and defeats Antony and Cleopatra at Actium and Alexandria
29	Virgil, *Georgics* published	29	Triple triumph of Caesar
20s	Earliest elegies of Propertius, Tibullus and (later) Ovid published	27	'Restoration of republic': Caesar assumes title of 'Augustus'
?23	Horace *Odes* 1–3 published		
20–19	Horace *Epistles* 1 published		
?19	Deaths of Virgil and Tibullus Publication of Virgil, *Aeneid*		

(*cont.*)

(*cont.*)

KEY LITERARY EVENTS		KEY HISTORICAL EVENTS	
		18–17	Moral legislation of Augustus
		17	Augustus celebrates Secular Games
?16	Propertius Book 4 published		
?13	Horace *Odes* 4 published		
		12 BC	Augustus becomes *pontifex maximus* (head of state religion)
After 12	Horace *Epistles* 2 and *Ars Poetica* published		
8 BC	Death of Horace		

WORKS CITED

Abel, W. (1930) *Die Anredeformen bei den römischen Elegiker: Untersuchungen zur elegischen Form*. Charlottenburg

Ableitinger-Grunberger, D. (1971) *Der junge Horaz und die Politik: Studien zur 7. und 16. Epode*. Heidelberg

Abraham, L., and Wilding, M. (1999) 'The Alchemical Republic: a reading of "An Horatian Ode upon Cromwell's return from Ireland"' in Chernaik and Dzelzainis (1999) 94–122

Acosta-Hughes, B., Kosmetatou, E., and Baumbach, M., eds. (2004) *Labored in Papyrus Leaves: Perspectives on an Epigram Collection Attributed to Posidippus (P. Mil. Vogl.* VIII *309)*. Cambridge, MA, and London

Adair, T. (1998) 'Shakespeare's Horatian poet', *Notes and Queries* 45: 353–5

Adorno, T. (1991) 'On lyric poetry and society', in *Notes to Literature* I, trans. S. W. Nicholsen. New York (originally published 1958)

Ahern, C. F. (1991) 'Horace's rewriting of Homer in *Carmen* 1.6', *Classical Philology* 86: 301–14.

Allen, A. W., Jr, et al. (1970) 'The addressees in Horace's first book of *Epistles*', *Studies in Philology* 67: 255–66

(1972) 'Horace's first book of *Epistles* as letters', *Classical Journal* 68: 119–33

Allen, C., Haskell, Y., and Muecke, F. (2005) *Charles-Alphonse Dufresnoy, De arte graphica: Edited with Introductory Essays and Commentary*. Geneva.

Allott, K., and Allott, M. (1979) *Arnold: The Complete Poems*. London

Almond, M. (2004) *The Works*. Washington

Alphanus of Salerno (1974) *I carmi di Alfano I, arcivescovo di Salerno*, ed. A. Lentini and F. Avagliano (Miscellanea Cassinense 38). Montecassino

Ancona, R. (1994) *Time and the Erotic in Horace's Odes*. Durham and London

(2002) 'The untouched self: Sapphic and Catullan muses in Horace, *Odes* 1.22', in Spentzou and Fowler, 161–86

Anderson, W. S. (1963) 'Pompey, his friends, and the literature of the first century BC', *University of California Publications in Classical Philology* 19: 1–88

(1966) 'Horace "Carm." 1.14: What kind of ship?', *Classical Philology* 61: 84–98

(1982) *Essays on Roman Satire*. Princeton

André J.-M. (1967) *Mécène: essai de biographie spirituelle*. Paris

Angeli, A. (1993) 'Frammenti di lettere di Epicuro nei papiri d'Ercolano', *Cronache Ercolanesi* 23: 11–27

Anon., ed. (1740) *Poetarum ex Academia Gallica, qui Latinè, aut Graecè scripserunt, Carmina*. 2nd edn. The Hague
Arkins, B. (1993) 'The cruel joke of Venus: Horace as love poet', in Rudd (1993b) 106–19
(2000) 'Athens no longer dies: Greek and Roman themes in MacNeice', *Classics Ireland* 7: 1–15
Armstrong, D. (1964) 'Horace, *Satires* I, 1–3: a structural study', *Arion* 3: 86–96
(1989) *Horace*. New Haven
(2004) 'Horace's *Epistles* 1 and Philodemus', in Armstrong et al. (2004) 267–98
Armstrong, D., Fish, J., Johnston, P. A., Skinner, M. B., eds. (2004) *Vergil, Philodemus, and the Augustans*. Austin
Arnold, M. (1970). *Selected Prose*. Harmondsworth
Arrighetti, G. (1960) *Epicuro: Opere*. Turin
Ashmore, J. (1621) *Certain selected Odes of Horace Englished, and their Arguments annexed*. London
Auhagen, U. (ed.) (2000) *Horaz und Celtis*. Tübingen
Bacon, H. (2001) 'Frost and the ancient muses', in Faggen (2001) 75–100
Badian, E. (1985) 'A phantom marriage law', *Philologus* 129: 82–98
Baldwin, T. W. (1944) *William Shakspere's small Latin and lesse Greeke*, 2 vols. Urbana
Ballaster, R. (1998) 'John Wilmot, earl of Rochester', in Zwicker (1998) 204–24
Barchiesi, A. (1993) 'Insegnare ad Augusto: Orazio, Epistole 2,1 e Ovidio, Tristia II', in Schiesaro et al. (1993) 79–103. English translation in A. Barchiesi (2001b) 79–103
(1994) 'Alcune difficoltà nella carriera di un poeta giambico: giambo ed elegia nell' epodo XI', in Cortés Tovar and Fernández Corte (1994) 127–38.
(1996) 'Poetry, praise and patronage: Simonides in Book 4 of Horace's *Odes*', *Classical Antiquity* 15: 5–47
(1997) 'Elegia', in Mariotti (1996–8) II. 42–4
(2000) 'Rituals in ink: Horace on the Greek lyric tradition', in Depew and Obbink (2000), 167–82
(2001a) 'Horace and iambos: the poet as literary historian', in Cavarzere et al. (2001) 141–64
(2001b) *Speaking Volumes: Narrative and Intertext in Ovid and Other Latin Poets*. London
(2001c) 'The crossing', in S. J. Harrison (2001b) 142–63
(2002) 'The uniqueness of the *Carmen Saeculare* and its tradition', in Woodman and Feeney (2002) 107–23
(2005) 'Lane-switching and jughandles in contemporary interpretations of Roman poetry', *Transactions of the American Philological Association* 135: 135–62
Barchiesi, M. (1987) *Il testo e il tempo: studi su Dante e Flaubert*. Urbino
Barclay, J. (2004) *Argenis*, ed. M. Riley and D. Prichard Huber. 2 vols. Assen and Tempe
Barthes, R. (1968) 'L'effet de réel', *Communications* 11: 84–9
Barton, A. (1984) *Ben Jonson: Dramatist*. Cambridge
Basson, A. F., and Dominik, W. J., eds. (2003) *Literature, Art, History: Studies on Classical Antiquity and Tradition in Honour of W. J. Henderson*. Frankfurt-am-Main

Battezzato, L. (2003) 'Song, performance, and text in the new Posidippus', *Zeitschrift für Papyrologie und Epigraphik* 145: 31–43
Bell, David (2002) 'Goethe's orientalism', in Boyle and Guthrie (2002) 199–212
Bennett, C. E. (1927) *Horace: The Odes and Epodes*. Cambridge, MA
Bernstein, M. A. (1987) '"O totiens servus": satire and servitude in Augustan Rome', *Critical Inquiry* 13: 450–74
Besomi, O., and Caruso, C., eds. (1992) *Il commento ai testi*. Basel, Boston and Berlin
Beugnot, B. (1999) 'La Lyre et le précepte: notes sur la réception de *L'Art Poétique* d'Horace', *Rivista di letterature moderne e comparate* 52.3: 197–211
Bijker, A., ed. (1996) *Riedel Horatiana: A Catalogue of the Horace Collection in Groningen University Library*. Nieuwkoop
Binns, J. W. (1990) *Intellectual Culture in Elizabethan and Jacobean England: The Latin Writings of the Age*. Leeds
Bischoff, B. (1971) 'Living with the satirists', in Bolgar (1971) 83–95. Reprinted in Bischoff (1981) 260–70
(1981) *Mittelalterliche Studien* III. Stuttgart
(1994) *Manuscripts and Libraries in the Age of Charlemagne*, trans. M. M. Gorman. Cambridge
Bolgar, R. R., ed. (1971) *Classical Influences on European Culture* AD *500–1500*. Cambridge
Bond, D. F., ed. (1965) *The Spectator*. 5 vols. Oxford
Bonfante, G. (1994) *La lingua parlata in Orazio*. Venosa
Borges, J. L. (2000) *Selected Poems*, ed. A. Coleman. New York
Bosco, U. (1965) *Francesco Petrarca*, 3rd edn. Bari
Bowditch, P. L. (2001) *Horace and the Gift Economy of Patronage*. Berkeley
Bowie, E. L. (1986) 'Early Greek elegy, symposium and public festival', *Journal of Hellenic Studies* 106: 13–35
(2001) 'Early Greek iambic poetry: the importance of narrative', in Cavarzere et al. (2001) 1–27
Bowman, A. K., Champlin, E., Lintott, A., eds. (1996) *The Cambridge Ancient History,* X: *The Augustan Empire,* 43 BC–AD 69, 2nd edn. Cambridge
Boyle, A. J. (1973) 'The edict of Venus: an interpretive essay on Horace's amatory odes', *Ramus* 2: 163–88
Boyle, N., and Guthrie, J., eds. (2002) *Goethe and the English-Speaking World*. Rochester, New York and Woodbridge
Boys-Stones, G., ed. (2002) *Metaphor, Allegory and the Classical Tradition*. Oxford
Braden, G. (1978) *The Classics and English Renaissance Poetry: Three Case Studies*. New Haven
(1994) 'Ancients and moderns' [review of Martindale and Hopkins (1993) and other works], *Translation and Literature* 3: 131–7
Bradner, L. (1940) *Musae Anglicanae: A History of Anglo-Latin Poetry, 1500–1925*. New York and London
Bradshaw, A. (1970) 'Horace, *Odes* 4.1', *Classical Quarterly* 20: 142–53
(1989) 'Horace *in Sabinis*', in Deroux (1989) 160–86.
Bramble, J. C. (1974) *Persius and the Programmatic Satire*. Cambridge
Braund, D., and Gill, C., eds. (2003) *Myth, History and Culture in Republican Rome*. Exeter

Braund, S. H. (1989) 'City and country in Roman satire', in S. H. Braund, ed., *Satire and Society in Ancient Rome*, Exeter, 23–48.
Braund, S. M., ed. (1996) *Juvenal: Satires Book I*. Cambridge
Bremer, J. M, Taalman Kip, A. M. van Erp, and Slings, S. R., eds. (1987) *Some Recently Found Greek Poems*. Leiden.
Bremmer, J. (1983) 'Scapegoat rituals in ancient Greece', *Harvard Studies in Classical Philology* 87: 299–320.
Brink, C. O. (1963) *Horace on Poetry: Prolegomena to the Literary Epistles*. Cambridge
(1971) *Horace on Poetry: The 'Ars Poetica'*. Cambridge
(1982) *Horace on Poetry: Epistles Book* II: *The Letters to Augustus and Florus*. Cambridge
(1986) *English Classical Scholarship: Historical Reflections on Bentley, Porson, and Housman*. Cambridge and New York
(1995) 'Three Horatian puzzles', in S. J. Harrison (1995d) 267–78
Brower, R. A. (1959) *Alexander Pope: The Poetry of Allusion*. Oxford
(1963) *The Poetry of Robert Frost*. Oxford
Brown, C. C. (1991) 'Horatian signatures: Milton and civilised community', in M. A. Di Cesare, ed., *Milton in Italy*, Binghamton, New York, 329–44
Brown, C. G. (1997) 'Iambos', in D. E. Gerber, ed., *A Companion to the Greek Lyric Poets* (*Mnemosyne* Suppl. 173) 11–88. Leiden, New York and Cologne
Brown, M. E. D. (1993) 'The Horatian view of the poet', in Jackson and Yoder (1993) 96–100
Brown, P. M. (1993) *Horace Satires* I. Warminster
Brunt, P. A. (1980a) *The Fall of the Roman Republic and Related Essays*. Oxford
(1980b) '*Amicitia* in the Roman Republic', in Brunt (1980a) 351–81
(1980c) '*Clientela*', in Brunt (1980a) 382–442
Buchheit, V. (1961) 'Horazens programmatische *Epode* (VI)', *Gymnasium* 68: 102–12
Büchner, K. (1970a) *Studien zur romischen Literatur* VIII: *Werkanalysen*. Wiesbaden
(1970b) 'Die Epoden des Horaz', in Büchner (1970a) 50–96
(1982) *Fragmenta Poetarum Latinorum Epicorum et Lyricorum*. Leipzig
Bunting, B. (1968) *Collected Poems*. London.
(2000) *Complete Poems*. Newcastle
Burrow, C. (1993) 'Horace at home and abroad: Wyatt and sixteenth-century Horatianism', in Martindale and Hopkins (1993) 27–49
Burzacchini, G. (1976) 'Alc. 130b~Hor. *Carm.* I 22', *Quaderni Urbinati di Cultura Classica* 22: 39–58
(1985) 'Some further observations on Alcaeus fr. 130b Voigt', *Proceedings of the Liverpool Latin Seminar* 5: 373–81
Busch, W. (1964) *Horaz in Russland*. Munich
Cain, T., ed. (1995) *Ben Jonson: Poetaster*. Manchester
Cairns, F. (1972) *Generic Composition in Greek and Roman Poetry*. Edinburgh
(1975) 'Horace, *Epode* 2, Tibullus 1, 1 and rhetorical praise of the countryside', *Museum Philologum Londiniense* 1: 79–91
(1992) 'The power of implication: Horace's invitation to Maecenas (*Odes* 1.20)', in Woodman and Powell (1992) 94–109
Cambridge University (1641) *Irenodia Cantabrigiensis ob paciferum serenissimi Regis Caroli e Scotia reditum mense Novembri 1641*. Cambridge

(1697) *Gratulatio Academiae Cantabrigiensis de Reditu serenissimi Regis Gulielmi III post Pacem et Libertatem Europae feliciter restitutam*. Cambridge
(1748) *Gratulatio Academiae Cantabrigiensis de Reditu serenissimi Regis Georgii II post Pacem et Libertatem Europae feliciter restitutam*. Cambridge
Campbell, D. A. (1982–1993) *Greek Lyric, with an English Translation*. 5 vols. Cambridge, MA, and London
Carey, C. (1986) 'Archilochus and Lycambes', *Classical Quarterly* 36: 60–7
Carne-Ross, D. S., and Haynes, K., eds. (1996) *Horace in English*. Harmondsworth
Carrubba, R. W. (1969) *The Epodes of Horace*. The Hague
Cauer, P. (1906) 'Zur Abgrenzung und Verbindung der Theile in Horazens *Ars Poetica*', *Rheinisches Museum* 61: 232–43
Cavarzere, A. (1992) *Orazio: il libro degli Epodi*. Venice
(1996) *Sul limitare: il 'motto' e la poesia di Orazio*. Bologna
Cavarzere, A., Aloni, A., and Barchiesi, A., eds. (2001) *Iambic Ideas*. Lanham
Cavenaile, R. (1958) *Corpus Papyrorum Latinarum*. Wiesbaden
Chatelain, E. (1884–1900) *Paléographie des classiques latins*. 2 vols. Paris
Chernaik, W. (2000) '"I loath the Rabble": friendship, love and hate in Rochester', in Fisher (2000) 7–19
Chernaik, W., and Dzelzainis, M., eds. (1999) *Marvell and Liberty*. Basingstoke
Citroni, M. (1995a) *Poesia e lettori in Roma antica: Forme della comunicazione letteraria*. Rome and Bari
(1995b) 'I piani di destinazione nella lirica di Orazio (con qualche considerazione su satire ed epistole)', in Citroni (1995a), 271–375
Citroni Marchetti, S. (2004) 'I precetti paterni e le lezioni dei filosofi: Demea, il padre di Orazio, e altri padri e figli', *Materiali e discussioni per l'analisi dei testi classici* 53: 9–63
Clark, J. (2002) 'Religion and political identity: Samuel Johnson as a nonjuror', in Clark and Erskine-Hill (2002) 79–145
Clark, J., and Erskine-Hill, H., eds. (2002) *Samuel Johnson in Historical Context*. Basingstoke
Classe, O., ed. (2000) *Encyclopaedia of Literary Translation into English*. London and Chicago
Cody, J. V. (1976) *Horace and Callimachean Aesthetics*. Brussels
Coffey, M. (1976) *Roman Satire*. London
Collinge, N. E. (1961) *The Structure of Horace's Odes*. London
Commager, S. (1957) 'The function of wine in Horace's *Odes*', *Transactions of the American Philological Association* 88: 68–80
(1962) *The Odes of Horace: A Critical Study*. Yale
Conte, G. B. (1994) *Genres and Readers: Lucretius, Love Elegy, Pliny's Encyclopedia*. Baltimore
(1996) *The Hidden Author: An Interpretation of Petronius' Satyricon*. Berkeley
(2002) *Virgilio: l'epica di sentimento*. Turin.
Corns, T. N., ed. (1993) *The Cambridge Companion to English Poetry: Donne to Marvell*. Cambridge
Cortés Tovar, R., and J. C. Fernández Corte, eds. (1994) *Bimilenario de Horacio*. Salamanca
Costa, C. D. N., ed. (1973) *Horace*. London
Courtney, E. (1993) *The Fragmentary Latin Poets*. Oxford

Creech, T. (1718) *The Works of Horace, in Latin and English*. 2 vols. 5th edn. London

Cucchiarelli, A. (2001) *La satira e il poeta: Orazio tra Epodi e Sermones*. Pisa

Cugusi, P. (1997–9) *Epistolographi Latini Minores*, I: *Aetatem anteciceronianam amplectens;* II: *Aetatem Ciceronianam et Augusteam amplectens*. Turin

Culler, J. (1997) *Literary Theory*. Oxford

(1981) *The Pursuit of Signs*. Ithaca

Curcio, G. (1913) *Q. Orazio Flacco studiato in Italia dal secolo XIII al XVIII*. Catania

Curran, J. (1996) 'Wieland's revival of Horace', *International Journal of the Classical Tradition* 3: 171–84

Daintree, D. (2000) 'Non omnis moriar: the lyrical tradition of Horace in the Middle Ages', *Latomus* 59: 889–902

Damon, C. (1997) *The Mask of the Parasite: A Pathology of Roman Patronage*. Ann Arbor

D'Arms, J. (1995) 'Heavy drinking and drunkenness in the Roman world: four questions for historians', in Murray and Tecusan (1995) 304–17

Davidson, J. N. (1998) *Courtesans and Fishcakes: The Consuming Passions of Classical Athens*. New York

Davies, M. (1991) *Poetarum Melicorum Graecorum Fragmenta*, I. Oxford

Davis, G. (1975) 'The persona of Licymnia: a revaluation of Horace *Carm.* 2.12', *Philologus* 119: 70–83

(1991) *Polyhymnia: The rhetoric of Horatian lyric discourse*. Berkeley

Davis, P. J. (2001) 'Horace, Augustus and the Secular Games', *Ramus* 30: 111–27

Davis, R. B. (1955) *George Sandys, Poet-Adventurer: A Study in Anglo-American Culture*. London

Dawson, C. M. (1950) 'The *Iambi* of Callimachus: a Hellenistic poet's experimental laboratory', *Yale Classical Studies* 11: 1–168

Dawson, T., and Dupree, R. S. (1994) *Seventeenth-Century English Poetry: An Annotated Anthology*. Hemel Hempstead

De Pretis, A. (2002) *'Epistolarity' in the First Book of Horace's Epistles*. Totowa

Degani, H. (1991) *Hipponactis testimonia et fragmenta*. 2nd edn. Stuttgart and Leipzig

Delhaye, P. (1958) '"Grammatica" et "ethica" au XIIe siècle', *Recherches de théologie ancienne et médiévale* 25: 59–110

Della Corte, F. (1973) 'Fra "Statilio Flacco" e Orazio', *Rivista de Filologia e di istruzione classica* n.s. 101: 442–50

Depew, M., and Obbink, D., eds. (2000), *Matrices of Genre: Authors, Canons and Society*. Cambridge

Deroux, C., ed. (1989) *Studies in Latin Literature and Roman History*, v. Brussels

Derrida, J. (1981) 'The law of genre', in Mitchell (1981) 51–77

Desbordes, F. (1979) 'Masculin/feminin: notes sur les *Odes* d'Horace', *Etudes de littérature ancienne* 1: 51–80

Desjardins, M.-C. [called de Villedieu] (1679) *The Unfortunate Heroes [Englished by a Gentleman for his Diversion]*. London

Dickie, M. W. (1981) 'The disavowal of *invidia* in Roman iamb and satire', *Proceedings of the Liverpool Latin Seminar* 3: 183–208

Diggle, J., Hall, J. B., and Jocelyn, H. D., eds. (1989), *Studies in Latin Literature and Its Tradition, in Honour of C. O. Brink* (*Proceedings of the Cambridge Philological Society* Suppl. 15). Cambridge
Dilke, O. A. W. (1958) 'When was the *Ars Poetica* written?', *Bulletin of the Institute of Classical Studies* 5: 49–57
(1973) 'Horace and the verse letter', in Costa (1973) 94–112
(1981) The interpretation of Horace's *Epistles*', *Aufstieg und Niedergang der römischen Welt* II. 31.3: 1837–57
Doblhofer, E. (1966) *Die Augustuspanegyrik des Horaz in formalhistorischer Sicht*. Heidelberg
(1981) 'Horaz und Augustus', *Aufstieg und Niedergang der römischen Welt* II. 31.3: 1922–86
(1992) *Horaz in der Forschung nach 1957*. Darmstadt
Donahue, J., ed. (2003) *American Journal of Philology* 124.3. (Special issue: *Roman Dining*)
Donaldson, I. (1997) *Jonson's Magic Houses: Essays in Interpretation*. Oxford
Doody, M. A. (1998) 'Gender, literature, and gendering literature in the Restoration', in Zwicker (1998) 58–81
Dorsch, T., and Murray, P. (2000) *Classical Literary Criticism*. Harmondsworth
Drant, T. (1566) *Medicinable morall . . .* London
Drexler, H. (1935) 'Interpretationen zu Horaz, 16. *Epode*', *Studi italiani di filologia classica* 12: 119–50
Dronke, P. (1976) 'Peter of Blois and poetry at the court of Henry II', *Mediaeval Studies* 38: 185–235
Du Quesnay, I. M. Le M. (1984) 'Horace and Maecenas: the propaganda value of *Sermones* 1', in Woodman and West (1984) 19–58
(1995) 'Horace, *Odes* 4.5: *Pro Reditu Imperatoris Caesaris Divi Filii Augusti*', in S. J. Harrison (1995d) 128–87
(2002) '*Amicus certus in re incerta cernitur*: *Epode* 1', in Woodman and Feeney (2002) 17–37
Duemmler, E. (1881) *Poetae Latini Aevi Carolini* I. Berlin
Dunbabin, K. (2003) *The Roman Banquet*. Cambridge
Duncan, D. (1979) *Ben Jonson and the Lucianic Tradition*. Cambridge
Dunn, F. M. (1995) 'Rhetorical approaches to Horace's *Odes*', *Arethusa* 28: 165–76
Dutton, R. (1996) *Ben Jonson: Authority, Criticism*. Basingstoke
Dyson, S., and Prior, R. (1995) 'Horace, Martial, and Rome: two poetic outsiders read the ancient city', *Arethusa* 28: 245–64
Eco, U. (1993) *Misreadings*. London
Edden, V. (1973) 'The best of lyric poets', in Costa (1973) 135–59
Edmunds, L. (1992) *From a Sabine Jar*. Chapel Hill
(2001) *Intertextuality and the Reading of Roman Poetry*. Baltimore and London
Eilers, C. (2002) *Roman Patrons of Greek Cities*. Oxford
Elsner, J., ed. (1996) *Art and Text in Roman Culture*. Cambridge
Enciclopedia oraziana: see Mariotti (1996–8)
Enck, J. J. (1966) *Jonson and the Comic Truth*. Madison, Wisconsin
Erickson, W. (1996) *Mapping* The Faerie Queene. *Quest Structures and the World of the Poem*. New York

Ernout, A., and Meillet, A. (1939) *Dictionnaire étymologique de la langue latine*. Paris
Erskine-Hill, H. (1981) 'Satire and self-portrayal: The first satire of the second book of Horace, imitated, and Pope's reception of Horace', in Killy (1981b) 153–71
(1983) *The Augustan Idea in English Literature*. London
(1996a) *Poetry and the Realm of Politics: Shakespeare to Dryden*. Oxford
(1996b) *Poetry of Opposition and Revolution: Dryden to Wordsworth*. Oxford
ed. (2000) *Alexander Pope: Selected Letters*. Oxford
Evans, H. B. (1978) 'Horace, *Satires* 2.7: saturnalia and satire', *Classical Journal* 73: 307–12
Faggen, R., ed. (2001) *The Cambridge Companion to Robert Frost*. Cambridge
Fairclough, H. R. (1929) *Horace: Satires, Epistles and Ars Poetica*. Cambridge, MA
Fara, P., and Money, D. (2004) 'Isaac Newton and Augustan Anglo-Latin poetry', *Studies in History and Philosophy of Science* 35.3: 549–71
Fedeli, P. (1978) 'Il V epodo e i giambi d'Orazio come espressione d'arte alessandrina', *Museum Philologum Londiniense* 3: 67–138
(1980) *Sesto Properzio. Il primo libro delle elegie*. Florence
(1997a) *Quinto Orazio Flacco: Le opere*, II.3: *Le epistole*. Rome
(1997b) 'Vino', in Mariotti (1996–8) II. 262–9. Rome
Feeney, D. C. (1991) *The Gods in Epic*. Oxford
(1993) 'Horace and the Greek lyric poets', in Rudd (1993b) 41–63
(1998) *Literature and Religion at Rome*. Cambridge
(2002) 'VNA CVM SCRIPTORE MEO: poetry, Principate and the traditions of literary history in the Epistle to Augustus', in Woodman and Feeney (2002) 172–87
Feo, M. (1998) 'Petrarca', in Mariotti (1996–8) III. 405–7
Ferraro, J. (1993) 'The satirist, the text and "the world beside": Pope's *First satire of the second book of Horace imitated*', *Translation and Literature* 2: 37–63
(2000) 'Pope, Rochester, and Horace', in Fisher (2000) 119–31
Ferri, R. (1993) *I dispiaceri di un epicureo: uno studio sulla poetica delle epistole oraziane*. Pisa
(1996) 'Epistola', in Mariotti (1996–8) I. 54–7
Ferry, D., trans. (1997) *The Odes of Horace*. New York
trans. (2001) *The Epistles of Horace*. New York
Finley, John H. (1937) 'Milton and Horace: a study of Milton's sonnets', *Harvard Studies in Classical Philology* 48: 29–73
Fisher, N., ed. (2000) *That Second Bottle: Essays on John Wilmot, Earl of Rochester*. Manchester
Fiske, G. C. (1920) *Lucilius and Horace*. Madison
Fitzgerald, W. (1988) 'Power and impotence in Horace's *Epodes*', *Ramus* 17: 176–91
(1995) *Catullan Provocations*. Berkeley
(2000) *Slavery and the Roman Literary Imagination*. Cambridge
Fleischmann, W. (1974) 'Classicism', in Preminger (1974) 136–41
Forster, H. (1982) 'The rise and fall of the Cambridge Muses (1603–1763)', *Transactions of the Cambridge Bibliographical Society* 8: 141–72
Forster, L. (1981) 'Die Emblemata Horatiana des Otho Vaenius', in Killy (1981b) 117–28
Foscolo, U. (1953) *Edizione nazionale delle opere di Ugo Foscolo* X. Florence

Fowler, D. (1991) 'Narrate and describe: the problem of ekphrasis', *Journal of Roman Studies* 81: 23–35. Reprinted in Fowler (2000) 64–85

(1993) 'Postscript: images of Horace in twentieth-century scholarship', in Martindale and Hopkins (1993) 268–76.

(1995) 'Horace and the aesthetics of politics', in S. J. Harrison (1995d) 248–66

(2000) *Roman Constructions: Readings in Postmodern Latin*. Oxford

Foxon, D. F. (1975) *English Verse 1701–1750*. 2 vols. Cambridge

Fraenkel, E. (1957) *Horace*. Oxford

France, P. (2000) *The Oxford Guide to Literature in English Translation*. Oxford

Francis, P. (1753) *A Poetical Translation of the Works of Horace*. 4 vols. 5th edn. London

Franssen, P., and Hoenselaars, T. (1999) *The Author as Character: Representing Historical Writers in Western Literature*. Teaneck and Madison

Freudenburg, K. (1993) *The Walking Muse: Horace on the Theory of Satire*. Princeton

(2001) *Satires of Rome: Threatening Poses from Lucilius to Juvenal*. Cambridge

ed. (2005) *The Cambridge Companion to Roman Satire*. Cambridge

Friedman, D. M. (1993) 'Andrew Marvell', in Corns (1993) 275–303

Friis-Jensen, K. (1988) 'Horatius liricus et ethicus: Two twelfth-century school texts on Horace's poems', *Cahiers de l'Institut du Moyen-Age Grec et Latin (Université de Copenhague)* 57: 81–147

(1990) 'The *Ars Poetica* in twelfth-century France: the Horace of Matthew of Vendôme, Geoffrey of Vinsauf, and John of Garland', *Cahiers de l'Institut du Moyen-Age Grec et Latin (Université de Copenhague)* 60: 319–88

(1993) 'The medieval Horace and his lyrics', in Ludwig (1993b) 257–303

(1995a) 'Horace and the early writers of arts of poetry', in S. Ebbesen, ed., *Sprachtheorien in Spätantike und Mittelalter* (Geschichte der Sprachtheorie 3) 360–401. Tübingen

(1995b) 'Commentaries on Horace's *Art of Poetry* in the incunable period', *Renaissance Studies* 9: 228–39

(1997a) 'Medieval commentaries on Horace', in Mann and Munk Olsen (1997) 51–73

(1997b) 'Petrarch and the medieval Horace', in M. Pade, H. Ragn Jensen and L. Waage Petersen, eds., *Avignon and Naples: Italy in France: France in Italy in the Fourteenth Century* (Analecta Romana Instituti Danici. Suppl. 25), Rome, 83–98

Friis-Jensen, K., Munk Olsen, B., and Smith, O. L. (1997) 'Bibliography of classical scholarship in the Middle Ages and the early Renaissance (9th to 15th centuries)', in Mann and Munk Olsen (1997) 197–251

Frischer, B. (1991) *Shifting Paradigms: New Approaches to Horace's Ars Poetica*. Atlanta

Gage, J. (1973) 'Horatian reminiscences in two twelfth-century art critics', *Journal of the Warburg and Courtauld Institutes* 36: 359–60

Gaisser, J. H. (1994) 'The Roman Odes at school', *Classical World* 87: 443–56

Gale, M. (1997) 'Propertius 2.7: *Militia amoris* and the ironies of elegy', *Journal of Roman Studies* 87: 77–91

Galinsky, K. (1996) *Augustan Culture*. Princeton

(2003) 'Horace's Cleopatra and Virgil's Dido', in Basson and Dominik (2003) 17–23

Galland-Hallyn, P. (2001) 'L'Ode latine comme genre "tempéré": le lyrisme familial de Macrin dans les *Hymnes* de 1537', *Humanistica Lovaniensia* 50: 221–65
Garland, H. and M. (1997) *The Oxford Companion to German Literature*. 3rd edn. Oxford
Gärtner, U. (2001) 'Lucilius und die Freundschaft', in Manuwald (2001) 90–110
Gaskell, P. (1952) 'Printing the classics in the eighteenth century', *The Book Collector* 1: 98–111
Genette, G. (1982) *Figures of Literary Discourse*. Oxford
Gerber, D. E. (1999) *Greek Iambic Poetry*. Cambridge, MA, and London
Gigon, O. (1980) 'Der Brief in der griechischen Philosophie', *Didactica Classica Gandensia* 20: 117–32
Gillespie, S. (1992) 'A checklist of Restoration English translations and adaptations of classical Greek and Roman poetry 1660–1700', *Translation and Literature* 1: 52–67
(1993) 'Horace's *Ode* 3.29: Dryden's "Masterpiece in English"', in Martindale and Hopkins (1993) 148–58
Gillespie, S., and Hopkins, D., eds. (2005) *The Oxford History of Literary Translation in English*, III: *1660–1790*. Oxford
Gladstone, W. E. (1894) *The Odes of Horace*. London
Glauche, G. (1970) *Schullektüre im Mittelalter* (Münchener Beiträge zur Mediävistik und Renaissance-Forschung). Munich
Glomski, J. (1987) 'The role of *imitatio* in J. Kochanowski's *Elegiae, Lyricorum libellus* and *Piesni*', *Oxford Slavonic Papers* 20: 34–59
Goad, C. (1918) *Horace in the English Literature of the Eighteenth Century*. New Haven. Reprinted New York, 1967
Godman, P., and Murray, O., eds. (1990) *Latin Poetry and the Classical Tradition*. Oxford
Gold, B. K., ed. (1982) *Literary and Artistic Patronage in Ancient Rome*. Austin
(1992) 'Openings in Horace's *Satires* and *Odes*: poet, patron, and audience', *Yale Classical Studies* 29: 161–85
Gowers, E. (1993a) *The Loaded Table*. Oxford
(1993b) 'Horace *Satires* 1. 5: an inconsequential journey', *Proceedings of the Cambridge Philological Society* 39: 48–66
(2003) 'Fragments of autobiography in Horace *Satires* 1', *Classical Antiquity* 22: 55–91
(2005) 'The restless companion: Horace, *Satires* 1 and 2', in Freudenburg (2005) 48–61
Grabher, C. (1967) *La poesia minore dell' Ariosto: la lirica latina, la lirica volgare, le satire e una nota sul carattere dell' Ariosto*. Rome
Gradel, I. (2002) *Emperor Worship and Roman Religion*. Oxford
Grassmann, V. (1966) *Die erotischen Epoden des Horaz: literarischer Hintergrund und sprachliche Tradition*. Munich
Gray, D. (1979) *Robert Henryson*. Leiden
Gray, T. (1935) *Correspondence of Thomas Gray* 1, ed. P. Toynbee and L. Whibley. Oxford
Greason, A. L. (1977) 'The indebtedness of Pope's "Eloisa to Abelard" to Francis Fane and Horace', *Notes and Queries* n.s. 24.3 (222): 232–3

Griffin, J. (1984) 'Augustus and the poets: *Caesar qui cogere posset*', in Millar and Segal (1984) 189–218
(1985) *Latin Poets and Roman Life*. London
(1993) 'Horace in the thirties', in Rudd (1993b) 1–22
(1997) 'Cult and personality in Horace', *Journal of Roman Studies* 87 (1997) 54–69
(2002) 'Look your last on lyric', in T. P. Wiseman (ed.), *Classics in Progress*, London, 311–32
Grimal, P. (1961) 'A propos de la xvi^e "Epode" d'Horace', *Latomus* 20: 721–30
Grimm, J. (1969) *Die Einheit der Ariost'schen Satire*. Frankfurt-am-Main
Gronewald, M., and Daniel, R. W. (2004a) 'Ein neuer Sappho-Papyrus', *Zeitschrift für Papyrologie und Epigraphik* 147: 1–8
(2004b) 'Nachtrag zum neuen Sappho-Papyrus', *Zeitschrift für Papyrologie und Epigraphik* 149: 1–4
Grube, G. M. A. (1965) *The Greek and Roman Critics*. London
Gruber, J. (1997) 'Horaz im deutschen Renaissancehumanismus', *Gymnasium* 104: 227–44
Guerinot, J. V. (1969) *Pamphlet Attacks on Alexander Pope, 1711–1744*. London
Guillemin, A.-M. (1929) *Pline et la vie littéraire de son temps*. Paris
Gummere, Richard M. (1963) *The American Colonial Mind and the Classical Tradition*. Cambridge, MA
Haan, E. (2003) *Andrew Marvell's Latin Poetry: From Text to Context*. Brussels
Habinek, T., and Schiesaro, A., eds. (1997) *The Roman Cultural Revolution*. Cambridge
Haight, E. H. (1948) 'Epistula item quaevis non magna poema est', *Studies in Philology* 45: 525–40
Hajdú, I. (1993) 'Ein Zürcher Kommentar aus dem 12. Jahrhundert zur *Ars poetica* des Horaz', *Cahiers de l'Institut du Moyen-Age Grec et Latin (Université de Copenhague)* 63: 231–93
Hallett, J. P., and Skinner, M. B., eds. (1997) *Roman Sexualities*. Princeton
Hammond, P. (1993) 'Figures of Horace in Dryden's literary criticism', in Martindale and Hopkins (1993) 127–47
(1998) 'Classical texts: translations and transformations', in Zwicker (1998) 143–61
(2000) 'Rochester's homoeroticism', in Fisher (2000) 47–62
Hannes, E. (1721) 'Paulo Herman M. D. . . . ex India reverso, Ode', in *Musarum Anglicanarum Analecta* I. 263–6. 2 vols. 4th edn. London
Hardie, P. R. (1993) '*Ut pictura poesis*: Horace and the visual arts', in Rudd (1993b) 120–39
(1997) 'Fifth-century Athenian and Augustan images of the barbarian other', *Classics Ireland* 4: 46–56
(2002a) *Ovid's Poetics of Illusion*. Cambridge
ed. (2002b) *The Cambridge Companion to Ovid*. Cambridge
Hardin, R. F. (1973) *Michael Drayton and the Passing of Elizabethan England*. Lawrence, KA
Harp, R., and Stewart, S. (eds.) (2000) *The Cambridge Companion to Ben Jonson*. Cambridge
Harris, W. V. (2003) 'The anger of women', *Yale Classical Studies* 32: 121–43

Harrison, G. (1987) 'The confessions of Lucilius (Horace *Sat.* 2.1.30–34): A Defense of Autobiographical Satire?', *Classical Antiquity* 6: 38–52
Harrison, S. J. (1988) 'Deflating the *Odes*: Horace *Epistles* 1.20', *Classical Quarterly* n.s. 38: 473–6
(1990) 'The praise singer: Horace, Censorinus and *Odes* 4.8', *Journal of Roman Studies* 80: 31–43
(1993) 'The literary form of Horace's Odes', in Ludwig (1993b) 131–62
(1995a) 'Horace, Pindar, Iullus Antonius, and Augustus: *Odes* 4.2', in S. J. Harrison (1995d) 108–27
(1995b) 'Poetry, philosophy, and letter-writing in Horace *Epistles* 1', in Innes et al. (1995) 47–61
(1995c) 'Some twentieth-century views of Horace', in S. J. Harrison (1995d) 1–16
ed. (1995d) *Homage to Horace: A Bimillenary Celebration*. Oxford
(1997) 'Archpoet, Poem VI and some Horatian intertexts', *Mittellateinisches Jahrbuch* 32: 37–42
(2001a) 'Some generic problems in Horace's *Epodes*: or, on (not) being Archilochus', in Cavarzere et al. (2001) 165–86
ed. (2001b) *Texts, Ideas and the Classics*. Oxford
(2002a) 'Ovid and genre: evolutions of an elegist', in Hardie (2002b) 79–94
(2002b) Review of E. A. Schmidt, *Zeit und Form: Dichtungen des Horaz*, *Bryn Mawr Classical Review* 11.10
(2002c) 'A. E. Housman's Latin Elegy to Moses Jackson', *Transactions of the American Philological Association* 132: 209–14
(2003) Review of McClatchy (2002), *Bryn Mawr Classical Review* 2003.03.05
(2004) 'Lyric middles: the turn at the centre in Horace's *Odes*', in Kyriakidis and De Martino (2004) 81–102
(2005a), 'Nostalgia and decline', in S. J. Harrison (2005b) 287–99
ed. (2005b) *A Companion to Latin Literature*. Oxford
(forthcoming, a) *Generic Enrichment in Vergil and Horace*. Oxford
(forthcoming, b) 'Horace and the construction of the Victorian gentleman', forthcoming in *Helios*
(forthcoming, c), 'Horace *Epistles* 2: the last Horatian book of sermones?', *Proceedings of the Liverpool Latin Seminar* 13 (2007)
Hawkins, Sir Thomas (1625) *Odes of Horace, the best of Lyrick Poets, contayning much morallity, and sweetnesse. Selected and Translated by Sr T. H.* London
Haye, T. (2003) 'Der Satiriker Francesco Filelfo – ein Lucilius der Renaissance', *Philologus* 147: 129–50
Haynes, J. (1986) *The Humanist as Traveller. G. Sandys's Relation of a Journey Begun an. dom. 1610 . . .* Rutherford, NJ
Heinze, R. (1919) 'Horazens Buch der Briefe', *Neue Jahrbücher für das klassische Altertum* 43: 305–15
(1972) *Vom Geist des Römertums*. Darmstadt
Heiserman, A. R. (1961) *Skelton and Satire*. Chicago
Helgerson, R. (1993) 'Ben Jonson', in Corns (1993) 148–70
Henderson, J. (1987) 'Suck it and see (Horace, *Epode* 8)', in Whitby et al. (1987) 105–18
(1999) *Writing Down Rome: Comedy, Satire, and Other Offences in Latin Poetry*. Oxford

Herford, C. H., and Simpson, P., eds. (1925) *Ben Jonson*, 1: *The Man and His Work*. Oxford
Herrick, M. T. (1946) *The Fusion of Horatian and Aristotelian Literary Criticism, 1531–1555*. Urbana
Hester, M. T. (1982) *Kinde Pitty and Brave Scorn: John Donne's Satires*. Durham, NC
Heyworth, S. J. (1993) 'Horace's *Ibis*: on the titles, unity, and contents of the *Epodes*', *Proceedings of the Liverpool Latin Seminar* 7: 85–96
(2001) 'Catullan iambics, Catullan *iambi*', in Cavarzere, Aloni and Barchiesi (2001) 117–40
Highet, G. (1949) *The Classical Tradition*. Oxford
Hills, P. D. (2001) 'Ennius, Suetonius and the genesis of Horace, *Odes* 4', *Classical Quarterly* 51: 613–6
Hils, G. (1953) *The Odes of Casimire, translated by G. H. (1646)*, ed. M.-S. Røstvig. Los Angeles
Hinds, S. (2002) 'Landscape with figures: the aesthetics of place in the *Metamorphoses* and its tradition', in Hardie (2002a) 122–49
Hingley, R. (2000), *Roman Officers and English Gentlemen*. London
Holder, A. (1894) *Pomponi Porfyrionis commentum in Horatium Flaccum*. Pfaffenhofen
Hooley, D. (1997) *The Knotted Thong: Structures of Mimesis in Persius*. Ann Arbor
Hopkins, D. (1993) 'Cowley's Horatian mice', in Martindale and Hopkins (1993) 103–26
Hopkins, L. (2001), 'A possible source for "An Horatian Ode upon Cromwell's return from Ireland"', *Notes and Queries* n.s. 48: 19–20
Hornblower, S., and Spawforth, A., eds. (1996) *The Oxford Classical Dictionary*, 3rd edn. Oxford
Horsfall, N. M. (1979a) 'Horace, *Sermones* 3?' *Liverpool Classical Monthly* 4.6: 117–9
(1979b) 'Horace, *Sermones* 3; *epilegomena*', *Liverpool Classical Monthly* 4.8: 169–71
(1993) *La villa sabina di Orazio: il galateo della gratitudine*. Venosa
(1998) 'The first person singular in Horace's *Carmina*', in Knox and Foss (1998) 40–54
Housman, A. E. (1907) 'Luciliana', *Classical Quarterly* 1: 148–59
Housman, A. E., Diggle, J., and Goodyear F. R. D., eds. (1972), *The Classical Papers of A. E. Housman*. 3 vols. Cambridge
Hubbard, M. (1995) 'Pindarici fontis qui non expalluit haustus: Horace, *Epistle* 1.3', in S. J. Harrison (1995d) 219–27
Hunt, T. (1991) *Teaching and Learning Latin in Thirteenth-Century England*, 1: *Texts*. Woodbridge
Hunter, M., and Money, D. (2005) 'Robert Boyle's first encomium: two Latin poems by Samuel Collins (1647)', *The Seventeenth Century* 20: 223–41
Hunter, R. L. (1985) 'Horace on friendship and free speech (*Epistles* 1.18 and *Satires* 1.4)', *Hermes* 113: 480–90
Hutchinson, G. O. (1988) *Hellenistic Poetry*. Oxford
(2001) *Greek Lyric Poetry: A Commentary on Selected Larger Pieces*. Oxford
(2002) 'The publication and individuality of Horace's *Odes* Books 1–3', *Classical Quarterly* 52: 517–37

Ijsewijn, J. (1990) *Companion to Neo-Latin Studies*. 2nd edn, part 1. Leuven
Ijsewijn, J., and Sacré, D. (1998) *Companion to Neo-Latin Studies*. 2nd edn, part 2. Leuven
Innes, D. (1989) 'Augustan critics', in G. A. Kennedy (1989) 254–67
(1995) 'Longinus: structure and unity', in J. G. Abbenes, S. R. Slings and I. Sluiter, eds., *Greek Literary Theory after Aristotle: A Collection of Papers in Honour of D. M. Schenkeveld*, 111–24. Amsterdam. Reprinted in Laird (2006)
(2002) 'Metaphor, simile and allegory as ornaments of style', in Boys-Stones (2002) 7–27
Innes, D., Hine, H., and Pelling, C., eds. (1995) *Ethics and Rhetoric: Classical Essays for Donald Russell on His Seventy-Fifth Birthday*. Oxford
Jackson, W., and Yoder, R. P., eds. (1993) *Approaches to Teaching Pope's Poetry*. New York
Jacobsen, P. C. (1978) 'Sextus Amarcius: un imitateur des satires d'Horace vers 1100', in H. Baader, ed., *Onze études sur l'esprit de la satire*, 197–219. Tübingen
Jaeger, C. S. (1994) *The Envy of Angels: Cathedral Schools and Social Ideals in Medieval Europe, 950–1200*. Philadelphia
Jaeger, M. (1995) 'Reconstructing Rome: the Campus Martius and Horace, *Ode* 1.8', *Arethusa* 28: 177–92
Janko, R. (2000) *Philodemus On Poems Book 1*. Oxford
Jasanoff, J., Melchert, H. C., and Oliver, L., eds. (1998) *Mír Curad: Studies in Honor of Calvert Watkins*. Innsbruck
Jocelyn, H. D. (1979) 'Horace, *Epistles* 1', *Liverpool Classical Monthly* 4.7: 145–7
(1982) 'Boats, women, and Horace *Odes* 1.14', *Classical Philology* 77: 330–5
(1995) 'Horace and the reputation of Plautus in the late first century BC', in S. J. Harrison (1995d) 228–47
John of Garland (1974) *The Parisiana Poetria of John of Garland*, ed. T. Lawler (Yale Studies in English 182). New Haven and London
Johnson, T. S. (2003) 'Locking-in and locking-out Lydia: lyric form and power in Horace's C. 1.25 and III.9', *Classical Journal* 99: 113–34
(2004) *A Symposion of Praise*. Madison
Johnson, W. R. (1982) *The Idea of Lyric*. Berkeley
(1993) *Horace and the Dialectic of Freedom*. Ithaca and London
Jones, P., ed. (2001) *Imagist Poetry*. London
Josifovic, S. (1966) *Horaz in der älteren serbokroatischen Literatur*. Skopje
Judson, A. C. (1945) *The Life of Edmund Spenser*. Baltimore
Kaiser, L. M. (1965) 'The first American translation of the *Odes* and *Epodes* of Horace', *Classical Journal* 60: 220–30
(1981) 'A census of American Latin verse, 1625–1825', *Proceedings of the American Antiquarian Society* 91.2: 197–299
(1984) *Early American Latin Verse, 1625–1825: An Anthology*. Chicago
Kaster, R. A., ed. (1995) *C. Suetonius Tranquillus: De grammaticis et rhetoribus*. Oxford
Keil, H. (1874) *Grammatici latini* VI. Leipzig
Kennedy, D. (1992) '"Augustan" and "anti-Augustan": reflections on terms of reference', in A. Powell (1992) 26–58
Kennedy, G. A., ed. (1989), *The Cambridge History of Literary Criticism* I. Cambridge

Kenney, E. J. (1977) 'A question of taste: Horace, *Epistles* 1.14.6–9', *Illinois Classical Studies* 2: 229–39
Kerkhecker, A. (1999) *Callimachus' Book of Iambi*. Oxford
Kiessling, A., and Heinze, R. (1964) *Q. Horatius Flaccus: Oden und Epoden*. Berlin. (First published 1930)
(1967) *Horaz: Satiren*. Berlin. (First published 1930)
Killy, W. (1981a) 'Über den deutschen Horaz', in Killy (1981b) 243–59
ed. (1981b) *Geschichte des Textverständnisses am Bespiel von Pindar und Horaz*. Munich
Kilpatrick, R. S. (1986) *The Poetry of Friendship: Horace, Epistles I*. Edmonton
(1990) *The Poetry of Criticism: Horace Epistles II and Ars Poetica*. Edmonton
Kindermann, U. (1978) *Satyra: Die Theorie der Satire im Mittellateinischen: Vorstudie zu einer Gattungsgeschichte*. Nuremberg
Kindstrand, J. F. (1976) *Bion of Borysthenes*. Uppsala
Kissel, W. (1981) 'Horaz 1936–1975', *Aufstieg und Niedergang der römischen Welt* II. 31.3: 1403–1558
(1994) 'Horazbibliographie 1976–91' in Koster (1994) 115–92
Klein, L. E. (1994) *Shaftesbury and the Culture of Politeness: Moral Discourse and Cultural Politics in Eighteenth-Century England*. Cambridge
Kleinzahler, A. (2003) *The Strange Hours Travelers Keep*. New York
Klingner, F. (1965) *Römische Geisteswelt*. Munich
Knoche, U. (1975) *Roman Satire*, trans. E. Ramage. Bloomington
Knox, P. E., and Foss, C., eds. (1998) *Style and Tradition: Studies in Honour of Wendell Clausen*. Stuttgart and Leipzig
Konstan, D. (1995) 'Patrons and friends (in Horace *Epist.* 1.18 and Juvenal 5)', *Classical Philology* 90: 328–42
(1997) *Friendship in the Classical World*. Cambridge
Koster, S., ed. (1994) *Horaz-Studien*. Erlangen
Kraggerud, E. (1984) *Horaz und Actium: Studien zu den politischen Epoden*. Oslo
Krasser, H., and Schmidt, E. A., eds. (1996) *Zeitgenosse Horaz: Der Dichter und seine Leser seit zwei Jahrtausenden*. Tübingen
Krevans, N. (1984) 'The Poet as Editor: Callimachus, Virgil, Horace, Propertius and the Development of the Poetic Book'. Dissertation, Princeton
Kroll, W. (1924) *Studien zum Verständnis der römischen Literatur*. Stuttgart
Krostenko, B. A. (2001) *Cicero, Catullus and the Language of Social Performance*. Chicago and London
Kupersmith, W. (1985) *Roman Satirists in Seventeenth-Century England*. Lincoln, Nebraska and London
(1995) 'William Diaper and two others imitate Swift imitating Horace', *Swift Studies* 10: 26–36
Kyriakidis, S., and De Martino, F., eds. (2004) *Middles in Latin Poetry*. Bari
La Penna, A. (1949) 'Schizzo di una interpretazione di Orazio, partendo dal primo libro delle *Epistole*', *Annali della Scuola Normale Superiore di Pisa* 18:14–48
(1963) *Orazio e l'ideologia del principato*. Turin
(1969) 'Orazio e la morale mondana europea', in *Orazio: tutte le opere*, Florence. Reprinted in La Penna (1993) 1–238
(1993) *Saggi e studi su Orazio*. Florence

(1995) 'Il vino di Orazio: nel *modus* e contro il *modus*', in Murray and Tecusan (1995) 266–82
Labate, M. (1994) 'La forma dell'amore: appunti sulla poesia erotica oraziana', in *Atti degli Convegni Bimillenario Oraziano*, 69–87. Venosa
Laird, A. (1996) '*Vt figura poesis*: writing art and the art of writing in Augustan poetry', in Elsner (1996) 75–102
(1999) *Powers of Expression, Expressions of Power*. Oxford
(2000) 'Design and designation', in Sharrock and Morales (2002) 143–70
ed. (2006) *Ancient Literary Criticism*. Oxford
(forthcoming) 'Fiction, philosophy, and logical closure', in S. Heyworth, ed., *Classical Constructions*. Oxford
Lamberton, R., and Keaney, J., eds. (1992) *Homer's Ancient Readers*. Princeton
Lana, I. (1989) *Il I libro delle Epistole di Orazio*. Turin
Le Moyne, N.-T. [called Des Essarts] (1800) *Les Siècles littéraires de la France*. Paris. Reprinted Geneva, 1971
Leach, E. W. (1971) 'Horace's *Pater Optimus* and Terence's Demea: autobiographical fiction and comedy in *Serm.* 1.4', *American Journal of Philology* 92: 616–32
(1974) *Vergil's Eclogues: Landscapes of Experience*. Ithaca
(1994) 'Horace *Carmen* 1.8: Achilles, the Campus Martius, and the articulation of gender roles in Augustan Rome', *Classical Philology* 89: 334–43
Lebègue, R. (1936) 'Horace en France pendant la Renaissance', *Bibliothèque d'humanisme et Renaissance* 3: 141–64, 289–308, 384–419
Lee, G. (1998) *The Odes of Horace*. Leeds
Lee, R. W. (1967) *Ut Pictura Poesis: The Humanistic Theory of Painting*. New York
Lefèvre, E. (1993) *Horaz: Dichter in augusteischen Rom*. Munich
Lefkowitz, M. (1981) *The Lives of the Greek Poets*. London
(1991) *First-Person Fictions: Pindar's Poetic 'I'*. Oxford
Lejay, E. (1911) *Oeuvres d'Horace: Satires*. Paris
Leo, F. (1900) *De Horatio et Archilocho*. Göttingen
(1901) review of H. Peter (1901), *Göttinger gelehrte Anzeigen* 163: 318–25
Leonardi, C., ed. (1980–) *Medioevo latino: bollettino bibliografico* 1 – . Spoleto
ed. (1998) *Gli umanesimi medievali*. Florence
Leonhardt, J. (1989) *Dimensio syllabarum: Studien zur lateinischen Prosodie- und Verslehre von der Spätantike bis zur frühen Renaissance*. Göttingen
Levi, P. (1997) *Horace: A Life*. London
Levine, J. M. (1991) *The Battle of the Books: History and Literature in the Augustan Age*. Ithaca
(2002) 'Why neoclassicism? Politics and culture in eighteenth-century England', *British Journal for Eighteenth-Century Studies* 25.1: 74–93. (Response by R. Cummings 93–9; summary by K. O'Brien 99–101)
Liberman, G. (1999) *Alcée: fragments: texte établi, traduit et annoté*. 2 vols. Paris
Lissarrague, F. (1990) *The Aesthetics of the Greek Banquet: Images of Wine and Ritual* (English trans. of *Un Flot d'images: une esthétique du banquet grec*, Paris, 1987). Princeton
Londry, M. (2004a) 'On the use of first-line indices for researching English poetry of the long eighteenth century, c. 1660–1830, with special reference to women poets', *The Library*, 7th series 5.1: 12–38

(2004b) 'The poems of Elizabeth Tollet: a critical edition'. Unpublished DPhil thesis. Oxford
Long, A. A. (1986) *Hellenistic Philosophy: Stoics, Epicureans, Sceptics*. 2nd edn. Berkeley and Los Angeles
(1992) 'Stoic readings of Homer', in Lamberton and Keaney (1992) 51–66 (= Long (1996) 88–94)
(1996) *Stoic Studies*. Cambridge
Long, A. A., and Sedley, D. N. (1987) *The Hellenistic Philosophers*. 2 vols. Cambridge
Longley, M. (1995) *The Ghost Orchid*. London
Lonsdale, R., ed. (1984) *The New Oxford Book of Eighteenth-Century Verse*. Oxford
(1989) *Eighteenth-Century Women Poets*. Oxford
Loveling, B. (1741) *Latin and English Poems, by a Gentleman of Trinity College, Oxford*. London
Lowe, E. A. (1950) *Codices Latini Antiquiores* v. Oxford
Lowrie, M. (1992) 'A sympotic Achilles: Horace *Epode* 13', *American Journal of Philology* 113: 413–33
(1995) 'A parade of lyric predecessors: Horace *C.* 1.12–1.18', *Phoenix* 49: 33–48
(1997) *Horace's Narrative Odes*. Oxford
Loxley, J. (1994) 'Marvell, Villiers and Royalist verse', *Notes and Queries* n.s. 41.2: 170–2
Ludwig, W. (1968) 'Die Komposition der beiden Satirenbücher des Horaz', *Poetica* 2: 304–22
(1990) 'The origin and development of the Catullan style in neo-Latin poetry', in Godman and Murray (1990) 183–97
(1993a) 'Horazrezeption in der Renaissance oder die Renaissance des Horaz', in Ludwig (1993b) 305–71 (discussion 372–9)
ed. (1993b) *Horace: L'oeuvre et les imitations: Un siècle d'interprétation* (Fondation Hardt: Entretiens 49). Geneva
Lyne, R. O. A. M. (1980) *The Latin Love Poets: From Catullus to Ovid*. Oxford
(1995) *Horace: Behind the Public Poetry*. New Haven
(2005a) 'Horace *Odes* Book 1 and the Alexandrian edition of Alcaeus', *Classical Quarterly* 55: 542–58
(2005b) 'Structure and allusion in Horace's book of *Epodes*', *Journal of Roman Studies* 95: 1–19
Lytton, Lord (1869) *The Odes and Epodes of Horace*. Edinburgh and London
McCanles, M. (1992) *Jonsonian Discriminations*. Toronto
McClatchy, J. D., ed. (2002) *Horace: The Odes: New Translations by Contemporary Poets*. Princeton
McFarlane, I. D. (1981) *Buchanan*. London
McGann, M. J. (1969) *Studies in Horace's First Book of Epistles*. Brussels
(1995) 'Reading Horace in the quattrocento: the *Hymn to Mars* of Michael Marullus', in S. J. Harrison (1995d) 329–47
(2004) 'Politian's ode to Horace (a translation)' in Mullett (2004) 287–88
MacKenzie, Niall (2002) 'A Jacobite undertone in "While Ladies interpose"?', in Clark and Erskine-Hill (2002) 265–94
McKitterick, R. (1989) *The Carolingians and the Written Word*. Cambridge
Macleod, C. (1979) 'The poetry of ethics: Horace, *Epistles* 1', *Journal of Roman Studies* 69: 16–27. Reprinted in Macleod (1983) 280–91

(1983) *Collected Essays*. Oxford
(1986) *Horace: The Epistles: Translated into English Verse with Brief Comment*. Rome
McNeill, R. L. B. (2001) *Horace: Image, Identity, and Audience*. Baltimore
Maddison, C. (1960) *Apollo and the Nine: A History of the Ode*. London
Maehler, H. (1982–97) *Die Lieder des Bakchylides*. 2 vols. Leiden
(1987–9) *Pindari Carmina cum Fragmentis*. 2 vols. Leipzig
Maggini, F. (1950) 'Un'ode di Orazio nella poesia di Petrarca', *Studi petrarcheschi* 3: 7–12
Manitius, M. (1893) *Analekten zur Geschichte des Horaz im Mittelalter (bis 1300)*. Göttingen
Mankin, D. (1995) *Horace: Epodes*. Cambridge
Mann, N., and Munk Olsen, B., eds. (1997) *Medieval and Renaissance Scholarship*. Leiden
Manuwald, G., ed. (2001) *Der Satiriker Lucilius und seine Zeit*. Munich
Marbod of Rennes (1984) *Liber decem capitulorum*, ed. R. Leotta. Rome
Marchesi, S. (2004) *Stratigrafie decameroniane*. Florence
Marchionni, R., (ed.) (2003) *Der Sciendum-Kommentar zu den Satiren des Horaz*. Munich
Mariotti, S., ed. (1996–8) *Orazio: Enciclopedia oraziana*. 3 vols. Rome
Marmier, J. (1962) *Horace en France, au dix-septième siècle*. Paris
Martignac, Etienne de (1696) *Horace*. 2 vols. Paris (1st edn 1678)
Martin, T. (1860) *The Odes of Horace*. London
Martindale, C. A., ed. (1997) *The Cambridge Companion to Virgil*. Cambridge
Martindale, C., and Hopkins, D., eds. (1993) *Horace Made New*. Cambridge
Martindale, C. and M. (1990) *Shakespeare and the Uses of Antiquity: An Introductory Essay*. London
Martindale, C., and Taylor, C. B., eds. (2004) *Shakespeare and the Classics*. Cambridge
Martindale, J. (1993) 'The best master of virtue and wisdom: the Horace of Ben Jonson and his heirs', in Martindale and Hopkins (1993) 50–85
Mastrogianni, A. (2002) *Die Poemata des Petrus Crinitus und ihre Horazimitation* (Hamburger Beiträge zur neulateinischen Philologie 3). Münster
Matthew, H. C. G., and Harrison, B., eds. (2004) *The Oxford Dictionary of National Biography*. 60 vols. Oxford
Maurach, G. (1968) 'Der Grundriss von Horazens erstem Epistelbuch', *Acta Classica* 11: 73–124
Mayer, R. (1986) 'Horace's Epistles I and Philosophy', *American Journal of Philology* 107: 55–73
(1994) *Horace. Epistles Book I*. Cambridge
(1995) 'Horace's *Moyen de Parvenir*', in S. J. Harrison (1995d) 279–95
(2005) 'Sleeping with the enemy: satire and philosophy', in Freudenburg (2005) 146–59
Mazzoli, G. (1997) 'Antecedenti e modelli letterari latini', in Mariotti (1996–8), II. 5–11
Medcalf, S. (1993) 'Kipling's Horace', in Martindale and Hopkins (1993) 217–39
Menéndez Pelayo, M. (1951) *Bibliografía hispano-latina clásica*, IV–VI. Santander

Metellus of Tegernsee (1965) *Die Quirinalien des Metellus von Tegernsee*, ed. P. C. Jacobsen. Leiden and Cologne

Mette, H. J. (1961) 'Genus tenue und mensa tenuis bei Horaz', *Museum Helveticum* 18: 136–9 (= Mette (1988) 188–91)

(1988) *Kleine Schriften*. Frankfurt

Millar, F. (1977) *The Emperor in the Roman World*. London

Millar, F., and Segal, E., eds. (1984) *Caesar Augustus: Seven Aspects*. Oxford

Miller, P. A. (1994) *Lyric Texts and Lyric Consciousness*. London and New York

Mills College (1938) *Quintus Horatius Flaccus: Editions in the US and Canada as They Appear in the Union Catalog of the Library of Congress*. Mills College, CA.

Milosz, C. (1969) *The History of Polish Literature*. New York

Mindt, N. (2006) Die meta-sympotischen Oden und Epoden des Horaz. Göttingen

Minnis, A. J., and Scott, A. B., eds. (1988) *Medieval Literary Theory and Criticism c. 1100–c. 1375: The Commentary-Tradition*. Oxford

Miralles, C., and Pòrtulas, J. (1983) *Archilochus and the Iambic Tradition*. Rome

(1988) *The Poetry of Hipponax*. Rome

Mitchell, W., ed. (1981) *On Narrative*. Chicago

Moles, J. (1995) Review of R. Mayer, *Horace: Epistles I*, *Bryn Mawr Classical Review* 95.02.37

(2002) 'Poetry, philosophy, politics, and play: *Epistles* 1', in Woodman and Feeney (2002) 141–57

Money, D. K. (1997) 'A Diff'rent-sounding lyre: Oxford commemorative verse in English, 1613–1834', *Bodleian Library Record* 16: 42–92

(1998) *The English Horace: Anthony Alsop and the Tradition of British Latin Verse*. Oxford

(2002) 'Samuel Johnson and the neo-Latin tradition', in Clark and Erskine-Hill (2002) 199–221

(2003) 'The politics of poetry: a quick look at Robert Walpole, and two thousand other Cambridge Latin poets', in R. Schnur et al., eds., *Acta Conventus Neo-Latini Cantabrigiensis* 361–9. Tempe

(2004a) 'John Ashmore', in Matthew and Harrison (2004) 2. 666–7

(2004b) 'James Alban Gibbes', in Matthew and Harrison (2004) 22.2–3

(2004c) 'Corbet Owen', in Matthew and Harrison (2004) 42.187–8

(2006) 'Aspects of Sarbiewski's reception in England: from Hils, Vaughan, and Watts to Coleridge, Bowring, Walker, and Coxe' in Urbanksi (2006), 157–87

Money, D. K., and Olszowy, J. (1995) 'Hebrew commemorative poetry in Cambridge, 1564–1763', *Transactions of the Cambridge Bibliographical Society* 10: 549–76

Morris, E. P. (1931) 'The form of the epistle in Horace', *Yale Classical Studies* 2: 81–114

Morrissette, B. A. (1947) *The Life and Works of Marie-Catherine Desjardins (Mme de Villedieu) 1632–1683*. St Louis

Most, G. W., Petersmann, H., and Ritter, A. M., eds. (1993) *Philanthropia kai eusebeia: Festschrift für Albrecht Dihle zum 70. Geburtstag*. Göttingen

Muecke, F. (ed.) (1993) *Horace: Satires II*. Warminster

(1997) 'Lingua e stile', in Mariotti (1996–8) II. 755–87

Mullett, M. (ed.) (2004) *Metaphrastes, or Gained in Translation: Essays and Translations in Honour of Robert H. Jordan*. Belfast
Munk Olsen, B. (1979) 'Les Classiques latins dans les florilèges médiévaux antérieurs au XIIIe siècle', *Revue d'Histoire des Textes* 9: 47–121
(1982–9) *L'étude des auteurs classiques latins aux XIe et XIIe siècles*, vols. 1–3:2. Paris
(1991) *I classici nel canone scolastico altomedievale*. Spoleto
(1991–2002) 'Chronique des manuscrits classiques latins (IXe–XIIe siècles), I–V' *Revue d'histoire des textes* 21: 37–76 (I), 24: 199–249 (II), 27: 29–85 (III), 30: 123–88 (IV), 32: 73–106 (V)
(1996) 'The production of the classics in the eleventh and twelfth centuries', in C. A. Chavannes-Mazel and M. M. Smith, eds., *Medieval Manuscripts of the Latin Classics: Production and Use*, 1–17. Los Altos Hills and London
Murav'ev, M. N. (1995) *Institutiones Rhetoricae: A Treatise of a Russian Sentimentalist*, ed. A. Kahn. Oxford
Murray, O. (1985) 'Symposium and genre in the poetry of Horace', *Journal of Roman Studies* 75: 39–50. (Reprinted in Rudd (1993b) 89–105)
ed. (1990) *Sympotica*. Oxford
Murray, O., and Tecusan, M., eds. (1995) *In Vino Veritas*. London
Murray, R. (1974) 'Neoclassical poetics', in Preminger (1974) 559–64
Nagy, G. (1976) '*Iambos*: typologies of invective and praise', *Arethusa* 9: 191–205
Nesselrath, H.-G. (1992) *Ungeschehenes Geschehen: 'Beinahe-Episoden' im griechischen und römischen Epos von Homer bis zur Spätantike*. Stuttgart
Nisbet, R. G. M. (1959) 'Notes on Horace, *Epistles* 1', *Classical Quarterly* 9: 73–6. Reprinted in Nisbet (1995a) 1–5
(1961) *Cicero: In Pisonem*. Oxford
(1969) Review of Doblhofer (1966), *Classical Review* 19: 173–5
(1984) 'Horace's *Epodes* and History', in Woodman and West (1984) 1–18
(1995a) *Collected Papers on Latin Literature*, ed. S. J. Harrison. Oxford
(1995b) 'The survivors: old-style literary men in the triumviral period', in Nisbet (1995a) 390–413
Nisbet, R. G. M., and Hubbard, M. (1970) *A Commentary on Horace, Odes I*. Oxford
(1978) *A Commentary on Horace, Odes II*. Oxford
Nisbet, R. G. M., and Rudd, N. (2004) *A Commentary on Horace, Odes III*. Oxford
Nitchie, E. J. (1918) 'Horace and Thackeray', *Classical Journal* 13: 393–418
Noferi, A. (1962) *L'esperienza poetica del Petrarca*. Florence
Noggle, J. (2000) 'Skeptical *ataraxia* and selfhood in Pope's *Imitations of Horace*', *1650–1850: Ideas, Aesthetics and Inquiries in the Early Modern Era* 5: 63–92
Norbrook, D. (1999) *Writing the English Republic: Poetry, Rhetoric and Politics 1627–60*. Cambridge
Norton, G. P., ed. (1999) *The Cambridge History of Literary Criticism* III: *The Renaissance*. Cambridge
Nuttall, A. D. (1993) 'Marvell and Horace: colour and translucency', in Martindale and Hopkins (1993) 86–102
Obbink, D., ed. (1995) *Philodemus and Poetry*. Oxford
(2005) 'Archilochus, *Elegies*', *Oxyrhynchus Papyri* 69: 18–42

Ogilvie, R. M. (1981) 'Translations of Horace in the seventeenth and eighteenth centuries', in Killy (1981b) 71–80
Ogilvy, J. D. A. (1967) *Books Known to the English*. Cambridge, MA
O'Higgins, L. (2003) *Women and Humor in Classical Greece*. Cambridge
Oksala, T. (1973) *Religion und Mythologie bei Horaz*. Helsinki
Oliensis, E. (1991) 'Canidia, Canicula, and the decorum of Horace's *Epodes*', *Arethusa* 24: 107–38
(1995) 'Life after publication: Horace, *Epistles* 1.20', *Arethusa* 28: 208–24
(1997) 'The erotics of *amicitia*: readings in Tibullus, Propertius, and Horace', in Hallett and Skinner (1997) 151–71
(1998) *Horace and the Rhetoric of Authority*. Cambridge
(2002) 'Feminine endings, lyric seductions', in Woodman and Feeney (2002) 93–106
Opelt, I. (1970) 'Prudentius und Horaz', in Wimmel (1970) 206–13
Otis, B. (1945) 'Horace and the elegists', *Transactions of the American Philological Association* 76: 177–90
Oxford University (1613) *Epithalamia sive Lusus Palatini in nuptias celsissimi Principis Domini Friderici Comitis Palatini ad Rhenum etc. et serenissimae Elisabethae Iacobi potentissimae Britanniae Regis Filiae Primogenitae*. Oxford
Oxford University (1619) *Academiae Oxoniensis Funebria sacra aeternae memoriae serenissimae Reginae Annae potentissimi monarchae Iacobi . . . sponsae dicata*. Oxford
Oxford University (1700) *Exequiae desideratissimo Principi Gulielmo Glocestriae Duci ab Oxoniensi Academia solutae*. Oxford
Oxford University (1736) *Gratulatio Academiae Oxoniensis in nuptias auspicatissimas illustrissimorum principum Frederici Principis Walliae et Augustae Principissae de Saxo-Gotha*. Oxford
Oxford University (1762) *Gratulatio Solennis Universitatis Oxoniensis ob celsissimum Georgium Fredericum Augustum Principem Walliae . . . auspicatissime natum*. Oxford
Page, D. L. (1962) *Poetae Melici Graeci*. Oxford
(1968) *Lyrica Graeca Selecta*. Oxford
(1974) *Supplementum Lyricis Graecis*. Oxford
(1978) *The Epigrams of Rufinus*. Cambridge
Page, T. E. (1890) *Q. Horati Flacci Carminum Libri* IV. London
Palmer, A.-M. (1989) *Prudentius on the Martyrs*. Oxford
Pardini, A. (1991) 'La ripartizione in libri dell'opera di Alceo', *Rivista di filologia e di istruzione classica* 119: 257–84
Parfitt, G. (1976) *Ben Jonson: Public Poet and Private Man*. London
Paschalis, M., ed. (2002) *Horace and Greek Lyric Poetry*. Rethymnon
Pasquali, G. (1964) *Orazio lirico*. Firenze. (1st edn 1920)
Pearcy, L. T. (1994) 'The personification of the text and Augustan poetics in *Epistles* 1.20', *Classical World* 87: 457–64
Pecere, O., and Reeve, M., eds. (1995) *Formative Stages of Classical Traditions*. Spoleto
Pellizer, E. (1990) 'Outlines of a morphology of sympotic entertainment', in O. Murray (1990) 177–84

Perutelli, A. (1993) 'Destinazioni delle Epistole', in *Atti del convegno nazionale di studi su Orazio*, Turin, 205–18
Peter, H. (1901) *Der Brief in der römischen Litteratur*. Leipzig
Peter, J. (1956) *Complaint and Satire in Early English Literature*. Oxford
Peterson, R. S. (1981) *Imitation and Praise in the Poems of Ben Jonson*. New Haven
Petrarca, F. (1933–42) *Familiarium Rerum Libri*, 4 vols., ed. V. Rossi. Florence
Petrie, J. (1983) *Petrarch: The Augustan Poets, the Italian Tradition and the Canzoniere*. Dublin
Pfeiffer, R. (1968) *A History of Classical Scholarship* I. Oxford
Pighi, J. B. (1965) *De Ludis Saecularibus*. Amsterdam
Pigman III, G. W. (1990) 'Neo-Latin imitation of the Latin classics', in Godman and Murray (1990) 199–210
Pomeroy, A. J. (1980) 'A man at a spring: Horace *Odes* 1.1', *Ramus* 9: 34–50
Poole, A., and Maule, J., eds. (1995) *The Oxford Book of Classical Verse*. Oxford
Popham, E., ed. (1779) *Selecta Poemata Anglorum Latina*. 2nd edn. London
Porro, A. (1994) *Vetera Alcaica: L'esegesi di Alceo dagli Alessandrini all'età imperiale*. Milan
Porter, D. H. (1995) '*Quo quo scelesti ruitis*: the downward momentum of Horace's *Epodes*', *Illinois Classical Studies* 20: 107–30
(2002) 'Playing the game: Horace, *Epistles* 1', *Classical World* 96: 21–60
Porter, J. I. (2006) *Classical Pasts: The Classical Traditions of Greece and Rome* (Princeton)
Pöschl, V. (1991) *Horazische Lyrik: Interpretationen*. Heidelberg
Pound, E. (1970) *Translations*. New York
Powell, A., ed. (1992) *Roman Poetry and Propaganda in the Age of Augustus*. London
Powell, A., and Welch, K., eds. (2002) *Sextus Pompeius*. Swansea
Powell, J. (1995) 'Friendship and its problems in Greek and Roman thought', in Innes et al. (1995) 31–45
Powell, M. (1983) *Fabula Docet: Studies in the Background and Interpretation of Henryson's Morall Fabillis*. Odense
Preminger A., ed. (1974) *Princeton Encyclopedia of Poetry and Poetics*. Princeton
Puelma-Piwonka, M. (1949) *Lucilius und Kallimachos*. Frankfurt
Purcell, N. (1983) 'The *Apparitores*: a study in social mobility', *Papers of the British School at Rome* 51: 125–73
Putnam, M. C. J. (1986) *Artifices of Eternity: Horace's Fourth Book of Odes*. Ithaca
(1990) 'Horace *Carm.* 2.9: Augustus and the ambiguities of encomium', in Raaflaub and Toher (1990) 212–38
(1995) 'From lyric to letter: Iccius in Horace *Odes* 1.29 and *Epistles* 1.12', *Arethusa* 28: 193–207
(1996) 'Pastoral satire', *Arion* 3: 303–16
(2000) *Horace's Carmen Saeculare*. New Haven
(2006) *Poetic Interplay: Catullus and Horace*. Princeton
Quadlbauer, F. (1962) *Die antike Theorie der genera dicendi im lateinischen Mittelalter.* Vienna
Questa, C. (1996) 'Questioni codicologiche', in Mariotti (1996–8) I. 329–44
Quinn, K. (1980) *Horace: Odes*. London
Quint, M.-B. (1988) *Untersuchungen zur mittelalterlichen Horaz-Rezeption*. Frankfurt

Raaflaub, K. A., and Toher, M., eds. (1990) *Between Republic and Empire*. Berkeley
Radcliffe, D. H. (2000) 'The poetry professors: eighteenth-century Spenserianism and Romantic concepts of culture', *1650–1850: Ideas, Aesthetics and Inquiries in the Early Modern Era* 5: 121–50
Rand, E. K. (1937a) 'Horace and the spirit of comedy', *The Rice Institute Pamphlet* 24: 39–117
(1937b) *A Toast to Horace*. Cambridge, MA
Raven, J. (2002) *London Booksellers and American Customers: Transatlantic Literary Community and the Charleston Library Society 1748–1811*. Columbia
Rawson, E. (1985) *Intellectual Life in the Late Roman Republic*. London
Reading, P. (1997) *Work in Regress*. Newcastle
Reckford, K. J. (1959) 'Some studies in Horace's odes on love', *Classical Journal* 55: 25–33
(1997) 'Horatius: the man and the hour', *American Journal of Philology* 118: 538–612
Reynen, H. (1964) 'Klima und Krankheit auf den Inseln der Seligen', in H. Reynen, *Interpretationen*, 77–104. Heidelberg
Reynolds, L. D., ed. (1983) *Texts and Transmission: A Survey of the Latin Classics*. Oxford
Reynolds, L. D., and Wilson, N. G. (1991) *Scribes and Scholars* (3rd edn; 1st edn 1968). Oxford
Reynolds, S. (1996) *Medieval Reading. Grammar, Rhetoric and the Classical Text*. Cambridge
Richardson, J. (2000) 'Defending the self: Pope and his Horatian poems', *Modern Language Review* 95: 623–33
Richlin, A. (1992) *The Garden of Priapus: Sexuality and Aggression in Roman Humor*, revised edn. New York and Oxford
Richmond, H. M. (1964) *The School of Love: The Evolution of the Stuart Love Lyric*. Princeton
Ricks, C. (2002) *Allusion to the Poets*. Oxford
Riggs, C. (1989) *Ben Jonson: A Life*. Cambridge, MA
Rivers, I., ed. (1982) *Books and Their Readers in Eighteenth-Century England*. Leicester
Roberts, M. (1993) *Poetry and the Cult of the Martyrs: The Liber Peristephanon of Prudentius*. Ann Arbor
Robortello, F. (1548) *In librum Aristotelis de arte poetica explicationes. Paraphrasis in librum Horatii, qui vulgo de arte poetica ad Pisones inscribitur*. Florence. Reprinted Munich 1968
Rodulfus Glaber (1989) *Rodolfo il Glabro: Cronache dell'anno mille (Storie)*, ed. G. Cavallo and G. Orlandi. Milan
Rogers, Pat (1992) 'Pope and Creech's Horace', *Notes and Queries* n.s. 39: 468–9
Roller, M. (2001) *Constructing Autocracy*. Princeton
(2003) 'Horizontal women: posture and sex in the Roman *convivium*', *American Journal of Philology* 124: 377–422
Romano, E. (1991) *Q. Orazio Flacco: Le Opere: Odi e Carme Secolare*. Rome
Ronnick, M. V. (1994) 'A Horatian influence on the verse of Samuel Danforth', *English Language Notes* 32: 37–9
Rosenmeyer, P. A. (2001) *Ancient Epistolary Fictions*. Cambridge

Rossetti, C. (2001) *The Complete Poems*. Harmondsworth
Rossi, L. E. (1998) 'Orazio, un lirico greco senza musica', *Seminari Romani di Cultura Greca* 1: 163–81
Rosslyn, F. (1993) 'Good humour and the agelasts: Horace, Pope and Gray', in Martindale and Hopkins (1993) 184–98
Rostagni, A. (1944) *Suetonio De Poetis e biografi minori*. Turin
(1946) *Arte poetica di Orazio*. Turin
Rostagno, E. (1933) *L'Orazio Laurenziano già di Francesco Petrarcha*. Rome
Røstvig, M.-S. (1954–8) *The Happy Man: Studies in the Metamorphosis of a Classical Ideal*. 2 vols. Oslo and Oxford (2nd edn 1962)
Roth, C. (1964) *A History of the Jews in England*. 3rd edn. Oxford
Rudd, N. (1966) *The Satires of Horace*. Cambridge
(1976) *Lines of Enquiry: Studies in Latin Poetry*. Cambridge
(1979a) '*Epistles* and *Sermones*', *Liverpool Classical Monthly* 4.7: 147
(1979b) *Horace, Satires and Epistles; Persius, Satires*. Harmondsworth
(1989) *Horace Epistles Book II and Epistle to the Pisones ('Ars Poetica')*. Cambridge
(1991) 'Two invitations', *Hermathena* 150: 4–17. Reprinted in Rudd (2005) 177–90
(1993a) 'Horace as moralist', in Rudd (1993b) 64–88
ed. (1993b) *Horace 2000: A Celebration. Essays for the Bimillennium*. London
(1994) *The Classical Tradition in Operation*. Toronto
(2004) *Horace: Odes and Epodes*. Cambridge, MA
(2005) *The Common Spring: Essays On Latin and English Poetry*. Bristol
Ruffell, I. A. (2003) 'Beyond satire: Horace, popular invective and the segregation of literature', *Journal of Roman Studies* 93: 35–65
Rupprich, H. (1970) *Geschichte der deutschen Literatur von den Anfängen bis zur Gegenwart* IV: *Die deutsche Literatur vom späten Mittelalter bis zum Barock*, part 1. Munich
Russell, D. A. (1973) '*Ars Poetica*', in Costa (1973) 113–34. Reprinted in Laird (2006) 325–45
(1979) 'De Imitatione', in Woodman and West (1979) 1–16
(1989) *Classical Literary Criticism*. Oxford
(1993) 'Self-disclosure in Plutarch and in Horace', in Most, Petersmann and Ritter (1993) 426–37
(2001) *Quintilian: The Orator's Education*, 5 vols. Cambridge, MA
Russell, D. A., and Winterbottom, M. (1972) *Ancient Literary Criticism: The Principal Texts in New Translations*. Oxford
Rutherford, I. (2000) *Pindar's Paeans*. Oxford
Rutherford, R. B. (2005) *Classical Literature: A Concise History*. Oxford
Saller, R. (1982) *Personal Patronage under the Early Empire*. Cambridge
Sandys, G. (1973) *A relation of a journey begun An. Dom. 1610. . . .* (facsimile of 1615 edn). Amsterdam
Santini, C. (2001) *Heinze e il suo saggio sull'ode oraziana*. Perugia
Santirocco, M. (1986) *Unity and Design in Horace's Odes*. Chapel Hill and London
(1995) 'Horace and Augustan Ideology', *Arethusa* 28: 225–43
Schäfer, E. (1970) 'Erasmus und Horaz', *Antike und Abendland* 16: 54–67

(1976) *Deutscher Horaz: Conrad Celtis. Georg Fabricius. Paul Melissus. Jacob Balde. Die Nachwirkung des Horaz in der neulateinischen Dichtung Deutschlands*. Wiesbaden
Schakel, P. J. (1993) 'Horace in modern dress', in Jackson and Yoder (1993) 169–76
(2001) 'Swift's voices: innovation and complication in the poems written at Market Hill', in Weinbrot et al. (2001) 114–32
Schiesaro, A., Mitsis, P., Strauss Clay, J., eds. (1993) *Mega nepios: il destinatario nell'epos didascalico: The Addressee in Didactic Epic* (*Materiali e discussioni per l'analisi dei testi classici* 31). Pisa
Schlegel, C. (2000) 'Horace and his fathers: *Satires* 1.4 and 1.6', *American Journal of Philology* 121: 93–119
Schmidt, E. A. (1977) '*Amica vis pastoribus*: der Jambiker Horaz in seinem Epodenbuch' *Gymnasium* 84: 401–21
(2002a) *Zeit und Form: Dichtungen des Horaz*. Heidelberg
(2002b) 'Horaz und die Erneuerung der deutschen Lyrik im 18. Jahrhundert', in E. A. Schmidt (2002a) 380–428
Schmidt, P. L. (1972) 'Catos *Epistula ad Marcum Filium* und die Anfänge der römischen Briefliteratur', *Hermes* 100: 568–76
Schmitz, T. (1994) 'L'Ode latine pendant la Renaissance française: un catalogue des odes publiées au seizième siècle', *Humanistica Lovaniensia* 43: 173–219
Schnegg-Köhler, B. (2002) *Die augusteischen Säkularspiele*. Munich
Scodel, J. (1998) 'Lyric forms', in Zwicker (1998) 120–42
(2002) *Excess and the Mean in Early Modern English Literature*. Princeton
Scodel, R. S. (1987) 'Horace, Lucilius, and Callimachean Polemic', *Harvard Studies in Classical Philology* 91: 199–215
Seager, R. (1993) 'Horace and Augustus: poetry and policy', in Rudd (1993b) 23–40
Setaioli, A. (1981) 'Gli "Epodi" di Orazio nella critica dal 1937 al 1972 (con un appendice fino al 1978)', *Aufstieg und Niedergang der römischen Welt* II. 31.3: 1674–1788
Sextus Amarcius (1969) *Sextus Amarcius. Sermones*, ed. K. Manitius (Monumenta Germanicae Historiae: Quellen zur Geistesgeschichte des Mittelalters 6). Weimar
Shackleton Bailey, D. R. (1965) *Cicero's Letters to Atticus* I. (Cambridge)
(1982) *Profile of Horace*. London
(1984) *Horatius: Opera*. Stuttgart
Sharpe, K., and Zwicker, S. N., eds. (1987) *Politics of Discourse: The Literature and History of Seventeenth-Century England*. Berkeley
(1998) *Refiguring Revolutions: Aesthetics and Politics from the English Revolution to the Romantic Revolution*. Berkeley
(2003) *Reading, Society, and Politics in Early Modern England*. Cambridge
Sharrock, A., and Morales, H., eds. (2000) *Intratextuality*. Oxford
Shepherd, S. (1989) *Spenser*. London
Sherbo, A., ed. (1979) *Christopher Smart's Verse Translation of Horace's Odes*. Victoria, BC
Sherburne, Sir Edward (1696) *The Comparison of Pindar and Horace, written in French by Mr Blondel*. London
Showerman, G. (1922) *Horace and His Influence*. London
Siewert, K. (1986) *Die althochdeutsche Horazglossierung*. Göttingen

Slings, S. R., ed. (1990) *The Poet's 'I' in Archaic Greek Lyric*. Amsterdam
Smith, B. H. (1978) *On the Margins of Discourse*. Chicago
Smith, C. (1993) *The Poems*, ed. S. Curran. New York and Oxford
Snell, B. (1938) 'Die 16. Epode von Horaz und Vergils 4. Ekloge', *Hermes* 73: 237–42
Sowerby, R. (1993) 'Pope and Horace', in Martindale and Hopkins (1993) 159–83
(1994) *The Classical Legacy in Renaissance Poetry*. London
Spentzou, E., and Fowler, D. P., eds., *Cultivating the Muse*. Oxford and New York
Stack, F. (1985) *Pope and Horace: Studies in Imitation*. Cambridge
Stapleton, F. L. (1993) '"He nothing common did or mean": Marvell's Charles I and Horace's *non humilis mulier*', *English Language Notes* 30.3: 31–40
Steggle, M. (1998) *Wars of the Theatres*. Victoria, BC
(1999) 'Horace the Second, or, Ben Jonson, Thomas Dekker and the battle for Augustan Rome', in Franssen and Hoenselaars (1999) 118–30
Steiner, T. R. (1975) *English Translation Theory 1650–1800*. Assen
Steinruck, M. (2000) *Iambos: Studien zum Publikum einer Gattung in der fruhgriechischen Literatur*. Hildesheim, Zurich and New York
Stella, F. (1998) 'Carolingi, scrittori', in Mariotti (1996–8) III. 159–67
Stemplinger, E. (1906) *Das Fortleben der horazischen Lyrik seit der Renaissance*. Leipzig
(1921) *Horaz im Urteil der Jahrhunderte*. Leipzig
Stephenson, R. H. (2002) 'Weimar classicism's debt to the Scottish Enlightenment', in Boyle and Guthrie (2002) 61–70
Stewart, S. (2000) 'Jonson's criticism', in Harp and Stewart (2000) 175–87
Stillers, R. (1988) *Humanistische Deutung: Studien zu Kommentar und Literaturtheorie in der italienischen Renaissance*. Düsseldorf
Stirewalt, M. L. (1993) *Studies in Ancient Greek Epistolography*. Atlanta
Storch, H. (1970) 'Freundschaft, Freundlichkeit und Liebe in den Oden des Horaz', *Altsprachliche Unterricht* 13: 5–26
Stotz, P. (1998) '*Safficum carmen*: Was hat die sapphische Dichtung des lateinischen Mittelalters mit Horaz zu tun?', in Leonardi (1998) 707–26
Stray, C. A. (1998) *Classics Transformed: Schools, Universities and Society in England, 1830–1960*. Oxford
Susanetti, D. (1992) *Sinesio di Cirene: introduzione, traduzione e commento*. Bari
Sutherland, E. (1997) 'Vision and desire in Horace, C. 2.5', *Helios* 24: 23–43
Swafford, J. (1997) *Johannes Brahms: A Biography*. New York
Sykutris, J. (1931) 'Epistolographie', *Paulys Real-Encyclopädie der klassischen Altertumswissenschaft* Supplementband 5: 185–220
Syme, R. (1939) *The Roman Revolution*. Oxford
(1964) *Sallust*. Berkeley and Los Angeles
(1978) *History in Ovid*. Oxford
(1979a) *Roman Papers* I. Oxford
(1979b) 'Problems about Janus', *American Journal of Philology* 100: 188–212
(1984) *Roman Papers* III. Oxford
(1986) *The Augustan Aristocracy*. Oxford
(1989) 'Janus and Parthia in Horace', in Diggle et al. (1989) 113–24
(1991) *Roman Papers* VI. Oxford
Syndikus, H. P. (1972–3) *Die Lyrik des Horaz*. 2 vols. (3rd edn 2001). Darmstadt
(1995) 'Some structures in Horace's *Odes*', in S. J. Harrison (1995d) 17–31

Szövérffy, J. (1964) *Die Annalen der lateinischen Hymnendichtung*, I. Berlin
Talbert, E. W. (1945) 'The purpose and teaching of Jonson's *Poetaster*', *Studies in Philology* 42: 225–52
Talbot, J. (2001) 'A Horatian pun in *Paradise Lost*', *Notes and Queries* n.s. 48: 21–3
Tarditi, G. (1968) *Archiloco/Archilochus*. Rome
Tarrant, R. J. (1976) *Seneca: Agamemnon*. Cambridge
(1983) 'Horace', in L. D. Reynolds (1983) 182–6
(1995) '*Da Capo* structure in some *Odes* of Horace', in S. J. Harrison (1995d) 32–49
(1997) 'Aspects of Virgil's reception in antiquity', in C. A. Martindale (1997) 56–72
(2002) 'Ovid and ancient literary history', in Hardie (2002b) 13–33
Tarteron, J. (1694) *Traduction nouvelle des Satyres, des Epistres, et de L'Art Poëtique d'Horace*. Paris
Tatum, W. J. (1997) 'Friendship, politics and literature in Catullus' poems: 65 and 66, 116', *Classical Quarterly* 47: 482–500
Tedeschi, A. (1985) 'L'invio del carme nella poesia lirica arcaica: Pindaro e Bacchilide', *Studi italiani di filologia classica* 3: 29–54
Terry, R. (2001) *Poetry and the Making of the English Literary Past, 1660–1781*. Oxford
Thill, A., and Banderier, G., eds. (1999) *La Lyre jésuite: anthologie de poèmes latins (1620–1730)*. Geneva
Thomas, P. (1964) *Sir Thomas Wyatt and His Background*. Stanford
Thomas, R. F. (1998) 'Voice, poetics, and Virgil's sixth Eclogue', in Jasanoff et al. (1998) 669–76. Reprinted in Thomas (1999) 288–96
(1999) *Reading Virgil and His Texts: Studies in Intertextuality*. Ann Arbor
(2004) '"Drownded in the tide": The *Nauagika* and some "problems" in Augustan poetry', in Acosta-Hughes et al. (2004) 259–75
Thomson, J. A. K. (1952) *Shakespeare and the Classics*. London
Tollet, E. (1755) *Poems on Several Occasions*. 2nd edn. London. (1st edn 1755; previous anonymous publication, 1724)
Tomlinson, C. (1993) 'Some aspects of Horace in the twentieth century', in Martindale and Hopkins (1993) 240–57
Traina, A. (1973) 'Semantica del *carpe diem*', *Rivista di filologia e di istruzione classica* 101: 5–21
(1985) 'Introduzione', in E. Mandruzzato, *Orazio: Odi ed Epodi*, Milan, 5–45
(1986) *Poeti latini (e neolatini)*. Bologna
(1991) 'Orazio e Aristippo: Le *Epistole* e l'arte di convivere', *Rivista di filologia e di istruzione classica* 119: 285–305
(1993) *Autoritratto di un poeta*. Venosa
Trapp, M. (2003) *Greek and Latin Letters: An Anthology with Translation*. Cambridge
Traube, L., ed. (1896) *Poetae Latini Aevi Carolini*, III. Berlin
Trimpi, W. (1962) *Ben Jonson's Poems: A Study of the Plain Style*. Stanford
Troxler-Keller, I. (1964) *Die Dichterlandschaft des Horaz*. Heidelberg
Turner, P. (1989) *Victorian Poetry, Drama and Miscellaneous Prose 1832–1890*. Oxford
Ulcinaite, E., ed. (1998) *Mathias Casimirus Sarbievius in cultura Lithuaniae, Poloniae, Europae*. Vilnius

Urban VIII (1634) *Poemata*. Antwerp
(1726) *Poemata*, ed. J. Brown. Oxford
Urbanski, P. (2000) *Theologia Fabulosa: Commentationes Sarbievianae*. Szczecin
(2006) *Pietas Humanistica*. Frankfurt am Main
Vance, N. (1997) *The Victorians and Ancient Rome*. Oxford
Vetta, M. (1991) *Poesia e simposio nella Grecia antica*. Rome and Bari
Vidal, J. L. (1994) 'La poesía augustea de Horacio', in Cortés Tovar and Fernández Corte (1994) 151–68
Villa, C. (1979) '"*Denique Terenti dultia legimus acta . . .*": una "Lectura Terenti" a S. Faustino di Brescia nel secolo IX', *Italia medioevale e umanistica* 22: 1–44
(1992) 'Per una tipologia del commento mediolatino: *l'Ars Poetica* di Orazio', in Besomi and Caruso (1992) 19–46
(1992–4) 'I manoscritti di Orazio', *Aevum* 66: 95–135; 67: 55–103; 68: 117–146
Voigt, E.-M. (1971) *Sappho et Alcaeus: Fragmenta*. Amsterdam
Vollmann, B. K. (1996) 'Erziehung zur Humanität: Horaz und die Satire des 11. Jahrhunderts', in Krasser and Schmidt (1996) 36–51
Vratovic, Vladimir, ed. (1998) *The Croatian Muses in Latin: Musae Croaticae Latini Sermonis: Hrvatske Muze na Latinskom*. Zagreb
Wagenvoort, H. (1956) 'The Crime of Fratricide (Hor. *Epod.* 7, 18)', in H. Wagenvoort, *Studies in Roman Literature, Culture and Religion*, 169–83. Leiden
Waldapfel, I. [later Trencsényi-Waldapfel] (1935) *Magyar Horatius*. Budapest
Walker, G. (1988) *John Skelton and the Politics of the 1520s*. Cambridge
Wallace-Hadrill, A. (1997) '*Mutatio morum*: the idea of a cultural revolution', in Habinek and Schiesaro (1997) 3–22
Wälli, S. (2002) *Melodien aus mittelalterlichen Horaz-Handschriften*. Kassel
Walsh, P. G. (1999) *Boethius: The Consolation of Philosophy*. Oxford
Washington, P., ed. (1997) *Roman Odes, Elegies and Epigrams*. London
Watson, L. (1983) 'Problems in *Epode* 11', *Classical Quarterly* 33: 229–38
(1991) *Arae: The Curse Poetry of Antiquity*. Leeds
(1995) 'Horace's *Epodes*: the Impotence of *Iambos?*', in S. J. Harrison (1995d) 188–202
(2001) '*Epode* 14: Horace's *Carmen Inconditum?*', in Cavarzere et al. (2001) 187–204
(2002) 'Horace and the pirates', in Powell and Welch (2002) 213–28
(2003) *A Commentary on Horace's Epodes*. Oxford
Watson, P. (1985) 'Axelson revisited: the selection of vocabulary in Latin poetry', *Classical Quarterly* 35: 430–58
Wedde, I. (2003) *The Commonplace Odes*. Auckland
Weinberg, B. (1961) *A History of Literary Criticism in the Italian Renaissance*. Chicago
Weinbrot, H. D. (1978) *Augustus Caesar in 'Augustan' England: The Decline of a Classical Norm*. Princeton
(1988) *Eighteenth-Century Satire: Essays on Text and Context from Dryden to Peter Pindar*. Cambridge
(2001) '"What must the world think of me?": Pope, Madame Dacier, and Homer – the anatomy of a quarrel', in Weinbrot et al. (2001) 183–206
Weinbrot, H. D., Schakel, P. J., and Karian, S. E., eds. (2001) *Eighteenth-Century Contexts: Historical Enquiries in Honour of Philip Harth*. Madison

West, D. (1967) *Reading Horace*. Edinburgh
(1995) *Horace Odes I: Carpe Diem*. Oxford
(1997) *Horace: Odes and Epodes*. Oxford
(1998) *Horace Odes II: Vatis Amici*. Oxford
(2002) *Horace Odes III: Aere Perennius*. Oxford
West, M. L. (1974) *Studies in Greek Elegy and Iambus*. Berlin and New York
(1989–92) *Iambi et Elegi Graeci ante Alexandrum Cantati*, 2nd edn. 2 vols. Oxford
(1990) 'The *Anacreontea*', in O. Murray (1990) 272–6
(2005) 'The new Sappho', *Zeitschrift für Papyrologie und Epigraphik* 151: 1–9
Westbrook, P. D. (1947) 'Horace's influence on Shakespeare's *Antony and Cleopatra*', *Proceedings of the Modern Language Association* 62: 392–98
Whitby, M., Hardie, P., and Whitby, M., eds. (1987) *Homo Viator: Classical Essays for John Bramble*. Bristol
White, P. (1991) 'Maecenas' retirement', *Classical Philology* 86: 130–8
(1993) *Promised Verse: Poets in the Society of Augustan Rome*. Cambridge, MA
Wickham, E. C. (1874) *The Works of Horace* I. Oxford
Wiggins, P. D. (1976) *The Satires of Ludovico Ariosto: A Renaissance Autobiography*. Athens, OH
Wilamowitz-Moellendorf, U. von (1913) *Sappho und Simonides*. Berlin
Wili, W. (1948) *Horaz und die augusteische Kultur*. Bern
Wilkinson, L. P. (1945) *Horace and His Lyric Poetry*. Cambridge
Willett, J., ed. (1964) *Brecht on Theatre: The Development of an Aesthetic*. London
Williams, G. (1962) 'Poetry in the moral climate of Augustan Rome', *Journal of Roman Studies* 52: 28–46
(1968) *Tradition and Originality in Roman Poetry*. Oxford
(1969) *The Third Book of Horace's Odes*. Oxford
(1972) *Horace* (Greece and Rome: New Surveys in the Classics 6). Oxford
(1990) 'Did Maecenas "fall from favor"? Augustan literary patronage', in Raaflaub and Toher (1990) 258–75
(1994) 'Public policies, private affairs, and strategies of address in the poetry of Horace', *Classical World* 87: 395–408
(1995) '*Libertino patre natus*: true or false?' in S. J. Harrison (1995d) 296–313
Williams, R. G. (1976) *The De Arte Poetica of Marco Girolamo Vida*. New York
Wilson, A. J. N. (1969) 'Andrew Marvell's "An Horatian Ode upon Cromwell's return from Ireland": the thread of the poem and its use of classical allusion', *Critical Quarterly* 11.4: 325–41
Wilson, P. (1982) 'Classical poetry and the eighteenth-century reader', in Rivers (1982) 69–96
Wimmel, W. (1953) 'Über das Verhältnis der 4. Ekloge zur 16. Epode', *Hermes* 81: 317–44
(1960) *Kallimachos in Rom*. Wiesbaden
ed. (1970) *Forschungen zur römischen Literatur: Festschrift zum 60. Geburtstag von Karl Büchner*. Wiesbaden
Winterfeld, P. von (1905) 'Wie sah der Codex Blandinius vetustissimus des Horaz aus?', *Rheinisches Museum* 60: 31–7
Wiseman, T. P. (1988) 'Satyrs in Rome? The background to Horace's *Ars Poetica*', *JRS* 78: 29–37

Wistrand, E. (1958) *Horace's Ninth Epode and Its Historical Background*. Gothenburg

(1972) *Opera Selecta*. Stockholm

Witke, C. (1968) 'Prudentius and the tradition of Latin poetry', *Transactions of the American Philological Association* 99: 509–25

Womersley, D., ed. (1997) *Augustan Critical Writing*. Harmondsworth

Wood, A. G. (1985) *Literary Satire and Theory: A Study of Horace, Boileau, and Pope*. New York and London

Woodman, A. J. (1980) 'The craft of Horace in *Odes* 1.14', *Classical Philology* 75: 60–7

(1981) Review of Nisbet and Hubbard (1978), *Liverpool Classical Monthly* 6: 159–66

(1983) 'Juvenal 1 and Horace', *Greece and Rome* 30: 81–4

(2002) '*Biformis Vates*: The *Odes*, Catullus and Greek lyric', in Woodman and Feeney (2002) 53–64

(2003) 'Poems to historians: Catullus 1 and Horace *Odes* 2.1', in Braund and Gill (2003) 191–216

Woodman, A. J. [Tony], and Feeney, D., eds. (2002) *Traditions and Contexts in the Poetry of Horace*. Cambridge

Woodman, A. J. [Tony], and Powell, J., eds. (1992) *Author and Audience in Latin Literature*. Cambridge

Woodman, A. J. [Tony], and West, D., eds. (1979) *Creative Imitation and Latin Literature*. Cambridge

Woodman, A. J. [Tony], and West, D., eds. (1984) *Poetry and Politics in the Age of Augustus*. Cambridge

Woods, M. C. (1991) 'A medieval rhetoric goes to school – and to the university. The commentaries on the *Poetria nova*', *Rhetorica* 9: 55–65

Wray, D. (2001) *Catullus and the Poetics of Roman Manhood*. Cambridge

Wright, F. A. (1933) *Select Letters of St Jerome*. Cambridge, MA

Wu, D. (1993) *Wordsworth's Reading 1770–1799*. Cambridge

Wyke, M. (1992) 'Augustan Cleopatras: female power and poetic authority', in A. Powell (1992) 98–140

Zanker, P. (1988) *The Power of Images in the Age of Augustus*. Ann Arbor

Zechmeister, J. (1877) *Scholia Vindobonensia ad Horatii Artem poeticam*. Vienna

Zetzel, J. E. G. (1980) 'Horace's *Liber Sermonum*: the structure of ambiguity', *Arethusa* 13: 59–77

(1982) 'The poetics of patronage in the late first century BC', in Gold (1982), 87–102

(2002) 'Dreaming about Quirinus: Horace's *Satires* and the development of Augustan poetry', in Woodman and Feeney (2002) 38–52

Zingerle, A. (1869–71) *Ovidius und sein Verhältniss zu den Vorgängern und gleichzeitigen römischen Dichtern*. Innsbruck

Ziolkowski, J. (2000) '*Nota bene*: why the classics were neumed in the Middle Ages', *Journal of Medieval Latin* 10: 74–102

(forthcoming) 'Il libro e la nota: il ruolo della musica nei manoscritti medievali (secc. X–XII) dell' "Orazio lirico"'

Zwicker, S. N., ed. (1998) *The Cambridge Companion to English Literature 1650–1740*. Cambridge

INDEX

Academic sceptics 175
accessus (introduction), medieval 292
Actium, battle of 11–12, 26, 82
addressees, poetic 155, 173–4, 177, 203–4
Alcaeus 25, 34, 40–6
Alexandrianism 50
Almond, Maureen 346
Alphanus of Salerno 297–8
Alsop, Anthony
apostrophe (address) 151
Archilochus 8, 25, 37–9, 93–104
Ariosto 310
Aristippus 175–7
aristocrats, young 16
Arnold, Matthew 336
Ars Poetica 132–43
  dating of 20
  Renaissance reception of 305
Auden, W. H. 340–1
Augustan poets, contemporary 71–2
Augustus 13–14, 15–16, 45, 65, 77–89, 115–16, 125, 198, 257–8

Bacchus 218–19
Bentley, Richard, edition of Horace 323
Bion 165–8, 178
Boethius 283
bowdlerisation 207–19
Brutus 8
Bunting, Basil 343–4
Byron, Lord 334

Caecilius Epirota, Q. 64
Callimachus 50–6, 93, 95, 99, 102, 181–2, 184, 245, 253–4
Canidia 10, 101–2, 169
Carmen Saeculare 86, 190, 227–8
  dating of 15
Carolingian transmission 285
carpe diem, slogan 154, 172, 243
Catullus 57, 69–71, 95, 102–3, 181–2, 267
Celtis, Conrad 306
civil war 82
Cleopatra 16–17
Clough, Arthur Hugh 336–7
commentaries on Horace
  ancient 282
  medieval 293–6
countryside, nature 235–47
Cynicism 165–8, 169–70

Dante Alighieri 304
death, presentation of 43–4
deixis 156
diatribe 107, 167–8, 171
Dowson, Ernest 338–9

editions of Horace, ancient 283
elegy, Latin 74–6, 255
Epicureanism 119, 168, 170–1, 172–4, 175–7, 178–9, 214, 224, 239–41, 242
epigram, Hellenistic 56–60
epinician (literary genre) 47
Epistles Book 1 85–6, 121–9
  dating of 14–15
Epistles Book 2 88–9, 129–30, 257–8
  dating of 18–20
Epodes 93–104
  dating of 9–12
epyllion 61–2

Fitzgerald, Edward 337
Florus 18–19

friendship 195–206
Frost, Robert 342–3

gender 222–8
genre, poetic 250–3
Gray, Thomas 328

Heiric of Auxerre 287–8
Hellenistic poetry/aesthetics 50–60
Hesiod 54
hetairai 210
Hipponax 37–9, 99–100, 102
Homer 112, 249
homosexuality 230–2
Hopkins, Gerard Manley 337
Horace
 ancient editions of 283
 bowdlerisation in reception of 207–19
 commentaries on 282, 293–6
 future fame, own predictions of 30
 imitations of 305–10, 321–5, 336–9
 life of 7–21
 physical appearance of 21
 self-representation of 22–35, 38, 106–9, 190, 222
 style of 262–72
 temperament of 21
 translations of 318–20, 335–6
 and wine 207–19
 and women 221–34
Housman, A. E. 339
hymnic form 182

imagery, poetic 204–6, 262
imitatio (literary imitation) 140–1
initiation/inspiration, poetic 55, 244–5

Janus, temple, closures of 19–20
Jerome and pagan literature 292
Jonson, Ben 313–16
Juvenal 279

Keats, John 335
Kipling, Rudyard 339

letter-form, ancient 121–30
letters, philosophical, ancient 126–8
life/art analogy 253–5
literary criticism 132–43, 248–61
Longley, Michael 345
love, desire 158–9, 221–34

Lucilius 67–8, 110–20, 129, 251, 256, 279
Lucretius 68–9, 168, 245

MacNeice, Louis 341–2
Maecenas 10, 11, 15, 16, 26, 53, 80–1, 97, 106, 115, 129, 168, 197–8, 199, 203, 232, 233–4, 241
magic 101–2
magister bibendi (sympotic president) 210
Marbod of Rennes 303–4
Marvell, Andrew 329–30
'mean', the 215–16
Mercury 24
Metellus of Tegernsee 298
metres, poetic 36–48, 94, 146–9, 262, 280
militia amoris (love as war) 34
Milton, John 328
mouse, town and country 236–7
music, medieval 288–9, 296

Naulochus, battle of 25–6
Neoptolemus of Parium 133–4
Newbolt, Henry 339–40

Odes Books 1–3 40–6, 82–5, 144–60
 dating of 12–14
Odes Book 4 82–5, 144–60
 dating of 16–17
Ovid 277–8
Owen, Wilfred 340

paean (literary genre) 46–7
Panaetius 165, 175, 176
panegyric 79, 84
Parke, John 324
Parthians 17
patronage 195–206
perfectionism 255–8
Persius 279
Petrarch 289, 299–300, 305–10
pharmakos (scapegoat) 100
Philippi, battle of 84
Philodemus 57, 118, 134–5, 168
philosophy 117–20, 158, 159
Pindar 46, 47, 252
Plautus 65–6
poets, position in society 258–60
politics 10, 115–17
polyeideia (generic variety) 56
Pope, Alexander 330–1
Pound, Ezra 343
Prior, Matthew 328–9

Propertius 51, 277
Prudentius 282, 284–5

readers, audience 256–7
reception of Horace
in Carolingian writers 297
in medieval writers 294–304
in Oxford and Cambridge in 18th cent. 326–7
in prose fiction 321–5
in 20th cent. 340–6
in 21st cent. 344–6
in Victorian writers 334–9
See also under individual authors
recusatio (poetic refusal) 19, 251–2
religion 194
Roman Odes 84, 193
Rossetti, Christina 337–8

Sabine estate 11, 16, 24, 26, 198, 199, 235, 237, 246–7
Sandys, George 316
Sappho 40–5
Sarbiewski, Casimir 325–6
Satires 105–20
dating of 9–12
dialogue technique in 113–14
Saxo Grammaticus 198
school curriculum 288, 291–2
Seneca 281, 284
Sextus Amaricius 302
Shakespeare, William 307
Skelton, John 306
Smith, Charlotte 331–2
Spenser, Edmund 307
sphragis (seal-poem) 15, 30
Statius 281
Stoicism 119–20, 170–1, 172–4, 175–7, 179, 239–40
structure, poetic 267
symposium 159, 172–3, 207–19, 242–4

Tennyson, Alfred Lord 337
Terence 66, 72–4
Thackeray, William 337
Tiberius 85, 87
time and space, presentation of 153–5
translations of Horace 318–20, 335–6

Urban VIII, Pope 325

Valerius Cato, P. 64, 68
Virgil 9, 16, 141–2, 211–12, 250

Wedde, Ian 345
wine 207–19
women 221–34
Wordsworth, William 334
Wyllys, Benjamin 327

Cambridge Companions to...

AUTHORS

Homer edited by Robert Fowler
Virgil edited by Charles Martindale
Ovid edited by Philip Hardie
Dante edited by Rachel Jacoff
Cervantes edited by Anthony J. Cascardi
Goethe edited by Lesley Sharpe
Dostoevskii edited by W. J. Leatherbarrow
Tolstoy edited by Donna Tussing Orwin
Chekhov edited by Vera Gottlieb and Paul Allain
Ibsen edited by James McFarlane
Flaubert edited by Timothy Unwin
Pushkin edited by Andrew Kahn
Proust edited by Richard Bales
Thomas Mann edited by Ritchie Robertson
Kafka edited by Julian Preece
Brecht edited by Peter Thomson and Glendyr Sacks
Walter Benjamin edited by David S. Ferris
Lacan edited by Jean-Michel Rabaté
Nabokov edited by Julian W. Connolly
Albert Camus edited by Edward J. Hughes
Chaucer, second edition edited by Piero Boitani and Jill Mann
Shakespeare edited by Margareta de Grazia and Stanley Wells
Christopher Marlowe edited by Patrick Cheney
Ben Jonson edited by Richard Harp and Stanley Stewart
John Donne edited by Achsah Guibbory
Spenser edited by Andrew Hadfield
Milton, second edition edited by Dennis Danielson
John Dryden edited by Steven N. Zwicker
Molière edited by David Bradby and Andrew Calder
Aphra Behn edited by Derek Hughes and Janet Todd
Samuel Johnson edited by Greg Clingham
Jonathan Swift edited by Christopher Fox
Mary Wollstonecraft edited by Claudia L. Johnson
William Blake edited by Morris Eaves
Wordsworth edited by Stephen Gill
Coleridge edited by Lucy Newlyn
Byron edited by Drummond Bone
Keats edited by Susan J. Wolfson
Shelley edited by Timothy Morton
Mary Shelley edited by Esther Schor
Jane Austen edited by Edward Copeland and Juliet McMaster
The Brontës edited by Heather Glen
Charles Dickens edited by John O. Jordan
Wilkie Collins edited by Jenny Bourne Taylor
George Eliot edited by George Levine
Thomas Hardy edited by Dale Kramer
Oscar Wilde edited by Peter Raby
George Bernard Shaw edited by Christopher Innes
W. B. Yeats edited by Marjorie Howes and John Kelly
Joseph Conrad edited by J. H. Stape
D. H. Lawrence edited by Anne Fernihough
Virginia Woolf edited by Sue Roe and Susan Sellers
James Joyce, second edition edited by Derek Attridge
T. S. Eliot edited by A. David Moody
Ezra Pound edited by Ira B. Nadel
W. H. Auden edited by Stan Smith
Beckett edited by John Pilling
Harold Pinter edited by Peter Raby
Tom Stoppard edited by Katherine E. Kelly
Brian Friel edited by Anthony Roche
Herman Melville edited by Robert S. Levine
Nathaniel Hawthorne edited by Richard Millington
Harriet Beecher Stowe edited by Cindy Weinstein
Theodore Dreiser edited by Leonard Cassuto and Claire Virginia Eby
Willa Cather edited by Marilee Lindermann
Edith Wharton edited by Millicent Bell
Henry James edited by Jonathan Freedman
Walt Whitman edited by Ezra Greenspan
Ralph Waldo Emerson edited by Joel Porte and Saundra Morris
Henry David Thoreau edited by Joel Myerson
Mark Twain edited by Forrest G. Robinson
Edgar Allan Poe edited by Kevin J. Hayes

Emily Dickinson edited by Wendy Martin
William Faulkner edited by Philip M. Weinstein
Ernest Hemingway edited by Scott Donaldson
F. Scott Fitzgerald edited by Ruth Prigozy
Wallace Stevens edited by John N. Serio
Robert Frost edited by Robert Faggen
Sylvia Plath edited by Jo Gill
Ralph Ellison edited by Ross Posnock
Eugene O'Neill edited by Michael Manheim
Tennessee Williams edited by Matthew C. Roudané
Arthur Miller edited by Christopher Bigsby
David Mamet edited by Christopher Bigsby
Sam Shepard edited by Matthew C. Roudané
Edward Albee edited by Stephen J. Bottoms
Philip Roth edited by Timothy Parrish

TOPICS

Greek Tragedy edited by P. E. Easterling
Roman Satire edited by Kirk Freudenburg
Old English Literature edited by Malcolm Godden and Michael Lapidge
Medieval Women's Writing edited by Carolyn Dinshaw and David Wallace
Medieval Romance edited by Roberta L. Krueger
Medieval English Theatre edited by Richard Beadle
English Renaissance Drama, second edition edited by A. R. Braunmuller and Michael Hattaway
Renaissance Humanism edited by Jill Kraye
English Poetry, Donne to Marvell edited by Thomas N. Corns
English Literature, 1500–1600 edited by Arthur F. Kinney
English Literature, 1650–1740 edited by Steven N. Zwicker
English Literature, 1740–1830 edited by Thomas Keymer and Jon Mee
Writing of the English Revolution edited by N. H. Keeble
English Restoration Theatre edited by Deborah C. Payne Fisk
British Romanticism edited by Stuart Curran
Eighteenth-Century Poetry edited by John Sitter
The Eighteenth-Century Novel edited by John Richetti
Gothic Fiction edited by Jerrold E. Hogle
Victorian Poetry edited by Joseph Bristow
The Victorian Novel edited by Deirdre David
Crime Fiction edited by Martin Priestman
Science Fiction edited by Edward James and Farah Mendlesohn
Travel Writing edited by Peter Hulme and Tim Youngs
American Realism and Naturalism edited by Donald Pizer
Nineteenth-Century American Women's Writing edited by Dale M. Bauer and Philip Gould
Victorian and Edwardian Theatre edited by Kerry Powell
The Literature of the First World War edited by Vincent Sherry
The Classic Russian Novel edited by Malcolm V. Jones and Robin Feuer Miller
The French Novel: from 1800 to the Present edited by Timothy Unwin
The Spanish Novel: from 1600 to the Present edited by Harriet Turner and Adelaida López de Martínez
The Italian Novel edited by Peter Bondanella and Andrea Ciccarelli
The Irish Novel edited by John Wilson Foster
The Modern German Novel edited by Graham Bartram
The Latin American Novel edited by Efraín Kristal
Jewish American Literature edited by Hana Wirth-Nesher and Michael P. Kramer
Native American Literature edited by Joy Porter and Kenneth M. Roemer
The African American Novel edited by Maryemma Graham
Canadian Literature edited by Eva-Marie Kröller
Contemporary Irish Poetry edited by Matthew Campbell
Modernism edited by Michael Levenson
American Modernism edited by Walter Kalaidjian
Postmodernism edited by Steven Connor
Postcolonial Literary Studies edited by Neil Lazarus
Feminist Literary Theory edited by Ellen Rooney
Australian Literature edited by Elizabeth Webby
American Women Playwrights edited by Brenda Murphy

Modern British Women Playwrights edited by Elaine Aston and Janelle Reinelt

Twentieth-Century Irish Drama edited by Shaun Richards

Shakespeare on Film edited by Russell Jackson

Shakespearean Comedy edited by Alexander Leggatt

Shakespeare on Stage edited by Stanley Wells and Sarah Stanton

Shakespeare's History Plays edited by Michael Hattaway

Shakespearean Tragedy edited by Claire McEachern

CAMBRIDGE COMPANION TO CULTURE

Modern German Culture edited by Eva Kolinsky and Wilfried van der Will

Modern Russian Culture edited by Nicholas Rzhevsky

Modern Spanish Culture edited by David T. Gies

Modern Italian Culture edited by Zygmunt G. Barański and Rebecca J. West

Modern French Culture edited by Nicholas Hewitt

Modern Latin American Literature edited by John King

Modern Irish Culture edited by Joe Cleary and Claire Connolly

Modern American Culture edited by Christopher Bigsby